Modern Database Management

Fifth Edition

FRED R. McFADDEN
University of Colorado–Colorado Springs

JEFFREY A. HOFFER
University of Dayton

MARY B. PRESCOTT
University of South Florida

 ADDISON-WESLEY

An imprint of Addison Wesley Longman, Inc.

Reading, Massachusetts • Menlo Park, California • New York • Harlow, England
Don Mills, Ontario • Sydney • Mexico City • Madrid • Amsterdam

■ In memory of my valued colleague Daniel Couger. — *F. R. M.*

■ To Patty, for her sacrifices, encouragement, and support.
To my students, for being receptive and critical, and challenging me to
be a better teacher. — *J. A. H.*

■ To Larry, Mike, and Ivan. Their love and support provide a foundation
to my life which makes efforts such as writing this book possible. And
to Jeff and Fred, who gave me the opportunity to write with them and
patiently provided invaluable guidance along the way. — *M. B. P.*

Executive Editor: Michael Roche
Developmental Editor: Maureen Allaire Spada
Assistant Editor: Ruth Berry
Editorial Assistant: Adam Hamel
Senior Marketing Manager: Tom Ziolkowski
Senior Marketing Coordinator: Deanna Storey
Senior Production Supervisor: Patty Mahtani
Manufacturing Buyer: Sheila Spinney
Design Director: Regina Hagen
Cover Designer: Linda Manly Wade
Text Designer: Sandra Rigney
Composition and Project Coordination: Elm Street Publishing Services, Inc.
Cover Image: © **Mick Tarel for Artville**

Library of Congress Cataloging-in-Publication Data

McFadden, Fred R., 1933–
    Modern database management / Fred R. McFadden, Jeffrey A. Hoffer,
Mary B. Prescott. — 5th ed.
        p.   cm.
    Includes bibliographical references and index.
    ISBN 0-8053-6054-9
    1. Database management.   I. Hoffer, Jeffrey A.   II. Prescott, Mary B.
    III. Title.
    QA76.9.D3M395   1999
    005.74—dc21

                                                                                98-4120
                                                                                   CIP

Reprinted with corrections, May 1999

    5 6 7 8 9 10 WCT 02 01 00

Contents

Preface   xix

Part I   The Context of Database Management   1

PART I OVERVIEW   2

Chapter 1   **The Database Environment**   3
Learning Objectives   3
Introduction   3
Basic Concepts and Definitions   4
    Data   4
    Data versus Information   5
    Metadata   5
Traditional File Processing Systems   7
    File Processing Systems at Pine Valley Furniture Company   7
    Disadvantages of File Processing Systems   8
        Program-Data Dependence   8
        Duplication of Data   9
        Limited Data Sharing   9
        Lengthy Development Times   9
        Excessive Program Maintenance   10
The Database Approach   10
    The Database Approach at Pine Valley Furniture Company   10
        Enterprise Data Model   10
        Relational Databases   11
        Implementing the Relational Databases   13
        A Database Application   14
The Range of Database Applications   15
    Personal Computer Databases   15
    Workgroup Databases   16
    Department Databases   18
    Enterprise Databases   19
    Summary of Database Applications   20
Advantages of the Database Approach   20
    Program–Data Independence   21
    Minimal Data Redundancy   21

Improved Data Consistency   22
Improved Data Sharing   22
Increased Productivity of Application Development   22
Enforcement of Standards   22
Improved Data Quality   23
Improved Data Accessibility and Responsiveness   23
Reduced Program Maintenance   23
Cautions About Database Benefits   23

Costs and Risks of the Database Approach   24
New, Specialized Personnel   24
Installation and Management Cost and Complexity   24
Conversion Costs   25
Need for Explicit Backup and Recovery   25
Organizational Conflict   25

Components of the Database Environment   25

Evolution of Database Systems   27
1960s   28
1970s   28
1980s   28
1990s   29
2000 and Beyond   29

Summary   29

Chapter Review   30
Key Terms   30
Review Questions   31
Problems and Exercises   31
Field Exercises   33
References   34
Further Reading   34

Project Case: Mountain View Community Hospital   35

Chapter 2   **Database Development Process   37**
Learning Objectives   37

Introduction   37

Database Development Within Information Systems
Development   38
Information Systems Architecture   39
Information Engineering   40
Information Systems Planning   40
Identifying Strategic Planning Factors   41
Identifying Corporate Planning Objects   41
Developing an Enterprise Model   41

Database Development Process   44
Systems Development Life Cycle   45
Enterprise Modeling   46
Conceptual Data Modeling   47
Logical Database Design   47
Physical Database Design and Creation   48
Database Implementation   48
Database Maintenance   48

Alternative IS Development Approaches   48
The Role of CASE and a Repository   50

Managing the People Involved in Database Development   51

Three-Schema Architecture for Database Development   53

Three-Tiered Database Location Architecture   56

Developing a Database Application for Pine Valley
   Furniture   58
   Matching User Needs to the Information Systems
      Architecture   59
   Analyzing Database Requirements   61
   Designing the Database   64
   Using a Database   67
   Administering a Database   69

Summary   70

Chapter Review   71
   Key Terms   71
   Review Questions   71
   Problems and Exercises   72
   Field Exercises   75
   References   75
   Further Reading   76

Project Case: Mountain View Community Hospital   77

Part II   Database Analysis   83

PART II OVERVIEW   84

Chapter 3   The Entity-Relationship Model   85

Learning Objectives   85

Introduction   85

The E-R Model   87
   Sample E-R Diagram   87
   E-R Model Notation   89

Entity-Relationship Model Constructs   89
   Entities   89

Entity Type Versus Entity Instance   91

Entity Type Versus System Input, Output, or User   91
   Strong Versus Weak Entity Types   92
   Attributes   93
      Simple Versus Composite Attributes   94
      Single-Valued Versus Multivalued Attributes   95
      Stored Versus Derived Attributes   95

Relationships   97
   Basic Concepts and Definitions in Relationships   98
      Attributes on Relationships   99
      Associative Entities   99
   Degree of a Relationship   101
      Unary Relationship   101

Binary Relationship   104
Ternary Relationship   104
Cardinality Constraints   105
Minimum Cardinality   106
Maximum Cardinality   106
Some Examples   106
A Ternary Relationship   107
Modeling Time-Dependent Data   107
Multiple Relationships   110

E-R Modeling Example: Pine Valley Furniture Company   111

Database Processing at Pine Valley Furniture   114
Showing Product Information   114
Showing Customer Information   115
Showing Customer Order Status   115
Showing Product Sales   117

Summary   117

Chapter Review   118
Key Terms   118
Review Questions   119
Problems and Exercises   119
Field Exercises   124
References   124
Further Reading   125

Project Case: Mountain View Community Hospital   126

Chapter 4   **The Enhanced E-R Model and Business Rules   129**
Learning Objectives   129

Introduction   129

Representing Supertypes and Subtypes   130
Basic Concepts and Notation   130
An Example   131
Attribute Inheritance   133
When to Use Supertype/Subtype Relationships   133
Representing Specialization and Generalization   133
Generalization   133
Specialization   136
Combining Specialization and Generalization   137

Specifying Constraints in Supertype/Subtype
Relationships   137
Specifying Completeness Constraints   137
Total Specialization Rule   138
Partial Specialization Rule   138
Specifying Disjointness Constraints   138
Disjoint Rule   139
Overlap Rule   139
Defining Subtype Discriminators   141
Disjoint Subtypes   141
Overlapping Subtypes   142
Defining Supertype/Subtype Hierarchies   143
An Example   143
Summary of Supertype/Subtype Hierarchies   145

Business Rules: An Overview   145
   The Business Rules Paradigm   146
   Scope of Business Rules   146
   Classification of Business Rules   147

Business Rules: Defining Structural Constraints   148
   Definitions   148
      Facts   148
      Derived Facts   149
      Definitions for Data Model   150
      Importance of Precise Definitions   150
   Domain Constraints   153

Business Rules: Defining Operational Constraints   154
   Declarative Approach to Business Rules   154
      Constraint Specification Language   155
   Constrained Objects and Constraining Objects   155
      Sample Business Rules   156

Summary   159

Chapter Review   160
   Key Terms   160
   Review Questions   160
   Problems and Exercises   161
   Field Exercises   163
   References   164
   Further Reading   164

Project Case: Mountain View Community Hospital   165

Chapter 5   **Object–Oriented Modeling   167**

Learning Objectives   167

Introduction   167

The Unified Modeling Language   170

Object-Oriented Modeling   171
   Representing Objects and Classes   171
   Types of Operations   173
   Representing Associations   174
   Representing Association Classes   177
   Representing Derived Attributes, Derived Associations, and
      Derived Roles   180
   Representing Generalization   181
   Interpreting Inheritance and Overriding   186
   Representing Multiple Inheritance   187
   Representing Aggregation   187

Business Rules   191

Object Modeling Example: Pine Valley Furniture
   Company   191

Summary   194

Chapter Review   195
   Key Terms   195
   Review Questions   196
   Problems and Exercises   197

Field Exercises 201
References 201
Project Case: Mountain View Community Hospital 202

Part III   Database Design   205

PART III OVERVIEW 206

Chapter 6   Logical Database Design and the Relational Model 207
Learning Objectives 207

Introduction 207

The Relational Data Model 208
Basic Definitions 208
Relational Data Structure 209
Relational Keys 209
Properties of Relations 210
Removing Multivalued Attributes from Tables 210
Example Database 211

Integrity Constraints 213
Domain Constraints 213
Entity Integrity 213
Referential Integrity 214
Operational Constraints 215
Creating Relational Tables 215
Well-Structured Relations 217

Transforming EER Diagrams into Relations 218
Step 1: Map Regular Entities 219
Composite Attributes 219
Multivalued Attributes 220
Step 2: Map Weak Entities 221
Step 3: Map Binary Relationships 222
Map Binary One-to-Many Relationships 222
Map Binary Many-to-Many Relationships 223
Map Binary One-to-One Relationships 224
Step 4: Map Associative Entities 224
Identifier Not Assigned 224
Identifier Assigned 225
Step 5: Map Unary Relationships 227
Unary One-to-Many Relationships 227
Unary Many-to-Many Relationships 228
Step 6: Map Ternary (and n-ary) Relationships 229
Step 7: Map Supertype/Subtype Relationships 231

Introduction to Normalization 232
Steps in Normalization 233
Functional Dependencies and Keys 235
Determinants 235
Candidate Keys 235

The Basic Normal Forms 237
First Normal Form 237
Second Normal Form 237

Third Normal Form   238
Normalizing Summary Data   241

Merging Relations   241
An Example   241
View Integration Problems   241
Synonyms   242
Homonyms   242
Transitive Dependencies   242
Supertype/Subtype Relationships   243

Summary   243

Chapter Review   244
Key Terms   244
Review Questions   244
Problems and Exercises   245
Field Exercises   249
References   250
Further Reading   250

Project Case: Mountain View Community Hospital   251

Chapter 7   **Physical Database Design   253**
Learning Objectives   253

Introduction   253

Physical Database Design Process   254
Data Volume and Usage Analysis   255

Designing Fields   257
Choosing Data Types   257
Coding and Compression Techniques   257
Controlling Data Integrity   259
Handling Missing Data   260

Designing Physical Records and Denormalization   260
Handling Fixed-Length Fields   261
Handling Variable-Length Fields   261
Denormalization   261

Designing Physical Files   267
Pointer   267
Access Methods   267
File Organizations   268
Sequential File Organizations   268
Indexed File Organizations   268
Hashed File Organizations   272
Summary of File Organizations   272
Clustering Files   272
Designing Controls for Files   274

Using and Selecting Indexes   274
Creating a Primary Key Index   274
Creating a Secondary Key Index   275
When to Use Indexes   275

RAID: Improving File Access Performance by Parallel
Processing   276

Choosing Among RAID Levels   278
RAID-0   278
RAID-1   278
RAID-2   281
RAID-3   281
RAID-4   281
RAID-5   281
RAID Performance   281
Designing Databases   282
Choosing Database Architectures   282
Optimizing for Query Performance   285
Summary   286
Chapter Review   288
Key Terms   288
Review Questions   288
Problems and Exercises   289
Field Exercises   291
References   292
Further Reading   292
Project Case: Mountain View Community Hospital   293

Part IV   Implementation   295

PART IV OVERVIEW   296

Chapter 8   Client/Server and Middleware   297
Learning Objectives   297
Introduction   297
Client/Server Architectures   298
File Server Architectures   299
Limitations of File Servers   300
Database Server Architectures   301
Three-Tier Architectures   302
Partitioning an Application   304
Role of the Mainframe   305
Using Parallel Computer Architectures   306
Multiprocessor Hardware Architectures   307
Business Related Uses of SMP and MPP Architectures   308
Using Middleware   309
Establishing Client/Server Security   311
Client/Server Issues   312
Summary   314
Chapter Review   315
Key Terms   315
Review Questions   316
Problems and Exercises   316

Field Exercises   317
References   318
Project Case: Mountain View Community Hospital   319

Chapter 9   **SQL   323**

Learning Objectives   323

Introduction   323

History of the SQL Standard   324

The Role of SQL in a Database Architecture   325

The SQL Environment   327

Defining a Database in SQL   331
Generating SQL Database Definitions   332
Creating Tables   332
Creating Data Integrity Controls   334
Changing Table Definitions   336
Removing Tables   336
Establishing Synonyms   336

Inserting, Updating, and Deleting Data   337
Batch Input   337
Deleting Database Contents   338
Changing Database Contents   338

Internal Schema Definition in RDBMSs   338
Creating Indexes   339

Processing Single Tables   340
Clauses of the SELECT Statement   340
Using Expressions   342
Using Functions   343
Using Wildcards   345
Comparison Operators   345
Using Boolean Operators   346
Ranges   347
Distinct   348
IN and NOT IN Lists   350
Sorting Results: The ORDER BY Clause   350
Categorizing Results: The GROUP BY Clause   351
Qualifying Results by Categories: The HAVING Clause   352

Processing Multiple Tables   354
Equi-join   354
Natural Join   355
Outer Join   356
Subqueries   358
Correlated Subqueries   361

View Definitions   363

Ensuring Transaction Integrity   366

Data Dictionary Facilities   368

Triggers and Procedures   369

SQL3   371

Summary   372

Chapter Review   373
Key Terms   373
Review Questions   373
Problems and Exercises   374
Field Exercises   377
References   378
Web Site References   378
Further Reading   379

Project Case: Mountain View Community Hospital   380

Chapter 10   Database Access from Client Applications   381

Learning Objectives   381

Introduction   381

Survey of Desktop Database Technology   382

Using Query-by-Example   383
The History and Importance of QBE   384
QBE: The Basics   384
Database Definition   386
Relationships   387
Building Queries Using QBE   388
Single-Table Queries   388
Selecting Qualified Records   390
Multiple-Table Queries   390
Self-Join   392
Basing a Query on Another Query   393
Access97 Query Types   394

Building a Client Application   396
Application Menus   396
Form Development   397
Report Development   399

Using OLE, COM, and ActiveX Controls for Database
    Access   401

Embedding SQL in Programs   403

Using Visual Basic for Applications (VBA) in Client
    Applications   406

Building Internet Database Servers   407

Summary   409

Chapter Review   410
Key Terms   410
Review Questions   410
Problems and Exercises   411
Field Exercises   413
References   414

Project Case: Mountain View Community Hospital   415

Chapter 11   Distributed Databases   417

Learning Objectives   417

Introduction   417
    Objectives and Trade-offs   421
Options for Distributing a Database   422
    Data Replication   423
        Snapshot Replication   424
        Near Real-Time Replication   425
        Pull Replication   425
        Database Integrity with Replication   425
        When to Use Replication   426
    Horizontal Partitioning   426
    Vertical Partitioning   427
    Combinations of Operations   429
    Selecting the Right Data Distribution Strategy   430
Distributed DBMS   431
    Location Transparency   433
    Replication Transparency   434
    Failure Transparency   435
    Commit Protocol   435
    Concurrency Transparency   436
        Timestamping   437
    Query Optimization   437
    Evolution of Distributed DBMS   440
        Remote Unit of Work   440
        Distributed Unit of Work   441
        Distributed Request   441
Distributed DBMS Products   442
    IBM Corporation and DB2   442
    Sybase Inc.   443
    Oracle Corporation   444
    Computer Associates International and Ingres   444
    Microsoft Corporation and SQL Server   445
Summary   445
Chapter Review   447
    Key Terms   447
    Review Questions   447
    Problems and Exercises   448
    Field Exercises   450
    References   451
Project Case: Mountain View Community Hospital   452

Chapter 12   **Object–Oriented Database Development   453**
Learning Objectives   453
Introduction   453
Object Definition Language   454
    Defining a Class   454
    Defining an Attribute   455
    Defining User Structures   456
    Defining Operations   456
    Defining a Range for an Attribute   457
    Defining Relationships   457
    Defining an Attribute with an Object Identifier as Its Value   459

Defining Many-to-Many Relationships, Keys, and Multivalued
Attributes   460
Defining Generalization   462
Defining an Abstract Class   464
Defining Other User Structures   464

OODB Design for Pine Valley Furniture Company   466

Creating Object Instances   467

Object Query Language   468
Basic Retrieval Command   469
Including Operations in Select Clause   469
Finding Distinct Values   470
Querying Multiple Classes   470
Writing Subqueries   471
Calculating Summary Values   471
Calculating Group Summary Values   472
Qualifying Groups   472
Using a Set in a Query   473

Current ODBMS Products and Their Applications   474

Summary   474

Chapter Review   475
Key Terms   475
Review Questions   476
Problems and Exercises   476
Field Exercises   477
References   478

Project Case: Mountain View Community Hospital   479

Part V   Data Administration   481

PART V OVERVIEW   482

Chapter 13   **Data and Database Administration   483**

Learning Objectives   483

Introduction   483

The Changing Roles of Data and Database
Administrators   484
Data Administration   484
Database Administration   485
Changing Approaches to Data Administration   488

Modeling Enterprise Data   490

Planning for Databases   491

Managing Data Security   492
Threats to Data Security   492
Views   494
Authorization Rules   495
User-Defined Procedures   497
Encryption   497
Authentication Schemes   497

Backing Up Databases   498
  Basic Recovery Facilities   499
    Backup Facilities   499
    Journalizing Facilities   499
    Checkpoint Facility   500
    Recovery Manager   500
  Recovery and Restart Procedures   500
    Switch   501
    Restore/Rerun   501
    Transaction Integrity   501
    Backward Recovery   502
    Forward Recovery   503
  Types of Database Failure   503
    Aborted Transactions   503
    Incorrect Data   504
    System Failure   504
    Database Destruction   505

Controlling Concurrent Access   505
  The Problem of Lost Updates   505
  Serializability   506
  Locking Mechanisms   507
    Locking Level   507
    Types of Locks   508
    Deadlock   508
    Managing Deadlock   510
  Versioning   510

Managing Data Quality   511
  Security Policy and Disaster Recovery   512
  Personnel Controls   513
  Physical Access Controls   513
  Maintenance Controls   514
  Data Protection and Privacy   514

Data Dictionaries and Repositories   514
  Repositories   515

Overview of Tuning the Database for Performance   516
  Installation of the DBMS   517
  Memory Usage   517
  Input/Output (I/O) Contention   518
  CPU Usage   518
  Application Tuning   518

Summary   519

Chapter Review   520
  Key Terms   520
  Review Questions   520
  Problems and Exercises   522
  Field Exercises   525
  References   525

Project Case: Mountain View Community Hospital   527

Chapter 14   **Data Warehouse   529**
Learning Objectives   529

Introduction   529

Basic Concepts of Data Warehousing   531
    A Brief History   531
    The Need for Data Warehousing   532
      Need for a Company-Wide View   532
      Need to Separate Operational and Information
      Systems   533

Data Warehouse Architectures   534
    Generic Two-Level Architecture   534
    An Expanded Data Warehouse Architecture   534
    Three-Layer Data Architecture   537
      Role of the Enterprise Data Model   537
      Role of Metadata   537

Some Data Characteristics   538
    Status versus Event Data   538
    Transient versus Periodic Data   539
    An Example of Transient and Periodic Data   540
      Transient Data   541
      Periodic Data   542

The Reconciled Data Layer   542
    Characteristics of Reconciled Data   543
    The Data Reconciliation Process   543
      Capture   544
      Scrub   544
      Load and Index   545

Data Transformation   546
    Data Transformation Functions   547
      Record-Level Functions   547
      Field-Level Functions   548
      More Complex Transformations   550
    Tools to Support Data Reconciliation   550
      Data Quality Tools   550
      Data Conversion Tools   550
      Data-Cleansing Tools   550

The Derived Data Layer   551
    Characteristics of Derived Data   551
    The Star Schema   552
      Fact Tables and Dimension Tables   552
      Example Star Schema   552
      Grain of a Fact Table   554
      Size of the Fact Table   554
    Variations of the Star Schema   556
      Multiple Fact Tables   556
      Snowflake Schema   556
      Proprietary Databases   557
    Independent versus Dependent Data Marts   558

The User Interface   559
    Role of Metadata   559
    On-Line Analytical Processing (OLAP) Tools   560
      Slicing a Cube   561
      Drill-Down   561

Data-Mining Tools   562
    Data-Mining Techniques   562
    Data-Mining Applications   562
Data Visualization   563

Summary   563

Chapter Review   565
    Key Terms   565
    Review Questions   565
    Problems and Exercises   566
    Field Exercises   568
    References   568
    Further Reading   569

Project Case: Mountain View Community Hospital   570

Appendix A   Object-Relational Databases   573

Basic Concepts and Definitions   573
    Features of an ORDBMS   574
    Complex Data Types   574

Enhanced SQL   575
    A Simple Example   575
    Content Addressing   576

Advantages of the Object-Relational Approach   576

ORDBMS Vendors and Products   577

References   577

Appendix B   Advanced Normal Forms   579

Boyce-Codd Normal Form   579
    Anomalies in STUDENT_ADVISOR   579
    Definition of Boyce-Codd Normal Form (BCNF)   580
    Converting a Relation to BCNF   580

Fourth Normal Form   582
    Multivalued Dependencies   583

Higher Normal Forms   584

References   584

Appendix C   Data Structures   585

Pointers   585

Data Structure Building Blocks   587

Linear Data Structures   589
    Stacks   590
    Queues   590
    Sorted Lists   591
    Multilists   593

Hazards of Chain Structures   594

Trees   594
    Balanced Trees   595

References   598

Glossary of Terms   599

Glossary of Acronyms   611

Index   613

Preface

This text is designed for an introductory course in database management. Such a course is usually required as part of an information systems curriculum in business schools, computer technology programs, and applied computer science departments. The Association of Information Technology Professionals (AITP), Association for Computing Machinery (ACM), and International Federation of Information Processing Societies (IFIPS) curriculum guidelines (for example, IS '97) all outline this type of database management course. Previous editions of our text have been used successfully for more than a decade at both the undergraduate and graduate levels, as well as in management and professional development programs.

This text represents an extensive revision and updating of the fourth edition of *Modern Database Management.* These revisions are necessary to accommodate the technical, managerial, and methodological changes occurring at an ever-increasing pace in this field. However, we have endeavored to retain the best features of our previous editions. We have made every effort to justify the title *Modern Database Management,* which was introduced in the fourth edition.

In this fifth edition we welcome a third co-author, Mary Prescott of the University of South Florida. Mary has served both as a reviewer and user of the previous editions of our text in numerous database courses and professional development programs. She brings valuable new insights to the preparation of a new edition of this text.

NEW TO THIS EDITION

The fifth edition of *Modern Database Management* updates and expands materials in areas undergoing rapid change due to improved managerial practices, database design tools and methodologies, and database technology. This section presents a chapter-by-chapter description of the major changes in this edition. Each chapter description presents a one-sentence statement of the purpose of that chapter, followed by a description of the changes and revisions that have been made since the fourth edition. This paragraph concludes with a one-sentence description of the strengths that have been retained from the fourth edition.

Chapter 1: The Database Environment This chapter discusses the role of databases in organizations and previews the major topics in the remainder of the text. The chapter introduces a new classification scheme that recognizes four types of databases:

personal, work group, departmental, and enterprise. It also introduces a discussion of the evolution of database technologies from pre-database files to modern object-relational systems. The chapter continues to present a well-organized comparison of database technology compared to conventional file-processing systems.

Chapter 2: Database Development Process   This chapter presents a detailed discussion of the role of database development within the broader context of information systems development. It is a synthesis of the material presented in Chapters 2 and 3 of the fourth edition. The chapter presents an expanded description of the systems development life cycle and the role of database development within that cycle. It also presents a new description of the prototyping methodology and its impact on database development. In addition, the chapter discusses important issues in database development, including management of the diverse group of people involved in database development and frameworks for understanding database architectures and technologies. The chapter continues to emphasize the information engineering methodology in database development, including the role of the enterprise data model.

Chapter 3: The Entity-Relationship Model   This chapter presents a thorough introduction to conceptual data modeling with the entity-relationship model. The chapter contains an expanded discussion of several important topics, including weak entities, associative entities, and ternary relationships. The chapter continues to proceed from simple to more complex examples, and it concludes with a comprehensive E-R diagram for Pine Valley Furniture Company.

Chapter 4: The Enhanced E-R Model and Business Rules   This is a new chapter for the fifth edition. It presents an expanded discussion of supertype/subtype relationships, which were covered in a single section in the fourth edition. It also provides an expanded discussion of business rules and their role, with an emphasis on the Ronald Ross graphical notation.

Chapter 5: Object-Oriented Modeling   This chapter presents an introduction to object-oriented modeling using the Unified Modeling Language (UML) of Booch, Jacobson, and Rumbaugh. This chapter has been thoroughly updated. Using the UML provides an industry-standard notation for representing classes and objects. The chapter continues to emphasize basic O-O concepts such as inheritance and aggregation.

Chapter 6: Logical Database Design and the Relational Model   This chapter describes the process of converting a conceptual data model to the relational data model. It features an improved logical organization compared to the fourth edition, with the process of transforming E-R diagrams into relations preceding the discussion of data normalization. There is also an expanded discussion of integrity constraints, including the representation of constraints using SQL code. The discussion of functional dependencies and normalization has been somewhat simplified. The chapter continues to emphasize the basic concepts of the relational data model and the role of the database designer in the logical design process.

Chapter 7: Physical Database Design   This chapter describes the steps that are essential in achieving an efficient database design. The chapter contains several important new topics, including controlling data integrity, designing physical records and denormalization, optimizing for query performance, bitmap indexes, and RAID. The chapter continues to emphasize the physical design process and the goals of that process.

Chapter 8: Client/Server and Middleware   This is a predominantly new chapter in the fifth edition (the chapter does contain an updated version of some client/server topics that appeared at the beginning of Chapter 13 in the fourth edition). The purpose of the chapter is to provide a thoroughly modern discussion of the client/server architecture, applications, and middleware in contemporary database environments. Important new topics include the three-tier client/server architecture, application partitioning, role of the mainframe, and use of parallel computer architectures. Symmetric multiprocessing (SMP) and massively parallel processing (MPP) architectures are described and compared. The chapter concludes with a discussion of the role of middleware and connecting databases to the Internet.

Chapter 9: SQL   This chapter presents a thorough introduction to the SQL language using the most recently released standard (SQL-92). New topics include integrity control statements, outer joins, an expanded discussion of correlated subqueries, maintenance of transaction integrity, and triggers and stored procedures. The chapter continues to use the Pine Valley Furniture Company case to illustrate a wide variety of practical queries and query results.

Chapter 10: Database Access from Client Applications   The purpose of this chapter is to describe the use of visually oriented data manipulation languages. This chapter is a thorough update of Chapter 10 in the fourth edition. It describes accessing databases and building applications using Microsoft Access97 Query-by-Example. The chapter also describes the use of object-oriented features such as Object Linking and Embedding (OLE), Component Object Model, and ActiveX controls. It also describes embedding SQL in programs and the use of Visual Basic for Applications (VBA). As in the fourth edition, this chapter facilitates the comparison of visual languages with SQL through the use of common examples.

Chapter 11: Distributed Databases   This chapter extensively updates and expands the material on distributed databases from Chapter 13 in the fourth edition. There is significant new coverage of the objectives and trade-offs for distributed databases, data replication alternatives, factors in selecting a data distribution strategy, and distributed database vendors and products. This chapter, along with Chapter 13 on data and database administration, provides thorough coverage of database concurrent access controls.

Chapter 12: Object-Oriented Database Development   The purpose of this totally new chapter is to show how to translate object-oriented models (explained in Chapter 5) into class, object, relationship, and operation definitions for an object-oriented DBMS. The chapter also introduces object query language (OQL), the OO equivalent to SQL 5 and the standard query language for ODBMSs. The chapter concludes with a survey of ODBMSs—both vendors and products.

Chapter 13: Data and Database Administration   This chapter presents a thorough discussion of the importance and roles of data and database administration and describes a number of the key issues that arise when these functions are being performed. Updating and extending much of the material from Chapter 12 in the fourth edition, this chapter emphasizes the changing roles and approaches of data and database administration. It contains an expanded discussion of database backup procedures and data security threats and responses and provides a new description of managing data quality. There is also a new discussion of measures for tuning database performance. The chapter continues to emphasize the critical importance of data and database management in managing data as a corporate asset.

Chapter 14: Data Warehouse   This chapter is completely new to the fifth edition. Its purpose is to describe the basic concepts of data warehousing and the reasons data warehousing is regarded as critical to competitive advantage in many organizations. Topics include alternative data warehouse architectures, techniques for data transformation and reconciliation, and the dimensional data model (or star schema) for data warehouses. User interfaces, including on-line analytical processing (OLAP) and data mining, are also described.

Appendices

The fifth edition contains four appendices intended for persons who wish to explore certain topics in greater depth.

Appendix A: Object-Relational Databases   This appendix presents a description of object-relational database management systems (ORDBMS). This material is new to the fifth edition. Topics include features of an ORDBMS, enhanced SQL, advantages of the object-relational approach, and a summary of ORDBMS vendors and products.

Appendix B: Advanced Normal Forms   This appendix presents a description (with examples) of Boyce/Codd and Fourth normal forms. This is an update of material that was presented in Chapter 6 of the fourth edition.

Appendix C: Data Structures   This appendix describes several data structures that often underlie database implementations. Topics include the use of pointers, stacks, queues, sorted lists, inverted lists, and trees.

Appendix D: Legacy DBMS   This appendix, located on the Web site for this text (http://hepg.awl.com, keyword: McFadden), presents a brief summary of the hierarchical and network database models.

PEDAGOGY

A number of additions and improvements have been made to chapter-end materials to provide a wider and richer range of choices for the user. The most important of these improvements are the following:

1. **Problems and exercises**   This section has been expanded in every chapter and contains a majority of new problems and exercises to support updated chapter material.

2. **Field exercises**   This new section provides a set of "hands-on" minicases that can be assigned to individual students or to small teams of students. Field exercises range from directed field trips to Internet searches and other types of research exercises.

3. **Project case**   The Mountain View Community Hospital case (which was used in the fourth edition as an expository case) has been totally restructured in the fifth edition as a student project. In each chapter the case begins with a brief description of the project as it relates to that chapter. The case then presents a series of project questions and exercises to be completed by individual students

or by small project teams. This case provides an excellent means for students to gain hands-on experience with the concepts and tools they have studied.

We have also updated the pedagogical features that helped make the fourth edition widely accessible to instructors and students. These features include the following:

1. **Learning objectives** appear at the beginning of each chapter to preview the major concepts and skills students will learn from that chapter. The learning objectives also provide a great study review aid for students as they prepare for assignments and examinations.

2. **Chapter introductions and summaries** both encapsulate the main concepts of each chapter and link material to related chapters, providing students with a comprehensive conceptual framework for the course.

3. The **chapter review**, which includes the problems, exercises, and field exercises discussed above, also contains **key terms** and **review questions** to test the student's grasp of important concepts, basic facts, and significant issues.

4. A **running glossary** defines key terms in the page margins as they are discussed in text. These terms are also defined at the end of the text in the **glossary of terms**. Also included is an end-of-book **glossary of acronyms** for abbreviations commonly used in database management.

ORGANIZATION

We encourage instructors to customize their use of this book to meet the needs of both their curriculum and student career paths. The modular nature of the text, its broad coverage, extensive illustrations, and inclusion of advanced topics and emerging issues make customization easy. The many references to current publications and Web sites can help instructors develop supplemental reading lists or expand classroom discussion beyond material presented in the text. The use of appendices for several advanced topics allow instructors to easily include or omit these topics.

The modular nature of the text allows the instructor to omit certain chapters or to cover chapters in a different sequence. For example, an instructor who wishes to emphasize object-oriented database concepts may cover Chapter 5 and then skip to Chapter 12. Another instructor who wishes to cover only basic entity/relationship concepts (but not the enhanced E-R model or business rules) may skip Chapter 4.

CASE TOOLS ORACLE EDITION OF *MODERN DATABASE MANAGEMENT*

Modern Database Management, fifth edition is the first database book on the market to offer students an outstanding CASE tools software package from Oracle. For a few dollars more than the price of the text alone, students can purchase this book along with the full editions of **Oracle Designer/2000 2.1**, **Oracle Developer/2000 2.1**, and **Personal Oracle7, release 7.3.4**. We are proud to offer such a highly valued, powerful software package to students at such a low cost.

SUPPLEMENTS

- **Instructor's Manual/Test Bank**   This volume provides chapter-by-chapter instructor objectives, classroom ideas, and answers to review questions, problems and exercises, field exercises, and project case questions. The Test Bank contains multiple-choice, true-false, and short-answer questions ranked according to level of difficulty and referenced with page numbers and topic headings from the text.

- **Instructor's Resource CD-ROM**   This Windows-based CD contains PowerPoint presentation slides, the complete Instructor's Manual, and a computerized version of the Test Bank in Addison Wesley Longman's **TestGen-EQ test generating software**. TestGen-EQ enables instructors to view, edit, and add Test Bank questions and create highly customized tests in a variety of formats. The program's built-in question editor allows the user to create graphs, import graphics, and insert mathematical symbols and templates. The online testing component—**QuizMaster-EQ**—is fully networkable and automatically grades quizzes, stores results, and allows the instructor to view or print several types of grading reports.

- **Web Site**   The Web site to accompany *Modern Database Management*, fifth edition includes Appendix D on Legacy DBMS, data sets for use with the Pine Valley Furniture case, and other useful resources and links for students and instructors. Please go to http://hepg.awl.com and use the keyword McFadden to check the site for the most current information and updates.

ACKNOWLEDGMENTS

We are grateful to numerous individuals who contributed to the preparation of *Modern Database Management*, fifth edition. First, we wish to thank our reviewers for their detailed suggestions and insights, characteristic of their thoughtful teaching style. Because of the extensive changes made from the fourth edition of *Modern Database Management*, analysis of topics and depth of coverage provided by the reviewers were crucial. Our reviewers include the following:

Cyrus Azarbod, *Mankato State University*

Michael Barrett, *Clarion University of Pennsylvania*

Douglas Bock, *Southern Illinois University, Edwardsville*

Sue Brown, *Indiana University*

I-Shien Chien, *Creighton University*

Sergio Davalos, *University of Portland, OR*

Mark Gillenson, *University of Memphis*

Bernard Han, *Washington State University*

Myron Hatcher, *California State University–Fresno*

Chang Hsieh, *University of Southern Mississippi*

Ram Kumar, *University of North Carolina, Charlotte*

Kathleen Moser, *Iowa State University*

Heidi Owens, *Portland State University*

David Paradice, *Texas A&M University*

Fred Prose, *Glendale Community College*

Siva Sankaran, *California State University–Northridge*

Werner Schenk, *University of Rochester*

Maureen Thommes, *Bemidja State University*

Charles Wertz, *State University of New York, Buffalo*

Surya Yadav, *Texas Tech University*

Ahmed Zaki, *College of William & Mary*

We extend special thanks to Mark Gillenson and his students, who have used the manuscript for *Modern Database Management*, fifth edition and provided excellent suggestions for improving the book. We also thank the undergraduate MIS students at the University of Dayton who extensively tested the manuscript as it was being prepared. Students at the University of Colorado–Colorado Springs and the University of South Florida were also instrumental in making suggestions that shaped the structure and content of this book.

We also thank Joe Valacich at Washington State University and Joey George at Louisiana State University for their great insights on the relationship of database development to the overall development of information systems. Their careful attention helps make our book compatible with books used in systems analysis and design courses, such as *Modern Systems Analysis and Design,* by Hoffer, George, and Valacich (Addison Wesley Longman).

We also thank Atish Sinha at the University of Dayton, who authored Chapters 5 and 12 on object-oriented database modeling and implementation. We sincerely appreciate all his efforts to integrate these chapters into the whole text by using the Pine Valley Furniture and Mountain View Community Hospital cases, to create parallel exercises which contrast OO approaches with entity-relationship and relational approaches, and to provide suggestions concerning all chapters. We also wish to acknowledge James Stanton, a student at University of Colorado–Colorado Springs, who prepared most of the PowerPoint graphics for Chapters 1, 3, 4, 6, and 14.

We are also very grateful to the staff and associates of Addison Wesley Longman for their support and guidance throughout this project. In particular, we wish to thank Executive Editor Mike Roche, who coordinated the planning for the text, Assistant Editor Ruth Berry, Senior Production Supervisor Patty Mahtani, Senior Marketing Manager Michelle Hudson, and Technical Art Supervisor Joe Vetere. We extend special thanks to our consulting editor, Maureen Allaire Spada, who has worked with us through several editions of *Modern Database Management* and has helped to integrate everyone's work on the project.

We are most grateful to Oracle Corporation for making their powerful modeling and development tools—Designer/2000, Developer/2000, and Personal Oracle7— available for use with the fifth edition of *Modern Database Management*. We believe students will benefit greatly from having such easy access to these important CASE tools. We particularly wish to thank Rene Bonvanie and Randy Baker of Oracle Corporation, as well as Maureen Dorhety, Diane Shorts, Marie Schmitt, Susan Andolsek, and other Oracle employees who worked behind the scenes to make this partnership a reality.

Finally, we give immeasurable thanks to our families—spouses, children, and parents—who endured many evenings and weekends of solitude for the thrill of seeing a book cover hang on a den wall. In particular, we marvel at the commitment of Evelyn McFadden and Patty Hoffer, who have lived the lonely life of a textbook author's spouse through five editions. We welcome Larry Prescott to this presainthood group. Much of the value of this text is due to their patience, encouragement, and love, but we alone bear the responsibility for any errors or omissions between the covers.

Fred R. McFadden
Jeffrey A. Hoffer
Mary B. Prescott

PART

I

The Context of Database Management

CHAPTER 1

The Database Environment

CHAPTER 2

Database Development Process

Part I Overview

Part I (consisting of two chapters) provides the context and basic definitions that are used throughout the remainder of the text. In this part, we portray database management as an exciting, challenging, and rapidly growing field that provides numerous career opportunities for students of information systems. We interact with databases (directly or indirectly) when performing the simplest daily tasks such as making a telephone call, using a credit card, or registering for a course. Organizations rely on databases in processing these transactions, as well as for providing information to managers for decision making. Until recently only the largest organizations could afford to build and maintain the large databases that are required for these applications. However, today even smaller organizations can quickly build up large databases by capturing transactions from point-of-sale systems, web servers, and other sources.

Chapter 1 (The Database Environment) provides the basic definitions of data, databases, metadata, and other terms associated with this environment. We compare databases with the older file management systems they replaced and describe several important advantages that are enabled by the carefully planned use of databases. We describe typical database applications and their characteristics for personal computers, workgroups, departments, and the entire enterprise. We also describe several typical costs and risks associated with the database environment. We describe the major components of the database environment, which are all described in greater detail later in the text. Finally, we provide a brief history of the evolution of database systems and the forces that have driven (and continue to drive) their development. The Pine Valley Furniture Company case is introduced and used to illustrate many of the principles and concepts of database management. This case is used in subsequent chapters as a continuing example of the use of database management.

Chapter 2 (Database Development Process) describes the general steps followed in the analysis, design, implementation, and administration of databases. This chapter also describes how the database development process fits into the overall information systems development process. We introduce enterprise data modeling, which sets the range and general contents of organizational databases, and is therefore often the first step in database development. We also present the concept of an information systems architecture that may be used as a blueprint for information systems in organizations. We describe and illustrate information engineering, which is a data-oriented methodology to create and maintain information systems.

We describe and illustrate the systems development life cycle in this chapter, as well as the alternative use of prototyping, which is an iterative development process. We describe the importance and use of computer-aided software engineering (CASE) tools and a repository in the information systems development process. We introduce the concept of schemas and a three-schema architecture, which is the dominant approach in modern database systems. Finally, we describe the roles of the various persons who are typically involved in a database development project.

It is essential that you understand clearly the various concepts and definitions that are presented in the chapters in Part I, because these concepts and definitions are used throughout the remainder of the text. You should answer a number of the review questions and exercises, and ask your instructor to clarify any concepts that remain unclear.

The Database Environment

After studying this chapter, you should be able to:

■ Define the following key terms: **database**, **data**, **information**, **metadata**, **enterprise data model**, **database application**, **data warehouse**, **data independence**, **repository**, **user view**, and **constraint**.

■ Explain why databases will continue to grow in number and into the next century.

■ Name several limitations of conventional file processing systems.

■ Identify four categories of databases, and several key decisions that must be made for each category.

■ Explain at least six advantages of the database approach, compared to traditional file processing.

■ Identify several costs and risks of the database approach.

■ List and briefly describe nine components of a typical database environment.

■ Briefly describe the evolution of database systems.

INTRODUCTION

The past two decades have witnessed enormous growth in the number and importance of database applications. Databases are used to store, manipulate, and retrieve data in nearly every type of organization including business, health care, education, government, and libraries. Database technology is routinely used by individuals on personal computers, by workgroups accessing databases on network servers, and by all employees using enterprise-wide distributed applications.

Following this period of rapid growth, will the demand for databases and database technology level off? Certainly not. In the highly competitive environment of the late 1990s there is every indication that database technology will assume even greater importance. Managers are seeking to use knowledge derived from databases for competitive advantage. For example, detailed sales databases can be mined to determine customer buying patterns as a basis for advertising and marketing campaigns. Many organizations today are building separate databases, called "data warehouses," for this type of decision support application (Lambert, 1996).

Although the future of databases is assured, much work remains to be done. Many organizations have a proliferation of incompatible databases that were developed to meet immediate needs, rather than based on a planned strategy or a well-managed evolution. Much of the data are trapped in older, "legacy" systems, and the data are often of poor quality. New skills are required to design data warehouses, and there is a critical shortage of skills in areas such as database analysis, database design, data administration, and database administration. We address these and other important issues in this textbook.

A course in database management has emerged as one of the most important courses in the information systems curriculum today. As an information systems professional, you must be prepared to analyze database requirements and design and implement databases within the context of information systems development. You must be prepared as well to consult with end users and show them how they can use databases (or data warehouses) to build decision support systems and executive information systems for competitive advantage.

In this chapter we introduce the basic concepts of databases and database management systems (DBMS). We describe traditional file management systems and some of their shortcomings that led to the database approach. We describe the range of database applications, from personal computers to workgroup, departmental, and enterprise databases. Next we consider the benefits, costs, and risks of using the database approach. We conclude the chapter with a summary of the evolution of database systems and of the range of technologies used to build, use, and manage databases. This chapter is intended to serve as a preview of the topics in the remainder of the text.

BASIC CONCEPTS AND DEFINITIONS

Database: An organized collection of logically related data.

We define a **database** as an organized collection of logically related data. A database may be of any size and complexity. For example, a salesperson may maintain a small database of customer contacts on her laptop computer that consists of a few megabytes of data. A large corporation may build a very large database consisting of several terabytes of data (a *terabyte* is a trillion bytes) on a large mainframe computer that is used for decision support applications (Winter, 1997). (We assume throughout the text that all databases are computer-based.)

Data

Historically, the term *data* referred to known facts that could be recorded and stored on computer media. For example in a salesperson's database, the data would include facts such as customer name, address, and telephone number. This definition now needs to be expanded to reflect a new reality. Databases today are used to store objects such as documents, photographic images, sound, and even video segments, in addition to conventional textual and numeric data. For example, the salesperson's database might include a photo image of the customer contact. It might also include a sound recording or video clip of the most recent conversation with the customer. To reflect this reality, we use the following broadened definition: **Data** consist of facts, text, graphics, images, sound, and video segments that have meaning in the users' environment.

Data: Facts, text, graphics, images, sound, and video segments that have meaning in the users' environment.

We have defined a database as an organized collection of related data. By *organized* we mean that the data are structured so as to be easily stored, manipulated, and retrieved by users. By related we mean that the data describe a domain of interest to a group of users and that the users can use the data to answer questions concerning that domain. For example a database for an automobile repair shop contains data identifying customers (the data items it lists include each customer's name, address, work phone number, home phone number, and preferred credit card number), automobiles belonging to those customers (the data items include make, model, and year), and repair histories for each of those automobiles (e.g., date of service, name of person who worked on vehicle, type of repair performed, and dollar amount of work performed).

Data Versus Information

The terms *data* and *information* are closely related, and in fact are often used interchangeably. However, it is often useful to distinguish between data and information. We define **information** as data that has been processed in such a way that it can increase the knowledge of the person who uses it. For example, consider the following list of facts:

Information: Data that have been processed in such a way as to increase the knowledge of the person who uses the data.

Baker, Kenneth D.	324917628
Doyle, Joan E.	476193248
Finkle, Clive R.	548429344
Lewis, John C.	551742186
McFerran, Debra R.	409723145
Sisneros, Michael	392416582

These facts satisfy our definition of data, but most persons would agree that the data are useless in their present form. Even if we guess that this is a list of persons' names together with their Social Security numbers, the data remain useless since we have no idea what the entries mean. Notice what happens when we place the same data in a context, as shown in Figure 1-1a. By adding a few additional data items and providing some structure, we recognize a class roster for a particular course. This is useful information to some users, such as the course instructor and the registrar's office.

Another way to convert data into information is to summarize it or otherwise process and present it for human interpretation. For example, Figure 1-1b shows summarized student enrollment data presented as graphical information. This information could be used as a basis for deciding whether to add new courses or to hire new faculty members.

In practice, databases today may contain either data or information (or both), according to our definitions. For example, a database may contain an image of the class roster document shown in Figure 1-1a. Also, data are often preprocessed and stored in summarized form in databases that are used for decision support. Throughout this text we use the term *database* without distinguishing its contents as data or information.

Figure 1-1
Converting data to
information

(a) Data in context

(b) Summarized data

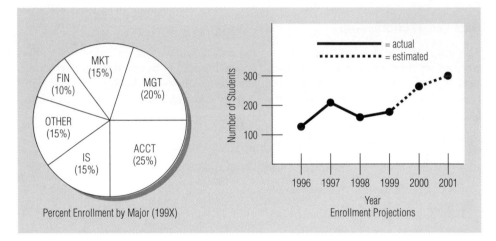

Metadata

As we have indicated, data only become useful when placed in some context. The primary mechanism for providing context for data is metadata. **Metadata** are data that describe the properties or characteristics of other data. Some of these properties include data definitions, data structures, and rules or constraints.

Metadata: Data that describe the properties or characteristics of other data.

Some sample metadata for the Class Roster (Figure 1-1a) are listed in Table 1-1. For each data item that appears in the Class Roster, the metadata show the data item name, the data type, length, minimum and maximum allowable values (where appropriate), and a brief description of each data item. Notice the distinction between data and metadata: Metadata are once removed from data. That is, metadata describe the properties of data but do not include that data. Thus, the metadata shown in Table 1-1 do not include any sample data from the Class Roster of Figure 1-1a. Metadata allow database designers and users to understand what data exist, what the data mean, and what the fine distinctions are between seemingly similar data items. The management of metadata is at least as crucial as managing the associated data since data without clear meaning can be confusing, misinterpreted, or erroneous.

Table 1-1   Example Metadata for Class Roster

| Data Item | | | Value | | |
Name	Type	Length	Min	Max	Description
Course	Alphanumeric	30			Course ID and name
Section	Integer	1	1	9	Section number
Semester	Alphanumeric	10			Semester and year
Name	Alphanumeric	30			Student name
ID	Integer	9			Student ID (SSN)
Major	Alphanumeric	4			Student major
GPA	Decimal	3	0.0	4.0	Student grade point average

TRADITIONAL FILE PROCESSING SYSTEMS

In the beginning of computer-based data processing, there were no databases. Computers that were considerably less powerful than today's personal computer filled large rooms and were used almost exclusively for scientific and engineering calculations. Gradually computers were introduced into the business world. To be useful for business applications, computers must be able to store, manipulate, and retrieve large files of data. Computer file processing systems were developed for this purpose. Although these systems have evolved over time, their basic structure and purpose have changed little over several decades.

As business applications became more complex, it became evident that traditional file processing systems had a number of shortcomings and limitations (described below). As a result, these systems have been replaced by database processing systems in most critical business applications today. Nevertheless, you should have at least some familiarity with file processing systems for the following reasons:

1. File processing systems are still widely used today, especially for backing up database systems.

2. Understanding the problems and limitations inherent in file processing systems can help us avoid these same problems when designing database systems.

In the remainder of this section we describe file processing systems and discuss their limitations by means of a realistic case example. In the next section we use the same case example to introduce and compare database processing systems.

File Processing Systems at Pine Valley Furniture Company

Pine Valley Furniture Company manufactures high-quality, all-wood furniture and distributes it to retail stores nationwide. Among the firm's several product lines are computer desks, entertainment centers, dinette sets, bookcases, and wall units. Customers submit orders to Pine Valley Furniture by any of several means: telephone, mail, fax, or electronic forms via the Internet. The company employs a total of about 100 persons at the present time and is experiencing rapid growth.

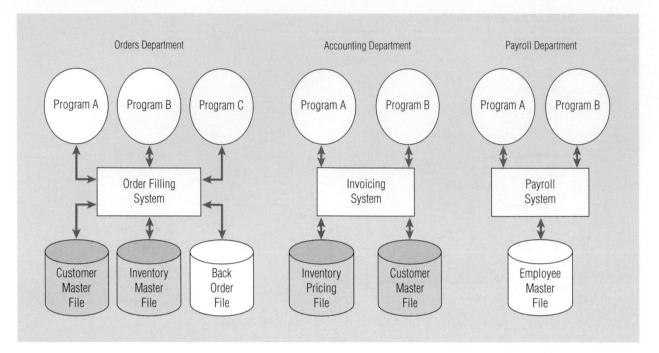

Figure 1-2
Three file processing systems at Pine Valley Furniture

Early computer applications at Pine Valley Furniture used the traditional file processing approach. This approach to information systems design focused on the data processing needs of individual departments, instead of evaluating the overall information needs of the organization. The information systems group typically responds to users' requests for new systems by developing (or acquiring) new computer programs for individual applications such as inventory control, accounts receivable, or human resource management. Each application program or system that is developed is designed to meet the needs of the particular requesting department or user group. Thus there is no overall map, plan, or model to guide the growth of applications.

Three of the computer applications based on the file processing approach are shown in Figure 1-2. The systems illustrated are Order Filling, Invoicing, and Payroll. The figure also shows the major data files associated with each application. A *file* is a collection of related records. For example, the Order Filling System has three files: Customer Master, Inventory Master, and Back Order. Notice that there is duplication of some of the files used by the three applications, which is typical of file processing systems.

Disadvantages of File Processing Systems

Several disadvantages are associated with conventional file processing systems. These disadvantages are listed in Table 1-2 and described briefly below.

Program-Data Dependence   File descriptions are stored within each application program that accesses a given file. For example, in the Invoicing System in Figure 1-2, Program A accesses both the Inventory Pricing File and the Customer Master File.

Table 1-2 Disadvantages of File-Processing Systems

Program-data dependence

Duplication of data

Limited data sharing

Lengthy development times

Excessive program maintenance

Therefore, this program contains a detailed file description for both of these files. As a consequence, any change to a file structure requires changes to the file descriptions for all programs that access the file.

Notice in Figure 1-2 that the Customer Master File is used in both the Order Filling System and the Invoicing System. Suppose it is decided to change the customer address field length in the records in this file from 30 to 40 characters. The file descriptions in each program that is affected (up to five programs) would have to be modified. It is often difficult even to locate all programs affected by such changes. What is worse, errors are often introduced when making changes.

Duplication of Data   Since applications are often developed independently in file processing systems, unplanned duplicate data files are the rule rather than the exception. For example, in Figure 1-2 the Order Filling System contains an Inventory Master File, while the Invoicing System contains an Inventory Pricing File. These files undoubtedly both contain data describing Pine Valley Furniture Company's products, such as product description, unit price, and quantity on hand. This duplication is wasteful since it requires additional storage space and increased effort to keep all files up to date. Unfortunately, duplicate data files often result in loss of data integrity since either the data formats may be inconsistent or data values may not agree (or both). Such unplanned and uncontrolled redundancy also can lead to loss of metadata integrity. For example, the same data item may have different names in different files, or conversely the same name may be used for different data items in different files.

Limited Data Sharing   With the traditional file processing approach, each application has its own private files and users have little opportunity to share data outside their own applications. Notice in Figure 1-2, for example, that users in the Accounting Department have access to the Invoicing System and its files, but they probably do not have access to the Order Filling System or the Payroll System and their files. It is often frustrating to managers to find that a requested report will require a major programming effort to obtain data from several incompatible files in separate systems. In addition, a major management effort may also be required since different organizational units may own these different files.

Lengthy Development Times   With traditional file processing systems, there is little opportunity to leverage previous development efforts. Each new application requires that the developer essentially start from scratch by designing new file formats and descriptions, and then writing the file access logic for each new program. The lengthy development times required are often inconsistent with today's fast-paced business environment, in which time to market (or time to production for an information system) is a key business success factor.

Excessive Program Maintenance   The preceding factors all combine to create a heavy program maintenance load in organizations that rely on traditional file processing systems. In fact, as much as 80 percent of the total information systems development budget may be devoted to program maintenance in such organizations. This of course leaves little opportunity for developing new applications.

It is important to note that many of the disadvantages of file processing we have mentioned can also be limitations of databases if an organization does not properly apply the database approach. For example, if an organization develops many separately managed databases (say, one for each department or business function) with little or no coordination of the metadata, then uncontrolled data duplication, limited data sharing, lengthy development time, and excessive program maintenance can occur. Thus, the database approach, which is explained in the next section, is as much a way to manage organizational data as it is a set of technology for defining, creating, maintaining, and using these data.

THE DATABASE APPROACH

The database approach emphasizes the integration and sharing of data throughout the organization (or at least across major segments of the organization). This approach requires a fundamental reorientation or shift in thought process, starting with top management. Such a reorientation is difficult for most organizations; still, many are making this shift today and learning that information can be used as a competitive weapon.

The Database Approach at Pine Valley Furniture Company

By the early 1990s competition in furniture manufacturing had intensified, and competitors seemed to respond more rapidly than Pine Valley Furniture to new business opportunities. While there were many reasons for this trend, managers felt that the computer information systems they had been using (based on traditional file processing) had become outmoded. The company started a development effort that eventually led to adopting a database approach for the company. This approach is described briefly in this chapter and in greater detail in Chapter 2.

Enterprise Data Model   Pine Valley Furniture Company's first step in converting to a database approach was to develop a list of the high-level entities that support the business activities of the organization. An *entity* is an object or concept that is important to the business. Some of the high-level entities identified at Pine Valley Furniture are the following: CUSTOMER, PRODUCT, EMPLOYEE, CUSTOMER ORDER, and DEPARTMENT.

After these entities were identified and defined, the company proceeded to develop an enterprise data model. An **enterprise data model** is a graphical model that shows the high-level entities for the organization and associations among those entities. A segment of the enterprise data model containing four entities and three pertinent associations is shown in Figure 1-3. The entities shown in this model segment are the following:

Enterprise data model: A graphical model that shows the high-level entities for the organization and the relationships among those entities.

- CUSTOMER   People and organizations that buy or may potentially buy products from Pine Valley Furniture

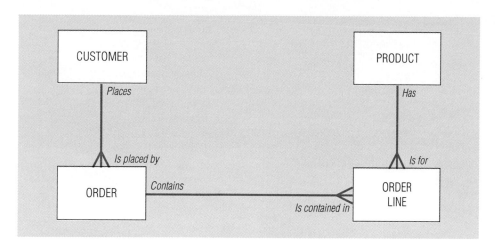

Figure 1-3
Segment from enterprise
data model (Pine Valley
Furniture Company)

- CUSTOMER ORDER   The purchase of one or more products by a customer

- PRODUCT   The items Pine Valley Furniture makes and sells

- ORDER LINE   Details about each product sold on a particular customer order (such as quantity and price)

The three associations (called *relationships* in database terminology) shown in the figure (represented by the three lines connecting entities) capture three fundamental business rules, as follows:

1. Each CUSTOMER *Places* any number of CUSTOMER ORDERs. Conversely, each CUSTOMER ORDER *Is placed by* exactly one CUSTOMER.

2. Each CUSTOMER ORDER *Contains* any number of ORDER LINEs. Conversely, each ORDER LINE *Is contained in* exactly one CUSTOMER ORDER.

3. Each PRODUCT *Has* any number of ORDER LINEs. Conversely, each ORDER LINE *Is for* exactly one PRODUCT.

The type of diagram shown in Figure 1-3 is referred to as an *entity-relationship diagram*. Entity-relationship (or E-R) diagrams are of such importance in database applications that we devote two chapters (3 and 4) to this type of model. Chapter 3 describes basic E-R diagrams, while Chapter 4 describes enhanced E-R diagrams. Both of these chapters also describe the various types of business rules and how they are captured and modeled.

Notice the following characteristics of the enterprise data model:

1. It is a model of the organization that provides valuable information about how the organization functions, as well as important constraints.

2. The enterprise data model stresses the *integration* of data and processes by focusing on entities, relationships, and business rules.

Relational Databases   The results of preliminary studies convinced management of the potential advantages of the database approach. The company decided to implement a modern relational database management system that views all data in the form of tables (we describe relational databases in Chapter 6). Figure 1-4 shows the following four tables with sample data: Customer, Product, Order, and Order_Line.

Figure 1-4
Four relations (Pine Valley
Furniture Company)

(a) Order and Order_Line
tables

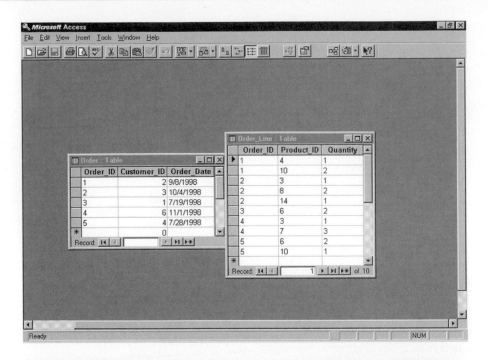

(b) Product and Customer
tables

Notice that these tables represent the four entities shown in the enterprise data model (Figure 1-3).

Each column of a table represents an attribute (or characteristic) of an entity. For example, the attributes shown for Customer are Customer_ID, Customer_Name, Address, City, State, and Postal_Code. Each row of a table represents an instance (or occurrence) of the entity. An important property of the relational model is that it represents relationships between entities by values stored in the columns of the corresponding tables. For example, notice that Customer_ID is an attribute of both the

Customer table and the Order table. As a result, we can easily link an order to its associated customer. For example, we can determine that Order_ID 3 is associated with Customer_ID 1. Can you determine which Product_IDs are associated with Order_ID 2? In subsequent chapters, you will learn how to retrieve data from these tables by using a powerful query language that exploits these linkages.

Implementing the Relational Databases   The database approach offers a number of potential advantages compared to the older file processing systems. However, few of these advantages will be realized if the organization simply implements a series of stand-alone databases, since this approach does not permit sharing of data by various members of the organization. In fact, stand-alone databases exhibit many of the same disadvantages common to file processing systems.

To facilitate data sharing, Pine Valley Furniture Company installed a local area network that links the personal computers in the various departments to a database server, as shown in Figure 1-5. When the Sales Department receives a new customer order, for example, the order is captured and entered into this database. An accountant can view the most recent monthly financial statements by querying the portion of the database that contains financial information.

Although the database quite adequately supports daily operations at Pine Valley Furniture Company, managers soon learned that the same database is often inadequate for decision support applications. For example, following are some types of questions that cannot be easily answered:

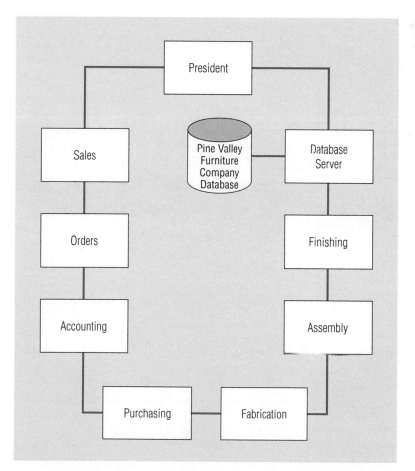

Figure 1-5
Client/server system for Pine Valley Furniture Company

1. What is the pattern of furniture sales this year, compared to the same period last year?

2. Who are our 10 largest customers, and what are their buying patterns?

3. What types of furniture tend to be sold together (for example, tables with chairs)?

To answer these and other questions, an organization often needs to build a separate database that contains historical and summarized information. Such a database is usually called a *data warehouse,* or in some cases a *data mart.* Also, analysts need specialized decision support tools to query and analyze the database. One class of tools used for this purpose is called *on-line analytical processing* (or *OLAP*) tools. We describe data warehouses, data marts, and related decision support tools in Chapter 14.

Database application:
An application program (or set of related programs) that is used to perform a series of database activities (create, read, update, and delete) on behalf of database users.

A Database Application   A **database application** is an application program (or set of related programs) that is used to perform a series of activities on behalf of database users. Each database application performs some combination of the following basic operations:

1. *Create*   Add new data to the database.

2. *Read*   Read current database data (often presented in a useful format on a computer screen or on a printed report).

3. *Update*   Update (or modify) current database data.

4. *Delete*   Delete current data from the database.

Figure 1-6
Customer invoice (Pine Valley Furniture Company)

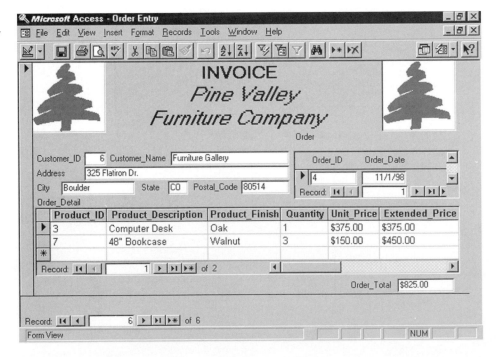

One of the important database applications at Pine Valley Furniture creates a customer invoice. When an order is ready to be shipped to a customer, an invoice is prepared that summarizes the items included on the order and computes the total dollar amount due for the order. A typical customer invoice is shown in Figure 1-6. Unless the original order has changed, the invoice is prepared automatically from data stored in the database (see Figure 1-4).

THE RANGE OF DATABASE APPLICATIONS

Databases range from those for a single user with a desktop computer to those on mainframe computers with thousands of users. The range of database applications can be divided into four categories, from simplest to most complex: personal computer (or PC) databases, workgroup databases, department databases, and enterprise databases. We introduce each category with a typical example, followed by some issues that generally arise within the category of use.

Personal Computer Databases

Personal computer (PC) databases are designed to support one user with a standalone personal computer (for example, a desktop or laptop computer). For example, consider a company that has a number of salespersons who call on actual or prospective customers. Each salesperson might carry a laptop computer with a simple database application to record customer information and the details of contacts with each customer. A typical user view of data from that application is shown in Figure 1-7.

Some of the key decisions that must be made in developing personal computer databases are the following:

1. Should the application be purchased from an outside vendor or developed within the organization?

2. If the database application is developed internally, should it be developed by the end user or by a professional within the information systems (IS) department?

3. What data are required by the user and how should the database be designed?

4. What commercial DBMS product should be used for the application?

5. How should data in the personal computer database be synchronized with data in other databases?

6. Who is responsible for the accuracy of the data in the personal computer database?

Personal computer databases are widely used because they can often improve personal productivity. However, they entail a risk: the data cannot easily be shared with other users. For example, suppose the sales manager wants a consolidated view of customer contacts. This cannot be quickly or easily provided from an individual salesperson's databases. This illustrates a very common problem: if data are of interest to one person, they probably are (or will soon become) of interest to others as well. For this reason, personal computer databases should be limited to those rather special situations (such as in a very small organization) where the need to share the data among users of the personal computer database is unlikely to arise.

Figure 1-7
Typical data from a personal
computer database

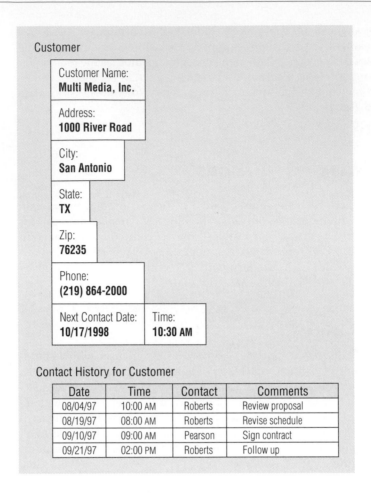

Customer

Customer Name:
Multi Media, Inc.

Address:
1000 River Road

City:
San Antonio

State:
TX

Zip:
76235

Phone:
(219) 864-2000

Next Contact Date: Time:
10/17/1998   **10:30 AM**

Contact History for Customer

Date	Time	Contact	Comments
08/04/97	10:00 AM	Roberts	Review proposal
08/19/97	08:00 AM	Roberts	Revise schedule
09/10/97	09:00 AM	Pearson	Sign contract
09/21/97	02:00 PM	Roberts	Follow up

Workgroup Databases

A *workgroup* is a relatively small team of people who collaborate on the same project or application or on a group of similar projects or applications. A workgroup typically comprises fewer than 25 persons. These persons might be engaged (for example) with a construction project or with developing a new computer application. A workgroup database is designed to support the collaborative efforts of such a team.

Consider a workgroup that develops both standard and custom objects (or software components) that are sold to software vendors as well as to end users. Table 1-3 is a list of some of the software objects that have been developed recently. Typically one or more persons work on a given object or component at a given time. The group needs a database that will track each item as it is developed and allow the data to be easily shared by the team members.

The method of sharing the data in this database is shown in Figure 1-8. Each member of the workgroup has a desktop computer and the computers are linked by means of a local area network (LAN). The database is stored on a central device called the *database server*, which is also connected to the network. Thus each member of the workgroup has access to the shared data. Different types of group member (e.g., developer or project manager) may have different user views of this shared database. Notice that this arrangement overcomes the principal objection to PC databases, which is that the data are not easily shared (at least data are easily shared

Table 1-3 List of Software Objects in an Example Workgroup Database

Object Place, Inc. 400 Magnolia St. Atlanta, GA 02103			
Name	**Language**	**Description**	**Price**
123Xtender	Visual Basic	Spreadsheet wrapper	595
DSSObjects	C++	Decision support generator	595
ObjectSuite	Smalltalk	Set of 6 generic objects	5000
OrderObject	Smalltalk	Generic order object	1000
PatientObject	Smalltalk	Generic patient object	1000

within the workgroup). This arrangement, however, introduces many data management issues not present with personal computer (single-user) databases, such as data security and data integrity with concurrent user data updating. Also, since an organization is composed of many workgroups, and an individual may be part of many different workgroups at the same or different times, it is possible to generate many databases, just as in the situation of personal computer databases.

In establishing a workgroup database, the organization must answer the same questions that applied to personal computer databases. In addition, the following database management questions arise:

1. How can the design of the database be optimized for a variety of group members' information requirements?

2. How can the various members use the database concurrently without compromising the integrity of the database?

3. Which database processing operations should be performed at a workstation and which should occur on the server?

Figure 1-8
Workgroup database with local area network

Figure 1-9

An example departmental
database (Personnel
Department)

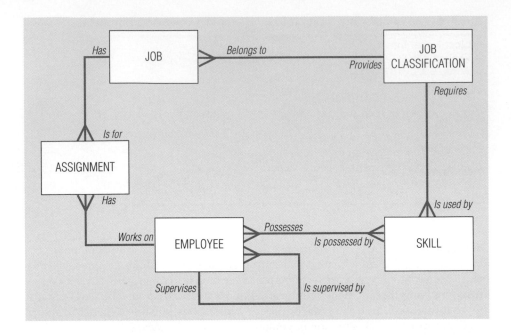

Department Databases

A *department* is a functional unit within an organization. Typical examples of departments are personnel, marketing, manufacturing, and accounting. A department is
generally larger than a workgroup (typically between 25 and 100 persons) and is
responsible for a more diverse range of functions.

   Department databases are designed to support the various functions and activities of a department. They are the most common of the four types of databases
described in this section. For example, consider a personnel database that is designed
to track data concerning employees, jobs, skills, and job assignments. A simplified
diagram of this database is shown in Figure 1-9. With the data entities and relationships shown in this diagram, users can query the database to obtain answers to questions such as the following:

1. For a particular job classification (such as Software Engineer), what job opportunities exist in the company at the present time?

2. For that same job classification, what skill (or skills) are required?

3. What skills are possessed by a particular employee? Conversely, which
   employees possess a particular skill (such as C++ programming)?

4. Which employees have held a particular job assignment? Conversely, what is
   the job history for a particular employee?

5. Which employees are supervised by a particular manager?

   Typical questions that must be addressed when designing and implementing
department databases (besides those already described) include the following:

1. How can the database and its environment be designed to produce adequate
   performance, given the large number of users and user transactions?

2. How can adequate security be provided to protect against unauthorized disclosure or distribution of sensitive data?

3. What database and application development tools should be used in this complex environment?

4. Do other departments maintain the same type of data, and if so, how can data redundancy and consistency of data and metadata best be managed?

5. Are the users of the database geographically dispersed or the size of the database so great that data must be stored on several computer systems, thus creating a *distributed database?*

Enterprise Databases

An enterprise database is one whose scope is the entire organization or enterprise (or, at least, many different departments). Such databases are intended to support organization-wide operations and decision making. Note that an organization may have several enterprise databases, so such a database is not inclusive of all organizational data. A single, operational, enterprise database is impractical for many medium to large organizations due to difficulties in performance for very large databases, diverse needs of different users, and the complexity of achieving a single definition of data (metadata) for all database users. An enterprise database does, however, support information needs from many departments. Arguably the most important type of enterprise database today is called a data warehouse. A **data warehouse** is an integrated decision support database whose content is derived from the various operational databases (such as personal computer, workgroup, and department databases). We describe data warehouses in detail in Chapter 14.

Data warehouse: An integrated decision support database whose content is derived from the various operational databases.

Consider a large health care organization that operates a group of medical centers including hospitals, clinics, and nursing homes. As shown in Figure 1-10, each of these medical centers has a separate database (or databases) to support the various operations at that facility. These databases contain data concerning patients, physicians, medical services, business operations, and other related entities.

The databases provide adequate support for most functions at each individual medical center. However, the organization has increasingly realized the need for a single, consolidated view of the entire organization; for example, to see the total activities with a single patient or supplier. This body of data (and information) is required for a variety of reasons: corporate decision making, dealing with external suppliers (such as insurance companies), and reporting to various agencies. To satisfy these requirements, the organization has created a data warehouse that is maintained at the corporate office. Data in the data warehouse are derived by extracting and summarizing data from the individual databases on a periodic basis and transmitting those data by means of a telecommunications network to the corporate data warehouse.

Several questions that often arise in the context of an enterprise database are the following:

1. How should the data be distributed among the various locations in the corporate structure?

2. How can the organization develop and maintain standards concerning data names, definitions, formats, and related issues?

Figure 1-10
An enterprise data
warehouse

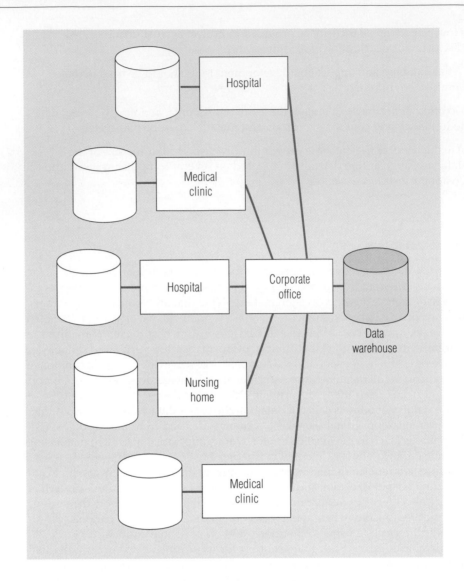

Summary of Database Applications

A summary of the various types of database applications that we have described in this section is shown in Table 1-4. For each type of database, the table shows the typical number of users, the typical database architecture (client/server architectures explained in Chapter 8), and the typical range of database size.

ADVANTAGES OF THE DATABASE APPROACH

The database approach offers a number of potential advantages compared to traditional file processing systems. The primary advantages are summarized in Table 1-5 and described below.

Table 1-4 Summary of Database Applications (adapted from White, 1995)

Type of Database	Typical Number of Users	Typical Architecture	Typical Size of Database
Personal computer	1	Desktop computer	Megabytes
Workgroup	5–25	Client/server (two-tier)	Megabytes–gigabytes
Department	25–100	Client/server (three-tier)	Gigabytes
Enterprise	>100	Client/server (distributed or parallel server)	Gigabytes–terabytes

Program–Data Independence

The separation of data descriptions (metadata) from the application programs that use the data is called **data independence**. With the database approach, data descriptions are stored in a central location called the *repository*. This property of database systems allows an organization's data to change and evolve (within limits) without changing the application programs that process the data.

Data independence: The separation of data descriptions from the application programs that use the data.

Minimal Data Redundancy

The design goal with the database approach is that previously separate (and redundant) data files are integrated into a single, logical structure. Each primary fact is recorded (ideally) in only one place in the database. For example, the fact that the product with Product_ID 3 is an oak computer desk with a unit price of $375.00 is recorded in one place in the Product table (see Figure 1-4a). The database approach does not eliminate redundancy entirely, but it allows the designer to carefully control the type and amount of redundancy. For example, each order in the Order table (Figure 1-4b) contains a Customer_ID to represent the relationship between orders and customers. At other times it may be desirable to include some limited redundancy to improve database performance, as we will see in later chapters.

Table 1-5 Advantages of the Database Approach

Program-data independence

Minimal data redundancy

Improved data consistency

Improved data sharing

Increased productivity of application development

Enforcement of standards

Improved data quality

Improved data accessibility and responsiveness

Reduced program maintenance

Improved Data Consistency

By eliminating (or controlling) data redundancy, we greatly reduce the opportunities for inconsistency. For example, if a customer address is stored only once, we cannot have disagreement on the stored values. Also, updating data values is greatly simplified when each value is stored in one place only. Finally, we avoid the wasted storage space that results from redundant data storage.

Improved Data Sharing

A database is designed as a shared corporate resource. Authorized users are granted permission to use the database, and each user (or group of users) is provided one or more user views to facilitate this use. A **user view** is a logical description of some portion of the database that is required by a user to perform some task. For example, each table in the Pine Valley Furniture database (Figure 1-4) can constitute a user view. However, a user view is often a form or report that comprises data from more than one table. For example, the customer invoice (Figure 1-6) also is a user view of the same database.

User view: A logical description of some portion of the database that is required by a user to perform some task.

Increased Productivity of Application Development

A major advantage of the database approach is that it greatly reduces the cost and time for developing new business applications. There are two important reasons that database applications can often be developed much more rapidly than conventional file applications:

1. Assuming that the database and the related data capture and maintenance applications have already been designed and implemented, the programmer can concentrate on the specific functions required for the new application, without having to worry about file design or low-level implementation details.

2. The database management system provides a number of high-level productivity tools such as forms and report generators and high-level languages that automate some of the activities of database design and implementation. We describe many of these tools in subsequent chapters.

Enforcement of Standards

When the database approach is implemented with full management support, the database administration function should be granted single-point authority and responsibility for establishing and enforcing data standards. These standards will include naming conventions, data quality standards, and uniform procedures for accessing, updating, and protecting data. The data repository provides database administrators with a powerful set of tools for developing and enforcing these standards. Unfortunately, the failure to implement a strong database administration function is perhaps the most common source of database failures in organizations. We describe the database administration (and related data administration) functions in Chapter 13.

Improved Data Quality

Concern with poor quality of data is a common theme in database administration today (Redman, 1995). The database approach provides a number of tools and processes to improve data quality. Two of the more important are the following:

1. Database designers can specify integrity constraints that are enforced by the DBMS. A **constraint** is a rule that cannot be violated by database users. We describe numerous types of constraints (also called business rules) in Chapters 3 and 4.

2. One of the objectives of a data warehouse environment is to clean up (or "scrub") operational data before they are placed in the data warehouse (Jordan, 1996). We describe data warehouses and the potential for improving data quality in Chapter 14.

Constraint: A rule that cannot be violated by database users.

Improved Data Accessibility and Responsiveness

With a relational database, end users without programming experience can often retrieve and display data, even when it crosses traditional departmental boundaries. For example, an employee can display information about computer desks at Pine Valley Furniture Company with the following query:

```
SELECT *
FROM PRODUCT
WHERE Product_Name = "Computer Desk";
```

The language used in this query is called Structured Query Language, or SQL (you will study this language in detail in Chapter 9).

Reduced Program Maintenance

Stored data must be changed frequently for a variety of reasons: new data item types are added, data formats are changed, and so on. A celebrated (or rather dreaded) example of this problem results from the well-known "year 2000" problem, in which common two-digit year fields will have to be extended to four digits to accommodate the rollover from the year 1999 to the year 2000.

In a file processing environment, the descriptions of data and the logic for accessing data are built into individual application programs (this is the program-data dependence issue described earlier). As a result, changes to data formats and access methods inevitably result in the need to modify application programs. In a database environment, data are more independent of the application programs that use them. Within limits, we can change either the data or the application programs that use the data without necessitating a change in the other factor. As a result, program maintenance can be significantly reduced in a modern database environment.

Cautions About Database Benefits

This section has identified nine major potential benefits of the database approach. However, we must caution you that many organizations have been frustrated in attempting to realize some of these benefits. For example, the goal of data independence (and therefore reduced program maintenance) has proven elusive due to the limitations of older data models and database management software. Fortunately, the relational model (as well as the newer object-oriented model) provide a significantly better environment for achieving these benefits. Another reason for failure to achieve the intended benefits is poor organizational planning and database implementation—even the best data management software cannot overcome such deficiencies. For this reason, we stress database planning and design in this text.

COSTS AND RISKS OF THE DATABASE APPROACH

As with any business decision, the database approach entails some additional costs and risks that must be recognized and managed when implementing this approach (see Table 1-6).

New, Specialized Personnel

Frequently, organizations that adopt the database approach need to hire or train individuals to design and implement databases, provide database administration services, and manage a staff of new people. Further, because of the rapid changes in technology these new people will have to be retrained or upgraded on a regular basis. This personnel increase may be more than offset by other productivity gains, and an organization should not minimize the need for these specialized skills, which are required to obtain the most from the potential benefits. We discuss the staff requirements for database management in Chapter 13.

Installation and Management Cost and Complexity

A multiuser database management system is a large and complex suite of software that has a high initial cost, requires a staff of trained personnel to install and operate, and also has substantial annual maintenance and support costs. Installing such a system may also require upgrades to the hardware and data communications systems in the organization. Substantial training is normally required on an ongoing basis to keep up with new releases and upgrades. Additional or more sophisticated and costly database software may be needed to provide security and to ensure proper concurrent updating of shared data.

Table 1-6   Costs and Risks of the Database Approach

New, specialized personnel
Installation and management cost and complexity
Conversion costs
Need for explicit backup and recovery
Organizational conflict

Conversion Costs

The term *legacy systems* is widely used to refer to older applications in an organization that are based on file processing and/or older database technology. The cost of converting these older systems to modern database technology—measured in terms of dollars, time, and organizational commitment—may often seem prohibitive to an organization. As will be shown in Chapter 14, the use of data warehouses is one strategy for continuing to use older systems while at the same time exploiting modern database technology and techniques.

Need for Explicit Backup and Recovery

A shared corporate database must be accurate and available at all times. This requires that comprehensive procedures be developed and used for providing backup copies of data and for restoring a database when damage occurs. A modern database management system normally automates many more of the backup and recovery tasks than a file system. We describe procedures for security, backup, and recovery in Chapter 13.

Organizational Conflict

A shared database requires a consensus on data definitions and ownership as well as responsibilities for accurate data maintenance. Experience has shown that conflicts on data definitions, data formats and coding, rights to update shared data, and associated issues are frequent and often difficult to resolve. Handling these issues requires organizational commitment to the database approach, organizationally astute database administrators, and a sound evolutionary approach to database development.

If strong top management support of and commitment to the database approach is lacking, end-user development of stand-alone databases is likely to proliferate. These databases do not follow the general database approach that we have described, and they are unlikely to provide the benefits described earlier.

COMPONENTS OF THE DATABASE ENVIRONMENT

The major components of a typical database environment and their relationships are shown in Figure 1-11. You have already been introduced to some (but not all) of these components in previous sections. Following is a brief description of the nine components shown in Figure 1-11.

1. **Computer-aided software engineering (CASE) tools**   Automated tools used to design databases and application programs. We describe the use of CASE tools for database design and development throughout the text.

2. **Repository**   Centralized storehouse for all data definitions, data relationships, screen and report formats, and other system components. A repository contains an extended set of metadata important for managing databases as well as other components of an information system. We describe the repository in Chapter 13.

Repository: A centralized knowledge base of all data definitions, data relationships, screen and report formats, and other system components.

Figure 1-11

Components of the database environment

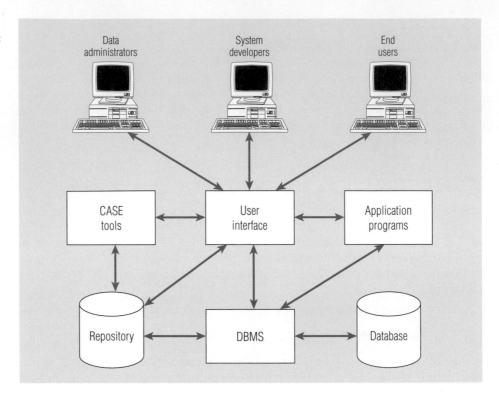

Database management system (DBMS): A software application that is used to create, maintain, and provide controlled access to user databases.

3. **Database management system (DBMS)**   Commercial software (and occasionally, hardware and firmware) system used to define, create, maintain, and provide controlled access to the database and also to the repository. We describe the functions of a DBMS in Chapters 11 and 13.

4. **Database**   An organized collection of logically related data, usually designed to meet the information needs of multiple users in an organization. It is important to distinguish between the database and the repository. The repository contains *definitions* of data, whereas the database contains *occurrences* of data. We describe the activities of database design in Chapters 3–7 and of implementation in Chapters 8–12.

5. **Application programs**   Computer programs that are used to create and maintain the database and provide information to users. Key database programming skills are described in Chapters 8 through 12.

6. **User interface**   Languages, menus, and other facilities by which users interact with various system components, such as CASE tools, application programs, the DBMS, and the repository. User interfaces are illustrated throughout this text.

7. **Data administrators**   Persons who are responsible for the overall information resources of an organization. Data administrators use CASE tools to improve the productivity of database planning and design. We describe the functions of data administration in detail in Chapter 13.

8. **System developers**   Persons such as systems analysts and programmers who design new application programs. System developers often use CASE tools for system requirements analysis and program design.

9. **End users**   Persons throughout the organization who add, delete, and modify data in the database and who request or receive information from it. All user interactions with the database must be routed through the DBMS.

With advances in software, the user interface is becoming increasingly user-friendly. Examples of such advances are menu-driven systems, use of a mouse, and voice-recognition systems. These systems promote end-user computing, which means that users who are not computer experts can define their own reports, displays, and simple applications. Of course, in such an environment, database administration must ensure the enforcement of adequate security measures to protect the database.

In summary, the DBMS operational environment shown in Figure 1-11 is an integrated system of hardware, software, and people that is designed to facilitate the storage, retrieval, and control of the information resource and to improve the productivity of the organization.

EVOLUTION OF DATABASE SYSTEMS

Database management systems were first introduced during the 1960s and have continued to evolve during subsequent decades. Figure 1-12 sketches this evolution by highlighting the database technology (or technologies) that tended to be in the forefront during each decade. In most cases the period of introduction was quite long, and the technology was first introduced during the decade preceding the one shown in the figure. For example, the relational model was first defined by E. F. Codd, an IBM research fellow, in a paper published in 1970 (Codd, 1970). However, the relational model did not realize widespread commercial success until the 1980s.

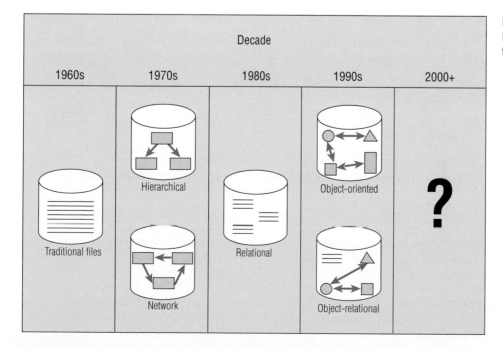

Figure 1-12
Evolution of database technologies

Database management systems were developed to overcome the limitations of file processing systems, described in a previous section. To summarize, some combination of the following three objectives always drove the development and evolution of database technology:

1. The need to provide greater independence between programs and data, thereby reducing maintenance costs

2. The desire to manage increasingly complex data types and structures

3. The desire to provide easier and faster access to data for users who have neither a background in programming languages nor a detailed understanding of how data are stored in databases

1960s

File processing systems were still dominant during this period. However, the first database management systems were introduced during that decade and were used primarily for large and complex ventures such as the Apollo moon-landing project. We can regard this as an experimental "proof-of-concept" period in which the feasibility of managing vast amounts of data with a DBMS was demonstrated. Also, the first efforts at standardization were taken with the formation of the Data Base Task Group in the late 1960s.

1970s

During this decade the use of database management systems became a commercial reality. The hierarchical and network database management systems were developed largely to cope with increasingly complex data structures such as manufacturing bills of materials that were extremely difficult to manage with conventional file processing methods. The hierarchical and network models are generally regarded as first-generation DBMS. Both approaches were widely used, and in fact many of these systems continue to be used today. However, there are some major disadvantages:

1. Difficult access to data, based on navigational record-at-a-time procedures. As a result, complex programs have to be written to answer even simple queries.

2. Very limited data independence, so that programs are not insulated from changes to data formats

3. No widely accepted theoretical foundation for either model, unlike the relational data model

We present a brief introduction to the hierarchical and network models in Appendix D, which is available on the Web at http://hepg.awl.com—keyword: McFadden.

1980s

To overcome these limitations, E. F. Codd and others developed the relational data model during the 1970s. This model, considered second-generation DBMS, received widespread commercial acceptance and diffusion during the 1980s. With the relational model, all data are represented in the form of tables. A relatively simple fourth-generation language called SQL (for Structured Query Language) is used for data retrieval. Thus the relational model provides ease of access for nonprogrammers, overcoming one of the major objections to first-generation systems.

1990s

The decade of the 1990s ushered in a new era of computing, first with client/server computing, then Internet applications becoming increasingly important. Whereas the data managed by a DBMS during the 1980s was largely structured (such as accounting data), multimedia data (including graphics, sound, images, and video) became increasingly common during the 1990s. To cope with these increasingly complex data, object-oriented databases (considered third generation) were introduced during the late 1980s. These databases are becoming increasingly important during the 1990s (David, 1997). We describe object-oriented databases in detail in Chapter 12 and how to model these databases in Chapter 5.

Since organizations must manage a vast amount of both structured and unstructured data, both relational and object-oriented databases are of great importance today. In fact, some vendors are developing combined object-relational DBMSs that can manage both types of data. We describe object-relational databases in Appendix A.

2000 and Beyond

We are naturally led to speculate what directions database technology will take during the next decade. While there will undoubtedly be some surprises, we can expect several well-established trends to continue:

1. The ability to manage increasingly complex data types. These types include multidimensional data, which have already assumed considerable importance in data warehouse applications. We discuss multidimensional data in Chapter 14.

2. The continued development of "universal servers." Based on object-relational DBMS, these are database servers that can manage a wide range of data types transparently to users. They will become especially important to Internet applications.

3. Fully distributed databases will become a reality. Thus an organization will be able to physically distribute its databases to multiple locations and update them automatically, transparent to the user community.

4. Content-addressable storage will become more popular. With this approach, users can retrieve data by specifying what data they desire, rather than how to retrieve them. For example, a user can scan a photograph and have the computer search for the closest match to that photo.

5. Database and other technologies, such as artificial intelligence and television-like information services will make database access much easier for untrained users. For example, users will be able to request data in a more natural language, and database technology will anticipate users' data needs based on past queries and relevant database changes.

SUMMARY

The past two decades have witnessed an enormous growth in the number and importance of database applications. Databases are used to store, manipulate, and retrieve data in every type of organization. In the highly competitive environment of the 1990s, there is every indication that database technology will assume even greater importance. A course in modern database management is one of the most important courses in the information systems curriculum.

A database is an organized collection of related data. We define data as known facts or objects that have meaning in the user environment. The term *organized* means that the data are structured so as to be easily stored, manipulated, and retrieved by users. The term *related* means that the data describe a domain of interest to a group of users, and that those users can use the data to answer questions concerning the domain. Information is data that have been placed in a context, or processed and presented in a form suitable for human interpretation.

Metadata are data that describe the properties or characteristics of other data. A database management system is a general-purpose commercial software system used to define, create, maintain, and provide controlled access to the database. A DBMS stores metadata in a repository, which is a central storehouse for all data definitions, data relationships, screen and report formats, and other system components.

Computer file processing systems were developed early in the computer era so that computers could store, manipulate, and retrieve large files of data. These systems (still in use today) have a number of important limitations such as dependence between programs and data, data duplication, limited data sharing, and lengthy development times. The database approach was developed to overcome these limitations. This approach emphasizes the integration and sharing of data across the organization. Advantages of this approach include program-data independence, improved data sharing, minimal data redundancy, and improved productivity of application development.

Database applications can be described in the following categories: personal computer databases, workgroup databases, departmental databases, and enterprise databases. The most important type of enterprise database today is called a data warehouse, which is an integrated decision support database whose content is derived from the various operational databases.

Database technology has evolved steadily since it was first introduced during the 1960s. The major objectives driving this evolution have included the desire to provide greater program-data independence, the need to manage increasingly complex data structures, and the desire to provide faster and easier access to all users. During the decade of the 1990s, both object-oriented and object-relational databases are increasingly being used to satisfy these objectives.

CHAPTER REVIEW

KEY TERMS

Constraint
Data
Data independence
Data warehouse
Database

Database application
Database management
  system (DBMS)
Enterprise data model
Information

Metadata
Repository
User view

REVIEW QUESTIONS

1. Define each of the following key terms:
   a. data
   b. information
   c. metadata
   d. database application
   e. data warehouse
   f. constraint
   g. database

2. Contrast the following terms:
   a. data dependence; data independence
   b. data warehouse; data mining
   c. data; information
   d. repository; database
   e. entity; enterprise data model

3. List and briefly describe four categories of databases and give an example of each type.

4. Why has the definition of data been expanded in today's environment?

5. List the nine major components in a database system environment.

6. How are relationships between tables expressed in a relational database?

7. List some key questions that must typically be answered for each of the following types of databases: personal computer; workgroup; departmental; enterprise.

8. What does the term *data independence* mean and why is it an important goal?

9. List six potential benefits of the database approach compared to conventional file systems.

10. List five additional costs or risks associated with the database approach.

11. For each decade from the 1960s to the 1990s, list the database technology (or technologies) that was dominant. Indicate the generation generally associated with each technology.

PROBLEMS AND EXERCISES

1. Match the following terms and definitions:

   _____ data
   _____ database application
   _____ constraint
   _____ repository
   _____ metadata
   _____ data warehouse
   _____ information
   _____ user view

   a. data placed in a context or summarized
   b. application program(s)
   c. facts, text, graphics, images, etc.
   d. integrated decision support database
   e. organized collection of related data
   f. includes data definitions and constraints
   g. centralized storehouse for all data definitions

_____ data independence

_____ database

h. separation of data descriptions from programs

i. a rule that cannot be violated

j. logical description of portion of database

2. For each of the following, indicate whether (under typical university circumstances) there is a one-to-many or a many-to-many relationship. Then using the shorthand notation introduced in the text, draw a diagram for each of the relationships.

    a. STUDENT and COURSE (students register for courses)

    b. BOOK and BOOK COPY (books have copies)

    c. COURSE and SECTION (courses have sections)

    d. SECTION and ROOM (sections are scheduled in rooms)

    e. INSTRUCTOR and COURSE

3. Refer to Figure 1-4 and answer the following questions:

    a. What order(s) do we have outstanding for Customer_ID 6? (Give the Order_ID and Order_Date.)

    b. What products are included on Order_ID 2? (Give the Product_ID and Quantity for each item.)

    c. What products are included on Order_ID 2? (Give the Product_ID, Product_Name, and Unit_Price for each item.)

4. Examine the personal computer database for customer contacts (Figure 1-7). Is the relationship between CUSTOMER and CONTACT HISTORY one-to-many or many-to-many? Using the shorthand notation introduced in the text, draw a diagram showing this relationship.

5. Examine the diagram for the Personnel database (Figure 1-9) and identify which relationship (or relationships) shown in the diagram is used to answer each of the following questions.

    a. What SKILLs are associated with the JOB CLASSIFICATION Software Engineer?

    b. Who are the EMPLOYEEs that work for Shannon Doyle?

    c. What JOBs currently have openings for the JOB CLASSIFICATION Database Administrator?

    d. What job ASSIGNMENTs have been given to the EMPLOYEE Steve Jones?

6. Using the shorthand notation introduced in the chapter, draw a single diagram to represent the following situation. A BANK has one or more BRANCHes (a BRANCH always belongs to exactly one BANK). Each BRANCH may have one or more CUSTOMERs (but a CUSTOMER is assigned to only one BRANCH). Each CUS-TOMER may own one or more ACCOUNTs, but each ACCOUNT is owned by only one CUSTOMER. Also each CUSTOMER may submit one or more TRANSACTIONs (but each TRANSACTION is submitted by one CUSTOMER). Finally, each ACCOUNT may have many TRANSACTIONs, and a TRANSACTION may be for more than one ACCOUNT.

7. Reread the definitions for data and database in this chapter. Database management systems only recently included the capability to store and retrieve more than numeric and textual data. What special data storage, retrieval, and maintenance capabilities do images, sound, video, and other advanced data types require that are not required or are simpler with numeric and textual data?

8. Table 1-1 shows example metadata for a set of data items. Identify three other columns for these data (that is, three other metadata characteristics for the listed attributes) and complete the entries of the table in Table 1-1 for these three additional columns.

9. In the section on "Disadvantages of File Processing Systems" the statement is made that the disadvantages of file processing systems can also be limitations of databases, depending on how an organization manages its databases. First, why do organizations create multiple databases, not just one all-inclusive database supporting all data processing needs? Second, what organizational and personal factors are at work that might lead an organization to having multiple, independently managed databases (and, hence, not completely following the database approach)?

10. Consider a student club or organization in which you are a member. What are the data entities of this enterprise? List and define each entity. Then, develop an enterprise data model (such as Figure 1-3) showing these entities and important relationships between them.

11. In the section of this chapter titled "The Range of Database Applications" four different categories of databases are introduced. For each category, a series of key decisions are outlined. Later in the text you will learn how to deal with these and other decisions; however, you should be able to anticipate partial responses for these decisions from your reading of this chapter and your overall familiarity with computer technologies. For the categories and key decisions listed below, explain what choice you think should be made or what factors should be considered in making a choice within any organization.

    a. *Personal computer database:* Who is responsible for the accuracy of the data in the personal computer database?

    b. *Workgroup database:* Which database processing operations should be performed at a workstation and which should occur on the server?

    c. *Department database:* How can adequate security be provided to protect against unauthorized disclosure or distribution of sensitive data?

    d. *Enterprise database:* How can the organization develop and maintain standards concerning data names, definitions, formats, and related issues?

FIELD EXERCISES

1. Choose an organization with a fairly extensive information systems department and set of information system applications. Investigate whether the organization follows more of a traditional file processing approach or the database approach to organizing data. How many different databases does the organization have? Try to draw a figure, similar to Figure 1-2, to depict some or all of the files and databases in this organization.

2. For the same organization as Field Exercise 1 or a different organization, talk with a database administrator or designer. What type of metadata does this organization maintain about its databases? Why did the organization choose to keep track of these and not other metadata? What tools are used to maintain these metadata?

3. For the same organization as Field Exercises 1 or 2 or a different organization, identify, if possible, one database of each of the four types of databases listed in this

chapter: personal computer, workgroup, department, and enterprise. Does this organization have a data warehouse? If so, how is the data warehouse formed from data in all the other databases?

4. Choose a small organization that is just beginning to use computer-based information systems. What, if any, database technologies is this organization using? In your opinion, should this organization follow the file processing or database approach? Why? Draw an enterprise data model for this organization.

5. You may want to keep a personal journal of ideas and observations about database management while you are studying this book. Use this journal to record comments you hear, summaries of news stories or professional articles you read, original ideas or hypotheses you create, URLs for and comments about Web sites related to databases, and questions that require further analysis. Keep your eyes and ears open for anything related to database management. Your instructor may ask you to turn in a copy of your journal from time to time in order to provide feedback and reactions. The journal is an unstructured set of personal notes that will supplement your class notes and can stimulate you to think beyond the topics covered within the time limitations of most courses.

REFERENCES

Codd, E. F. 1970. "A Relational Model of Data for Large Relational Databases." *Communications of the ACM* 13 (June): 377–87.

David, M. 1997. "Multimedia Database: Through the Looking Glass." *Database Programming & Design* 10:5 (May): 26–35.

Jordan, A. 1996. "Data Warehouse Integrity: How Long and Bumpy the Road?" *Data Management Review* 6:3 (March): 35–37.

Lambert, B. 1996. "Data Warehousing Fundamentals: What You Need to Succeed." *Data Management Review* 6:3 (March): 24–30.

Redman, T. C. 1995. "Improve Data Quality for Competitive Advantage." *Sloan Management Review* 36:2 (Winter): 99–107.

White, C. 1995. "Database Technology: Sorting Out the Options." *Supplement to Database Programming and Design* 8 (December): 41–44, 46.

Winter, R. 1997. "What, After All, Is a Very Large Database?" *Database Programming & Design* 10:1 (January): 23–26.

FURTHER READING

Hoffer, J. A., J. F. George, and J. S. Valacich. 1999. *Modern Systems Analysis and Design.* 2nd ed. Reading, MA: Addison-Wesley.

Project Case

INTRODUCTION

This case is included to provide you an opportunity to apply the concepts and techniques you have learned in each chapter. We have selected a hospital for this case since it is a type of organization that is at least somewhat familiar to most persons and because health care institutions are of such importance in our society today. A segment of the case is included at the end of each chapter in this text. Each segment includes a brief description of the case as it relates to the material in the chapter followed by questions and exercises related to the material.

PROJECT DESCRIPTION

Mountain View Community Hospital is a not-for-profit, short-term, acute care general hospital. It is a relatively small hospital, with some 150 beds at the present time.

The basic goal of Mountain View Community is to provide high-quality health care for its surrounding community while containing costs that have been rising in accordance with national trends in recent years.

Mountain View Community has computer applications that support the following areas (among others): patient care administration, clinical services, financial management, and administrative services. Most of these applications have been purchased from outside vendors, but a few have been developed internally. The computer applications are based on the use of client/server technology, such as illustrated in Figure 1-5. Most of the computer applications are implemented using relational database technology. Most of the databases (as well as the applications) are departmental, using the classification introduced in this chapter.

The relational databases at Mountain View Community Hospital contain a number of tables. Two of these tables, with some sample data, are shown in Figure 1. The PATIENT table contains data concerning

Figure 1
Two database tables

PATIENT

Patient Name	Patient Number	Patient Address
Dimas, Salena	8379	617 Valley Vista
Dolan, Mark	4238	818 River Run
Larreau, Annette	3047	127 Sandhill
Wiggins, Brian	5838	431 Walnut
Thomas, Wendell	6143	928 Logan

PATIENT CHARGES

Item Description	Item Code	Patient Number	Amount
Room Semi-Priv	200	4238	1600
Speech Therapy	350	3047	750
Radiology	275	4238	150
Physical Therapy	409	5838	600
EKG Test	500	8379	200
Room Semi-Priv	200	3047	800
Standard IV	470	8379	150
EEG Test	700	4238	200

current or recent patients at the hospital, while the PATIENT CHARGES table contains data describing charges that have been incurred by those patients. These tables have been simplified for this chapter but will be expanded in later chapters.

PROJECT QUESTIONS

1. What are some of the important benefits that Mountain View Community should seek in using databases? Relate your response to the hospital environment, as much as possible.

2. What are some of the costs and risks of using databases that the hospital must manage carefully?

3. At the present time, Mountain View Community is using relational database technology. Although this technology is appropriate for structured data such as patient or accounting data, it is less well suited to complex data such as graphical data and images. Can you think of some types of data maintained by a hospital that fit this latter category? What types of database technology might be better suited to these data types than relational?

4. How are data in the PATIENT and PATIENT CHARGES tables related? That is, how can a user find the relevant charges for a particular patient?

PROJECT EXERCISES

1. Using the shorthand notation introduced in this chapter, draw a diagram showing the relationship between PATIENT and PATIENT CHARGES.

2. Develop a metadata chart (see Table 1-1) for the data attributes in the PATIENT and PATIENT CHARGES tables. Use at least those columns shown in Table 1-1, but you may include other metadata characteristics, as you think are appropriate for the management of data at Mountain View Community Hospital.

3. One of the important database views for the hospital is the Patient Bill. Following is a highly simplified version of this view. Fill in the missing data in this view, using the data from Figure 1.

Patient Name: Dolan, Mark

Patient Number: _____

Patient Address: _____

Item Code	Item Description	Amount
_____	_____	_____
_____	_____	_____
_____	_____	_____

4. Using the shorthand notation introduced in this chapter, draw a single diagram that represents the following relationships in the hospital environment.

- A HOSPITAL has on its staff one or more PHYSICIANs. A PHYSICIAN is on the staff of only one HOSPITAL.

- A PHYSICIAN may admit one or more PATIENTs. A PATIENT is admitted by only one PHYSICIAN.

- Each PATIENT may incur any number of CHARGEs. A particular CHARGE may be incurred by any number of PATIENTs.

- A HOSPITAL has one or more WARDs. Each WARD is located in exactly one HOSPITAL.

- A WARD has any number of EMPLOYEEs. An EMPLOYEE may work in one or more WARDs.

5. The goal of Mountain View Community Hospital is to provide high-quality health care for its surrounding community, while containing costs that have been rising in accordance with national trends in recent years. How would a well-managed database help the hospital achieve its mission? Give some examples of how the use of databases in the hospital might improve health care quality or contain costs.

2

Database Development Process

After studying this chapter, you should be able to:

■ Define the following key terms: **enterprise data modeling, information systems architecture (ISA),** information engineering, top-down planning, business functions, functional decomposition, systems development life cycle (SDLC), prototyping, computer-aided software engineering (CASE), repository, project, incremental commitment, **conceptual schema, physical schema,** and **client/server architecture.**

■ Describe the life cycle of a systems development project, with emphasis on the purpose of database analysis, design, and implementation activities.

■ Explain the prototyping approach to database and application development.

■ Explain the roles of individuals who design, implement, use, and administer databases.

■ Explain the differences between conceptual, external, and physical schemas and the reasons for a three-schema architecture for databases.

■ Explain the three-tiered location architecture for databases and database processing.

■ Explain the scope of a database design and development class project.

■ Draw simple data models, which show the scope of a database.

INTRODUCTION

Chapter 1 introduced the database approach to information systems and the database application environment found in many organizations. An example organization, Pine Valley Furniture Company, was used to illustrate many of the principles and concepts of the database approach to information systems. You will again see Pine

Valley Furniture in this, as well as subsequent chapters, as a continuing example of the application of database management.

Chapter 2 presents an overview of the general steps followed in the analysis, design, implementation, and administration of databases. Because a database is one part of an information system, you will see in this chapter how the database development process fits into the overall information systems development process. The chapter emphasizes the need to coordinate database development with all the other activities in the development of a complete information system. The chapter includes highlights from a hypothetical database development process in Pine Valley Furniture. In this example, the chapter introduces tools for developing databases on personal computers and the process of extracting data from enterprise databases for use in stand-alone applications.

There are several reasons for discussing database development at this point. First, although you may have used the basic capabilities of a database management system, such as Microsoft Access®, you may not yet have developed an understanding of how the database was developed. The primary goal of this text is to introduce you to the concepts and many of the skills you will use to design and build database applications. Using simple examples, this chapter briefly illustrates what you will be able to do after you complete a database course using this text. Thus, this chapter helps you to develop a vision and context for each topic developed in detail in subsequent chapters.

Second, many students learn best from a text full of concrete examples. Although all of the chapters in this text contain numerous examples, illustrations, and actual database designs and code, each chapter concentrates on a specific aspect of database management. We have designed this chapter to help you to understand how all of these individual aspects of database management are related. Although we keep the technical details to a minimum, we hope you will develop a thirst to learn the data modeling and development skills presented thoroughly in subsequent chapters.

Finally, many instructors want you to begin the initial steps of a database development group or individual course project early in your database course. Because of the logical progression of topics in this book, you will study many pages before you see your target for the project. This chapter gives you an idea of how to structure a database development project, sufficient to begin on a course exercise. Obviously, since this is only Chapter 2, many of the examples and notations we will use will be much simpler than required on your project, in other course assignments, or in a real organization.

One note of caution: You will not learn how to design or develop databases just from this chapter. We have purposely kept the content of this chapter introductory and simplified. Many of the notations used in this chapter are not exactly like the ones you will learn in subsequent chapters. Our purpose in Chapter 2 is to give you a general understanding of the key steps and types of skills, not to teach you specific techniques. You will, however, develop an intuition and motivation for the skills and knowledge presented in later chapters.

DATABASE DEVELOPMENT WITHIN INFORMATION SYSTEMS DEVELOPMENT

Enterprise data modeling:
The first step in database development, in which the scope and general contents of organizational databases are specified.

In many organizations, database development begins with **enterprise data modeling**, which establishes the range and general contents of organizational databases. This step typically occurs during information systems planning for an organization. Its purpose is to create an overall picture or explanation of organizational data, not the

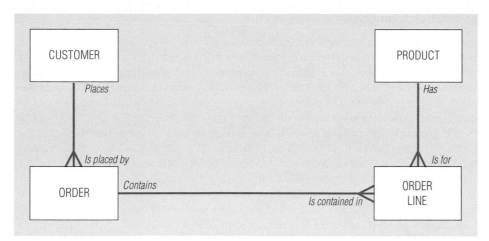

Figure 2-1
Segment from enterprise
data model (Pine Valley
Furniture Company)

design for a particular database. A particular database provides the data for one or more information systems, whereas an enterprise data model, which may encompass many databases, describes the scope of data maintained by the organization. In enterprise data modeling you review current systems, analyze the nature of the business areas to be supported, describe the data needed at a very high level of abstraction, and plan one or more database development projects. Figure 2-1, a duplicate of Figure 1-4, shows a segment of an enterprise data model for Pine Valley Furniture using a simplified version of the notation you will learn in Chapters 3 and 4.

Information Systems Architecture

A high-level data model, such as Figure 2-1, is only one part of an overall **information systems architecture (ISA)**, or blueprint, for information systems in an organization. You would develop an enterprise data model as part of developing the total information systems architecture during information systems planning. According to Zachman (1987) and Sowa and Zachman (1992), an information systems architecture consists of six key components:

Information systems architecture (ISA):
A conceptual blueprint or plan that expresses the desired future structure for the information systems in an organization.

1. *Data* (which can be represented as in Figure 2-1, but there are other representations, some of which are depicted in the next section on information systems planning)

2. *Processes* that manipulate data (these can be represented by data flow diagrams, object-models with methods, or other notations)

3. *Network,* which transports data around the organization and between the organization and its key business partners (which can be shown by a schematic of the network links and topology)

4. *People,* who perform processes and are the source and receiver of data and information (people can be shown on process models as senders and receivers of data)

5. *Events and points in time* when processes are performed (these can be shown by state-transition diagrams and other means)

6. *Reasons* for events and rules that govern the processing of data (often shown in textual form, but some diagramming tools exist for rules, such as decision tables)

Information Engineering

Information engineering:
A formal, top-down
methodology that uses a data
orientation to create and
maintain information systems.

An information systems architecture is developed by information systems planners following a particular methodology for IS planning. One such formal and popular methodology is information engineering. **Information engineering** is a data-oriented methodology to create and maintain information systems. Because of its data orientation, a brief explanation of information engineering can be helpful as you begin to understand how databases are identified and defined. Information engineering follows a **top-down planning** approach in which specific information systems are deduced from a broad understanding of information needs (for example, we need data about our customers, products, suppliers, salespersons, work centers, etc.) rather than from consolidating many specific information requests (such as an order entry screen or sales summary by territory report). Top-down planning offers the advantages of a broad perspective, a way to look at integration of individual system components, an understanding of the relationship of information systems to business objectives, and an understanding of the impact of information systems across the whole organization.

Top-down planning: A
generic information systems
planning methodology that
attempts to gain a broad
understanding of the
information system needs of
the entire organization.

Information engineering includes four steps: planning, analysis, design, and implementation. The planning phase of information engineering results in an information systems architecture, including an enterprise data model. We review the planning phase of information engineering in the next section. Although this book does not follow the information engineering methodology per se, the remaining chapters address activities that fall under the remaining three phases of information engineering.

Information Systems Planning

The goal of information systems planning is to align information technology with the business strategies of the organization. Such an alignment is important in order to achieve the maximum benefits from investments in information systems and technologies. As depicted in Table 2-1, the planning phase of the information engineering methodology includes three steps, which are discussed in the following three sections.

Table 2-1   Information Engineering Planning Phase

Step	Explanation
1.	Identify strategic planning factors a. Goals b. Critical success factors c. Problem areas
2.	Identify corporate planning objects a. Organizational units b. Locations c. Business functions d. Entity types
3.	Develop enterprise model a. Functional decomposition b. Entity-relationship diagram c. Planning matrixes

Table 2-2 Example Results of Information Engineering Planning Phase

Planning Factor	Examples
Goals	Maintain 10% per year growth rate Maintain 15% before-tax return on investment Avoid employee layoffs Be a responsible corporate citizen
Critical success factors	High-quality products On-time deliveries of finished products High productivity of employees
Problem areas	Inaccurate sales forecasts Increasing competition Stockouts of finished products

Identifying Strategic Planning Factors The strategic planning factors are organization goals, critical success factors, and problem areas. The purpose of identifying these factors is to develop the planning context and to link information systems plans to the strategic business plans. Table 2-2 shows some possible strategic planning factors for Pine Valley Furniture. These factors help information system managers to set priorities to address requests for new information systems, and hence the development of databases. For example, the problem area of inaccurate sales forecasts might cause information system managers to place additional historical sales data, new market research data, or data concerning results from test trials of new products in organizational databases.

Identifying Corporate Planning Objects The corporate planning objects define the business scope. The scope limits subsequent systems analysis and where information system changes can occur. Five key planning objects are as follows (see Table 2-3 for examples of these for Pine Valley Furniture):

- *Organizational units* The various departments of the organization

- *Organizational locations* The places where business operations occur

- *Business functions* Related groups of business processes that support the mission of the organization. Note that business functions are different from organizational units; in fact, a function may be assigned to more than one organizational unit (for example, product development, a function, may be the joint responsibility of the Sales and Manufacturing departments).

- *Entity types* Major categories of data about the people, places, and things managed by the organization

- *Information systems* The application software and supporting procedures for handling sets of data

Business function: A related group of business processes that support some aspect of the mission of an enterprise.

Developing an Enterprise Model A comprehensive enterprise model consists of a functional breakdown (or decomposition) model of each business function, an enterprise data model, and various planning matrixes. **Functional decomposition** is the process of breaking down the functions of an organization into progressively greater levels of detail. Functional decomposition is a classical process employed in systems analysis in order to simplify problems, isolate attention, and identify components. An

Functional decomposition: An iterative process of breaking down the description of a system into finer and finer detail in which one function is described in greater detail by a set of other, supporting functions.

Table 2-3   Example Corporate Planning Objects
(for Pine Valley Furniture Company)

Planning Object	Examples

Organizational units	Sales Department
	Orders Department
	Accounting Department
	Manufacturing
	    Fabrication Department
	    Assembly Department
	    Finishing Department
	Purchasing Department

Organizational locations	Corporate Headquarters Durango Plant Western Regional Sales Office Lumber Mill

Business functions	Business planning
	Product development
	Materials management
	Marketing and sales
	    Order fulfillment
	    Order shipment
	    Sales summarization
	Production operations
	Finance and accounting

Entity types	CUSTOMER PRODUCT RAW MATERIAL ORDER WORK CENTER INVOICE EQUIPMENT EMPLOYEE

Information systems	Transaction processing
	    Order tracking
	    Order processing
	    Plant scheduling
	    Payroll
	Management information systems
	    Sales management
	    Inventory control
	    Production scheduling

example of decomposition of an order fulfillment function for Pine Valley Furniture appears in Figure 2-2. Often many databases are necessary to handle the full set of business functions and supporting functions (for example, all of the functions and subfunctions listed in Table 2-3), whereas a particular database may support only a subset of the supporting functions (for example, those in Figure 2-2). It is helpful, however, to have a total, high-level enterprise view in order to minimize redundancy of data and make the data purposeful.

An enterprise data model is described using a particular notation. Figure 2-1 uses a general notation that could be employed, although a popular format is entity-relationship diagramming, which is explained in Chapters 3 and 4. Besides such a graph-

Figure 2-2 Example process decomposition of an order fulfillment function (Pine Valley Furniture Company)

ical depiction of the entity types, a thorough enterprise data model would also include descriptions of each entity type and a compendium of various statements about how the business operates, called *business rules,* which govern the validity of data. Business rules are also defined and illustrated in Chapters 3 and 4.

An enterprise data model shows not only the entity types but also the relationships between data entities. Other relationships, between various planning objects, are also depicted during enterprise modeling. A common format for showing the interrelationships between planning objects is matrixes. A wide variety of planning matrixes can be used; several common ones are:

- *Location-to-function*   Indicates which business functions are being performed at which business locations

- *Unit-to-function*   Identifies which business functions are performed by or are the responsibility of which business units

- *Information system-to-data entity*   Explains how each information system interacts with each data entity (e.g., whether each system creates, retrieves, updates, or deletes data in each entity)

- *Supporting function-to-data entity*   Identifies which data are captured, used, updated, or deleted within each function

- *Information system-to-objective*   Shows which information systems support each business objective

Figure 2-3 illustrates a possible function–to–data entity matrix. Such a matrix could be used for various purposes, including the following three:

1. *Identify orphans*   Indicate which data entities are not used by any function, or which functions do not use any entities

2. *Spot missing entities*   Employees involved with each function who examine the matrix can identify any entities that may have been missed

3. *Prioritize development*   If a given function has a high priority for systems development (maybe because it is related to important organizational

Figure 2-3
Example business function–to–data entity matrix

Business Functions \ Data Entity Types	Customer	Product	Raw Material	Order	Work Center	Work Order	Invoice	Equipment	Employee
Business Planning	X	X						X	X
Product Development		X	X		X			X	
Materials Management		X	X	X	X	X		X	
Order Fulfillment	X	X	X	X	X	X	X	X	X
Order Shipment	X	X		X	X		X		X
Sales Summarization	X	X		X			X		X
Production Operations		X	X	X	X	X		X	X
Finance and Accounting	X	X	X	X	X		X	X	X

X = data entity (column) is used within business function (row)

objectives), then the entities used by that area also have a high priority in database development

See Hoffer, George, and Valacich (1999) for a more thorough description of how to use planning matrixes for information engineering and systems planning.

DATABASE DEVELOPMENT PROCESS

Information systems planning, based on information engineering, is one source of database development projects. Such projects develop new databases often to meet strategic organizational needs, such as improved customer support, better production and inventory management, or more accurate sales forecasting. Many database development projects arise, however, more in a *bottom-up* fashion. In this case, projects are requests by information system users, who need certain information to do their job, or from other information systems professionals, who see a need to improve data management in the organization. Even in the bottom-up case, enterprise data modeling still must be done in order to understand whether existing databases can provide the desired data, and if not, what new databases, data entities, and attributes need to be added to the current organizational data resource.

Whether identified from strategic or operational information needs, each database development project usually focuses on one database. Some database projects concentrate only on defining, designing, and implementing a database as a foundation for subsequent information systems development. In most cases, however, a database and the associated information processing functions are developed together as part of a comprehensive information systems development project.

Systems Development Life Cycle

A traditional process for conducting an information systems development project is called the **systems development life cycle (SDLC)**. The SDLC is a complete set of steps that a team of information systems professionals, including database designers and programmers, follow in an organization to specify, develop, maintain, and replace information systems. This process is often viewed as a cascade of steps, as depicted in Figure 2-4 (Hoffer, George, and Valacich, 1999). The metaphor of a cascade or waterfall is used since each step flows into the next; that is, the total specification of the information system is developed in pieces, and the output from one piece is used as input to subsequent pieces. As depicted in the figure, however, the steps are not purely linear: steps overlap in time (thus steps can be conducted in parallel), and it is possible to backtrack to previous steps when prior decisions need to be reconsidered (thus, the water can run back up the waterfall!).

Systems development life cycle (SDLC): The traditional methodology used to develop, maintain, and replace information systems.

Figure 2-4
Systems development life cycle (SDLC)

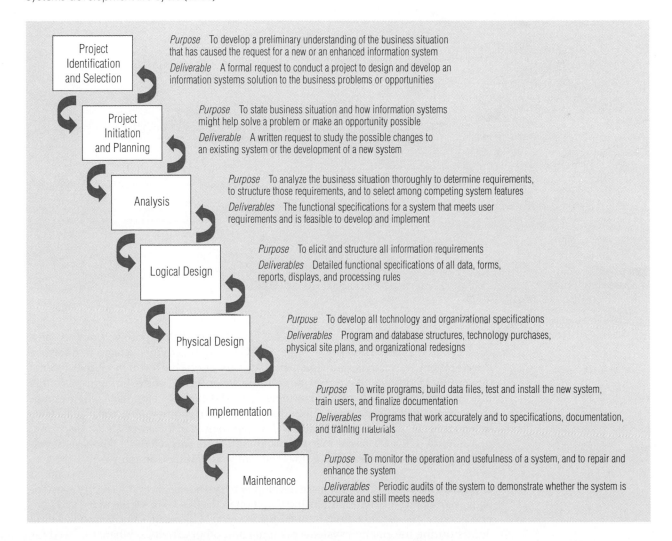

Project Identification and Selection

Purpose To develop a preliminary understanding of the business situation that has caused the request for a new or an enhanced information system

Deliverable A formal request to conduct a project to design and develop an information systems solution to the business problems or opportunities

Project Initiation and Planning

Purpose To state business situation and how information systems might help solve a problem or make an opportunity possible

Deliverable A written request to study the possible changes to an existing system or the development of a new system

Analysis

Purpose To analyze the business situation thoroughly to determine requirements, to structure those requirements, and to select among competing system features

Deliverables The functional specifications for a system that meets user requirements and is feasible to develop and implement

Logical Design

Purpose To elicit and structure all information requirements

Deliverables Detailed functional specifications of all data, forms, reports, displays, and processing rules

Physical Design

Purpose To develop all technology and organizational specifications

Deliverables Program and database structures, technology purchases, physical site plans, and organizational redesigns

Implementation

Purpose To write programs, build data files, test and install the new system, train users, and finalize documentation

Deliverables Programs that work accurately and to specifications, documentation, and training materials

Maintenance

Purpose To monitor the operation and usefulness of a system, and to repair and enhance the system

Deliverables Periodic audits of the system to demonstrate whether the system is accurate and still meets needs

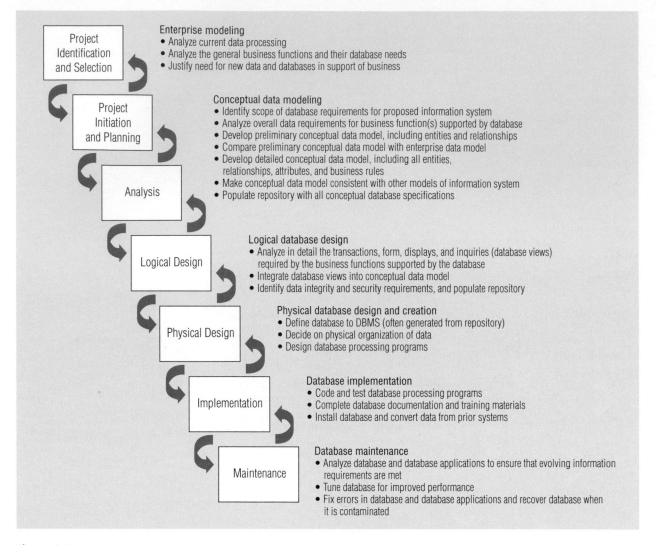

Figure 2-5
Database development activities during the systems development life cycle (SDLC)

Figure 2-4 is annotated with a brief explanation of the purpose and deliverables of each SDLC phase. Each phase of the SDLC includes activities related to database development, so database management issues are pervasive throughout the systems development process. We repeat these same seven SDLC steps in Figure 2-5, this time annotating the figure with an outline of the database development activities typically included in each phase. Note that there is not a one-to-one correspondence between SDLC phases and database development steps: *conceptual data modeling* occurs in two SDLC phases. We will briefly illustrate each of these database development steps later in this chapter for Pine Valley Furniture Company.

Enterprise Modeling   The database development process begins with enterprise modeling (part of Project Identification and Selection in the SDLC) to set the range and general contents of organizational databases. As you will recall, enterprise modeling occurs during information systems planning and other activities, where the need for information system changes and enhancements is identified and the scope of all organizational data is outlined. In this step you review current databases and information systems, analyze the nature of the business area that is the subject of the development project, and describe, in very general terms, the data needed for each information system under consideration for development. Only selected projects move into the next phase based on the projected value of each project to the organization.

Conceptual Data Modeling   For an information system project that is initiated, in conceptual data modeling you analyze the overall data requirements of the proposed information system. This is done in two stages. First, during the Project Initiation and Planning phase, you develop a diagram similar to Figure 2-1 as well as other documentation to outline the scope of data involved in this particular development project without consideration of what databases already exist. Only high-level categories of data (entities) and major relationships are included at this point. Then during the Analysis phase of the SDLC, you produce a detailed data model, which identifies all the organizational data that must be managed for this information system. You define every data attribute, list all categories of data, represent every business relationship between data entities, and specify every rule that dictates the integrity of data. It is also during the analysis phase that you check the conceptual data model (also called a *conceptual schema* later in this chapter) for consistency with other types of models developed to explain other dimensions of the target information system, such as processing steps, rules for handling data, and the timing of events. However, even this detailed conceptual data model is preliminary, since subsequent SDLC activities may find missing elements or errors when designing specific transactions, reports, displays, and inquiries. Thus it is often said that conceptual data modeling is done in a top-down fashion, driven from a general understanding of the business area, not from specific information processing activities.

Logical Database Design   In logical database design you approach database development from two perspectives. First, you transform the conceptual data model into a standard notation called relations, based on relational database theory. You will learn how to conduct this important process in Chapter 6. Then, as each computer program in the information system is designed, including the program's input and output formats, you perform a detailed review of the transactions, reports, displays, and inquiries supported by the database. During this so-called bottom-up analysis you verify exactly what data are to be maintained in the database and the nature of those data as needed for each transaction, report, and so forth.

The analysis of each individual report, transaction, and so on considers a particular, limited, but thorough, view of the database. It may be possible to change, as needed, the conceptual data model as each report, transaction, and so on is analyzed. Especially on larger projects, different teams of analysts and systems developers may work independently on different programs or sets of programs. The details of all of their work may not be revealed until well into the logical design phase. In this case, you must combine, or integrate, the original conceptual data model along with these individual *user views* into a comprehensive design during logical database design. It is also possible that additional information processing requirements will be identified during logical information systems design, in which case these new requirements must be integrated into the previously identified logical database design.

The final step in logical database design is to transform the combined and reconciled data specifications into basic, or atomic, elements following well-established rules for well-structured data specifications. For most databases today, these rules come from relational database theory and a process called *normalization*, which we will describe in detail in Chapter 6. The result is a complete picture of the database without any reference to a particular database management system for managing these data. With a final logical database design in place, you can begin to specify the logic of the particular computer programs and queries needed to maintain and report the database contents.

Physical Database Design and Creation   In physical database design and creation, you decide on the organization of the database in computer storage (usually disk) and define the physical structure of the database management system. You outline the programs to process transactions and to generate anticipated management information and decision-support reports. The goal is to design a database that will efficiently and securely handle all data processing against it. Thus, physical database design is done in close coordination with the design of all other aspects of the physical information system: programs, computer hardware, operating systems, and data communications networks.

Database Implementation   In database implementation, you write, test, and install the programs that process the database. You might program in standard programming languages (like COBOL, C, or Visual Basic), in special database processing languages (like SQL), or using special-purpose nonprocedural languages to produce stylized reports and displays, possibly including graphs. Also during implementation, you finalize all database documentation, users are trained, and you put procedures into place for the ongoing support of information system (and database) users. The last step is to load data from existing information sources (files and databases from legacy applications plus new data now needed). Loading is often done by first unloading data from existing files and databases into a neutral format (such as binary or text files) and then loading these data into the new database. Finally, you put the database and its associated applications into production for data maintenance and retrieval by the actual users. During production, you will periodically back up the database and recover the database in case of contamination or destruction.

Database Maintenance   In database maintenance, you evolve the database. In this step, you add, delete, or change characteristics of the structure of a database in order to meet changing business conditions, to correct errors in database design, or to improve the processing speed of database applications. You might also need to rebuild a database if it becomes contaminated or destroyed due to a program or computer system malfunction. This is typically the longest step of database development, since it lasts throughout the life of the database and its associated applications. You can view each time the database evolves as an abbreviated database development process, in which conceptual data modeling, logical and physical database design, and database implementation occur to deal with the proposed changes.

Alternative IS Development Approaches

The systems development life cycle or slight variations on it are often used to guide the development of information systems and databases. The SDLC is a methodical, highly structured approach, which includes many checks and balances to insure that each step produces accurate results and the new or replacement information system is consistent with existing systems with which it must communicate or for which there needs to be consistent data definitions. Consequently, the SDLC is often criticized for the length of time needed until a working system is produced, which occurs only at the end of the process. Increasingly, organizations use more rapid application development (RAD) methods, which follow an iterative process of rapidly repeating

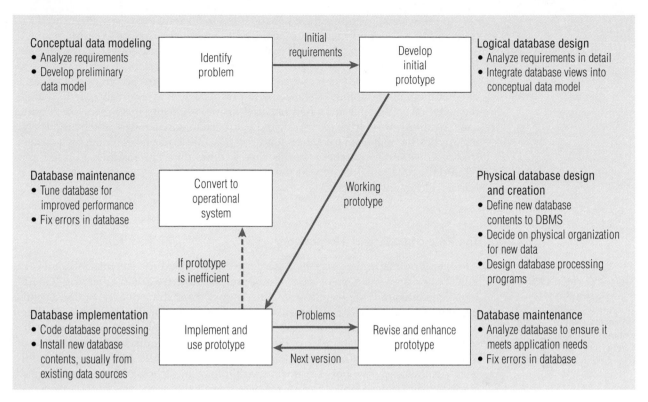

Figure 2-6
The prototyping methodology and database development process

analysis, design, and implementation steps until you converge on the system the user wants. These RAD methods work best when most of the database needed already exists, and hence for systems that primarily retrieve data, rather than for those that populate and revise databases.

One of the most popular RAD methods is **prototyping**. Prototyping is an iterative process of systems development in which requirements are converted to a working system that is continually revised through close work between analysts and users. Figure 2-6 shows the prototyping process. We have included on this figure annotations to indicate roughly which database development activities occur in each prototyping phase. You typically do only a very cursory attempt at conceptual data modeling when the information system problem is identified. During the development of the initial prototype, you simultaneously design the displays and reports the user wants while understanding any new database requirements and defining a database to be used by the prototype. This is typically a new database, which is a copy of portions of existing databases, possibly with new content. If new contents are required, they will usually come from external data sources, such as market research data, general economic indicators, or industry standards.

You repeat database implementation and maintenance activities as new versions of the prototype are produced. Often security and integrity controls are minimal since the emphasis is on getting working prototype versions ready as quickly as possible. Also, documentation tends to be delayed until the end of the project, and user training occurs from hands-on use. Finally, once an accepted prototype is created, you and the user decide if the final prototype, and its database, can be put into production

Prototyping: An iterative process of systems development in which requirements are converted to a working system that is continually revised through close work between analysts and users.

as is. If the system, including the database, is too inefficient, then the system and database will be reprogrammed and reorganized to meet performance expectations.

With the increasing popularity of visual programming tools (such as Visual Basic, Java, Visual C++, and fourth-generation languages) in which it is easy to modify the interface between user and system, prototyping is becoming the systems development methodology of choice. With prototyping it is relatively easy to change the contents and layout of user reports and displays. During this process, new database requirements may be identified, and hence existing databases used by the evolving application will need to change. It is even possible to use prototyping for a system that requires a new database. In this case, sample data are acquired to build and rebuild the database prototype as the system requirements evolve through the iterative development process.

The Role of CASE and a Repository

Computer-aided software engineering (CASE):
Software tools that provide automated support for some portion of the systems development process.

At several points in the preceding section we mentioned the role of CASE tools in information systems development. **Computer-aided software engineering (CASE)** tools are software that provides automated support for some portion of the systems development process. For our purposes in the study of database development, there are three relevant features of CASE tools. First is the ability to help us draw data models using entity-relationship and other notations (see Figure 2-1 for an example of a form of E-R notation). A CASE tool's drawing capabilities are "database intelligent" in that each symbol represents specific data modeling constructs, and these symbols can be used only in ways consistent with the properties of the associated constructs. Database drawing tools are used in enterprise modeling, conceptual data modeling, logical database design, and physical data modeling. CASE tools can help us insure consistency across diagrams. For example, a CASE tool will make sure that each use of the PRODUCT entity on any diagram has exactly the same meaning. CASE drawing tools enforce unique names for each data object and may be able to automatically redraw a data model when characteristics of data objects change.

Often, different drawing tools and associated methods are used for different stages of the database development process. For example, one tool is used for enterprise modeling to draw high-level diagrams and matrixes. Still another tool may be used in conceptual data modeling, and yet another in logical database design.

The second important feature of CASE tools is the ability to generate code. Most often, this code contains the database definition commands to be given to a database management system. During database implementation, the CASE tool will refer to all the conceptual, logical, and physical data specifications and compose SQL commands to create relational tables, define each attribute of each table, and define key indexes. Although less frequently a capability of CASE tools, some CASE tools can generate C or other language code for the rudiments of database retrieval and updating programs.

As with drawing tools, many organizations use separate tools ("best of breed") for code generation as well as drawing. If these tools and methods are to be effective, they must be integrated. In particular, the tools must be able to share the metadata that are developed during each stage of the process. Unfortunately, the ability to share such information among CASE tools has not been common, especially among tools from different vendors. A so-called *integrated-CASE* (or *I-CASE*) tool provides support across the whole life cycle, but such tools are rarely used since they tend to be strong in supporting certain phases and weak in supporting other phases of the systems development process. Tools that support the SDLC from the Project Identification and Selection phase through Physical Design are called *upper CASE tools;* tools that support the Implementation and Maintenance phases are called *lower CASE tools.*

Tool integration depends on a formal, detailed architecture for building and maintaining information systems. This architecture includes formal definitions of interfaces between tools, data model standards among tools, and common controls across the life cycle. This leads to the third feature of CASE tools important to our discussion of the database development process: an information repository (or *repository* for short). A **repository** is a knowledge base of information about the facts that an enterprise must be able to access and the processes it must perform to be successful (Moriarty, 1991). Thus, for example, all of the information that is collected during the six stages of database development is maintained in a repository. In a sense, a repository is a database itself, which contains information needed to generate all the diagrams, form and report definitions, and other system documentation. A repository helps systems and database analysts achieve a seamless integration of data from several CASE tools.

> **Repository:** A knowledge base of information about the facts that an enterprise must be able to access and the processes it must perform to be successful.

MANAGING THE PEOPLE INVOLVED IN DATABASE DEVELOPMENT

As implied in Figure 2-5, a database is developed as part of a project. A **project** is a planned undertaking of related activities to reach an objective that has a beginning and an end. A project begins with the first steps of the Project Initiation and Planning phase and ends with the last steps of the Implementation phase. A senior systems or database analyst will be assigned to be project leader, who is responsible for creating detailed project plans as well as staffing and supervising the project team. A good project leader will possess skills in leadership, management, customer relations and communications, technical problem solving, conflict management, team building, and risk and change management.

> **Project:** A planned undertaking of related activities to reach an objective that has a beginning and an end.

A project is initiated and planned in the Project Initiation and Planning phase, executed during Analysis, Logical Design, Physical Design, and Implementation phases, and closed down at the end of implementation. During initiation the project team is formed. A systems or database development team can include one or more each of the following:

- *Systems analysts*   Analyze the business situation and identify the need for information and information services to meet the problems or opportunities of the business

- *Database analysts*   Concentrate on determining the requirements and design for the database component of the information system

- *Users*   Provide assessment of their information needs and monitor that the developed system meets their needs

- *Programmers*   Design and write computer programs that have embedded in them commands to maintain and access data in the database

- *Database and data administrators*   Have responsibility for existing and future databases and ensure consistency and integrity across databases, and as experts on database technology, provide consulting and training to other project team members

- *Other technical experts*   E.g., networking, operating systems, testing, and documentation

Figure 2-7

Graphical diagrams for depicting project plans

(a) Gantt chart

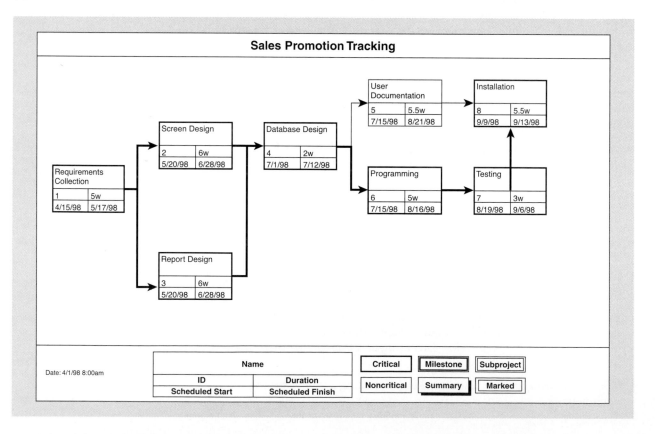

(b) PERT chart

It is the responsibility of the of the project leader to select and manage all of these people as an effective team. See Hoffer, George, and Valacich (1999) for details on how to manage a systems development project team.

Project close down occurs when the project is naturally or unnaturally terminated. An unnatural termination occurs when the system no longer appears to have business value, when the performance of the system or the development team is unacceptable, or the project runs out of time, funding, or support. To determine whether a project is progressing on time and within budget, the project leader develops detailed schedules of project activities. Often these schedules are depicted in graphical form, such as shown in the sample charts in Figure 2-7. These charts show when project activities begin and end, who is responsible for doing each activity, how much effort is required to do each activity, and the precedence relationships between activities (that is, which activities depend on the output of other activities).

A characteristic of successful systems development projects is frequent review points, when project team members report the results of the project to date. Often these results are reported to people outside the project team, including other users, those who are providing the funding for the project, and senior information systems and possibly general management. The reasons for these review points are to

- Validate that the project is progressing in a satisfactory way.

- Step back from the details of daily activities and verify that all the parts of the project are coming together.

- Gain renewed commitment from all parties to the project (especially important for projects which last more than a few months).

Central to the third reason is the concept of incremental commitment. **Incremental commitment** is a strategy in systems development projects in which the project is reviewed after each phase and continuation of the project is rejustified in each of these reviews. Incremental commitment allows those interested in the project to commit only to the next phase (with limited time and cost) and then to reassess whether further commitment of resources (people and money) is warranted after some results are shown. Thus, significant resources are not wasted when the original concept for the system does not prove valuable. Incremental commitment also allows a project to be easily redirected or killed.

Incremental commitment: A strategy in systems development projects in which the project is reviewed after each phase and continuation of the project is rejustified in each of these reviews.

THREE-SCHEMA ARCHITECTURE FOR DATABASE DEVELOPMENT

The explanation earlier in this chapter of the database development process referred to several different, but related, views or models of databases that you will develop on a systems development project:

- Conceptual schema (during the Analysis phase),

- External schema or user view (during the Analysis and Logical Design phases), and

- Physical or internal schema (during the Physical Design phase)

Figure 2-8 depicts the relationship between these three views of a database. It is important to keep in mind that these are all views or models of the same organizational database; that is, each organizational database has one physical and one conceptual

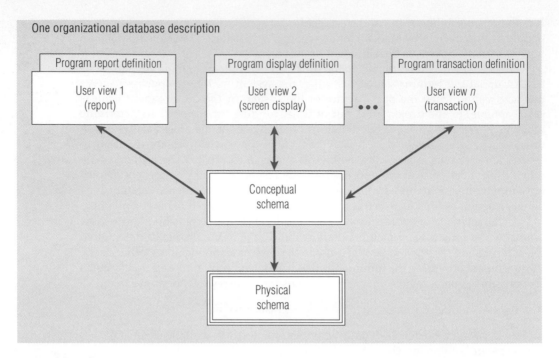

Figure 2-8
Three-schema database architecture

schema and one or more user views. Thus, the three-schema architecture defines one database, with multiple ways to look at this one set of data.

Conceptual schema: A detailed, technology independent specification of the overall structure of a database.

A **conceptual schema** is a detailed specification of the overall structure of organizational data, while being independent of any database management technology. A conceptual schema defines the whole database without reference to how data are stored in a computer's secondary memory. As a database developer you will usually depict a conceptual schema in graphical format using entity-relationship or object modeling notations; we have called this type of conceptual schema a *data model.* In addition, you will store the specifications for the conceptual schema as metadata in a repository or data dictionary.

A *user view* was defined in Chapter 1 as a logical description of some portion of the database that is required by a user to perform some task. Thus, a user view (or external schema) is also independent of database technology but typically contains a subset of the associated conceptual schema, relevant to a particular user or group of users (for example, an inventory manager or accounts receivable department). A user view is also the version of the schema used in a particular program (for example, an order entry program), because a program is used by a particular user or group of users. Thus, a user view is defined in both logical (technology-independent) terms as well as programming language terms (that is, consistent with the syntax of the program's language). Often the original depiction of a user view is a computer screen display, business transaction (such as a subscription renewal form), or a report since each of these often depicts all of the data needed by a program that processes that display, transaction, or report. A logical version of a user view can be represented as an E-R or object diagram or as relations. The process of translating an E-R diagram into relations and then merging relations (view integration) into one complete relational description of a database is described in Chapter 6.

A **physical schema** contains the specifications for how data from a conceptual schema are stored in a computer's secondary memory. Of importance to you as a database analyst and designer is the *definition* of the physical database (the physical schema), which provides all the specifications to the database technology to allocate and manage physical secondary memory space where data are to be stored and accessed.

Database development and database technologies are based on encouraging the distinction among these three views of databases. Your role on a database development project may deal exclusively with tasks associated with only one of these three views. For example, early in your career, you may design external schemas used in one or more programs. Later, with experience, you will be asked to design physical schemas or conceptual schemas. Database design issues vary across the levels. For this reason, this text is organized to focus your attention on the issues in the design of each of these three representations of databases:

- *Conceptual*   Chapters 3–5 discuss entity-relationship modeling and object-oriented modeling, which are two different graphical notations for depicting conceptual schemas or data models.

- *External*   Chapter 6 discusses relational databases, normalization, translating E-R diagrams into relations, and merging sets of relations; all of these topics assist in the development and analysis of external schemas.

- *Physical*   Chapter 7 discusses the decisions you have to make in designing a physical database, and Chapter 9 reviews how to specify these decisions in one language used to define physical schemas and databases—SQL.

Together, conceptual, external, and physical schemas form the three-schema architecture for databases. Note that even though Figure 2-8 shows external schemas at the top, external schemas are not necessarily developed before the conceptual schema. In fact, you will typically develop conceptual and external schemas iteratively (see Figure 2-9). Often, you develop a first cut at the conceptual schema based on the organization's enterprise data model and the general understanding of database requirements on a project. Then you develop external schemas (user views) for each transaction, report, screen display, and other system use. In most cases, an analysis of the external schemas will yield new attributes and possibly entities and relationships not shown in the conceptual schema. So, next you will augment the conceptual schema with these requirements identified from so-called bottom-up sources, thus making the conceptual and external schemas consistent. When new user views are identified, this process of evolving both the conceptual and external schemas repeats.

When you are ready to begin developing the database and its associated application programs, you then write the specifications for the associated physical schema. Besides the conceptual and external schemas, you additionally consider hardware and software characteristics and users' database performance expectations while designing the physical database with its associated physical schema. It is possible that when you design the physical database you will encounter inconsistencies or other issues with the conceptual schema or user views, so it is possible to cycle back to these design steps (not shown on Figure 2-9). When additional user requirements are identified later, the process begins again. Usually new requirements are batched and considered together in a new cycle of external and conceptual schema design, so that the database is not constantly changing. Periodic revisions of the database occur during the Maintenance phase of systems development.

Physical schema:
Specifications for how data from a conceptual schema are stored in a computer's secondary memory.

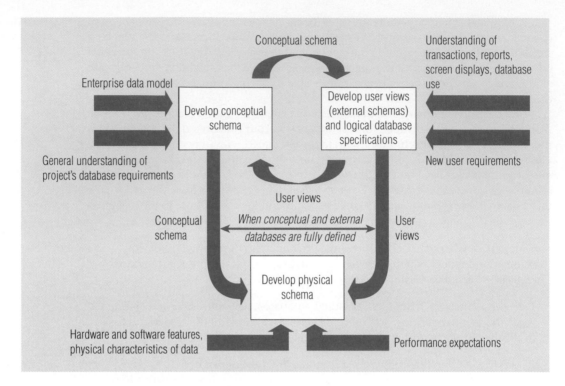

Figure 2-9
Process of developing three-schema architecture for a database project

THREE-TIERED DATABASE LOCATION ARCHITECTURE

Apparently, all good (database) things come in threes!

When designing a database, you have choices about where to store the data. These choices are made during physical database design. We will consider a wide range of physical database design decisions in Chapter 7, but in this section we want to outline a major database architectural choice that can affect the database development process.

In Chapter 1 you learned that there are personal computer, workgroup, department, and enterprise databases. Personal computer databases are often designed and developed by end users themselves, with only training and consulting help from database professionals, if the database contains data of interest only to its end user. Sometimes a personal computer database is an extract from a workgroup or enterprise database, in which case database professionals often write the extracting routines to create the local database. Workgroup and department databases are often developed in combination by end users, systems professionals working in business units, and central database professionals. A combination of people is necessary since a wide variety of issues must be balanced in the design of shared databases: processing speed, ease of use, differences in data definitions, and the like. Enterprise databases, because of their organization-wide impact and extensive size, tend to be developed by highly trained database professionals, often in a centralized database development group.

This view of database location, which implies that a database is located strictly at one of these four levels, is somewhat simplified for many modern organizations. In fact, the data for a given information system may reside in multiple locations or tiers of computers, in order to balance various organizational and technical factors. Also, different types of processing of data from a database may occur at different locations, in order to take advantage of the processing speed, ease of use, or ease of programming on different computer platforms. Although four (and even more) tiers are possible (that is, data on a desktop or laptop microcomputer, on a workgroup server, on a department server, and on a corporate mainframe), three tiers are more commonly considered:

1. *Client tier*   A desktop or laptop computer, which concentrates on managing the user–system interface and localized data—also called the presentation tier

2. *Department (or workgroup) minicomputer server tier*   Performs calculations and provides access to data shared within the workgroup—also called the process services tier

3. *Enterprise server (minicomputer or mainframe) tier*   Performs sophisticated calculations and manages the merging of data from multiple sources across the organization—also called the data services tier

This three-tiered architecture is depicted in Figure 2-10. A limited view of the client/server architecture considers only the client tier and a general server tier.

The tiered architecture for databases and information systems is related to the concept of a client/server architecture for distributed computing in an organization.

Figure 2-10
Three-tiered client/server database architecture

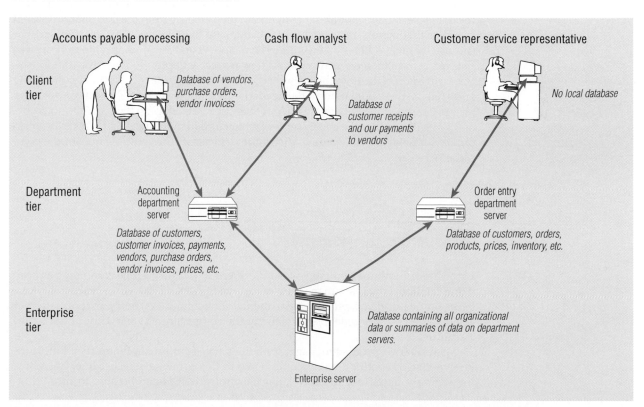

Client/server architecture:
A local area network–based
environment in which
database software on a server
(called a database server or
database engine) performs
database commands sent to it
from client workstations, and
application programs on each
client concentrate on user
interface functions.

In a **client/server architecture**, which is based on a local area network, database software on a server (called a *database server* or *database engine*) performs database commands sent to it from client workstations, and application programs on each client concentrate on user interface functions. In practice, the total conceptual database (as well as the application processing routines that access this database) can be distributed across the local PC workstation, an intermediate server (workgroup or department), and a centralized server (department or enterprise) as one distributed database or as separate but related physical databases. Hoffer, George, and Valacich (1999) and Thompson (1997) outline why this type of architecture is increasingly popular. Briefly, the reasons for the use of a client/server architecture are:

- It allows for simultaneous processing on multiple processors for the same application, thus improving application response time and data processing speed.

- It is possible to take advantage of the best data processing features of each computer platform (e.g., the advanced user interface capabilities of PCs versus the computational speed of minicomputers and mainframes).

- You can mix client technologies (personal computers with Intel or Motorola processors, network computers, information kiosks, etc.) and, yet, share common data; in addition, you can change technologies at any tier with limited impact on the system modules on other tiers.

- Processing can be performed close to the source of processed data, thereby improving response times and reducing network traffic.

- It allows for and encourages the acceptance of open system standards.

The most significant implication for database development from the use of a multiple-tiered client/server architecture is the ease of separating the development of the database and the modules that maintain the database from the information system modules that present the contents of the database to end users. Presentation routines can use languages like PowerBuilder, Java, and Visual Basic to provide easy-to-use, graphic user interfaces. Through middleware (see Chapter 8), the presentation routines can interact through the tiers to access the routines that access the required data and analyze these data to form the needed information. As a database developer and programmer, you might work at any of these tiers, developing the requisite software.

We will consider the client/server architecture in more detail in Chapter 7, which outlines how to decide where to distribute data across the multiple tiers of the computer network.

DEVELOPING A DATABASE APPLICATION FOR PINE VALLEY FURNITURE

Pine Valley Furniture Company was introduced in Chapter 1. The company has been using relational database management technology since 1990, with a variety of databases on personal computers, departmental minicomputers, and a corporate server (see Figure 1-6 for a general schematic of the computer network within Pine Valley Furniture).

Helen Jarvis, product manager for home office furniture at Pine Valley Furniture, knows that competition has become fierce in this growing product line. Thus, it is increasingly important to Pine Valley Furniture that Helen be able to more thoroughly analyze sales of her products. Often these analyses are ad hoc, driven by rapidly changing and unanticipated business conditions, comments from furniture store managers, trade industry gossip, or experience. Helen has requested that she be given direct access to sales data with an easy-to-use interface so that she can search for answers to the various marketing questions she will generate.

Chris Martin is a systems analyst in Pine Valley Furniture's information systems development area. Chris has worked at Pine Valley Furniture for five years, and has experience with information systems from several business areas within Pine Valley. From the various systems development projects Chris has worked on, his information systems education at Western Florida University, and the extensive training Pine Valley has given Chris, he has become one of Pine Valley's best systems developers. Chris is skilled in data modeling and is familiar with several relational database management systems used within the firm. Because of his experience, expertise, and availability, the head of information systems has assigned Chris to work with Helen on her request for a marketing support system.

Since Pine Valley Furniture has been careful in the development of their systems, especially since adopting the database approach, the company already has a fairly complete information systems architecture, including databases for all operational business functions. Thus, it is likely that Chris will be able to extract the data Helen needs from existing databases. Pine Valley's information system architecture calls for such systems as Helen is requesting to be built on stand-alone databases, so the unstructured and unpredictable use of data will not interfere with the access to the operational databases needed to support efficient transaction processing systems.

Further, since Helen's needs are for data analysis, not creation and maintenance, and are personal, not institutional, Chris decides to follow a combination of prototyping and life cycle approaches to developing the system Helen has requested. By a combination, Chris means that he will follow all the life cycle steps, but he will conduct very quickly and in a cursory way those steps not integral to prototyping. Thus, he will very quickly address project initiation and planning (including placing this project within the company's information system architecture), then use an iterative cycle of analysis, design, and implementation to work closely with Helen to develop a working prototype of the system she needs. Because the system will be personal and likely will require a database with limited scope, Chris hopes the prototype will end up being the actual system Helen will use. Chris has chosen to develop the system using Microsoft Access®, Pine Valley's preferred technology for personal computer databases.

Matching User Needs to the Information Systems Architecture

Chris begins the project to develop the database and associated marketing support system for the home office furniture area by interviewing Helen. Chris asks Helen about her business area, taking notes about business area objectives, business functions, data entity types, and other business objects with which she deals. At this point, Chris listens more than talks, so that he can concentrate on understanding Helen's business area; he interjects questions and makes sure that Helen does not try to jump ahead to talk about what she thinks she needs as computer screens and reports from the information system. Chris asks very general questions, using, as much as possible, business and marketing terminology. For example, Chris asks Helen what issues she faces managing the home office products; what people, places, and things are of interest to her in her job; how far back in time does she need data to do her analyses; and what events occur in the business that are of interest to her.

Table 2-4   Business Objects for Product Line Marketing Support System

Planning Object	Objects for Home Office Product Line Tracking	Does Object Exist in Pine Valley Information Systems Architecture?
Objectives	Increase annual sales ($) of home office products by at least 16%	No
	Increase annual profit margin of home office product line by at least 10%	No
	Increase same customer repeat sales ($) of home office products by at least 5%	No
	Exceed sales goals for each product finish category of home office products	No
	Have home office products perform above average for all Pine Valley products	No
	Reduce time to fill office product orders by 5%	No
	Reduce time to receive final payment on office product invoices by 5%	No
Organizational units	Marketing Department	Yes
	Office Furniture Product Line Management	No
	Accounting Department	Yes
	Orders Department	Yes
Organizational locations	Regional Sales Offices	Yes
	Corporate Headquarters	Yes
Business functions	Payment receipt	Yes
	Product development	—
	Demographics analysis	No
	Target market analysis	Yes
	Marketing and sales	—
	Order fulfillment	Yes
	Sales summarization	Yes
	Order taking	Yes
Entity types	CUSTOMER	Yes
	PRODUCT	Yes
	PRODUCT LINE	Yes
	ORDER	Yes
	INVOICE	Yes
	PAYMENT	Yes
Information systems	Order processing	Yes
	Sales management	Yes

Table 2-4 summarizes what Chris learns from this initial interview. This table lists the various business objects Helen mentioned and indicates which of these are already in Pine Valley Furniture's information systems architecture. There are a few entries in the figure that are not in the information systems architecture. However, all of the major categories of data Helen mentioned are covered in the architecture and are managed in existing information systems. Thus, Chris is confident that most, if not all, of the data Helen might want already exist within company databases.

Chris does two quick analyses before talking with Helen again. First, he identifies all of the databases that contain data associated with the data entities Helen

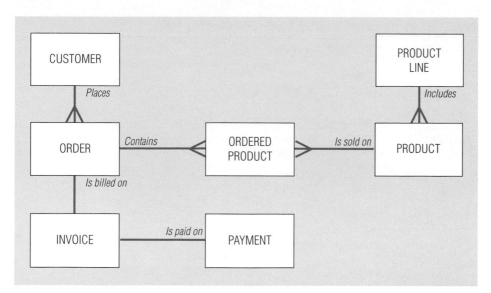

Figure 2-11
Preliminary data model for
product line marketing
support system

mentioned. From these databases, Chris makes a list of all of the data attributes from these data entities which he thinks might be of interest to Helen in her analyses of the home office furniture market. Chris's previous involvement in projects that developed Pine Valley's standard sales tracking and forecasting system and cost accounting system helps him extrapolate from the information in Table 2-4 to speculate about the kinds of data Helen might want. For example, the objective to exceed sales goals for each product finish category of office furniture suggests that Helen wants product annual sales goals in her system; also, the objective of achieving at least a 16 percent annual sales growth means that the prior year's orders for each product need to be included. He also concludes that Helen's database must include all products, not just those in the office furniture line, because she wants to compare her line to others. He is able to eliminate, however, many data attributes kept on each data entity. For example, Helen does not appear to need various customer data such as address, phone number, contact person, store size, and salesperson. He does, though, include a few attributes, customer type and zip code, which are not obvious from Table 2-4. He includes these because they were important attributes in the sales forecasting system.

Second, from this list, Chris draws a graphic data model that represents the data entities with the associated data attributes as well as the major relationships between these data entities. Chris's hope is that he can reduce the time for the analysis phase of the systems development process (and hence the time to do conceptual data modeling) by presenting this data model to Helen. A graphic of the data model for the preliminary database that Chris produces appears in Figure 2-11. Table 2-5 lists the data attributes about each entity Chris thinks Helen wants for the system. Chris lists in Table 2-5 only basic data attributes from existing databases, since Helen will likely want to combine these data in various ways for the analyses she will want to do.

Analyzing Database Requirements

Chris's initial meeting with Helen lasted only 45 minutes, but he feels that it resulted in a lot of ideas to share with Helen from the data he collected then and his subsequent work. He schedules a longer session, two hours, with Helen to go over these

Table 2-5   Data Attributes for Entities in Preliminary Data Model

Entity Type	Attribute
CUSTOMER	Customer_Identifier Customer_Name Customer_Type Customer_ZIPCODE
PRODUCT	Product_Identifier Product_Finish Product_Price Product_Cost Product_Annual_Sales_Goal Product_Line_Name
PRODUCT LINE	Product_Line_Name Product_Line_Annual_Sales_Goal
ORDER	Order_Number Order_Placement_Date Order_Fulfillment_Date Customer_Identifier
ORDERED PRODUCT	Order_Number Product_Identifier Order_Quantity
INVOICE	Invoice_Number Order_Number Invoice_Date
PAYMENT	Invoice_Number Payment_Date

findings. Prior to the meeting, he sends Helen a rough project schedule outlining the steps he plans to follow and the estimated length of each step. Because prototyping is a user-driven process, in which the user says when to stop iterating on the new prototype versions, Chris can provide only rough estimates of the duration of certain project steps. For this reason, Chris's boss has decided that this project should be billed to Helen on a consulting time basis, not at a fixed cost.

Chris does more of the talking at this second meeting. He methodically walks through each data entity in Figure 2-11 explaining what it means, what each data attribute associated with it (in Table 2-5) means, and what business policies and procedures are represented by each line between entities. For example, Chris explains that each order is billed on one invoice and each invoice is a bill for exactly one order. An Order_Number uniquely identifies each order, and an order is placed by one customer. Other data about an order Chris thinks Helen might want to know include the date when the order was placed and the date when the order was filled (this would be the latest shipment date for the products on the order). Chris also explains that the Payment_Date attribute represents when the customer paid in full for the order; that is, the PAYMENT entity aggregates any partial payments a customer might make to indicate when the final payment is made.

During this discussion, Helen tells Chris about some additional data she wants (the number of years a customer has purchased products from Pine Valley Furniture and the number of shipments necessary to fill each order). Helen also notes that Chris has only one year of sales goals indicated for a product line. She reminds him that she wants these data for both the past and current years. As she reacts to the data model, Chris asks her how she intends to use the data she wants. Chris does not try to be thorough at this point, since he knows that Helen has not worked with an information set like the one being developed; thus, she may not yet be positive what data she wants or what she wants to do with the data. Rather, Chris's objective is to understand a few ways in which Helen intends to use the data so he can develop an initial prototype, including the database and several computer displays or reports. The final list of attributes that Helen agrees she needs appears in Table 2-6.

Table 2-6 Data Attributes for Entities in Final Data Model

Entity Type	Attribute*
CUSTOMER	Customer_Identifier
	Customer_Name
	Customer_Type
	Customer_ZIPCODE
	Customer_Years
PRODUCT	Product_Identifier
	Product_Finish
	Product_Price
	Product_Cost
	Product_Prior_Year_Sales_Goal
	Product_Current_Year_Sales_Goal
	Product_Line_Name
PRODUCT LINE	Product_Line_Name
	Product_Line_Prior_Year_Sales_Goal
	Product_Line_Current_Year_Sales_Goal
ORDER	Order_Number
	Order_Placement_Date
	Order_Fulfillment_Date
	Order_Number_of_Shipments
	Customer_Identifier
ORDERED PRODUCT	Order_Number
	Product_Identifier
	Order_Quantity
INVOICE	Invoice_Number
	Order_Number
	Invoice_Date
PAYMENT	Invoice_Number
	Payment_Date

* Changes from preliminary list of attributes appear in italics.

Designing the Database

Since Chris is following a prototyping methodology and since the first two sessions with Helen quickly identified the data Helen might need, Chris is able to begin immediately to build the prototype. First, Chris creates extracts from the corporate databases for the data entities and attributes Helen suggested. Chris is able to create all of these files using the SQL query language. Some of the data Helen wants are computed from raw, operational data (e.g., Customer_Years), but SQL makes it easy for Chris to specify these calculations. This extracting results in a single ASCII file for each data entity; each row in a file contains all of the data attributes associated with that data entity in the data model, and the rows are different instances of the entity. For example, each row of the ASCII file for the PRODUCT LINE data entity contains data for product line name and the annual sales goals for the past and current years.

Second, Chris translates the final data model from his discussion with Helen into a set of tables for which the columns are data attributes and the rows are different sets of values for those attributes. Tables are the basic building blocks of a relational database, which is the database style for Microsoft Access. The definitions of the PRODUCT LINE, PRODUCT, ORDER, and ORDERED PRODUCT tables Chris created, including associated data attributes, are shown in Figures 2-12 through 2-15. Chris did this translation so that each table had one or more attributes, called the table's *primary key*, which will be distinct for each row in the table (these attributes have a key symbol next to them in the figures). The other major properties of each table are that there is only one value for each attribute in each row and if we know the value of the whole identifier and nothing but the identifier, there can be only one value for each of the other attributes. For example, for any product line, there can be only one value for the current year's sales goal.

Figure 2-12
Definition of PRODUCT
LINE table

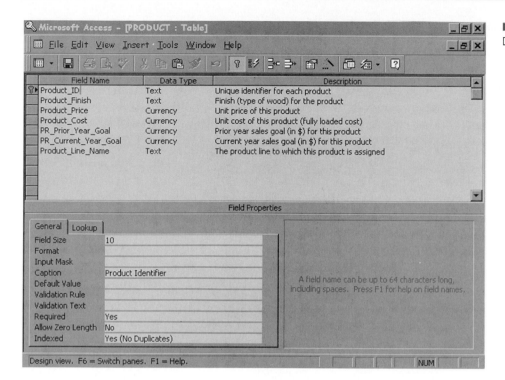

Figure 2-13
Definition of PRODUCT table

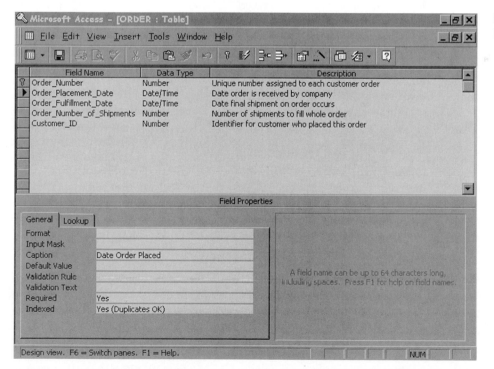

Figure 2-14
Definition of ORDER table

Figure 2-15

Definition of ORDERED
PRODUCT table

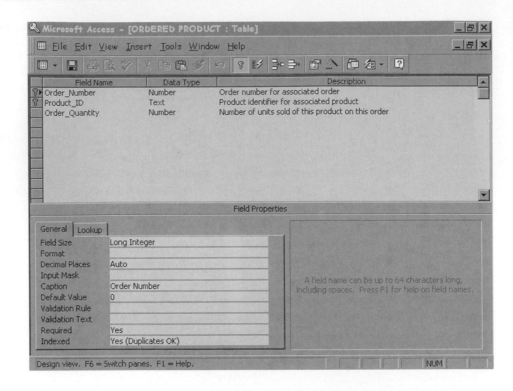

The design of the database includes specifying the format, or properties, for each attribute (Access calls attributes fields). These design decisions were easy in this case because most of the attributes were already specified in the corporate data dictionary. In Figures 2-12 through 2-15 the field properties for one field are shown for each table: PRODUCT LINE (Product_Line_Name), PRODUCT (Product_ID), ORDER (Order_Placement_Date), and ORDERED PRODUCT (Order_Number)—indicated by the arrow to the left of the field name. A few attributes, such as Order_Number_of_Shipments on the ORDER table, were computed from raw data in Pine Valley databases, so Chris had to create the specifications for such attributes.

The other major decision Chris has to make about database design is how to physically organize the database to respond the fastest to the queries Helen will write. Since the database will be used for decision support, neither Chris nor Helen can anticipate all of the queries that will arise; thus, Chris must make the physical design choices from experience rather than precise knowledge of the way the database will be used. The key physical database design decision that Microsoft Access allows a database designer to make is on which attributes to create indexes (an index is like a card catalog in the library, through which rows with common characteristics can be quickly located). All primary key attributes (like Order_Number for the ORDER table), those with unique values across the rows of the table, are indexed. In addition to this, Chris uses a general rule of thumb: create an index for any attribute that has more than 10 different values and which Helen might use to segment the database. For example, Helen indicated that one of the ways she wanted to use the database is to look at sales by product finish. Thus, it might make sense to create an index on the PRODUCT table using the Product_Finish attribute. However, Pine Valley uses only six product finishes, or types of wood, so this is not a useful index candidate. On the other hand, Order_Placement_Date (called a secondary key since there may be more than one row in the ORDER table with the same

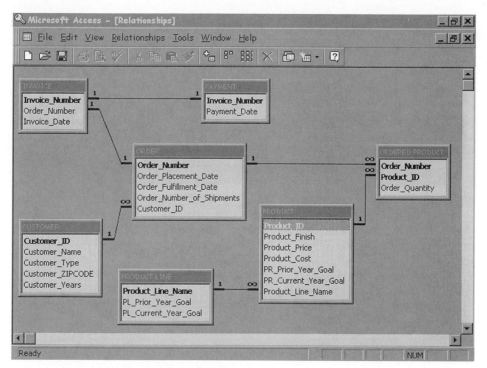

Figure 2-16
Database definition for Home
Office product line marketing
support system—final
Access data model

value of this attribute), which Helen also wants to use to analyze sales in different type periods, is a good index candidate. Look in Figures 2-12 through 2-15 for entries in the Indexed box near the bottom of the screen to see if the selected attribute is indexed and, if so, whether the index allows duplicates (a primary key may not have duplicates).

Figure 2-16 shows the final data model used by Access for the home office marketing database. Each box represents one table in the database; the attributes of a table are listed inside the associated box. Although the notation for relationships is slightly different from Figure 2-11, the meaning is the same. For example, the line from the CUSTOMER entity to the ORDER entity in Figure 2-16 shows a 1 near CUSTOMER and an infinity symbol next to ORDER, which has the same meaning as the Places relationship in Figure 2-11.

Using a Database

Helen will use the database Chris has built mainly for ad hoc questions, so Chris will train her on Microsoft Access, especially the database query features. Chris wants to wait to do this training after the system is better specified and Helen has learned about the database and Microsoft Access from the prototyping process. Helen has indicated, however, a few standard questions she expects to ask periodically. Microsoft Access provides capabilities for Chris to develop several types of prewritten routines that can make it easier for Helen to answer these standard questions (so she does not have to program these questions from scratch):

• *Form*   A set of attributes, in a predetermined format, all based on a single database record. Thus, a form might contain the data about a given customer, or

Figure 2-17

Home Office sales-to-goal
comparison query

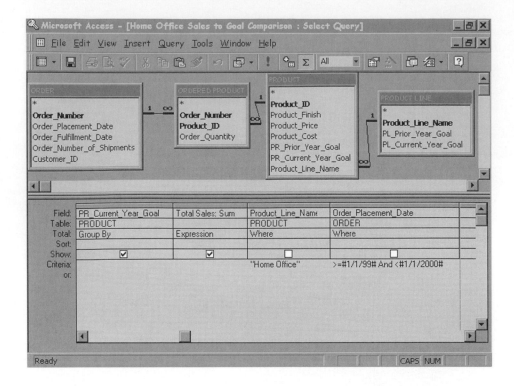

might contain the data about a specific order and the customer attributes for the customer associated with the order.

- *Report*   A set of attributes, in a predetermined format, based on many unrelated records. A report usually contains the same attributes about each record. For example, a report might list the product identifier, current year sales, and current year sales goal for all the products for which sales are below goal. A report usually includes page numbers, titles on each page, the date the report was printed, and other descriptive information.

- *Query*   A question to be answered from the database as posed in a particular querying language, Query-by-Example. The result of a query is a table in which the columns are the attributes the user wants to see and the rows are different instances of those attributes which satisfy the qualification entered by the user.

During the prototyping development process Chris may develop many examples of each of these routines as Helen communicates more clearly what she wants the system to be able to do. At this early stage of development, however, Chris wants to develop one routine to create the first prototype. One of the standard sets of information Helen says she wants is a list of each of the products in the Home Office line showing each product's total sales to date compared to its current year sales goal. An Access query can produce this result. Helen may want the results of this query to be displayed in a more stylized fashion—an opportunity to use a report—but for now Chris will present this feature to Helen only as a query.

The query to produce this list of products appears in Figure 2-17, with sample output in Figure 2-18. The query in Figure 2-17 shows the relationship of the data model needed for this query at the top and the Query-by-Example code below. If a field is checked in the Show box, then that field is to be included in the result. Two

Product Identifier	Current Year Product Sales Goal	Total Sales
3	$37,500.00	$3,000.00
5	$22,000.00	$650.00
6	$17,500.00	$6,000.00
8	$55,000.00	$3,250.00

Figure 2-18
Home Office product line sales comparison

fields, Product_Line_Name and Order_Placement_Date, are only used to select the Home Office furniture and orders in the current year, 1999. The Group By phase on the PR_Current_Year_Goal (and also on the Product_ID field not shown on this screen capture) tells Access to sum the total sales for each product. Not all of the query can be seen in Figure 2-17 due to screen size limitations. The missing pieces are

- The Product_ID field is also included to the left of the PR_Current_Year_Goal field.

- The expression to calculate the total sales for each product is missing after the word Sum. This missing expression is:

    Total Sales: Sum([Order_Quantity]*[Product_Price])

Only limited data are included for this example, so the Total Sales results in Figure 2-18 are fairly small, but the format is the result of the query in Figure 2-17.

Chris is now ready to meet with Helen again to see if the prototype is beginning to meet her needs. Chris shows Helen the system (by running Access and displaying screens like those in Figures 2-16 through 2-18). As Helen makes suggestions, Chris is able to make a few changes online, but many of Helen's observations will have to wait for more careful work at his desk.

Space does not permit us to review the whole project to develop the Home Office marketing support system. Chris and Helen ended up meeting about a dozen times before Helen was satisfied that all the attributes she needed were in the database; that the standard queries, forms, and reports Chris wrote were of use to her; and that she knew how to write queries for unanticipated questions. Chris will be available to Helen at any time to provide consulting support when she has trouble with the system, including writing more complex queries, forms, or reports. One final decision that Chris and Helen made was that the performance of the final prototype was efficient enough that the prototype did not have to be rewritten or redesigned. Helen was now ready to use the system.

Administering a Database

The administration of the Home Office marketing support system is fairly simple. Helen decided that she could live with weekly downloads of new data from Pine Valley's operational databases into her Access database. Chris wrote a C program with SQL commands embedded in it to perform the necessary extracts and wrote an Access program in Visual Basic to rebuild the Access tables from these extracts; he scheduled these jobs to run every Sunday evening. Chris also updated the corporate information systems architecture model to include the Home Office marketing support system. This step was important so that when changes occurred to formats for data included in Helen's system, the corporate CASE tool could alert Chris that changes might have to be made also in her system.

SUMMARY

This chapter discussed the process of developing databases and the applications that used them. Database development begins with enterprise data modeling, where the range and general contents of organizational databases are established. Enterprise data modeling is part of an overall process that develops an information systems architecture (including data, processes, network, people, events, and reasons) for an organization. One popular methodology for developing an information systems architecture is information engineering, a top-down information systems planning approach.

Information systems planning must consider organization goals, critical success factors, and problem areas of the organization. During information systems planning, data entities need to be related to other organizational planning objects: organizational units, locations, business functions, and information systems. Business functions can be represented at various levels of detail by breaking them down through a process called functional decomposition. Relationships between data entities and the other organizational planning objects can be represented at a high level by planning matrixes, which can be manipulated to understand patterns of relationships.

Once the need for a database is identified either from information systems planning or from a specific request (such as the one from Helen Jarvis for a Home Office products marketing support system), a project team is formed to develop all elements. The project team follows a systems development process, such as the systems development life cycle or prototyping. The systems development life cycle can be represented by seven methodical steps: (1) project identification and selection, (2) project initiation and planning, (3) analysis, (4) logical design, (5) physical design, (6) implementation, and (7) maintenance. Database development activities occur in each of these overlapping phases, and feedback may occur which causes a project to return to a prior phase. In prototyping, a database and its applications are iteratively refined through a close interaction of systems developers and users. Prototyping works best when the database application is small and stand-alone, and a small number of users exist.

Throughout the systems development process, CASE tools are used to develop data models and to maintain the metadata for the database and applications. A repository maintains all of the documentation. Various people might use the CASE tools and associated repository during a database development project: systems analysts, database analysts, users, programmers, database and data administrators, and other technical specialists. As a significant new portion of a project is completed and entries are made in the repository, a review point occurs so that those working on the project and funding the human and capital resources of the project can assess progress and renew commitment based on incremental achievements.

Those working on a database development project deal with three views, or schemas, for a database: (1) conceptual schema, which provides a complete, technology-independent picture of the database; (2) physical or internal schema, which specifies the complete database as it will be stored in computer secondary memory; and (3) external schemas or user views, which describe a subset of the database relevant to a specific set of users.

A modern database and the applications that use it may be located on multiple computers. Although any number from one to many tiers may exist, three tiers of computers relate to the client/server architecture for database processing: (1) the client tier, where database contents are presented to the user; (2) the workgroup tier, where analyses on database contents are made; and (3) the enterprise server tier, where the data from across the organization are merged into an organizational asset.

We closed the chapter with the review of a hypothetical database development project in Pine Valley Furniture Company. This system to support marketing a Home Office furniture product line illustrated the use of a personal computer database management system, Microsoft Access, for developing a retrieval-only database. The database in this application contained data extracted from the enterprise databases and then stored in a separate database on the client tier. Prototyping was used to develop this database application because the user, Helen Jarvis, had rather unstructured needs that could best be discovered through an iterative process of developing and refining the system.

CHAPTER REVIEW

KEY TERMS

Business function
Client/server
  architecture
Computer-aided
  software engineering
  (CASE)
Conceptual schema
Enterprise data
  modeling

Functional
  decomposition
Incremental
  commitment
Information
  engineering
Information systems
  architecture (ISA)
Physical schema

Project
Prototyping
Repository
Systems development
  life cycle (SDLC)
Top-down planning

REVIEW QUESTIONS

1. Define each of the following key terms:
   a. Information systems architecture (ISA)
   b. Systems development life cycle (SDLC)
   c. Client/server architecture
   d. Incremental commitment
   e. Enterprise data model
   f. Conceptual data modeling

2. Contrast the following terms:
   a. physical schema; conceptual schema
   b. systems development life cycle; prototyping
   c. top-down planning; functional decomposition
   d. enterprise data modeling; information engineering
   e. repository; computer-aided software engineering

3. List and explain the four steps of information engineering.

4. Describe the three steps in the information engineering planning phase.

5. List and explain the three information engineering strategic planning factors.

6. List and define the five key corporate planning objects.

7. Explain the significance of functional decomposition in information systems and database development.

8. Explain the use of information system planning matrixes in information systems development.

9. Name the seven phases of the traditional systems development life cycle, and explain the purpose and deliverables of each phase.

10. In which of the seven phases of the SDLC do database development activities occur?

11. Define the steps in the prototyping systems development process. Which database development activities occur in each prototyping step?

12. Explain the differences between user views, a conceptual schema, and a physical schema as different views of the same database.

13. Are the design of external schemas and a conceptual schema done in a particular sequence? Why or why not?

14. Define the three-tiered database architecture.

15. In the three-tiered database architecture, is it possible for there to be no database on a particular tier? If not, why? If yes, give an example.

16. List the six key components of an information systems architecture (ISA). Which of these components relate to database design? Why?

17. What is the significance of the waterfall metaphor for the systems development life cycle (SDLC)?

18. When during the database development process might an entity-relationship diagram be drawn? How are these different diagrams of the same database different from one another?

19. What are the reasons for implementing a client/server database architecture?

PROBLEMS AND EXERCISES

1. Match the following terms and definitions:

_____ conceptual schema	a. repeatedly breaking a function into finer and finer detail
_____ business function	
_____ prototyping	b. periodic review points in a systems development project
_____ systems development life cycle	c. a rapid approach to systems development
_____ functional decomposition	d. a comprehensive description of business data
_____ top-down planning	
_____ incremental commitment	e. gains a broad understanding of information system needs
_____ physical schema	f. a related group of business processes

g. the structure of data stored in secondary memory

h. a structured, step-by-step approach to systems development

2. Is the waterfall metaphor a good representation of the systems development life cycle? Explain any problems you have with this metaphor.

3. Rearrange the rows and columns of Figure 2-3 into a more useful sequence. Why did you choose this new sequence of rows and columns? For what purpose can you now use the rearranged matrix?

4. List three additional entities that might appear in an enterprise data model for Pine Valley Furniture (Figure 2-1).

5. Consider your business school or other academic unit as a business enterprise.

   a. Define several functions and do a functional decomposition to at least three levels.

   b. Define several major data entity types, and draw a preliminary enterprise data model (similar in notation to Figure 2-1).

   c. Develop a planning matrix with the lowest level functions from part a of the exercise as rows and data entity types from part b as columns. Fill in the cells of this matrix similar to Figure 2-3.

   d. Define four critical success factors (CSFs) for the academic unit.

   e. Would your business school or academic unit benefit from a multiple-tiered architecture for data? Why or why not?

6. Consider a student club in which you are involved.

   a. Define several information systems (manual or automated) used by this club.

   b. Define several major data entity types, and draw a preliminary enterprise data model (similar in notation to Figure 2-1).

   c. Develop an Information System–to–Data Entity planning matrix. Fill in the cells to show how each information system interacts with each data entity (code the cell with a C for create new instances of that entity, R for retrieves data about that entity, U for updates values of data for that entity, and D for deletes instances of that entity.

   d. Reorganize the rows and columns of your answer to part c of this exercise to create, as best you can, a matrix with cells with entries along the main diagonal and empty cells off the main diagonal. What does this reorganized matrix tell you?

7. Imagine a planning matrix of Business Functions–to–Data Entities. Suppose that by studying this matrix you determine that three of the business functions provide the bulk of the use of five of the data entities. What implications might this have for identifying databases for development?

8. Consider Table 2-3. Develop a hypothetical Information System–to–Entity Type matrix from the information in this table. Make assumptions about which information systems create, retrieve, update, and delete data from each data entity. Code the cells to indicate create (C), retrieve (R), update (U), and delete (D). Since the information systems listed include both transaction processing and management information systems, what patterns of entity usage do you observe?

9. Consider Table 2-3. Develop a hypothetical functional decomposition of the Product development business function, similar to what is shown for the Order fulfillment function in Figure 2-2. Do any of the same subfunctions appear in both Figure 2-2 and your diagram? Why?

10. Explain the differences between an enterprise data model and a conceptual data model. How many databases does each represent? What scope of the organization does each address? What are other salient differences?

11. Is it possible that during the physical database design and creation step of database development you might want to return to the logical database design activity? Why or why not? If it is possible, give an example of what might arise during physical database design and creation that would cause you to want to reconsider the conceptual and external database designs from prior steps.

12. Contrast the top-down nature of database development during conceptual data modeling with the bottom-up nature of database development during logical database design. What major differences exist in the type of information considered in each of these two database development steps?

13. The objective of the prototyping systems development methodology is to rapidly build and rebuild an information system as the user and systems analyst learn from use of the prototype what features should be included in the evolving information system. Since the final prototype does not have to become the working system, where do you think would be an ideal location to develop a prototype: on a personal computer, workgroup computer, department computer, or enterprise server? Does your answer depend on any assumptions?

14. Consider an organization with which you frequently interact, such as a bank, credit card company, university, or insurance company, from which you receive several computer-generated messages, such as monthly statements, transaction slips, and so forth. Depict the data included in each message you receive from the organization as its own user view; use the notation of Figure 2-1 to represent these views. Now, combine all of these user views together into one conceptual data model, also using the notation of Figure 2-1. What did you observe about the process of combining the different user views? Were there inconsistencies across the user views? Once you have created the conceptual data model, would you like to change anything about any of the user views?

15. Consider Figure 2-10, which depicts a hypothetical three-tiered database architecture. Identify potential duplications of data across all the databases listed on this figure. What problems might arise because of this duplication? Does this duplication violate the principles of the database approach outlined in Chapter 1? Why or why not?

16. Consider Figure 2-11. Explain the meaning of the line which connects ORDER to INVOICE and the line which connects INVOICE to PAYMENT. What does this say about how Pine Valley does business with its customers?

17. Answer the following questions concerning Figures 2-12 through 2-15:

    a. Why is the data type of PL_Prior_Year_Goal and other goal fields currency?

    b. What will be the field size for the Product_Line_Name field in the PRODUCT table? Why?

    c. Why is the Product_ID field in the PRODUCT table specified to be required?

    d. Investigate the format of a Date/Time field, such as Order_Placement_Date, in the ORDER table. How does Access handle the change from the twentieth to the twenty-first centuries?

    e. Why do two fields, Order_Number and Product_ID, have keys next to them for the ORDERED PRODUCT table?

18. Consider the Access query in Figure 2-17.

    a. Why is it necessary to include the Order_Placement_Date field in this query even though it is not displayed in the query result?

b. How would the query have to change if Helen Jarvis wanted to see the results for all of the product lines, not just Home Office?

FIELD EXERCISES

1. Interview systems and database analysts at several organizations. Ask them to describe their systems development process. Does it resemble more the systems development life cycle or prototyping? Do they use methodologies similar to both? When do they use their different methodologies?

2. Choose an organization with which you are familiar, possibly where you work, your university, or an organization where a friend works. For this organization, describe its information systems architecture (ISA). Does it have a formally prepared architecture, or did you have to create one? Interview information system managers in this organization to find out why they do or do not have a formally recognized information systems architecture.

3. Choose an organization with which you are familiar, possibly your employer, your university, or an organization where a friend works. Consider a major database in this organization, such as one supporting customer interactions, accounting, or manufacturing. What is the architecture for this database? Is the organization using some form of client/server architecture? Interview information system managers in this organization to find out why they chose the architecture for this database.

4. Choose an organization with which you are familiar, possibly your employer, your university, or an organization where a friend works. Interview a systems analyst or database analyst and ask questions about the typical composition of an information systems development team. Specifically, what role does a database analyst play in project teams? Is a database analyst used throughout the systems development process or is the database analyst used only at selected points?

5. Choose an organization with which you are familiar, possibly your employer, your university, or an organization where a friend works. Interview a systems analyst or database analyst and ask questions about how that organization uses CASE tools in the systems development process. Concentrate your questions on how CASE tools are used to support data modeling and database design and how the CASE tool's repository maintains the information collected about data, data characteristics, and data usage. If multiple CASE tools are used on one or many projects, ask how the organization attempts to integrate data models and data definitions. Finally, inquire how satisfied the systems and database analysts are with CASE tool support for data modeling and database design.

REFERENCES

Hoffer, J. A., J. F. George, and J. S. Valacich. 1999. *Modern Systems Analysis and Design.* 2nd ed. Reading, MA: Addison-Wesley.

Moriarty, T. 1991. "Framing Your System." *Database Programming & Design* 4 (June): 38–43.

Sowa, J. F., and J. A. Zachman. 1992. "Extending and Formalizing the Framework for Information Systems Architecture." *IBM Systems Journal* 31 (3): 590–616.

Thompson, C. 1997. "Committing to Three-Tier Architecture." *Database Programming & Design* 10 (August): 26–30, 32, 33.

Zachman, J. A. 1987. "A Framework for Information Systems Architecture." *IBM Systems Journal* 26 (March): 276–92.

FURTHER READING

Finkelstein, C. 1989. *An Introduction to Information Engineering.* Reading, MA: Addison-Wesley.

Shank, M. E., A. C. Boynton, and R. W. Zmud. 1985. "Critical Success Factor Analysis as a Methodology for IS Planning." *MIS Quarterly* 9 (June): 121–29.

Project Case

PROJECT DESCRIPTION

You were introduced to Mountain View Community Hospital in Chapter 1. Figure 1 shows an organizational chart for Mountain View Community Hospital as of January 1, 1999. Like most general hospitals, Mountain View Community is divided into two primary organizational groups. The physicians, headed by Dr. Browne (chief of staff), are responsible for the quality of medical care provided to their patients. The group headed by Ms. Baker (administrator) provides the nursing, clinical, and administrative support the physicians need to serve their patients.

Goals and Critical Success Factors As stated in Chapter 1, Mountain View Community Hospital's basic goal is to provide high-quality health care for its surrounding community while containing costs that have been rising in accordance with national trends in recent years. Mountain View Community Hospital serves a community of about 50,000 with an annual growth rate of 10 percent, a trend that is expected to continue since the surrounding area is attracting many retirees. Thus, Mountain View Community Hospital has a goal to expand its capacity (adding another 50 beds in five years) and opening a managed care retirement center with independent apartments to assisted living facili-

Figure 1 Organization chart, January 1999

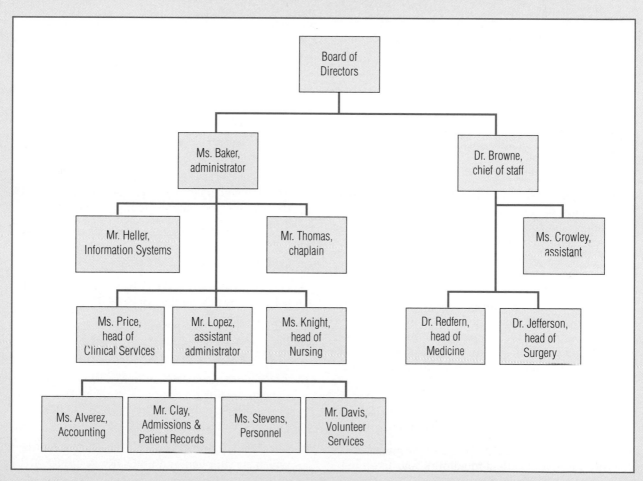

ties. Adequate land exists for expansion adjacent to the current hospital facilities. Because of this expansion, Mountain View Community Hospital plans to increase the size of both administrative and medical staff, create a new department of Retirement Living under Ms. Baker, and create a new department of Geriatric Medicine under Dr. Browne.

In response to the steady growth and expansion plans at Mountain View Community Hospital, a special study team including Mr. Heller, Mr. Lopez, Dr. Jefferson, and a consultant has been developing a long-term business plan, including an information systems plan for the Hospital. Their work is not complete, but they have begun to identify many of the elements necessary to build the plan. In order to meet the goals of high-quality health care, cost containment, and expansion into new services, the team concluded that the Hospital has four critical success factors: quality of medical care, control of operating costs, control of capital costs, and recruitment and retention of skilled personnel (especially nurses). The development of improved information systems is an enabler in dealing with each of these CSFs.

The team is currently at work to generate two to four short- or long-term objectives for each CSF. So far they have developed the following four objectives related to the control of operating costs CSF:

1. Reduce costs for purchased items

2. More efficiently schedule staff

3. Lower cost of liability insurance

4. Expand volunteer services

The study team described each of these CSFs and objectives in more detail and stored these descriptions in a repository managed by the CASE tool used by the information systems department.

Enterprise Modeling   The study team also has developed a preliminary list of business functions that describe the administrative and medical activities within the Hospital. These functions consider the organizational goals and CSFs explained in the prior section. At this point, the study team has identified five major business functions that cut across all of the organizational units:

*   *Patient care administration*   Manages the logistical and record-keeping aspects of patient care.

*   *Clinical services*   Provide laboratory testing and procedures, and patient monitoring and screening.

*   *Patient care services*   Provide patients with medical care and support services.

*   *Financial management*   Manage the financial resources and operations of the hospital.

*   *Administrative services*   Provide general management and support services not directly related to patient care.

The study team has been able to break each of these high-level functions into lists of more detailed functions (see Figure 2), but the team knows that these lists are not complete nor well defined at this point.

The study team initially has a preliminary set of 10 entity types that describe the data required by the hospital for its operation and administration: FACILITY, PHYSICIAN, PATIENT, WARD, STAFF, LABORATORY, TEST, MEDICAL/SURGICAL ITEM, SUPPLY ITEM, and VENDOR. From discussions with hospital staff, reviewing hospital documents, and studying existing information systems, the study team developed a list of business rules that describe the policies of the hospital and nature of the hospital's operation which govern the relationships between these entities. Some of these rules are:

1. A FACILITY maintains a number of LABORATORY(ies): radiology, electrodiagnosis, hematology, and so on.

2. A FACILITY contains a number of WARDs (obstetrics, emergency, rehabilitation, geriatrics, etc.).

3. Each WARD is assigned a certain number of STAFF members (nurses, secretaries, etc.); a STAFF member may be assigned to multiple WARDs.

4. A FACILITY staffs a number of PHYSICIANs on its medical staff. A PHYSICIAN may be on the staff of more than one FACILITY.

5. A PHYSICIAN treats PATIENTs, and a PATIENT is treated by any number of PHYSICIANs.

6. A PHYSICIAN diagnoses PATIENTs, and a PATIENT is diagnosed by any number of PHYSICIANs.

7. A PATIENT may be assigned to a WARD (outpatients are not assigned to a WARD). The hospital cares only about the current WARD a patient is assigned to (if assigned at all).

8. A PATIENT uses MEDICAL/SURGICAL ITEMS, which are supplied by VENDORs. A VENDOR

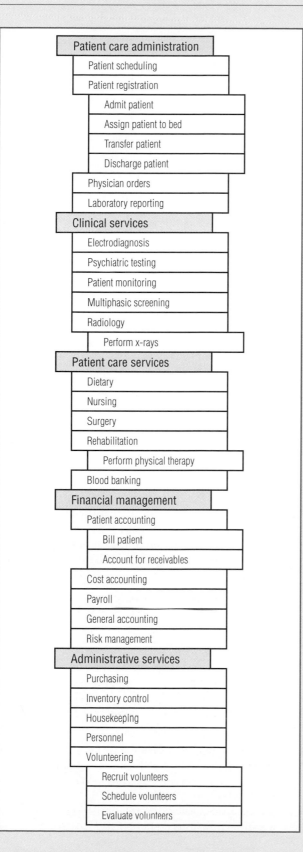

Figure 2
Business functions

also provides SUPPLY ITEMs that are used for housekeeping and maintenance purposes.

9. A LABORATORY performs TESTs about PATIENTs.

They recognized that certain business functions, such as risk management and volunteering, were not adequately represented in the set of data entities and business rules, but they decided to deal with these and other areas later. The study team stored descriptions of these data entities and the business rules in the CASE repository for later analysis. Using the identified entities and business rules, the study team developed a preliminary enterprise data model (see Figure 3). Again, this data model is preliminary since it does not follow all the conventions used in the information systems department for drawing data models, but the purpose of this enterprise model is to give only a general overview of organizational data.

Developing Planning Matrixes   The study team used the CASE tool to produce a first version of a function-to-entity type matrix (see Figure 4). This matrix maps the business functions from Figure 2 with the 10 data entities. The cells of the matrix are coded as follows:

M = function maintains instances of entity (creates, updates, and deletes)

R = function uses data about entity

As an initial pass at this matrix, the study team decided not to separately code data creation, update, and deletion activities.

The study team also used the CASE tool to relate business functions to the four critical success factors (see Figure 5 for the result of their work). In this figure the cells indicate:

E = doing the function well is essential in achieving the CSF

D = doing the function well helps in achieving the CSF

The study team is looking for ways to combine the results shown in Figures 4 and 5 to help them set some priorities for information systems development.

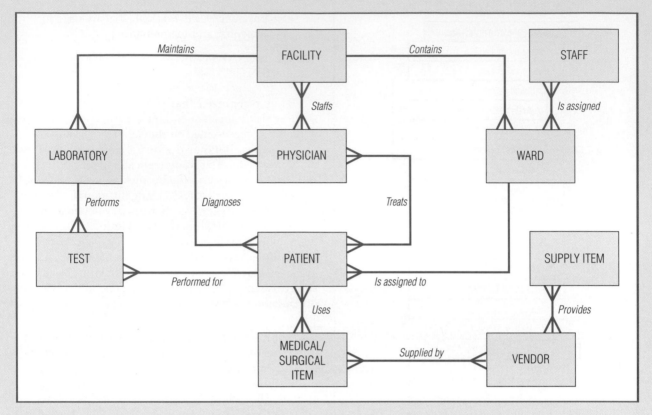

Figure 3
Preliminary enterprise data model

PROJECT QUESTIONS

1. Which information system planning matrixes (among those shown in this case study or others not shown) might assist the study team at Mountain View Community Hospital to determine a tiered location plan for databases? Why?

2. In the project description above, objectives are listed for one of the four critical success factors, operating cost control. Write plausible objectives, given the structure and plans of the hospital, for the other three CSFs.

3. What additional activities might occur within the "volunteering" business function?

4. What activities might occur within the "risk management" business function?

5. What additional data entities, besides the 10 entities mentioned in this case, might the risk management business function need?

6. Do you think that the study team will be able to identify all the data entities by doing the kind of analysis they have been doing? If not, what other database development steps will need to be done and when?

7. Why do you think the people on the business planning study team were selected for this assignment? Would you have chosen different or additional people?

8. In the case description above, nine business rules are listed. The study team used these rules to develop Figure 3. What other business rules, besides these nine, are implied by or depicted in Figure 3?

9. Even though capital cost control is a critical success factor, only two business functions in Figure 5 mention this CSF. Why? What would need to be done to enhance this figure so that more entries indicated a relationship between business functions and this CSF?

Figure 4
Business function–to–data entity matrix

Business Functions \ Data Entity Types	Facility	Physician	Patient	Ward	Staff	Laboratory	Test	Medical/ Surgical Item	Supply Item	Vendor
Patient Scheduling		R	R			R				
Patient Registration			M	R						
Physician Orders		R	R				R			
Laboratory Reporting			R			R	R			
Electrodiagnosis							M			
Psychiatric Testing							M			
Patient Monitoring			R							
Multiphasic Screening			R			R	M			
Radiology						R	M			
Dietary			R							
Nursing			R							
Surgery		R	R							
Rehabilitation			R							
Blood Banking			R			R				
Patient Accounting			R	R		R	R			
Cost Accounting	R		R	R			R			
Payroll		R		R	R					
General Accounting	M			M		M				
Risk Management	R	R	R					R		R
Purchasing								M	M	M
Inventory Control								R	R	
Housekeeping									R	
Personnel		M			M				R	
Volunteering	R		R	R		R				

M = data entity (column) is maintained by business function (row)
R = data entity (column) is used by business function (row)

PROJECT EXERCISES

1. Rearrange the rows and columns of Figure 4 so that the entries form a block diagonal pattern. What conclusions do you reach from analyzing this pattern?

2. Redraw Figure 1 to reflect the structure of the hospital after its planned future expansion and growth. Given this expansion and growth, what else would need to change about Figures 2, 3, and 4?

3. Based on Figures 4 and 5, determine which data entities are essential for operating cost control. What implications does this result have for information systems development?

4. In Project Question 5 you listed additional data entities needed for the risk management business

Business Functions \ Critical Success Factors	Quality Care	Operating Cost Control	Capital Cost Control	Staff Recruitment and Retention
Patient Scheduling	D			
Patient Registration				
Physician Orders	D			
Laboratory Reporting	D			
Electrodiagnosis			D	
Psychiatric Testing	D			
Patient Monitoring	E			
Multiphasic Screening	E			
Radiology	D			
Dietary	E			
Nursing	E	E		E
Surgery	D	D	E	
Rehabilitation	E			
Blood Banking	D			
Patient Accounting	D	E		
Cost Accounting		E		
Payroll				D
General Accounting				
Risk Management		E		D
Purchasing		E		
Inventory Control		E		
Housekeeping		D		
Personnel				E
Volunteering		E		E

E = business function (row) is essential in achieving CSF (column)
D = business function (row) is desirable in achieving CSF (column)

Figure 5
Business function–to–CSF matrix

function. Modify Figure 3 to include these additional entities and the relevant relationships among all data entities.

5. One of the important outputs from the "bill patient" business function is the Patient Bill. Project Exercise 2 in Chapter 1 introduced a reduced version of this bill, which is repeated below. That exercise asked you to add missing data that would typically appear on a patient bill. Using your result from that exercise, verify that the enterprise data model in Figure 3 contains the data necessary to generate a patient bill. Explain what you have to do to perform this verification. What did you discover from your analysis?

Patient Name: Dolan, Mark

Patient Number: _____

Patient Address: _____

Item Code	Item Description	Amount
_____	_____	_____
_____	_____	_____
_____	_____	_____

6. The study team activities described in this case study have related to very early stages of information system and database development. Outline the next steps that should be followed within the Information Systems unit to align current systems and databases to the future information systems needs of the hospital.

7. The manager of the risk management area is anxious to receive computerized support for his activities. The hospital is increasingly facing malpractice claims and litigation, and he does not believe he can wait for improved information services until the information systems and database plans are set. What this manager wants is a system that will track claims, legal suits, lawyers, judges, medical staff, disbursements against claims, and judgments. How would you proceed to deal with this request for improved information services? What methodology would you apply to design the systems and databases he needs? Why?

8. Consider again the request of the manager of risk management from Project Exercise 7. On what tier or tiers would you recommend the system and database he needs be developed? Why?

PART

II

Database Analysis

CHAPTER 3

The Entity-Relationship Model

CHAPTER 4

The Enhanced E-R Model and Business Rules

CHAPTER 5

Object-Oriented Modeling

Part II Overview

The first step in database development is database analysis, in which we determine user requirements for data and develop data models to represent those requirements. Part II (consisting of three chapters) describes alternative techniques for *conceptual* data modeling. A conceptual data model is one that represents data from the viewpoint of the user, independent of any technology that will be used to implement the model.

Chapter 3 (The Entity-Relationship Model) presents the main features of this popular data model. The entity-relationship (or E-R) model has become the *de facto* standard for conceptual data modeling during the past two decades. This chapter introduces the notation and main constructs of this modeling technique including entities, relationships, and attributes. We distinguish between strong and weak entity types and the use of identifying relationships. We describe different types of attributes including simple versus composite attributes, single-valued versus multivalued attributes, derived attributes, and identifiers. We contrast relationship types and instances and introduce associative entities. We describe and illustrate relationships of various degrees including unary, binary, and ternary relationships. We also describe the various relationship cardinalities that arise in modeling situations. We discuss the common problem of how to model time-dependent data. Finally, we describe the situation where multiple relationships are defined between a given set of entities. The E-R modeling concepts are illustrated with an extended example for Pine Valley Furniture Company.

Chapter 4 (The Enhanced E-R Model and Business Rules) presents advanced concepts in entity-relationship modeling and introduces recently developed notation for capturing more complex business rules on E-R diagrams. These additional modeling features are often required to cope with the increasingly complex business environment encountered in organizations today.

The most important new modeling construct incorporated in the enhanced entity-relationship (or EER) diagram is supertype/subtype relationships. This facility allows us to model a general entity type (called a supertype) and then subdivide it into several specialized entity types called subtypes. For example, sports cars and sedans are subtypes of automobiles. We introduce a simple notation for representing supertype/subtype relationships. We also introduce generalization and specialization as two contrasting techniques for identifying supertype/subtype relationships. We introduce notation to further refine the basic supertype/subtype relationships.

Business rules are statements that define or constrain some aspect of the business. We develop a classification for the different types of business rules that are commonly encountered. We then describe and illustrate a declarative approach for expressing business rules, together with a notation for the rules that is superimposed on the EER diagram.

Chapter 5 (Object-Oriented Modeling) introduces an alternative set of concepts and models for expressing user requirements. The object-oriented model is becoming increasingly popular because of its ability to represent complex data types and complex relationships. This chapter uses the Unified Modeling Language (or UML) developed by Booch, Rumbaugh, and Jacobson to express a logical model of user requirements.

In the object-oriented model, the user domain is modeled in objects. An object is an entity that has three properties: state, behavior, and identity. The behavior of an object is determined by one or more operations that are encapsulated in the object. Associations between objects are expressed using notation that is similar to that on E-R diagrams. Important properties associated with the object-oriented model include generalization, inheritance, and polymorphism. This chapter presents an object-oriented version (in the form of a class diagram) of the Pine Valley Furniture case (from Chapter 3) so that you can compare these two approaches.

The conceptual data modeling concepts presented in the three chapters in Part II provide the foundation for your career in database analysis and design. As a database analyst you will be expected to apply one or more of these techniques in modeling user requirements for data and information.

The Entity-Relationship Model

LEARNING OBJECTIVES

After studying this chapter, you should be able to:

- Concisely define each of the following key terms: **entity-relationship model (E-R model)**, **entity-relationship diagram (E-R diagram)**, **entity**, **entity type**, **entity instance**, **strong entity type**, **weak entity type**, **identifying owner**, **attribute**, **composite attribute**, **simple attribute**, **multivalued attribute**, **derived attribute**, **identifier**, **composite identifier**, **relationship**, **relationship instance**, **associative entity**, **degree of a relationship**, **unary relationship**, **binary relationship**, **ternary relationship**, **cardinality constraint**, **minimum and maximum cardinality**, and **time stamp**.

- State reasons why many system developers believe that data modeling is the most important part of the system development process.

- Distinguish unary, binary, and ternary relationships and give a common example of each.

- Model each of the following constructs in an E-R diagram: composite attribute, multivalued attribute, derived attribute, associative entity, and identifying relationship.

- Draw an entity-relationship (E-R) diagram to represent common business situations.

- Model minimum and maximum cardinality constraints on an E-R diagram.

- Convert a many-to-many relationship to an associative entity type.

- Model simple time-dependent data using time stamps in an E-R diagram.

INTRODUCTION

You have already been introduced to the entity-relationship model through simplified examples of its use in the first two chapters of this text. In this chapter we describe the entity-relationship (E-R) model in detail. After some years of use, the

E-R model remains the mainstream approach for conceptual data modeling. Its popularity stems from factors such as relative ease of use, widespread CASE tool support, and the belief that entities and relationships are natural modeling concepts in the real world.

The E-R model is most often used as a tool for communications between database designers and end users during the analysis phase of database development (described in Chapter 2). The E-R model is used to construct a *conceptual* data model, which is a representation of the structure and constraints of a database that is independent of the software (such as a database management system) and its associated data model that will be used to implement the database.

Some authors introduce terms and concepts peculiar to the relational data model when discussing E-R modeling. In particular, they recommend that the E-R model be completely normalized, with full resolution of primary and foreign keys. However, we believe that this forces a premature commitment to the relational data model. In today's database environment, it is equally likely that the database will be implemented with object-oriented technology, or with a mixture of object-oriented and relational. Therefore, we defer discussion of normalization concepts to Chapter 6.

The entity-relationship model was introduced in a key article by Chen (1976), in which he described the main constructs of the E-R model—entities and relationships—and their associated attributes. The model has subsequently been extended to include additional constructs by Chen and others; for example, see Teorey, Yang, and Fry (1986) and Storey (1991). The E-R model continues to evolve, but unfortunately there is not yet a standard notation for E-R modeling. Song, Evans, and Park (1995) present a side-by-side comparison of 10 different E-R modeling notations, explaining the major advantages and disadvantages of each approach. Many systems developers believe that data modeling is the most important part of the systems development process. This belief is based on three important reasons (Hoffer, George, and Valacich, 1999):

1. The characteristics of data captured during data modeling are crucial in the design of databases, programs, and other system components. The facts and rules captured during the process of data modeling are essential in assuring data integrity in an information system.

2. Data rather than processes are the most complex aspects of many modern information systems and hence require a central role in structuring system requirements. Often the goal is to provide a rich data resource that might support any type of information inquiry, analysis, and summary.

3. Data tend to be more stable than the business processes that use that data. Thus an information system design that is based on a data orientation should have a longer useful life than one based on a process orientation.

In this chapter we present the main features of E-R modeling, using common notation and conventions. We begin by defining the basic constructs of the E-R model: entities, attributes, and relationships. We define three types of entities that are common in E-R modeling: strong entities, weak entities, and associative entities. We also define several important types of attributes, including single- and multivalued attributes, derived attributes, and composite attributes. We then introduce three important concepts associated with relationships: the degree of a relationship, the cardinality of a relationship, and participation constraints in a relationship. We conclude with an extended example of an E-R diagram for Pine Valley Furniture Company.

THE E-R MODEL

An **entity-relationship model** (or **E-R model**) is a detailed, logical representation of the data for an organization or for a business area. The E-R model is expressed in terms of entities in the business environment, the relationships (or associations) among those entities, and the attributes (or properties) of both the entities and their relationships. An E-R model is normally expressed as an **entity-relationship diagram** (or **E-R diagram**), which is a graphical representation of an E-R model.

Entity-relationship model: A logical representation of the data for an organization or for a business area.

Entity-relationship diagram (E-R diagram): A graphical representation of an entity-relationship model.

Sample E-R Diagram

To jump start your understanding of E-R diagrams, Figure 3-1 presents a simplified E-R diagram for a small manufacturing company. This company purchases items from a number of different vendors, who then ship the items to the manufacturer. The items are assembled into products that are sold to customers who order the products. Each customer order may include one or more lines corresponding to the products appearing on that order.

Figure 3-1
Sample E-R diagram

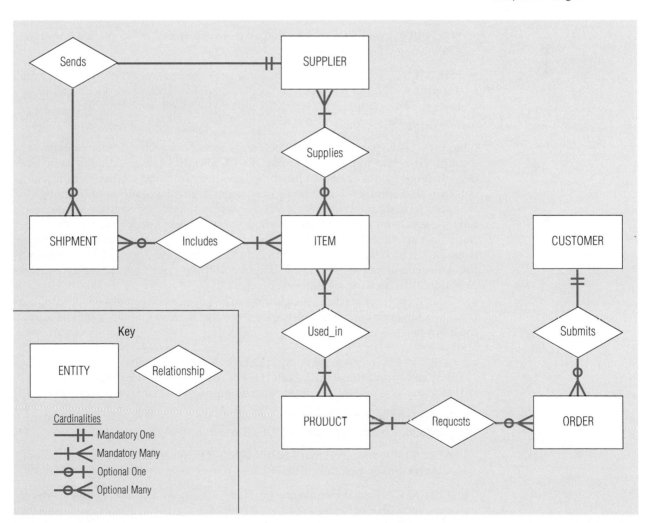

The diagram in Figure 3-1 shows the entities and relationships for this company (attributes are omitted to simplify the diagram for now). Entities are represented by the rectangle symbol, while relationships between entities are represented by the diamond symbol connected by lines to the related entities. The entities in Figure 3-1 are:

- CUSTOMER   A person or organization who has ordered or might order products. *Example:* L. L. Fish Furniture.

- PRODUCT   A type of furniture made by Pine Valley Furniture which may be ordered by customers. Note that a product is not a specific bookcase since individual bookcases do not need to be tracked. *Example:* A 6-foot, 5-shelf, oak bookcase called O600.

- ORDER   The transaction associated with the sale of one or more products to a customer and identified by a transaction number from sales or accounting. *Example:* The event of L. L. Fish buying one product O600 and four products O623 on September 10, 1997.

- ITEM   A type of component which goes into making one or more products, which can be supplied by one or more suppliers. *Example:* A 4-inch, ball-bearing caster called I-27-4375.

- SUPPLIER   Another company that may provide items to Pine Valley Furniture. *Example:* Sure Fasteners, Inc.

- SHIPMENT   Items received in the same package by Pine Valley Furniture from a supplier. All items in a shipment appear on one bill-of-lading document. *Example:* The receipt of 300 I-27-4375 and 200 I-27-4380 items from Sure Fasteners, Inc. on September 9, 1997.

Note that it is important to clearly define, as metadata, each category of entity. For example, it is important to know that the CUSTOMER entity includes persons or organizations that have not yet purchased products from Pine Valley Furniture. It is common that different departments in an organization have different meanings for the same term (homonyms). For example, Accounting may designate as customers only those persons or organizations who have ever made a purchase, thus excluding potential customers, whereas Marketing designates as customers anyone they have contacted or who has purchased from Pine Valley Furniture or any known competitor. An accurate and thorough E-R diagram without clear metadata may be interpreted in different ways by different people.

The symbols at the end of each line on an E-R diagram represent relationship cardinalities. On examining Figure 3-1, we can see that these cardinality symbols express the following business rules:

1. A SUPPLIER may supply many ITEMs (by "may supply" we mean the supplier may not supply any items). Each ITEM is supplied by any number of SUPPLIERs (by "is supplied" we mean must be supplied by at least one supplier).

2. Each ITEM must be used in at least one PRODUCT, and may be used in many products. Conversely, each PRODUCT must use one or more ITEMs.

3. A SUPPLIER may send many SHIPMENTs. On the other hand, each shipment must be sent by exactly one SUPPLIER.

4. A SHIPMENT must include one (or more) ITEMs. An ITEM may be included on several SHIPMENTs.

5. A CUSTOMER may submit any number of ORDERs. However, each ORDER must be submitted by exactly one CUSTOMER.

6. An ORDER must request one (or more) PRODUCTs. A given PRODUCT may not be requested on any ORDER, or may be requested on one or more orders.

Note that each of these business rules roughly follows a certain grammar:

      <entity> <minimum cardinality> <relationship> <maximum cardinality>
        <entity>

For example, rule 5 is:

      <CUSTOMER> <may> <submit> <any number> <ORDER>

This grammar gives you a standard way to put each relationship into an English statement.

E-R Model Notation

The basic notation we use for E-R diagrams is shown in Figure 3-2. As indicated in the previous section, there is no industry standard notation (in fact, you saw a slightly simpler notation in Chapters 1 and 2). However, we believe that the notation in Figure 3-2 combines most of the desirable features of the different notations that are commonly used, and also allows us to accurately model most situations that are encountered in practice. We introduce additional notation for enhanced entity-relationship models (including class-subclass relationships) in Chapter 4.

ENTITY-RELATIONSHIP MODEL CONSTRUCTS

The basic constructs of the entity-relationship model are entities, relationships, and attributes. As shown in Figure 3-2, the model allows numerous variations for each of these constructs. The richness of the E-R model allows designers to model real-world situations accurately and expressively, which helps account for the popularity of the model.

Entities

An **entity** is a person, place, object, event, or concept in the user environment about which the organization wishes to maintain data. Some examples of each of these *types* of entities follow:

Person: EMPLOYEE, STUDENT, PATIENT

Place: CITY, STATE, COUNTRY

Object: MACHINE, BUILDING, AUTOMOBILE

Event: SALE, REGISTRATION, RENEWAL

Concept: ACCOUNT, COURSE, WORK CENTER

Entity: A person, place, object, event, or concept in the user environment about which the organization wishes to maintain data.

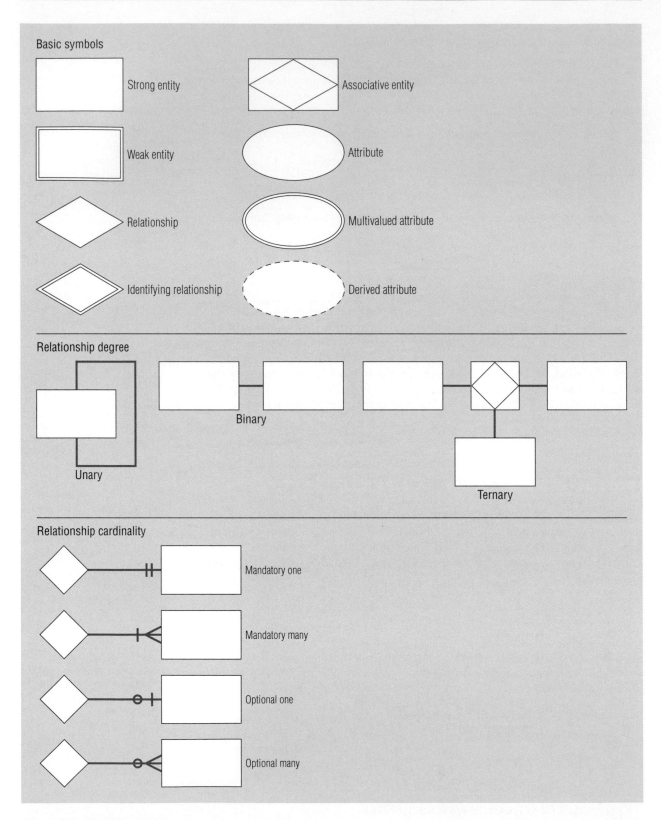

Figure 3-2 Basic E-R notation

Figure 3-3
Entity type (EMPLOYEE) with two instances

Entity type: EMPLOYEE

Attributes:

EMPLOYEE NUMBER	CHAR (10)
NAME	CHAR (25)
ADDRESS	CHAR (30)
CITY	CHAR (20)
STATE	CHAR (2)
ZIP	CHAR (9)
DATE HIRED	DATE
BIRTHDATE	DATE

Two Instances of EMPLOYEE:

642-17-8360	534-10-1971
Michelle Brady	David Johnson
100 Pacific Avenue	450 Redwood Drive
San Francisco	Redwood City
CA	CA
98173	97142
03-21-1992	08-16-1994
06-19-1968	09-04-1975

Entity Type Versus Entity Instance   There is an important distinction between entity types and entity instances. An **entity type** is a collection of entities that share common properties or characteristics. Each entity type in an E-R model is given a name. Since the name represents a collection (or set) of items, it is always singular. We use capital letters for names of entity type(s). In an E-R diagram the entity name is placed inside the box representing the entity type (see Figure 3-2).

> **Entity type:** A collection of entities that share common properties or characteristics.

An **entity instance** is a single occurrence of an entity type. Figure 3-3 illustrates the distinction between an entity type and two of its instances. An entity type is described just once (using metadata) in a database, while many instances of that entity type may be represented by data stored in the database. For example, there is one EMPLOYEE entity type in most organizations, but there may be hundreds (or even thousands) of instances of this entity type stored in the database. We often use the single term "entity" rather than entity instance, when the meaning is clear from the context of our discussion.

> **Entity instance:** A single occurrence of an entity type.

Entity Type Versus System Input, Output, or User   A common mistake made when you are just learning to draw E-R diagrams, especially if you already are familiar with data process modeling (such as data flow diagramming), is to confuse data entities with other elements of an overall information systems model. A simple rule to avoid such confusion is that a true data entity will have many possible instances, each with a distinguishing characteristic, as well as one or more other descriptive pieces of data.

Consider Figure 3-4a, which might be drawn to represent a database needed for a college sorority's expense system. In this situation, the sorority treasurer manages accounts, receives expense reports, and records expense transactions against each account. However, do we need to keep track of data about the Treasurer (the TREASURER entity type) and her supervision of accounts (the Manages relationship) and receipt of reports (the Gives_to relationship)? The Treasurer is the person entering data about accounts and expenses and receiving expense reports. That is, she is a *user*

Figure 3-4
Example of inappropriate
entities

(a) System user (Treasurer)
and output (Expense Report)
shown as entities

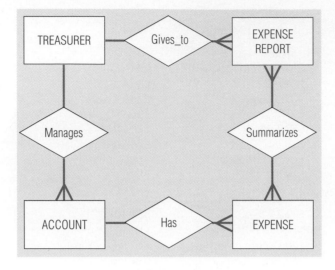

(b) E-R model with only the
necessary entities

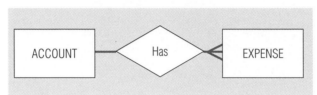

of the database. Since there is only one Treasurer, TREASURER data do not need to be kept. Further, is the EXPENSE REPORT entity necessary? Since an expense report is computed from expense transactions and account balances, it is the result of extracting data from the database. Even though there will be multiple instances of expense reports given to the Treasurer over time, data needed to compute the report contents each time are already represented by the ACCOUNT and EXPENSE entity types.

Another key to understanding why the E-R diagram in Figure 3-4a might be in error is the nature of the *relationship names* Gives_to and Summarizes. These relationship names refer to business activities that transfer or translate data, not to simply the association of one kind of data with another kind of data. The simple E-R model in Figure 3-4b shows entities and a relationship that would be sufficient to handle the sorority expense system as described here.

Strong Versus Weak Entity Types

Strong entity type: An entity that exists independently of other entity types.

Most of the basic entity types to identify in an organization are classified as strong entity types. A **strong entity type** is one that exists independently of other entity types. Examples include STUDENT, EMPLOYEE, AUTOMOBILE, and COURSE. Instances of a strong entity type always have a unique characteristic (called an *identifier*)—that is, an attribute or combination of attributes that uniquely distinguish each occurrence of that entity.

Weak entity type: An entity type whose existence depends on some other entity type.

Identifying owner: The entity type on which the weak entity type depends.

In contrast, a **weak entity type** is an entity type whose existence depends on some other entity type. A weak entity type has no business meaning and is not needed in the E-R diagram without the entity on which it depends. The entity type on which the weak entity type depends is called the **identifying owner** (or simply **owner** for short). A weak entity type does not have its own identifier. Generally on an

Figure 3-5
Example of a weak entity

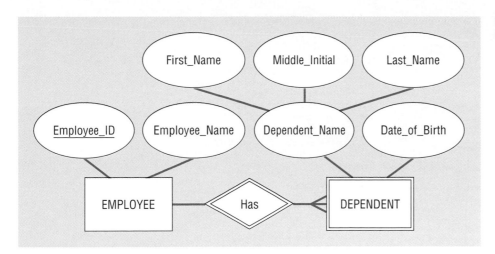

E-R diagram a weak entity type has an attribute that serves as a *partial* identifier. During a later design stage (described in Chapter 6), a full identifier will be formed for the weak entity by combining the partial identifier with the identifier of its owner.

An example of a weak entity type with an identifying relationship is shown in Figure 3-5. EMPLOYEE is a strong entity type with identifier Employee_ID (we note the identifier attribute by underlining it). DEPENDENT is a weak entity type, as indicated by the double-lined rectangle. The relationship between a weak entity type and its owner is called an **identifying relationship**. In Figure 3-5, "Has" is the identifying relationship (indicated by the double-lined diamond symbol). The attribute Dependent_Name serves as a *partial* identifier (Dependent_Name is a composite attribute that can be broken into component parts, as we describe below). During a later design stage, Dependent_Name will be combined with Employee_ID (the identifier of the owner) to form a full identifier for DEPENDENT.

Identifying relationship:
The relationship between a weak entity type and its owner.

Attributes

Each entity type has a set of attributes associated with it. An **attribute** is a property or characteristic of an entity type that is of interest to the organization. Following are some typical entity types and their associated attributes:

Attribute: A property or characteristic of an entity type that is of interest to the organization.

STUDENT   Student_ID, Student_Name, Address, Phone_Number, Major

AUTOMOBILE   Vehicle_ID, Color, Weight, Horsepower

EMPLOYEE   Employee_ID, Employee_Name, Address, Skill

In naming attributes, we use an initial capital letter followed by lowercase letters. If an attribute name consists of two words, we use an underscore character to connect the words and we start each word with a capital letter; for example: Employee_Name. In E-R diagrams, we represent an attribute by placing its name in an ellipse with a line connecting it to its associated entity. Attributes may also be associated with relationships, as described below. Note that an attribute is associated with exactly one entity or relationship.

Each entity (or instance of an entity type) has a value associated with each of the attributes of that entity type. For example, Figure 3-6 shows two entities with their respective attribute values. A database is, in essence, the collection of all of these attribute values for all of the entities. Thus, each entity has an identifying attribute

Figure 3-6
Two entity instances with attribute values

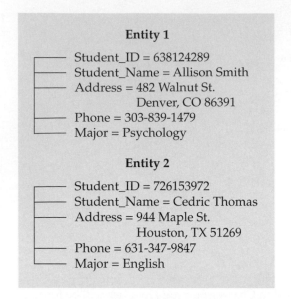

plus one or more other attributes. If you try to create an entity that has only an identifier, then that entity is likely not legitimate. Such a data structure may simply hold a list of legal values for some attribute, which is better kept outside the database.

Simple Versus Composite Attributes   Some attributes can be broken down into meaningful component parts. The most common example is Address, which can usually be broken down into the following components: Street_Address, City, State, and Postal_Code. A **composite attribute** is an attribute (such as Address) that can be broken down into component parts. Figure 3-7 shows the notation that we use for composite attributes applied to this example. The component attributes may appear above or below the composite attribute on an E-R diagram.

Composite attribute: An attribute that can be broken down into component parts.

Composite attributes provide considerable flexibility to users, who can either refer to the composite attribute as a single unit or else refer to individual components of that attribute. Thus, for example, a user can either refer to Address or refer to one of its components, such as Street_Address. The decision whether to subdivide an attribute into its component parts depends on whether users will need to refer to

Figure 3-7
A composite attribute

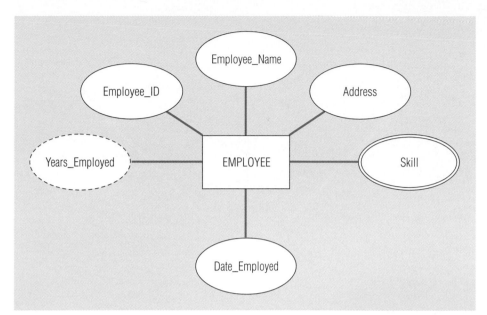

those individual components. Of course the designer must always attempt to anticipate possible future usage patterns for the database.

A **simple** (or **atomic**) **attribute** is an attribute that cannot be broken down into smaller components. For example, all of the attributes associated with AUTOMOBILE are simple: Vehicle_ID, Color, Weight, and Horsepower.

Simple attribute: An attribute that cannot be broken down into smaller components.

Single-Valued Versus Multivalued Attributes   Figure 3-6 shows two entities with their respective attribute values. For each entity instance, each of the attributes in the figure has one value. It frequently happens that there is an attribute that may have more than one value for a given instance. For example, the EMPLOYEE entity type has an attribute named Skill, whose values record the skill (or skills) for that employee. Of course, some employees may have more than one skill (such as COBOL Programmer and C++ Programmer). A **multivalued attribute** is an attribute that may take on more than one value for a given entity instance. We indicate a multivalued attribute with an ellipse with double lines, as shown for the Skill attribute in the EMPLOYEE example in Figure 3-8.

Multivalued attribute: An attribute that may take on more than one value for a given entity instance.

Stored Versus Derived Attributes   Some attribute values that are of interest to users can be calculated or derived from other related attribute values that are stored in the database. For example, suppose that for an organization, the EMPLOYEE entity type has a Date_Employed attribute. If users need to know how many years a person has been employed, that value can be calculated using Date_Employed and today's date. A **derived attribute** is an attribute whose values can be calculated from related attribute values (plus possibly data not in the database, such as today's date, the current time, or a security code provided by a system user). We indicate a derived attribute in an E-R diagram by using an ellipse with a dashed line, as shown in Figure 3-8.

Derived attribute: An attribute whose values can be calculated from related attribute values.

In some situations the value of an attribute can be derived from attributes in related entities. For example, consider the invoice created for each customer at Pine Valley Furniture Company (see Figure 1-6). Order_Total is an attribute of the INVOICE entity, which indicates the total dollar amount that is billed to the customer. The value of Order_Total can be computed by summing the Extended_Price values

Figure 3-9
Simple and composite
key attributes

(a) Simple key attribute

(b) Composite key attribute

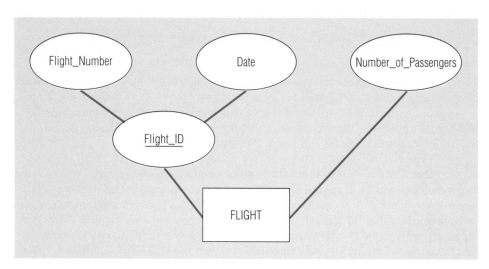

for the various line items that are billed on the invoice. Formulas for computing values such as this are one type of business rule, and we discuss business rules in the next chapter.

Identifier: An attribute (or combination of attributes) that uniquely identifies individual instances of an entity type.

An **identifier** is an attribute (or combination of attributes) that uniquely identifies individual instances of an entity type. The identifier for the STUDENT entity type introduced earlier is Student_ID, while the identifier for AUTOMOBILE is Vehicle_ID. Notice that an attribute such as Student_Name is not a candidate identifier or key, since many students may potentially have the same name and students, like all people, can change their names. To be a candidate identifier, each entity instance must have a single value for the attribute and the attribute must be associated with the entity. We underline identifier names on the E-R diagram, as shown in the example in Figure 3-9a.

Composite identifier: An identifier that consists of a composite attribute.

For some entity types, there is no single (or atomic) attribute that can serve as the identifier (that is, will ensure uniqueness). However, two (or more) attributes used in combination may serve as the identifier. A **composite identifier** is an identifier that consists of a composite attribute. Figure 3-9b shows the entity FLIGHT with the composite identifier Flight_ID. Flight_ID in turn has component attributes

Flight_Number and Date. This combination is required to uniquely identify individual occurrences of FLIGHT. We use the convention that the composite attribute (Flight_ID) is underlined to indicate it is the identifier, while the component attributes are not underlined.

Some entities may have more than one candidate identifier. If there is more than one candidate identifier, the designer must choose one of them as the identifier. Bruce (1992) suggests the following criteria for selecting identifiers:

1. Choose an identifier that will not change its value over the life of each instance of the entity type. For example, the combination of Employee_Name and Address (even if unique) would be a poor choice as an identifier for EMPLOYEE because the values of Employee_Name and Address could easily change during an employee's term of employment.

2. Choose an identifier such that for each instance of the entity, the attribute is guaranteed to have valid values and not be null (or unknown). If the identifier is a composite attribute (such as Flight_ID in Figure 3-9), make sure that all parts of the identifier will have valid values.

3. Avoid the use of so-called intelligent identifiers (or keys), whose structure indicates classifications, locations, and so on. For example, the first two digits of an identifier may indicate the warehouse location. Such codes are often changed as conditions change, which renders the identifier values invalid.

4. Consider substituting single-attribute surrogate identifiers for large composite identifiers. For example, an attribute called Game_Number could be used for the entity type GAME instead of the combination of Home_Team and Visiting_Team.

RELATIONSHIPS

Relationships are the glue that holds together the various components of an E-R model. Intuitively, a *relationship* is an association among the instances of one or more entity types that is of interest to the organization. But to understand this definition more clearly we must distinguish between relationship types and relationship instances. To illustrate, consider the entity types EMPLOYEE and COURSE, where COURSE represents training courses that may be taken by employees. To track courses that have been completed by particular employees, we define a relationship called Completes between the two entity types (see Figure 3-10a). This is a many-to-many relationship, since each employee may complete any number of courses, while a given course may be completed by any number of employees. For example, in Figure 3-10b, the employee Melton has completed three courses (C++, COBOL, and Perl). The SQL course has been completed by two employees (Celko and Gosling).

In this example, there are two entity types (EMPLOYEE and COURSE) that participate in the relationship named Completes. In general, any number of entity types (from one to many) may participate in a relationship.

We use in this and subsequent chapters the convention of a diamond with a single verb phrase label to represent a relationship. Because relationships often occur because of an organizational event, entity instances are related because an action was taken; thus a verb phrase is appropriate for the label. This verb phrase should be in the present tense and descriptive. There are, however, many ways to represent a relationship. In Chapter 1 (e.g., Figure 1-3) we used another popular notation of just

Figure 3-10   Relationship type and instances

(a) Relationship type (Completes)

(b) Relationship instances

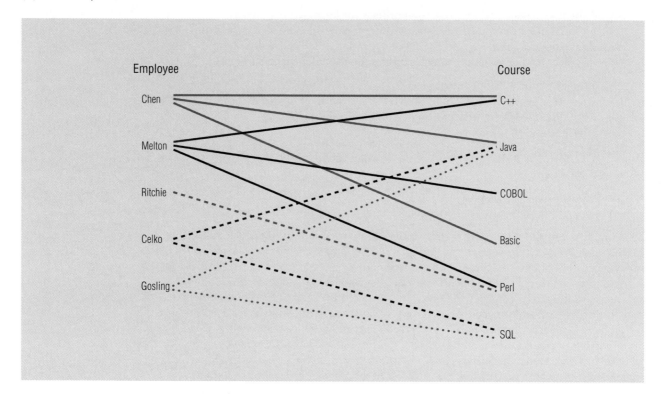

a line without a diamond, but with two relationship names, one for each direction of the relationship. Some data modelers prefer the format with two relationship names. These two notations have the same structural meaning, so you may use either format.

Basic Concepts and Definitions in Relationships

Relationship type: A meaningful association between (or among) entity types.

A **relationship type** is a meaningful association between (or among) entity types. The phrase "meaningful association" implies that the relationship allows us to answer questions that could not be answered given only the entity types. A relationship type

Table 3-1   Instances Showing Date_Completed

Employee_Name	Course_Title	Date_Completed
Chen	C++	06/1998
Chen	Java	09/1998
Chen	Basic	10/1998
Melton	C++	06/1998
Melton	COBOL	02/1999
Melton	SQL	03/1999
Ritchie	Perl	11/1998
Celko	Java	03/1998
Celko	SQL	03/1999
Gosling	Java	09/1998
Gosling	Perl	06/1998

is denoted by a diamond symbol containing the name of the relationship, as in the example shown in Figure 3-10a. We suggest you use a short, descriptive verb phrase that is meaningful to the user in naming the relationship.

A **relationship instance** is an association between (or among) entity instances, where each relationship instance includes exactly one entity from each participating entity type (Elmasri and Navathe, 1994). For example, in Figure 3-10b, each line in the figure represents a relationship instance between one employee and one course, indicating that the employee has completed that course.

Relationship instance: An association between (or among) entity instances, where each relationship instance includes exactly one entity from each participating entity type.

Attributes on Relationships   Attributes may be associated with a many-to-many (or one-to-one) relationship, as well as with an entity. For example, suppose the organization wishes to record the date (month and year) when an employee completes each course. This attribute is named Date_Completed. For some sample data, see Table 3-1.

Where should the attribute Date_Completed be placed on the E-R diagram? Referring to Figure 3-10a, you will notice that Date_Completed has not been associated with either the EMPLOYEE or COURSE entity. That is because Date_Completed is a property of the *relationship* Completes, rather than a property of either entity. In other words, for each instance of the relationship Completes, there is a value for Date_Completed. One such instance (for example) shows that the employee named Melton completed the course titled C++ on 06/1998.

A revised version of the E-R diagram for this example is shown in Figure 3-11a. In this diagram the attribute Date_Completed is connected to the relationship symbol joining the two entities. Other attributes might be added to this relationship if appropriate, such as Course_Grade, Instructor, and Room_Location.

Associative Entities   The presence of one or more attributes on a relationship suggests to the designer that the relationship should perhaps instead be represented as an entity type. An **associative entity** is an entity type that associates the instances of one or more entity types and contains attributes that are peculiar to the relationship

Associative entity: An entity type that associates the instances of one or more entity types and contains attributes that are peculiar to the relationship between those entity instances.

Figure 3-11   An associative entity

(a) Attribute on a relationship

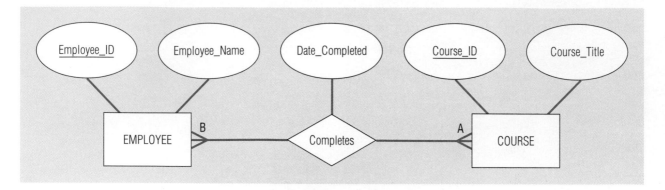

(b) An associative entity (CERTIFICATE)

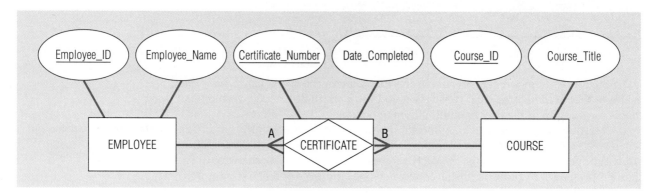

between those entity instances. An *associative* entity is represented with the diamond relationship symbol enclosed within the entity box, as shown in Figure 3-11b. The purpose of this special symbol is to preserve the information that the entity was initially specified as a relationship on the E-R diagram. Associative entities are sometimes referred to as *gerunds*, since the relationship name (a verb) is usually converted to an entity name that is a noun (an *-ing* form of the verb). Note in Figure 3-11b that there is no relationship diamond on the line between an associative entity and a strong entity. This is because the associative entity represents the relationship.

How do you know whether or not to convert a relationship to an associative entity type? Following are four conditions that should exist:

1. All of the relationships for the participating entity types are "many" relationships.

2. The resulting associative entity type has independent meaning to end users, and preferably can be identified with a single-attribute identifier.

3. The associative entity has one or more attributes, in addition to the identifier.

4. The associative entity participates in one or more relationships independent of the entities related in the associated relationship.

Figure 3-11b shows the relationship Completes converted to an associative entity type. In this case, the training department for the company has decided to award a certificate to each employee who completes a course. Thus the entity is named CERTIFICATE, which certainly has independent meaning to end users. Also, each certificate has a number (Certificate_Number) which serves as the identifier. The attribute Date_Completed is also included.

Notice that converting a relationship to an associative entity has caused the relationship notation to move. That is, the "many" cardinality now terminates at the associative entity, rather than at each participating entity type. In Figure 3-11, this shows that an employee, who may complete one or more courses (notation A in Figure 3-11a), may be awarded more than one certificate (notation A in Figure 3-11b); and that a course, which may have one or more employees complete it (notation B in Figure 3-11a), may have many certificates awarded (notation B in Figure 3-11b).

Degree of a Relationship

The **degree** of a relationship is the number of entity types that participate in that relationship. Thus, the relationship Completes is of degree 2, since there are two entity types: EMPLOYEE and COURSE. The three most common relationships in E-R models are unary (degree 1), binary (degree 2), and ternary (degree 3). Higher-degree relationships are possible, but they are rarely encountered in practice, so we restrict our discussion to these three cases. Examples of unary, binary, and ternary relationships appear in Figure 3-12.

Degree: The number of entity types that participate in a relationship.

As you look at Figure 3-12, understand that any particular data model represents a specific situation, not a generalization. For example, consider the Manages relationship in Figure 3-12a. In some organizations, it may be possible for one employee to be managed by many other employees (e.g., in a matrix organization). It is important when you develop an E-R model that you understand the rules of the particular organization you are modeling.

Unary Relationship   A **unary relationship** is a relationship between the instances of a *single* entity type (unary relationships are also called *recursive* relationships). Two examples are shown in Figure 3-12a. In the first example, "Is_married_to" is shown as a one-to-one relationship between instances of the PERSON entity type. In the second example, "Manages" is shown as a one-to-many relationship between instances of the EMPLOYEE entity type. Using this relationship, we could identify (for example) the employees who report to a particular manager. (*Note:* In these examples, we ignore whether these are mandatory- or optional-cardinality relationships, as shown in the notation of Figure 3-2; we will introduce these concepts in a later section of this chapter.) Figure 3-13 shows an example of another unary relationship, called a *bill-of-materials structure.* Many manufactured products are made of assemblies, which in turn are composed of subassemblies and parts, and so on. As shown in Figure 3-13a, we can represent this structure as a many-to-many unary relationship. In this figure, the entity type ITEM is used to represent all types of components, and we use "Has_components" for the name of the relationship type that associates lower-level items with higher-level items.

Unary relationship: A relationship between the instances of a single entity type.

Two occurrences of this bill-of-materials structure are shown in Figure 3-13b. Each of these diagrams shows the immediate components of each item as well as the quantities of that component. For example, item X consists of item U (quantity 3) and item V (quantity 2). You can easily verify that the associations are in fact many-to-many. Several of the items have more than one component type (for example, item A

Figure 3-12
Examples of relationships
of different degrees

(a) Unary relationships

(b) Binary relationships

(c) Ternary relationships

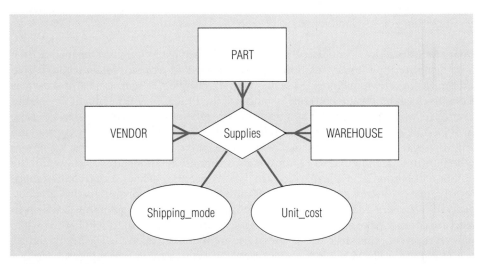

has three immediate component types: V, X, and Y). Also, some of the components are used in several higher-level assemblies. For example, item X is used in both item A and item B. The many-to-many relationship guarantees that, for example, the same sub-assembly structure of X is used each time item X goes into making some other item.

The presence of the attribute Quantity on the relationship suggests that the analyst consider converting the relationship "Has_components" to an associative entity. Figure 3-13c shows the entity type BOM_STRUCTURE, which forms an association

Figure 3-13 Representing a bill-of-materials structure

(a) Many-to-many relationship

(b) Two instances

(c) Associative entity

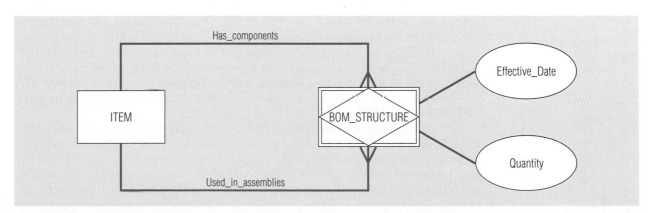

between instances of the ITEM entity type. A second attribute (named Effective_Date) has been added to BOM_STRUCTURE to record the date when this component was first used in the related assembly.

Binary relationship: A relationship between the instances of two entity types.

Binary Relationship   A **binary relationship** is a relationship between the instances of two entity types and is the most common type of relationship encountered in data modeling. Figure 3-12b shows three examples. The first (one-to-one) indicates that an employee is assigned one parking place, and each parking place is assigned to one employee. The second (one-to-many) indicates that a product line may contain several products, and each product belongs to only one product line. The third (many-to-many) shows that a student may register for more than one course, and that each course may have many student registrants.

Ternary relationship: A simultaneous relationship among the instances of three entity types.

Ternary Relationship   A **ternary relationship** is a *simultaneous* relationship among the instances of three entity types. A typical business situation that leads to a ternary relationship is shown in Figure 3-12c. In this example, vendors can supply various parts to warehouses. The relationship Supplies is used to record the specific parts that are supplied by a given vendor to a particular warehouse. Thus there are three entity types: VENDOR, PART, and WAREHOUSE. There are two attributes on the relationship Supplies: Shipping_Mode, and Unit_Cost. For example, one instance of Supplies might record the fact that vendor X can ship part C to warehouse Y, that the shipping mode is next-day air, and that the cost is $5 per unit.

Note that a ternary relationship is not the same as three binary relationships. For example, Unit_Cost is an attribute of the Supplies relationship in Figure 3-12c. Unit_Cost cannot be properly associated with any one of the three possible binary relationships among the three entity types (such as that between PART and WAREHOUSE). Thus, for example, if we were told that vendor X can ship part C for a unit cost of $8, those data would be incomplete since they would not indicate to what warehouse the parts would be shipped.

As usual, the presence of an attribute on the relationship Supplies in Figure 3-12c suggests converting the relationship to an associative entity type. Figure 3-14 shows an alternative (and equally correct) representation of the ternary relationship shown in Figure 3-12c. In Figure 3-14, the (associative) entity type SUPPLY SCHEDULE is used to replace the Supplies relationship from Figure 3-12c. Clearly the entity type SUPPLY SCHEDULE is of independent interest to users. However, notice that an identifier has not yet been assigned to SUPPLY SCHEDULE. This is acceptable. If no identifier is assigned to an associative entity during E-R modeling, an identifier (or key) will be assigned during logical modeling (discussed in Chapter 6). This will be a composite identifier whose components will consist of the identifier for each of the participating entity types (in this example, PART, VENDOR, and WAREHOUSE). Can you think of other attributes that might be associated with SUPPLY SCHEDULE?

As noted earlier, we do not use diamond symbols on the lines from SUPPLY SCHEDULE to the three entities. This is because these lines do not represent binary relationships. To keep the same meaning as the ternary relationship of Figure 3-12c, we cannot break the Supplies relationship into three binary relationships, as we have already mentioned.

We strongly recommend that you convert all ternary (or higher) relationships to associative entities, as in this example. Song, Evans, and Park (1995) show that participation constraints (described in the next section) cannot be accurately represented for a ternary relationship, given the notation that we use in this chapter. However, by converting to an associative entity, the constraints can be accurately represented.

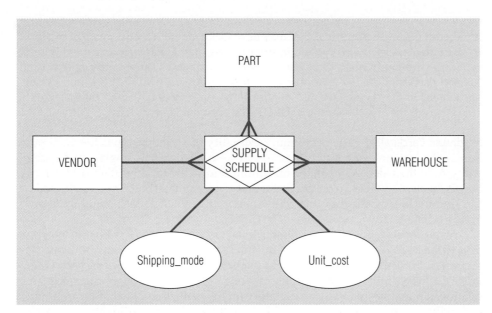

Figure 3-14
Ternary relationship as an associative entity

Cardinality Constraints

Suppose there are two entity types, A and B, that are connected by a relationship. A **cardinality constraint** specifies the number of instances of entity B that can (or must) be associated with each instance of entity A. For example, consider a video store that rents videotapes of movies. Since the store may stock more than one videotape for each movie, this is intuitively a "one-to-many" relationship as shown in Figure 3-15a. Yet it is also true that the store may not have any tapes of a given movie in stock at a particular time (for example, all copies may be checked out). We need a more precise notation to indicate the *range* of cardinalities for a relationship. This notation was introduced in Figure 3-2, which you may want to review at this time.

Cardinality constraint:
Specifies the number of instances of one entity that can (or must) be associated with each instance of another entity.

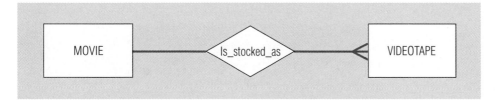

Figure 3-15
Introducing cardinality constraints

(a) Basic relationship

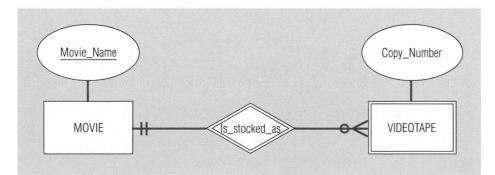

(b) Relationship with cardinality constraints

Minimum cardinality: The minimum number of instances of one entity that may be associated with each instance of another entity.

Minimum Cardinality   The **minimum cardinality** of a relationship is the minimum number of instances of entity B that may be associated with each instance of entity A. In our videotape example, the minimum number of videotapes for a movie is zero. When the minimum number of participants is zero, we say that entity type B is an *optional* participant in the relationship. In this example, VIDEOTAPE is an optional participant in the "Is_stocked_as" relationship. This fact is indicated by the symbol zero through the arrow near the VIDEOTAPE entity in Figure 3-15b.

Maximum cardinality: The maximum number of instances of one entity that may be associated with a single occurrence of another entity.

Maximum Cardinality   The **maximum cardinality** of a relationship is the maximum number of instances of entity B that may be associated with a single occurrence of entity A. In the video example, the maximum cardinality for the VIDEOTAPE entity type is "many"—that is, an unspecified number greater than one. This is indicated by the "crow's foot" symbol on the arrow next to the VIDEOTAPE entity symbol in Figure 3-15b.

A relationship is, of course, bidirectional, so there is also cardinality notation next to the MOVIE entity. Notice that the minimum and maximum are both one (see Figure 3-15b). This is called a *mandatory one* cardinality. In other words, each video-tape of a movie must be a copy of exactly one movie. In general, participation in a relationship may be optional or mandatory for the entities involved. If the minimum cardinality is zero, participation is optional; if the minimum cardinality is 1, participation is mandatory.

In Figure 3-15b, some attributes have been added to each of the entity types. Notice that VIDEOTAPE is represented as a weak entity. This is because a videotape cannot exist unless the owner movie also exists. The identifier of MOVIE is Movie_Name. VIDEOTAPE does not have a unique identifier. However, Copy_Number is a *partial* identifier which, together with Movie_Name, would uniquely identify an instance of VIDEOTAPE.

Some Examples   Examples of three relationships that show all possible combinations of minimum and maximum cardinalities appear in Figure 3-16. Each example states the business rule for each cardinality constraint, and shows the associated E-R notation. Each example also shows some relationship instances, to clarify the nature

Figure 3-16
Examples of cardinality constraints

(a) Mandatory cardinalities

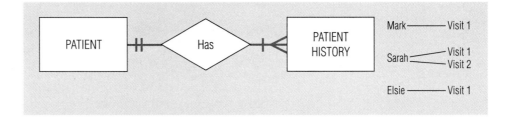

(b) One optional, one mandatory cardinality

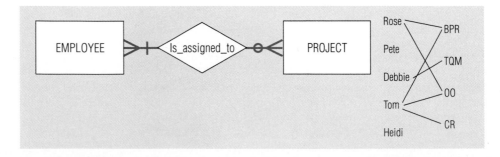

(c) Optional cardinalities

of the relationship. You should study each of these examples carefully. Following are the business rules for each of the examples in Figure 3-16:

1. PATIENT Has PATIENT HISTORY (Figure 3-16a). Each patient has one or more patient histories (the initial patient visit is always recorded as an instance of PATIENT HISTORY). Each instance of PATIENT HISTORY "belongs to'" exactly one PATIENT.

2. EMPLOYEE Is_assigned_to PROJECT (Figure 3-16b). Each PROJECT has at least one EMPLOYEE assigned to it (some projects have more than one). Each EMPLOYEE may or (optionally) may not be assigned to any existing PROJECT (e.g., employee 'Pete'), or may be assigned to one or more PROJECTs.

3. PERSON Is_married_to PERSON (Figure 3-16c). This is an optional zero or one cardinality in both directions, since a person may or may not be married.

It is possible for the maximum cardinality to be a fixed number, not an arbitrary "many" value. For example, suppose corporate policy states that an employee may work on at most five projects at the same time. We could show this business rule by placing a 5 above or below the crow's foot next to the PROJECT entity in Figure 3-16b.

A Ternary Relationship We showed the ternary relationship with the associative entity type SUPPLY SCHEDULE in Figure 3-14. Now let's add cardinality constraints to this diagram, based on the business rules for this situation. The E-R diagram, with the relevant business rules, is shown in Figure 3-17. Notice that PART and WARE-HOUSE are mandatory participants in the relationship, while VENDOR is an optional participant. The cardinality at each of the participating entities is mandatory one, since each SUPPLY SCHEDULE instance must be related to exactly one instance of each of these participating entity types.

As noted earlier, a ternary relationship is not equivalent to three binary relationships. Unfortunately, you are not able to draw ternary relationships with many CASE tools; instead, you are forced to represent ternary relationships as three binaries. If you are forced to do this, then do not draw the binary relationships with diamonds, and be sure to make the cardinality next to the three strong entities mandatory one.

Modeling Time-Dependent Data

Database contents vary over time. For example, in a database that contains product information, the unit price for each product may be changed as material and labor costs and market conditions change. If only the current price is required, then Price

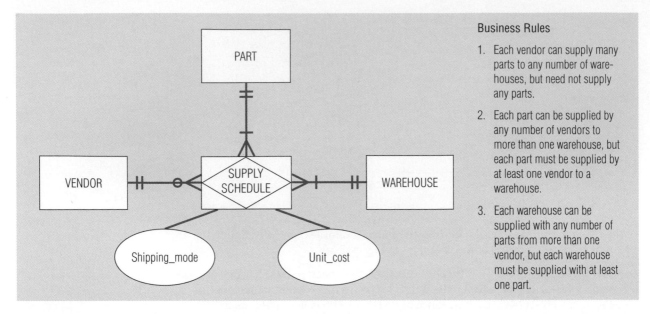

Business Rules

1. Each vendor can supply many parts to any number of ware-houses, but need not supply any parts.

2. Each part can be supplied by any number of vendors to more than one warehouse, but each part must be supplied by at least one vendor to a warehouse.

3. Each warehouse can be supplied with any number of parts from more than one vendor, but each warehouse must be supplied with at least one part.

Figure 3-17
Cardinality constraints in a ternary relationship

can be modeled as a single-valued attribute. However for accounting, billing, and other purposes, we are likely to need to preserve a history of the prices and the time period over which each was in effect. As Figure 3-18 shows, we can conceptualize this requirement as a series of prices and the effective date for each price. This results in the (composite) multivalued attribute named Price_History. The components of Price_History are Price and Effective_Date. An important characteristic of such a composite, multivalued attribute is that the component attributes go together. Thus, in Figure 3-18, each Price is paired with the corresponding Effective_Date.

In Figure 3-18, each value of the attribute Price is time stamped with its effective date. A **time stamp** is simply a time value (such as date and time) that is associated with a data value. A time stamp may be associated with any data value that changes over time when we need to maintain a history of those data values. Time stamps may be recorded to indicate the time the value was entered (transaction time), the time the value becomes valid or stops being valid, or the time when critical actions were performed (such as updates, corrections, or audits).

Time stamp: A time value that is associated with a data value.

Figure 3-18
Simple example of time stamping

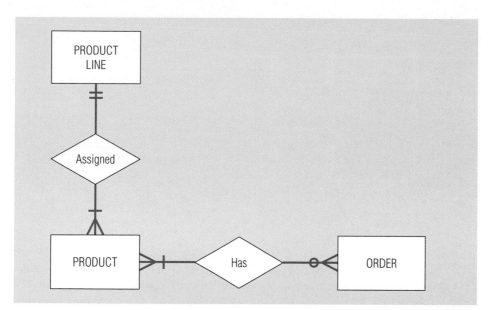

Figure 3-19
Pine Valley Furniture product
database

(a) E-R diagram not recognizing product reassignment

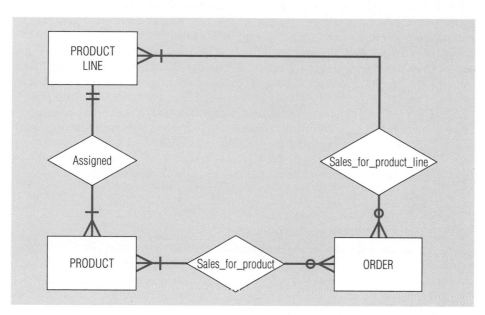

(b) E-R diagram recognizing
product reassignment

The use of simple time stamping (as in the preceding example) is often adequate for modeling time-dependent data. However, time often introduces subtler complexities in data modeling. For example, Figure 3-19a represents a portion of an E-R diagram for Pine Valley Furniture Company. Each product is assigned to a product line (or related group of products). Customer orders are processed throughout the year, and monthly summaries are reported by product line and by product within product line.

Suppose that in the middle of the year, due to a reorganization of the sales function, some products are reassigned to different product lines. The model shown in Figure 3-19a is not designed to track the reassignment of a product to a new product line. Thus, all sales reports will show cumulative sales for a product based on its *current* product line, rather than the one at the time of the sale. For example, a product

Figure 3-20
Examples of multiple
relationships

(a) Employees and
departments

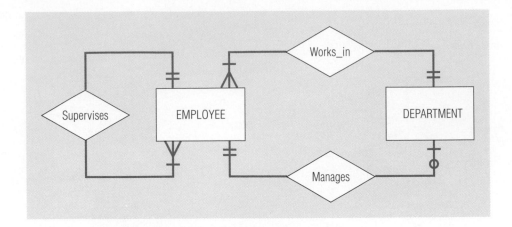

may have total year-to-date sales of $50,000 and be associated with product line B, yet $40,000 of those sales may have occurred while the product was assigned to product line A. This fact will be lost using the model of Figure 3-19a. The simple design change shown in Figure 3-19b will correctly recognize product reassignments. A new relationship (called Sales_for_product_line) has been added between ORDER and PRODUCT LINE. As customer orders are processed, they are credited to both the correct product and product line as of the time of the sale.

We have discussed the problem of time-dependent data with managers in several organizations who are considered leaders in the use of data modeling and database management. These discussions revealed that current data models (and database management systems based on those models) are generally inadequate in handing time-dependent data, and that organizations often ignore this problem and hope that the resulting inaccuracies balance out. However, data warehousing applications are designed to remove many of these uncertainties by providing explicit designs for time-dependent data. You need to be alert to the complexities posed by time-dependent data as you develop data models in your organization.

Multiple Relationships

In some situations an organization may wish to model more than one relationship between the same entity types. Two examples are shown in Figure 3-20. Figure 3-20a shows two relationships between the entity types EMPLOYEE and DEPARTMENT. The relationship Works_in associates employees with the department in which they work. This relationship is one-to-many and is mandatory in both directions. That is, a department must have at least one employee who works there (perhaps the department manager), and each employee must be assigned to exactly one department. (*Note:* These are specific business rules which we assume for this illustration. It is crucial when you develop an E-R diagram for a particular situation that you understand the business rules that apply for that setting. For example, if EMPLOYEE were to include retirees, then each employee may not be currently assigned to exactly one department; further, the E-R model in Figure 3-20a assumes that the organization needs to remember in which DEPARTMENT each EMPLOYEE currently works, rather than remembering the history of department assignments. Again, the structure of the data model reflects the information the organization needs to remember.)

The second relationship between EMPLOYEE and DEPARTMENT (named "Manages") associates each department with the employee who manages that department. The relationship from DEPARTMENT to EMPLOYEE is mandatory one,

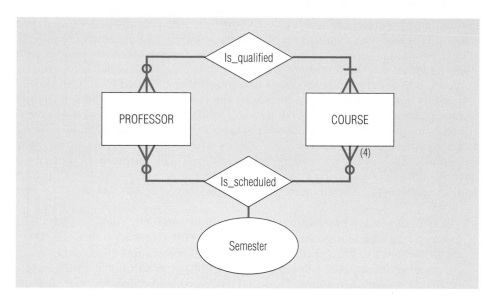

indicating that a department must have exactly one manager. From EMPLOYEE to DEPARTMENT the relationship is optional one since a given employee either is or is not a department manager.

Figure 3-20a also shows the unary relationship Supervises that associates each employee with his or her supervisor, and vice versa. This relationship records the business rule that each employee must have exactly one supervisor. Conversely, each employee may supervise any number of employees, or may not be a supervisor.

The example in Figure 3-20b shows two relationships between the entity types PROFESSOR and COURSE. The relationship Is_qualified associates professors with the courses they are qualified to teach. A given course may have more than one qualified instructor, or (optionally) may not have any qualified instructors. This might happen (for example) if the course is new and has just been entered in the catalog. Conversely, each instructor must be qualified to teach at least one course (a reasonable expectation!).

The second relationship in this figure associates professors with the courses they are actually scheduled to teach during a given semester. Notice that the maximum cardinality for courses scheduled for an instructor during a semester is four. This is an example of how you can record a fixed constraint (upper or lower) on an E-R diagram. The attribute Semester (which could be a composite attribute with components Semester_Name and Year) is on the relationship Is_scheduled.

The E-R diagram in Figure 3-20b captures the basic cardinality constraints. Often, however, there are other business rules that cannot easily be captured on a basic E-R diagram. Consider the following rule for the example shown in Figure 3-20b: An instructor who is scheduled to teach a course must be qualified to teach that course (another reasonable rule!). In Chapter 4 we discuss techniques for capturing such rules as part of the overall modeling process.

E-R MODELING EXAMPLE: PINE VALLEY FURNITURE COMPANY

Developing an entity-relationship diagram can proceed from one (or both) of two perspectives. With a top-down perspective, the designer proceeds from basic descriptions of the business, including its processes and environment. This approach is most appropriate for developing a high-level E-R diagram with only the major entities and relationships and with a limited set of attributes (such as just the entity identifiers). With a bottom-up approach, the designer proceeds from detailed discussions with users, and from a detailed study of documents, screens, and other data sources. This approach is necessary for developing a detailed, "fully attributed" E-R diagram.

In this section we develop a high-level E-R diagram for Pine Valley Furniture Company, based largely on the first of these approaches (see Figure 3-21). We reference the customer invoice (from Chapter 1) to add some detail and illustrate how the two approaches can be combined.

From a study of the business processes at Pine Valley Furniture Company, we have identified the following entity types. An identifier is also suggested for each entity, together with selected important attributes.

- The company sells a number of different furniture products. These products are grouped into several product lines. The identifier for a product is Product_ID, while the identifier for a product line is Product_Line_ID. Referring to the customer invoice (Figure 1-5), we identify the following additional attributes for product: Product_Description, Product_Finish, and Unit_Price. Another attribute for product line is Product_Line_Name. A product line may group any number of products, but must group at least one product. Each product must belong to exactly one product line.

- Customers submit orders for products. The identifier for an order is Order_ID, and another attribute is Order_Date. A customer may submit any number of orders, but need not submit any orders. Each order is submitted by exactly one customer. The identifier for a customer is Customer_ID. Other attributes include Customer_Name and Customer_Address.

- A given customer order must request at least one product. Any product sold by Pine Valley Furniture may not be requested on any order, or may be requested on one or more orders. An attribute associated with each order and product is Quantity, which is the number of units requested.

- Pine Valley Furniture has established sales territories for its customers. Each customer does business in one or more of these sales territories. The identifier for a sales territory is Territory_ID. A sales territory may have any number of customers, or may not have any customers doing business.

- Pine Valley Furniture Company has several salespersons. The identifier for a salesperson is Salesperson_ID. Other attributes include Salesperson_Name, Salesperson_Telephone, and Salesperson_Fax. A salesperson serves exactly one sales territory. Each sales territory is served by one or more salespersons.

- Each product is assembled from one or more raw materials. The identifier for the raw material entity is Material_ID. Other attributes include Unit_of_Measure and Unit_Price. Each raw material may be assembled into one or more products.

- Raw materials are supplied by vendors. The identifier for a vendor is Vendor_ID. Other attributes include Vendor_Name and Vendor_Address. Each raw material can be supplied by one or more vendors. A vendor may supply any number of raw materials, or may not supply any raw materials to Pine Valley Furniture. An attribute of the relationship between vendor and raw material is Unit_Price.

- Pine Valley Furniture has established a number of work centers. The identifier for a work center is Work_Center_ID. Another attribute is Location. Each

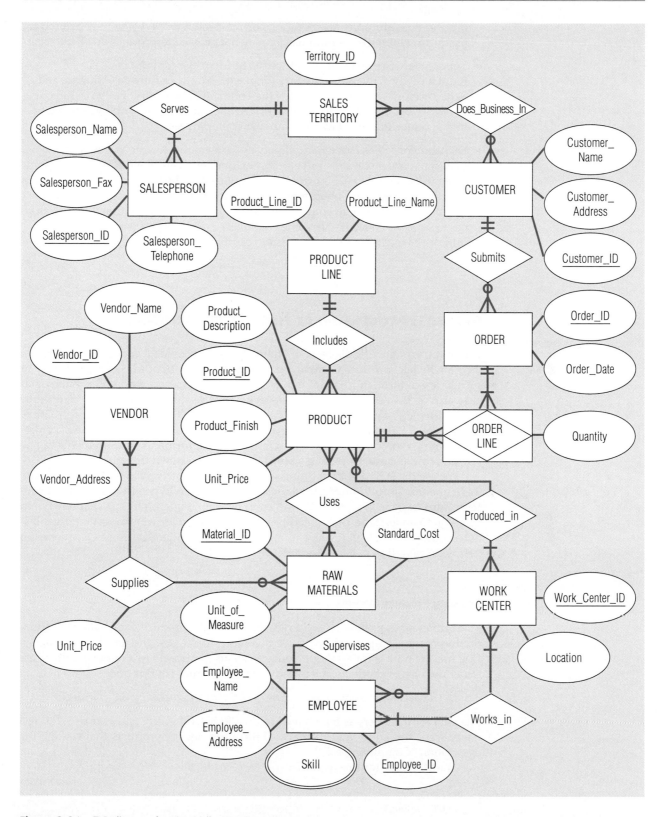

Figure 3-21   E-R diagram for Pine Valley Furniture Company

product is produced in one or more work centers. A work center may be used to produce any number of products, or may not be used to produce any products.

- The company has over 100 employees. The identifier for employee is Employee_ID. Other attributes are Employee_Name, Employee_Address, and Skill. An employee may have more than one skill. Each employee works in one or more work centers. A work center must have at least one employee working in that center, but may have any number of employees.

- Each employee has exactly one supervisor. An employee who is a supervisor may supervise any number of employees, but not all employees are supervisors. (*Note:* This business rule is actually ambiguous, but the E-R diagram notation we have introduced so far obscures the ambiguity. We cannot tell from the rule or the diagram whether an employee may be a supervisor but without any employees to supervise, or whether some employees are not supervisors. Notation introduced in Chapter 4 can be used to clarify this distinction.)

DATABASE PROCESSING AT PINE VALLEY FURNITURE

The purpose of the E-R diagram in Figure 3-21 is to provide a conceptual design for the Pine Valley Furniture Company database. It is important to check the quality of such a design through frequent interaction with the persons who will use the database after it is implemented. An important type of quality check is to determine whether the E-R model can easily satisfy user requests for data and/or information. Employees at Pine Valley Furniture have many data retrieval and reporting requirements. In this section we show how a few of these information requirements can be satisfied by database processing against the database shown in Figure 3-21.

We use the SQL database processing language (explained in Chapter 9) to state these queries. To fully understand these queries, you will need to understand concepts introduced in Chapter 6. However, a few simple queries in this chapter should help you to understand the capabilities of a database to answer important organizational questions and give you a jump start toward understanding SQL queries in Chapter 6 as well as in later chapters.

Showing Product Information

Many different users have a need to see data about the products Pine Valley Furniture produces; for example, salespersons, inventory managers, and product managers. One specific need is for a salesperson who wants to respond to a request from a customer for a list of products of a certain type. An example of this query is:

List all details for the various computer desks that are stocked by the company.

The data for this query is maintained in the PRODUCT entity (see Figure 3-21). The query scans this entity and displays all the attributes for products that contain the description "Computer Desk."

The SQL code for this query is:

```
SELECT *
FROM PRODUCT
WHERE Product_Description LIKE "Computer Desk%";
```

Typical output for this query is:

```
Product_ID    Product_Description    Product_Finish    Unit_Price
        3     Computer Desk 48"      Oak                   375.00
        8     Computer Desk 64"      Pine                  450.00
```

SELECT * FROM PRODUCT says display all attributes of PRODUCT entities. The WHERE clause says to limit the display to only products whose description begins with the phrase "Computer Desk."

Showing Customer Information

Another common information need is to show data about Pine Valley Furniture customers. One specific type of person who needs this information is a territory sales manager. The following is a typical query from a territory sales manager:

List the details of customers in the Northwest sales territory.

The data for this query are maintained in the CUSTOMER entity. As we explain in Chapter 6, the attribute Territory_ID will be added to the CUSTOMER entity when the E-R diagram in Figure 3-21 is translated into a database which can be accessed via SQL. The query scans that entity and displays all attributes for customers who are in the selected territory.

The SQL code for this query is:

```
SELECT *
FROM CUSTOMER
WHERE Territory_ID = "Northwest";
```

Typical output for this query is:

```
Customer_ID    Customer_Name       Customer_Address                           Territory
          5    Value Furniture     394 Rainbow Dr., Seattle, WA 97954         Northwest
          9    Furniture Gallery   816 Peach Rd., Santa Clara, CA 96915       Northwest
```

The explanation of this SQL query is similar to the previous one.

Showing Customer Order Status

The previous two queries were relatively simple, involving data from only one table in each case. Often, data from multiple tables are needed in one information request. Although the query was simple, we did have to look through the whole database to find the entity and attributes needed to satisfy the request.

To simplify query writing and for other reasons many database management systems support creating restricted views of a database suitable for the information needs of a particular user. For queries related to customer order status, Pine Valley utilizes such a user view "orders for customers" shown in Figure 3-22a. This user view allows users to see only CUSTOMER and ORDER entities in the database, and only the attributes of these entities shown in the figure. As we explain in Chapter 6, the attribute Customer_ID will be added to the ORDER entity (as shown in Figure 3-22a). A typical order status query is:

How many orders have we received from "Value Furniture"?

Figure 3-22

Two user views for Pine Valley Furniture

(a) User View 1: Orders for customers

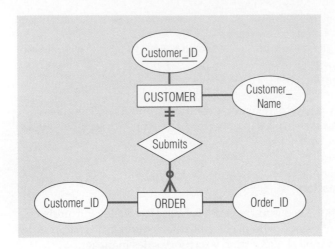

(b) User View 2: Orders for products

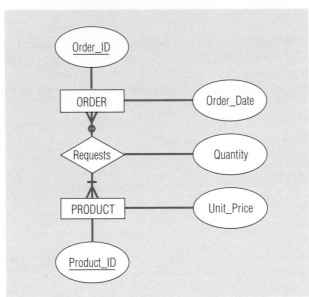

We can write the SQL code for this query in several ways. The way we have chosen is to compose a query within a query, called a subquery. The query is performed in two steps. First, the subquery (or inner query) scans the CUSTOMER entity to determine the Customer_ID for the customer named "Value Furniture" (the ID for this customer is 5, as shown in the output for the previous query). Then the query (or outer query) scans the ORDER entity and counts the order instances for this customer.

The SQL code for this query against the "orders for customer" user view is:

```
SELECT COUNT (Order_ID)
FROM ORDER
WHERE Customer_ID =
  (SELECT Customer_ID
   FROM CUSTOMER
   WHERE Customer_Name = "Value Furniture");
```

Typical output for this query is:

```
COUNT(Order_ID)
        4
```

Showing Product Sales

Salespersons, territory managers, product managers, production managers, and others have a need to know the status of product sales. One kind of sales question is what products are having an exceptionally strong sales month. Typical of this question is the following query:

> *What products have had total sales exceeding $25,000 during the past month (June, 1998)?*

This query can be written using the user view "orders for products" shown in Figure 3-22b. Data to respond to the query are obtained from the following sources:

- Order_Date from the ORDER entity (to find only orders in the desired month).

- Quantity for each product on each order from the associative entity ORDER LINE for an ORDER entity in the desired month.

- Unit_Price for the product ordered from the PRODUCT entity associated with the ORDER LINE entity.

For each item that has been ordered during the month of June 1998, the query needs to multiply Quantity times Unit_Price to get the dollar value of a sale. The total amount is then obtained for that item by summing over all orders. Data are displayed only if the total exceeds $25,000.

The SQL code for this query is beyond the scope of this chapter, since it requires techniques introduced in Chapter 6. We show this SQL query in that chapter. We introduce this query now only to suggest the power that a database such as shown in Figure 3-21 has to find information for management from detailed data.

SUMMARY

This chapter has described the basic entity relationship (E-R) model and the use of this tool within the context of conceptual data modeling. An E-R model is a detailed, logical representation of the data for an organization. An E-R model is usually expressed in the form of an E-R diagram, which is a graphical representation of an E-R model. The E-R model was introduced by Chen in 1976, and has become the most commonly used technique for describing the logical structure of data. However, at the present time there is no standard notation for E-R modeling.

The basic constructs of an E-R model are entity types, relationships, and related attributes. An entity is a person, place, object, event, or concept in the user environment about which the organization wishes to maintain data. An entity type is a collection of entities that share common properties, while an entity instance is a single occurrence of an entity type. A strong entity type is an entity that has its own identifier and can exist without other entities. A weak entity type is an entity whose existence depends on the existence of a strong entity type. Weak entities do not have their own identifier, although they normally have a partial identifier. Weak entities are identified through an identifying relationship with their owner entity type.

An attribute is a property or characteristic of an entity or relationship that is of interest to the organization. There are several types of attributes. A simple attribute is one that has no component parts. A composite attribute is an attribute that can be broken down into component parts. For example, Person_Name can be broken down into the parts First_Name, Middle_Initial, and Last_Name. A multivalued attribute is one that can have multiple values for a single instance of an entity. For example, the attribute College_Degree might have multiple values for an individual. A derived attribute is one whose values can be calculated from other attribute values. For example, Average_Salary can be calculated from values of Salary for all employees.

An identifier is an attribute that uniquely identifies individual instances of an entity type. Identifiers should be chosen carefully to ensure stability and ease of use. Identifiers may be simple attributes, or they may be composite attributes with component parts.

A relationship type is a meaningful association between (or among) entity types. A relationship instance is an association between (or among) entity instances. The degree of a relationship is the number of entity types that participate in the relationship. The most common relationship types are unary (degree 1), binary (degree 2), and ternary (degree 3).

In developing E-R diagrams, we sometimes encounter many-to-many (and one-to-one) relationships that have one or more attributes associated with the relationship, rather than with one of the participating entity types. This suggests that we consider converting the relationship to an associative entity. This type of entity associates the instances of one or more entity types and contains attributes that are peculiar to the relationship. Associative entity types may have their own simple identifier, or they may be assigned a composite identifier during logical design.

A cardinality constraint is a constraint that specifies the number of instances of entity B that may (or must) be associated with each instance of entity A. Cardinality constraints normally specify the minimum and maximum number of instances. The possible constraints are mandatory one, mandatory many, optional one, optional many, and a specific number. The minimum cardinality constraint is also referred to as the participation constraint. A minimum cardinality of zero specifies optional participation, while a minimum cardinality of one specifies mandatory participation.

CHAPTER REVIEW

KEY TERMS

Associative entity	Entity-relationship	Minimum cardinality
Attribute	diagram (E-R	Multivalued attribute
Binary relationship	diagram)	Relationship instance
Cardinality constraint	Entity-relationship	Relationship type
Composite attribute	model (E-R model)	Simple attribute
Composite identifier	Entity type	Strong entity type
Degree	Identifier	Ternary relationship
Derived attribute	Identifying owner	Time stamp
Entity	Identifying relationship	Unary relationship
Entity instance	Maximum cardinality	Weak entity type

R E V I E W   Q U E S T I O N S

1. Define each of the following terms:
   a. entity type
   b. entity-relationship model
   c. entity instance
   d. attribute
   e. relationship type
   f. identifier
   g. multivalued attribute
   h. associative entity
   i. cardinality constraint
   j. weak entity
   k. identifying relationship
   l. derived attribute
   m. multivalued attribute

2. Contrast the following terms:
   a. stored attribute; derived attribute
   b. entity type; entity instance
   c. simple attribute; composite attribute
   d. entity type; relationship type
   e. strong entity type; weak entity type
   f. degree; cardinality

3. Give three reasons why many system designers believe that data modeling is the most important part of the system development process.

4. State four criteria for selecting identifiers for entities.

5. State three conditions that suggest the designer should model a relationship as an associative entity type.

6. List the four types of cardinality constraints, and draw an example of each.

7. Give an example of a weak entity type, other than those described in this chapter.

8. What is the degree of a relationship? List the three types of relationship degrees described in the chapter, and give an example of each.

9. Give an example (other than those described in this chapter) for each of the following:
   a. Derived attribute
   b. Multivalued attribute
   c. Composite attribute

10. Give an example of each of the following, other than those described in this chapter.
    a. Ternary relationship
    b. Unary relationship

P R O B L E M S   A N D   E X E R C I S E S

1. Match the following terms and definitions.
   _____ composite attribute
   _____ associative entity
   _____ unary relationship
   _____ weak entity
   _____ attribute

   a. uniquely identifies entity instances
   b. relates instances of a single entity type
   c. specifies maximum and minimum number of instances
   d. relationship modeled as an entity type
   e. association between entity types

_____ entity	f. collection of similar entities
_____ relationship type	g. number of participating entity types in relationship
_____ cardinality constraint	
_____ degree	h. property of an entity
_____ identifier	i. can be broken into component parts
_____ entity type	j. depends on the existence of another entity type
_____ ternary	
_____ bill-of-materials	k. relationship of degree three
	l. many-to-many unary relationship
	m. person, place, object, concept, event

2. There is a bulleted list on pages 112 and 114 describing Figure 3-21. For each of the 10 points in the list, identify the subset of Figure 3-21 described by that point.

3. Draw an E-R diagram for each of the following situations (if you believe that you need to make additional assumptions, clearly state them for each situation):

   a. A company has a number of employees. The attributes of EMPLOYEE include Employee_ID (identifier), Name, Address, and Birthdate. The company also has several projects. Attributes of PROJECT include Project_ID (identifier), Project_Name, and Start_Date. Each employee may be assigned to one or more projects, or may not be assigned to a project. A project must have at least one employee assigned, and may have any number of employees assigned. An employee's billing rate may vary by project, and the company wishes to record the applicable billing rate (Billing_Rate) for each employee when assigned to a particular project.

   b. A university has a large number of courses in its catalog. Attributes of COURSE include Course_Number (identifier), Course_Name, and Units. Each course may have one or more different courses as prerequisites, or may have no prerequisites. Similarly, a particular course may be a prerequisite for any number of courses, or may not be prerequisite for any other course.

   c. A laboratory has several chemists who work on one or more projects. Chemists also may use certain kinds of equipment on each project. Attributes of CHEMIST include Employee_ID (identifier), Name, and Phone_ No. Attributes of PROJECT include Project_ID (identifier) and Start_Date. Attributes of EQUIPMENT include Serial_No and Cost. The organization wishes to record Assign_Date—that is, the date when a given equipment item was assigned to a particular chemist working on a specified project. A chemist must be assigned to at least one project and one equipment item. A given equipment item need not be assigned, and a given project need not be assigned either a chemist or an equipment item.

   d. A college course may have one or more scheduled sections, or may not have a scheduled section. Attributes of COURSE include Course_ID, Course_Name, and Units. Attributes of SECTION include Section_Number and Semester_ID. Semester_ID is composed of two parts: Semester, and Year. Section_Number is an integer (such as "1" or "2") that distinguishes one section from another for the same course but does not uniquely identify a section.

   e. A hospital has a large number of registered physicians. Attributes of PHYSICIAN include Physician_ID (the identifier) and Specialty. Patients are admitted to the hospital by physicians. Attributes of PATIENT include Patient_ID (the identifier) and Patient_Name. Any patient who is admitted must have exactly one admitting physician. A physician may optionally admit any number of patients. Once admitted, a given patient must be treated by at least one physician. A particular physician may treat any number of patients, or may not treat any patients. Whenever a patient is treated by a physician, the hospital wishes to record the details of the

Figure 3-23
Grade report

```
                        MILLENNIUM COLLEGE
                        GRADE REPORT
                        FALL SEMESTER 199X
─────────────────────────────────────────────────────────────
NAME:                  Emily Williams          ID: 268300458
CAMPUS ADDRESS:        208 Brooks Hall
MAJOR:                 Information Systems
─────────────────────────────────────────────────────────────
COURSE      TITLE         INSTRUCTOR    INSTRUCTOR    GRADE
  ID                        NAME          LOCATION
─────────────────────────────────────────────────────────────
IS 350    Database Mgt.     Codd           B104          A
IS 465    System Analysis   Parsons        B317          B
```

treatment (Treatment_Detail). Components of Treatment_Detail include Date, Time, and Results.

4. Figure 3-23 shows a Grade Report that is mailed to students at the end of each semester. Prepare an E-R diagram reflecting the data contained in Grade Report. Assume that each course is taught by one instructor.

5. The entity type STUDENT has the following attributes: Student_Name, Address, Phone, Age, Activity, and No_of_Years. Activity represents some campus-based student activity, while No_of_Years represents the number of years the student has engaged in this activity. A given student may engage in more than one activity. Draw an E-R diagram for this situation.

6. Prepare an E-R diagram for a real estate firm that lists property for sale. The following describes this organization:

   - The firm has a number of sales offices in several states. Attributes of sales office include Office_Number (identifier) and Location.

   - Each sales office is assigned one or more employees. Attributes of employee include Employee_ID (identifier) and Employee_Name. An employee must be assigned to only one sales office.

   - For each sales office, there is always one employee assigned to manage that office. An employee may manage only the sales office to which she is assigned.

   - The firm lists property for sale. Attributes of property include Property_ID (identifier) and Location. Components of Location include Address, City, State, and Zip_Code.

   - Each unit of property must be listed with one (and only one) of the sales offices. A sales office may have any number of properties listed, or may have no properties listed.

   - Each unit of property has one or more owners. Attributes of owners are Owner_ID (identifier) and Owner_Name. An owner may own one or more units of property. An attribute of the relationship between property and owner is Percent_Owned.

7. Add minimum and maximum cardinality notation to each of the following figures, as appropriate:

   a. Figure 3-5.   d. Figure 3-12 (all parts).
   b. Figure 3-10a.   e. Figure 3-13c.
   c. Figure 3-11b.   f. Figure 3-14.

8. After completing a course in database management, you have been asked to develop a preliminary E-R diagram for a symphony orchestra. You discover the following entity types should be included:

   - CONCERT SEASON   The season during which a series of concerts will be performed. Identifier is Opening_Date, which includes Month, Day, and Year.
   - CONCERT   A given performance of one or more compositions. Identifier is Concert_Number. Another important attribute is Concert_Date, which consists of the following: Month, Day, Year, and Time. Each concert typically has more than one concert date.
   - COMPOSITION   Compositions to be performed at each concert. Identifier is Composition_ID, which consists of the following: Composer_Name, and Composition_Name. Another attribute is Movement_ID, which consists of two parts: Movement_Number, and Movement_Name. Many, but not all, compositions have multiple movements.
   - CONDUCTOR   Person who will conduct the concert. Identifier is Conductor_ID. Another attribute is Conductor_Name.
   - SOLOIST   Solo artist who performs a given composition on a particular concert. Identifier is Soloist_ID. Another attribute is Soloist_Name.

   During further discussions you discover the following:

   - A concert season schedules one or more concerts. A particular concert is scheduled for only one concert season.
   - A concert includes the performance of one or more compositions. A composition may be performed at one or more concerts, or may not be performed.
   - For each concert there is one conductor. A conductor may conduct any number of concerts, or may not conduct any concerts.
   - Each composition may require one or more soloists, or may not require a soloist. A soloist may perform one or more compositions at a given concert, or may not perform any composition. The symphony orchestra wishes to record the date when a soloist last performed a given composition (Date_Last_Performed).

   Draw an E-R diagram to represent what you have discovered, as explained above.

9. Obtain a common user view such as a credit card statement, phone bill, or some other common document. Prepare an E-R diagram for this document.

10. Draw an E-R diagram for some organization that you are familiar with—boy scouts/ girl scouts, sports team, etc.

11. Draw an E-R diagram for the following situation (Batra, Hoffer, and Bostrom, 1988). Projects, Inc., is an engineering firm with approximately 500 employees. A database is required to keep track of all employees, their skills, projects assigned, and departments worked in. Every employee has a unique number assigned by the firm, required to store his or her name and date of birth. If an employee is currently married to another employee of Projects, Inc., the date of marriage and who is married to whom must be stored; however, no record of marriage is required if an employee's spouse is not also an employee. Each employee is given a job title (for example, engineer, secretary, and so on). An employee does only one type of job at any given time, and we only need to retain information for an employee's current job.

    There are 11 different departments, each with a unique name. An employee can report to only one department. Each department has a phone number.

    To procure various kinds of equipment, each department deals with many vendors. A vendor typically supplies equipment to many departments. We are required to store the name and address of each vendor and the date of the last meeting between a department and a vendor.

Many employees can work on a project. An employee can work on many projects (for example, Southwest Refinery, California Petrochemicals, and so on) but can only be assigned to at most one project in a given city. For each city, we are interested in its state and population. An employee can have many skills (preparing material requisitions, checking drawings, and so on), but she or he may use only a given set of skills on a particular project. (For example, an employee MURPHY may prepare requisitions for the Southwest Refinery project and prepare requisitions as well as check drawings for California Petrochemicals.) Employees use each skill that they possess in at least one project. Each skill is assigned a number, and we must store a short description of each skill. Projects are distinguished by project numbers, and we must store the estimated cost of each project.

12. Draw an E-R diagram for the following situation (state any assumptions you believe you have to make in order to develop a complete diagram): Stillwater Antiques buys and sells one-of-a-kind antiques of all kinds (for example, furniture, jewelry, china, and clothing). Each item is uniquely identified by an item number and is also characterized by a description, asking price, condition, and open-ended comments. Stillwater works with many different individuals, called clients, who sell items to and buy items from the store. Some clients only sell items to Stillwater, some only buy items, and some others both sell and buy. A client is identified by a client number and is also described by a client name and client address. When Stillwater sells an item in stock to a client, the owners want to record the commission paid, the actual selling price, sales tax (tax of zero indicates a tax exempt sale), and date sold. When Stillwater buys an item from a client, the owners want to record the purchase cost, date purchased, and condition at time of purchase.

13. Draw an E-R diagram for the following situation (state any assumptions you believe you have to make in order to develop a complete diagram): The H. I. Topi School of Business operates international business programs in 10 locations throughout Europe. The School had its first class of 9000 graduates in 1965. The School keeps track of each graduate's student number, name when a student, country of birth, current country of citizenship, current name, current address, and the name of each major the student completed (each student has one or two majors). In order to maintain strong ties to its alumni, the School holds various events around the world. Events have a title, date, location, and type (for example, reception, dinner, or seminar). The School needs to keep track of which graduates have attended which events. For an attendance by a graduate at an event, a comment is recorded about information School officials learned from that graduate at that event. The School also keeps in contact with graduates by mail, e-mail, telephone, and fax interactions. As with events, the School records information learned from the graduate from each of these contacts. When a School official knows that he or she will be meeting or talking to a graduate, a report is produced showing the latest information about that graduate and the information learned during the past two years from that graduate from all contacts and events the graduate attended.

14. Assume that at Pine Valley Furniture each product (described by product number, description, and cost) comprises at least three components (described by component number, description, and unit of measure) and components are used to make one or many products. In addition, assume that components are used to make other components and that raw materials are also considered to be components. In both cases of components, we need to keep track of how many components go into making something else. Draw an E-R diagram for this situation, and place minimum and maximum cardinalities on the diagram.

15. Stock brokerages sell stocks and the prices are continually changing. Draw an E-R diagram that takes into account the changing nature of stock price.

16. Each semester, each student must be assigned an advisor who counsels students about degree requirements and helps students register for classes. Each student must register for classes with the help of an advisor, but if the student's assigned advisor is not available, the student may register with any advisor. We must keep track of students, the assigned advisor for each, and the name of the advisor with whom the student registered for the current term. Represent this situation of students and advisors with an E-R diagram.

FIELD EXERCISES

1. Interview a friend or family member to elicit the entities, attributes, and relationships the person comes in contact with at work. Use this information to construct and present to this person an entity-relationship diagram. Revise the diagram until it seems appropriate to you and to your friend or family member.

2. Visit two local small businesses, one in the service sector (such as a dry cleaner, auto repair shop, veterinarian, or bookstore) and one that manufactures tangible goods. Interview employees from these organizations to elicit from them the entities, attributes, and relationships that are commonly encountered in these organizations. Use this information to construct entity-relationship diagrams. What differences and similarities are there between the diagrams for the service- and the product-oriented companies? Does the entity-relationship diagramming technique handle both situations equally well? Why or why not?

3. Ask a database or systems analyst to give you examples of unary, binary, and ternary relationships that the analyst has dealt with personally at his or her company. Ask which is most common and why.

4. Ask a database or systems analyst in a local company to show you an E-R diagram for one of the organization's primary databases. Ask questions to be sure you understand what each entity, attribute, and relationship means. Does this organization use the same E-R notation used in this text? If not, what other or alternative symbols are used and what do these symbols mean? Does this organization model associative entities on the E-R diagram? If not, how are associative entities modeled?

5. For the same E-R diagram used in Field Exercise 4 or for a different database in the same or a different organization, identify any uses of time stamping or other means to model time-dependent data. Why are time-dependent data necessary for those who use this database? Would the E-R diagram be much simpler if it were not necessary to represent the history of attribute values?

REFERENCES

Batra, D., J. A. Hoffer, and R. B. Bostrom. 1988. "A Comparison of User Performance Between the Relational and Extended Entity Relationship Model in the Discovery Phase of Database Design." *Proceedings of the Ninth International Conference on Information Systems.* Minneapolis, Nov. 30–Dec. 3: 295–306.

Bruce, T. A. 1992. *Designing Quality Databases with IDEF1X Information Models.* New York: Dorset House.

Chen, P. P.-S. 1976. "The Entity-Relationship Model—Toward a Unified View of Data." *ACM Transactions on Database Systems* 1 (March): 9–36.

Elmasri, R. and S. B. Navathe. 1994. *Fundamentals of Database Systems.* 2nd ed. Menlo Park, CA: Benjamin/Cummings.

Hoffer, J. A., J. F. George, and J. S. Valacich. 1999. *Modern Systems Analysis and Design.* 2nd ed. Reading, MA: Addison-Wesley.

Song, I.-Y., M. Evans, and E. K. Park. 1995. "A Comparative Analysis of Entity-Relationship Diagrams." *Journal of Computer & Software Engineering* 3 (4): 427–59.

Storey, V. C. 1991. "Relational Database Design Based on the Entity-Relationship Model." *Data and Knowledge Engineering* 7 (1991): 47–83.

Teorey, T. J., D. Yang, and J. P. Fry. 1986. "A Logical Design Methodology for Relational Databases Using the Extended Entity-Relationship Model." *Computing Surveys* 18 (June): 197–221.

FURTHER READING

Batini, C., S. Ceri, and S. B. Navathe. 1992. *Conceptual Database Design: An Entity-Relationship Approach.* Menlo Park, CA: Benjamin/Cummings.

Keuffel, W. 1996. "Battle of the Modeling Techniques." *DBMS* 9 (August): 83, 84, 86, 97.

Moody, D. 1996. "The Seven Habits of Highly Effective Data Modelers." *Database Programming & Design* 9 (October): 57, 58, 60–62, 64.

Tillman, G. 1994. "Should You Model Derived Data?" *DBMS* 7 (November): 88, 90.

Tillman, G. 1995. "Data Modeling Rules of Thumb." *DBMS* 8 (August): 70, 72, 74, 76, 80–82, 87.

Project Case

PROJECT DESCRIPTION

After completing a course in database management, you have been hired as a summer intern by Mountain View Community Hospital. Your first assignment is to work as part of a team of three persons to develop a high-level E-R diagram for the hospital. You conduct interviews with a number of hospital administrators and staff to identify the key entities for the hospital. After a short time your team has identified the following entities:

- Ward—a treatment center within the hospital. Examples of wards are maternity and emergency care. Each ward has a ward number (identifier) and a ward name.

- Patient—a person who is either admitted to the hospital or is registered in an outpatient program. Each patient has a patient number (identifier) and name.

- Physician—a member of the hospital medical staff who may admit patients to the hospital and who may administer medical treatments. Each physician has a physician ID (identifier) and name.

- Bed—a hospital bed that may be assigned to a patient who is admitted to the hospital. Each bed has a bed number (identifier), a room number, and a ward number.

- Item—any medical or surgical item that may be used in treating a patient. Each item has an item number (identifier), description, and unit cost.

- Employee—any person employed as part of the hospital staff. Each employee has an employee number and name.

- Treatment—any test or procedure performed by a physician on behalf of a patient. Each treatment has a treatment ID that consists of two parts: treatment number, and treatment name.

The team next recorded the following information concerning relationships:

- Each hospital employee is assigned to work in one or more wards. Each ward has at least one employ-

ee, and may have any number of employees. The hospital records the number of hours per week that a given employee works in a particular ward.

- Each ward has exactly one employee who is designated nurse in charge for that ward.

- A given patient may or may not be assigned to a bed (since some patients are outpatients). A bed may or may not be assigned to a patient.

- A patient must be referred to the hospital by exactly one physician. A physician may refer any number of patients, or may not refer any patients.

- Physicians may perform any number of treatments on behalf of any number of patients, or may not perform any treatments. A patient may have treatments performed by any number of physicians. For each treatment performed on behalf of a given patient by a particular physician, the hospital records the following information: treatment date, treatment time, and results.

- A patient may optionally consume any number of items. A given item may be consumed by one or more patients, or may not be consumed. For each item consumed by a patient, the hospital records the following: date, time, quantity, and total cost (which can be computed by multiplying quantity times unit cost).

PROJECT QUESTIONS

1. Why would Mountain View Community Hospital want to use entity-relationship modeling to understand its data requirements? What other ways might the hospital want to model its information requirements?

2. Do there appear to be any weak entities in the description of the Mountain View Community Hospital data requirements? If so, what are they?

3. What is the significance in developing an E-R diagram for Mountain View Community Hospital to the third entry in the preceding list, which states that some patients are assigned to a bed, but outpatients are not assigned to a bed?

4. Is Mountain View Community Hospital itself an entity type in a data model to represent its data requirements?

PROJECT EXERCISES

1. Study the project description very closely. What other questions would you like to ask in order to better understand the data requirements at Mountain View Community Hospital?

2. Develop an E-R diagram for Mountain View Community Hospital. State any assumptions you had to make in developing the diagram.

3. The project description describes an entity type called Item. Given your answer to Project Exercise 2, will this entity type also be able to represent in-room TVs as a billable item to patients? Why or why not?

4. Suppose the attribute bed number were a composite attribute, composed of ward number, room number, and individual bed number. Redraw any parts of your answer to Project Exercise 2 that would have to change to handle this composite attribute.

5. Consider your new E-R diagram for Mountain View Community Hospital after changing your answer to Project Exercise 2 to handle the situation in Project Exercise 4. Now, additionally assume that a ward contains many rooms, and each room may contain items that are billed to patients assigned to that room. Redraw your E-R diagram to accommodate this new assumption.

6. Does your answer to Project Exercise 2 allow more than one physician to perform a treatment on a patient at the same time? If not, redraw your answer to Project Exercise 2 to accommodate this situation. Make any additional assumptions you consider necessary in order to represent this situation.

7. Does your answer to Project Exercise 2 allow the same treatment to be performed more than once on the same patient by the same physician? If not, redraw your answer to Project Exercise 2 to accommodate this situation. Make any additional assumptions you consider necessary in order to represent this situation.

CHAPTER

4

The Enhanced E-R Model
and Business Rules

LEARNING OBJECTIVES

After studying this chapter, you should be able to:

■ Concisely define each of the following key terms: **enhanced entity-relationship (EER) model, subtype, supertype, attribute inheritance, generalization, specialization, subtype discriminator, business rule, term, fact,** and **domain constraint.**

■ Recognize when to use subtype/supertype relationships in data modeling.

■ Use both specialization and generalization as techniques for defining supertype/subtype relationships.

■ Specify both completeness constraints and disjointness constraints in modeling supertype/subtype relationships.

■ Develop a supertype/subtype hierarchy for a realistic business situation.

■ State several premises related to a business rules paradigm.

■ Name the various categories of business rules.

■ Define a simple operational constraint using a graphical model or structured English statement.

INTRODUCTION

The basic E-R model described in Chapter 3 was first introduced during the mid-1970s. It has been suitable for modeling most common business problems and has enjoyed widespread use. However, the business environment has changed dramatically since that time. Business relationships are more complex and as a result, business data are much more complex as well. For example organizations must be prepared to segment their markets and to customize their products, which places much greater demands on organizational databases.

To better cope with these changes, researchers have continued to enhance the E-R model so that it can more accurately represent the complex data encountered in

129

Enhanced entity-relationship model:
The model that has resulted from extending the original E-R model with new modeling constructs.

today's business environment. The term **enhanced entity-relationship (EER) model** is used to identify the model that has resulted from extending the original E-R model with these new modeling constructs.

The most important new modeling construct incorporated in the EER model is supertype/subtype relationships. This facility allows us to model a general entity type (called the *supertype*) and then subdivide it into several specialized entity types called *subtypes*. Thus, for example, the entity type CAR can be modeled as a supertype, with subtypes SEDAN, SPORTS CAR, COUPE, and so on. Each subtype inherits attributes from its supertype and in addition may have special attributes of its own. Adding new notation for modeling supertype/subtype relationships has greatly improved the flexibility of the basic E-R model.

Enhanced E-R diagrams are used to capture important business rules such as constraints in supertype/subtype relationships. However, most organizations use a multitude of business rules to guide behavior. Many of these rules cannot be expressed with basic E-R diagrams, or even with enhanced E-R diagrams. Promising research at present is directed at developing new ways of expressing business rules, which would allow end users with some training to define their own rules to the system. These rules then automatically become constraints that are enforced by the database management system and are used to maintain the database in a consistent or valid state. This business rules approach allows organizations to respond much more quickly to changing business conditions than previous approaches to systems development.

REPRESENTING SUPERTYPES AND SUBTYPES

Recall from Chapter 3 that an entity type is a collection of entities that share common properties or characteristics. While the entity instances that compose an entity type are similar, we do not expect them to be identical. One of the major challenges in data modeling is to recognize and clearly represent entities that are almost the same; that is, entity types that share common properties but also have one or more distinct properties that are of interest to the organization.

Subtype: A subgrouping of the entities in an entity type that is meaningful to the organization and that shares common attributes or relationships distinct from other subgroupings.

Supertype: A generic entity type that has a relationship with one or more subtypes.

For this reason, the E-R model has been extended to include supertype/subtype relationships. A **subtype** is a subgrouping of the entities in an entity type that is meaningful to the organization. For example, STUDENT is an entity type in a university. Two subtypes of STUDENT are GRADUATE STUDENT and UNDERGRADUATE STUDENT. In this example, we refer to STUDENT as the supertype. A **supertype** is a generic entity type that has a relationship with one or more subtypes.

Basic Concepts and Notation

The basic notation that we use for supertype/subtype relationships is shown in Figure 4-1. The supertype is connected with a line to a circle, which in turn is connected by a line to each subtype that has been defined. The U-shaped symbol on each line connecting a subtype to the circle indicates that the subtype is a subset of the supertype. It also indicates the direction of the subtype/supertype relationship.

Attributes that are shared by all entities (including the identifier) are associated with the supertype. Attributes that are unique to a particular subtype are associated with that subtype. Other components will be added to this notation to provide additional meaning in supertype/subtype relationships as we proceed through the remainder of this chapter.

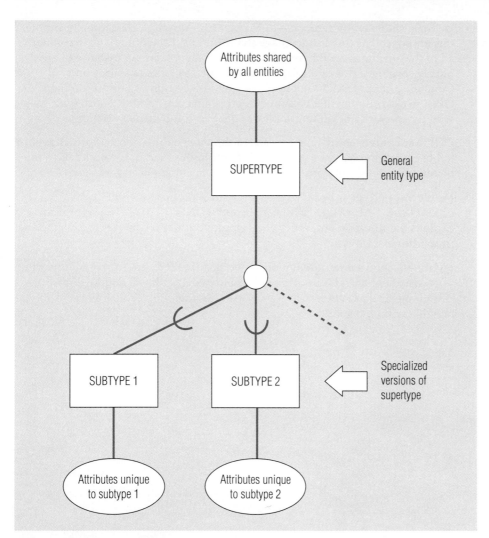

Figure 4-1
Basic notation for supertype/
subtype relationships

An Example   Let us illustrate supertype/subtype relationships with a simple yet common example. Suppose that an organization has three basic types of employees: hourly employees, salaried employees, and contract consultants. Some of the important attributes for each of these types of employees are the following:

- *Hourly employees*   Employee_Number, Employee_Name, Address, Date_Hired, Hourly_Rate

- *Salaried employees*   Employee_Number, Employee_Name, Address, Date_Hired, Annual_Salary, Stock_Option

- *Contract consultants*   Employee_Number, Employee_Name, Address, Date_Hired, Contract_Number, Billing_Rate

Notice that all of the employee types have several attributes in common: Employee_Number, Employee_Name, Address, and Date_Hired. In addition, each type has one or more attributes distinct from the attributes of other types (for example, Hourly_Rate is unique to hourly employees). If you were developing a conceptual data model in this situation, you might consider three choices:

1. Define a single entity type called EMPLOYEE. Although conceptually simple, this approach has the disadvantage that EMPLOYEE would have to contain all of the attributes for the three types of employees. For an instance of an hourly employee (for example), attributes such as Annual_Salary and Contract_Number would not apply and would be null or not used. When taken to a development environment, programs that use this entity type would necessarily be quite complex to deal with the many variations.

2. Define a separate entity type for each of the three entities. This approach would fail to exploit the common properties of employees, and users would have to be careful to select the correct entity type when using the system.

3. Define a supertype called EMPLOYEE, with subtypes for HOURLY EMPLOYEE, SALARIED EMPLOYEE, and CONSULTANT. This approach exploits the common properties of all employees, yet recognizes the distinct properties of each type.

Figure 4-2 shows a representation of the EMPLOYEE supertype with its three subtypes, using enhanced ER notation. Attributes shared by all employees are associated with the EMPLOYEE entity type. Attributes that are peculiar to each subtype are included with that subtype only.

Figure 4-2
Employee supertype with three subtypes

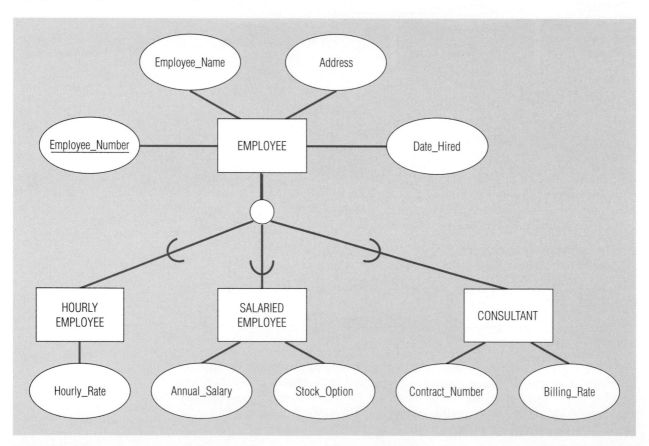

Attribute Inheritance   A subtype is an entity type in its own right. An entity instance of a subtype represents the *same* entity instance of the supertype. For example, if 'Therese Jones' is an occurrence of the CONSULTANT subtype, then this same person is necessarily an occurrence of the EMPLOYEE supertype. As a consequence, an entity in a subtype must possess not only values for its own attributes, but also values for its attributes as a member of the supertype.

Attribute inheritance is the property by which subtype entities inherit values of all attributes of the supertype. This important property makes it unnecessary to include supertype attributes redundantly with the subtypes. For example, Employee_Name is an attribute of EMPLOYEE (Figure 4-2), but not of the subtypes of EMPLOYEE. Thus the fact that the employee's name is 'Therese Jones' is inherited from the EMPLOYEE supertype. However, the Billing_Rate for this same employee is an attribute of the subtype CONSULTANT.

> **Attribute inheritance:**
> A property that subtype entities inherit values of all attributes of the supertype.

We have established that a member of a subtype *must* be a member of the supertype. Is the converse also true—that is, is a member of the supertype also a member of one (or more) of the subtypes? This may or may not be true, depending on the business situation. We discuss the various possibilities later in this chapter.

When to Use Supertype/Subtype Relationships   Whether to use supertype/subtype relationships or not is a decision that the data modeler must make in each situation. You should consider using subtypes when either (or both) of the following conditions are present:

1. There are attributes that apply to some (but not all) of the instances of an entity type. For example, see the EMPLOYEE entity type in Figure 4-2.

2. The instances of a subtype participate in a relationship unique to that subtype.

Figure 4-3 is an example of the use of subtype relationships that illustrates both of these situations. The hospital entity type PATIENT has two subtypes: OUTPATIENT and RESIDENT PATIENT (the primary key is Patient_ID). All patients have an Admit_Date attribute, as well as a Patient_Name. Also, every patient is cared for by a RESPONSIBLE PHYSICIAN who develops a treatment plan for the patient.

Each subtype has an attribute that is unique to that subtype. Outpatients have a Checkback_Date, while resident patients have a Date_Discharged. Also, resident patients have a unique relationship that assigns each patient to a bed (notice that this is a mandatory relationship). Each bed may or may not be assigned to a patient.

Earlier we discussed the property of attribute inheritance. Thus each outpatient and each resident patient inherits the attributes of the parent supertype PATIENT: Patient_ID, Patient_Name, and Admit_Date. Figure 4-3 also illustrates the principle of relationship inheritance. Each outpatient and each inpatient are also instances of PATIENT; therefore, each Is_cared_for by a RESPONSIBLE PHYSICIAN.

Representing Specialization and Generalization

We have described and illustrated the basic principles of supertype/subtype relationships, including the characteristics of "good" subtypes. But in developing real-world data models, how can you recognize opportunities to exploit these relationships? There are two processes—specialization and generalization—that serve as mental models in developing supertype/subtype relationships.

Generalization   A unique aspect of human intelligence is the ability and propensity to classify objects and experiences and to generalize their properties. In data

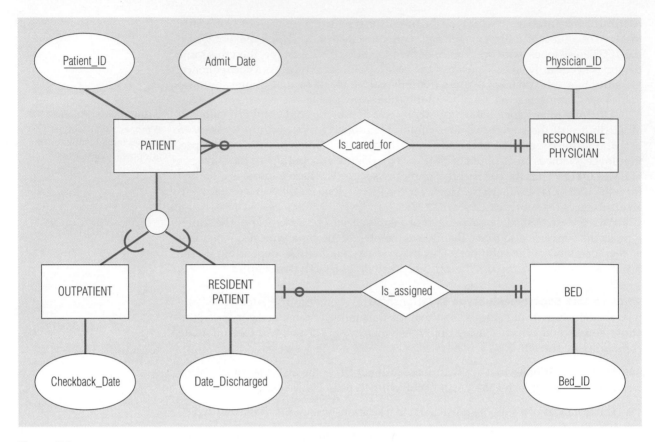

Figure 4-3
Supertype/subtype relationships in a hospital

Generalization: The process of defining a more general entity type from a set of more specialized entity types.

modeling, **generalization** is the process of defining a more general entity type from a set of more specialized entity types. Thus generalization is a bottom-up process.

An example of generalization is shown in Figure 4-4. In Figure 4-4a, three entity types have been defined: CAR, TRUCK, and MOTORCYCLE. At this stage, the data modeler intends to represent these separately on an E-R diagram. However, on closer examination we see that the three entity types have a number of attributes in common: Vehicle_ID (identifier), Vehicle_Name (with components Make and Model), and Engine_Displacement. This fact (reinforced by the presence of a common identifier) suggests that each of the three entity types is really a version of a more general entity type.

This more general entity type (named VEHICLE) together with the resulting supertype/subtype relationships is shown in Figure 4-4b. The entity CAR has the specific attribute No_of_Passengers, while TRUCK has two specific attributes: Capacity and Cab_Type. Thus, generalization has allowed us to group entity types along with their common attributes, while at the same time preserving specific attributes that are peculiar to each subtype.

Notice that the entity type MOTORCYCLE is not included in the relationship. Is this simply an omission? No—instead, it is deliberately not included because it does not satisfy the conditions for a subtype discussed earlier. Comparing Figure 4-4 parts a and b, you will notice that the only attributes of MOTORCYCLE are those that are common to all vehicles; there are no attributes specific to motorcycles. Further,

Figure 4-4 Example of generalization

(a) Three entity types: CAR, TRUCK, and MOTORCYCLE

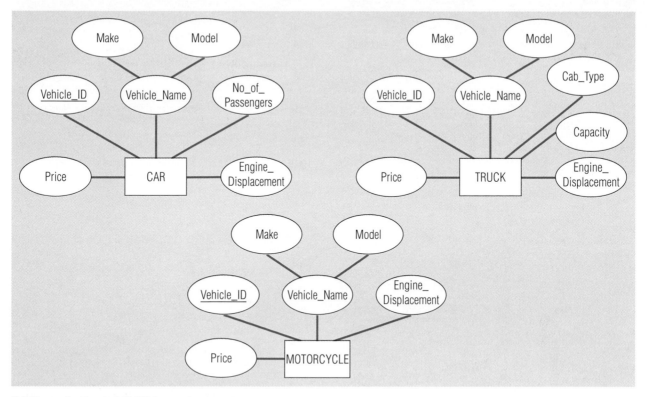

(b) Generalization to VEHICLE supertype

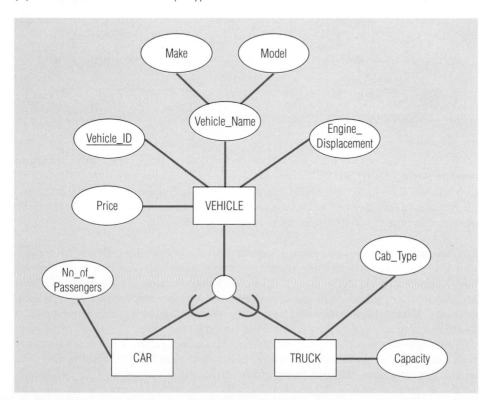

Figure 4-5
Example of specialization

(a) Entity type PART

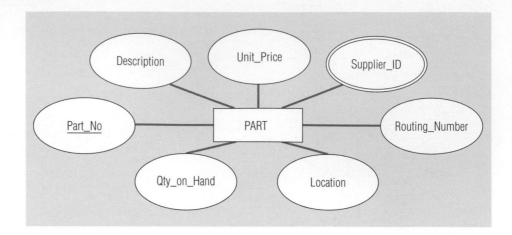

(b) Specialization to
MANUFACTURED PART and
PURCHASED PART

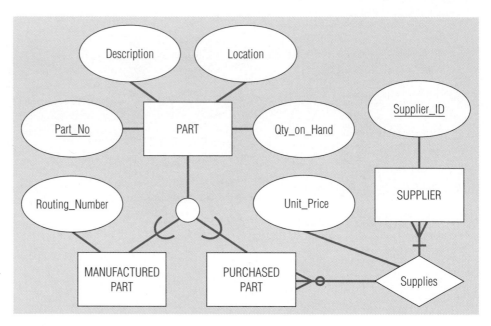

MOTORCYCLE does not have a relationship to another entity type. Thus there is no need to create a MOTORCYCLE subtype.

The fact that there is no MOTORCYCLE subtype suggests that it must be possible to have an instance of VEHICLE that is not a member of any of its subtypes. We discuss this type of constraint in the next section.

Specialization: The process of defining one or more subtypes of the supertype, and forming supertype/subtype relationships.

Specialization   As we have seen, generalization is a bottom-up process. Specialization is a top-down process, the direct reverse of generalization. Suppose that we have defined an entity type with its attributes. **Specialization** is the process of defining one or more subtypes of the supertype, and forming supertype/subtype relationships. Each subtype is formed based on some distinguishing characteristic such as attributes or relationships specific to the subtype.

An example of specialization is shown in Figure 4-5. Figure 4-5a shows an entity type named PART, together with several of its attributes. The identifier is Part_No, and other attributes include Description, Unit_Price, Location, Qty_on_Hand,

Routing_Number, and Supplier_ID (the last attribute is multivalued since there may be more than one supplier for a part).

In discussions with users, we discover that there are two possible sources for parts: some are manufactured internally, while others are purchased from outside suppliers. Further, we discover that some parts are obtained from both sources. In this case the choice depends on factors such as manufacturing capacity, unit price of the parts, and so on.

Some of the attributes in Figure 4-5a apply to all parts, regardless of source. However, others depend on the source. Thus Routing_Number applies only to manufactured parts, while Supplier_ID and Unit_Price apply only to purchased parts. These factors suggest that PART should be specialized by defining the subtypes MANUFACTURED PART and PURCHASED PART (see Figure 4-5b).

In Figure 4-5b, Routing_Number is associated with MANUFACTURED PART. The data modeler initially planned to associate Supplier_ID and Unit_Price with PURCHASED PART. However, in further discussions with users she suggested instead that they create a new relationship between PURCHASED PART and SUPPLIER. This relationship (named Supplies in Figure 4-5b) allows users to more easily associate purchased parts with their suppliers. Notice that the attribute Unit_Price is now associated with the relationship Supplies, so that the unit price for a part may vary from one supplier to another. In this example, specialization has permitted a preferred representation of the problem domain.

Combining Specialization and Generalization   Specialization and generalization are both valuable techniques for developing supertype/subtype relationships. Which technique you use at a particular time depends on several factors such as the nature of the problem domain, previous modeling efforts, and personal preference. You should be prepared to use both approaches and to alternate back and forth as dictated by the preceding factors.

SPECIFYING CONSTRAINTS IN SUPERTYPE/SUBTYPE RELATIONSHIPS

So far we have discussed the basic concepts of supertype/subtype relationships and introduced some basic notation to represent these concepts. We have also described the processes of generalization and specialization which assist a data modeler recognize opportunities for exploiting these relationships. In this section we introduce additional notation to represent constraints on supertype/subtype relationships. These constraints allow us to capture some of the important business rules that apply to these relationships. The two most important types of constraints that are described in this section are completeness and disjointness constraints (Elmasri and Navathe, 1994).

Specifying Completeness Constraints

A **completeness constraint** addresses the question whether an instance of a supertype must also be a member of at least one subtype. The completeness constraint has two possible rules: total specialization and partial specialization. The **total specialization rule** specifies that each entity instance of the supertype *must* be a member of some subtype in the relationship. The **partial specialization rule** specifies that an entity instance of the supertype is allowed not to belong to any subtype. We illustrate each of these rules with earlier examples from this chapter (see Figure 4-6).

Completeness constraint:
A type of constraint that addresses the question whether an instance of a supertype must also be a member of at least one subtype.

Total specialization rule:
Specifies that each entity instance of the supertype *must* be a member of some subtype in the relationship.

Partial specialization rule:
Specifies that an entity instance of the supertype is allowed not to belong to any subtype.

Figure 4-6 Examples of completeness constraints

(a) Total specialization rule

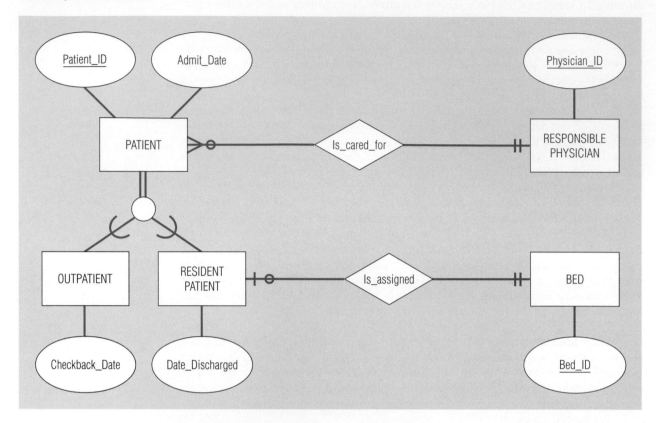

Total Specialization Rule Figure 4-6a repeats the example of PATIENT (Figure 4-3), and introduces the notation for total specialization. In this example, the business rule is the following: A patient must be either an outpatient or a resident patient (there are no other types of patient in this hospital). Total specialization is indicated by the *double* line extending from the PATIENT entity type to the circle.

In this example, every time a new instance of PATIENT is inserted into the supertype, a corresponding instance is inserted into either OUTPATIENT or RESIDENT PATIENT. If the instance is inserted into RESIDENT PATIENT, an instance of the relationship Is_assigned is created to assign the patient to a hospital bed.

Partial Specialization Rule Figure 4-6b repeats the example of VEHICLE and its subtypes CAR and TRUCK from Figure 4-4. Recall that in this example motorcycle is a type of vehicle, but that it is not represented as a subtype in the data model. Thus if a vehicle is a car, it must appear as an instance of CAR, and if it is a truck, it must appear as an instance of TRUCK. However, if the vehicle is a motorcycle, it cannot appear as an instance of any subtype. This is an example of partial specialization, and it is specified by the *single* line from the VEHICLE supertype to the circle.

Disjointness constraint:
A constraint that addresses the question whether an instance of a supertype may simultaneously be a member of two (or more) subtypes.

Disjoint rule: Specifies that if an entity instance (of the supertype) is a member of one subtype, it cannot simultaneously be a member of any other subtype.

Specifying Disjointness Constraints

A **disjointness constraint** addresses the question whether an instance of a supertype may simultaneously be a member of two (or more) subtypes. The disjointness constraint has two possible rules: the disjoint rule and the overlap rule. The **disjoint rule**

(b) Partial specialization rule

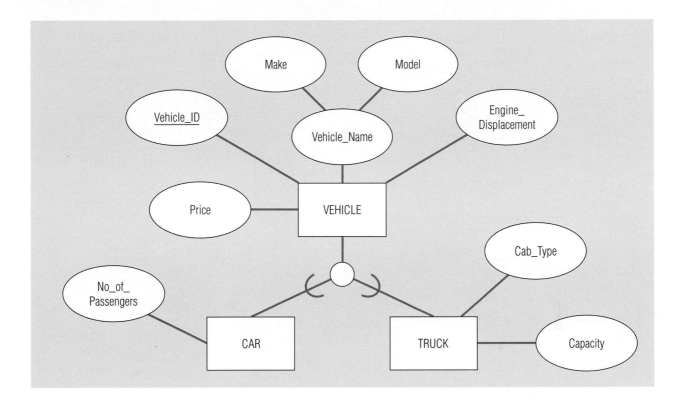

specifies that if an entity instance (of the supertype) is a member of one subtype, it cannot simultaneously be a member of any other subtype. The **overlap rule** specifies that an entity instance can simultaneously be a member of two (or more) subtypes. An example of each of these rules is shown in Figure 4-7.

Overlap rule: Specifies that an entity instance can simultaneously be a member of two (or more) subtypes.

Disjoint Rule Figure 4-7a shows the PATIENT example from Figure 4-6a. The business rule in this case is the following: *At any given time,* a patient must be either an outpatient or a resident patient but cannot be both. This is the disjoint rule, as specified by the letter '**d**' in the circle joining the supertype and its subtypes. Note in this figure, the subclass of a PATIENT may change over time, but at a given time, a PATIENT is of only one type.

Overlap Rule Figure 4-7b shows the entity type PART with its two subtypes, MANUFACTURED PART and PURCHASED PART (from Figure 4-5b). Recall from our discussion of this example that some parts are both manufactured and purchased. Some clarification of this statement is required. In this example an instance of PART is a particular part number (that is, a *type of part*), not an individual part (this is indicated by the identifier, which is Part_No). For example, consider part number 4000. At a given time the quantity on hand for this part might be 250, of which 100 are manufactured and the remaining 150 are purchased parts. In this case, it is not important to keep track of individual parts. When tracking individual parts is important, then each part is assigned a serial number identifier, and the quantity on hand is 1 or 0, depending on whether that individual part exists or not.

Figure 4-7 Examples of disjointness constraints

(a) Disjoint rule

(b) Overlap rule

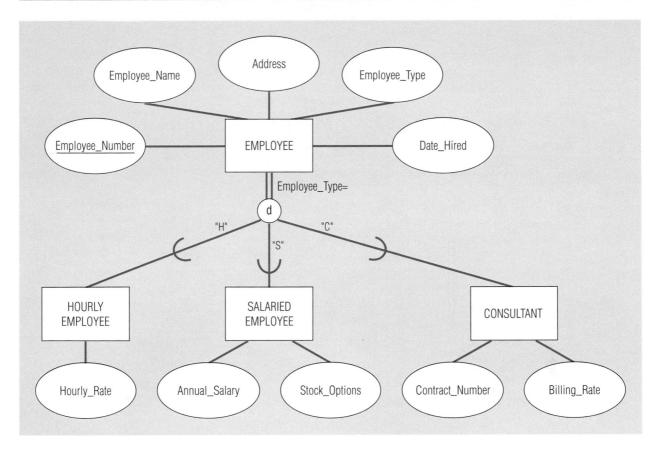

Figure 4-8
Introducing a subtype discriminator (disjoint rule)

The overlap rule is specified by placing the letter 'o' in the circle, as shown in Figure 4-7b. Notice in this figure that the total specialization rule is also specified, as indicated by the double line. Thus any part must be either a purchased part or a manufactured part, or it may simultaneously be both of these.

Defining Subtype Discriminators

Given a supertype/subtype relationship, consider the problem of inserting a new instance of the supertype. Into which of the subtypes (if any) should this instance be inserted? We have already discussed the various possible rules that apply to this situation. We need a simple mechanism to implement these rules, if one is available. Often this can be accomplished by using a subtype discriminator. A **subtype discriminator** is an attribute of the supertype whose values determine the target subtype or subtypes.

Subtype discriminator: An attribute of the supertype whose values determine the target subtype or subtypes.

Disjoint Subtypes An example of the use of a subtype discriminator is shown in Figure 4-8. This example is for the EMPLOYEE supertype and its subtypes, introduced in Figure 4-2. Notice that the following constraints have been added to this figure: total specialization and disjoint subtypes. Thus each employee must be either hourly, salaried, or a consultant.

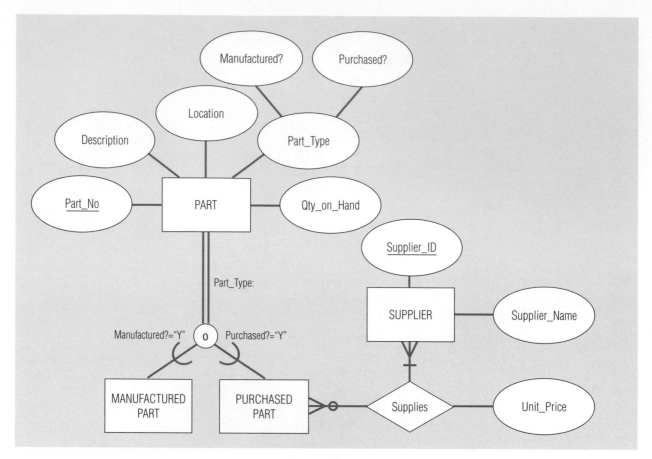

Figure 4-9
Subtype discriminator (overlap rule)

A new attribute (Employee_Type) has been added to the supertype, to serve as subtype discriminator. When a new employee is added to the supertype, this attribute is coded with one of three values, as follows: "H" (for Hourly), "S" (for Salaried), or "C" (for Consultant). Depending on this code, the instance is then assigned to the appropriate subtype.

The notation we use to specify the subtype discriminator is also shown in Figure 4-8. The expression "Employee_Type=" (which is the left-hand side of a condition statement) is placed next to the line leading from the supertype to the circle. The value of the attribute that selects the appropriate subtype (in this example, either "H", "S", or "C") is placed adjacent to the line leading to that subtype. Thus for example, the condition "Employee_Type= "S" causes an entity instance to be inserted into the SALARIED EMPLOYEE subtype.

Overlapping Subtypes   When subtypes overlap, a slightly modified approach must be applied for the subtype discriminator. The reason is that a given instance of the supertype may require that we create an instance in more than one subtype.

An example of this situation is shown in Figure 4-9 for PART and its overlapping subtypes. A new attribute named Part_Type has been added to PART. Part_Type is a composite attribute with components Manufactured? and Purchased? Each of these attributes is a Boolean variable (that is, it takes on only the values yes,

'Y', and no, 'N'). When a new instance is added to PART, these components are coded as follows:

Type of Part	Manufactured?	Purchased?
Manufactured only	'Y'	'N'
Purchased only	'N'	'Y'
Purchased and manufactured	'Y'	'Y'

The method for specifying the subtype discriminator for this example is shown in Figure 4-9. Notice that this approach can be used for any number of overlapping subtypes.

Defining Supertype/Subtype Hierarchies

We have considered a number of examples of supertype/subtype relationships in this chapter. It is possible for any of the subtypes in these examples to have other subtypes defined on it (in this case, the subtype becomes a supertype for the newly defined subtypes). A **supertype/subtype hierarchy** is a hierarchical arrangement of supertypes and subtypes, where each subtype has only one supertype (Elmasri and Navathe, 1994).

We present an example of a supertype/subtype hierarchy in this section (see Figure 4-10). This example includes most of the concepts and notation we have used in this chapter to this point. It also presents a methodology (based on specialization) that you can use in many data modeling situations.

Supertype/subtype hierarchy: A hierarchical arrangement of supertypes and subtypes, where each subtype has only one supertype.

An Example Suppose that you are asked to model the human resources in a university. Using specialization (top-down approach) you might proceed as follows. Starting at the top of a hierarchy, model the most general entity type first. In this case, the most general entity type is PERSON. List and associate all attributes of PERSON. The attributes shown in Figure 4-10 are: SSN (identifier), Name, Address, Gender, and Date_of_Birth. The entity type at the top of a hierarchy is sometimes called the *root*.

Next, define all major subtypes of the root. In this example, there are three subtypes of PERSON: EMPLOYEE (persons who work for the university), STUDENT (persons who attend classes), and ALUMNUS (persons who have graduated). Since there are no other types of persons of interest to the university the total specialization rule applies, as shown in the figure. A person might belong to more than one subtype (for example, ALUMNUS and EMPLOYEE), so the overlap rule is used. Note, overlap allows for any overlap (a PERSON may be simultaneous in any pair or in all three subtypes). If certain combinations are not allowed, then a more refined supertype/subtype hierarchy would have to be developed to eliminate the prohibited combinations.

Attributes that apply specifically to each of these subtypes are shown in the figure. Thus each instance of EMPLOYEE has a value for Date_Hired and Salary. Major_Dept is an attribute of STUDENT, and Degree (with components Year, Degree, and Date) is an attribute of ALUMNUS.

The next step is to evaluate whether any of the subtypes already defined qualify for further specialization. In this example, EMPLOYEE is partitioned into two subtypes: FACULTY and STAFF. FACULTY has the specific attribute Rank, while STAFF

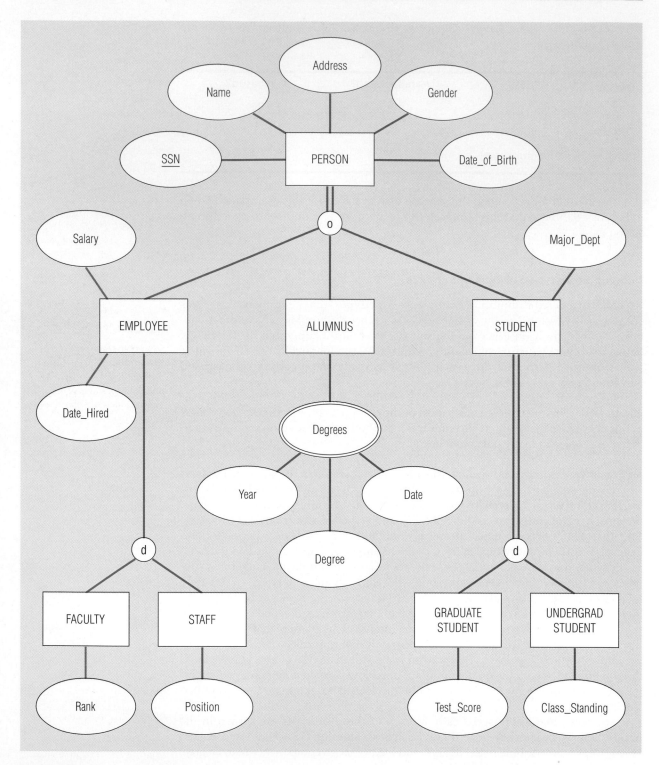

Figure 4-10
Example of supertype/subtype hierarchy

has the specific attribute Position. Notice that in this example, the subtype EMPLOYEE becomes a supertype to FACULTY and STAFF. Because there may be types of employees other than faculty and staff (such as student assistants), the partial specialization rule is indicated. However, an employee cannot be both faculty and staff at the same time. Therefore, the disjoint rule is indicated in the circle.

Two subtypes are also defined for STUDENT: GRADUATE STUDENT and UNDERGRADUATE STUDENT. UNDERGRADUATE STUDENT has the attribute Class_Standing, while GRADUATE STUDENT has the attribute Test_Score. Notice that total specialization and the disjoint rule are specified; you should be able to state the business rules for these constraints.

Summary of Supertype/Subtype Hierarchies   We note two features concerning the attributes contained in the hierarchy shown in Figure 4-10.

1. Attributes are assigned at the highest logical level that is possible in the hierarchy. For example, since SSN (that is, Social Security Number) applies to all persons, it is assigned to the root. On the other hand, Date_Hired applies only to employees so it is assigned to EMPLOYEE. This approach ensures that attributes can be shared by as many subtypes as possible.

2. Subtypes that are lower in the hierarchy inherit attributes not only from their immediate supertype, but from all supertypes higher in the hierarchy, up to the root. Thus for example, an instance of faculty has values for all of the following attributes: SSN, Name, Address, Sex, and Date_of_Birth (from PERSON), Date_Hired and Salary (from EMPLOYEE), and Rank (from FACULTY).

In the student case at the end of this chapter, we ask you to develop an enhanced E-R diagram for Mountain View Community Hospital using the same procedure we outlined in this section.

BUSINESS RULES: AN OVERVIEW

We have seen that E-R diagrams (and enhanced E-R diagrams) are a useful means for expressing certain types of business rules. Thus, for example, the participation and disjointness constraints associated with supertypes and subtypes discussed in this chapter are an expression of the business rules associated with those relationships. However, there are many other types of business rules in an organization that cannot be expressed with this notation. In this section we develop a general framework for business rules and show how to express some important types of rules that elude the standard E-R (and enhanced E-R) notation.

A **business rule** is "a statement that defines or constrains some aspect of the business. It is intended to assert business structure or to control or influence the behavior of the business" (Guide Business Rules Project, 1995). For example, the following two statements are common expressions of business rules:

Business rule: A statement that defines or constrains some aspect of the business. It is intended to assert business structure or to control or influence the behavior of the business.

- "A student may register for a section of a course only if he or she has successfully completed the prerequisites for that course."

- "A preferred customer qualifies for a 10% discount, unless he has an overdue account balance."

Most organizations today (and their employees) are guided by thousands of combinations of such rules. In the aggregate these rules influence behavior and determine how the organization responds to its environment (Gottesdiener, 1997).

The Business Rules Paradigm

The concept of business rules has been used in information systems for some time. However, it has been more common to use the related term "integrity constraint" when referring to such rules. The intent of this term is generally somewhat more limited in scope, usually referring to maintaining valid data values and relationships in the database.

Today the term "business rules" has a much broader scope, so that it includes all rules (such as the two examples quoted above) that have an impact on the databases in an organization. In fact, a business rules approach has been advocated by a number of authors as a new paradigm for specifying information systems requirements (von Halle, 1997). This approach is based on the following premises:

- Business rules are a core concept in an enterprise since they are an expression of business policy and guide individual and aggregate behavior.

- Business rules can be expressed in terms that are familiar to end users. Thus users can define then maintain their own rules.

- Business rules are highly maintainable. They are stored in a central repository, and each rule is expressed only once, then shared throughout the organization.

- Enforcement of business rules can be automated, through the use of software that can interpret the rules and enforce them using the integrity mechanisms of the database management system.

Although much progress has been made, the industry has not realized all of these objectives to date. Research is continuing (especially on automating business rules), and the business rules approach holds considerable promise for the future. Possibly the premise with greatest potential benefit is "Business rules are highly maintainable." The ability to specify and maintain the requirements for information systems as a set of rules has considerable power when coupled with an ability to automatically generate information systems from a repository of rules. Automatic generation and maintenance of systems not only will simplify the systems development process but also will improve the quality of systems.

Scope of Business Rules

In this chapter we are concerned only with business rules that impact an organization's databases. Most organizations have a host of rules and/or policies that fall outside this definition. For example, the rule "Friday is dress-down day" may be an important policy statement, but it has no immediate impact on databases. On the other hand the rule "A student may register for a section of a course only if he or she has successfully completed the prerequisites for that course" is within our scope since it constrains the transactions that may be processed against the database. In particular, it causes any transaction to be rejected that attempts to register a student who does not have the necessary prerequisites.

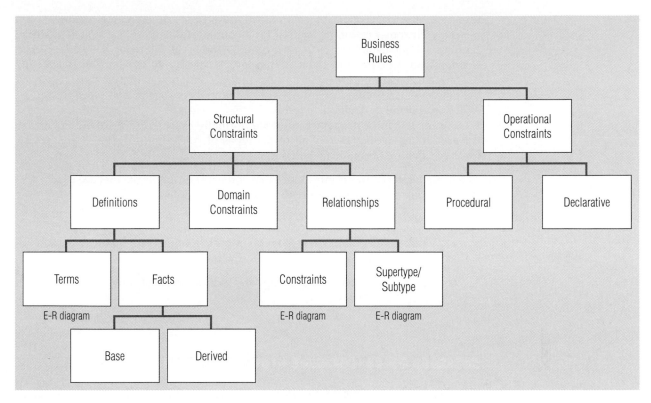

Figure 4-11
Classification of business rules

Certain forms of integrity constraints that are specific to a certain data model (such as the relational model) are also ignored in this chapter. For example, key constraints (which require primary keys for all relations) are specific to the relational model. Also, referential integrity constraints (which maintain the integrity of references between related tables or relations) are a property of the relational data model. We describe these constraints in Chapter 6.

Classification of Business Rules

An attempt to classify the various important types of business rules is shown in Figure 4-11. In this diagram, business rules are divided into two broad categories: structural constraints and operational constraints. There is no consensus on the use of these terms (or the grouping of rules within each category), but this diagram provides a useful framework for discussion.

Structural constraints are rules that define the static structure of the organization. Three primary types of structural constraints are shown in Figure 4-11: definitions, domains, and relationships. Definitions are further subdivided into terms and facts. Associated with relationships are constraints and supertype/subtype relationships.

Operational constraints are rules that constrain the ongoing operations of the organization. These operations are often characterized by a series of transactions that

Structural constraints:
Business rules that define the static structure of the organization. The three primary types are definitions, domains, and relationships.

Operational constraints:
Business rules that constrain the ongoing operations of the organization. These operations are often characterized by a series of transactions that represent business events.

represent business events. Typical transactions include adding a new customer, processing a customer order, registering for a course, and purchasing shares of stock. Each transaction usually leads to some combination of the following database actions: Create, Read, Update, and Delete. From the perspective of database management, operational constraints are integrity rules that are designed to protect the integrity of the database. As shown in Figure 4-11, operational constraints can be expressed in either procedural or declarative terms.

Figure 4-11 indicates which rules are normally captured in E-R (and enhanced E-R) diagrams. Notice that of all of the types of rules that are shown, only three types of rules are normally included in these diagrams:

1. *Terms*   E-R diagrams introduce most of the important terms that are used, including the names of entity types, attributes, and relationships.

2. *Relationship structures*

    a. Constraints: minimum cardinality (or participation constraints) and maximum cardinality.

    b. Supertype/subtype relationships and associated constraints.

BUSINESS RULES: DEFINING STRUCTURAL CONSTRAINTS

In this section we describe definitions and domains, which are structural constraints not previously described in the context of E-R diagrams. We use a simple data model for class scheduling to illustrate these constraints, as well as the operational constraints described in the next section. The data model segment for this example is shown in Figure 4-12.

The data model in Figure 4-12 contains four entity types: FACULTY, COURSE, SECTION, and STUDENT. It also shows the relationships between these entity types. Notice that SECTION is a weak entity type, since it cannot exist without the COURSE entity type. The identifying relationship for SECTION is named "Is_scheduled" and the partial identifier is Section_ID (a composite attribute with components Section_No and Semester). Only selected attributes are shown for the various entities to simplify the diagram.

Definitions

Term: A word or phrase that has a specific meaning for the business.

As shown in Figure 4-11, definitions consist of two components: terms and facts. A **term** is a word or phrase that has a specific meaning for the business. Examples of terms are: course, section, rental car, flight, reservation, and passenger. Such terms must be defined carefully and concisely. However, there is no need to define common terms such as day, month, person, or television since these terms are understood by most persons without ambiguity.

Fact: An association between two or more terms.

Facts   Definitions are facts (the reason for the distinction is that while definitions are facts, some facts are not definitions). A **fact** is an association between two or more terms. Examples of facts that are definitions are the following (the defined terms are underlined):

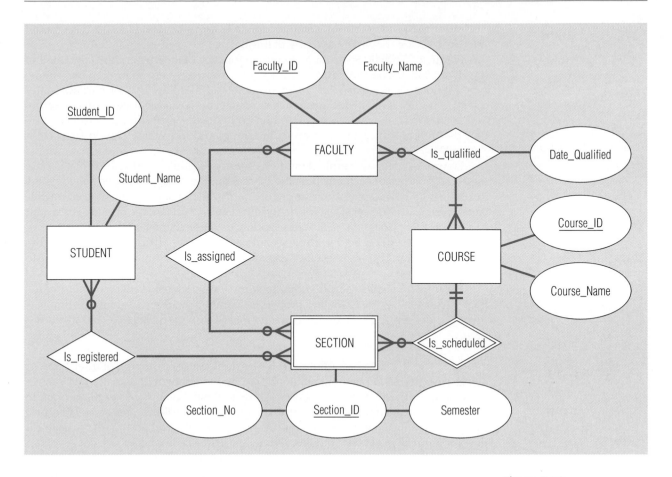

Figure 4-12
Data model segment for
class scheduling

- A course is a module of instruction in a particular subject area. This definition associates two terms: module of instruction, and subject area. We assume that these are common terms that do not need to be further defined.

- A *customer* may request a *model of car* from a *rental branch* on a particular *date*. This fact, which is a definition of <u>model rental request</u>, associates the four terms in italics (Guide Business Rules Project, 1995). Three of these terms are business-specific terms that would need to be defined individually (date is a common term).

Derived Facts   The type of facts described above are called *base* facts—that is, they are fundamental facts that cannot be derived from other terms or facts. Another type of fact (shown in Figure 4-11) is called the derived fact. A **derived fact** is a fact that is derived from other facts or rules, using an algorithm or inference. Following are two examples of derived facts:

Derived fact: A fact that is derived from other facts or rules, using an algorithm or inference.

- rental charge = base rental price + optional insurance + refueling charge

- GPA = quality points/total hours taken

    where quality points = sum[for all courses attempted]
        (hours/course*numerical grade assigned)

Definitions for Data Model   Definitions for the terms contained in the data model (Figure 4-12) are shown in Figures 4-13 through 4-15.

Figure 4-13 provides a sample definition for each of the four entities contained in the data model. The properties recorded for each entity are the following: name, type (regular, weak, or associative), definition, and identifier (full or partial). Many other properties could be included such as source, organizational steward, and so on. You should examine each entity definition and note the terms that are associated by that definition. Which of these are common terms, and which should be further defined?

Figure 4-14 shows sample definitions for the attributes that appear in the data model. Properties of each attribute are: name, domain, definition, and whether the attribute may be null (empty). You might expect the definition to include characteristics of each attribute such as type, length, and so on. Instead, the domain constraint is a name that "points to" a full description of these characteristics. Domain constraints are described below. Some people say that the attribute is a role for the domain constraint, so that domain constraints can play many roles (be related to many attributes).

Figure 4-15 shows sample definitions for the relationships in the data model. Each definition has the following properties: name, type (degree and maximum cardinality), description, constraints (such as mandatory participation), and attributes (if any).

Importance of Precise Definitions   E-R diagrams consist primarily of three types of objects: entities, attributes, and relationships. We have shown how to identify each of these items but have deferred discussing how to define such objects until this section on structural constraints. Although that approach simplified the discussion and allowed us to focus on the E-R diagrams, we do not recommend that approach for developing real-world data models. In fact, the opposite is true:

Figure 4-13
Sample entity definitions

1. Name: **FACULTY**
    Type: Regular
    Definition: a university employee who is academically qualified to teach courses and perform other designated duties
    Identifier: Faculty_ID

2. Name: **COURSE**
    Type: Regular
    Definition: a module of instruction in a particular subject area
    Identifier: Course_ID

3. Name: **SECTION**
    Type: Weak
    Definition: an offering of a course during a particular semester
    Identifier: Section_ID (partial only)

4. Name: **STUDENT**
    Type: Regular
    Definition: a person who has been admitted to the school and who has registered for at least one course during the past year
    Identifier: Student_ID

1. Name: **Faculty_ID**
   Domain: Person_IDs
   Definition: unique identifier of
     a faculty member
   Null: no

2. Name: **Faculty_Name**
   Domain: Person_Names
   Definition: name of a faculty member
   Null: no

3. Name: **Course_ID**
   Domain: Course_ID
   Definition: unique identifier of a course
   Null: no

4. Name: **Course_Name**
   Domain: Course_Names
   Definition: name of a course
   Null: no

5. Name: **Section_ID**
   Components: Section_No, Semester
   Definition: partial identifier of a section
   Null: no

6. Name: **Student_ID**
   Domain: Person_IDs
   Definition: unique identifier of a student
   Null: no

7. Name: **Student_Name**
   Domain: Person_IDs
   Definition: name of a student
   Null: no

8. Name: **Section_No**
   Domain:Section_Nos
   Definition: number of a section
   Null: no

9. Name: **Semester**
   Domain: Semesters
   Definition: semester when a course
     section is offered
   Null: no

10. Name: **Date_Qualified**
    Domain: Date
    Definition: Date a faculty member becomes
      qualified to teach a particular course
    Null: yes

Figure 4-14
Sample attribute definitions

A term should not be added to the E-R diagram until *after* it has been carefully defined, and agreement has been obtained on this definition.

It might seem that obtaining concurrence in an organization on the definitions to be used for the various terms should be relatively easy. However, this is usually far from the case. In fact, it is likely to be one of the most difficult challenges you will face in data modeling or, for that matter, in any other endeavor. It is not unusual for an organization to have multiple definitions (perhaps a dozen or more) for common terms such as "customer" or "order."

To illustrate the problems inherent in developing definitions, consider the entity STUDENT in Figure 4-12. The sample definition we use in Figure 4-13 is: "a person who has been admitted to the school and who has registered for at least one course during the past year." This definition is certain to be challenged, since it is probably too narrow. A person who is a student typically proceeds through several stages in relationship with the school, such as the following:

1. Prospect: some formal contact, indicating an interest in the school.

2. Applicant: applies for admission.

3. Admitted applicant: admitted to the school and perhaps to a degree program.

4. Matriculated student: registers for at least one course.

5. Continuing student: registers for courses on an ongoing basis
   (no substantial gaps).

Figure 4-15

Sample relationship definitions

Name: **Is_qualified**
Type: Binary M:N
Description: associates each faculty member with the course(s) he or she is qualified to teach based on academic preparation and experience.
Constraints: each faculty must be qualified to teach at least one course.
Attributes: Date_Qualified

Name: **Is_scheduled**
Type: Binary M:N
Description: associates each course with the sections that have been scheduled for that course.
Constraints: identifying relationship (mandatory).
Attributes: none

Name: **Is_registered**
Type: Binary M:N
Description: associates each student with the course sections for which he or she is registered during the *current* semester.
Constraints: none
Attributes: none

Name: **Is_assigned**
Type: Binary M:N
Description: associates each faculty member with the course section(s) he or she is assigned to teach during the *current* semester.
Constraints: none
Attributes: none

6. Former student: fails to register for courses during some stipulated period (now may reapply).

7. Graduate: satisfactorily completes some degree program (now may apply for another program).

Imagine the difficulty of obtaining consensus on a single definition in this situation! It would seem you might consider three alternatives:

1. Use multiple definitions to cover the various situations. This is likely to be highly confusing and is not recommended.

2. Use a very general definition that will cover most situations. Add a status attribute to the student entity type to record a given student's actual status.

3. Consider using specialization to develop several subtypes for STUDENT. We describe the conditions that suggest the use of subtypes earlier in this chapter.

Note the futility of attempting to include the STUDENT entity type on an E-R diagram before a precise definition has been developed. Depending on how the term has been defined, you might arrive at any of the following representations:

1. A single entity type with a status attribute.

2. Multiple entity types.

3. A supertype with several subtypes.

1. Name: **Person_IDs**
   Data Type: Character
   Allowable Characters: digits

2. Name: **Person_Names**
   Data Type: Character
   Max. Length: 30

3. Name: **Course_IDs**
   Data Type: Character
   Format: ssss nnnn
          ssss = subject
          nnnn = course number

4. Name: **Course_Names**
   Data Type: Character
   Max. Length: 30

5. Name: **Section_Nos**
   Data Type: Integer
   Length: 1

6. Name: **Semesters**
   Data Type: Character
   Format: pppp yyyy
         pppp = period
         allowable values = 'Fall', Sprg', 'Summ'
         yyyy = year

7. Name: **Dates**
   Data Type: Date

Figure 4-16
Sample domain constraints

Domain Constraints

A **domain constraint** (sometimes simply called *domain*) is a specification of the characteristics of the data values that can be associated with one or more attributes. In other words, a domain constraint states the collection of values from which each of the values of one or more attributes are taken. A domain constraint typically specifies characteristics such as the data type, length, and range of acceptable values. Other possible characteristics are default value and number of decimal places.

Figure 4-16 shows sample domain constraints for the attributes previously defined in Figure 4-14. Properties of the domain constraints shown in this figure include domain name, data type, and (where appropriate) allowable characters, maximum length, and format. Other properties such as minimum or maximum value, default value, or number of decimal places might also be included.

The relationship between attributes and domains is shown using E-R notation in Figure 4-17. Each attribute is assigned to one domain constraint (called DOMAIN for

Domain constraint: A specification of the characteristics of the data values that can be associated with one or more attributes.

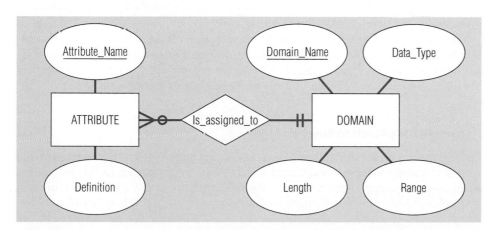

Figure 4-17
Relationship between attributes and domains

short in the figure). A given domain may be assigned to any number of attributes. As a simple example, notice that the attributes Faculty_Name and Student_Name in Figure 4-14 are both assigned to the domain constraint named Person_Names.

The use of domain constraints represents a major step forward in terms of data independence and ease of maintenance. Productivity is improved during system definition since the developer need define only a limited number of domains, then assign attributes to those domains. An even greater improvement results from reduced maintenance costs. Suppose that a definition of a data type changes as a result of a business change. Rather than having to change countless attribute definitions, the database administrator need only change the data definition in the domain that has changed.

To understand the importance of this change, consider the celebrated "Year 2000" problem that was mentioned in Chapter 1. This is basically a domain problem, since the rollover to the year 2000 requires that the Year subfield in the Date field be extended from two to four digits. Unfortunately, in most contemporary systems these data type definitions are buried in countless application programs. The use of domains (such as shown in Figure 4-16) would greatly simplify correcting this problem.

Unfortunately, few contemporary database management systems support domains at the present time. Object-oriented systems are a major exception, since domains are implemented as classes in these systems. However, support for domains will soon be provided by relational and object-relational systems as well.

BUSINESS RULES: DEFINING OPERATIONAL CONSTRAINTS

The most active (and also most promising) area of business rules development is in the realm of operational constraints. As stated previously, operational constraints are rules that constrain the ongoing operations of the business. Most organizations have hundreds (or thousands) of such rules. However, until recently the business rules have been managed in a largely haphazard manner that has prevented a rules-based approach to systems development.

Business rules have traditionally been implemented in procedural logic buried deep within *individual* application programs—in a form that is virtually unrecognizable, and far removed from original business intent (Ross, 1994). This approach places a heavy burden on the programmer, who must know all the constraints that a transaction may violate and must include checks for each of these constraints. An omission, misunderstanding, or error by the programmer will likely leave the database in an inconsistent state (Elmasri and Navathe, 1994).

The procedural approach also makes it extremely difficult to modify and maintain business rules. Business rules change rapidly as a business organization and its environment change. Unfortunately, with the procedural approach the relevant rules are difficult to find and change, and the process is highly error-prone.

Declarative Approach to Business Rules

To help overcome the difficulties of the procedural approach, the modern approach uses declarations for specifying business rules. With this approach each rule is stated as an assertion concerning the intent of the rule, without specifying how the rule will be implemented. A further distinction of the declarative approach is that all rules are stored in a constraint base. A **constraint base** is an organized collection of rules (or constraints), usually stored in a repository. When the database management system processes a transaction, it accesses the appropriate rules in the constraint base to apply the constraints to the affected transaction. Some database management systems call these declarations integrity constraints or triggers; triggers will be discussed in Chapter 9.

Constraint base: An organized collection of rules (or constraints), usually stored in a repository.

Constraint Specification Language   With the declarative approach, each rule is specified using a particular language syntax. There are two desirable features for such a language:

1. It should be relatively simple so that end users not only can understand the rule statements, but also can define the rules themselves.

2. The language should be sufficiently structured to be automatically convertible to the necessary computer code.

At the present time there are two main candidates for a constraint specification language: a graphical syntax and structured grammar (such as English). Ronald Ross, a database expert who has taken a leading role in business rules development, has developed an extensive graphical syntax for specifying business rules (Ross, 1994). Other researchers are pursuing a structured grammar approach. In the remainder of this section we illustrate both of these approaches.

Constrained Objects and Constraining Objects

Most business rules are assertions that constrain objects you have already defined on your E-R diagram. In other words, the assertions constrain the entities, attributes, and/or relationships on the E-R diagram.

Consider the following simple business rule for the rental car industry:

"A person can rent a car only if he or she possesses a valid driver's license."

From this statement, you can infer three entity types: PERSON, CAR, and DRIVER'S LICENSE. Figure 4-18a shows these entity types, with two relationships. The relationship Rents (one-to-many optional) associates a person with a car he or she has rented (if any). The relationship Possesses (one-to-one optional) associates a person with a (valid) driver's license, if any.

Figure 4-18a captures the *structural* aspects of the objects in the business rule. However, it does not capture the constraint on those objects. Figure 4-18b adds a new symbol (using the Ross notation) that expresses a constraint relationship. The dashed line at the tail of this symbol is connected to the *constrained* object. A **constrained object** is an entity, attribute, or relationship on which operations (such as add, delete, update, or read) are limited. In this example, the relationship Rents is the constrained object. Notice that neither PERSON nor CAR is the constrained object. Rather, it is the ability of a person to rent a car (create a new instance of this relationship) that is constrained.

Constrained object: An entity, attribute, or relationship on which operations (such as create, delete, update, or read) are limited.

In this same figure, the *constraining* object is the relationship Possesses (indicated by the dashed line at the head of the symbol). A **constraining object** is an entity, attribute, or relationship that influences the ability to perform an operation (create, delete, update, or read) on another object. The letter 'R' inside the symbol represents 'Restricted', which is one of the many options for this type of constraint. Notice in Figure 4-18b that neither PERSON nor DRIVER'S LICENSE is the constraining object.

Constraining object: An entity, attribute, or relationship that influences the ability to perform an operation (create, delete, update, or read) on another object.

Figure 4-18
Representing a business rule

(a) Simple E-R diagram segment

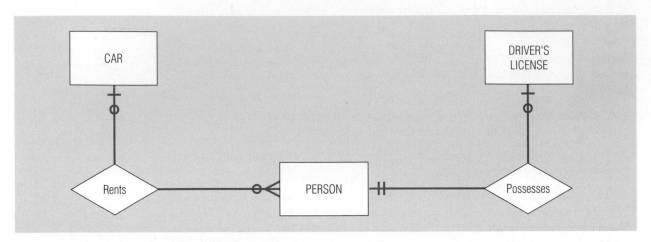

(b) Adding symbol to enforce business rule

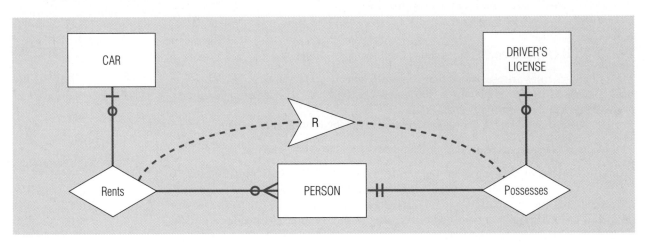

Rather, it is the relationship Possesses that is the constraining object since it indicates whether or not a person possesses a valid driver's license.

In this example there is only one constraining object. However, as we will see in the next example, there may be more than one constraining object in a business rule. The business rule in this example has the following syntax:

{(constrained object) (condition) (constraining object(s))}

Most business rules can be expressed using this syntax, and Ross's notation is essentially a graphical version.

Sample Business Rules   Now let's return to the data model for class scheduling (Figure 4-12) and add two business rules that relate to that model. We ask you to add additional rules in the chapter exercises.

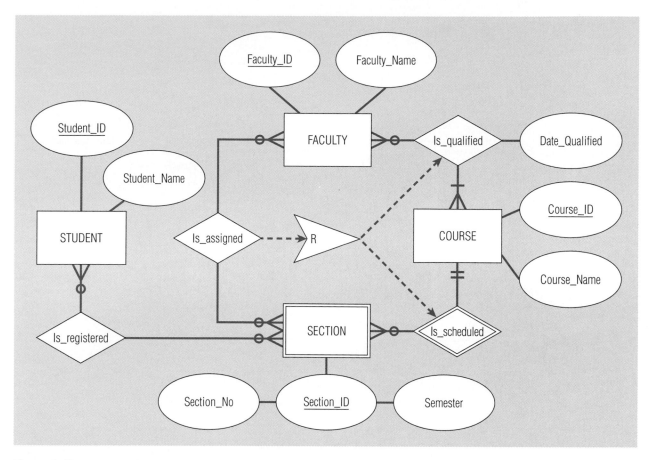

Figure 4-19
Business Rule 1: For a faculty member to be assigned to teach a section of a course, the faculty member must be qualified to teach the course for which that section is scheduled.

Business Rule 1 For a faculty member to be assigned to teach a section of a course, the faculty member must be qualified to teach the course for which that section is scheduled.

This rule refers to three entity types in Figure 4-12: FACULTY, SECTION, and COURSE. The question is whether a faculty member can be assigned to teach a section (of a course). Thus the constrained object is the relationship Is_assigned. We are not constraining the faculty member, nor are we constraining the section. Rather, we are constraining the assignment of the faculty member to the section. Figure 4-19 shows the dashed line from Is_assigned to the constraint relationship symbol.

What is the constraining object in this rule? For a faculty member to be assigned to teach a section of a course, *two* conditions are necessary:

1. The faculty member must be qualified to teach the course (this information is recorded by the Is_qualified relationship), and

2. The section must be scheduled for the course (this information is recorded by the Is_scheduled relationship).

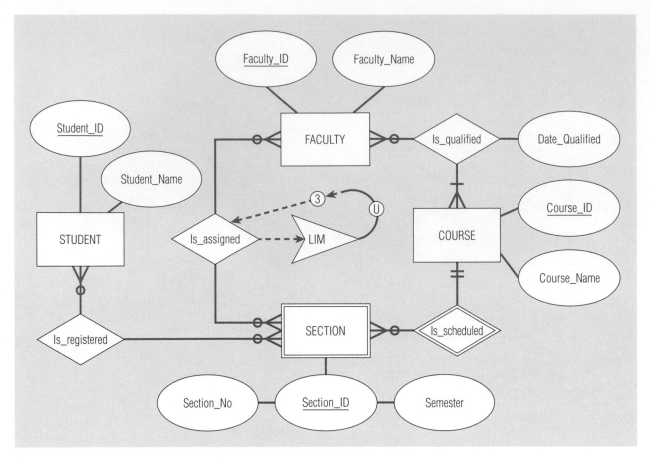

Figure 4-20
Business Rule 2: For a faculty member to be assigned to teach a section of a course, the faculty member must not be assigned to teach a total of more than three course sections.

Thus in this case there are two constraining objects. This fact is represented by the dashed lines from the constraint relationship symbol to each of the two relationships.

Business Rule 2   For a faculty member to be assigned to teach a section of a course, the faculty member must not be assigned to teach a total of more than three course sections.

This rule imposes a limitation on the *total* number of sections a faculty member may teach at a given time. Since the rule involves a total, it requires a modification of the previous notation.

As shown in Figure 4-20, the constrained object is again the relationship Is_assigned. However, in this case, the constraining object is also the relationship Is_assigned! In particular, it is a count of the total sections assigned to the faculty member. The letters 'LIM' in the constraint relationship symbol stand for 'limit'. The arrow leaving this symbol then points to a circle with the letter 'U', which stands for 'upper'. The second circle then contains the number 3, which is the upper limit. Thus the constraint is read as follows: "the constraining object is a count of the number of sections assigned to the faculty member, which has an upper limit of three." If a faculty member is already assigned three sections, any transaction that attempts to add another section will be rejected.

You can implement business rules such as those above using the SQL language, and store the rules as part of the database definitions. One way to implement a rule with SQL is to use the **CREATE ASSERTION** statement, which is included in the most recent version of this language (SQL2). For example, consider Business Rule 2. The following statement creates an assertion named 'Overload_Protect':

```
CREATE ASSERTION Overload_Protect
CHECK (SELECT COUNT(*)
  FROM ASSIGNED
  WHERE Faculty_ID = '12345') <= 3;
```

This statement checks whether the total number of course sections assigned to a particular faculty member is less than or equal to the limit (three). The database management system is responsible for ensuring that this constraint is not violated.

Many other business rules, besides the few examples of this section, are possible. See Ross (1994) for a comprehensive list and associated notation.

SUMMARY

This chapter has described how the basic E-R model has been extended to include supertype/subtype relationships. A *supertype* is a generic entity type that has a relationship with one or more subtypes. A *subtype* is a grouping of the entities in an entity type that is meaningful to the organization. For example, the entity type PERSON is frequently modeled as a supertype. Subtypes of PERSON may include EMPLOYEE, VOLUNTEER, and CLIENT. Subtypes inherit the attributes and relationships associated with their supertype.

Supertype/subtype relationships should normally be considered in data modeling with either (or both) of the following conditions present: First, there are attributes that apply to some (but not all) of the instances of an entity type. Second, the instances of a subtype participate in a relationship unique to that subtype.

The techniques of generalization and specialization are important guides in developing supertype/subtype relationships. Generalization is the bottom-up process of defining a generalized entity type from a set of more specialized entity types. Specialization is the top-down process of defining one or more subtypes of a supertype that has already been defined.

The EER notation allows us to capture the important business rules that apply to supertype/subtype relationships. The completeness constraint allows us to specify whether an instance of a supertype must also be a member of at least one subtype. There are two cases: with total specialization, an instance of the supertype *must* be a member of at least one subtype. With partial specialization, an instance of a supertype may or may not be a member of any subtype. The disjointness constraint allows us to specify whether an instance of a supertype may simultaneously be a member of two or more subtypes. Again, there are two cases. With the disjoint rule, an instance can be a member of only *one* subtype *at a given time.* With the overlap rule, an entity instance can simultaneously be a member of two (or more) subtypes.

A subtype discriminator is an attribute of a supertype whose values determine to which subtype (or subtypes) a supertype instance belongs. A supertype/subtype hierarchy is a hierarchical arrangement of supertypes and subtypes, where each subtype has only one supertype.

A business rule is a statement that defines or constrains some aspect of the business. It is intended to assert business structure or to control or influence the behavior of the business. Business rules can be divided into two major categories: structural constraints and operational constraints. Structural constraints define the static structure of the organization, while operational constraints are rules that constrain the ongoing operations of the organization.

The most important types of structural constraints described in this chapter are definitions and domain constraints. Definitions consist of two components: terms and facts. A term is a word or phrase that has a specific meaning for the business. A fact is an association between two or more terms. A derived fact is a a fact that can be derived from other facts or rules.

A domain constraint is a specification of the data values that can be associated with an attribute. The use of domain constraints improves productivity and helps improve the quality of data definitions.

The most active (and also most promising) area of business rules development is in the area of operational constraints. The modern approach uses declarations to specify this type of business rule. With this approach, each rule is specified using either a graphical syntax or a structured grammar. Each business rule consists of a constrained object and one or more constraining objects. A constraint base is an organized collection of rules, usually stored in a repository.

CHAPTER REVIEW

KEY TERMS

Attribute inheritance	Domain constraint	Specialization
Business rule	Enhanced entity-	Structural constraint
Completeness constraint	relationship (EER)	Subtype
Constrained object	model	Subtype discriminator
Constraining object	Fact	Supertype
Constraint base	Generalization	Supertype/subtype
Derived fact	Operational constraint	hierarchy
Disjoint rule	Overlap rule	Term
Disjointness constraint	Partial specialization rule	Total specialization rule

REVIEW QUESTIONS

1. Define each of the following terms:

   a. supertype   g. subtype discriminator

   b. subtype   h. constraint base

   c. specialization   i. generalization

   d. business rule   j. disjoint rule

   e. term   k. overlap rule

   f. fact

2. Contrast the following terms:

   a. supertype; subtype

  b. generalization; specialization

  c. constrained object; constraining object

  d. disjoint rule; overlap rule

  e. structural constraint; operational constraint

  f. total specialization rule; partial specialization rule

3. State two conditions that indicate when a designer should consider using supertype/subtype relationships.

4. State four premises that form the basis for the business rules paradigm.

5. Give an example (other than those discussed in the chapter) of a supertype/subtype relationship.

6. Give an example (other than those discussed in the chapter) of each of the following:

  a. structural constraint

  b. operational constraint

7. What is attribute inheritance? Why is it important?

8. Give an example of each of the following:

  a. supertype/subtype relationship where the disjoint rule applies

  b. supertype/subtype relationship where the overlap rule applies

9. What types of business rules are normally captured in an EER diagram?

10. What is the purpose of a subtype discriminator?

PROBLEMS AND EXERCISES

1. Match the following terms and definitions.

_____ supertype	a. subset of supertype
_____ business rule	b. entity belongs to two subtypes
_____ domain constraint	c. subtype gets supertype attributes
_____ subtype	d. organized collection of rules
_____ specialization	e. association between terms
_____ constraint base	f. word with business meaning
_____ term	g. calculated using an algorithm
_____ subtype discriminator	h. generalized entity type
_____ attribute inheritance	i. specifies allowable data values
_____ overlap rule	j. creating subtypes for an entity type
_____ fact	k. influences behavior of a business
_____ derived fact	l. locates target subtype for an entity

2. Examine the hierarchy for the university EER diagram (Figure 4-10). As a student, you are an instance of one of the subtypes: either UNDERGRADUATE STUDENT or GRADUATE STUDENT. List the names of all the attributes that apply to you, and then for each attribute record the data value that applies to you.

3. Add a subtype discriminator for each of the supertypes shown in Figure 4-10. Show the discriminator values that assign instances to each subtype. Use the following subtype discriminator names and values:

   a. PERSON: Person_Type (Employee?, Alumnus?, Student?)

   b. EMPLOYEE: Employee_Type (Faculty, Staff)

   c. STUDENT: Student_Type (Grad, Undergrad)

4. Draw an EER diagram for the following problem. A nonprofit organization depends on a number of different types of persons for its successful operation. The organization is interested in the following attributes for all of these persons: SSN, Name, Address, City/State/Zip, and Telephone. Three types of persons are of greatest interest: employees, volunteers, and donors. Employees only have a Date_Hired attribute, and volunteers only have a Skill attribute. Donors only have a relationship (named Donates) with an Item entity type. A donor must have donated one or more items, and an item may have no donors, or one or more donors.

   There are persons other than employees, volunteers, and donors who are of interest to the organization, so that a person need not belong to any of these three groups. On the other hand, at a given time a person may belong to two or more of these groups (for example, employee and donor).

5. Add a subtype discriminator (named Person_Type) to the EER diagram you created in Problem and Exercise 4.

6. A rental car agency classifies the vehicles it rents into four categories: compact, mid-size, full-size, and sport utility. The agency wants to record the following data for all vehicles: VID, Make, Model, Year, and Color. There are no unique attributes for any of the four classes of vehicle. The entity type vehicle has a relationship (named Rents) with a customer entity type. None of the four vehicle classes has a unique relationship with an entity type. Would you consider creating a supertype/subtype relationship for this problem? Why or why not?

7. At a weekend retreat, the entity type PERSON has three subtypes: CAMPER, BIKER, and RUNNER. Draw a separate EER diagram segment for each of the following situations:

   a. At a given time, a person must be exactly one of these subtypes.

   b. A person may or may not be one of these subtypes. However, a person who is one of these subtypes cannot at the same time be one of the other subtypes.

   c. A person may or may not be one of these subtypes. On the other hand, a person may be any two (or even three) of these subtypes at the same time.

   d. At a given time, a person must be at least one of these subtypes.

8. A bank has three types of accounts: checking, savings, and loan. Following are the attributes for each type of account:

   CHECKING: Acct_No, Date_Opened, Balance, Service_Charge
   SAVINGS: Acct_No, Date_Opened, Balance, Interest_Rate
   LOAN: Acct_No, Date_Opened, Balance, Interest_Rate, Payment

   Assume that each bank account must be a member of exactly one of these subtypes. Using generalization, develop an EER model segment to represent this situation. Remember to include a subtype discriminator.

9. Refer to the employee EER diagram (Figure 4-2) to perform the following exercises. Make any assumptions that you believe are necessary.

   a. Develop a sample definition for each entity type, attribute, and relationship in the diagram.

   b. Develop sample domain definitions for all of the attributes in the figure.

10. Refer to the data model for class scheduling (Figure 4-12). Add graphical notation to the figure to express each of the following business rules:

    a. For a section of a course to be scheduled, there must be a faculty member who is qualified to teach that course (*Hint:* See Figure 4-19.)

    b. For a student to register in a section of a course, that student may not be registered in a total of more than six course sections at a given time (*Hint:* See Figure 4-20.)

11. Refer to the EER diagram for car rental (Figure 4-18a). Modify the diagram and add notation as needed to express the following business rule: A person can rent a car only if he or she possesses a valid driver's license and a valid credit card. In this example, what is (are):

    a. the constrained object?   b. the constraining object(s)?

12. Refer to the EER diagram for hospital relationships (Figure 4-3). Add notation to express the following business rule: A resident patient can be assigned a bed only if that patient has been assigned a responsible physician. In this example, what is (are):

    a. the constrained object?   b. the constraining object(s)?

13. Consider the following "business" rule: "A student may attend a concert only if that student has completed his (her) homework."

    a. Draw an EER diagram segment to portray the entities and relationships implied in this rule.

    b. Add suitable notation to express the business rule constraint.

    c. Identify each of the following: (i) constrained object; (ii) constraining object(s).

14. Refer to the EER diagram for patients (Figure 4-3) and perform the following exercises. Make any assumptions you believe are necessary.

    a. Develop sample definitions for each entity type, attribute, and relationship in the diagram.

    b. Develop sample domain definitions for each attribute in the diagram.

FIELD EXERCISES

1. Interview a friend or family member to elicit common examples of the following things they may come in contact with at work.

    a. *Supertype/subtype relationships.* You will have to explain the meaning of this term to the person you are interviewing and provide a common example, such as: PROPERTY: RESIDENTIAL, COMMERCIAL; or BONDS: CORPORATE, MUNICIPAL. Use the information the person provides to construct an EER diagram segment and present it to the person. Revise if necessary until it seems appropriate to you and your friend or family member.

    b. *Business rules.* Give the person you are interviewing examples of business rules, using the ones provided in this chapter (Figures 4-18, 4-19, and 4-20). When your informant gives you a rule from his or her environment, restructure it if necessary to conform to the syntax of this chapter.

2. Visit two local small businesses, one in the service sector and one in manufacturing. Interview employees from these organizations to obtain examples of both supertype/subtype relationships and operational business rules (such as "A customer can return merchandise only with a valid sales slip"). In which of these environments is it easier to find examples of these constructs? Why?

3. Schedule an interview with a senior administrator in the registrar's office or office of admissions and records in your school. Obtain definitions that are used for common terms such as student, course, section, and instructor, and compare them with the definitions given in this chapter. Ask this person for examples of errors or misunderstandings that may have occurred as a result of lack of agreement on common definitions.

4. Ask a database administrator or database or systems analyst in a local company to show you an EER (or E-R) diagram for one of the organization's primary databases. Does this organization model supertype/subtype relationships? If so, what notation is used and does the CASE tool the company uses support these relationships? Also, what types of business rules are included during the EER modeling phase? How are business rules represented, and how and where are they stored?

5. Read the summary of business rules published by the Guide Business Rules Project (1995) and the article by Gottesdiener (1997). Then write a three-page executive summary of current directions in business rules and their potential impact on systems development and maintenance.

REFERENCES

Elmasri, R. and S. B. Navathe. 1994. *Fundamentals of Database Systems.* Menlo Park, CA: Benjamin/Cummings.

Gottesdiener, E. 1997. "Business Rules Show Power, Promise." *Application Development Trends* 4 (3) (March): 36–54.

Guide Business Rules Project, Final Report. 1995. "Defining Business Rules—What Are They Really?" *Go to:* http://www.guide.org/ap/apbrc1.htm#s1.

Ross, R. G. 1994. *The Business Rule Book.* Boston: Database Research Group, Inc.

von Halle, B. 1997. "Digging for Business Rules." *Database Programming & Design* 8 (11) (November): 11–13.

FURTHER READING

Schmidt, B. 1997. "A Taxonomy of Domains." *Database Programming & Design* 10 (9) (September): 95, 96, 98, 99.

von Halle, B. 1996. "Object-Oriented Lessons." *Database Programming & Design* 9 (1) (January): 13–16.

von Halle, B., and R. Kaplan. "Is IT Falling Short?" *Database Programming & Design* 10 (6) (June): 15–17.

Project Case

PROJECT DESCRIPTION

As a large service organization, Mountain View Community Hospital depends on a large number of persons for its continued success. There are four groups of persons on whom the hospital is most dependent: employees, physicians, patients, and volunteers. Of course some common attributes are shared by all of these persons: Person_ID (identifier), Name, Address, City/State/Zip, Birth_Date, and Phone.

Each of the four groups of persons has at least one unique attribute of its own. Employees have a Date_Hired, Volunteers have a Skill, Physicians have a Specialty and a Pager# (pager number), and Patients have a Contact_Date (date of first contact with the hospital).

Some other persons in the hospital community do not belong to one of these four groups (their numbers are relatively small). However, a particular person may belong to two (or more) of these groups at a given time (for example, Patient and Volunteer).

Each patient has one (and only one) physician responsible for that patient. A given physician may not be responsible for a patient at a given time or may be responsible for one or more patients. Patients are divided into two groups: resident and outpatient. Each resident patient has a Date_Admitted attribute. Each outpatient is scheduled for zero or more visits. The entity visit has two attributes: Date (partial identifier) and Comments. Notice that an instance of visit cannot exist without an outpatient owner entity.

Employees are subdivided into three groups: nurse, staff, and technician. Only nurse has the attribute Certificate, which indicates the qualification (RN, LPN, etc.). Only staff has the attribute Job_Class, and only technician has the attribute Skill. Each nurse is assigned to one (and only one) care center. Examples of care centers are Maternity, Emergency, and Cardiology (care centers were formerly called wards). Attributes of care center are Name (identifier) and Location. A care center may have one or more nurses assigned to it. Also for each care center, one of the nurses assigned to that care center is appointed nurse_in_charge. A nurse cannot be appointed nurse_in_charge of a care center unless she or he has an RN certificate.

Each technician is assigned to one or more laboratories. Attributes of laboratory include Name (identifier) and Location. A laboratory must have at least one technician assigned to it and may have any number of technicians assigned.

There may be no beds assigned to a care center, or a care center may have one or more beds (up to any number) assigned to it. The only attribute of bed is Bed_ID (identifier). Bed_ID is a composite attribute, with components Bed# and Room#. Each resident patient must be assigned to a bed. A bed may or may not have a resident patient assigned to it at a given time.

PROJECT QUESTIONS

1. Is the ability to model supertype/subtype relationships likely to be important in a hospital environment such as Mountain View Community Hospital? Why or why not?

2. Can the business rules paradigm and the ability to easily define, implement, and maintain business rules be used as a competitive advantage in a hospital environment such as Mountain View Community Hospital? Why or why not?

3. Do there appear to be any weak entities in the description of the data requirements in this project segment? If so, what are they?

4. Can you think of any business rules (other than the one explicitly described in the case) that are likely to be used in a hospital environment?

PROJECT EXERCISES

1. Draw an EER diagram to accurately represent this set of requirements, carefully following the notation from this chapter.

2. Develop definitions for each of the following types of objects in your EER diagram from Project Exercise 1. Consult with some member of the hospital or health-care community if one is

available; otherwise make reasonable assumptions based on your own knowledge and experience.

a. Entity types   b. Attributes

c. Relationships   d. Domain definitions

3. You should recognize the statement "a nurse cannot be appointed nurse_in_charge of a care center unless she or he has an RN certificate" as a statement of a business rule. However, this statement does not conform to the syntax we developed in this chapter for stating business rules in the form {constrained object, constraint condition, constraining object(s)}. Revise the statement so that it conforms to this syntax. Then answer the following questions:

a. What is the constrained object? Is it an entity, an attribute, a relationship, or some other object?

b. What is the constraining object (or objects, if more than one)? Is it an entity, an attribute, a relationship, or some other object?

4. Compare the EER diagram that you developed in this chapter with the E-R diagram you developed in Chapter 3 in Project Exercise 2. What are the differences between these two diagrams? Why are there differences?

5. Merge the two diagrams from Project Exercise 4 above and from Project Exercise 2 in Chapter 3 into a single diagram. Explain decisions you make during the merging.

5

Object-Oriented Modeling

After studying this chapter, you should be able to:

■ Define the following key terms: object, state, behavior, class, class diagram, object diagram, operation, encapsulation, constructor operation, query operation, update operation, association, association role, multiplicity, association class, abstract class, concrete class, class-scope attribute, abstract operation, method, polymorphism, overriding, multiple classification, aggregation, and composition.

■ Describe the activities in the different phases of the object-oriented development life cycle.

■ State the advantages of object-oriented modeling vis-à-vis structured approaches.

■ Compare and contrast the object-oriented model with the E-R and EER models.

■ Model a real-world application by using a UML class diagram.

■ Provide a snapshot of the detailed state of a system at a point in time using a UML object diagram.

■ Recognize when to use generalization, aggregation, and composition relationships.

■ Specify different types of business rules in a class diagram.

INTRODUCTION

In Chapters 3 and 4, you learned about data modeling using the E-R and EER models. In those chapters you learned how to model the data needs of an organization using entities, attributes, and a wide variety of relationships. In this chapter,

This chapter was written by Professor Atish P. Sinha, University of Dayton.

you will be introduced to the object-oriented model, which is becoming increasingly popular because of its ability to thoroughly represent complex relationships, as well as to represent data and data processing in a consistent notation. Fortunately, most of the concepts you learned in those chapters correspond to concepts in object-oriented modeling, but as you will see, the object-oriented model has even more features than the EER model.

As you learned in Chapters 3 and 4, a data model is an abstraction of the real world. It allows you to deal with the complexity inherent in a real-world problem by focusing on the essential and interesting features of the data an organization needs. An object-oriented model is built around *objects,* just as the E-R model is built around entities. However, as we shall see later, an object *encapsulates* both data and *behavior,* implying that we can use the object-oriented approach not only for data modeling, but also for process modeling. To thoroughly model any real-world application, you need to model both the data and the processes that act on the data (recall the discussion in Chapter 2 about information planning objects). By allowing you to capture them together within a common representation, and by offering benefits such as *inheritance* and code reuse, the object-oriented modeling approach provides a powerful environment for developing complex systems.

The object-oriented development life cycle, depicted in Figure 5-1, consists of progressively developing object representation through three phases—analysis, design, and implementation—similar to the heart of the systems development life cycle explained in Chapter 2. In the early stages of development, the model you develop is abstract, focusing on external qualities of the system. As the model evolves, it becomes more and more detailed, the focus shifting to how the system will be built and how it should function. The emphasis in modeling should be on analysis and design, focusing on front-end conceptual issues, rather than back-end implementation issues, which unnecessarily restrict design choices (Rumbaugh et al., 1991).

In the analysis phase, you develop a model of the real-world application showing its important properties. The model abstracts concepts from the application domain and describes *what* the intended system must do, rather than *how* it will be done. It specifies the functional behavior of the system, independently of concerns relating to the environment in which it is to be finally implemented. You need to devote sufficient time to clearly understand the requirements of the problem. The

Figure 5-1

Phases of object-oriented systems development cycle

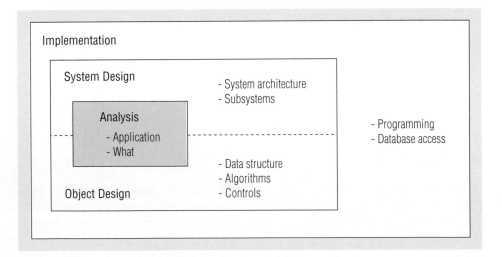

analysis model should capture those requirements completely and accurately. Remember that it is much easier and cheaper to make changes or fix flaws during analysis than during the later phases.

In the object-oriented design phase, you define *how* the application-oriented analysis model will be realized in the implementation environment. Jacobson et al. (1992) cite three reasons for using object-oriented design. These three reasons are:

1. The analysis model is not formal enough to be implemented directly in a programming language. To move seamlessly into the source code requires refining the objects by making decisions on what operations an object will provide, what the communication between objects should look like, what messages are to be passed, and so forth.

2. The actual system must be adapted to the environment in which the system will actually be implemented. To accomplish that, the analysis model has to be transformed into a design model, considering different factors such as performance requirements, real-time requirements and concurrency, the target hardware and systems software, the DBMS and programming language to be adopted, and so forth.

3. The analysis results can be validated using object-oriented design. At this stage, you can verify whether the results from the analysis are appropriate for building the system, and make any necessary changes to the analysis model.

To develop the design model, you must identify and investigate the consequences that the implementation environment will have on the design (Jacobson et al., 1992). All strategic design decisions—such as how the DBMS is to be incorporated, how process communications and error handling are to be achieved, what component libraries are to be reused—are made. Next, you incorporate those decisions into a first-cut design model that adapts to the implementation environment. Finally, you formalize the design model to describe how the objects interact with one another for each conceivable scenario (use case).

Rumbaugh et al. (1991) separate the design activity into two stages: system design and *object design*. As the system designer, you propose an overall system architecture, which organizes the system into components called subsystems and provides the context to make decisions such as identifying concurrency; allocation of subsystems to processors and tasks; handling access to global resources; selecting the implementation of control in software; and more.

During object design, you build a design model by adding implementation details—such as restructuring classes for efficiency, internal data structures and algorithms to implement each class, implementation of control, implementation of associations, and packaging into physical modules—to the analysis model in accordance with the strategy established during system design. The application-domain object classes from the analysis model still remain, but they are augmented with computer-domain constructs, with a view toward optimizing important performance measures.

The design phase is followed by the implementation phase. In this phase, you implement the design using a programming language and/or a database management system. Translating the design into program code is a relatively straightforward process, given that the design model already incorporates the nuances of the programming language and the DBMS.

Coad and Yourdon (1991b) identify several motivations and benefits of object-oriented modeling, which follow:

- The ability to tackle more challenging problem domains.

- Improved communication between the users, analysts, designers, and programmers.

- Increased consistency among analysis, design, and programming activities.

- Explicit representation of commonality among system components.

- Robustness of systems.

- Reusability of analysis, design, and programming results.

- Increased consistency among all the models developed during object-oriented analysis, design, and programming.

The last point needs further elaboration. In other modeling approaches, such as structured analysis and design (described in Chapter 2), the models that are developed (e.g., data flow diagrams during analysis and structure charts during design) lack a common underlying representation and, therefore, are very weakly connected. In contrast to the abrupt and disjoint transitions that those approaches suffer from, the object-oriented approach provides a continuum of representation from analysis to design to implementation (Coad and Yourdon, 1991a), engendering a seamless transition from one model to another (Jacobson et al., 1992). For instance, moving from object-oriented analysis to object-oriented design entails expanding the analysis model with implementation-related details, not developing a whole new representation.

In this chapter, we present object-oriented modeling as a high-level conceptual activity, focusing mainly on object-oriented analysis, especially data analysis. As you will learn in Chapter 12, a good conceptual model is invaluable for designing and implementing an object-oriented database application.

THE UNIFIED MODELING LANGUAGE

The Unified Modeling Language (UML) is "a language for specifying, visualizing, and constructing the artifacts of software systems, as well as for business modeling" (*UML Document Set*, 1997). It culminated from the efforts of three leading experts, Grady Booch, Ivar Jacobson, and James Rumbaugh, who have defined an object-oriented modeling language that is expected to become an industry standard in the near future. The UML builds upon and unifies the semantics and notations of the Booch (Booch, 1994), OOSE (Jacobson et al., 1992), and OMT (Rumbaugh et al., 1991) methods, as well as those of other leading methods.

The UML notation is useful for graphically depicting an object-oriented analysis or design model. It not only allows you to specify the requirements of a system and capture the design decisions, but it also promotes communication among key persons involved in the development effort. A developer can use an analysis or design model expressed in the UML notation as a means to communicate with domain experts, users, and other stakeholders.

For representing a complex system effectively, it is necessary that the model you develop has a small set of independent views or perspectives. UML allows you to represent multiple perspectives of a system by providing different types of graphical diagrams, such as the use-case diagram, class diagram, state diagram, interaction diagram, component diagram, and deployment diagram. The underlying model integrates those views so that the system can be analyzed, designed, and implemented in a complete and consistent fashion.

Because this text is about databases, we will describe only the *class diagram,* which addresses the data, as well some behavioral, aspects of a system. We will not describe the other diagrams because they provide perspectives that are not directly related to a database system, for example, the dynamic aspects of a system. But keep in mind that a database system is usually part of an overall system, whose underlying model should encompass all the different perspectives.

OBJECT-ORIENTED MODELING

In this section, we introduce you to object-oriented modeling. We describe the main concepts and techniques involved in object-oriented modeling, including: objects and classes; encapsulation of attributes and operations; association, generalization, and aggregation relationships; cardinalities and other types of constraints; polymorphism; and inheritance. We show how you can develop class diagrams, using the UML notation, to provide a logical view of the system being modeled.

Representing Objects and Classes

In the object-oriented approach, we model the world in objects. Before applying the approach to a real-world problem, therefore, we need to understand what an object really is. An **object** is an entity that has a well-defined role in the application domain, and has state, behavior, and identity. An object is a concept, abstraction, or thing that makes sense in an application context (Rumbaugh et al., 1991). An object could be a tangible or visible entity (e.g., a person, place, or thing); it could be a concept or event (e.g., Department, Performance, Marriage, Registration, etc.); or it could be an artifact of the design process (e.g., User Interface, Controller, Scheduler, etc.).

> **Object:** An entity that has a well-defined role in the application domain, and has state, behavior, and identity.

You might be wondering how objects are different from entities in the E-R model you studied in Chapter 3. Clearly, entities in the E-R model can be represented as objects in the object model. But, in addition to storing a state (information), an object also exhibits behavior, through operations that can examine or affect its state.

The **state** of an object encompasses its properties (attributes and relationships) and the values those properties have, and its **behavior** represents how an object acts and reacts (Booch, 1994). An object's state is determined by its attribute values and links to other objects. An object's behavior depends on its state and the operation being performed. An operation is simply an action that one object performs upon another in order to get a response. You can think of an operation as a service provided by an object (supplier) to its clients. A client sends a message to a supplier, which delivers the desired service by executing the corresponding operation.

> **State:** Encompasses an object's properties (attributes and relationships) and the values those properties have.

> **Behavior:** Represents how an object acts and reacts.

Consider an example of a student, by the name of Mary Jones, represented as an object. The state of this object is characterized by its attributes, say, name, date of birth, year, address, and phone, and the values these attributes currently have. For example, name is "Mary Jones," year is "junior," and so on. Its behavior is expressed through operations such as calc-gpa, which is used to calculate a student's current grade point average. The Mary Jones object, therefore, packages both its state and its behavior together.

All objects have an identity; that is, no two objects are the same. For example, if there are two Student instances with the same name and date of birth, they are essentially two different objects. Even if those two instances have identical values for all the attributes, the objects maintain their separate identities. At the same time, an object maintains its own identity over its life. For example, if Mary Jones gets married and changes her name, address, and phone, she will still be represented by the same object.

The term "object" is sometimes used to refer to a group of objects, rather than an individual object. The ambiguity can be usually resolved from the context. In the strict sense of the term, however, "object" refers to an individual object, not to a class of objects. That is the interpretation we follow in this text. If you want to eliminate any possible confusion altogether, you can use "object instance" to refer to an individual object, and **object class** (or simply **class**) to refer to a set of objects that share a common structure and a common behavior (just as we used entity type and entity instance in Chapter 3). In our example, therefore, *Mary Jones* is an object instance, while Student is an object class.

You can depict the classes graphically in a class diagram as in Figure 5-2a. A **class diagram** shows the static structure of an object-oriented model: the object classes, their internal structure, and the relationships in which they participate. In UML, a class is represented by a rectangle with three compartments separated by horizontal lines. The class name appears in the top compartment, the list of attributes in the middle compartment, and the list of operations in the bottom compartment of a box. The figure shows two classes, Student and Course, along with their attributes and operations.

The Student class is a group of Student objects that share a common structure and a common behavior. All students have in common the properties of name, date of birth, year, address, and phone. They also exhibit common behavior by sharing the calc-age, calc-gpa, and register-for(course) operations. A class, therefore, provides a template or schema for its instances. Each object knows to which class it belongs; for example, the Mary Jones object knows that it belongs to the Student class. Objects belonging to the same class may also participate in similar relationships with other objects; for example, all students register for courses and, therefore, the Student class can participate in a relationship called 'registers-for' with another class called Course (see the later section on Association).

An **object diagram**, also known as instance diagram, is a graph of instances that are compatible with a given class diagram. In Figure 5-2b, we have shown an object diagram with two instances, one for each of the two classes that appear in Figure 5-2a. A static object diagram, such as the one shown in the figure, is an instance of a class diagram, providing a snapshot of the detailed state of a system at a point in time (*UML Notation Guide*, 1997). We will provide examples of only static object diagrams, and not dynamic object diagrams (known as collaboration diagrams).

In an object diagram, an object is represented as a rectangle with two compartments. The names of the object and its class are underlined and shown in the top compartment using the following syntax:

objectname : classname

The object's attributes and their values are shown in the second compartment. For example, we have an object called Mary Jones that belongs to the Student class. The values of the name, dateOfBirth, and year attributes are also shown. Attributes whose values are not of interest to you may be suppressed; for example, we have not shown the address and phone attributes for Mary Jones. If none of the attributes are of interest, the entire second compartment may be suppressed. The name of the object may also be omitted, in which case the colon should be kept with the class name as we have done with the instance of Course. If the name of the object is shown, the class name, together with the colon, may be suppressed.

Object class: A set of objects that share a common structure and a common behavior.

Class diagram: Shows the static structure of an object-oriented model: the object classes, their internal structure, and the relationships in which they participate.

Object diagram: A graph of instances that are compatible with a given class diagram.

An **operation**, such as calc-gpa in Student (see Figure 5-2a), is a function or a service that is provided by all the instances of a class. It is only through such operations that other objects can access or manipulate the information stored in an object. The operations, therefore, provide an external interface to a class; the interface presents the outside view of the class without showing its internal structure or how its operations are implemented. This technique of hiding the internal, implementation details of an object from its external view is known as **encapsulation** or information hiding (Booch, 1994; Rumbaugh et al., 1991). So while we provide the abstraction of the behavior common to all instances of a class in its interface, we encapsulate within the class its structure and the secrets of the desired behavior.

Operation: A function or a service that is provided by all the instances of a class.

Encapsulation: The technique of hiding the internal, implementation details of an object from its external view.

Types of Operations

Operations can be classified into three types, depending on the kind of service requested by clients: (1) constructor, (2) query, and (3) update (*UML Notation Guide,* 1997). A **constructor operation** creates a new instance of a class. For example, you can have an operation called create-student within Student that creates a new student and initializes its state. Such constructor operations are available to all classes and are therefore not explicitly shown in the class diagram.

A **query operation** is an operation without any side effects; it accesses the state of an object but does not alter the state (Fowler, 1997; Rumbaugh et al., 1991). For example, the Student class can have an operation called get-year (not shown), which simply retrieves the year (freshman, sophomore, junior, or senior) of the Student

Constructor operation: An operation that creates a new instance of a class.

Query operation: An operation that accesses the state of an object but does not alter the state.

object specified in the query. Note that there is no need to explicitly show a query such as get-year in the class diagram since it retrieves the value of an independent, base attribute. Consider, however, the calc-age operation within Student. This is also a query operation because it does not have any side effects. Note that the only argument for this query is the target Student object. Such a query can be represented as a derived attribute (Rumbaugh et al., 1991); for example, we can represent "age" as a derived attribute of Student. Because the target object is always an implicit argument of an operation, there is no need to show it explicitly in the operation declaration.

Update operation: An operation that alters the state of an object.

An **update operation** has side effects; it alters the state of an object. For example, consider an operation of Student called promote-student (not shown). The operation promotes a student to a new year, say, from junior to senior, thereby changing the Student object's state (value of the year attribute). Another example of an update operation is register-for(course), which, when invoked, has the effect of establishing a connection from a Student object to a specific Course object. Note that, in addition to having the target Student object as an implicit argument, the operation has an explicit argument called "course," which specifies the course for which the student wants to register. Explicit arguments are shown within parentheses.

Representing Associations

Association: A relationship between object classes.

Parallel to the definition of a relationship for the E-R model, an **association** is a relationship among object classes. As in the E-R model, the degree of an association relationship may be one (unary), two (binary), three (ternary), or higher (*n*-ary). In Figure 5-3, we use the examples from Figure 3-12 to illustrate how the object-oriented model can be used to represent association relationships of different degrees. An association is shown as a solid line between the participating classes. The end of an association where it connects to a class is called an **association role** (*UML Notation Guide*, 1997). Each association has two or more roles. A role may be explicitly named with a label near the end of an association (see the "manager" role in Figure 5-3a). The role name indicates the role played by the class attached to the end near which the name appears. Use of role names is optional. You can specify role names in place of, or in addition to, an association name.

Association role: The end of an association where it connects to a class.

Figure 5-3a shows two unary relationships, *Is-married-to* and *Manages*. At one end of the *Manages* relationship, we have named the role as "manager," implying that an employee can play the role of a manager. We have not named the other roles, but we have named the associations. When the role name does not appear, you may think of the role name as being that of the class attached to that end (Fowler, 1997). For example, you may call the role for the right end of the *Is-assigned* relationship in Figure 5-3b as Parking Place.

Multiplicity: Indicates how many objects participate in a given relationship.

Each role has a **multiplicity**, which indicates how many objects participate in a given relationship. In a class diagram, a multiplicity specification is shown as a text string representing an interval (or intervals) of integers in the following format:

lower-bound..upper-bound

The interval is considered to be closed, which means that the range includes both the lower and upper bounds. For example, a multiplicity of 2..5 denotes that a minimum of 2 and a maximum of 5 objects can participate in a given relationship. Multiplicities, therefore, are nothing but cardinality constraints that were discussed in Chapter 3. In addition to integer values, the upper bound of a multiplicity can be a star character (*), which denotes an infinite upper bound. If a single integer value is specified, it means that the range includes only that value.

Figure 5-3
Examples of association
relationships of different
degrees

(a) Unary relationship

(b) Binary relationship

(c) Ternary relationship

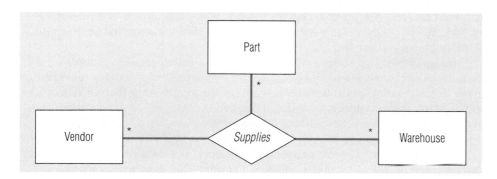

The most common multiplicities in practice are 0..1, *, and 1. The 0..1 multiplicity indicates a minimum of 0 and a maximum of 1 (optional one), while * (or equivalently, 0..*) represents the range from 0 to infinity (optional many). A single 1 stands for 1..1, implying that exactly one object participates in the relationship (mandatory one).

The multiplicities for both roles in the *Is-married-to* relationship are 0..1, indicating that a person may be single or married to one person. The multiplicity for the manager role in the *Manages* relationship is 0..1 and that for the other role is *, implying that an employee may be managed by only one manager, but a manager may manage many employees.

Figure 5-4

Examples of binary
association relationships

(a) University example

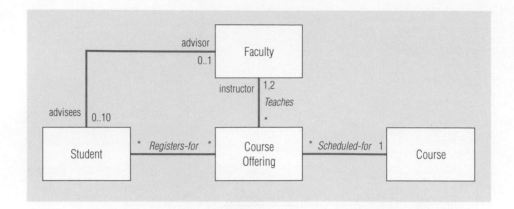

Figure 5-3b shows three binary relationships: *Is-assigned* (one-to-one), *Contains* (one-to-many), and *Registers-for* (many-to-many). A binary association is inherently bidirectional, though in a class diagram, the association name can be read in only one direction (Rumbaugh et al., 1991). For example, the *Contains* association is read from Product Line to Product. (*Note:* As in this example, you may show the direction explicitly by using a solid triangle next to the association name.) Implicit, however, is an inverse traversal of *Contains*, say, *Belongs-to*, which denotes that a product belongs to a particular product line. Both directions of traversal refer to the same underlying association; the name simply establishes a direction.

The diagram for the *Is-assigned* relationship shows that an employee is assigned a parking place or not assigned at all (optional one). Reading in the other direction, we say that a parking place has either been allocated for a single employee or not allocated at all (optional one again). Similarly, we say that a product line contains many products, but at least one, whereas a given product belongs to exactly one product line (mandatory one). The diagram for the third binary association states that a student registers for multiple courses, but it is possible that he or she does not register at all, and a course, in general, has multiple students enrolled in it (optional many in both directions).

In Figure 5-3c, we show a ternary relationship called *Supplies* among Vendor, Part, and Warehouse. As in the E-R diagram, we represent a ternary relationship using a diamond symbol and place the name of the relationship there. The relationship is many-to-many-to-many, and as discussed in Chapter 3, it cannot be replaced by three binary relationships without loss of information.

The class diagram in Figure 5-4a shows binary associations between Student and Faculty, between Course and Course Offering, between Student and Course Offering, and between Faculty and Course Offering. The diagram shows that a student may have an advisor, while a faculty member may advise up to a maximum of 10 students. Also, while a course may have multiple offerings, a given course offering is scheduled for exactly one course. UML allows you to numerically specify any multiplicity. For example, the diagram shows that a course offering may be taught by one or two instructors (1, 2). You can specify a single number (e.g., 2 for the members of a bridge team), a range (e.g., 11..14 for the players of a soccer team who participated in a particular game), or a discrete set of numbers and ranges (e.g., 3, 5, 7 for the number of committee members, and 20..32, 35..40 for the workload in hours per week of the employees of a company).

Figure 5-4a also shows that a faculty member plays the role of an instructor, as well as that of an advisor. While the advisor role identifies the Faculty object associated with a Student object, the advisees role identifies the set of Student objects asso-

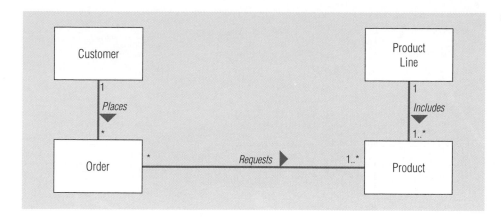

ciated with a Faculty object. We could have named the association as, say, *Advises*, but, in this case, the role names are sufficiently meaningful to convey the semantics of the relationship.

Figure 5-4b shows another class diagram for a customer order. The corresponding object diagram is presented in Figure 5-5; it shows some of the instances of the classes and the links among them. (*Note:* Just as an instance corresponds to a class, a link corresponds to a relationship.) In this example, we see the orders placed by two customers, Joe and Jane. Joe has placed two orders, Ord 20 and Ord 56. In Ord 20, Joe has ordered product P93 from the sports product line. In Ord 56, he has ordered the same sports product again, as well as product P50 from the hardware product line. Notice that Jane has ordered the same hardware product as Joe, in addition to two other products (P9 and P10) from the cosmetics product line.

Representing Association Classes

When an association itself has attributes or operations of its own, or when it participates in relationships with other classes, it is useful to model the association as an
association class (just as we used an "associative entity" in Chapter 3). For example,
in Figure 5-6a, the attributes term and grade really belong to the many-to-many association between Student and Course. The grade of a student for a course cannot be
determined unless both the student and the course are known. Similarly, to find the
term(s) in which the student took the course, both student and course must be
known. The checkEligibility operation, which determines if a student is eligible to
register for a given course, also belongs to the association, rather than to any of the
two participating classes. We have also captured the fact that, for some course registrations, a computer account is issued to a student. For these reasons, we model
Registration as an association class, having its own set of features and an association
with another class (Computer Account). Similarly, for the unary *Tutors* association,
beginDate and numberOfHrs (number of hours tutored) really belong to the association, and, therefore, appear in a separate association class.

You have the option of showing the name of an association class on the association path, or the class symbol, or both. When an association has only attributes, but
does not have any operations or does not participate in other associations, the recommended option is to show the name on the association path, but to omit it from
the association class symbol, to emphasize its "association nature" (*UML Notation
Guide,* 1997). That is how we have shown the *Tutors* association. On the other hand,

Association class: An association that has attributes or operations of its own or that participates in relation-ships with other classes.

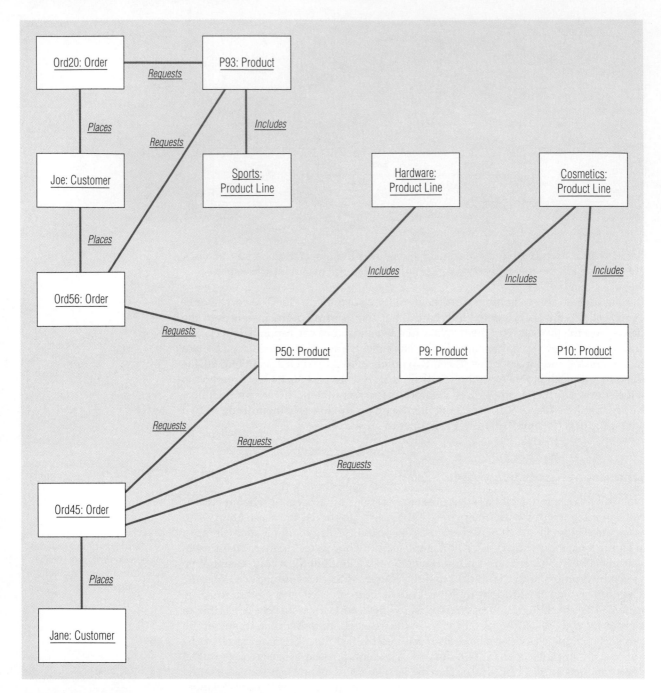

Figure 5-5
Object diagram for customer order example

we have displayed the name of the Registration association—which has two attributes and one operation of its own, as well as an association called *Issues* with Computer Account—within the class rectangle to emphasize its "class nature."

Figure 5-6b shows a part of the object diagram representing a student, Mary Jones, and the courses she has registered for in the fall 1999 term: MKT350 and

Figure 5-6
Association class and
link object

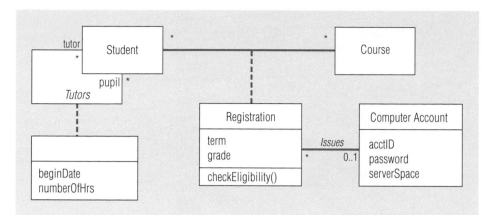

(a) Class diagram showing
association classes

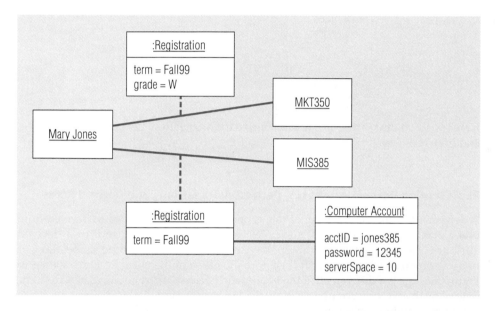

(b) Object diagram showing
link objects

MIS385. Corresponding to an association class in a class diagram, link objects are present in an object diagram. In this example, there are two link objects (shown as :Registration) for the Registration association class, capturing the two course registrations. The diagram also shows that for the MIS385 course, Mary Jones has been issued a computer account with an ID, a password, and a designated amount of space on the server. She still has not received a grade for this course, but, for the MKT350 course, she received a grade of W because she withdrew from the course.

Figure 5-7 shows a ternary relationship among the Student, Software, and Course classes. It captures the fact that students use various software tools for different courses. For example, we could store the information that Mary Jones used Microsoft Access and Oracle for the Database Management course, Rational Rose and Visual C++ for the Object-Oriented Modeling course, and Level5 Object for the Expert Systems Course. Now suppose we want to estimate the number of hours per week Mary will spend using Oracle for the Database Management course. This process really belongs to the ternary association, and not to any of the individual classes. Hence we have created an association class called Log, within which we have declared an operation called estimateUsage. In addition to this operation, we

Figure 5-7
Ternary relationship with
association class

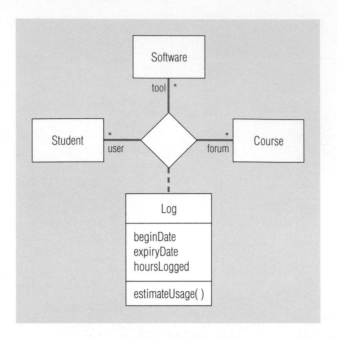

have specified three attributes that belong to the association: beginDate, expiryDate, and hoursLogged.

Representing Derived Attributes, Derived Associations, and Derived Roles

A derived attribute, association, or role is one that can be computed or derived from other attributes, associations, and roles, respectively (the concept of a derived attribute was introduced in Chapter 3). A derived element (attribute, association, or role) is shown by placing a slash (/) before the name of the element. For instance, in Figure 5-8, age is a derived attribute of Student, because it can be calculated from the date of birth and the current date (the calculation is shown on this diagram within {} below the Student object class). Also, the *Takes* relationship between Student and Course is derived, because it can be inferred from the *Registers-for* and *Scheduled-for*

Figure 5-8
Derived attribute,
association, and role

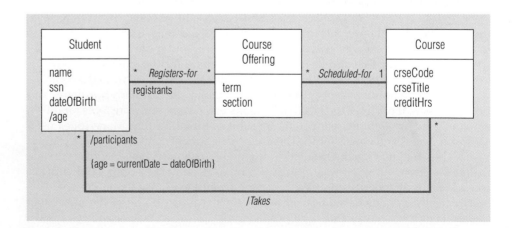

relationships. By the same token, participants is a derived role because it can be derived from other roles.

Representing Generalization

You were introduced to *generalization* and *specialization* in Chapter 4. Using the enhanced E-R model, you learned how to abstract the common attributes of two or more entities, as well as the common relationships in which they participate, into a more general entity supertype, while keeping the attributes and relationships that are not common in the entities (subtypes) themselves. In the object-oriented model, we apply the same notion, but with one difference. In generalizing a set of object classes into a more general class, we abstract not only the common attributes and relationships, but the common operations as well. The attributes and operations of a class are collectively known as the features of the class. The classes that are generalized are called subclasses, and the class they are generalized into is called a superclass, in perfect correspondence to subtypes and supertype for EER diagramming.

Consider the example shown in Figure 5-9a (see Figure 4-8 for the corresponding EER diagram). There are three types of employees: hourly employees, salaried employees, and consultants. The features that are shared by all employees—empName, empNumber, address, dateHired, and printLabel—are stored in the Employee superclass, while the features that are peculiar to a particular employee type are stored in the corresponding subclass (e.g., hourlyRate and computeWages of Hourly Employee). A generalization path is shown as a solid line from the subclass to the superclass, with a hollow triangle at the end of, and pointing toward, the superclass. You can show a group of generalization paths for a given superclass as a tree with multiple branches connecting the individual subclasses, and a shared segment with a hollow triangle pointing toward the superclass. In Figure 5-9b (corresponding to Figure 4-3), for instance, we have combined the generalization paths from Outpatient to Patient, and from Resident Patient to Patient, into a shared segment with a triangle pointing toward Patient.

You can indicate the basis of a generalization by specifying a discriminator next to the path. A discriminator (corresponding to the subtype discriminator defined in Chapter 4) shows which property of an object class is being abstracted by a particular generalization relationship (Rumbaugh et al., 1991). You can discriminate on only one property at a time. For example, in Figure 5-9a, we discriminate the Employee class on the basis of employment type (hourly, salaried, consultant). To disseminate a group of generalization relationships as in Figure 5-9b, we need to specify the discriminator only once. Although we discriminate the Patient class into two subclasses, Outpatient and Resident Patient, based on residency, we show the discriminator label only once next to the shared line.

An instance of a subclass is also an instance of its superclass. For example in Figure 5-9b, an Outpatient instance is also a Patient instance. For that reason, a generalization is also referred to as an *Is-a* relationship. Also, a subclass inherits all the features from its superclass. For example in Figure 5-9a, in addition to its own special features—hourlyRate and computeWages—the Hourly Employee subclass inherits empName, empNumber, address, dateHired, and printLabel from Employee. An instance of Hourly Employee will store values for the attributes of Employee and Hourly Employee, and, when requested, will apply the printLabel and computeWages operations.

Generalization and inheritance are transitive across any number of levels of a superclass/subclass hierarchy. For instance, we could have a subclass of Consultant

Figure 5-9
Examples of generalization,
inheritance, and constraints

(a) Employee superclass with
three subclasses

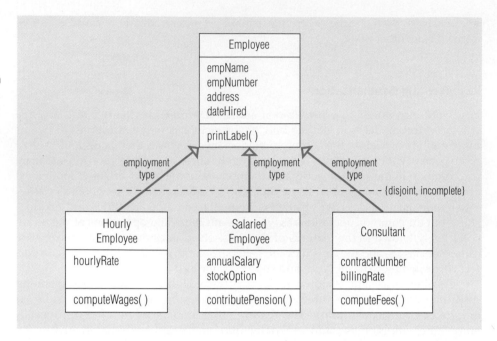

(b) Abstract Patient class
with two concrete
subclasses

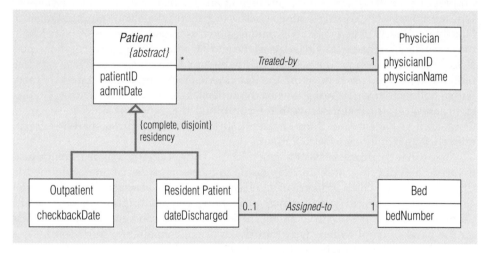

called Computer Consultant, which would inherit the features of Employee and Consultant. An instance of Computer Consultant would be an instance of Consultant and, therefore, an instance of Employee too. Employee is an ancestor of Computer Consultant, while Computer Consultant is a descendant of Employee; these terms are used to refer to generalization of classes across multiple levels (Rumbaugh et al., 1991).

Inheritance is one of the major advantages of using the object-oriented model. It allows code reuse: There is no need for a programmer to write code that has already been written for a superclass. The programmer only writes code that is unique to the new, refined subclass of an existing class. In actual practice, object-oriented programmers typically have access to large collections of class libraries in their respective domains. They identify those classes that may be reused and refined to meet the demands of new applications. Proponents of the object-oriented model claim that code reuse results in productivity gains of several orders of magnitude.

Notice that in Figure 5-9b the *Patient* class is in italics, implying that it is an abstract class. An **abstract class** is a class that has no direct instances, but whose descendants may have direct instances (Booch, 1994; Rumbaugh et al., 1991). (*Note:* You can additionally write the word *abstract* within braces just below the class name. This is especially useful when you generate a class diagram by hand.) A class that can have direct instances (e.g., Outpatient or Resident Patient) is called a **concrete class**. In this example, therefore, Outpatient and Resident Patient can have direct instances, but *Patient* cannot have any direct instances of its own.

The *Patient* abstract class participates in a relationship called *Treated-by* with Physician, implying that all patients, outpatients and resident patients alike, are treated by physicians. In addition to this inherited relationship, the Resident Patient class has its own special relationship called *Assigned-to* with Bed, implying that only resident patients may be assigned to beds. So, in addition to refining the attributes and operations of a class, a subclass can also specialize the relationships in which it participates.

In Figure 5-9a and 5-9b, the words "complete," "incomplete," and "disjoint" have been placed within braces, next to the generalization. They indicate semantic constraints among the subclasses (complete corresponds to total specialization in the EER notation, whereas incomplete corresponds to partial specialization). In UML, a comma-separated list of keywords is placed either near the shared triangle as in Figure 5-9b, or near a dashed line that crosses all of the generalization lines involved as in Figure 5-9a (*UML Notation Guide,* 1997). Any of the following UML keywords may be used: overlapping, disjoint, complete, and incomplete. According to the UML Notation Guide (1997), these terms have the following meanings:

- *Overlapping*   A descendant may be descended from more than one of the subclasses (same as the overlapping rule in EER diagramming).

- *Disjoint*   A descendant may not be descended from more than one of the subclasses (same as the disjoint rule in EER diagramming).

- *Complete*   All subclasses have been specified (whether or not shown). No additional subclasses are expected (same as the total specialization rule in EER diagramming).

- *Incomplete*   Some subclasses have been specified, but the list is known to be incomplete. There are additional subclasses that are not yet in the model (same as the partial specialization rule in EER diagramming).

Both the generalizations in Figures 5-9a and 5-9b are disjoint. An employee can be an hourly employee, a salaried employee, or a consultant, but cannot, say, be both a salaried employee and a consultant. Similarly, a patient can be an outpatient or a resident patient, but not both. The generalization in Figure 5-9a is incomplete (a departure from what was shown in Figure 4-8), specifying that an employee might not belong to any of the three types. In such a case, an employee will be stored as an instance of Employee, a concrete class. In contrast, the generalization in Figure 5-9b is complete, implying that a patient has to be either an outpatient or a resident patient, and nothing else. For that reason, *Patient* has been specified as an abstract class.

In Figure 5-10, we show an example of an overlapping constraint. The diagram shows that research assistants and teaching assistants are graduate students. The overlapping constraint indicates that it is possible for a graduate student to serve as both a research assistant and a teaching assistant. For example, Sean Bailey, a graduate student, has a research assistantship of 12 hours/week and a teaching assistantship of 8 hours/week. Also notice that Graduate Student has been specified as a

Abstract class: A class that has no direct instances, but whose descendants may have direct instances.

Concrete class: A class that can have direct instances.

Figure 5-10
Example of overlapping
constraint

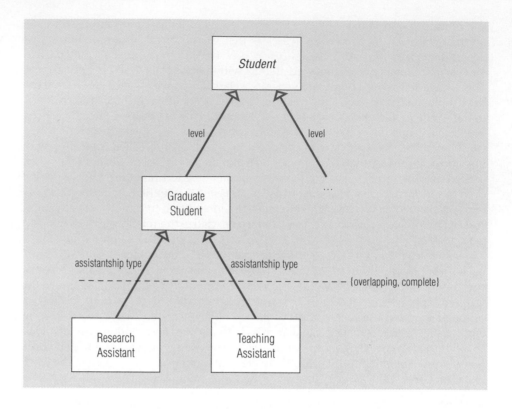

concrete class so that graduate students without an assistantship can be represented. The ellipsis (…) under the generalization line based on the "level" discriminator does not represent an incomplete constraint. It simply indicates that there are other subclasses in the model that have not been shown in the diagram. For example, although Undergrad Student is in the model, we have opted not to show it in the diagram since the focus is on assistantships. You may also use an ellipsis when there are space limitations.

In Figure 5-11, we represent both graduate and undergraduate students in a model developed for student billing. The calc-tuition operation computes the tuition a student has to pay; this sum depends on the tuition per credit hour (tuitionPerCred), the courses taken, and the number of credit hours (creditHrs) for each of those courses. The tuition per credit hour, in turn, depends on whether the student is a graduate or an undergraduate student. In this example, that amount is $300 for all graduate students, and $250 for all undergraduate students. To denote that, we have underlined the tuitionPerCred attribute in each of the two subclasses, along with its value. Such an attribute is called a **class-scope attribute**, which specifies a value common to an entire class, rather than a specific value for an instance (Rumbaugh et al, 1991).

You can also specify an initial default value of an attribute using an "=" sign after the attribute name. This is the initial attribute value of a newly created object instance. For example, in Figure 5-11, the creditHrs attribute has an initial value of 3, implying that when a new instance of Course is created, the value of creditHrs is set to 3 by default. You can write an explicit constructor operation to modify the initial default value. The value may also be modified later through other operations. The difference between an initial value specification and a class-scope attribute is that while the former allows the possibility of different attribute values for the instances of a class, the latter forces all the instances to share a common value.

Class-scope attribute: An attribute of a class which specifies a value common to an entire class, rather than a specific value for an instance.

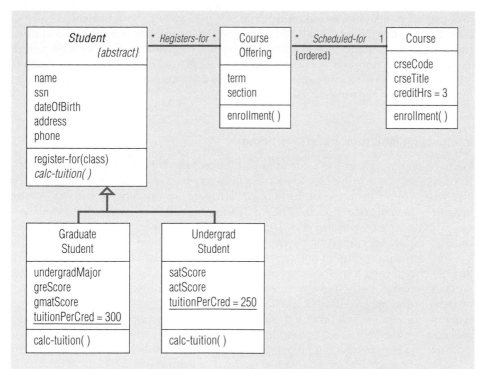

Figure 5-11
Polymorphism, abstract operation, class-scope attribute, and ordering

In addition to specifying the multiplicity of an association role, you can also specify other properties, for example, if the objects playing the role are ordered or not. In the figure, we placed the keyword constraint "{ordered}" next to the Course Offering end of the *Scheduled-for* relationship to denote the fact that the offerings for a given course are ordered into a list—say, according to term and section. It is obvious that it makes sense to specify an ordering only when the multiplicity of the role is greater than one. The default constraint on a role is "{unordered}"; that is, if you do not specify the keyword "{ordered}" next to the role, it is assumed that the related elements form an unordered set. For example, the course offerings are not related to a student who registers for those offerings in any specific order.

The Graduate Student subclass specializes the abstract Student class by adding four attributes—undergradMajor, greScore, gmatScore, and tuitionPerCred—and by refining the inherited *calc-tuition* operation. Notice that the operation is shown in italics within the Student class, indicating that it is an abstract operation. An **abstract operation** defines the form or protocol of the operation, but not its implementation (Rumbaugh et al., 1991). In this example, the Student class defines the protocol of the *calc-tuition* operation, without providing the corresponding **method** (the actual implementation of the operation). The protocol includes the number and types of the arguments, the result type, and the intended semantics of the operation. The two concrete subclasses, Graduate Student and Undergrad Student, supply their own implementations of the calc-tuition operation. Note that because these classes are concrete, they cannot store abstract operations.

It is important to note that although the Graduate Student and Undergraduate Student classes share the same calc-tuition operation, they might implement the operation in quite different ways. For example, the method that implements the operation for a graduate student might add a special graduate fee for each course the student takes. The fact that the same operation may apply to two or more classes in

Abstract operation: Defines the form or protocol of the operation, but not its implementation.

Method: The implementation of an operation.

Polymorphism: The same operation may apply to two or more classes in different ways.

different ways is known as **polymorphism**, a key concept in object-oriented systems (Booch, 1994; Rumbaugh et al., 1991). The enrollment operation in Figure 5-11 illustrates another example of polymorphism. While the enrollment operation within Course Offering computes the enrollment for a particular course offering or section, an operation with the same name within Course computes the combined enrollment for all sections of a given course.

Interpreting Inheritance and Overriding

We have seen how a subclass can augment the features inherited from its ancestors. In such cases, the subclass is said to use *inheritance for extension.* On the other hand, if a subclass constrains some of the ancestor attributes or operations, it is said to use *inheritance for restriction* (Booch, 1994; Rumbaugh et al., 1991). For example, a subclass called Tax-Exempt Company may suppress or block the inheritance of an operation called compute-tax from its superclass, Company.

Overriding: The process of replacing a method inherited from a superclass by a more specific implementation of that method in a subclass.

The implementation of an operation can also be overridden. **Overriding** is the process of replacing a method inherited from a superclass by a more specific implementation of that method in a subclass. The reasons for overriding include extension, restriction, and optimization (Rumbaugh et al., 1991). The name of the new operation remains the same as the inherited one, but it has to be explicitly shown within the subclass to indicate that the operation is overridden.

In *overriding for extension,* an operation inherited by a subclass from its superclass is extended by adding some behavior (code). For example, a subclass of Company called Foreign Company inherits an operation called compute-tax but extends the inherited behavior by adding a foreign surcharge to compute the total tax amount.

In *overriding for restriction,* the protocol of the new operation in the subclass is restricted. For example, an operation called place-student(job) in Student may be restricted in the International Student subclass by tightening the argument job (see Figure 5-12). While students in general may be placed in all types of jobs during the summer, international students may be limited to only on-campus jobs because of visa restrictions. The new operation overrides the inherited operation by tightening the job argument, restricting its values to only a small subset of all possible jobs.

Figure 5-12
Overriding inheritance

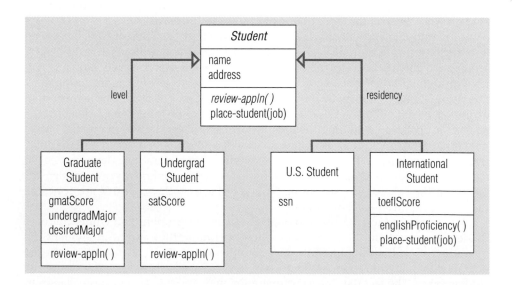

This example also illustrates the use of multiple discriminators. While the basis for one set of generalizations is a student's "level" (graduate or undergraduate), that for the other set is his or her "residency" status (U.S. or international).

In *overriding for optimization*, the new operation is implemented with improved code by exploiting the restrictions imposed by a subclass. Consider, for example, a subclass of Student called Dean's List Student, which represents all those students who are on the Dean's List. To qualify for the Dean's List, a student must have a grade point average greater than or equal to 3.50. Suppose Student has an operation called mailScholApps, which mails applications for merit- and means-tested scholarships to students who have a gpa greater than or equal to 3.00, and whose family's total gross income is less than $20,000. The method for the operation in Student will have to check the conditions, whereas the method for the same operation in the Dean's List Student subclass can improve upon the speed of execution by removing the first condition from its code. Consider another operation called findMinGpa, which finds the minimum gpa among the students. Suppose the Dean's List Student class is sorted in ascending order of the gpa, but the Student class is not. The method for findMinGpa in Student must perform a sequential search through all the students. In contrast, the same operation in Dean's List Student can be implemented with a method that simply retrieves the gpa of the first student in the list, thereby obviating the need for a time-consuming search.

Representing Multiple Inheritance

So far you have been exposed to single inheritance, where a class inherits from only one superclass. But sometimes, as we saw in the example with research and teaching assistants, an object may be an instance of more than one class. This is known as **multiple classification** (Fowler, 1997; *UML Notation Guide*, 1997). For instance, Sean Bailey, who has both types of assistantships, has two classifications: one as an instance of Research Assistant and the other as an instance of Teaching Assistant. Multiple classification, however, is discouraged by experts. It is not supported by the ordinary UML semantics and many object-oriented languages.

> **Multiple classification:** An object is an instance of more than one class.

To get around the problem, we can use multiple inheritance, which allows a class to inherit features from more than one superclass. For example, in Figure 5-13, we have created Research & Teaching Assistant, which is a subclass of both Research Assistant and Teaching Assistant. All students who have both research and teaching assistantships may be stored under the new class. We may now represent Sean Bailey as an object belonging to only the Research & Teaching Assistant class, which inherits features from both its parents, such as researchHrs and assignProject(proj) from Research Assistant and teachingHrs and assignCourse(crse) from Teaching Assistant.

Representing Aggregation

An **aggregation** expresses a *Part-of* relationship between a component object and an aggregate object. It is a stronger form of association relationship (with the added "part-of" semantics) and is represented with a hollow diamond at the aggregate end. For example, Figure 5-14 shows a personal computer as an aggregate of CPU (up to four for multiprocessors), hard disks, monitor, keyboard, and other objects. Note that aggregation involves a set of distinct object instances, one of which contains or is composed of the others. For example, a Personal Computer object is related to

> **Aggregation:** A part-of relationship between a component object and an aggregate object.

Figure 5-13
Multiple inheritance

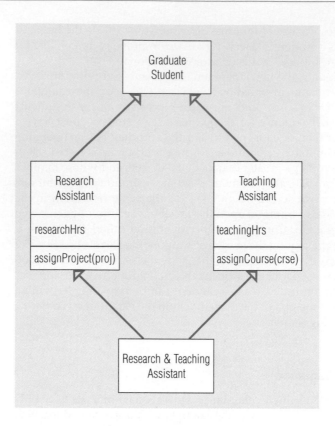

(consists of) CPU objects, one of its parts. In contrast, generalization relates object classes: an object (e.g., Mary Jones) is simultaneously an instance of its class (e.g., Undergrad Student) and its superclass (e.g., Student). Only one object (e.g., Mary Jones) is involved in a generalization relationship. This is why multiplicities are indicated at the ends of aggregation lines, whereas there are no multiplicities for generalization relationships.

Figure 5-14
Example of aggregation

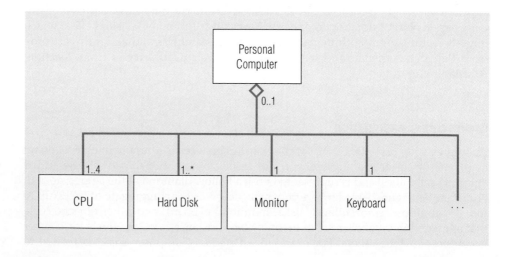

Figure 5-15
Aggregation and composition

(a) Class diagram

(b) Object diagram

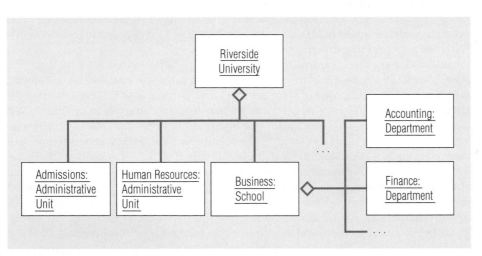

Figure 5-15a shows an aggregation structure of a university. The object diagram in Figure 5-15b shows how Riverside University, a University object instance, is related to its component objects, which represent administrative units (e.g., Admissions, Human Resources, etc.) and schools (e.g., Arts and Science, Business, etc.). A school object (e.g., Business), in turn, comprises several department objects (e.g., Accounting, Finance, etc.).

Notice that the diamond at one end of the relationship between Building and Room is not hollow, but solid. A solid diamond represents a stronger form of aggregation, known as composition (Fowler, 1997; *UML Notation Guide*, 1997). In **composition**, a part object belongs to only one *whole* object; for example, a room is part of only one building. Therefore, the multiplicity on the aggregate end may not exceed 1. Parts may be created after the creation of the whole object; for example, rooms may

Composition: A part object that belongs to only one whole object, and that lives and dies with the whole object.

Figure 5-16

Recursive aggregation

be added to an existing building. However, once a part of a composition is created, it lives and dies with the whole; deletion of the aggregate object cascades to its components. If a building is demolished, for example, so are all its rooms. However, it is possible to delete a part before its aggregate dies, just as it is possible to demolish a room without bringing down a building.

Consider another example of aggregation, the bill-of-materials structure presented earlier in Chapter 3. Many manufactured products are made up of assemblies, which in turn are composed of subassemblies and parts, and so on. We saw how we could represent this type of structure as a many-to-many unary relationship (called Has_components) in an E-R diagram (see Figure 3-13). When the relationship has an attribute of its own, such as Quantity, the relationship can be converted to an associative entity. Note that though the bill-of-materials structure is essentially an aggregation, we had to represent it as an association because the E-R model does not support the semantically stronger concept of aggregation. In the object-oriented model, we can explicitly show the aggregation.

In Figure 5-16, we have represented the bill-of-materials structure. To distinguish between an assembly and a primitive part (one without components), we have created two classes, Assembly and Simple Part, both of which are subclasses of a class called Part. The diagram captures the fact that a product consists of many parts, which themselves can be assemblies of other parts, and so on; this is an example of *recursive* aggregation. Because Part is represented as an abstract class, a part is either an assembly or a primitive part. An Assembly object is an aggregate of instances of the Part superclass, implying that it is composed of other assemblies (optional) and primitive parts. Note that we can easily capture an attribute, such as the quantity of parts in an assembly, inside an association class attached to the aggregation relationship.

When you are unsure whether a relationship between two objects is an association or an aggregation, try to figure out if one object is really part of the other object. That is, is there a whole/part relationship? Note that an aggregation does not necessarily have to imply physical containment, such as that between Personal Computer and CPU. The whole/part relationship may be conceptual, for example, the one between a mutual fund and a certain stock that is part of the fund. In an aggregation, an object may or may not exist independently of an aggregate object. For example, a stock exists irrespective of whether it is part of a mutual fund or not, while a department does not exist independently of an organization. Also, an object may be part of several aggregate objects (e.g., many mutual funds may contain IBM stocks in their portfolios). Remember, however, that while this is possible in aggregation, composition does not allow an object to be part of more than one aggregate object.

Another characteristic of aggregation is that some of the operations on the whole automatically apply to its parts. For example, an operation called ship in the Personal Computer object class applies to CPU, Hard Disk, Monitor, etc., because whenever a computer is shipped, so are its parts. The ship operation on Personal Computer is said to *propagate* to its parts (Rumbaugh et al., 1991).

BUSINESS RULES

Business rules were discussed in detail earlier in Chapter 4. You saw how to express different types of rules in an E-R diagram. In the examples provided in this chapter, we captured many business rules as constraints—implicitly, as well as explicitly—on classes, instances, attributes, operations, relationships, etc. For example, you saw how to specify cardinality constraints and ordering constraints on association roles. You also saw how to represent semantic constraints (e.g., overlapping, disjoint, etc.) among subclasses. Many of the constraints that were discussed so far in this chapter were imposed by including a set of UML keywords within braces—for example, {disjoint, complete} and {ordered}—and placing them close to the elements the constraints apply to. For example, in Figure 5-11, we expressed a business rule that offerings for a given course are ordered. But if you cannot represent a business rule using such a predefined UML constraint, you can define the rule in plain English, or in some other language such as formal logic.

When you have to specify a business rule involving two graphical symbols (such as those representing two classes or two associations), you can show the constraint as a dashed arrow from one element to the other, labeled by the constraint name in braces (*UML Notation Guide,* 1997). In Figure 5-17, for example, we have stated the business rule that the chair of a department must be a member of the department by specifying the *Chair-of* association as a subset of the *Member-of* association.

When a business rule involves three or more graphical symbols, you can show the constraint as a note and attach the note to each of the symbols by a dashed line (*UML Notation Guide,* 1997). In Figure 5-17, we have captured the business rule that "each faculty member assigned to teach a section of a course must be qualified to teach that course" within a note symbol. Because this constraint involves all three association relationships, we have attached the note to each of the three association paths.

OBJECT MODELING EXAMPLE: PINE VALLEY FURNITURE COMPANY

In Chapter 3, you saw how to develop a high-level E-R diagram for the Pine Valley Furniture Company (see Figure 3-21). We identified the entity types, as well as their keys and other important attributes, based on a study of the business processes at the company. We will now show you how to develop a class diagram for the same

Figure 5-17
Representing business rules

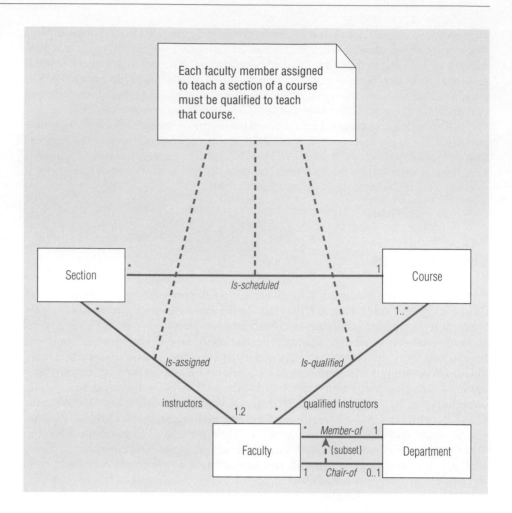

Each faculty member assigned to teach a section of a course must be qualified to teach that course.

application using the object-oriented approach. The class diagram is shown in Figure 5-18. We discuss the commonalities, as well as the differences, between this diagram and the E-R diagram.

As you would expect, the entity types are represented as object classes and all the attributes are shown within the classes. Note, however, that you do not need to show explicit identifiers in the form of primary keys, because, by definition, each object has its own identity. The E-R model, as well as the relational data model (see Chapter 6), requires you to specify explicit identifiers because there is no other way of supporting the notion of identity. In the object-oriented model, the only identifiers you should represent are attributes that make sense in the real world, such as salespersonID, customerID, orderID, and productID, which are represented as keys in the class diagram. Notice that we have not shown an identifier for Product Line, based on the assumption that Product_Line_ID was merely included in the E-R diagram as an internal identifier, not as a real-world attribute such as orderID or productID. If Pine Valley Furniture Company does not actually use vendorID or, for that matter, any other attribute, to support its business processes, you should not include that attribute in the class diagram. For that reason, we have not shown identifiers for classes such as Vendor, Order Line, and Skill.

In the E-R diagram, "Skill" was shown as a multivalued attribute of Employee. In the class diagram, we have shown Skill as a separate object class, because, accord-

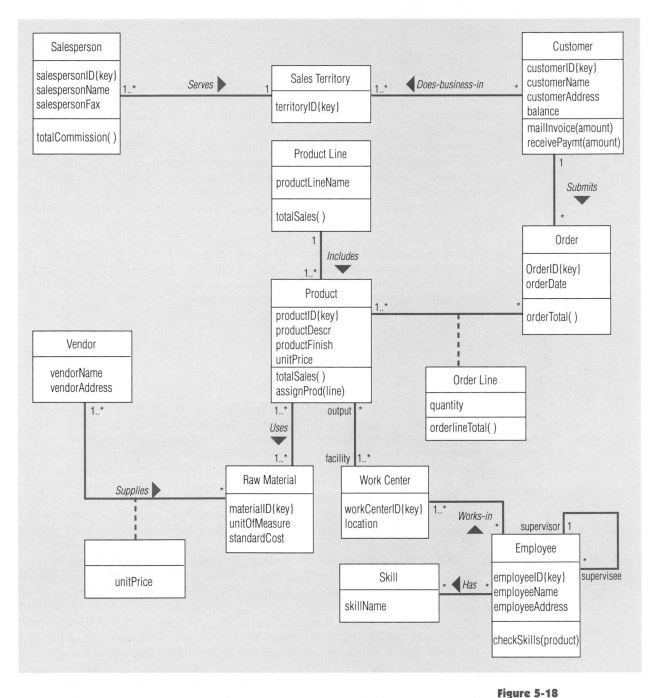

Figure 5-18
Class diagram for Pine Valley
Furniture Company

ing to Fowler (1997), in a conceptual object oriented model, an attribute should always be single-valued. Order Line is shown as an association class, as is *Supplies.* Note that while we have displayed the name of the Order Line association within the class symbol to emphasize its "class nature," we have shown the name of the *Supplies* association on the association path to emphasize its "association nature."

The class diagram of Figure 5-18 shows several processes, represented as operations, that could not be captured in a E-R diagram. For example, Customer has an operation called mailInvoice, which, when executed, mails an invoice to a customer who has placed an order, specifying the total order amount in dollars, and increases the customer's outstanding balance by that amount. On receipt of payment from the customer, the receivePaymt operation adjusts the balance by the amount received. The orderlineTotal operation of Order Line computes the total dollar amount for a given order line of an order, whereas the orderTotal operation of Order computes the total amount for an entire order (i.e., the sum total of the amounts on all the order lines).

Figure 5-18 also illustrates polymorphism. The totalSales operation appears within both the Product and Product Line classes, but is implemented as two different methods. While the method in Product computes the total sales for a given product, the one in Product Line computes the total sales of all products belonging to a given product line.

The following operations—totalSales, totalCommission, orderTotal, orderlineTotal, and checkSkills—are all query operations, because they do not have any side effects. In contrast, mailInvoice, receivePaymt, and assignProd are all update operations because they alter the state of some object(s). For example, the assignProd operation assigns a new product to the product line specified in the "line" argument, thereby changing the state of both the product (which becomes assigned) and the product line (which includes one more product).

SUMMARY

In this chapter, we introduced the object-oriented modeling approach, which is becoming increasingly popular because it supports effective representation of a real-world application—both in terms of its data and processes—using a common underlying representation. We described the activities involved in the different phases of the object-oriented development life cycle, and emphasized the seamless nature of the transitions that an object-oriented model undergoes as it evolves through the different phases, from analysis to design to implementation. This is in sharp contrast to other modeling approaches, such as structured analysis and design, which lack a common underlying representation and, therefore, suffer from abrupt and disjoint model transitions.

We presented object-oriented modeling as a high-level conceptual activity, especially as it pertains to data analysis. We introduced the concept of objects and classes, and discussed object identity and encapsulation. Throughout the chapter, we developed several class diagrams, using the UML notation, to show you how to model various types of situations. You also learned how to draw an object diagram that corresponds to a given class diagram. The object diagram is an instance of the class diagram, providing a snapshot of the actual objects and links present in a system at some point in time.

We showed how to model the processes underlying an application using operations. We discussed three types of operations: constructor, query, and update. The E-R model (as well as the enhanced E-R model) does not allow you to capture processes; it only allows you to model the data needs of an organization. In this chapter, we emphasized several similarities between the E-R model and the object-oriented model, but, at the same time, highlighted those features that make the latter more powerful than the former.

We showed how to represent association relationships of different degrees—unary, binary, and ternary—in a class diagram. An association has two or more roles; each role has a multiplicity, which indicates the number of objects that participate in the relationship. Other types of constraints can be specified on association roles, such as forming an ordered set of objects. When an association itself has attributes or operations of its own, or when it participates in other associations, the association is modeled as a class; such a class is called an association class. Links and link objects in an object diagram correspond to associations and association classes, respectively, in a class diagram. Derived attributes, derived relationships, and derived roles can also be represented in a class diagram.

The object-oriented model expresses generalization relationships using super-classes and subclasses, similar to supertypes and subtypes in the enhanced E-R model. The basis of a generalization path can be denoted using a discriminator label next to the generalization path. Semantic constraints among subclasses can be specified using UML keywords such as overlapping, disjoint, complete, and incomplete. When a class does not have any direct instances, it is modeled as an abstract class. An abstract class may have an abstract operation, whose form, but not method, is provided.

In a generalization relationship, a subclass inherits features from its superclass, and by transitivity, from all its ancestors. Inheritance is a very powerful mechanism because it supports code reuse in object-oriented systems. We discussed ways of applying inheritance of features, as well as reasons for overriding inheritance of operations in subclasses. We also introduced another key concept in object-oriented modeling, that of polymorphism, which means that an operation can apply in different ways across different classes. The concepts of encapsulation, inheritance, and polymorphism in object-oriented modeling provide system developers with powerful mechanisms for developing complex, robust, flexible, and maintainable business systems.

The object-oriented model supports aggregation, while the E-R or the enhanced E-R model does not. Aggregation is a semantically stronger form of association, expressing the *Part-of* relationship between a component object and an aggregate object. We distinguished between aggregation and generalization, and provided you with tips for choosing between association and aggregation in representing a relationship. We discussed a stronger form of aggregation, known as composition, in which a part object belongs to only one whole object, living and dying together with it.

In this chapter, you also learned how to state business rules implicitly, as well as explicitly, in a class diagram. UML provides several keywords that can be used as constraints on classes, attributes, relationships, etc. In addition, user-defined constraints may be used to express business rules. When a business rule involves two or more elements, you saw how to express the rule in a class diagram, such as by using a note symbol. We concluded the chapter by developing a class diagram for Pine Valley Furniture Company, illustrating how to apply the object-oriented approach to model both the data and the processes underlying real-world business problems.

CHAPTER REVIEW

KEY TERMS

Abstract class	Association class	Class-scope attribute
Abstract operation	Association role	Composition
Aggregation	Behavior	Concrete class
Association	Class diagram	Constructor operation

Encapsulation   Object class (class)   Query operation
Method   Object diagram   State
Multiple classification Operation   Update operation
Multiplicity   Overriding
Object   Polymorphism

R E V I E W   Q U E S T I O N S

1. Define each of the following terms:
   a. object class
   b. state
   c. behavior
   d. encapsulation
   e. operation
   f. method
   g. constructor operation
   h. query operation
   i. update operation
   j. abstract class
   k. concrete class
   l. abstract operation
   m. multiplicity
   n. class-scope attribute
   o. association class
   p. polymorphism
   q. overriding
   r. multiple classification
   s. composition
   t. recursive aggregation

2. Contrast the following terms:
   a. class; object
   b. attribute; operation
   c. state; behavior
   d. operation; method
   e. query operation; update operation
   f. abstract class; concrete class
   g. class diagram; object diagram
   h. association; aggregation
   i. generalization; aggregation
   j. aggregation; composition
   k. overriding for extension; overriding for restriction

3. State the activities involved in each of the following phases of the object-oriented development life cycle: object-oriented analysis, object-oriented design, and object-oriented implementation.

4. Compare and contrast the object-oriented model with the enhanced E-R model.

5. State the conditions under which a designer should model an association relationship as an association class.

6. Using a class diagram, give an example for each of the following types of relationships: unary, binary, and ternary. Specify the multiplicities for all the relationships.

7. Add role names to the association relationships you identified in Review Question 6.

8. Add operations to some of the classes you identified in Review Question 6.

9. Give an example of generalization. Your example should include at least one super-class and three subclasses, and a minimum of one attribute and one operation for each of the classes. Indicate the discriminator and specify the semantic constraints among the subclasses.

10. If the diagram you developed for Review Question 9 does not contain an abstract class, extend the diagram by adding an abstract class that contains at least one abstract operation. Also, indicate which features of a class are inherited by other classes.

11. Using (and, if necessary, extending) the diagram from your solution to Review Question 10, give an example of polymorphism.

12. Give an example of aggregation. Your example should include at least one aggregate object and three component objects. Specify the multiplicities at each end of all the aggregation relationships.

PROBLEMS AND EXERCISES

1. Match the following terms to the appropriate definitions:

_____ concrete class	a. operation applied in different ways
_____ abstract operation	b. form, not implementation
_____ aggregation	c. direct instances
_____ overriding	d. belongs to only one whole object
_____ polymorphism	e. method replacement
_____ association class	f. part-of relationship
_____ composition	g. a set of objects
_____ object class	h. equivalent to associative entity

2. Draw a class diagram, showing the relevant classes, attributes, operations, and relationships, for each of the following situations (if you believe that you need to make additional assumptions, clearly state them for each situation):

   a. A company has a number of employees. The attributes of Employee include employeeID (primary key), name, address, and birthdate. The company also has several projects. Attributes of Project include projectName and startDate. Each employee may be assigned to one or more projects, or may not be assigned to a project. A project must have at least one employee assigned, and may have any number of employees assigned. An employee's billing rate may vary by project, and the company wishes to record the applicable billing rate for each employee when assigned to a particular project. At the end of each month, the company mails a check to each employee who has worked on a project during that month. The amount of the check is based on the billing rate and the hours logged for each project assigned to the employee.

   b. A university has a large number of courses in its catalog. Attributes of Course include courseNumber (primary key), courseName, and units. Each course may have one or more different courses as prerequisites, or may have no prerequisites. Similarly, a particular course may be a prerequisite for any number of courses, or may not be prerequisite for any other course. The university adds or drops a prerequisite for a course only when the director for the course makes a formal request to that effect.

c. A laboratory has several chemists who work on one or more projects. Chemists also may use certain kinds of equipment on each project. Attributes of Chemist include name and phoneNo. Attributes of Project include projectName and startDate. Attributes of Equipment include serialNo and cost. The organization wishes to record assignDate—that is, the date when a given equipment item was assigned to a particular chemist working on a specified project—as well as totalHours, that is, the total number of hours the chemist has used the equipment for the project. The organization also wants to track the usage of each type of equipment by a chemist. It does so by computing the average number of hours the chemist has used that equipment on all assigned projects. A chemist must be assigned to at least one project and one equipment item. A given equipment item need not be assigned, and a given project need not be assigned either a chemist or an equipment item.

d. A college course may have one or more scheduled sections, or may not have a scheduled section. Attributes of Course include courseID, courseName, and units. Attributes of Section include sectionNumber and semester. The value of sectionNumber is an integer (such as "1" or "2") that distinguishes one section from another for the same course, but does not uniquely identify a section. There is an operation called findNumSections that finds the number of sections offered for a given course in a given semester.

e. A hospital has a large number of registered physicians. Attributes of Physician include physicianID (primary key) and specialty. Patients are admitted to the hospital by physicians. Attributes of Patient include patientID (primary key) and patientName. Any patient who is admitted must have exactly one admitting physician. A physician may optionally admit any number of patients. Once admitted, a given patient must be treated by at least one physician. A particular physician may treat any number of patients, or may not treat any patients. Whenever a patient is treated by a physician, the hospital wishes to record the details of the treatment, by including the date, time, and results of the treatment.

3. A student, whose attributes include studentName, address, phone, and age, may engage in multiple campus-based activities. The university keeps track of the number of years a given student has participated in a specific activity and, at the end of each academic year, mails an activity report to the student showing his participation in various activities. Draw a class diagram for this situation.

4. Prepare a class diagram for a real estate firm that lists property for sale. The following describes this organization:

- The firm has a number of sales offices in several states; location is an attribute of sales office.

- Each sales office is assigned one or more employees. Attributes of employee include employeeID and employeeName. An employee must be assigned to only one sales office.

- For each sales office, there is always one employee assigned to manage that office. An employee may manage only the sales office to which she is assigned.

- The firm lists property for sale. Attributes of property include propertyName and location.

- Each unit of property must be listed with one (and only one) of the sales offices. A sales office may have any number of properties listed, or may have no properties listed.

- Each unit of property has one or more owners. Attributes of owner are ownerName and address. An owner may own one or more units of property. For each property that an owner owns, an attribute called percentOwned indicates what percentage of the property is owned by the owner.

Add a subset constraint between two of the associations you identified in your class diagram.

5. Draw a class diagram for some organization that you are familiar with—boy scouts/girl scouts, sports team, etc. In your diagram, indicate names for at least four association roles.

6. Draw a class diagram for the following situation (state any assumptions you believe you have to make in order to develop a complete diagram): Stillwater Antiques buys and sells one of a kind antiques of all kinds (for example, furniture, jewelry, china, and clothing). Each item is uniquely identified by an item number and is also characterized by a description, asking price, condition, and open-ended comments. Stillwater works with many different individuals, called clients, who sell items to and buy items from the store. Some clients only sell items to Stillwater, some only buy items, and some others both sell and buy. A client is identified by a client number, and is also described by a client name and client address. When Stillwater sells an item in stock to a client, the owners want to record the commission paid, the actual selling price, sales tax (tax of zero indicates a tax exempt sale), and date sold. When Stillwater buys an item from a client, the owners want to record the purchase cost, date purchased, and condition at time of purchase.

7. Draw a class diagram for the following situation (state any assumptions you believe you have to make in order to develop a complete diagram): The H. I. Topi School of Business operates international business programs in 10 locations throughout Europe. The School had its first class of 9000 graduates in 1965. The School keeps track of each graduate's student number, name, country of birth, current country of citizenship, current name, current address, and the name of each major the student completed (each student has one or two majors). In order to maintain strong ties to its alumni, the School holds various events around the world. Events have a title, date, location, and type (for example, reception, dinner, or seminar). The School needs to keep track of which graduates have attended which events. For an attendance by a graduate at an event, a comment is recorded about information School officials learned from that graduate at that event. The School also keeps in contact with graduates by mail, e-mail, telephone, and fax interactions. As with events, the School records information learned from the graduate from each of these contacts. When a School official knows that he or she will be meeting or talking to a graduate, a report is produced showing the latest information about that graduate and the information learned during the past two years from that graduate from all contacts and events the graduate attended.

8. Assume that at Pine Valley Furniture each product (described by product number, description, and cost) comprises at least three components (described by component number, description, and unit of measure) and components are used to make one or many products. In addition, assume that components are used to make other components and that raw materials are also considered to be components. In both cases of components, we need to keep track of how many components go into making something else. Draw a class diagram for this situation; indicate the multiplicities for all the relationships you identified in the diagram.

9. Draw a class diagram for the following problem. A nonprofit organization depends on a number of different types of persons for its successful operation. The organization is interested in the following attributes for all of these persons: ssn, name,

address, and phone. There are three types of persons who are of greatest interest: employees, volunteers, and donors. In addition to the attributes for a person, an employee has an attribute called dateHired, and a volunteer has an attribute called skill. A donor is a person who has donated one or more items to the organization. An item, specified by a name, may have no donors, or one or more donors. When an item is donated, the organization records its price, so that at the end of the year, it can identify the top ten donors.

There are persons other than employees, volunteers, and donors who are of interest to the organization, so that a person need not belong to any of these three groups. On the other hand, at a given time a person may belong to two or more of these groups (for example, employee and donor).

10. A bank has three types of accounts: checking, savings, and loan. Following are the attributes for each type of account:

    CHECKING: Acct_No, Date_Opened, Balance, Service_Charge

    SAVINGS: Acct_No, Date_Opened, Balance, Interest_Rate

    LOAN: Acct_No, Date_Opened, Balance, Interest_Rate, Payment

    Assume that each bank account must be a member of exactly one of these subtypes. At the end of each month the bank computes the balance in each account and mails a statement to the customer holding that account. The balance computation depends on the type of the account. For example, a checking account balance may reflect a service charge, whereas a savings account balance may include an interest amount. Draw a class diagram to represent the situation. Your diagram should include an abstract class, as well as an abstract operation for computing balance.

11. Refer to the class diagram for hospital relationships (Figure 5-9b). Add notation to express the following business rule: A resident patient can be assigned a bed only if that patient has been assigned a physician who will assume responsibility for the patient's care.

12. An organization has been entrusted with developing a Registration and Title system that maintains information about all vehicles registered in a particular state. For each vehicle that is registered with the office, the system has to store the name, address, telephone number of the owner, the start date and end date of the registration, plate information (issuer, year, type, and number), sticker (year, type, and number), and registration fee. In addition, the following information is maintained about the vehicles themselves: the number, year, make, model, body style, gross weight, number of passengers, diesel-powered (yes/no), color, cost, and mileage. If the vehicle is a trailer, the parameters diesel-powered and number of passengers are not relevant. For travel trailers, the body number and length must be known. The system needs to maintain information on the luggage capacity for a car, maximum cargo capacity and maximum towing capacity for a truck, and horsepower for a motorcycle. The system issues registration notices to owners of vehicles whose registrations are due to expire after two months. When the owner renews the registration, the system updates the registration information on the vehicle.

    a. Develop an object-oriented model by drawing a class diagram that shows all the object classes, attributes, operations, relationships, and multiplicities. For each operation, show its argument list.

    b. Each vehicle consists of a drive train, which, in turn, consists of an engine and a transmission. (Ignore the fact that a trailer doesn't have an engine and a transmission.) Suppose that, for each vehicle, the system has to maintain the following information: the size and number of cylinders of its engine, and the type and weight of its transmission. Add classes, attributes, and relationships to the class diagram to capture this new information.

c. Give a realistic example (you may create one) of an operation that you override in a subclass or subclasses. Add the operation at appropriate places in the class diagram, and discuss the reasons for overriding.

FIELD EXERCISES

1. Interview a friend or family member to elicit from them common examples of superclass/subclass relationships. You will have to explain the meaning of this term and provide a common example, such as: PROPERTY: RESIDENTIAL, COMMERCIAL; or BONDS: CORPORATE, MUNICIPAL. Use the information they provide to construct a class diagram segment and present it to this person. Revise if necessary until it seems appropriate to you and your friend or family member.

2. Visit two local small businesses, one in the service sector and one in manufacturing. Interview employees from these organizations to obtain examples of both superclass/subclass relationships and operational business rules (such as "A customer can return merchandise only if the customer has a valid sales slip"). In which of these environments is it easier to find examples of these constructs? Why?

3. Ask a database administrator or database or systems analyst in a local company to show you an EER (or E-R) diagram for one of the organization's primary databases. Translate this diagram into a class diagram.

4. Interview a systems analyst in a local company who uses object-oriented programming and system development tools. Ask to see any analysis and design diagrams the analyst has drawn of the database and applications. Compare these diagrams to the ones in this chapter. What differences do you see? What additional features and notations are used and what are their purpose?

REFERENCES

Booch, G. 1994. *Object-Oriented Analysis and Design with Applications.* 2nd ed. Redwood City, CA: Benjamin/Cummings.

Coad, P., and E. Yourdon. 1991a. *Object-Oriented Analysis.* 2nd ed. Englewood Cliffs, NJ: Prentice-Hall.

Coad, P., and E. Yourdon. 1991b. *Object-Oriented Design.* Englewood Cliffs, NJ: Prentice-Hall.

Fowler, M. 1997. *UML Distilled: Applying the Standard Object Modeling Language.* Reading, MA: Addison-Wesley.

Jacobson, I., M. Christerson, P. Jonsson, and G. Overgaard. 1992. *Object-Oriented Software Engineering: A Use Case Driven Approach.* Reading, MA: Addison-Wesley.

Rumbaugh, J., M. Blaha, W. Premerlani, F. Eddy, and W. Lorensen. 1991. *Object-Oriented Modeling and Design.* Englewood Cliffs, NJ: Prentice-Hall.

UML Document Set. 1997. Version 1.0 (January). Santa Clara, CA: Rational Software Corp.

UML Notation Guide. 1997. Version 1.0 (January). Santa Clara, CA: Rational Software Corp.

Project Case

PROJECT DESCRIPTION

This project description is similar to the project description included with Chapter 4. After you complete this project, it will be useful for you to compare the data models developed in each of the project cases from Chapters 4 and 5.

As a large service organization, Mountain View Community Hospital depends on a large number of persons for its continued success. There are four groups of persons on whom the hospital is most dependent: employees, physicians, patients, and volunteers. Of course there are some common attributes shared by all of these persons: personID (identifier), name, address, city-state-zip, dateOfBirth, and phone.

Each of the four groups of persons has at least one unique attribute. Employees have a dateHired, Volunteers have a skill, Physicians have a specialty and a pagerNumber, and Patients have a dateOfContact (date of first contact with the hospital) and calc-age. There are also unique methods for each of the four groups of persons. Employees have calc-benefits, Volunteers have assign-to-Center(CareCenter), Physicians have treats(Patient), and Patients have calc-age and assignToLocation(Bed). An Employee or a Physician who is also a Patient also has an attribute specialService.

There are other persons in the hospital community who do not belong to one of these four groups (although their numbers are relatively small). On the other hand, a particular person may belong to two (or more) of these groups at a given time (for example, Patient and Volunteer).

Each patient has one (and only one) physician who is responsible for that patient. A given physician may not be responsible for a patient at a given time, or may be responsible for one or more patients. Patients are divided into two groups: resident, and outpatient. Each resident patient has a dateOfAdmission attribute and a method of assignToBed(Bed), which overrides the assignToLocation method of all patients. Each outpatient is scheduled for zero or more visits. The entity visit has two attributes: date (partial identifier) and comments. Notice that an instance of visit cannot exist without an outpatient owner entity.

Employees are subdivided into three groups: nurse, staff, and technician. Only nurse has the attribute cer-

tificate, which indicates the qualification (RN, LPN, etc.). Only staff has the attribute jobClass, while only technician has the attribute skill. Each nurse is assigned to one (and only one) care center. Examples of care centers are Maternity, Emergency, and Cardiology (care centers were formerly called wards). Attributes of care center are name (identifier) and location. A care center may have one or more nurses assigned to it. Also for each care center, one of the nurses assigned to that care center is appointed nurse_in_charge; however, a nurse cannot be appointed nurse_in_charge unless she or he has an RN certificate. Care centers are located in buildings, and a building is described by buildingNumber, buildingName, and buildingCode.

Each technician is assigned to one or more laboratories. Attributes of laboratory include name (identifier) and location. A laboratory must have at least one technician assigned to it and may have any number of technicians assigned. A laboratory is housed in one and only one building, and a building may house many laboratories. A laboratory includes equipment and the employees who work in that laboratory, and a laboratory also has a method numberOfEmployees.

There may be no beds assigned to a care center, or a care center may have one or more beds (up to any number) assigned to it. The only attribute of bed is bedID (identifier) and the only method of bed is utilization. bedID is a composite attribute, with components bedNumber and roomNumber. Each resident patient must be assigned to a bed. A bed may or may not have a resident patient assigned to it at a given time.

PROJECT QUESTIONS

1. Is the ability to model superclass/subclass relationships likely to be important in a hospital environment such as Mountain View Community Hospital? Why or why not?

2. Do there appear to be any link objects in the description of the data requirements in this project segment? If so, what are they?

3. Are there any abstract object classes in the description of this hospital? Why or why not?

PROJECT EXERCISES

1. Draw a class diagram to accurately represent this set of requirements, carefully following the notation from this chapter.

2. Develop definitions for each of the following types of objects in your class diagram from Project Exercise 1. Consult with some member of the hospital or health-care community if one is available; otherwise make reasonable assumptions based on your own knowledge and experience.

   a. Classes   c. Relationships

   b. Attributes   d. Methods

3. You should recognize the statement "A nurse cannot be appointed nurse_in_charge of a care center unless she or he has an RN certificate" as a statement of a business rule. How did you model this business rule differently from what you did in the project case in Chapter 4? What is the constrained object? Is it an entity, an attribute, a relationship, or some other object?

4. Compare the class diagram you developed in this chapter with the EER diagram that you developed in Chapter 4 with the E-R diagram you developed in Chapter 3 in Project Exercise 2. What are the differences between these two diagrams? Why are there differences?

5. Did you find any examples of aggregation or composition in the description of the project in this chapter? Why or why not?

PART

III

Database Design

CHAPTER 6

Logical Database Design and the Relational Model

CHAPTER 7

Physical Database Design

Part III Overview

By the end of the database analysis phase of database development, systems and database analysts have a fairly clear understanding of the data storage and access requirements of users. However, the model for data developed during analysis explicitly avoided any ties to database technologies. Before we can implement a database, the conceptual data model must be mapped into a data model that is compatible with the database management system to be used.

The activities of database design transform the requirements for data storage developed during database analysis into structured specifications to guide database implementation. There are two forms of specifications:

1. *Logical,* which maps the conceptual requirements into the data model associated with a specific database management system

2. *Physical,* which indicates all the parameters for data storage that are then input to database implementation, during which a database is actually defined using a data definition language.

In Chapter 6 we describe logical database design, with special emphasis on the relational data model. Logical database design is the process of transforming the conceptual data model (described in Chapters 3 and 4) into a logical data model. Most database management systems in use today use the relational data model, so this data model is the basis for our discussion of logical database design.

In this chapter, we first define the important terms and concepts for this model, including relation, foreign key, anomaly, normal form, normalization, functional dependency, partial functional dependency, and transitive dependency. We next describe and illustrate the process of transforming an E-R model to the relational model. Many CASE tools support this transformation today; however, it is important that you understand the underlying principles and procedures. We then describe the concepts of normalization in detail. Normalization, which is the process of designing well-structured relations, is an important component of logical design for

the relational model. Finally, we describe how to merge relations while avoiding common pitfalls that may occur in this process.

The purpose of physical database design, the topic of Chapter 7, is to translate the logical description of data into the technical specifications for storing and retrieving data. The goal is to create a design for storing data that will provide adequate performance and ensure database integrity, security, and recoverability. Physical database design produces the technical specifications that programmers and others involved in information systems construction will use during the implementation phase, which we discuss in Chapters 8 through 12.

In Chapter 7 you will learn key terms and concepts for physical database design, including data type, page, pointer, denormalization, partitioning, file organization, indexed file organization, and hashed file organization. You will study the basic steps required to develop an efficient physical database design. You will learn how to estimate the amount of data that users will require in the database, and how data are likely to be used. You will learn about choices for storing attribute values and how to select among these choices. You will also learn why normalized tables do not always form the best physical data files, and how you can denormalize the data to achieve data retrieval speed improvements. You will learn about different file organizations and about the use of indexes, which are important in speeding up the retrieval of data. Chapter 7 also addresses how to use redundant data storage schemes, RAID, to provide improved performance and reliability to databases. And you will learn the major differences between different architectures for databases.

You must carefully perform physical database design because decisions made during this stage have a major impact on data accessibility, response times, security, user friendliness, and similarly important information system design factors. Database administration (described in Chapter 13) plays a major role in physical database design, so we will return to some advanced design issues in that chapter, and Chapter 11 addresses distributed database design issues.

CHAPTER

6

Logical Database Design and the Relational Model

LEARNING OBJECTIVES

After studying this chapter, you should be able to:

■ Define the following key terms: relation, primary key, composite key, foreign key, null, entity integrity rule, referential integrity constraint, well-structured relation, anomaly, recursive foreign key, normalization, normal form, functional dependency, determinant, candidate key, first normal form, second normal form, partial functional dependency, third normal form, transitive dependency, synonyms, alias, and homonym.

■ List five properties of relations.

■ State two properties that are essential for a candidate key.

■ Give a concise definition of each of the following: first normal form, second normal form, and third normal form.

■ Briefly describe four problems that may arise when merging relations.

■ Transform an E-R (or EER) diagram to a logically equivalent set of relations.

■ Create relational tables that incorporate entity integrity and referential integrity constraints.

■ Use normalization to decompose a relation with anomalies into well-structured relations.

INTRODUCTION

In this chapter we describe logical database design, with special emphasis on the relational data model. Logical database design is the process of transforming the conceptual data model (described in Chapters 3 and 4) into a logical data model. Although there are other data models, we have two reasons for emphasizing in this chapter the relational data model. First, the relational data model is most commonly used in contemporary database applications. Second, some of the principles of logical database design for the relational model apply to the other logical models as well.

We have introduced the relational data model informally through simple examples in earlier chapters. In this chapter, we first define the important terms and concepts for this model. (We will often use the abbreviated term *relational model* when referring to the relational data model.) We next describe and illustrate the process of transforming an E-R model to the relational model. Many CASE tools support this transformation today; however, it is important that you understand the underlying principles and procedures. We then describe the concepts of normalization in detail. Normalization, which is the process of designing well-structured relations, is an important component of logical design for the relational model. Finally, we describe how to merge relations while avoiding common pitfalls that may occur in this process.

The objective of logical database design is to translate the conceptual design (which represents an organization's requirements for data) into a logical database design that can be implemented on a chosen database management system. The resulting databases must meet user needs for data sharing, flexibility, and ease of access. The concepts presented in this chapter are essential to your understanding of the database development process.

THE RELATIONAL DATA MODEL

The relational data model was first introduced in 1970 by E. F. Codd, then of IBM (Codd, 1970). Two early research projects were launched to prove the feasibility of the relational model and to develop prototype systems. The first of these, at IBM's San Jose Research Laboratory, led to the development of System R (a prototype relational DBMS–RDBMS) during the late 1970s. The second, at the University of California at Berkeley, led to the development of Ingres, an academically oriented RDBMS. Commercial RDBMS products from numerous vendors started to appear about 1980 (see the World Wide Web site for this book for links to RDBMS and other DBMS vendors). Today RDBMSs have become the dominant technology for database management, and there are literally hundreds of RDBMS products for computers ranging from personal computers to mainframes.

Basic Definitions

The relational data model represents data in the form of tables. The relational model is based on mathematical theory and therefore has a solid theoretical foundation. However, we need only a few simple concepts to describe the relational model, and it is therefore easily understood and used by those unfamiliar with the underlying theory. The relational data model consists of the following three components (Fleming and von Halle, 1989):

1. *Data structure*   Data are organized in the form of tables with rows and columns.

2. *Data manipulation*   Powerful operations (using the SQL language) are used to manipulate data stored in the relations.

3. *Data integrity*   Facilities are included to specify business rules that maintain the integrity of data when they are manipulated.

We discuss data structure and data integrity in this section. Data manipulation is discussed in Chapter 9.

EMPLOYEE1

Emp_ID	Name	Dept_Name	Salary
100	Margaret Simpson	Marketing	48,000
140	Allen Beeton	Accounting	52,000
110	Chris Lucero	Info Systems	43,000
190	Lorenzo Davis	Finance	55,000
150	Susan Martin	Marketing	42,000

Figure 6-1
EMPLOYEE1 relation with sample data

Relational Data Structure   A **relation** is a named, two-dimensional table of data. Each relation (or table) consists of a set of named columns and an arbitrary number of unnamed rows. An attribute, consistent with its definition in Chapter 3, is a named column of a relation. Each row of a relation corresponds to a record that contains data (attribute) values for a single entity. Figure 6-1 shows an example of a relation named EMPLOYEE1. This relation contains the following attributes describing employees: Emp_ID, Name, Dept_Name, and Salary. The five rows of the table correspond to five employees. It is important to understand that the sample data in Figure 6-1 are intended to illustrate the structure of the EMPLOYEE1 relation; they are not part of the relation itself. Even if we add another row of data to the figure, it is still the same EMPLOYEE1 relation. Nor does deleting a row change the relation. In fact, we could delete *all* of the rows shown in Figure 6-1, and the EMPLOYEE1 relation would still exist. Stated differently, Figure 6-1 is an instance of the EMPLOYEE1 relation.

> **Relation:** A named, two-dimensional table of data.

We can express the *structure* of a relation by a shorthand notation in which the name of the relation is followed (in parentheses) by the names of the attributes in that relation. For EMPLOYEE1 we would have:

EMPLOYEE1(Emp_ID,Name,Dept_Name,Salary).

Relational Keys   We must be able to store and retrieve a row of data in a relation, based on the data values stored in that row. To achieve this goal, every relation must have a primary key. A **primary key** is an attribute (or combination of attributes) that uniquely identifies each row in a relation. We designate a primary key by underlining the attribute name. For example, the primary key for the relation EMPLOYEE1 is Emp_ID. Notice that this attribute is underlined in Figure 6-1. In shorthand notation we express this relation as follows:

> **Primary key:** An attribute (or combination of attributes) that uniquely identifies each row in a relation.

EMPLOYEE1(Emp_ID,Name,Dept_Name,Salary)

The concept of a primary key is related to the term "identifier" defined in Chapter 3. In many cases, the same attribute (or attributes) indicated as an entity's identifier in an E-R diagram will be the same attributes that compose the primary key for the relation representing that entity. There are exceptions; for example, associative entities do not have to have an identifier and the identifier of a weak entity forms only part of a weak entity's primary key. In addition, there may be several attributes of an entity that may serve as the associated relation's primary key. All of these situations will be illustrated later in this chapter.

A **composite key** is a primary key that consists of more than one attribute. For example, the primary key for a relation DEPENDENT would likely consist of the combination Emp_ID and Dependent_Name. We show several examples of composite keys later in this chapter.

> **Composite key:** A primary key that consists of more than one attribute.

Foreign key: An attribute in a relation of a database that serves as the primary key of another relation in the same database.

Often we must represent the relationship between two tables or relations. This is accomplished through the use of foreign keys. A **foreign key** is an attribute (possibly composite) in a relation of a database that serves as the primary key of another relation in the same database. For example, consider the relations EMPLOYEE1 and DEPARTMENT:

EMPLOYEE1(Emp_ID,Name,Dept_Name,Salary)
DEPARTMENT(Dept_Name,Location,Fax)

The attribute Dept_Name is a foreign key in EMPLOYEE1. It allows a user to associate any employee with the department to which he or she is assigned. Some authors emphasize the fact that an attribute is a foreign key by using a dashed underline, such as

EMPLOYEE1(Emp_ID,Name,Dept_Name,Salary)

We provide numerous examples of foreign keys in the remainder of this chapter.

Properties of Relations   We have defined relations as two-dimensional tables of data. However, not all tables are relations. Relations have several properties that distinguish them from nonrelational tables. We summarize these properties below.

1. Each relation (or table) in a database has a unique name.

2. An entry at the intersection of each row and column is atomic (or single-valued). There can be no multivalued attributes in a relation.

3. Each row is unique; no two rows in a relation are identical.

4. Each attribute (or column) within a table has a unique name.

5. The sequence of columns (left to right) is insignificant. The columns of a relation can be interchanged without changing the meaning or use of the relation.

6. The sequence of rows (top to bottom) is insignificant. As with columns, the rows of a relation may be interchanged or stored in any sequence.

Removing Multivalued Attributes from Tables   The second property of relations above states that there can be no multivalued attributes in a relation. Thus a table that contains one or more multivalued attributes is not a relation. As an example, Figure 6-2a shows the employee data from the EMPLOYEE1 relation extended to include courses that may have been taken by those employees. Since a given employee may have taken more than one course, the attributes Course_Title and Date_Completed are multivalued attributes. For example, the employee with Emp_ID 100 has taken two courses. If an employee has not taken any courses, the Course_Title and Date_Completed attribute values are null (see employee with Emp_ID 190 for an example).

We show how to eliminate the multivalued attributes in Figure 6-2b by filling the relevant data values into the previously vacant cells of Figure 6-2a. As a result, the table in Figure 6-2b has only single-valued attributes and now satisfies the atomic property of relations. The name EMPLOYEE2 is given to this relation to distinguish it from EMPLOYEE1. However, as you will see below, this new relation does have some undesirable properties.

Figure 6-2
Eliminating multivalued attributes

(a) Table with repeating groups

Emp_ID	Name	Dept_Name	Salary	Course_Title	Date_Completed
100	Margaret Simpson	Marketing	48,000	SPSS	6/19/199X
				Surveys	10/7/199X
140	Alan Beeton	Accounting	52,000	Tax Acc	12/8/199X
110	Chris Lucero	Info Systems	43,000	SPSS	1/12/199X
				C++	4/22/199X
190	Lorenzo Davis	Finance	55,000		
150	Susan Martin	Marketing	42,000	SPSS	6/16/199X
				Java	8/12/199X

(b) EMPLOYEE2 relation

EMPLOYEE2

Emp_ID	Name	Dept_Name	Salary	Course_Title	Date_Completed
100	Margaret Simpson	Marketing	48,000	SPSS	6/19/199X
100	Margaret Simpson	Marketing	48,000	Surveys	10/7/199X
140	Alan Beeton	Accounting	52,000	Tax Acc	12/8/199X
110	Chris Lucero	Info Systems	43,000	SPSS	1/12/199X
110	Chris Lucero	Info Systems	43,000	C++	4/22/199X
190	Lorenzo Davis	Finance	55,000		
150	Susan Martin	Marketing	42,000	SPSS	6/19/199X
150	Susan Martin	Marketing	42,000	Java	8/12/199X

Example Database

A relational database consists of any number of relations. The structure of the database is described through the use of a conceptual schema (defined in Chapter 2), which is a description of the overall logical structure of the database. There are two common methods for expressing a (conceptual) schema:

a. Short text statements, in which each relation is named and the names of its attributes follow in parentheses (see EMPLOYEE1 and DEPARTMENT relations defined earlier in this chapter).

b. A graphical representation, in which each relation is represented by a rectangle containing the attributes for the relation.

Text statements have the advantage of simplicity. On the other hand, a graphical representation provides a better means of expressing referential integrity constraints (as you will see shortly). In this section we use both techniques for expressing a schema so that you can compare them.

Figure 6-3
Schema for four relations
(Pine Valley Furniture)

We developed an entity-relationship diagram for Pine Valley Furniture in Chapter 3 (see Figure 3-21). In Chapter 1 we showed the following four relations from this database (see Figure 1-4): CUSTOMER, ORDER, ORDER LINE, and PRODUCT. In this section we show a schema for these four relations. A graphical representation is shown in Figure 6-3.

Following is a text description for the relations:

CUSTOMER(Customer_ID,Customer_Name,Address,City,State,Zip)
ORDER(Order_ID,Order_Date,Customer_ID)
ORDER LINE(Order_ID,Product_ID,Quantity)
PRODUCT(Product_ID,Product_Description,Product_Finish,Unit_Price,On_Hand)

Notice that the primary key for ORDER LINE is a composite key consisting of the attributes Order_ID and Product_ID. Also Customer_ID is a foreign key in the ORDER relation; this allows the user to associate an order with the customer who submitted the order. ORDER LINE has two foreign keys: Order_ID, and Product_ID. These keys allow the user to associate each line on an order with the relevant order and product.

An instance of this database is shown in Figure 6-4. This figure shows four tables with sample data. Notice how the foreign keys allow us to associate the various tables. It is a good idea to create an instance of your relational schema with sample data for three reasons:

1. The sample data provide a convenient way to check the accuracy of your design.

2. The sample data help improve communications with users in discussing your design.

3. You can use the sample data to develop prototype applications and to test queries.

Figure 6-4
Instance of a relational schema

INTEGRITY CONSTRAINTS

The relational data model includes several types of constraints whose purpose is to facilitate maintaining the accuracy and integrity of data in the database. The major types of integrity constraints are domain constraints, entity integrity, referential integrity, and operational constraints.

Domain Constraints

All of the values that appear in a column of a relation must be taken from the same domain. A domain is the set of values that may be assigned to an attribute (domains were introduced in Chapter 4). A domain definition usually consists of the following components: domain name, meaning, data type, size (or length), and allowable values or allowable range (if applicable). Table 6-1 shows domain definitions for the domains associated with the attributes in Figure 6-3.

Entity Integrity

The entity integrity rule is designed to assure that every relation has a primary key, and that the data values for that primary key are all valid. In particular, it guarantees that every primary key attribute is non-null.

In some cases a particular attribute cannot be assigned a data value. There are two situations where this is likely to occur: Either there is no applicable data value, or the applicable data value is not known when values are assigned. Suppose for example that you fill out an employment form that has a space reserved for a fax number. If you have no fax number, you leave this space empty since it does not apply to you. Or suppose that you are asked to fill in the telephone number of your previous

Table 6-1 Domain Definitions for Selected Attributes

Attribute	Domain Name	Description	Domain
Customer_ID	Customer_IDs	Set of all possible customer IDs	character: size 5
Customer_Name	Customer_Names	Set of all possible customer names	character: size 25
Customer_Address	Customer_Addresses	Set of all possible customer addresses	character: size 30
Order_ID	Order_IDs	Set of all possible order IDs	character: size 5
Order_Date	Order_Dates	Set of all possible order dates	date format mm-dd-yy
Product_ID	Product_IDs	Set of all possible product IDs	character: size 5
Product_Description	Product_Descriptions	Set of all possible product descriptions	character size 25
Product_Finish	Product_Finishes	Set of all possible product finishes	character: size 12
Unit_Price	Unit_Prices	Set of all possible unit prices	monetary: 6 digits
On_Hand	On_Hands	Set of all possible on hands	integer: 3 digits

employer. If you do not recall this number, you may leave it empty since that information is not known.

The relational data model allows us to assign a null value to an attribute in the just described situations. A **null** is a value that may be assigned to an attribute when no other value applies, or when the applicable value is unknown. In reality, a null is not a value but rather the absence of a value. For example, it is not the same as a numeric zero or a string of blanks. The inclusion of nulls in the relational model is somewhat controversial, since it sometimes leads to anomalous results (Date, 1995). On the other hand, Codd advocates the use of nulls for missing values (Codd, 1990).

One thing on which everyone agrees is that primary key values must not be allowed to be null. Thus the **entity integrity rule** states the following: No primary key attribute (or component of a primary key attribute) may be null.

Null: A value that may be assigned to an attribute when no other value applies, or when the applicable value is unknown.

Entity integrity rule: No primary key attribute (or component of a primary key attribute) can be null.

Referential Integrity

In the relational data model, associations between tables are defined through the use of foreign keys. For example in Figure 6-4, the association between the CUSTOMER and ORDER tables is defined by including the Customer_ID attribute as a foreign key in ORDER. This of course implies that before we insert a new row in the ORDER table, the customer for that order must already exist in the CUSTOMER table. If you examine the rows in the ORDER table in Figure 6-4, you will find that every customer number for an order already appears in the CUSTOMER table.

A **referential integrity constraint** is a rule that maintains consistency among the rows of two relations. The rule states that if there is a foreign key in one relation, either each foreign key value must match a primary key value in the other relation or else the foreign key value must be null. You should examine the tables in Figure 6-4 to check whether the referential integrity rule has been enforced.

The graphical version of the relational schema provides a simple technique for identifying associations where referential integrity must be enforced. Figure 6-5 shows the schema for the relations introduced in Figure 6-3. An arrow has been

Referential integrity constraint: A rule that states that either each foreign key value must match a primary key value in the other relation or else the foreign key value must be null.

Figure 6-5
Referential integrity
constraints (Pine
Valley Furniture)

drawn from each foreign key to the associated primary key. A referential integrity constraint must be defined for each of these arrows in the schema.

Operational Constraints

In Chapter 4 we discussed business rules and introduced a new category of business rules we called operational constraints. For example, a typical operational constraint might state the following: "A person may purchase a ticket for the all-star game only if that person is a season-ticket holder." There are various techniques for defining and enforcing such rules. We discuss some of these techniques in later chapters.

Creating Relational Tables

In this section we create table definitions for the four tables shown in Figure 6-5. These definitions are created using **CREATE TABLE** statements from the SQL data definition language. In practice, these table definitions are actually created during the implementation phase later in the database development process. However, we show these sample tables in this chapter for continuity and especially to illustrate the way the integrity constraints described above are implemented in SQL.

The SQL table definitions are shown in Figure 6-6. One table is created for each of the four tables shown in the relational schema (Figure 6-5). Each attribute for a table is then defined. Notice that the data type and length for each attribute is taken from the domain definitions (Table 6-1). For example, the attribute Customer_Name in the CUSTOMER relation is defined as VARCHAR (variable character) data type with

```
CREATE TABLE CUSTOMER
                (CUSTOMER_ID            VARCHAR(5)      NOT NULL,
                 CUSTOMER_NAME          VARCHAR(25)     NOT NULL,
                 CUSTOMER ADDRESS       VARCHAR(30)     NOT NULL,
PRIMARY KEY (CUSTOMER_ID));

CREATE TABLE ORDER
                (ORDER_ID               CHAR(5)         NOT NULL,
                 ORDER DATE             DATE            NOT NULL,
                 CUSTOMER_ID            VARCHAR(5)      NOT NULL,
PRIMARY KEY (ORDER_ID),
FOREIGN KEY (CUSTOMER_ID) REFERENCES CUSTOMER (CUSTOMER_ID));

CREATE TABLE ORDER_LINE
                (ORDER_ID               CHAR(5)         NOT NULL,
                 PRODUCT_ID             CHAR(5)         NOT NULL,
                 QUANTITY               INT             NOT NULL,
PRIMARY KEY (ORDER_ID, PRODUCT_ID),
FOREIGN KEY (ORDER_ID) REFERENCES ORDER (ORDER_ID),
FOREIGN KEY (PRODUCT_ID) REFERENCES PRODUCT (PRODUCT_ID));

CREATE TABLE PRODUCT
                (PRODUCT_ID             CHAR(5)         NOT NULL,
                 PRODUCT_DESCRIPTION    VARCHAR(25),
                 PRODUCT_FINISH         VARCHAR(12),
                 UNIT_PRICE             DECIMAL(8,2)    NOT NULL,
                 ON_HAND                INT             NOT NULL,
PRIMARY KEY (PRODUCT_ID));
```

Figure 6-6
SQL table definitions

length 25. By specifying **NOT NULL**, each attribute can be constrained from being assigned a null value.

The primary key for each table is specified for each table using the **PRIMARY KEY** clause at the end of each table definition. The ORDER_LINE table illustrates how to specify a primary key when that key is a composite attribute. In this example, the primary key of ORDER_LINE is the combination of Order_ID and Product_ID. Each primary key attribute in the four tables is constrained with **NOT NULL**. This enforces the entity integrity constraint described in the previous section. Notice that the **NOT NULL** constraint can also be used with non–primary key attributes.

Referential integrity constraints are easily defined, using the graphical schema shown in Figure 6-5. An arrow originates from each foreign key and "points to" the related primary key in the associated relation. In the SQL table definition, a **FOREIGN KEY REFERENCES** statement corresponds to each of these arrows. Thus for the table ORDER, the foreign key CUSTOMER_ID references the primary key of CUS-TOMER, which is also CUSTOMER_ID. Although in this case the foreign key and primary keys have the same name, this need not be the case. For example, the foreign key attribute could be named CUST_NO instead of CUSTOMER_ID. However, the foreign and primary keys must be from the *same* domain.

The ORDER_LINE table provides an example of a table that has two foreign keys. Foreign keys in this table reference both the ORDER and PRODUCT tables.

Well-Structured Relations

To prepare for our discussion of normalization, we need to address the following question: What constitutes a well-structured relation? Intuitively, a **well-structured relation** contains minimal redundancy and allows users to insert, modify, and delete the rows in a table without errors or inconsistencies. EMPLOYEE1 (Figure 6-1) is such a relation. Each row of the table contains data describing one employee, and any modification to an employee's data (such as a change in salary) is confined to one row of the table. In contrast, EMPLOYEE2 (Figure 6-2b) is not a well-structured relation. If you examine the sample data in the table, you will notice considerable redundancy. For example, values for Emp_ID, Name, Dept_Name, and Salary appear in two separate rows for employees 100, 110, and 150. Consequently, if the salary for employee 100 changes, we must record this fact in two rows (or more, for some employees).

Redundancies in a table may result in errors or inconsistencies (called **anomalies**) when a user attempts to update the data in the table. Three types of anomalies are possible: insertion, deletion, and modification.

1. *Insertion anomaly* Suppose that we need to add a new employee to EMPLOYEE2. The primary key for this relation is the combination of Emp_ID and Course_Title (as noted earlier). Therefore, to insert a new row, the user must supply values for both Emp_ID and Course_Title (since primary key values cannot be null or nonexistent). This is an anomaly, since the user should be able to enter employee data without supplying course data.

2. *Deletion anomaly* Suppose that the data for employee number 140 are deleted from the table. This will result in losing the information that this employee completed a course (Tax Acc) on 12/8/199x. In fact, it results in losing the information that this course had an offering that completed on that date.

3. *Modification anomaly* Suppose that employee number 100 gets a salary increase. We must record the increase in each of the rows for that employee (two occurrences in Figure 6-2); otherwise the data will be inconsistent.

These anomalies indicate that EMPLOYEE2 is not a well-structured relation. The problem with this relation is that it contains data about two entities: EMPLOYEE and COURSE. We will use normalization theory (described below) to divide EMPLOYEE2 into two relations. One of the resulting relations is EMPLOYEE1 (Figure 6-1). The other we will call EMP_COURSE, which appears with sample data in Figure 6-7. The primary key of this relation is the combination of Emp_ID and Course_Title, and we underline these attribute names in Figure 6-7 to highlight this fact. Examine Figure 6-7 to verify that EMP_COURSE is free of the types of anomalies described above and is therefore well-structured.

Well-structured relation: A relation that contains minimal redundancy and allows users to insert, modify, and delete the rows in a table without errors or inconsistencies.

Anomalies: Errors or inconsistencies that may result when a user attempts to update a table that contains redundant data. There are three types of anomalies: insertion, deletion, and modification anomalies.

Emp_ID	Course_Title	Date_Completed
100	SPSS	6/19/199X
100	Surveys	10/7/199X
140	Tax Acc	12/8/199X
110	SPSS	1/12/199X
110	C++	4/22/199X
150	SPSS	6/19/199X
150	Java	8/12/199X

Figure 6-7
EMP_COURSE

TRANSFORMING EER DIAGRAMS INTO RELATIONS

During logical design you transform the E-R (and EER) diagrams that were developed during conceptual design into relational database schemas. The inputs to this process are the entity-relationship (and enhanced E-R) diagrams that you studied in Chapters 3 and 4. The outputs are the relational schemas described in the first two sections of this chapter.

Transforming (or mapping) E-R diagrams to relations is a relatively straightforward process with a well-defined set of rules. In fact, many CASE tools can automatically perform many of the conversion steps. However, it is important that you understand the steps in this process for three reasons:

1. CASE tools often cannot model more complex data relationships such as ternary relationships and supertype/subtype relationships. For these situations you may have to perform the steps manually.

2. There are sometimes legitimate alternatives where you will need to choose a particular solution.

3. You must be prepared to perform a quality check on the results obtained with a CASE tool.

In the following discussion we illustrate the steps in the transformation with examples taken from Chapters 3 and 4. It will help for you to recall that we discussed three types of entities in those chapters:

1. *Regular entities* are entities that have an independent existence and generally represent real-world objects such as persons and products. Regular entity types are represented by rectangles with a single line.

2. *Weak entities* are entities that cannot exist except with an identifying relationship with an owner (regular) entity type. Weak entities are identified by a rectangle with a double line.

Figure 6-8
Mapping the regular entity CUSTOMER

(a) CUSTOMER entity type

(b) CUSTOMER relation

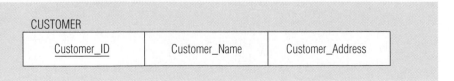

Figure 6-9 Mapping a composite attribute

(a) CUSTOMER entity type with composite attribute

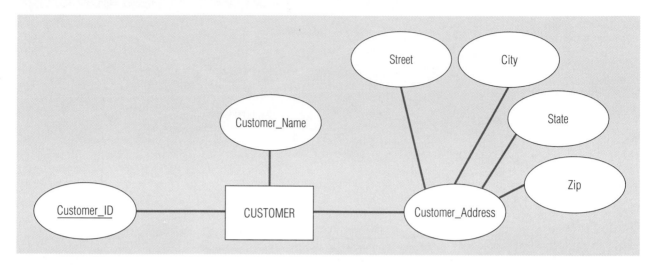

(b) CUSTOMER relation with address detail

CUSTOMER

Customer_ID	Customer_Name	Street	City	State	Zip

3. *Associative entities* (also called gerunds) are formed from many-to-many relationships between other entity types. Associative entities are represented by a rectangle with a single line that encloses the diamond relationship symbol.

Step 1: Map Regular Entities

Each regular entity type in an ER diagram is transformed into a relation. The name given to the relation is generally the same as the entity type. Each simple attribute of the entity type becomes an attribute of the relation. The identifier of the entity type becomes the primary key of the corresponding relation. You should check to make sure that this primary key satisfies the desirable properties of identifiers outlined in Chapter 3.

Figure 6-8a shows a representation of the CUSTOMER entity type for Pine Valley Furniture Company from Chapter 3 (see Figure 3-21). The corresponding CUSTOMER relation is shown in graphical form in Figure 6-8b. In this figure and those that follow in this section we show only a few key attributes for each relation to simplify the figures.

Composite Attributes   When a regular entity type has a composite attribute, only the simple component attributes of the composite attribute are included in the new relation. Figure 6-9 shows a variation on the example of Figure 6-8, where

Figure 6-10
Mapping an entity with a multivalued attribute

(a) Employee entity type with multivalued attribute

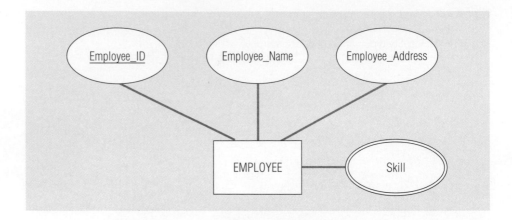

(b) Mapping a multivalued attribute

Customer_Address is represented as a composite attribute with components Street, City, State, and Zip (see Figure 6-9a). This entity is mapped to the CUSTOMER relation, which contains the simple address attributes, as shown in Figure 6-9b.

Multivalued Attributes When the regular entity type contains a multivalued attribute, two new relations (rather than one) are created. The first relation contains all of the attributes of the entity type except the multivalued attribute. The second relation contains two attributes that form the primary key of the second relation. The first of these attributes is the primary key from the first relation, which becomes a foreign key in the second relation. The second is the multivalued attribute. The name of the second relation should capture the meaning of the multivalued attribute.

An example of this procedure is shown in Figure 6-10. This is the EMPLOYEE entity type for Pine Valley Furniture Company (Figure 3-21). As shown in Figure 6-10a, EMPLOYEE has Skill as a multivalued attribute. Figure 6-10b shows the two relations that are created. The first (called EMPLOYEE) has the primary key Employee_ID. The second relation (called EMPLOYEE_SKILL) has the two attributes Employee_ID and Skill, which form the primary key. The relationship between foreign and primary keys is indicated by the arrow in the figure.

The relation EMPLOYEE_SKILL contains no nonkey attributes (also called *descriptors*). Each row simply records the fact that a particular employee possesses a particular skill. This provides an opportunity for you to suggest to users that new attributes can be added to this relation. For example, the attributes Years_Experience and/or Certification_Date might be appropriate new values to add to this relation.

Figure 6-11
Example of mapping
a weak entity

(a) Weak entity DEPENDENT

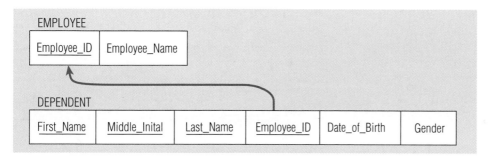

Step 2: Map Weak Entities

Recall that a weak entity type does not have an independent existence, but exists only through an identifying relationship with another entity type called the owner. A weak entity type does not have a complete identifier, but must have an attribute called a partial identifier that permits distinguishing the various occurrences of the weak entity for each owner entity instance.

The following procedure assumes that you have already created a relation corresponding to the owner entity type during Step 1. If you have not, you should create that relation now using the process described in Step 1.

For each weak entity type, create a new relation and include all of the simple attributes (or simple components of composite attributes) as attributes of this relation. Then include the primary key of the *owner* relation as a foreign key attribute in this new relation. The primary key of the new relation is the combination of this primary key of the owner and the partial identifier of the weak entity type.

An example of this process is shown in Figure 6-11. Figure 6-11a shows the weak entity type DEPENDENT and its owner entity type EMPLOYEE, linked by the identifying relationship Has (see Figure 3-5). Notice that the attribute Dependent_Name, which is the partial identifier for this relation, is a composite attribute with components First_Name, Middle_Initial, and Last_Name. Thus we assume that, *for a given employee,* these items will uniquely identify a dependent (a notable exception being the case of prizefighter George Foreman, who has named all his sons after himself!).

Figure 6-11b shows the two relations that result from mapping this E-R segment. The primary key of DEPENDENT consists of four attributes: Employee_ID,

Figure 6-12
Example of mapping a
1:M relationship

(a) Relationship between
customers and orders

(b) Mapping the relationship

First_Name, Middle_Initial, and Last_Name. Date_of_Birth and Gender are the nonkey attributes. The foreign key relationship with its primary key is indicated by the arrow in the figure.

Step 3: Map Binary Relationships

The procedure for representing relationships depends on both the degree of the relationships (unary, binary, ternary) and the cardinalities of the relationships. We describe and illustrate the important cases in the following discussion.

Map Binary One-to-Many Relationships For each binary 1:M relationship, first create a relation for each of the two entity types participating in the relationship,

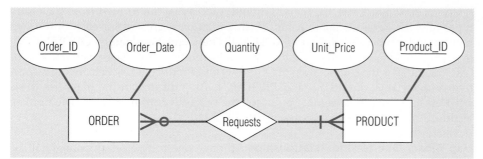

Figure 6-13
Example of mapping an
M:N relationship

(a) Requests relationship
(M:N)

(b) Three resulting relations

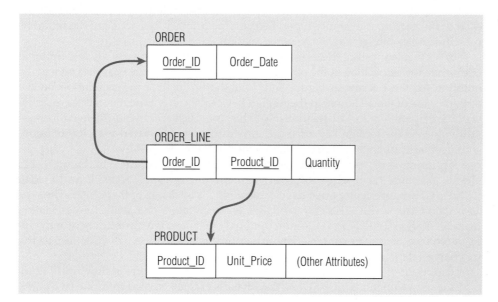

using the procedure described in Step 1. Next, include the primary key attribute (or attributes) of the entity on the one-side of the relationship as a foreign key in the relation that is on the many-side of the relationship (a mnemonic you can use to remember this rule is this: The primary key <u>m</u>igrates to the <u>m</u>any side).

To illustrate this simple process, we use the Submits relationship between customers and orders for Pine Valley Furniture Company (see Figure 3-21). This 1:M relationship is illustrated in Figure 6-12a. Figure 6-12b shows the result of applying the above rule to map the entity types with the 1:M relationship. The primary key Customer_ID of CUSTOMER (the one-side) is included as a foreign key in ORDER (the many-side). The foreign key relationship is indicated with an arrow.

Map Binary Many-to-Many Relationships   Suppose that there is a binary many-to-many (M:N) relationship between two entity types A and B. For such a relationship, we create a new relation C. Include as foreign key attributes in C the primary key for each of the two participating entity types. These attributes become the primary key of C. Any nonkey attributes that are associated with the M:N relationship are included with the relation C.

Figure 6-13 shows an example of applying this rule. Figure 6-13a shows the Requests relationship between the entity types ORDER and PRODUCT for Pine Valley Furniture Company (introduced in Figure 3-22b). Figure 6-13b shows the three relations (ORDER, PRODUCT, and ORDER_LINE) that are formed from the entity types and the Requests relationship. First, a relation is created for each of the two regular entity types ORDER and PRODUCT. Then a relation (named ORDER_LINE in Figure 6-13b) is created for the Requests relationship. The primary key of ORDER_LINE is the combination of Order_ID and Product_ID, which are the respective primary keys of ORDER and PRODUCT. As indicated in the diagram, these attributes are foreign keys that "point to" the respective primary keys. The nonkey attribute QUANTITY also appears in ORDER_LINE.

Map Binary One-to-One Relationships   Binary one-to-one relationships can be viewed as a special case of one-to-many relationships. The process of mapping such a relationship to relations requires two steps. First two relations are created, one for each of the participating entity types. Second, the primary key of one of the relations is included as a foreign key in the other relation.

In a 1:1 relationship, the association in one direction is nearly always optional one, while the association in the other direction is mandatory one (you can review the notation for these terms in Figure 3-1). You should include in the relation on the optional side of the relationship the foreign key of the entity type that has the mandatory participation in the 1:1 relationship. This approach will avoid the need to store null values in the foreign key attribute. Any attributes associated with the relationship itself are also included in the same relation as the foreign key.

An example of applying this procedure is shown in Figure 6-14. Figure 6-14a shows a binary 1:1 relationship between the entity types NURSE and CARE CENTER. Each care center must have a nurse who is in charge of that center. Thus the association from CARE CENTER to NURSE is a mandatory one, while the association from NURSE to CARE CENTER is an optional one (since any nurse may or may not be in charge of a care center). The attribute Date_Assigned is attached to the In_charge relationship.

The result of mapping this relationship to a set of relations is shown in Figure 6-14b. The two relations NURSE and CARE CENTER are created from the two entity types. Since CARE CENTER is the optional participant, the foreign key is placed in this relation. In this case the foreign key is called Nurse_in_Charge. It has the same domain as Nurse_ID, and the relationship with the primary key is shown in the figure. The attribute Date_Assigned is also located in CARE CENTER.

Step 4: Map Associative Entities

As explained in Chapter 3, when the data modeler encounters a many-to-many relationship, he or she may choose to model that relationship as an associative entity in the E-R diagram. This approach is most appropriate when the end user can best visualize the relationship as an entity type rather than as an M:N relationship. Mapping the associative entity involves essentially the same steps as mapping an M:N relationship, as described in Step 3.

The first step is to create three relations: one for each of the two participating entity types, and the third for the associative entity. We refer to the relation formed from the associative entity as the *associative relation*. The second step then depends on whether on the E-R diagram an identifier was assigned to the associative entity.

Identifier Not Assigned   If an identifier was not assigned, the default primary key for the associative relation consists of the two primary key attributes from the other two relations. These attributes are then foreign keys that reference the other two relations.

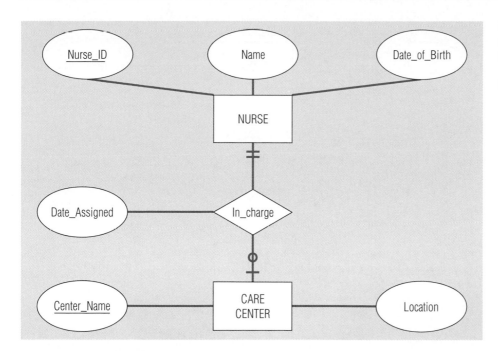

Figure 6-14
Mapping a binary 1:1
relationship

(a) Binary 1:1 relationship

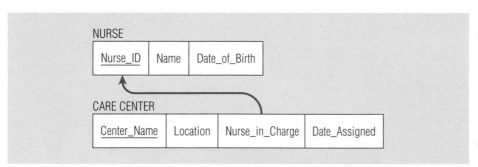

(b) Resulting relations

An example of this case is shown in Figure 6-15. Figure 6-15a shows the associative entity ORDER LINE that links the ORDER and PRODUCT entity types at Pine Valley Furniture Company (see Figure 3-21). Figure 6-15b shows the three relations that result from this mapping. Note the similarity of this example to that of an M:N relationship shown in Figure 6-13.

Identifier Assigned Sometimes the data modeler will assign an identifier (called a *surrogate* identifier or key) to the associative entity type on the E-R diagram. There are two reasons that may motivate this approach:

1. The associative entity type has a natural identifier that is familiar to end users.

2. The default identifier (consisting of the identifiers for each of the participating entity types) may not uniquely identify instances of the associative entity.

The process for mapping the associative entity in this case is now modified as follows. As before, a new (associative) relation is created to represent the associative entity. However, the primary key for this relation is the identifier assigned on the E-R diagram (rather than the default key). The primary keys for the two participating entity types are then included as foreign keys in the associative relation.

Figure 6-15
Mapping an associative entity

(a) An associative entity

(b) Three resulting relations

An example of this process is shown in Figure 6-16. Figure 6-16a shows the associative entity type SHIPMENT that links the CUSTOMER and VENDOR entity types. Shipment_No has been chosen as the identifier for SHIPMENT, for two reasons:

1. Shipment_No is a natural identifier for this entity that is very familiar to end users.

2. The default identifier consisting of the combination of Customer_ID and Vendor_ID does not uniquely identify the instances of SHIPMENT. In fact, a given vendor will make many shipments to a given customer. Even including the attribute Date does not guarantee uniqueness, since there may be more

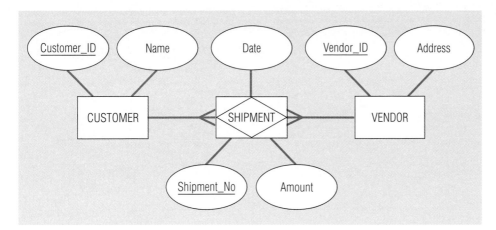

Figure 6-16
Mapping an associative entity with an identifier

(a) Associative entity (SHIPMENT)

(b) Three relations

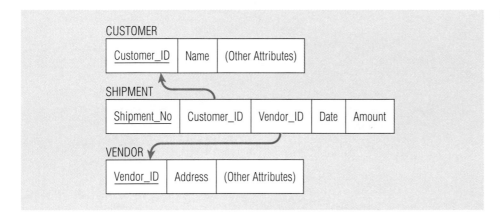

than one shipment by a particular vendor on a given date, but the surrogate key Shipment_No will uniquely identify each shipment.

Two nonkey attributes associated with SHIPMENT are Date and Amount.

The result of mapping this entity to a set of relations is shown in Figure 6-16b. The new associative relation is named SHIPMENT. The primary key is Shipment_No. Customer_ID and Vendor_ID are included as foreign keys in this relation, and Date and Amount are nonkey attributes.

Step 5: Map Unary Relationships

In Chapter 4 we defined a unary relationship as a relationship between the instances of a single entity type. Unary relationships are also called recursive relationships. The two most important cases of unary relationships are one-to-many and many-to-many. We discuss these two cases separately since the approach to mapping is somewhat different for the two types.

Unary One-to-Many Relationships   The entity type in the unary relationship is mapped to a relation using the procedure described in Step 1. Then a foreign key attribute is added *within* the same relation that references the primary key values (this

Figure 6-17
Mapping a unary 1:N
relationship

(a) EMPLOYEE entity with
Manages relationship

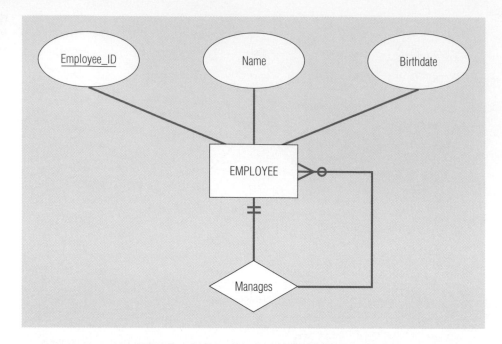

(b) EMPLOYEE relation with
recursive foreign key

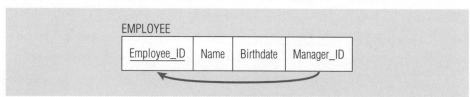

Recursive foreign key: A
foreign key in a relation that
references the primary key
values of that same relation.

foreign key must have the same domain as the primary key). A **recursive foreign key**
is a foreign key in a relation that references the primary key values of that same
relation.

Figure 6-17a shows a unary one-to-many relationship named Manages that associates each employee of an organization with another employee who is his or her
manager. Each employee has exactly one manager; a given employee may manage
zero to many employees.

The EMPLOYEE relation that results from mapping this entity and relationship
is shown in Figure 6-17b. The (recursive) foreign key in the relation is named
Manager_ID. This attribute has the same domain as the primary key Employee_ID.
Each row of this relation stores the following data for a given employee:
Employee_ID, Name, Birthdate, and Manager_ID (that is, the Employee_ID for this
employee's manager). Notice that since it is a foreign key, Manager_ID references
Employee_ID.

Unary Many-to-Many Relationships   With this type of relationship, two relations
are created: one to represent the entity type in the relationship and the other an associative relation to represent the M:N relationship itself. The primary key of the associative relation consists of two attributes. These attributes (which need not have the
same name) both take their values from the primary key of the other relation. Any
nonkey attribute of the relationship is included in the associative relation.

An example of mapping a unary M:N relationship is shown in Figure 6-18.
Figure 6-18a shows a bill-of-materials relationship among items that are assembled

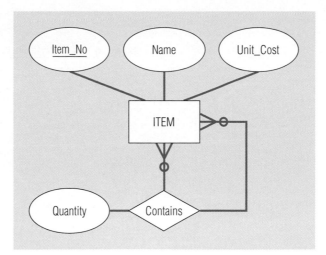

Figure 6-18
Mapping a unary M:N relationship

(a) Bill-of-materials relationships (M:N)

(b) ITEM and COMPONENT relations

from other items or components (this structure was described in Chapter 3 and an example appears in Figure 3-13). The relationship (called Contains) is M:N since a given item can contain numerous component items, and conversely an item can be used as a component in numerous other items.

The relations that result from mapping this entity and its relationship are shown in Figure 6-18b. The ITEM relation is mapped directly from the same entity type. COMPONENT is an associative relation whose primary key consists of two attributes that are arbitrarily named Item_No and Component_No. The attribute Quantity is a non-key attribute of this relation that for a given item, records the quantity of a particular component item used in that item. Notice that both Item_No and Component_No reference the primary key (Item_No) of the ITEM relation.

We can easily query the above relations to determine (for example) the components of a given item. The following SQL query will list the immediate components (and their quantity) for item number 100:

```
SELECT Component_No, Quantity
FROM COMPONENT
WHERE Item_No = 100;
```

Step 6: Map Ternary (and *n*-ary) Relationships

Recall from Chapter 3 that a ternary relationship is a relationship among three entity types. In that chapter we recommended that you convert a ternary relationship to an associative entity in order to represent participation constraints more accurately.

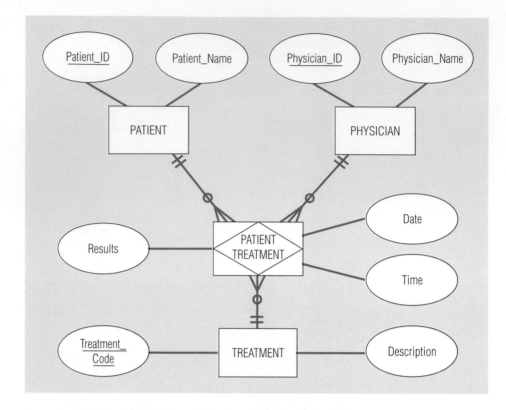

To map an associative entity type that links three regular entity types, we create a new associative relation. The default primary key of this relation consists of the three primary key attributes for the participating entity types (in some cases, additional attributes are required to form a unique primary key). These attributes then act in the role of foreign keys that reference the individual primary keys of the participating entity types. Any attributes of the associative entity type become attributes of the new relation.

An example of mapping a ternary relationship (represented as an associative entity type) is shown in Figure 6-19. Figure 6-19a is an E-R segment (or view) that represents a *patient* receiving a *treatment* from a *physician*. The associative entity type PATIENT TREATMENT has the attributes Date, Time, and Results; values are recorded for these attributes for each instance of PATIENT TREATMENT.

The result of mapping this view is shown in Figure 6-19b. The primary key attributes Patient_ID, Physician_ID, and Treatment_Code become foreign keys in PATIENT TREATMENT. These attributes are components of the primary key of PATIENT TREATMENT. However, they do not uniquely identify a given treatment, since a patient may receive the same treatment from the same physician on more than one occasion. Does including the attribute Date as part of the primary key (along with the other three attributes) result in a primary key? This would be so if a given patient receives only one treatment from a particular physician on a given date. However, this is not likely to be the case. For example, a patient may receive a treatment in the morning, then the same treatment in the afternoon. To resolve this issue, we include Time as part of the primary key. Therefore, the primary key of PATIENT TREATMENT consists of the five attributes shown in Figure 6-19b: Patient_ID, Physician_ID, Treatment_Code, Date, and Time. The only nonkey attribute in the relation is Results.

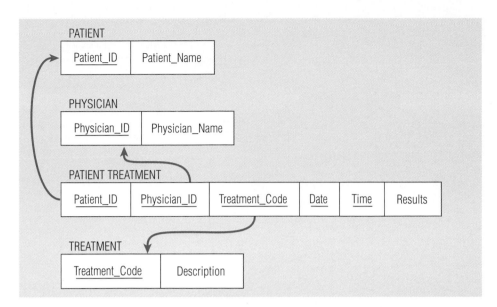

Step 7: Map Supertype/Subtype Relationships

The relational data model does not yet directly support supertype/subtype relationships. Fortunately, there are various strategies that database designers can use to represent these relationships with the relational data model (Chouinard, 1989). For our purposes we use the following strategy, which is the one most commonly employed:

1. Create a separate relation for the supertype and for each of its subtypes.

2. Assign to the relation created for the supertype the attributes that are common to all members of the supertype, including the primary key.

3. Assign to the relation for each subtype the primary key of the supertype, and only those attributes that are unique to that subtype.

4. Assign one (or more) attributes of the supertype to function as the subtype discriminator (the role of the subtype discriminator was discussed in Chapter 4).

An example of applying this procedure is shown in Figures 6-20 and 6-21. Figure 6-20 shows the supertype EMPLOYEE with subtypes HOURLY EMPLOYEE, SALARIED EMPLOYEE, and CONSULTANT (this example is described in Chapter 4, and Figure 6-20 is a repeat of Figure 4-8). The primary key of EMPLOYEE is Employee_Number, and the attribute Employee_Type is the subtype discriminator.

The result of mapping this diagram to relations using the above rules is shown in Figure 6-21. There is one relation for the supertype (EMPLOYEE) and one for each of the three subtypes. The primary key for each of the four relations is Employee_Number. A prefix is used to distinguish the name of the primary key for each subtype. For example, S_Employee_Number is the name for the primary key of the relation SALARIED_EMPLOYEE. Each of these attributes is a foreign key that references the supertype primary key, as indicated by the arrows in the diagram. Each subtype relation contains only those attributes peculiar to the subtype.

For each subtype, a relation can be produced that contains *all* of the attributes of that subtype (both specific and inherited) by using an SQL command that joins the subtype with its supertype. For example, suppose that we want to display a table

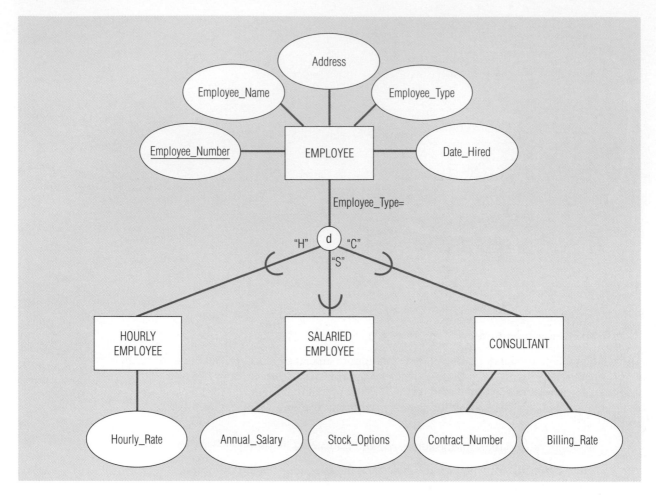

Figure 6-20
Supertype/subtype
relationships

that contains all of the attributes for SALARIED_EMPLOYEE. The following command is used:

```
SELECT *
FROM EMPLOYEE, SALARIED_EMPLOYEE
WHERE Employee_Number = S_Employee_Number;
```

Although you have not yet formally studied such commands, you can intuitively see that this command will join the two tables and produce a larger table that contains all of the attributes from both tables.

INTRODUCTION TO NORMALIZATION

Normalization is a formal process for deciding which attributes should be grouped together in a relation. In Chapters 3 and 4 you used common sense to group attributes into entity types during conceptual data modeling. In the previous section of this chapter you learned how to map E-R diagrams to relations. Before proceeding with physical design, we need a method to validate the logical design to this point.

Figure 6-21
Mapping supertype/subtype relationships to relations

Normalization is primarily a tool to validate and improve a logical design, so that it satisfies certain constraints that avoid unnecessary duplication of data.

We have presented an intuitive discussion of well-structured relations; however, we need formal definitions of such relations, together with a process for designing them. **Normalization** is the process of decomposing relations with anomalies to produce smaller, well-structured relations. For example, we used the principles of normalization to convert the EMPLOYEE2 table (with its redundancy) to EMPLOYEE1 (Figure 6-1) and EMP_COURSE (Figure 6-7).

Normalization: The process of decomposing relations with anomalies to produce smaller, well-structured relations.

Steps in Normalization

Normalization can be accomplished and understood in stages, each of which corresponds to a normal form (see Figure 6-22). A **normal form** is a state of a relation that results from applying simple rules regarding functional dependencies (or relationships between attributes) to that relation. We describe these rules briefly in this section and illustrate them in detail in the following sections.

Normal form: A state of a relation that results from applying simple rules regarding functional dependencies (or relationships between attributes) to that relation.

1. *First normal form* Any multivalued attributes (also called repeating groups) have been removed, so there is a single value (possibly null) at the intersection of each row and column of the table (as in Figure 6-2b).

2. *Second normal form* Any partial functional dependencies have been removed.

3. *Third normal form* Any transitive dependencies have been removed.

Figure 6-22
Steps in normalization

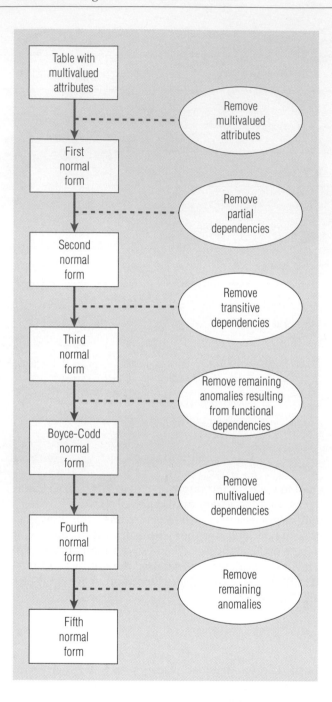

4. *Boyce/Codd normal form*   Any remaining anomalies that result from functional dependencies have been removed.

5. *Fourth normal form*   Any multivalued dependencies have been removed.

6. *Fifth normal form*   Any remaining anomalies have been removed.

We describe and illustrate first through third normal forms in this chapter. The remaining normal forms are described in Appendix B.

Functional Dependencies and Keys

Normalization is based on the analysis of functional dependencies. A **functional dependency** is a constraint between two attributes or two sets of attributes. For any relation R, attribute B is functionally dependent on attribute A if, for every valid instance of A, that value of A uniquely determines the value of B (Dutka and Hanson, 1989). The functional dependency of B on A is represented by an arrow, as follows: A → B. An attribute may be functionally dependent on two (or more) attributes, rather than on a single attribute. For example, consider the relation EMP_COURSE (Emp_ID,Course_Name,Date_Completed) shown in Figure 6-7. We represent the functional dependency in this relation as follows:

> Emp_ID,Course_Name → Date_Completed.

The functional dependency in this statement implies that the date a course is completed is completely determined by the identity of the employee and the name of the course. Common examples of functional dependencies are the following:

1. SSN → Name, Address, Birthdate   A person's name, address, and birthdate are functionally dependent on that person's Social Security number.

2. VIN → Make, Model, Color   The make, model, and color of a vehicle are functionally dependent on the vehicle identification number.

3. ISBN → Title, First_Author_Name   The title of a book and the name of the first author are functionally dependent on the book's international standard book number (ISBN).

Determinants   The attribute on the left-hand side of the arrow in a functional dependency is called a **determinant**. SSN, VIN, and ISBN are determinants (respectively) in the preceding three examples. In the EMP_COURSE relation (Figure 6-7) the combination of Emp_ID and Course_Name is a determinant.

Candidate Keys   A **candidate key** is an attribute, or combination of attributes, that uniquely identifies a row in a relation. A candidate key must satisfy the following properties (Dutka and Hanson, 1989), which are a subset of the six properties of a primary key previously listed:

1. *Unique identification*   For every row, the value of the key must uniquely identify that row. *This property implies that each nonkey attribute is functionally dependent on that key.*

2. *Nonredundancy*   No attribute in the key can be deleted without destroying the property of unique identification.

Let's apply the preceding definition to identify candidate keys in two of the relations described in this chapter. The EMPLOYEE1 relation (Figure 6-1) has the following schema: EMPLOYEE1(Emp_ID,Name,Dept_Name,Salary). Emp_ID is the only determinant in this relation. All of the other attributes are functionally dependent on Emp_ID. Therefore Emp_ID is a candidate key and (since there are no other candidate keys) also is the primary key.

We represent the functional dependencies for a relation using the notation shown in Figure 6-23. Figure 6-23a shows the representation for EMPLOYEE1. The horizontal line in the figure portrays the functional dependencies. A vertical line drops from the primary key (Emp_ID) and connects to this line. Vertical arrows then point to each of the nonkey attributes that are functionally dependent on the primary key.

Functional dependency: A constraint between two attributes or two sets of attributes.

Determinant: The attribute on the left-hand side of the arrow in a functional dependency.

Candidate key: An attribute, or combination of attributes, that uniquely identifies a row in a relation.

Figure 6-23
Representing functional dependencies

(a) Functional dependencies in EMPLOYEE1

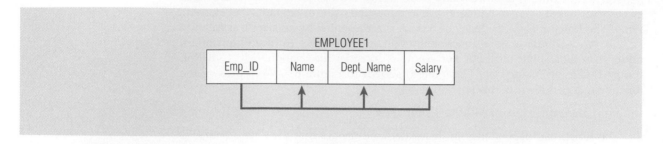

(b) Functional dependencies in EMPLOYEE2

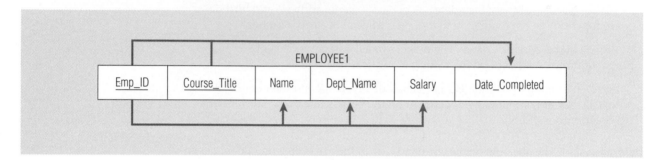

For the relation EMPLOYEE2 (Figure 6-2b), notice that (unlike EMPLOYEE1), Emp_ID does not uniquely identify a row in the relation. For example, there are two rows in the table for Emp_ID number 100. There are two functional dependencies in this relation:

1. Emp_ID → Name, Dept_Name, Salary

2. Emp_ID, Course_Title → Date_Completed

The functional dependencies indicate that the combination of Emp_ID and Course_Title is the only candidate key (and therefore the primary key) for EMPLOYEE2. In other words, the primary key of EMPLOYEE2 is a composite key. Neither Emp_ID nor Course_Title uniquely identifies a row in this relation, and therefore by property 1 cannot by itself be a candidate key. Examine the data in Figure 6-2b to verify that the combination of Emp_ID and Course_Title does uniquely identify each row of EMPLOYEE2. We represent the functional dependencies in this relation in Figure 6-23b. Notice that Date_Completed is the only attribute that is functionally dependent on the full primary key consisting of the attributes Emp_ID and Course_Title.

We can summarize the relationship between determinants and candidate keys as follows. A candidate key is always a determinant, while a determinant may or may not be a candidate key. For example, in EMPLOYEE2, Emp_ID is a determinant but not a candidate key. A candidate key is a determinant that uniquely identifies the remaining (nonkey) attributes in a relation. A determinant may be a candidate key (such as Emp_ID in EMPLOYEE1), part of a composite candidate key (such as Emp_ID in EMPLOYEE2), or a nonkey attribute. We will describe examples of this shortly.

THE BASIC NORMAL FORMS

Now that we have examined functional dependencies and keys, we are ready to describe and illustrate first through third normal forms. We also describe the normalization of summary data that appear in information bases.

First Normal Form

A relation is in **first normal form** (1NF) if it contains no multivalued attributes. Recall that the first property of a relation is that the value at the intersection of each row and column must be atomic. Thus a table that contains multivalued attributes or repeating groups is not a relation.

First normal form: A relation which contains no multivalued attributes.

In the previous section, in describing how to map E-R diagrams to relations, we described a procedure for removing multivalued attributes from entity types on the E-R diagram. Thus if you developed a logical design by transforming E-R diagrams to relations, there should not be any multivalued attributes remaining. However, many older, legacy systems written in languages such as COBOL supported multivalued attributes. Since you may participate in efforts to convert these older systems to relational databases, it is important that you understand how to eliminate multivalued attributes.

We illustrated a table with repeating groups in Figure 6-2a and then converted it to the relation EMPLOYEE2 in Figure 6-2b by removing the multivalued attributes. Thus EMPLOYEE2 is a relation in first normal form. A table with multivalued attributes is converted to a relation in first normal form by extending the data in each column to fill cells that are empty because of the multivalued attributes.

Second Normal Form

A relation is in **second normal form** (2NF) if it is in first normal form and every nonkey attribute is fully functionally dependent on the primary key. Thus no nonkey attribute is functionally dependent on part (but not all) of the primary key. A relation that is in first normal form will be in second normal form if any one of the following conditions applies:

Second normal form: A relation that is in first normal form and has every nonkey attribute fully functionally dependent on the primary key.

1. The primary key consists of only one attribute (such as the attribute Emp_ID in EMPLOYEE1).

2. No nonkey attributes exist in the relation (thus all of the attributes in the relation are components of the primary key).

3. Every nonkey attribute is functionally dependent on the full set of primary key attributes.

EMPLOYEE2 (Figure 6-2b) is an example of a relation that is not in second normal form. The primary key for this relation is the composite key Emp_ID, Course_Title. Therefore the nonkey attributes Name, Dept_Name, and Salary are functionally dependent on part of the primary key (Emp_ID) but not on Course_Title. These dependencies are shown graphically in Figure 6-23b.

A **partial functional dependency** is a functional dependency in which one or more nonkey attributes (such as Name) are functionally dependent on part (but not all) of the primary key. The partial functional dependency in EMPLOYEE2 creates redundancy in that relation, which results in anomalies when the table is updated as we noted in a previous section.

Partial functional dependency: A functional dependency in which one or more nonkey attributes (such as Name) are functionally dependent on part (but not all) of the primary key.

To convert a relation to second normal form, we decompose the relation into new relations that satisfy one (or more) of the conditions described above. EMPLOYEE2 is decomposed into the following two relations:

1. EMPLOYEE1(Emp_ID,Name,Dept_Name,Salary)   This relation satisfies condition 1 above and is in second normal form (sample data are shown in Figure 6-1).

2. EMP_COURSE(Emp_ID,Course_Title,Date_Completed)   This relation satisfies property 3 above and is also in second normal form (sample data appear in Figure 6-7).

You should examine these new relations to verify that they are free of the anomalies associated with EMPLOYEE2.

Third Normal Form

Third normal form: A relation that is in second normal form and has no transitive dependencies present.

A relation is in **third normal form** (3NF) if it is in second normal form and no transitive dependencies exist. A **transitive dependency** in a relation is a functional dependency between two (or more) nonkey attributes. For example, consider the relation

SALES(Cust_ID,Name,Salesperson,Region)

Transitive dependency: A functional dependency between two (or more) nonkey attributes.

(Sample data for this relation appear in Figure 6-24a.)

The functional dependencies in the SALES relation are shown graphically in Figure 6-24b. Cust_ID is the primary key, so that all of the remaining attributes are

Figure 6-24
Relation with transitive dependency

(a) SALES relation with sample data

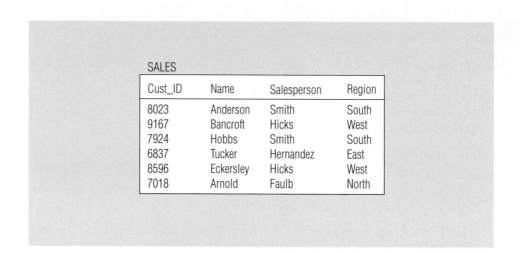

(b) Transitive dependency in SALES relation

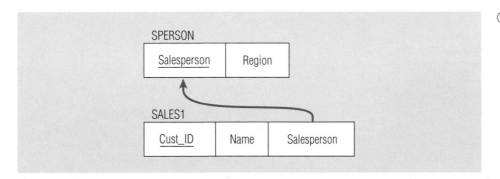

Figure 6-25
Removing a transitive
dependency

(a) Decomposing the
SALES relation

(b) Relations in 3NF

functionally dependent on this attribute. However, there is a transitive dependency (Region is functionally dependent on Salesperson and Salesperson is functionally dependent on Cust_ID). As a result, there are update anomalies in SALES.

1. *Insertion anomaly*   A new salesperson (Robinson) assigned to the North region cannot be entered until a customer has been assigned to that salesperson (since a value for Cust_ID must be provided to insert a row in the table).

2. *Deletion anomaly*   If customer number 6837 is deleted from the table, we lose the information that salesperson Hernandez is assigned to the East region.

3. *Modification anomaly*   If salesperson Smith is reassigned to the East region, several rows must be changed to reflect that fact (two rows are shown in Figure 6-24a).

These anomalies arise as a result of the transitive dependency. The transitive dependency can be removed by decomposing SALES into two relations, as shown in Figure 6-25a. Note that Salesperson, which is the determinant in the transitive dependency in SALES, becomes the primary key in SPERSON. Salesperson becomes a foreign key in SALES1.

As shown in Figure 6-25b, the new relations are now in third normal form, since no transitive dependencies exist. You should verify that the anomalies that exist in SALES are not present in SALES1 and SPERSON.

Transitive dependencies may also occur between sets of attributes in a relation. For example, the relation SHIPMENT(Snum,Origin,Destination,Distance) could be used to record shipments according to origin, destination, and distance (Dutka and Hanson, 1989). Sample data for this relation appear in Figure 6-26a. The functional

Figure 6-26
Another example of transitive dependencies

(a) SHIPMENT relation with sample data

SHIPMENT

Snum	Origin	Destination	Distance
409	Seattle	Denver	1,537
618	Chicago	Dallas	1,058
723	Boston	Atlanta	1,214
824	Denver	Los Angeles	1,150
629	Minneapolis	St. Louis	587

(b) Functional dependencies in SHIPMENT

(c) Relations in 3NF

SHIPTO

Snum	Origin	Destination
409	Seattle	Denver
618	Chicago	Dallas
723	Boston	Atlanta
824	Denver	Los Angeles
629	Minneapolis	St. Louis

DISTANCES

Origin	Destination	Distance
Seattle	Denver	1,537
Chicago	Dallas	1,058
Boston	Atlanta	1,214
Denver	Los Angeles	1,150
Minneapolis	St. Louis	587

dependencies in the SHIPMENT relation are shown in Figure 6-26b. The primary key of the SHIPMENT relation is the attribute Snum (for Shipment Number). As a result, we know that the relation is in second normal form (why?). However, there is a transitive dependency in this relation: the Distance attribute is functionally dependent on the *pair* of nonkey attributes Origin and Destination. As a result there are anomalies in SHIPMENT (as an exercise, you should examine Figure 6-26a and identify insertion, deletion, and modification anomalies). We can remove the transitive dependency in SHIPMENT by decomposing it into two relations (both in 3NF):

SHIPTO(Snum,Origin,Destination)
DISTANCES(Origin,Destination,Distance)

The first of these relations provides the origin and destination for any given shipment, while the second provides the distance between an origin and destination pair. Sample data for these relations appear in Figure 6-26c.

Normalizing Summary Data

Databases to support managerial decision making in an organization often contain subsets and summaries of data from operational databases. These "data warehouses" used to support higher levels of management are often normalized (at least to a certain extent) to avoid the same anomalies that arise in operational databases. We describe the issues associated with normalizing data in data warehouses in Chapter 14.

MERGING RELATIONS

In a previous section, we described how to transform E-R diagrams to relations. We then described how to check the resulting relations to determine whether they are in third normal form, and perform normalization steps if necessary.

As part of the logical design process, normalized relations may have been created from a number of separate E-R diagrams and (possibly) other user views. Some of the relations may be redundant; that is, they may refer to the same entities. If so, we should merge those relations to remove the redundancy. This section describes merging relations (also called *view integration*). An understanding of how to merge relations is important for three reasons:

1. On large projects, the work of several subteams comes together during logical design, so there is a need to merge relations.

2. Integrating existing databases with new information requirements often leads to the need to integrate different views.

3. New data requirements may arise during the life cycle, so there is a need to merge any new relations with what has already been developed.

An Example

Suppose that modeling a user view results in the following 3NF relation:

    EMPLOYEE1(Employee_ID,Name,Address,Phone)

Modeling a second user view might result in the following relation:

    EMPLOYEE2(Employee_ID,Name,Address,Jobcode,No_Years)

Since these two relations have the same primary key (Employee_ID), they likely describe the same entity and may be merged into one relation. The result of merging the relations is the following relation:

    EMPLOYEE(Employee_ID,Name,Address,Phone,Jobcode,No_Years).

Notice that an attribute that appears in both relations (such as Name in this example) appears only once in the merged relation.

View Integration Problems

When integrating relations as in the preceding example, the database analyst must understand the meaning of the data and must be prepared to resolve any problems that may arise in that process. In this section we describe and briefly illustrate four problems that arise in view integration: *synonyms, homonyms, transitive dependencies,* and *supertype/subtype relationships.*

Synonyms   In some situations, two (or more) attributes may have different names but the same meaning, as when they describe the same characteristic of an entity. Such attributes are called **synonyms**. For example, Employee_ID and Employee_No may be synonyms. When merging the relations that contain synonyms, you should obtain agreement (if possible) from users on a single, standardized name for the attribute and eliminate any other synonyms. (Another alternative is to choose a third name to replace the synonyms.) For example, consider the following relations:

> STUDENT1(Student_ID,Name)
> STUDENT2(Matriculation_No,Name,Address)

In this case, the analyst recognizes that both the Student_ID and Matriculation_No are synonyms for a person's Social Security number and are identical attributes. One possible resolution would be to standardize on one of the two attribute names, such as Student_ID. Another option is to use a new attribute name, such as SSN, to replace both synonyms. Assuming the latter approach, merging the two relations would produce the following result:

> STUDENT(SSN,Name,Address)

Often when there are synonyms, there is a need to allow some database users to refer to the same data by different names. Users may need to use familiar names that are consistent with terminology in their part of the organization. An **alias** is an alternative name used for an attribute. Many database management systems allow the definition of an alias that may be used interchangeably with the primary attribute label.

Homonyms   An attribute that may have more than one meaning is called a **homonym**. For example, the term "account" might refer to a bank's checking account, savings account, loan account, or other type of account (therefore, "account" refers to different data, depending on how it is used).

You should be on the lookout for homonyms when merging relations. Consider the following example:

> STUDENT1(Student_ID,Name,Address)
> STUDENT2(Student_ID,Name,Phone_No,Address)

In discussions with users, the analyst may discover that the attribute Address in STUDENT1 refers to a student's campus address, while in STUDENT2 the same attribute refers to a student's permanent (or home) address. To resolve this conflict, we would probably need to create new attribute names, so that the merged relation would become

STUDENT(Student_ID,Name,Phone_No,Campus_Address, Permanent_Address).

Transitive Dependencies   When two 3NF relations are merged to form a single relation, transitive dependencies (described earlier in this chapter) may result. For example, consider the following two relations:

> STUDENT1(Student_ID,Major)
> STUDENT2(Student_ID,Advisor)

Since STUDENT1 and STUDENT2 have the same primary key, the two relations may be merged:

Synonyms: Two (or more) attributes having different names but the same meaning, as when they describe the same characteristic of an entity.

Alias: An alternative name used for an attribute.

Homonym: An attribute that may have more than one meaning.

STUDENT(Student_ID,Major,Advisor)

However, suppose that each major has exactly one advisor. In this case, Advisor is functionally dependent on Major:

Major → Advisor

If the preceding functional dependency exists, then STUDENT is in 2NF but not in 3NF, since it contains a transitive dependency. The analyst can create 3NF relations by removing the transitive dependency (Major becomes a foreign key in STUDENT):

STUDENT(Student_ID,Major)
MAJOR ADVISOR(Major,Advisor)

Supertype/Subtype Relationships   These relationships may be hidden in user views or relations. Suppose that we have the following two hospital relations:

PATIENT1(Patient_ID,Name,Address)
PATIENT2(Patient_ID,Room_No)

Initially, it appears that these two relations can be merged into a single PATIENT relation. However, the analyst correctly suspects that there are two different types of patients: inpatients and outpatients. PATIENT1 actually contains attributes common to *all* patients. PATIENT2 contains an attribute (Room_No) that is a characteristic only of inpatients. In this situation, the analyst should create supertype/subtype relationships for these entities:

PATIENT(Patient_ID,Name,Address)
INPATIENT(Patient_ID,Room_No)
OUTPATIENT(Patient_ID,Date_Treated)

For an extended discussion of view integration in database design, see Navathe, Elmasri, and Larson (1986).

SUMMARY

Logical database design is the process of transforming the conceptual data model into a logical data model. The emphasis in this chapter has been on the relational data model, because of its importance in contemporary database systems. The relational data model represents data in the form of tables called relations. A relation is a named, two-dimensional table of data. A key property of relations is that they cannot contain multivalued attributes.

In this chapter, we described the major steps in the logical database design process. This process is based on transforming E-R diagrams to normalized relations. The three steps in this process are the following: Transform E-R (and EER) diagrams to relations, normalize the relations, and merge the relations. The result of this process is a set of relations in third normal form that can be implemented using any contemporary relational database management system.

Each entity type in the E-R diagram is transformed to a relation that has the same primary key as the entity type. A one-to-many relationship is represented by adding a foreign key to the relation that represents the entity on the many-side of the relationship. (This foreign key is the primary key of the entity on the one-side of the relationship.) A many-to-many relationship is represented by creating a separate relation. The primary key of this relation is a composite key, consisting of the primary key of each of the entities that participate in the relationship.

The relational model does not directly support supertype/subtype relationships, but we can model these relationships by creating a separate table (or relation) for the supertype and for each subtype. The primary key of each subtype is the same (or at least from the same domain) as for the supertype. The supertype must have an attribute called the subtype discriminator that indicates to which subtype (or subtypes) each instance of the supertype belongs. The purpose of normalization is to derive well-structured relations that are free of anomalies (inconsistencies or errors) that would otherwise result when the relations are updated or modified. Normalization is based on the analysis of functional dependencies, which are constraints between two attributes (or two sets of attributes). It may be accomplished in several stages. Relations in first normal form (1NF) contain no multivalued attributes or repeating groups. Relations in 2NF contain no partial dependencies, and relations in 3NF contain no transitive dependencies. We can use diagrams that show the functional dependencies in a relation to help decompose that relation (if necessary) to obtain relations in third normal form. Higher normal forms (beyond 3NF) have also been defined; we discuss these normal forms in Appendix B.

We must be careful when combining relations to deal with problems such as synonyms, homonyms, transitive dependencies, and class/subclass relationships.

CHAPTER REVIEW

KEY TERMS

Alias	Normal form	Second normal form
Anomaly	Normalization	Synonyms
Candidate key	Null	Third normal form
Composite key	Partial functional	Transitive dependency
Determinant	dependency	Well-structured relation
Entity integrity rule	Primary key	
First normal form	Recursive foreign key	
Foreign key	Referential integrity	
Functional dependency	constraint	
Homonym	Relation	

REVIEW QUESTIONS

1. Define each of the following terms:
   a. determinant
   b. functional dependency
   c. transitive dependency
   d. recursive foreign key
   e. normalization
   f. composite key
   g. relation
   h. normal form
   i. partial functional dependency

2. Contrast the following terms:
   a. normal form; normalization
   b. candidate key; primary key
   c. functional dependency; transitive dependency
   d. composite key; recursive foreign key
   e. determinant; candidate key

3. Summarize six important properties of relations.

4. Describe two properties that must be satisfied by candidate keys.

5. Describe three types of anomalies which can arise in a table.

6. Fill in the blanks in each of the following statements:
   a. A relation that has no partial functional dependencies is in _____ normal form.
   b. A relation that has no multivalued attributes is in _____ normal form.
   c. A relation that has no transitive dependencies is in _____ normal form.

7. What is a well-structured relation? Why are well-structured relations important in logical database design?

8. Describe how the following components of an E-R diagram are transformed to relations:
   a. regular entity type
   b. relationship (1:M)
   c. relationship (M:N)
   d. relationship (supertype/subtype)
   e. multivalued attribute
   f. weak entity
   g. composite attribute

9. Briefly describe four typical problems that often arise in merging relations, and common techniques for addressing those problems.

10. List three conditions that you can apply to determine whether a relation that is in first normal form is also in second normal form.

11. Explain how each of the following types of integrity constraints are enforced in the SQL CREATE TABLE commands:
    a. Entity integrity
    b. Referential integrity

12. How are relationships between entities represented in the relational data model?

13. How do you represent a 1:M unary relationship in a relational data model?

14. How do you represent a M:N ternary relationship in a relational data model?

15. What is the relationship between the primary key of a relation and the functional dependencies among all attributes within that relation?

PROBLEMS AND EXERCISES

---

1. Match the following terms to the appropriate definitions:
   _____ well-structured relation
   _____ anomaly
   _____ functional dependency

   a. constraint between two attributes
   b. functional dependency between nonkey attributes

_____ determinant	c. references primary key in same relation
_____ composite key	
_____ 1NF	d. multivalued attributes removed
_____ 2NF	e. inconsistency or error
_____ 3NF	f. contains little redundancy
_____ recursive foreign key	g. contains two (or more) attributes
_____ relation	h. contains no partial functional dependencies
_____ transitive dependency	i. transitive dependencies eliminated
	j. attribute on left-hand side of functional dependency
	k. named two-dimensional table of data

2. For each of the following E-R diagrams from Chapter 3:

   I. Transform the diagram to a relational schema that shows referential integrity constraints (see Figure 6-5 for an example of such a schema).

   II. For each relation, diagram the functional dependencies (see Figure 6-23 for an example).

   III. If any of the relations are not in 3NF, transform those relations to 3NF.

   a. Figure 3-8.   e. Figure 3-15b.

   b. Figure 3-9b.   f. Figure 3-18.

   c. Figure 3-11a.   g. Figure 3-21.

   d. Figure 3-11b

3. For each of the following EER diagrams from Chapter 4:

   I. Transform the diagram to a relational schema that shows referential integrity constraints (see Figure 6-5 for an example of such a schema).

   II. For each relation, diagram the functional dependencies (see Figure 6-23 for an example).

   III. If any of the relations are not in 3NF, transform those relations to 3NF

   a. Figure 4-6b.   d. Figure 4-10.

   b. Figure 4-7a.   e. Figure 4-20.

   c. Figure 4-9.

4. For each of the following relations, indicate the normal form for that relation. If the relation is not in third normal form, decompose it into 3NF relations. Functional dependencies (other than those implied by the primary key) are shown where appropriate.

   a. CLASS(Course_No,Section_No)

   b. CLASS(Course_No,Section_No,Room)

   c. CLASS(Course_No,Section_No,Room,Capacity)   Room → Capacity

   d. CLASS(Course_No,Section_No,Course_Name,Room,Capacity)
   Course_No → Course_Name,   Room → Capacity

5. Figure 6-27 shows a class list for Lakewood College. Convert this user view to a set of 3NF relations. Assume the following:

   • An instructor has a unique location.

   • A student has a unique major.

   • A course has a unique title.

MILLENNIUM COLLEGE
CLASS LIST
FALL SEMESTER 199X

COURSE NO.:   IS 460
COURSE TITLE: DATABASE
INSTRUCTOR NAME: NORMA L. FORM
INSTRUCTOR LOCATION: B 104

STUDENT NO	STUDENT NAME	MAJOR	GRADE
38214	Bright	IS	A
40875	Cortez	CS	B
51893	Edwards	IS	A

Figure 6-27
Class list
(Millennium College)

6. Figure 6-28 shows an E-R diagram for a simplified credit card environment. There are two types of card accounts: debit cards and credit cards. Credit card accounts accumulate charges with merchants. Each charge is identified by the date and amount of the charge.

a. Develop a relational schema (similar to Figure 6-5).

b. Show the functional dependencies (similar to Figure 6-23).

c. Develop a set of 3NF relations.

7. Table 6-2 contains sample data for parts and for vendors who supply those parts. In discussing these data with users, we find that part numbers (but not descriptions) uniquely identify parts, and that vendor names uniquely identify vendors.

a. Convert this table to a relation (named PART SUPPLIER) in first normal form. Illustrate the relation with the sample data in the table.

b. List the functional dependencies in PART SUPPLIER and identify a candidate key.

c. For the relation PART SUPPLIER, identify each of the following: an insert anomaly, a delete anomaly, and a modification anomaly.

d. Draw a relational schema for PART SUPPLIER (similar to Figure 6-23) and show the functional dependencies.

e. In what normal form is this relation?

f. Develop a set of 3NF relations from PART SUPPLIER.

Table 6-2   Sample Data for Parts and Vendors

Part_No.	Description	Vendor_Name	Address	Unit Cost
1234	Logic chip	Fast Chips	Cupertino	10.00
		Smart Chips	Phoenix	8.00
5678	Memory chip	Fast Chips	Cupertino	3.00
		Quality Chips	Austin	2.00
		Smart Chips	Phoenix	5.00

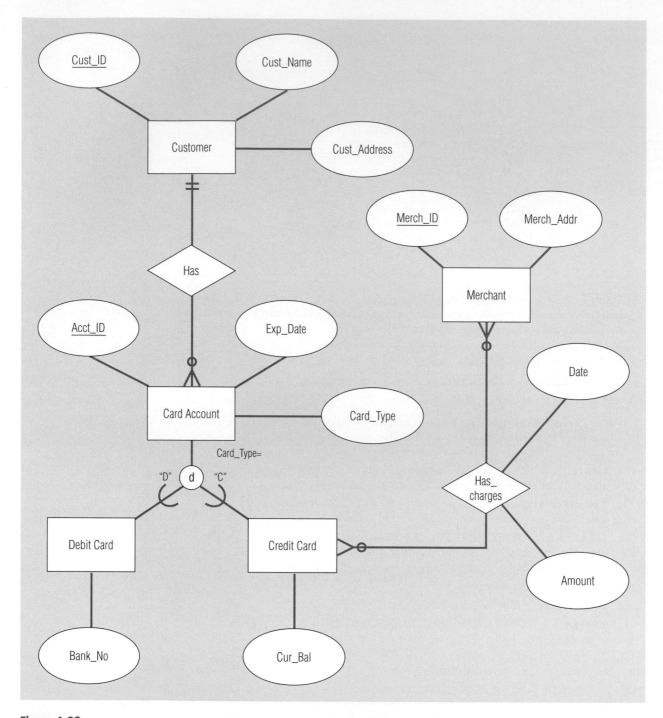

Figure 6-28
E-R diagram for bank cards

8. Table 6-3 shows a relation called GRADE REPORT for a university. Following is a description of the functional dependencies in GRADE REPORT:

- Student_ID → Student_Name,Campus_Address,Major
- Course_ID → Course_Title,Instructor_Name,Instructor_Location
- Student_ID,Course_ID → Grade
- Instructor_Name → Instructor_Location

Table 6-3   GRADE REPORT Relation

GRADE REPORT

Student_ID	Student_ Name	Campus_ Address	Major	Course_ID	Course_ Title	Instructor_ Name	Instructor_ Location	Grade
168300458	Williams	208 Brooks	IS	IS 350	Database Mgt	Codd	B 104	A
268300458	Williams	208 Brooks	IS	IS 465	Systems Analysis	Parsons	B 317	B
543291073	Baker	104 Phillips	Acctg	IS 350	Database Mgt	Codd	B 104	C
543291073	Baker	104 Phillips	Acctg	Acct 201	Fund Acctg	Miller	H 310	B
543291073	Baker	104 Phillips	Acctg	Mktg 300	Intro Mktg	Bennett	B 212	A

Following is your assignment:

a. Draw a relational schema (similar to Figure 6-23) and diagram the functional dependencies in the relation.

b. In what normal form is this relation?

c. Decompose GRADE REPORT into a set of 3NF relations.

d. Draw a relational schema for your 3NF relations (similar to Figure 6-5) and show the referential integrity constraints.

FIELD EXERCISES

1. Interview systems and database designers at several organizations. Ask them to describe the process they use for logical design. How do they transform their conceptual data models (e.g., E-R diagrams) to relational schema? What is the role of CASE tools in this process? Do they use normalization? If so, to what level?

2. Obtain a common document such as a sales slip, customer invoice from an auto repair shop, credit card statement, etc. Then do the following:

a. List the attribute names on the document.

b. List the functional dependencies among the attributes (make any assumptions you find necessary).

c. Draw a schema for the relation (similar to Figure 6-23) and diagram the functional dependencies.

d. Decompose the relation into a set of 3NF relations, and draw the relational schema (similar to Figure 6-5).

3. Obtain documentation for three popular PC-based CASE tools and compare the notation they use for representing relational schemas. You may use the following Internet addresses to obtain on-line information for the following three tools:

a. Microsoft Access: www.microsoft.com/Visual Tools/

b. Erwin: www.logicworks.com

c. EasyER: www.esti.com

4. Find a form or report from a business organization, possibly a statement, bill, or document you have received. Draw an EER diagram of the data in this form or report. Transform the diagram into a set of 3NF relations.

REFERENCES

Chouinard, P. 1989. "Supertypes, Subtypes, and DB2." *Database Programming & Design* 2 (October): 50–57.

Codd, E. F. 1970. "A Relational Model of Data for Large Relational Databases." *Communications of the ACM* 13 (June): 77–87.

Codd, E. F. 1990. *The Relational Model for Database Management Version 2.* Reading, MA: Addison-Wesley.

Date, C. J. 1995. *An Introduction to Database Systems.* 6th ed. Reading, MA: Addison-Wesley.

Dutka, A. F., and H. H. Hanson. 1989. *Fundamentals of Data Normalization.* Reading, MA: Addison-Wesley.

Fleming, C. C., and B. von Halle. 1989. *Handbook of Relational Database Design.* Reading, MA: Addison-Wesley.

Navathe, S., R. Elmasri, and J. Larson. 1986. "Integrating User Views in Database Design." *Computer* (January): 50–62.

FURTHER READING

Elmasri, R. and Navathe, S. 1994. *Fundamentals of Database Systems.* 2nd ed. Menlo Park, CA: Benjamin Cummings.

Hoffer, J. A., J. F. George, and J. S. Valacich. 1999. *Modern Systems Analysis and Design.* 2nd ed. Reading, MA: Addison-Wesley.

Storey, V. C. 1991. "Relational Database Design Based on the Entity-Relationship Model." *Data and Knowledge Engineering* 7: 47–83.

Project Case

You have been introduced to the Mountain View Community Hospital case in the preceding chapters. This chapter continues the case with special emphasis on logical design for the relational data model. Although the hospital will continue to evaluate newer technology such as object-oriented and object-relational, it is expected that relational technology will continue to dominate its systems development over the next few years.

PROJECT QUESTIONS

1. Why will Mountain View Community Hospital continue to use relational technology for systems development, despite the continuing emergence of newer technology?

2. Should Mountain View Community Hospital use normalization in designing its relational databases? Why or why not?

3. Why are entity integrity and referential integrity constraints of importance to the hospital?

4. Who in the hospital should be involved in data normalization?

PROJECT EXERCISES

Your assignment is to perform a logical design for the databases at Mountain View Community Hospital. In Chapters 3 and 4 you developed conceptual data

models for the hospital. Specifically, in those chapters you prepared the following:

- E-R diagram for the major entities and relationships in the hospital (see Project Exercise 2 in Chapter 3).

- EER diagram emphasizing the human resources in the hospital (see Project Exercise 1 in Chapter 4).

Your assignment in this chapter is to develop a logical design for one or both of these conceptual designs. For each logical design, you are to perform the following tasks:

1. Map the E-R (and/or EER) diagram to a relational schema, using the techniques described in this chapter. Be sure to underline all primary keys, include all necessary foreign keys, and indicate referential integrity constraints.

2. Diagram the functional dependencies in each relation.

3. If any relation is not in 3NF, decompose that relation into 3NF relations and revise the relational schema.

4. Write CREATE TABLE commands for each relation. Make reasonable assumptions concerning the data type for each attribute in each of the relations.

5. If you develop a logical design for the E-R diagram for both chapters, merge the relations into a single set of 3NF relations.

Physical Database Design

L E A R N I N G   O B J E C T I V E S

After studying this chapter, you should be able to:

■ Define the following key terms: field, data type, physical record, page, pointer, blocking factor, denormalization, horizontal partitioning, vertical partitioning, physical file, pointer, access method, file organization, sequential file organization, indexed file organization, hashed file organization, hashing algorithm, index, secondary key, and bitmap index.

■ Describe the physical database design process, its objectives, and deliverables.

■ Choose storage formats for attributes from a logical data model.

■ Select an appropriate file organization by balancing various important design factors.

■ Describe three important types of file organization.

■ Describe the purpose of indexes and the important considerations in selecting attributes to be indexed.

■ Translate a relational data model into efficient database structures, including knowing when and how to denormalize the logical data model.

INTRODUCTION

In Chapters 3 through 6 you learned how to describe and model organizational data during the conceptual data modeling and logical database design phases of the database development process. You learned how to use EER notation, object-oriented notation, and the relational data model and normalization to develop abstractions of organizational data that capture the meaning of data; however, these notations do not explain *how* data will be processed or stored. The purpose of physical database design is to translate the logical description of data into the technical specifications for storing and retrieving data. The goal is to create a design for storing data that will provide adequate performance and insure database integrity, security, and recoverability.

Physical database design does not include implementing files and databases (i.e., creating them and loading data into them). Physical database design produces the technical specifications that programmers and others involved in information systems construction will use during the implementation phase, which we discuss in Chapters 8 through 12.

In this chapter you will study the basic steps required to develop an efficient physical database design. We concentrate in this chapter on the design of a single, centralized database. Later in Chapter 11 you will learn about the design of databases that are stored at multiple, distributed sites. In Chapter 7 you will learn how to estimate the amount of data that users will require in the database, and how data are likely to be used. You will learn about choices for storing attribute values and how to select among these choices. You will also learn why normalized tables do not always form the best physical data files, and how you can denormalize the data to improve the speed of data retrieval. You will learn about different file organizations and about the use of indexes, which are important in speeding up the retrieval of data. And you will learn the major differences between different architectures for databases.

You must carefully perform physical database design, since the decisions made during this stage have a major impact on data accessibility, response times, securing, user friendliness, and similarly important information system design factors. Database administration (described in Chapter 13) plays a major role in physical database design, so we will return to some advanced design issues in that chapter.

PHYSICAL DATABASE DESIGN PROCESS

In most situations, many physical database design decisions are implicit or eliminated when you choose the database management technologies to use with the information system you are designing. Since many organizations have standards for operating systems, database management systems, and data access languages, you must deal only with those choices not implicit in the given technologies. Thus, we will cover only those decisions you will make most frequently, as well as other selected decisions that may be critical for some types of applications, such an on-line data capture and retrieval.

The primary goal of physical database design is data processing efficiency. Today, with ever-decreasing costs for computer technology per unit of measure (both speed and space measures), it is typically very important for you to design the physical database to minimize the time required by users to interact with the information system. Thus, we concentrate on how to make processing of physical files and databases efficient, with less attention on efficient use of space.

Designing physical files and databases requires certain information that should have been collected and produced during prior system development phases. The information needed for physical file and database design includes these requirements:

- Normalized relations, including volume estimates

- Definitions of each attribute

- Descriptions of where and when data are used: entered, retrieved, deleted, and updated (including frequencies)

- Expectations or requirements for response time and data security, backup, recovery, retention, and integrity

- Descriptions of the technologies (database management systems) used for implementing the database

Physical database design requires several critical decisions that will affect the integrity and performance of the application system. These key decisions include the following:

1. Choosing the storage format (called *data type*) for each attribute from the logical data model. The format is chosen to minimize storage space and to maximize data integrity.

2. Grouping attributes from the logical data model into *physical records*. You will discover that although the columns of a relational table are a natural definition for the contents of a physical record, this is not always the most desirable grouping of attributes.

3. Arranging similarly structured records in secondary memory (primarily hard disks) so that individual and groups of records (called *file organizations*) can be stored, retrieved, and updated rapidly. Consideration must be given also to protecting data and recovering data after errors are found.

4. Selecting structures (called *indexes* and *database architectures*) for storing and connecting files to make retrieving related data more efficient.

5. Preparing strategies for handling queries against the database that will optimize performance and take advantage of the file organizations and indexes that you have specified. Efficient database structures will be of benefit only if queries and the database management systems that handle those queries are tuned to intelligently use those structures.

Data Volume and Usage Analysis

As mentioned above, data-volume and frequency-of-use statistics are critical inputs to the physical database design process. Thus, either the final step you need to take in logical database design or the first step you need to take in physical database design is to estimate the size and usage patterns of the database.

An easy way to show the statistics about data volumes and usage is by adding notation to the EER diagram that represents the final set of normalized relations from logical database design. Figure 7-1 shows the EER diagram (without attributes) for a simple inventory database in Pine Valley Furniture Company. This EER diagram represents the normalized relations constructed during logical database design for the original conceptual data model of this situation depicted in Figure 4-7. The Supplies many-to-many relationship from Figure 4-7 is shown in Figure 7-1 as an associative entity, QUOTATION, corresponding to the relation created from this relationship.

Both data volume and access frequencies are shown in Figure 7-1. For example, there are 1000 PARTs in this database. The supertype PART has two subtypes, MANUFACTURED (40 percent of all PARTs are manufactured) and PURCHASED (70 percent are purchased—since some PARTs are of both subtypes, the percentages sum to more than 100 percent). The analysts at Pine Valley estimate that there are typically 50 SUPPLIERs, and Pine Valley receives on average 50 QUOTATIONs from each SUPPLIER, yielding a total of 2500 QUOTATIONs. The dashed arrows represent access frequencies. So, for example, across all applications that use this database, there

Figure 7-1
Composite usage map (Pine Valley Furniture Company)

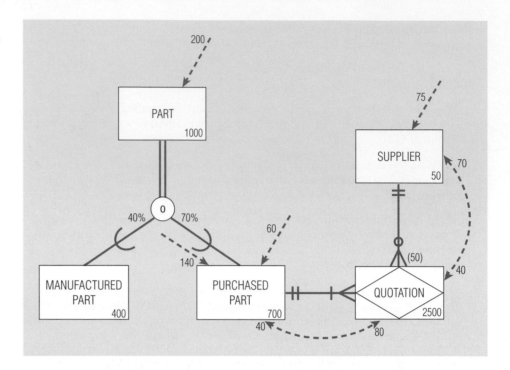

are on average 200 accesses per hour of PART data, and these then yield, based on subtype percentages, 140 accesses per hour to PURCHASED PART data. There are an additional 60 direct accesses to PURCHASED PART data. Of this total of 200 accesses to PURCHASED PART, 80 accesses then also require QUOTATION data and of these 80 accesses to QUOTATION, there are 70 subsequent accesses to SUPPLIER data.

The volume and frequency statistics are generated during the systems analysis phase of the systems development process when systems analysts are studying current and proposed data processing and business activities. The data-volume statistics represent the size of the business, and should be calculated assuming business growth over at least a several-year period. The access frequencies are estimated from the timing of events, transaction volumes, and reporting and querying activities. Since many databases support ad hoc accesses, and such accesses may change significantly over time, the access frequencies tend to be less certain than the volume statistics. Fortunately, precise numbers are not necessary. What is crucial is the relative size of the numbers, which will suggest where the greatest attention needs to be given in order to achieve the best possible performance.

It can be helpful for subsequent physical database design steps if you can also explain the nature of the access for the access paths shown by the dashed lines. For example, it can be helpful to know that of the 200 accesses to PART data, 150 ask for a part or a set of parts based on the primary key, Part_No (e.g., access a part with a particular number); the other 50 accesses qualify part data for access by the value of Qty_on_Hand (these specifics are not shown in Figure 7-1). This more precise description can help in selecting indexes, one of the major topics we discuss later in this chapter. It might also be helpful to know if an access results in data creation, retrieval, update, or deletion. Such a refined description of access frequencies can be handled by additional notation on a diagram such as in Figure 7-1 or by text and tables kept in other documentation.

DESIGNING FIELDS

A **field** is the smallest unit of application data recognized by system software, such as a programming language or database management system. A field corresponds to a simple attribute from the logical data model, so a field represents each component of a composite attribute.

Field: The smallest unit of named application data recognized by system software.

The basic decisions you must make in specifying each field concern the type of data (or storage type) used to represent values of this field, data integrity controls built into the database, and how the DBMS should handle missing values for the field. There are other field specifications, such as display format, which must be made as part of the total specification of the information system, but we will not be concerned here with those specifications typically handled by programs rather than the DBMS. See Hoffer, George, and Valacich (1999) for a thorough coverage of all field specifications.

Choosing Data Types

A **data type** is a detailed coding scheme recognized by system software, such as a DBMS, for representing organizational data. The bit pattern of the coding scheme is usually transparent to you, but the space to store data and the speed required to access data are of consequence in physical database design. The specific DBMS you will use will dictate which choices are available to you. For example, Table 7-1 lists the data types available in the Oracle DBMS, a typical DBMS that uses the SQL data definition and manipulation language. Additional data types might be available for currency, voice, image, and user defined for some DBMSs.

Data type: A detailed coding scheme recognized by system software, such as a DBMS, for representing organizational data.

Selecting a data type involves four objectives that will have different relative importances for different applications:

1. Minimize storage space.

2. Represent all possible values.

3. Improve data integrity.

4. Support all data manipulations.

The correct data type to choose for a field can, in minimal space, represent every possible value (but eliminate illegal values) for the associated attribute and can support the required data manipulation (e.g., numeric data types for arithmetic and character data types for string manipulation). Any attribute domain constraints from the conceptual data model are helpful in selecting a good data type for that attribute. Achieving these four objectives can be subtle. For example, consider a DBMS for which the SMALLINT data type (see Table 7-1) has a maximum width of 2 bytes. Suppose SMALLINT is sufficient to represent a quantity sold field. When quantity sold fields are summed, the sum may require a number larger than 2 bytes. If the DBMS uses the field's data type for results of any mathematics on that field, SMALLINT will not work. Some data types have special manipulation capabilities; for example, only the DATE data type allows true date arithmetic.

Coding and Compression Techniques   Some attributes have a sparse set of values or are so large that given data volumes, considerable storage space will be consumed (large data fields mean that data are farther apart, which yields slower data processing). A field with a limited number of possible values can be translated into a code

TABLE 7-1 Data Types in Oracle

Data Type	Description
CHAR(*size*)	Alphanumeric, where *size* is the maximum length. Padded to right with blanks. Maximum *size* is 255.
DATE	Valid calendar dates from January 1, 4712 B.C. to December 31, 4712 A.D.
DECIMAL	Same as NUMBER.
FLOAT	Same as NUMBER.
INTEGER	Same as NUMBER.
INTEGER(*size*)	Same as NUMBER with a specified number of digits (*size*).
LONG	Alphanumeric data of variable size up to 2 gigabytes in length. Only one LONG column may exist per table and a LONG column may be used only for display, not qualification, in queries.
LONG RAW	Binary data; otherwise, same as LONG.
LONG VARCHAR	Same as LONG.
MLSLABEL	4-byte representation of a secure operating system label.
NUMBER	Signed number up to 40 digits, plus decimal point and sign. Numbers may be specified with digits 0 to 9, + or − sign, and decimal point or in scientific notation in the range 1.0E–130 to 9.99..E125.
NUMBER(*size*)	Number with a specified number of digits (*size*).
NUMBER(*size,d*)	Number with total width of *size*, including a decimal point, and *d* digits after decimal point (e.g., NUMBER(5,2) can handle up to ±999.99)
NUMBER(*)	Same as NUMBER.
SMALLINT	Same as NUMBER.
RAW(*size*)	Binary data, *size* bytes long. Maximum size is 255 bytes.
RAW MLSLABEL	Binary format for a secure operating system label.
VARCHAR2(*size*)	Alphanumeric data having a maximum of *size* bytes (up to 200).
VARCHAR(*size*)	Same as VARCHAR2.

that requires less space. Consider the example of the product Finish field illustrated in Figure 7-2. Products at Pine Valley Furniture come in only a limited number of woods: Birch, Maple, and Oak. By creating a code or translation table, each Finish field value can be replaced by a code, a cross-reference to the look-up table, similar to a foreign key. This will decrease the amount of space for the Finish field, and hence for the PRODUCT file. There will be additional space for the FINISH look-up table, and when the Finish field value is needed, an extra access to this look-up table will be required. If the Finish field is infrequently used or the number of products very large, the relative advantages of coding may outweigh the costs. Note that the code table would not appear in the conceptual or logical model. The code table is a physical construct to achieve data processing performance improvements, not a set of data with business value.

A form of a code table is used by data compression techniques, such as file zip routines. A data compression technique looks for patterns in data and then codes frequently appearing patterns with fewer bits. Although such routines are typically used to compress a whole file, such a routine could be used with some DBMSs to compress specific fields. Related to data compression techniques are encryption tech-

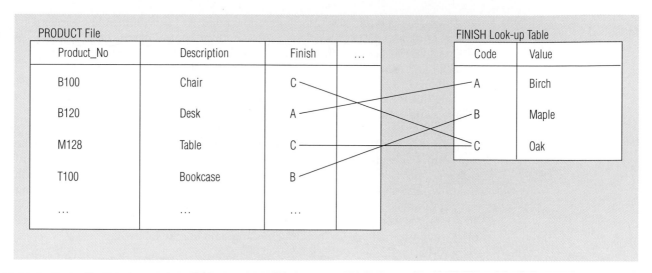

Figure 7-2
Example code look-up table (Pine Valley Furniture)

niques, which translate a field into a secure format. In both cases, for a user to see the actual field value, software must know the reverse translation process.

Controlling Data Integrity

For many DBMSs, data integrity controls (i.e., controls on the possible value a field can assume) can be built into the physical structure of the fields and controls enforced by the DBMS on those fields. The data type enforces one form of data integrity control since it may limit the type of data (numeric or character) and length of a field value. Some other typical integrity controls that a DMBS may support are the following:

- *Default value* A default value is the value a field will assume unless a user enters an explicit value for an instance of that field. Assigning a default value to a field can reduce data entry time since entry of a value can be skipped and it can also help to reduce data entry errors for the most common value.

- *Range control* A range control limits the set of permissible values a field may assume. The range may be a numeric lower to upper bound or a set of specific values. Range controls must be used with caution since the limits of the range may change over time. A combination of range controls and coding has led to the Year 2000 problem faced by many organizations, in which a field for year is represented by only the numbers 00 to 99. It is better to implement any range controls through a DBMS since range controls in programs may be inconsistently enforced and it is more difficult to find and change them.

- *Null value control* A null value was defined in Chapter 6 as an empty value. Each primary key must have an integrity control that prohibits a null value. Any other required field may also have a null value control placed on it if that is the policy of the organization. For example, a university may prohibit adding a course to its database unless that course has a title as well as a value of the primary key, Course_ID. Many fields legitimately may have a null value, so this control should be used only when truly required by business rules.

- *Referential integrity*   The term "referential integrity" was defined in Chapter 6. Referential integrity on a field is a form of range control in which the value of that field must exist as the value in some field in another row of the same or different table. That is, the range of legitimate values comes from the dynamic contents of a field in a database table, not from some prespecified set of values. Note that referential integrity guarantees that only some existing cross-referencing value is used, not that it is the correct one.

Handling Missing Data   When a field may be null, simply entering no value may be sufficient. For example, suppose a customer zip code field is null and a report summarizes total sales by month and zip code. How should sales to customers with unknown zip codes be handled? Two options for handling or preventing missing data have already been mentioned: using a default value and not permitting missing (null) values. Missing data are inevitable. According to Babad and Hoffer (1984), other possible methods for handling missing data are the following:

1. Substitute an estimate of the missing value. For example, for a missing sales value when computing monthly product sales, use a formula involving the mean of the existing monthly sales values for that product indexed by total sales for that month across all products. Such estimates must be marked so that users know that these are not actual values.

2. Track missing data so that special reports and other system elements cause people to quickly resolve unknown values. This can be done by setting up a trigger in the database definition. A trigger is a routine that will automatically execute when some event occurs or time period passes. One trigger could log the missing entry to a file when a null or other missing value is stored, and another trigger runs periodically to create a report of the contents of this log file.

3. Perform sensitivity testing so that missing data are ignored unless knowing a value might significantly change results; if, for example, total monthly sales for a particular salesperson are almost over a threshold that would make a difference in that person's compensation. This is the most complex of the methods mentioned and hence requires the most sophisticated programming, which must be written in application programs since DBMSs do not have the sophistication to handle this method.

DESIGNING PHYSICAL RECORDS AND DENORMALIZATION

Physical record: A group of fields stored in adjacent memory locations and retrieved together as a unit.

In a logical data model you grouped into a relation those attributes that are determined by the same primary key. In contrast, a **physical record** is a group of fields stored in adjacent memory locations and retrieved together as a unit. The design of a physical record involves choosing the sequencing of fields into adjacent storage locations to achieve two goals: efficient use of secondary storage and data processing speed.

Page: The amount of data read or written in one secondary memory (disk) input or output operation. For I/O with a magnetic tape, the equivalent term is record block.

The efficient use of secondary storage is influenced by both the size of the physical record and the structure of secondary storage. Computer operating systems read data from hard disks in units called pages, not physical records. A **page** is the amount of data read or written in one secondary memory input or output operation. The page size is fixed by system programmers and is selected to most efficiently use RAM across all applications. Depending on the computer system, a physical record may or may not be allowed to span two pages. Thus, if page length is not an integer multiple of the physical record length, wasted space may occur at the end of a page. The number of physical records per page is called the **blocking factor**. If storage space is scarce and physical records cannot span pages, creating multiple physical records from one logical relation will minimize wasted storage space.

Blocking factor: The number of physical records per page.

Handling Fixed-Length Fields

Designing a physical record to conserve storage space is easier if every field is of fixed length. In the case of fixed-length fields, fields are simply placed in sequence one after another. Trailing blanks pad character fields and leading zeros pad numeric fields. With this scheme, we know the exact location within a file for each field of each physical record. It is easy to find the position of the mth field in the nth record in this way:

> Address of beginning of file
> $+$ $(n-1)$*record length
> $+$ $\text{sum}(\text{length}_i)$
> $i = 1$ to $m - 1$
> ──────────────────────────
> $=$ Address of beginning of desired field

where length_i is the length of field i. Some other techniques for designing physical records with fixed-length fields are reviewed in Appendix C.

Handling Variable-Length Fields

A variable-length field makes the location of a particular field and of a particular record irregular. That is, depending on which records exist and the precise values for fields, different records and fields will be in different locations. A common way to handle variable-length fields is to break the relation into a fixed-length physical record containing all the fixed-length fields and one or more variable-length physical records (possibly a separate record for each variable-length field). This is the way many PC DBMSs handle a memo field, which is a variable-length field. Again, other techniques for designing physical records with variable-length fields are reviewed in Appendix C.

Denormalization

The preceding discussion of physical record design concentrated on efficient use of storage space. In most cases the second goal of physical record design—efficient data processing—dominates the design process. Efficient processing of data, just like efficient accessing of books in a library, depends on how close together related data (or books) are. Often all the attributes that appear within a relation are not used together, and data from different relations are needed together to answer a query or produce a report. Thus, although normalized relations solve data maintenance anomalies, normalized relations, if implemented one for one as physical records, may not yield efficient data processing.

The processing performance difference between totally normalized and partially normalized databases can be dramatic. Inmon (1988) reports of a study to quantify fully and partially normalized databases. A fully normalized database contained eight tables with about 50,000 rows each, another partially normalized one had four tables with roughly 25,000 rows each, and yet another partially normalized database had two tables. The result showed that the less than fully normalized databases could be as much as an order of magnitude faster than the fully normalized one. Although such results depend greatly on the database and the type of processing against it, these results suggest that you should carefully consider whether the physical records should exactly match the normalized relations for a database.

Denormalization: The process of transforming normalized relations into unnormalized physical record specifications.

Denormalization is the process of transforming normalized relations into unnormalized physical record specifications. We will review various forms and reasons for denormalization in this section. In general, denormalization may partition a relation into several physical records, may combine attributes from several relations together into one physical record, or may do a combination of both. As Finkelstein (1988) points out, denormalization can increase the chance of errors and inconsistencies and can force reprogramming systems if business rules change. Further, denormalization optimizes certain data processing at the expense of others, so if the frequencies of different processing activities change, the benefits of denormalization may no longer exist.

Rogers (1989) introduces several common denormalization opportunities (Figures 7-3 through 7-5 show examples of normalized and denormalized relations for each of these three situations):

1. *Two entities with a one-to-one relationship*   Even if one of the entities is an optional participant, if the matching entity exists most of the time, then it may be wise to combine these two relations into one record definition (especially if the access frequency between these two entity types is high). Figure 7-3 shows student data with optional data from a standard scholarship application a student may complete. In this case, one record could be formed with four fields from the STUDENT and SCHOLARSHIP APPLICATION normalized relations (assuming Application_ID is no longer needed). (*Note:* In this case, fields from the optional entity must have null values allowed.)

2. *A many-to-many relationship (associative entity) with nonkey attributes*   Rather than joining three files to extract data from the two basic entities in the relationship, it may be advisable to combine attributes from one of the entities into the record representing the many-to-many relationship, thus avoiding one join operation in many data access modules. Again, this would be most advantageous if this joining occurs frequently. Figure 7-4 shows price quotes for different items from different vendors. In this case, fields from ITEM and PRICE QUOTE relations might be combined into one record to avoid having to join all three files together. (*Note:* This may create considerable duplication of data—in the example, the ITEM fields, such as Description, would repeat for each price quote. This would necessitate excessive updating if duplicated data change.)

3. *Reference data*   Reference data exist in an entity on the one-side of a one-to-many relationship, and this entity participates in no other database relationships. You should seriously consider merging the two entities in this situation into one record definition when there are few instances of the entity on the many-side for each entity instance on the one-side. See Figure 7-5 in which several ITEMs have the same STORAGE INSTRUCTIONs and STORAGE INSTRUCTIONs only relate to ITEMs. In this case, the storage instruction data could be stored in the ITEM record creating, of course, redundancy and potential for extra data maintenance. (Instr_ID is no longer needed.)

Figure 7-3

A possible denormalization situation: two entities with one-to-one relationship *(Note:* We assume Application_ID is not necessary when all fields are stored in one record, but this field can be included if it is required application data.)

Figure 7-4
A possible denormalization situation: a many-to-many relationship with nonkey attributes

The opportunities just listed all deal with combining tables to avoid doing joins. In contrast, denormalization can also be used to create more tables by partitioning a relation into multiple tables. Both horizontal and vertical partitioning, or a combina-

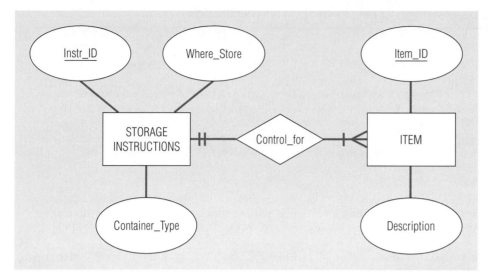

Figure 7-5
A possible denormalization
situation: reference data

tion, are possible. **Horizontal partitioning** breaks a relation into multiple record specifications by placing different rows into different records based upon common column values. In a library setting, horizontal partitioning is similar to placing the business journals in a business library, the science books in a science library, and so on. Each file created from the partitioning has the same record layout. For example, a customer relation could be broken into four regional customer files based on the value of a field Region.

Horizontal partitioning makes sense when different categories of rows of a table are processed separately; for example, for the customer table just mentioned, if a high percentage of the data processing needs to work with only one region at a time. Horizontal partitioning can also be more secure since file level security can be used to prohibit users from seeing certain rows of data. Also, each partitioned table can be organized differently, appropriate for how it is individually used. It is likely also

Horizontal partitioning:
Distributing the rows of a table into several separate files.

TABLE 7-2   Advantages and Disadvantages of Data Partitioning and Replication

Advantages of Partitioning

1. *Efficiency:* Data used together are stored close to one another and separate from data not used together.
2. *Local optimization:* Each partition of data can be stored to optimize performance for its own use.
3. *Security:* Data not relevant to one group of users can be segregated from data they are allowed to use.
4. *Recovery and uptime:* Smaller files will take less time to recover, and other files are still accessible if one file is damaged, so the effects of damage are isolated.
5. *Load balancing:* Files can be allocated to different storage areas (disks or other media), which minimizes contention for access to the same storage area or even allows for parallel access to the different areas.

Disadvantages of Partitioning

1. *Inconsistent access speed:* Different partitions may yield different access speeds, thus confusing users. Also, when data must be combined across partitions, users may have to deal with significantly slower response times.
2. *Complexity:* Partitioning is usually not transparent to programmers, who will have to write more complex programs due to the violations of third normal form.
3. *Anomalies:* Insertion, deletion, and update anomalies are possible and special programming is required to avoid these problems.
4. *Extra space and update time:* Data may be duplicated across the partitions, taking extra storage space compared to storing all the data in normalized files. Updates which affect data in multiple partitions can take more time than if one file were used.

faster to recover one of the partitioned files than one file with all the rows. In addition, taking one of the partitioned files out of service because it was damaged or so it can be recovered still allows processing against the other partitioned files to continue. Finally, each of the partitioned files can be placed on a separate disk drive to reduce contention for the same drive and hence improve performance across the database. These advantages of horizontal partitioning (actually all forms of partitioning), along with the disadvantages, are summarized in Table 7-2.

Note that horizontal partitioning is very similar to creating a supertype/subtype relationship because different types of the entity (where the subtype discriminator is the field used for segregating rows) are involved in different relationships, hence different processing. In fact, when you have a supertype/subtype relationship, you need to decide if you will create separate tables for each subtype or combine them in various combinations. Combining makes sense when all subtypes are used about the same way, whereas partitioning the supertype entity into multiple files makes sense when the subtypes are handled differently in transactions, queries, and reports. When a relation is partitioned horizontally, the whole set of rows can be reconstructed by the SQL UNION operator. Thus, for example, all customer data can be viewed together when desired.

Vertical partitioning:
Distributing the columns of a table into several separate files.

Vertical partitioning distributes the columns of a relation into separate files, repeating the primary key in each of the files. An example of vertical partitioning would be breaking apart a part relation by placing the part number along with accounting-related part data into one record specification, the part number along with engineering-related part data into another record specification, and the part number along with sales-related part data into yet another record specification. The advantages and disadvantages of vertical partitioning are similar to those for horizontal partitioning. When, for example, accounting-, engineering-, and sales-related part data need to be used together, these tables can be joined. Thus, neither horizontal nor vertical partitioning prohibits the ability to treat the original relation as a whole.

Combinations of horizontal and vertical partitioning are also possible. This form of denormalization—record partitioning—is especially common for a database whose files are distributed across multiple computers. Thus, you will study this topic again in Chapter 11.

The final form of denormalization we introduce is data replication. In data replication, the same data are purposely stored in multiple places in the database (the client/server database in Figure 2-10 shows a form of data replication). For example, consider again Figure 7-1. You learned earlier in this section that relations can be denormalized by combining data from an associative entity with data from one of the simple entities with which it is associated. So, in Figure 7-1, QUOTATION data might be stored with PURCHASED PART data in one expanded PURCHASED PART physical record specification. With data duplication, the same QUOTATION data might also be stored with its associated SUPPLIER data in another expanded SUPPLIER physical record specification. With this data duplication, once either a SUPPLIER or PURCHASED PART record is retrieved, the related QUOTATION data will also be available without any further access to secondary memory. This improved speed is worthwhile only if QUOTATION data are frequently accessed with SUPPLIER and with PURCHASED PART data and if the costs for extra secondary storage and data maintenance are not great.

DESIGNING PHYSICAL FILES

A **physical file** is a named portion of secondary memory (a magnetic tape or hard disk) allocated for the purpose of storing physical records. Some computer operating systems allow a physical file to be split into separate pieces. If this occurs, it typically will be transparent to you as the database designer. In subsequent sections, we will assume that a physical file is not split and each record in a file has the same structure.

> **Physical file:** A named portion of secondary memory (a magnetic tape or hard disk) allocated for the purpose of storing physical records.

Pointer

All files are organized by using two basic constructs to link one piece of data with another piece of data: sequential storage and pointers. With sequential storage one field or record is stored right after another field or record. Although simple to implement and use, sometimes sequential storage is not the most efficient way to organize data. A **pointer** is a field of data that can be used to locate a related field or record of data. In most cases, a pointer contains the address, or location, of the associated data. Pointers are used in a wide variety of data storage structures; however, we will see only a few of their uses in this chapter. The interested reader can read Appendix C for a broader coverage of the use of pointers.

> **Pointer:** A field of data that can be used to locate a related field or record of data.

Access Methods

All input/output operations are ultimately handled by the data management portion of the computer's operating system. Each operating system supports one or more algorithms for storing and retrieving data; these algorithms are called **access methods**. There are two basic types of access methods: relative and direct. A *relative* access method supports accessing data as an offset from the most recently referenced point in secondary memory. A *sequential* access method is a special case of this type since

> **Access method:** An operating system algorithm for storing and locating data in secondary memory.

the "next" record begins the distance of one record from the beginning of the current record. In general, a relative access method supports finding the nth record from the current position or from the beginning of the file. A direct access method uses a calculation to generate the beginning address of a record. The simplest form of a direct method is to tell the access method to go to a particular disk address. Another variation is to provide a record's primary key and the direct access method determines where this record should be located. We will discuss this access method under the more inclusive concept of file organizations in the next section.

File Organizations

File organization: A technique for physically arranging the records of a file on secondary storage devices.

A **file organization** is a technique for physically arranging the records of a file on secondary storage devices. In choosing a file organization for a particular file in a database, you should consider seven important factors:

1. Fast data retrieval

2. High throughput for processing data input and maintenance transactions

3. Efficient use of storage space

4. Protection from failures or data loss

5. Minimizing need for reorganization

6. Accommodating growth

7. Security from unauthorized use

Often these objectives conflict, and you must select a file organization that provides a reasonable balance among the criteria within resources available.

In this chapter we consider the following families of basic file organizations: sequential, indexed, and hashed. Figure 7-6 illustrates each of these organizations with the nicknames of some universities.

Sequential file organization: The records in the file are stored in sequence according to a primary key value.

Sequential File Organizations   In a **sequential file organization**, the records in the file are stored in sequence according to a primary key value (see Figure 7-6a). To locate a particular record, a program must normally scan the file from the beginning until the desired record is located. A common example of a sequential file is the alphabetical list of persons in the white pages of a telephone directory (ignoring any index that may be included with the directory). A comparison of the capabilities of sequential files with the other two types of files appears later in Table 7-3.

Indexed file organization: The records are stored either sequentially or nonsequentially and an index is created that allows software to locate individual records.

Index: A table or other data structure used to determine the location of rows in a file that satisfy some condition.

Secondary key: One field or a combination of fields for which more than one record may have the same combination of values.

Indexed File Organizations   In an **indexed file organization**, the records are stored either sequentially or nonsequentially and an index is created that allows the application software to locate individual records (see Figure 7-6b). Like a card catalog in a library, an **index** is a table that is used to determine the location of rows in a file that satisfy some condition. Each index entry matches a key value with one or more records. An index can point to unique records (a primary key index, such as on the Product_ID field of a product record) or to potentially more than one record. An index that allows each entry to point to more than one record is called a **secondary key** index. Secondary key indexes are important for supporting many reporting requirements and for providing rapid ad hoc data retrieval. An example would be an index on the Finish field of a product record.

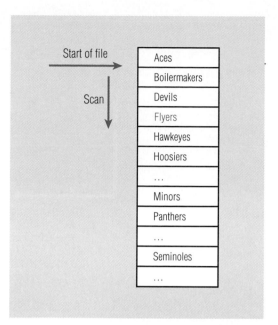

Figure 7-6
Comparison of file
organizations

(a) Sequential

(b) Indexed

(continues)

(c) Hashed

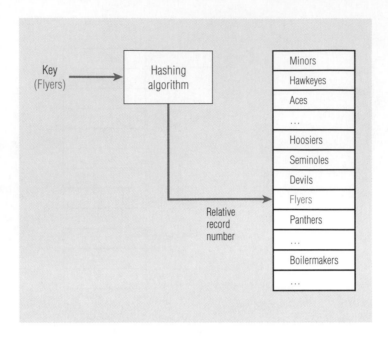

The example in Figure 7-6b illustrates that indexes can be built on top of indexes, creating a hierarchical set of indexes. This may be desirable since an index itself is a file and, if it is very large, it too can be organized by indexing the index. Each index entry in Figure 7-6b has a key value and a pointer to another index or to a data record. For example, to find the record with key 'Flyers', the file organization would start at the top index and take the pointer after the entry F, which points to another index for all keys that begin with the letters A through F in the alphabet. Then the software would follow the pointer after the F in this index, which represents all those records with keys that begin with the letters E through F. Eventually, the search through the indexes either locates the desired record or indicates that no such record exists.

Indexed sequential: Storage of records sequentially by primary key value (within each data block) using a simple index (called a *block index*).

The index structure in Figure 7-6b is called indexed sequential. In an **indexed sequential** organization the records are stored sequentially by primary key value; in Figure 7-6b, records are sequential within each block and the blocks are not necessarily adjacent, but an indexed sequential structure can store all the data records in one sequential file. One common variation of indexed sequential stores a pointer at the end of each index and data record block, and this point has as its value the address of the next block in sequence. For example, there would be another pointer in the first index block on the second level of Figure 7-6b, which would have the address of the index block that begins with the letter H; and the end of the data block with Aces and Boilermakers would have the address of the data block that begins with Flyers. This has been the most common approach to an indexed file organization. An indexed sequential index structure is a nice compromise between a purely sequential file organization and an **indexed nonsequential** file organization, in which each data record may be stored anywhere on disk. Indexed sequential in comparison to indexed nonsequential allows more efficient use of space and faster sequential data processing without much if any sacrifice in random data record accessing speed.

Indexed nonsequential: Storage of records in no particular order using an index to find each record.

One of the most powerful capabilities of indexed file organizations is the ability to create multiple indexes. Multiple indexes exist in a library, where there are indexes on title, author, and subject pointing to the same set of books and journals. Thus, we can virtually create another file by simply creating another index on the same set of data records, so the voluminous data are not replicated. Multiple indexes can be manipulated. For example, if we use the Finish index to find the addresses for the set of product records with the Birch finish and the Cost index to find the set of product records that cost under $500 to make, we can intersect these two sets to find the addresses of those products, and only those products, that are Birch and cost under $500. This ability to use multiple indexes in one query is important in processing queries against a relational database. Logical AND, OR, and NOT operations can be handled by simply manipulating results from an index scan, thus avoiding the more costly access to data records that do not meet all the qualifications of the query.

The general structure of a hierarchical index like that in Figure 7-6b is called a tree (with the root node at the top and leaf nodes at the bottom—yes, the tree is upside down!). The performance of a tree of index entries is greatly influenced by the properties of the tree structure used. The most common type of tree used by access methods and database management systems to store indexes is a balanced tree, or B-tree, and the most popular form of a B-tree is a B+-tree. In a B-tree, all the leaves (which typically contain the data records or pointers to each record) are stored at the same distance from the root, as in Figure 7-6b in which all the data records are stored two levels from the root. The operating system access methods and DBMS manage whatever index tree structure is used, and usually you have little choice on how the index is structured and the management of the tree is transparent to you as database designer or programmer. Appendix C includes a review of tree data structures and the parameters of a tree design over which you might have some control.

Of increasing popularity today is a variety of indexes called a bitmap index. A **bitmap index** (see Figure 7-7) assigns a bitmap for each key value. Suppose a Product table has 10 rows and the Price attribute has 4 different values in these 10 rows (this example is small for illustration purposes). A bitmap index on the Price field would have 4 entries with 10 bits per entry. Each bit in each bitmap entry matches a row in the Product table. If, for example, bit 8 is on for the entry for Price of $400, it indicates that row 8 of the Product table has Price $400 (each bit column will have only one bit on). A bitmap is ideal for attributes that have even a few possible values, which is not true for conventional tree indexes. A bitmap also often requires less storage space (possibly as little as 25 percent) than a conventional tree index (Schumacher, 1997), but for an attribute with many distinct values, a bitmap index can exceed the storage space of a conventional tree index.

An interesting feature of a bitmap index is that one bitmap can be used for multiple keys. For example, we could add another set of rows to the bottom of Figure 7-7

Bitmap index: A table of bits in which each row represents the distinct values of a key and each column is a bit, which when on indicates that the record for that bit column position has the associated field value.

Figure 7-7
Bitmap index on Product Price attribute

	Product Table Row Numbers									
Price	1	2	3	4	5	6	7	8	9	10
100	0	0	1	0	1	0	0	0	0	0
200	1	0	0	0	0	0	0	0	0	0
300	0	1	0	0	0	0	1	0	0	1
400	0	0	0	1	0	1	0	1	1	0

Products 3 and 5 have Price $100
Product 1 has Price $200
Products 2, 7, and 10 have Price $300
Products 4, 6, 8, and 9 have Price $400

for all the values of the Room attribute. Then, each bit column would have two bits on, one for the associated Product row's price and one for room. A query looking for $100 products for the dining room can intersect the bit pattern for the $100 price row with the dining room row to find only those products that satisfy both conditions. Bit manipulation of this nature can be very efficient.

Hashed file organization:
The address for each record is determined using a hashing algorithm.

Hashing algorithm:
A routine that converts a primary key value into a relative record number (or relative file address).

Hashed File Organizations   In a **hashed file organization**, the address of each record is determined using a hashing algorithm (see Figure 7-6c). A **hashing algorithm** is a routine that converts a primary key value into a record address. Although there are several variations of hashed files, in most cases the records are located nonsequentially as dictated by the hashing algorithm. Thus, sequential data processing is impractical.

A typical hashing algorithm uses the technique of dividing each primary key value by a suitable prime number and then using the remainder of the division as the relative storage location. For example, suppose that an organization has a set of approximately 1,000 employee records to be stored on magnetic disk. A suitable prime number would be 997, since it is close to 1,000. Now consider the record for employee 12396. When we divide this number by 997, the remainder is 432. Thus, this record is stored at location 432 in the file. Another technique (not discussed here) must be used to resolve duplicates (or overflow) that can occur with the division/remainder method when two or more keys hash to the same address (known as a "hash clash".)

Summary of File Organizations

The three families of file organizations cover most of the file organizations you will have at your disposal as you design physical files and databases. Although more complex structures can be built using the data structures outlined in Appendix C, you are unlikely to be able to use these with a database management system.

Table 7-3 summarizes the comparative features of sequential, indexed, and hashed file organizations. You should review this table and study from Figure 7-6 why each comparative feature is true.

Clustering Files

Some database management systems allow adjacent secondary memory space to contain rows from several tables. In this case, a physical file does not contain records with identical structures. For example, in Oracle, rows from one, two, or more related tables that are often joined together can be stored in the same area on disk. A cluster is defined by the tables and the column or columns by which the tables are usually joined. For example, a Customer table and a Customer_Order table would be joined by the common value of Customer_ID, or the rows of a Price_Quote table (which contains prices on items purchased from vendors) might be clustered by common values of Item_ID. Clustering reduces the time to access related records compared to the normal allocation of different files to different areas of a disk. Time is reduced since related records will be closer to each other than if the records are stored in separate files in separate areas of the disk. Defining a table to be in only one cluster reduces retrieval performance for only those tables stored in the same cluster.

The following Oracle database definition commands show how a cluster is defined and tables assigned to the cluster. First, the cluster (adjacent disk space) is specified, as in the following example:

Table 7-3 Comparative Features of Different File Organizations

Factor	File Organization		
	Sequential	**Indexed**	**Hashed**
Storage Space	No wasted space	No wasted space for data, but extra space for index	Extra space may be needed to allow for addition and deletion of records after initial set of records is loaded
Sequential Retrieval on Primary Key	Very fast	Moderately fast	Impractical
Random Retrieval on Primary Key	Impractical	Moderately fast	Very fast
Multiple Key Retrieval	Possible, but requires scanning whole file	Very fast with multiple indexes	Not possible
Deleting Records	Can create wasted space or require reorganizing	If space can be dynamically allocated, this is easy, but requires maintenance of indexes	Very easy
Adding New Records	Requires rewriting file	If space can be dynamically allocated, this is easy, but requires maintenance of indexes	Very easy, except multiple keys with same address require extra work
Updating Records	Usually requires rewriting file	Easy, but requires maintenance of indexes	Very easy

```
CREATE CLUSTER ORDERING (CLUSTERKEY CHAR(25));
```

The term ORDERING names the cluster space; the term CLUSTERKEY is required but not used again.

Then tables are assigned to the cluster when the tables are created, such as:

```
CREATE TABLE CUSTOMER (
  CUSTOMER_ID          VARCHAR2(25)  NOT NULL,
  CUSTOMER_ADDRESS     VARCHAR2(15)
  )
  CLUSTER ORDERING (CUSTOMER_ID);

CREATE TABLE ORDER (
  ORDER_ID             VARCHAR2(20)  NOT NULL,
  CUSTOMER_ID          VARCHAR2(25)  NOT NULL,
  ORDER_DATE           DATE
  )
  CLUSTER ORDERING (CUSTOMER_ID);
```

Access to records in a cluster can be specified in Oracle to be via an index on the cluster key or via a hashing function on the cluster key. Reasons for choosing an indexed versus a hashed cluster are similar to those for choosing between indexed and hashed files (see Table 7-3). Clustering records is best used when the records are fairly static; when records are frequently added, deleted, and changed, wasted space can arise and it may be difficult to locate related records close to one another after the initial loading of records, which defines the clusters. Clustering is, however, one option a file designer has to improve the performance of tables that are frequently used together in the same queries and reports.

Designing Controls for Files

One additional aspect of a database file about which you may have design options are the types of controls you can use to protect the file from destruction or contamination or to reconstruct the file if it is damaged. In addition, you may require security controls on fields, files, or databases. We address these options in detail in Chapters 9 and 13. Briefly, files will be damaged, so the key is the ability to rapidly restore a damaged file. Backup procedures provide a copy of a file and of the transactions that have changed the file. When a file is damaged, the file copy or current file along with the log of transactions are used to recover the file to an uncontaminated state. In terms of security, the most effective method is to encrypt the contents of the file so that only programs with access to the decryption routine will be able to see the file contents. Again, these important topics will be covered later when you study the relational data manipulation language SQL in Chapter 9 and the activities of data and database administration in Chapter 13.

USING AND SELECTING INDEXES

Most database manipulations require locating a row (or collection of rows) that satisfy some condition. For example, we may want to retrieve all customers in a given zip code or all students with a particular major. Scanning every row in a table looking for the desired rows may be unacceptably slow, particularly when tables are large, as they often are in real-world applications. Using indexes, as described above, can greatly speed up this process, and defining indexes is an important part of physical database design.

As described in the section on indexes above, indexes on a file can be created for either a primary or a secondary key or both. It is typical that an index would be created for the primary key of each table. The index is itself a table with two columns: the key and the address of the record or records that contain that key value. For a primary key, there will be only one entry in the index for each key value.

Creating a Primary Key Index

The Customer table defined in the section on clustering has a primary key of Customer_ID. A primary key index would be created on this field using the following SQL command:

```
CREATE UNIQUE INDEX CUSTINDEX ON CUSTOMER(CUSTOMER_ID);
```

In this command, CUSTINDEX is the name of the index file created to store the index entries. The ON clause specifies which table is being indexed and the column (or columns) that form the index key. The UNIQUE keyword makes the CUSTINDEX a primary key index. When this command is executed, any existing records in the Customer table would be indexed. If there are duplicate values of Customer_ID, the CREATE INDEX command will fail. Once the index is created, the DBMS will reject any insertion or update of data in the CUSTOMER table that would violate the uniqueness constraint on Customer_IDs.

When a composite primary key exists, you simply list all the elements of the primary key in the ON clause. For example, a table of line items on a customer order might have a composite primary key of Order_ID and Product_ID. The SQL command to create this primary key index for the Order_Line table would be as follows:

```
CREATE UNIQUE INDEX LINEINDEX ON ORDER_LINE(ORDER_ID,PRODUCT_ID);
```

Creating a Secondary Key Index

Database users often want to retrieve rows of a relation based on value for attributes other than the primary key. For example, in a Product table, users might want to retrieve records that satisfy any combination of the following conditions:

- All table products (Description = 'Table')

- All oak furniture (Finish = 'Oak')

- All dining room furniture (Room = 'DR')

- All furniture priced below $500 (Price<500)

To speed up such retrievals, we can define an index on each attribute that we use to qualify a retrieval. For example, we could create an index on the Description field of the Product table with the following SQL command:

```
CREATE INDEX DESCINDX ON PRODUCT(DESCRIPTION);
```

Notice that the term UNIQUE should not be used with secondary key attributes, since each value of the attribute may be repeated. As with primary keys, a secondary key index can be created on a combination of attributes.

To create a bitmap index, you follow a similar command structure. If we wanted a bitmap index for the Description field, the command would be:

```
CREATE BITMAP INDEX DESCBITINDX ON PRODUCT (DESCRIPTION);
```

When to Use Indexes

During physical database design, you must choose which attributes to use to create indexes. There is a trade-off between improved performance for retrievals through the use of indexes, and degraded performance for inserting, deleting, and updating the records in a file. Thus, indexes should be used generously for databases intended primarily to support data retrievals, such as for decision support applications. Indexes should be used judiciously for databases that support transaction processing and other applications with heavy updating requirements, since the indexes impose additional overhead.

Following are some rules of thumb for choosing indexes for relational databases.

1. Indexes are most useful on larger tables.

2. Specify a unique index for the primary key of each table.

3. Indexes are most useful for columns that frequently appear in WHERE clauses of SQL commands either to qualify the rows to select (e.g., WHERE

FINISH = 'Oak', for which an index on Finish would speed retrieval) or for linking (joining) tables (e.g., WHERE PRODUCT.PRODUCT_ID = ORDER_LINE.PRODUCT_ID, for which a secondary key index on Product_ID in the Order_Line table and a primary key index on Product_ID in the Product table would improve retrieval performance). In the latter case, the index is on a foreign key in the Order_Line table that is used in joining tables.

4. Use an index for attributes referenced in ORDER BY (sorting) and GROUP BY (categorizing) clauses. You do have to be careful, though, about these clauses. Be sure that the DBMS will, in fact, use indexes on attributes listed in these clauses (e.g., Oracle uses indexes on attributes in ORDER BY clauses but not GROUP BY clauses).

5. Use an index when there is significant variety in the values of an attribute. Oracle suggests that an index is not useful when there are fewer than 30 different values for an attribute, and an index is clearly useful when there are 100 or more different values for an attribute. Similarly, an index will be helpful only if the results of a query which uses that index do not exceed roughly 20 percent of the total number of records in the file (Schumacher, 1997).

6. Check your DBMS for the limit, if any, on the number of indexes allowable per table. Many systems permit no more than 16 indexes, and may limit the size of an index key value (e.g., no more than 2000 bytes for each composite value). If there is such a limit in your system, you will have to choose those secondary keys that will most likely lead to improved performance.

7. Be careful indexing attributes that have null values. For many DBMSs, rows with a null value will not be referenced in the index (so they cannot be found from an *index search* of ATTRIBUTE = NULL). Such a search will have to be done by scanning the file.

Selecting indexes is arguably the most important physical database design decision, but it is not the only way you can improve the performance of a database. Other ways address such issues as reducing the costs to relocate records, optimizing the use of extra or so-called free space in files, and optimizing query processing algorithms (see Viehman, 1994, for a discussion of these additional ways to enhance physical database design and efficiency). We briefly discuss the topic of query optimization in a later section of this chapter since such optimization can be used to overrule how the DBMS would use certain database design options included because of their expected improvement in data processing performance in most instances.

RAID: IMPROVING FILE ACCESS PERFORMANCE BY PARALLEL PROCESSING

In previous sections of this chapter you learned about denormalization and clustering, two schemes for placing data used together close to one another in disk storage. Denormalization and clustering work well to minimize data access time if data used together in a program can be located within one physical data page. For small records, this is certainly possible. However, data used together or immediately after one another may have to be stored in separate pages; in this case, multiple, sequential disk input/output operations will be required for reading and writing these data.

Thus, denormalization and clustering may not be sufficient schemes for significantly improving data read and write performance.

Two of the inevitable trends in computer technology are the constant reduction in cost and size of computer technologies. These two trends make redundancy of computer components both economically and physically feasible. The feasibility of using multiple, small computer components also allows parallel processing of data. The result of parallel processing of data is that, for example, four input/output operations, when done in parallel, take as long as only one such operation.

Parallel database processing can be accomplished by a database designer through using hardware and software technology called **Redundant Arrays of Inexpensive Disks (RAID)**. RAID storage uses a set, or array, of physical disk drives that appear to the database user (and programs) as if they form one large logical storage unit. Thus, RAID does not change the logical or physical structure of application programs or database queries.

In order to maximize input/output performance of RAID, all the disk drives need to be kept busy. Striping accomplishes the balancing of the workload across the disk drives. Segments of data, called **stripes**, cut across all of the disk drives, as illustrated in Figure 7-8. Logically sequential pages of data (for example, multiple pages for one record, a cluster of records, or several logically sequential records from one file) are stored in round robin fashion across the physical disk drives. Thus, for the hypothetical RAID storage illustrated in Figure 7-8, it would be possible to read four

Redundant Arrays of Inexpensive Disks (RAID): A set, or array, of physical disk drives that appear to the database user (and programs) as if they form one large logical storage unit.

Stripe: The set of pages on all disks in a RAID which are the same relative distance from the beginning of the disk drive.

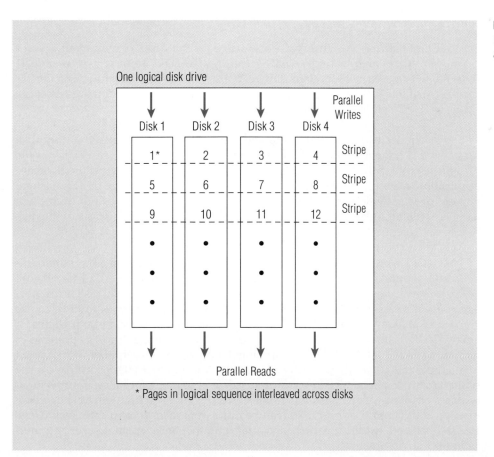

Figure 7-8
RAID with four disks and striping

logically sequential pages of data in parallel, in the elapsed time it takes to read just one page. A very long data record (containing possibly an audio or video field), which is stored in several physical pages, can be read in a fraction of the time it would take without RAID. Or multiple related records (a cluster) that span several pages can be read all at the same time.

Most multiuser operating systems today, including Microsoft NT, UNIX, and Novell NetWare, support some forms of RAID. Such operating systems initiate the parallel read operations and concatenate the results together into one logical record for the requesting program. These operating systems also permit multithreading, in which parallel input/output operations come from different user programs or tasks. RAID can also be implemented in hardware using special adapters, thus offloading from the host computer the work to break down input and output operations into parallel steps.

RAID has one important risk: the increased likelihood of a disk drive failure across the whole database. If the mean time between failures of an individual disk drive is, say, 1.2 million operations, then the mean time between failures of a RAID array with, say, four disk drives will be 1.2 million divided by 4, or every 300,000 parallel disk operations. To cope with this risk and to make disk storage fault tolerant, many types of RAID technologies redundantly store data so that at least one copy of the data is accessible when demanded, or store extra error correction codes so that damaged or lost data can be rebuilt.

Choosing Among RAID Levels

As a file and database designer, you likely will have five types of redundant or error correcting RAID architectures, RAID-1 through RAID-5, from which to choose. RAID-0, which uses no redundant storage, is also used since it has the fastest performance by utilizing the highest degree of parallelism. Figure 7-9 compares these six forms of RAID and lists a few key features of each form.

RAID-0   The fastest read/write time and most efficient data storage of any disk array type is achieved with RAID-0 (see Figure 7-9a). In RAID-0, every disk in the array is used to store application data. RAID-0 is typically used when the database application accesses very large records (thus requiring most of one or even several stripes) or is extremely input/output intensive. Since RAID-0 does not utilize any form of data redundancy or stripe error correction codes, a failure in any of the disk drives can corrupt the database.

RAID-1   One way to improve fault tolerance is to store application data redundantly. A fully redundant storage, or disk mirror, is accomplished in RAID-1 (see Figure 7-9b), in which each page is redundantly written. Although the total disk array storage space is effectively cut in half, the database has a high degree of fault tolerance since it is unlikely that exactly the same page will be damaged in both copies. A single RAID-1 array of two disk drives does not use striping, but it is possible to append several dual disk RAID-1 arrays together to form a larger array with striping (sometimes this alternative to RAID-1 is called RAID-10). In RAID-1, each page write operation is done in parallel to a pair of disk drives, so no performance improvement is achieved. However, two read operations, even if generated from separate database queries in different user programs, can be done in parallel *for each dual array.* Thus, RAID-1 has both excellent performance and fault tolerance for single-user and multiple-user environments.

Figure 7-9
Six levels of RAID

(a) RAID-0

(b) RAID-1 with two pairs of mirrored disks

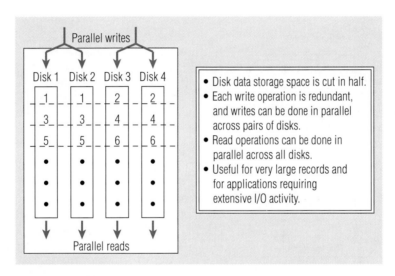

(c) RAID-2 with half the drives used for data

(d) RAID-3

- Each data record spans all data disks.
- ***One*** disk is used exclusively for error correction codes (ECCs) (so more data space than in RAID-2).
- ECC is used to recover damaged data or drive in stripe.
- Each write operation uses all drives in parallel.
- Each read operation uses all drives in parallel.
- Only one program accesses array at a time.

(e) RAID-4

- Potentially many records in one stripe.
- ***One*** disk is used exclusively for error correction codes (ECCs) (so more data space than in RAID-2), but this drive is very busy if frequent write operations.
- ECC is used to recover damaged data or drive in stripe.
- Write operations done in parallel.
- Read operations done in parallel.
- Accesses from several programs can be processed in parallel in the array.

(f) RAID-5

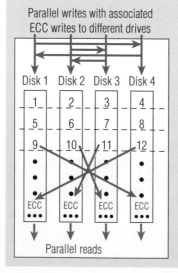

- Potentially many records in one stripe.
- ***All*** disks are used for data and error correction codes (ECCs), so no bottleneck to write ECCs.
- ECC is used to recover damaged data or drive in stripe.
- Write operations are done in parallel.
- Read operations are done in parallel.
- Accesses from several programs can be processed in parallel in the array.

RAID-2   In RAID-2 (see Figure 7-9c), some disks are used with data striping for parallel data processing (without redundant storage) and other disks are dedicated to storing error correction codes. The error correction codes are used to detect errors in the stripes and to reconstruct data when pages within the data stripes are damaged. Thus, whereas RAID-1 uses redundancy to allow recovery from damaged data, RAID-2 (and subsequent levels) uses more efficient error correction, or parity, codes. However, since most disk drives in computers today already store page-level error correction codes, or parity information, within each physical page, RAID-2 is less desirable than RAID-3.

RAID-3   As with RAID-2, RAID-3 stripes data across drives, but only one drive stores stripe-level error correction codes (see Figure 7-9d). Error correction codes embedded within each page are used to detect page errors, but a page's error correction code cannot be used to recover a damaged page. Assume that drive 3 in Figure 7-9c crashes. Then page 3 in each stripe can be recovered from the other data pages and the error correction page in its stripe by an exclusive OR calculation within the stripe. RAID-3 is usually used when very long records exist, such that one record requires one or more stripes. Thus, each logical input/output operation uses, or spans, all the drives in the array. Consequently, since each logical input/output operation utilizes the whole array, it is not possible to process in parallel requests from multiple users or programs. So, RAID-3 works best in single-user and uniprogramming environments.

RAID-4   In RAID-4, stripe-level error correction codes are stored on only one drive as in RAID-3, but multiple records are stored in a stripe (see Figure 7-9e). Thus, read operations to different records from the same or different programs can be done in parallel across the drives. The bottleneck is the parity drive, since it must be accessed to have an error correction page updated when any data record is rewritten. For databases with frequent record updates, such as for on-line transaction processing, this can create considerable contention (and hence delay) for the parity drive, reducing the advantages of parallel processing. This bottleneck can be avoided by using RAID-5.

RAID-5   Also called *Rotating Parity Array,* RAID-5 (see Figure 7-9f) does not use a dedicated parity drive. Each drive contains both data and parity pages. Read operations can be done in parallel on all drives. A write operation will access its one or more drives to write the new record plus the parity drive *for that record.* Different records store their error correction codes, for recovery purposes, on different drives. Thus, write operations can also be done in parallel with less likelihood of delay compared to RAID-4 since random record updates will generate random error correction page updates randomly distributed across the drives.

RAID Performance

As noted in the prior sections, RAID-1, RAID-3, and RAID-5 dominate the other forms of fault-tolerant RAID. Since RAID-3 is designed for single-user or data-intensive situations, this form of RAID has specialized applicability. For most database applications, this means that you will most likely choose between RAID-1 or RAID-5.

One RAID manufacturer, Distributed Processing Technology (http://www.dpt.com), has compared the performance of RAID-1 and RAID-5 for both read and write operations with various numbers of disk drives in the array and for disk drives with different transfer rates. As you might expect, RAID-5 more efficiently uses storage space since it does not store data redundantly. RAID-5 outperforms RAID-1 in read operations since greater parallelism is possible with the same number or disk drives in the array. However, write times with RAID-5 can be anywhere from 1.67 to 3 times those for RAID-1 (depending on the benchmark application and array configuration). Thus, RAID-5 is less desirable than RAID-1 for highly volatile files. DPT has also estimated that in order to make write operations twice as fast as on one drive, RAID-1 requires an array of four disk drives whereas RAID-5 requires from seven to twelve disk drives.

So, what form of RAID is best? RAID-1 is best for fault-tolerant, database maintenance applications (those requiring a high percentage of up-time) or when only two disk drives are affordable. RAID-5 is best for read-intensive applications against very large data sets and at least three (and more typically five) disk drives are affordable.

DESIGNING DATABASES

Most modern information systems utilize database technologies, either database management systems or data warehouse systems, for data storage and retrieval. Recall that a database is a collection of logically related data, designed to meet the information needs of multiple users in an organization. The relationship between files in a database is due to relationships identified in the conceptual and logical data models. The relationships imply access paths between data. Each type of database technology allows different types of access paths. So, the process of choosing the appropriate type of DBMS or data warehousing technology is one of matching the needed access paths with the capabilities of the database technology.

Choosing Database Architectures

There are different styles of database management and data warehousing systems, each characterized by the way data are defined and structured, called database architectures. Deciding which database architecture best suits your database is fundamental to database design. A particular database management or warehousing system supports one of five different architectures. Figure 7-10 compares these five architectures:

1. *Hierarchical database model*   In this model, files are arranged in a top-down structure that resembles a tree or genealogy chart. Data are related in a nested, one-to-many set of relationships. The top file is called the root, the bottom files are called leaves, and intermediate files have one parent, or owner, file and one or several children files. Among the oldest of the database architectures, many hierarchical databases exist in larger organizations today. This technology is best applied when the conceptual data model also resembles a tree and when most data access begins with the same (root) file. Hierarchical database technology is used for high-volume transaction processing and MIS applications. Few new databases are developed with hierarchical DBMSs since newer applications tend to have broader needs than simply transaction processing or summarization of transaction data.

2. *Network database model*   In this model, each file may be associated with an arbitrary number of files. Although very flexible because any relationships can be implemented (a hierarchy is a special case of a network), the form of implementation, usually using pointers between related records in different

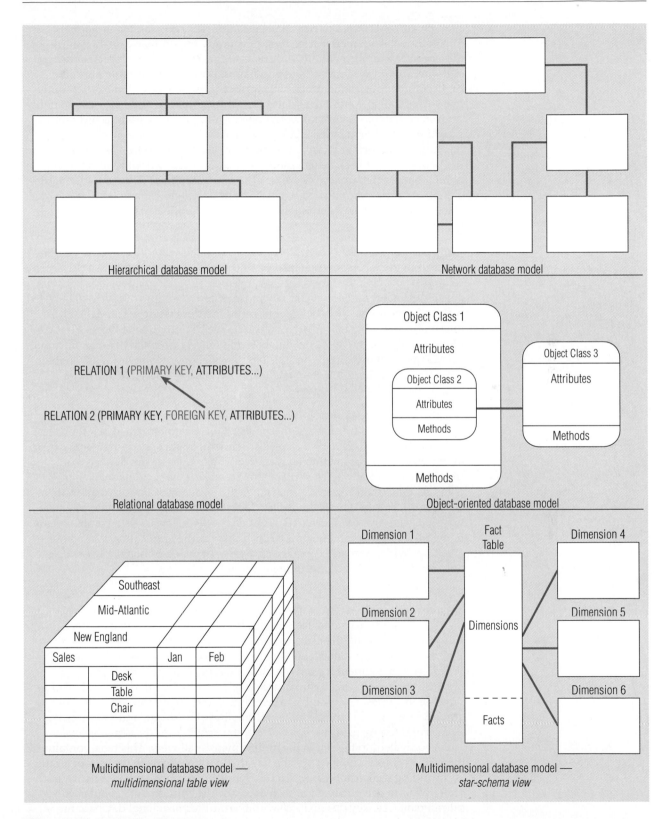

Hierarchical database model

Network database model

RELATION 1 (PRIMARY KEY, ATTRIBUTES...)

RELATION 2 (PRIMARY KEY, FOREIGN KEY, ATTRIBUTES...)

Relational database model

Object Class 1

Attributes

Object Class 2

Attributes

Methods

Methods

Object Class 3

Attributes

Methods

Object-oriented database model

Southeast
Mid-Atlantic
New England

Sales		Jan	Feb
Desk			
Table			
Chair			

Multidimensional database model —
multidimensional table view

Dimension 1

Dimension 2

Dimension 3

Fact Table

Dimensions

Facts

Dimension 4

Dimension 5

Dimension 6

Multidimensional database model —
star-schema view

Figure 7-10 Database architectures

files, creates significant overhead in storage space and maintenance time. Typically, network model systems support only one-to-many relationships along each arc in the network, but some support many-to-many relationships. Network model systems are still popular on powerful mainframes and for high-volume transaction processing applications. Since the database designer has such detailed control over data organizations, it is possible to design highly optimized databases with network systems. For example, each record type (a record type is shown by each box in the network) can be organized using hashing algorithms or located near another related record type—an early form of clustering. Network systems support a wider variety of processing requirements than do hierarchical database systems, but network systems still require significant programming and database design knowledge and time, and hence are used primarily in those organizations with significant expertise with such technologies.

3. *Relational database model*   The most common database model for new systems defines simple tables for each relation and many-to-many relationships. Cross-reference keys link the tables together, representing the relationships between entities. Primary and secondary key indexes provide rapid access to data based upon qualifications. Most new applications are built using relational DBMSs, and many relational DBMS products exist. See Chapter 6 for a thorough review of the features of the relational database model and Chapter 10 for an introduction to query-by-example, one style of relational query language and Chapter 9 for coverage of the SQL relational data manipulation language, the most widely used relational language.

4. *Object-oriented database model*   In this model, attributes and methods that operate on those attributes are encapsulated in structures called object classes. Relationships between object classes are shown, in part, by nesting or encapsulating one object class within another. New object classes are defined from more general object classes. A major advantage of this data model is that complex data types like graphics, video, and sound are supported as easily as simpler data types. This is the newest DBMS technology and larger organizations are gaining experience with it by selectively using it when complex data or event-driven programming is appropriate for the application. Chapters 5 and 12 provide extensive coverage of the use of the data model for conceptual data modeling and database implementation.

5. *Multidimensional database model*   This database model is used in data warehousing applications. Two ways of viewing this model exist. The first views data as a multidimensional table in which each cell contains one or more simple attributes and the dimensions are ways to categorize the raw data. These categories, or dimensions, are the factors on which users want to summarize or segment the data, such as time periods, geography, lines of business, or people. A cell contains data relevant to the intersection of all of its dimension values. For example, a cell might hold the number-of-units-sold attribute for a given time period, location, line of business, and salesperson. The second (equivalent) view is called a star schema. At the center is a fact table, equivalent to the cell in the multidimensional view. This table contains all the raw attributes and a composite key made up of the primary keys of all the surrounding dimension tables. The surrounding dimension tables define each of the ways to categorize data, such as all the description data about each salesperson. The key design issue with the multidimensional database model is identifying in advance the lowest common denominator of data, and hence all

the dimensions or categories by which users wish to summarize the raw facts. Although the multidimensional database model is a special case of both the relational and network data models, special DBMSs have been developed that optimize dimensional data processing. Chapter 14 deals with data warehousing and the multidimensional data model.

We have chosen to cover in greater detail in this textbook only the three newest of these database models: relational, object-oriented, and multidimensional. If you want to know more about hierarchical and network database models, refer to some of the sources listed in Further Reading at the end of this chapter.

OPTIMIZING FOR QUERY PERFORMANCE

The primary purpose today for physical database design is to optimize the performance of database processing. Database processing includes adding, deleting, and modifying a database, as well as a variety of data retrieval activities. For databases that have greater retrieval traffic than maintenance traffic, optimizing the database for query performance (producing online or off-line anticipated and ad hoc screens and reports for end users) is the primary goal. This chapter has already covered most of the decisions you can make to tune the database design to meet the need of database queries (clustering, indexes, file organizations, etc.). In this final section of this chapter we introduce a few additional advanced database design and processing options now available in many DBMSs.

One of the major computer architectural changes over the last few years is the increased use of multiple processors in database servers. Database servers frequently use symmetric multiprocessor (SMP) or massive parallel processor (MMP) technology (Schumacher, 1997). To take advantage of this parallel processing capability, some of the more sophisticated DBMSs include strategies for breaking apart a query into modules that can be processed in parallel by each of the related processors. The most common approach is to replicate the query so that each copy works against a portion of the database, usually a horizontal partition (sets of rows). The partitions need to be defined in advance by the database designer. The same query is run against each portion in parallel on separate processors, and the intermediate results from each processor are combined to create the final query result as if the query were run against the whole database.

Suppose you have an Order table with several million rows for which query performance has been slow. To ensure that subsequent scans of this table are performed in parallel using at least three processors, you would alter the structure of the table with the SQL command:

```
ALTER TABLE ORDER PARALLEL 3
```

You need to tune each table to the best degree of parallelism, so it is not uncommon to alter a table several times until the right degree is found.

A second option for using parallel scanning on a table occurs when the query is written. When the DBMS parses a query, it decides, based on statistics it keeps about the database structure, number of distinct values for fields, and the query what is the best strategy—called a query plan—for accessing each index and table. The DBMS includes rules that consider these statistics and the DMBS uses these rules to pick the best query plan. The module of the DMBS that does these calculations is called the cost-based optimizer. The query plan calculated by the cost-based optimizer says what table or index to use first and how to use it, then what table or index to use next, and so on. Oracle includes an ANALYZE command that collects these statistics and stores them for use by the DBMS.

It is possible in some DBMSs to give the DBMS a hint or suggestion within the query to force the DBMS to process the query in a certain way. For example, suppose we wanted to count the number of orders processed by a particular sales representative, Smith. In Oracle, parallel table processing works only when a table is scanned, not when it is accessed via an index. So, in Oracle, we need to force both a full table scan as well as scanning in parallel. The SQL command for this query would be as follows:

```
SELECT /*+ FULL(ORDER) PARALLEL(ORDER,3) */ COUNT(*)
   FROM ORDER
   WHERE SALESPERSON = "SMITH";
```

The clause inside the /* */ delimiters is the hint to Oracle. This hint overrides whatever query plan Oracle would naturally create for this query. Thus, a hint is specific to each query, but the use of such hints must be anticipated by altering the structure of tables to be handled with parallel processing.

Parallel query processing speed can be impressive. Schumacher (1997) reports of a test in which the time to perform a query was cut in half with parallel processing compared to a normal table scan. Since an index is a table, indexes can also be given the parallel structure, so that scans of an index are also faster. Again, Schumacher (1997) shows an example where the cost to create an index by parallel processing was reduced from approximately seven minutes to five seconds!

This concludes our discussion of advanced options for tuning the performance of a database. All options are not available with every DBMS, and each DBMS often has unique options due to its underlying design. You should refer to reference manuals for your DBMS to know what specific tuning options are available to you.

SUMMARY

During physical database design, you the designer translate the logical description of data into the technical specifications for storing and retrieving data. The goal is to create a design for storing data that will provide adequate performance and insure database integrity, security, and recoverability. In physical database design you consider normalized relations and data volume estimates, data definitions, data processing requirements and their frequencies, user expectations, and database technology characteristics to establish field specifications, record designs, file organizations, and a database architecture.

A field is the smallest unit of application data, corresponding to an attribute in the logical data model. You must determine the data type, integrity controls, and how to handle missing values for each field, among other factors. A data type is a detailed coding scheme for representing organizational data. Data may be coded or compressed to reduce storage space. Field integrity control includes specifying a default value, range of permissible values, null value permission, and referential integrity.

A physical record is a group of fields stored in adjacent memory locations and retrieved together as a unit. Physical records are usually stored in a page, which is the amount of data read or written in one secondary memory input or output operation. The number of records in a page is called the blocking factor. For efficiency reasons, the attributes of one relation and only those attributes may not be stored in one physical record. A process of denormalization transforms normalized relations into unnormalized physical record specifications. Denormalization is done to place in one physical record those attributes frequently needed together in an I/O operation. Denormalization includes horizontal partitioning, which breaks a relation into multiple record specifications by placing different rows into different records based upon common column values. Denormalization also includes vertical partitioning, which distributes the columns of a relation into separate files, repeating the primary key in each of the files.

A physical file is a named portion of secondary memory allocated for the purpose of storing physical records. Data within a physical file are organized through a combination of sequential storage and pointers. A pointer is a field of data that can be used to locate a related field or record of data. Operating access methods are algorithms that use the combination of sequential and pointer storage to place and find data.

A file organization uses operating access methods to arrange the records of a file on a secondary storage device. The three major categories of file organizations are: (1) sequential, which stores records in sequence according to a primary key value; (2) indexed, in which records are stored sequentially or nonsequentially and an index is used to keep track of where the records are stored; (3) hashed, in which the address of each record is determined using an algorithm that converts a primary key value into a record address. Physical records of several types can be clustered together into one physical file in order to place records frequently used together close to one another in secondary memory.

The indexed file organization is one of the most popular in use today. An index may be based on a primary key or a secondary key, which allows more than one record to be associated with the same key value. The newest form of an index, a bitmap index, creates a table of bits in which an on bit means that the related record has the related key value. Indexes are important in speeding up data retrieval, especially when multiple conditions are used for selecting, sorting, or relating data. Indexes are useful in a wide variety of situations, including for large tables, for columns that are frequently used to qualify the data to be retrieved, when a field has a large number of distinct values, and when data processing is dominated by data retrieval rather than data maintenance.

File access efficiency and file reliability can be enhanced by the use of Redundant Arrays of Inexpensive Disks, RAID. RAID allows blocks of data from one or several programs to be read and written in parallel to different disks, thus reducing the input/output days with traditional sequential I/O operations on a single disk drive. Six levels of RAID allow a file and database designer to choose the combination of access efficiency, space utilization, and fault tolerance best suited for the database applications.

Database architectures in use today are hierarchical, network, relational, object-oriented, and multidimensional. Hierarchical and network primarily appear in legacy applications, whereas relational, object-oriented, and multidimensional are used for new systems development.

The introduction of multiprocessor database servers has made possible new capabilities in database management systems. One major new feature is the ability to break a query apart and to process the query in parallel against segments of a table. Such parallel query processing can greatly improve the speed of query processing. Also, database programmers can improve database processing performance by providing the DBMS with hints about the sequence in which to perform table operations. These hints override the cost-based optimizer of the DBMS. Both the DBMS and programmers can look at statistics about the database to determine how to process a query.

This chapter concludes the section of this book on database design. Having developed complete physical data specifications, you are now ready to begin implementing the database with database technology. Implementation means defining the database and programming client and server routines to handle the queries, reports, and transactions against the database. These are primary topics of the next five chapters, which cover relational database implementation on client platforms, server platforms, client/server environments, and with object-oriented technologies.

CHAPTER REVIEW

KEY TERMS

Access method	Horizontal partitioning	Redundant Array of
Bitmap index	Index	Inexpensive Disks
Blocking factor	Indexed file organization	(RAID)
Data type	Indexed nonsequential	Secondary key
Denormalization	Indexed sequential	Sequential file
Field	Page	organization
File organization	Physical file	Stripe
Hashed file organization	Physical record	Vertical partitioning
Hashing algorithm	Pointer	

REVIEW QUESTIONS

1. Define each of the following terms:
   a. file organization
   b. sequential file organization
   c. indexed file organization
   d. hashing file organization
   e. denormalization
   f. index
   g. secondary key
   h. data type
   i. bitmap index
   j. RAID

2. Contrast the following terms:
   a. horizontal partitioning; vertical partitioning
   b. indexed sequential; indexed nonsequential
   c. physical record; physical file
   d. page; physical record
   e. secondary key; primary key

3. What are the major inputs to physical database design?

4. What are the key decisions in physical database design?

5. What information is shown on a composite usage map?

6. What decisions have to be made to develop a field specification?

7. What are the objectives of selecting a data type for a field?

8. Why are field values coded or compressed?

9. What options are available for controlling field integrity?

10. Describe three ways to handle missing field values.

11. Describe how to calculate the address of the beginning of a desired field for a file containing all fixed-length fields.

12. Explain why normalized relations may not be efficient physical records.

13. List three common situations that suggest denormalizing relations to form physical records.

14. What are the advantages and disadvantages of horizontal and vertical partitioning?

15. What two basic constructs are used to link one piece of data with another piece of data in physical files?

16. List seven important criteria in selecting a file organization.

17. Why is an indexed nonsequential structure for an indexed file organization desirable?

18. Under what circumstances is a bitmap index desirable?

19. What is the purpose of clustering of data in a file?

20. State seven rules of thumb for choosing indexes.

21. Contrast the two ways of viewing multidimensional databases.

22. Explain two options for optimizing query performance.

23. Which level of RAID is best? Why?

PROBLEMS AND EXERCISES

1. Match the following terms to the appropriate definitions:

   _____ bitmap index   a. data read in one I/O operation

   _____ hashing algorithm   b. the number of records in a page

   _____ page   c. a named area of secondary memory

   _____ physical record   d. a table of zeros and ones

   _____ pointer   e. a field not containing business data

   _____ blocking factor   f. converts a key value into an address

   _____ physical file   g. adjacent fields

2. Consider the following two relations for Lakewood College:

   ```
   STUDENT (Student_ID, Student_Name, Campus_Address, GPA)
   REGISTRATION (Student_ID, Course_ID, Grade)
   ```

   Following is a typical query against these relations:

   ```
   SELECT STUDENT.STUDENT_ID, STUDENT_NAME, COURSE_ID, GRADE
     FROM STUDENT, REGISTRATION
         WHERE    STUDENT.STUDENT_ID = REGISTRATION.STUDENT_ID
         AND      GPA > 3.0
     ORDER BY STUDENT_NAME;
   ```

    a. On what attributes should indexes be defined to speed up the above query? Give the reasons for each attribute selected.

    b. Write SQL commands to create indexes for each attribute you identified in (a).

3. Consider the composite usage map in Figure 7-1. After a period of time, the assumptions for this usage map have changed as follows:

    a. There is an average of 40 quotations (rather than 50) for each supplier.

    b. Manufactured parts represent only 30 percent of all parts and purchased parts represent 75 percent.

    c. The number of direct access to purchased parts increases to 75 per hour (rather than 60).

Draw a new composite usage map reflecting this new information to replace Figure 7-1.

4. Choose Oracle data types for the attributes in the normalized relations in Figure 7-4.

5. Suppose you were designing a default value for the age field in a student record at your university. What possible values would you consider and why? How might the default vary by other characteristics about the student, such as school within the university or degree sought?

6. When a student has not chosen a major at a university, the university often enters a value of "Undecided" for the major field. Is "Undecided" a default value or a way to represent the null value?

7. Consider the following normalized relations from a database in a large retail chain:

STORE (Store_ID, Region, Manager_ID, Square_Feet)

EMPLOYEE (Employee_ID, Where_Work, Employee_Name, Employee_Address)

DEPARTMENT (Department_ID, Manager_ID, Sales_Goal)

SCHEDULE (Department_ID, Employee_ID, Date)

What opportunities might exist for denormalizing these relations when defining the physical records for this database? Under what circumstances would you consider creating such denormalized records?

8. Assume that you have a hard disk file designated to accommodate a maximum of 1,000 records of 240 bytes each. Assume that a page is 4,000 bytes in length and that records may not span pages. How many bytes will be needed for this file?

9. What problems might arise from vertically partitioning a relation? Given these potential problems, what general conditions influence when to partition a relation vertically?

10. Is it possible with a sequential file organization to permit sequential scanning of the data based on several sorted orders? If not, why not? If it is possible, how?

11. Suppose each record in a file were connected to its prior and next record in key sequence using pointers. Thus, each record might have the following format:

Primary key, other attributes, pointer to prior record, pointer to next record.

    a. What would be the advantages of this file organization compared to a sequential file organization?

    b. In contrast to a sequential file organization, would it be possible to keep the records in multiple sequences? Why or why not?

12. Assume a student file in a university database had an index on Student_ID (the primary key) and indexes on Major, Age, Marital_Status, and Home_Zipcode (all secondary keys). Further, assume that the university wanted a list of students majoring

in MIS or Computer Science, over the age of 25, and married OR students majoring in Computer Engineering, single, and from the 45462 zipcode. How could indexes be used so that only records that satisfy this qualification are accessed?

13. Consider again the student file described in Problem and Exercise 12. For which of the indexes would it make sense to use a bitmap index? What conditions have to hold for a bitmap index to make sense? Choose one of the keys that is a likely candidate for a bitmap index and draw a figure similar to Figure 7-7 showing the structure of that index.

14. Consider Figure 7-6c. Assuming that the empty rows in the leaves of this index show space where new records can be stored, explain where the record for 'Sooners' would be stored. Where would the record for 'Flashes' be stored? What might happen when one of the leaves is full and a new record needs to be added to that leaf?

15. Consider Figure 7-10, which compared the general characteristics of the most popular database architectures. Write relations equivalent to the multidimensional table view database model.

16. Can clustering of files occur after the files are populated with records? Why or why not?

17. Parallel query processing, as described in this chapter, means that the same query is run on multiple processors and each processor accesses in parallel a different subset of the database. Another form of parallel query processing, not discussed in this chapter, would partition the query so that each part of the query runs on a different processor but that part accesses whatever part of the database it needs. Most queries involve a qualification clause that selects the records of interest in the query. In general, this qualification clause is of the form:

    (condition OR condition OR …) AND (condition OR condition OR …) AND …

    Given this general form, how might a query be broken apart so that each parallel processor handles a subset of the query, and then combines the subsets together after each part is processed?

18. In Figure 7-9f, suppose records 2, 3, 7, and 9 are being updated simultaneously by four different users. Which of these records could be updated in parallel? Design the scheduling of these updates to maximize parallel processing.

FIELD EXERCISES

---

1. Find out what database management systems are available at your university for student use. Investigate which data types these DBMSs support. Compare these DBMSs based upon data types supported and suggest which types of applications each DBMS is best suited for based on this comparison.

2. Using the Web site for this text and other Internet resources, investigate the parallel processing capabilities of several leading DBMSs. How do their capabilities differ?

3. Using the Web site for this text and other Internet resources, investigate the capabilities of object-oriented database products. How much do these DBMSs cost? For what types of applications do the vendors suggest using their products?

4. Contact a database designer or administrator in an organization with which you are familiar. Ask what file organizations are available in the various DBMSs used in that

organization. Interview this person to learn what factors he or she considers when selecting an organization for database files. For indexed files, ask how he or she decides what indexes to create. Are indexes ever deleted? Why?

5. Contact a database designer or administrator in an organization with which you are familiar. Ask if the person uses RAID technology with the organization's databases. Why or why not? If the person is using RAID, what level(s) are employed? Why?

REFERENCES

Babad, Y. M., and J. A. Hoffer. 1984. "Even No Data Has a Value." *Communications of the ACM* 27 (August): 748–56.

Finkelstein, R. 1988. "Breaking the Rules Has a Price." *Database Programming & Design* 1 (June): 11–14.

Hoffer, J., J. George, and J. Valacich. 1999. *Modern System Analysis and Design.* 2nd ed. Reading, MA: Addison-Wesley.

Inmon, W. H. 1988. "What Price Normalization." *ComputerWorld* (October 17): 27, 31.

Rogers, U. 1989. "Denormalization: Why, What, and How?" *Database Programming & Design* 2 (December): 46–53.

Schumacher, R. 1997. "Oracle Performance Strategies." *DBMS* 10 (May): 89–93.

Viehman, P. 1994. "24 Ways to Improve Database Peformance." *Database Programming & Design* 7 (February): 32–41.

FURTHER READING

Bontempo, C. J., and C. M. Saracco. 1996. "Accelerating Indexed Searching." *Database Programming & Design* 9 (July): 37–43.

Elmasri, R. and S. Navathe. 1994. *Fundamentals of Database Systems.* 2nd ed. Menlo Park, CA: Benjamin/Cummings.

Loney, K., E. Aronoff, and N. Sonawalla. 1996. "Big Tips for Big Tables." *Database Programming & Design* 9 (November): 58–62.

Project Case

You have been developing a database for Mountain View Community Hospital throughout the preceding chapters. In this project case you will make some physical database design decisions based on the conceptual and relational database you developed in Chapters 3 and 6.

PROJECT DESCRIPTION

Mountain View Community Hospital has decided to use a relational database management system (DBMS), Oracle, for this database. Thus, the design of the physical database must conform to the capabilities of this DBMS. (If you are not familiar with Oracle, you can alternatively assume that Mountain View Community Hospital chose another DBMS with which you are familiar, and then answer the following questions accordingly.)

PROJECT QUESTIONS

1. What additional kinds of information, besides the 3NF relations you developed in the Project Case in Chapter 6 for the conceptual database of Chapter 3, do you need to do physical database design for this database?

2. Are there opportunities for horizontal or vertical partitioning of this database? If you are not sure, what other information would you need to answer this question with greater certainty?

3. Case Figure 1 shows an initial composite usage map for a portion of the Mountain View Community Hospital database. Since the usage map was developed, a few assumptions about the use of the data have changed:

   • There is an average of 12 (rather than 10) item consumptions per patient.

   • There is an average of 40 (rather than 30) times per hour that performance data are accessed for patients, and each time, the corresponding treatment data are also accessed.

   Draw a new version of Figure 1 reflecting this new information.

PROJECT EXERCISES

1. In Project Exercise 4 from Chapter 6, you wrote CREATE TABLE commands for each relation in the logical database for the Mountain View Community Hospital conceptual database of Chapter 3. However, you did so not fully understanding the physical database design choices you might have available to you in Oracle (or whatever DBMS you are using for this project). Reconsider your previous CREATE TABLE commands in answering the following questions:

   a. Would you choose different data types for any fields? Why?

   b. Are any fields candidates for coding? If so, what coding scheme would you use for each of these fields?

   c. Which fields may take on a null value?

   d. Suppose the date of performing a treatment were not entered. What procedures would you use for handling these missing data? Can you and should you use a default value for this field? Why or why not?

2. In Project Question 2 above, you were asked to identify opportunities for data partitioning. Besides partitioning, do you see other opportunities for denormalization of the relations for this database? If not, why not? If yes, where and how might you denormalize?

3. In Project Question 3 above, you updated Figure 1, a composite usage map, for part of the Mountain View Community Hospital database. Referring to this updated version of Figure 1, do you see any opportunities for clustering rows from two or more tables? Why or why not?

4. Write CREATE INDEX commands for the primary key indexes of each table in the Mountain View Community Hospital database.

5. Consider the following query against the Mountain View Community Hospital database: For each treatment performance in the past two weeks, list in order by treatment ID and within ID

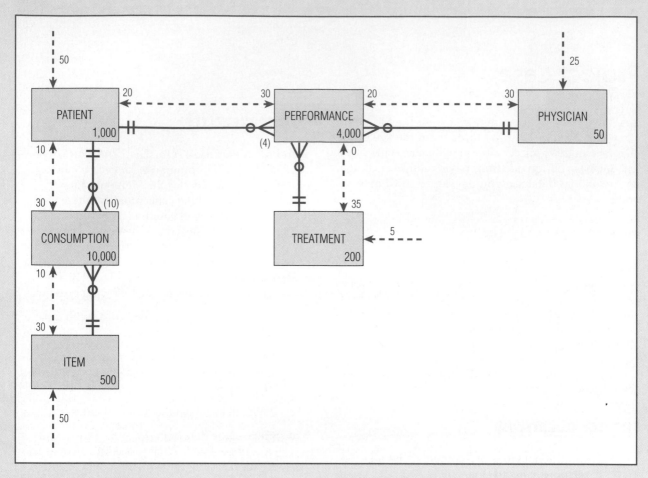

Figure 1
Composite usage map

by date in reverse chronological order, the physicians performing each treatment (grouped by treatment) and the number of times this physician performed that treatment that day.

Create secondary key indexes to optimize the performance of this query. Make any assumptions you need to answer this question.

PART

IV

Implementation

CHAPTER 8

Client/Server and Middleware

CHAPTER 9

SQL

CHAPTER 10

Database Access from Client Applications

CHAPTER 11

Distributed Databases

CHAPTER 12

Object-Oriented Database Development

Part IV Overview

Part IV considers topics associated with implementing relational and object-oriented database systems for one centralized and several distributed sites. Database implementation, as indicated in Chapter 2, includes coding and testing database processing programs, completing database documentation and training materials, and installing databases and converting data, as necessary, from prior systems. Here, at last, is the point in the systems development life cycle that the prior activities, enterprise modeling, conceptual data modeling, and logical and physical database design, have directed us toward. At the end of implementation we expect a functioning system that meets users' information requirements. After that, the system will be put into production use, and database maintenance will be necessary for the life of the system. The chapters in Part IV help you develop an initial understanding of the complexities and challenges of implementing a database system.

Chapter 8 covers client/server architectures and middleware. These architectures operate in networked environments, splitting application processing between front-end clients and back-end processors or servers. The potential for tailoring client/server architectures closely to business needs, thereby improving productivity while reducing costs, induces close attention to the development of effective client/server architectures. Current trends in client/server are included here, and an understanding of how middleware facilitates these trends is provided.

Chapter 9 describes SQL (Structured Query Language), which has become a standard language (especially on database servers) for creating and processing relational databases. In addition to a brief history of SQL that includes discussion of the present SQL-92 and the proposed SQL3 standards, the syntax of SQL is explored. Data definition language (DDL) commands used to create a database are included, as are data manipulation language (DML) commands used to query the database. A brief introduction to database triggers and stored procedures complete the chapter.

Chapter 10 provides an introduction to implementing client-side databases, emphasizing Microsoft Access, including graphical user interfaces (GUIs),

Query-by-Example (QBE), forms designers, and report generators. The Access QBE is contrasted with SQL coding. The components of a client application, including menus, forms, and reports are illustrated using Access97. More advanced topics, such as achieving database access from client applications, the use of embedded SQL or Visual Basic for Applications, and the access of databases through the Web, are also included.

Chapter 11 discusses approaches and problems to building distributed databases. We consider the potential risks and advantages associated with distributed databases, along with the business conditions which make development of distributed databases desirable. Strategies for design are included. Considerations such as synchronous and asynchronous data replication and partitioning are raised. Steps to take which result in optimal distributed query processing are also included.

Chapter 12 demonstrates the transformation of conceptual object-oriented models into logical schemas that can be implemented using object database management systems (ODBMSs). The introduction of object definition language (ODL) allows the reader to create logical object-oriented database schemas. Readers learn to transform the conceptual UML class diagrams presented in Chapter 5 into the logical ODL schemas of this chapter. Skills needed to accomplish this type specification for attributes, operation arguments, and operation returns, creation of different structure types, creation of objects, and specification of attribute values for objects. Object query language (OQL), which is similar to SQL, is also included, and the reader learns to formulate OQL queries in much the same fashion as SQL queries were formulated in Chapter 9.

As indicated by the brief synopses of the chapters, Part IV provides both a conceptual understanding of the issues involved in implementing database applications and a practical initial understanding of the procedures necessary to construct a database prototype. The introduction of recent strategies, such as client/server and distributed databases, as well as strategies which are only beginning to win acceptance, such as object-oriented database schemas, equips the reader to understand expected future developments in databases.

8

Client/Server and Middleware

After studying this chapter, you should be able to:

■ Define the following key terms: **client/server systems, file server, fat client, database server, stored procedure, three-tier architecture, thin client, application partitioning, symmetric multiprocessing (SMP), massively parallel processing/shared nothing multiprocessing (MPP), middleware,** and **application program interface (API)**.

■ List several major advantages of the client/server architecture, compared to other computing approaches.

■ Explain the three components of application logic: data presentation services, processing services, and storage services.

■ Distinguish among a file server, a database server, and a three-tiered architecture.

■ Describe middleware and explain how middleware facilitates client/server architectures.

■ Describe conceptually how to connect a database to the Internet.

INTRODUCTION

Client/server systems operate in networked environments, splitting the processing of an application between a front-end client and a back-end processor. Generally, the client process requires some resource, which the server provides to the client. Clients and servers can reside in the same computer, or they can be on different computers that are networked together. Both clients and servers are intelligent and programmable, so that the computing power of both can be used to devise effective and efficient applications.

It is difficult to overestimate the impact that client/server applications have had in the last 10 years. Advances in personal computer technology and the rapid evolution of graphical user interfaces (GUIs), networking, and communications have

Client/server systems: A networked computing model that distributes processes between clients and servers, which supply the requested services. In a database system, the database generally resides on a server that processes the DBMS. The clients may process the application systems or request services from another server that holds the application programs.

changed the way businesses use computing systems to meet ever more demanding business needs. Personal computers linked through networks that support work-group computing are the norm. Mainframe applications have been rewritten to run in client/server environments and take advantage of the greater cost effectiveness of networks of personal computers and workstations. The need for strategies that fit specific business environments is being filled by client/server solutions because they offer flexibility, scalability (the ability to upgrade a system without having to redesign it), and extensibility (the ability to define new data types and operations). As businesses become more global in their operations, they must devise distributed systems (these will be covered in Chapter 11); their plans often include client/server architectures. Recent business plans also call for client/server solutions that enable firms to represent themselves on the World Wide Web.

In this chapter we review developments in multiuser database management environments that have led to the development of various client/server strategies for data processing. These include LAN-based DBMSs, client/server DBMSs (including three-tiered architectures), parallel computing architectures, Internet and Intranet DBMSs, and middleware.

Driving the trend toward these database technologies are a variety of new opportunities and competitive pressures. Corporate restructurings, such as mergers, acquisitions, and consolidations, make it necessary to connect, integrate, or replace existing stand-alone applications. One consequence of corporate downsizing is that individual managers have broader control, necessitating access to a wider range of data. Applications are being downsized from expensive mainframes to networked microcomputers and workstations that are much more user friendly and sometimes more cost effective. Handling network traffic, which may become excessive with some architectures, is a key issue in developing successful client/server applications, especially as organizations place mission-critical applications in distributed environments. Establishing a good balance between centralized and decentralized systems is a matter of much current discussion, as organizations strive to gain maximum benefits from both client/server and mainframe-based DBMSs.

CLIENT/SERVER ARCHITECTURES

Client/server environments use a local area network to support a network of personal computers, each with its own storage, that are also able to share common devices (such as a hard disk or printer) and software (such as a DBMS) attached to the LAN. Each PC and workstation on a LAN is typically within 100 feet of the others, with a total network cable length of under 1 mile. At least one PC is designated as a file server, where the shared database is stored. The LAN modules of a DBMS add concurrent access controls, possibly extra security features, and query- or translation-queuing management to support concurrent access from multiple users of a shared database.

The several client/server architectures that have evolved can be distinguished by the distribution of application logic components across clients and servers. There are three components of application logic (see Figure 8-1). The first is the input/output (I/O) or presentation logic component. This component is responsible for formatting and presenting data on the user's screen or other output device, and for managing user input from a keyboard or other input device. The second component is the processing component. It handles data processing logic, business rules logic, and data management logic. Data processing logic includes such activities as data

Figure 8-1
Application logic
components

validation and identification of processing errors. Business rules that have not been coded at the DBMS level may be coded in the processing component. Data management logic identifies the data necessary for processing the transaction or query. The third component is storage, the component responsible for data storage and retrieval from the physical storage devices associated with the application. Activities of a DBMS occur in the storage component logic.

File Server Architectures

The first client/server architectures developed were file servers. In a basic file server environment (see Figure 8-2), all data manipulation occurs at the workstations where data are requested. The client handles the presentation logic, processing logic, and much of the storage logic (that part associated with a DBMS). One or more file servers are attached to the LAN. A **file server** is a device that manages file operations and is shared by each of the client PCs attached to the LAN. Each of these file servers acts as an additional hard disk for each of the client PCs. For example, your PC might recognize a logical F: drive, which is actually a disk volume stored on a file server on the LAN. Programs on your PC refer to files on this drive by the typical path specification, involving this drive and any directories, as well as the filename. With a file server, each client PC may be called a **fat client**, one where most processing occurs on the client rather than on a server.

In a file server environment, each client PC is authorized to use the DBMS when a database application program runs on that PC. Thus, there is one database but many concurrently running copies of the DBMS, one on each of the active PCs. The primary characteristic of file server architecture is that all data manipulation is performed at the client PCs, not at the file server. The file server acts simply as a shared data storage device. Software at the file server queues access requests, but it is up to the application program at each client PC, working with the copy of the DBMS on that PC, to handle all data management functions. For example, data security checks and file and record locking are initiated at the client PCs in this environment.

File server: A device that manages file operations and is shared by each of the client PCs attached to the LAN.

Fat client: A client PC that is responsible for processing, including presentation logic, extensive application logic and business rules logic, and many DBMS functions.

Figure 8-2
File server model

Limitations of File Servers

There are three limitations when using file servers on local area networks. First, considerable data movement is generated across the network. For example, when an application program running on a client PC in Pine Valley Furniture wants to access the oak products, the whole Product table is transferred to the client PC and then scanned at the client to find the few desired records. Thus, the server does very little work, the client is busy with extensive data manipulation, and the network is transferring large blocks of data. Consequently, a client-based LAN places considerable burden on the client PC to do functions that have to be performed on all clients, and creates a high network traffic load.

Second, each client workstation must devote memory to a full version of the DBMS. This means that there is less room in memory for application programs on the client PC. Also, increasing RAM on the PC will improve performance by increasing the total amount of data that can reside on the PC while a transaction is being processed. Further, because the client workstation does most of the work, each client must be rather powerful to provide a suitable response time. In contrast, the file server does not need much RAM and need not be a very powerful PC, since it does little work.

Third, and possibly most important, the DBMS copy in each workstation must manage the shared database integrity. In addition, each application program must recognize, for example, locks and take care to initiate the proper locks. Thus, application programmers must be rather sophisticated to understand various subtle conditions that can arise in a multiple-user database environment. They must understand how their application will interact with the DBMS's concurrency, recovery, and security controls, and sometimes must program such controls into their applications.

Database Server Architectures

An improvement in client/server architectures which followed the file server approach is the **database server**, where the client workstation is responsible for managing the user interface, including presentation logic, data processing logic, and business rules logic, and the database server is responsible for database storage, access, and processing. Figure 8-3 shows a typical database server architecture. With the DBMS placed on the database server, LAN traffic is reduced, because only those records that match the requested criteria are transmitted to the client station, rather than entire data files. Some people refer to the central DBMS functions as the *back-end functions,* whereas they call the application programs on the client PCs *front-end programs.*

Moving the DBMS to the database server has several advantages. With this architecture, only the database server requires processing power adequate to handle the database, and the database is stored on the server, not on the clients. Therefore, the database server can be tuned to optimize database-processing performance. Since less data are sent across the LAN, the communication load is reduced. User authorization, integrity checking, data dictionary maintenance, and query and update processing are all performed in one location, on the database server.

Client/server projects that use file server and database server architectures tend to be departmental applications, supporting a relatively small number of users. Such applications are not mission critical and have been most successful where transaction volumes are low, immediate availability is not critical, and security is not of the highest concern. As companies have sought to gain expected benefits from client/server projects, such as scalability, flexibility, and lowered costs, they have had to develop new approaches to client/server architectures.

The use of **stored procedures**, modules of code that implement application logic, which are included on the database server, pushed the database server architecture

Database server: A computer that is responsible for database storage, access, and processing in a client/server environment. Some people also use this term to describe a two-tier client/server environment.

Stored procedure: A module of code, usually written in a proprietary language such as Oracle's PL/SQL or Sybase's Transact-SQL, that implements application logic or a business rule and is stored on the server, where it runs when it is called.

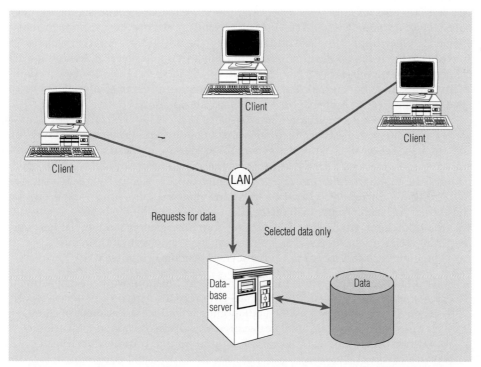

Figure 8-3
Database server architecture

toward being able to handle more critical business applications (Quinlan, 1995). As pointed out by Quinlan, stored procedures have the following advantages:

- Performance improves for compiled SQL statements.

- Network traffic decreases as processing moves from the client to the server.

- Security improves if the stored procedure is accessed rather than the data and code is moved to the server, away from direct end-user access.

- Data integrity improves as multiple applications access the same stored procedure.

- Stored procedures result in a thinner client and a fatter database server.

However, writing stored procedures takes more time than using Visual Basic or Powerbuilder to create an application. Also, the proprietary nature of stored procedures reduces their portability and may make it difficult to change DBMSs without having to rewrite the stored procedures.

Also, each client must be loaded with the applications that will be used at that location. Upgrades to an application will require that each client be upgraded separately. These drawbacks to database server architectures have led to the popularity of three-tier architecture.

THREE-TIER ARCHITECTURES

Three-tier architecture:
A client/server configuration that includes three layers: a client layer and two server layers. While the nature of the server layers differs, a common configuration is an application server.

In general, a **three-tier architecture** includes another server layer in addition to the client and database server layers previously mentioned (see Figure 8-4). Such configurations are also referred to as *n*-tier, multitier, or enhanced client/server architectures. The additional server in a three-tier architecture may be used for different purposes. Often application programs reside on the additional server, in which case it is referred to as an application server. But the additional server may hold a local database while another server holds the enterprise database. Each of these configurations is likely to be referred to as a three-tier architecture, but the functionality of each differs, and each is appropriate for a different situation.

In some three-tier architectures, most application code is stored on the application server. This case realizes the same benefits as come from putting stored procedures on the database server in a two-tier architecture. Using an application server can also improve performance by the use of true machine code, easier portability of the application code to other platforms, and less reliance on proprietary languages such as SQL/PLUS (Quinlan, 1995). In many situations, most business processing occurs on the application server rather than on the client workstation or database server, resulting in a **thin client**. Upgrading application programs requires loading the new version only on the application server, rather than on every client workstation.

Thin client: A PC configured for handling user interfaces and some application processing, usually with no or limited local data storage.

Three-tier architectures can provide several benefits (Thompson, 1997):

- *Scalability*   Three-tier architectures are more scalable than two-tier architectures. For example, the middle tier can be used to reduce the load on a database server by using a transaction processing (TP) monitor to reduce the number of connections to a server, and additional application servers can be added to distribute application processing. A TP monitor is a program that controls data transfer between clients and servers in order to provide a consistent environment for online transaction processing (OLTP).

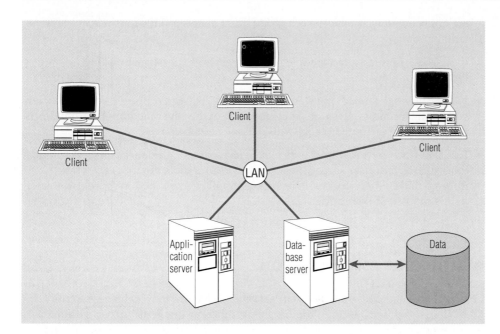

Figure 8-4
Three-tier architecture

- *Technological flexibility*   It is easier to change DBMS engines, though triggers and stored procedures will need to be rewritten, with a three-tier architecture. The middle tier can even be moved to a different platform. Simplified presentation services make it easier to implement various desired interfaces such as Web browsers or kiosks.

- *Lower long-term costs*   Use of off-the-shelf components or services in the middle tier can reduce costs, as can substitution of modules within an application rather than an entire application.

- *Better match of systems to business needs*   New modules can be built to support specific business needs rather than building more general, complete applications.

- *Improved customer service*   Multiple interfaces on different clients can access the same business processes.

- *Competitive advantage*   The ability to react to business changes quickly by changing small modules of code rather than entire applications can be used to gain a competitive advantage.

- *Reduced risk*   Again, the ability to implement small modules of code quickly and combine them with code purchased from vendors limits the risk assumed with a large-scale development project.

Three-tier and *n*-tier architectures are the most recent developments in client/server approaches. Challenges associated with moving to a three-tier or more complicated environment include (Thompson, 1997).

- *High short-term costs*   Implementing a three-tier architecture requires that the presentation component be split from the process component. Accomplishing this split requires more programming in a 3GL language such as C than is required in implementing a two-tier architecture.

- *Tools and training*   Because three-tier architectures are relatively new, tools for implementing them are not yet well developed. Also, because training programs are not yet widely available, companies must develop skills for their implementation in-house.

- *Experience*   Similarly, few people have as yet had experience building three-tier systems.

- *Incompatible standards*   Few standards have as yet been proposed for transaction processing monitors. It is not yet clear which of the several competing standards proposed for distributed objects will prevail.

- *Lack of end-user tools that work with middle-tier services*   Widely available generic tools such as end-user spreadsheets and reporting tools do not yet operate through middle-tier services. This problem will be explained in more detail later in this chapter, in the middleware section.

PARTITIONING AN APPLICATION

Application partitioning:
The process of assigning portions of application code to client or server partitions after it is written, in order to achieve better performance and interoperability (ability of a component to function on different platforms).

Clearly there is no one optimal client/server architecture that is the best solution for all business problems. Rather, the flexibility inherent in client/server architectures offers organizations the possibility of tailoring their configurations to fit their particular processing needs. **Application partitioning** helps in this tailoring. It gives developers the opportunity to write application code they can later place either on a client workstation or on a server, depending which location will give the best performance. It is not necessary to include the code that will place the process being partitioned, or to write the code that will establish the connections to the process. Those activities are handled by application partitioning tools. Current examples of such tools are Dynasty (by Dynasty Technologies), Fort— (Fort—Software), and Visual Gen (IBM) (Quinlan, 1995).

The application code can be developed and tested on a client workstation and decisions about partitioning that code and placing it can be made later. This capability is likely to increase developers' productivity. Application modules can be placed on a client or server late in the design phase. However, the developer must understand how and where each process will need to run in order to synchronize each process or transaction correctly across databases and platforms. Decisions about placing code on the application or database server will depend partly on the DBMS capabilities. For example, a DBMS that supports static SQL (completely prewritten SQL code) through stored procedures and triggers that are located on the database server may give a performance decrement if dynamic SQL code (SQL code created at run time) is located on the application server. Each dynamic SQL statement will generate a dynamic bind (or linkage to database objects) at the database server as it is processed. The performance impact will depend on how intensively dynamic SQL statements are used. Whether to concentrate processing on the application server or the database server is a decision that must be made by the developer, who understands the hardware environment available, the interactions of the hardware and DBMS software, and the demands of the application.

It is also possible to add transaction processing monitors to client/server systems in order to improve performance. Where multiple application servers and database servers are available, TP monitors can balance the workload, directing transactions to servers that are not busy. TP monitors are also useful in distributed environments, where distributed transactions from a single unit of work can be managed across a heterogeneous environment.

ROLE OF THE MAINFRAME

The role of the mainframe has been uncertain over the last decade as distributed, client/server, and PC computing capabilities have developed. As mentioned above, mission-critical systems, which were resident on mainframe systems a decade ago, have tended to remain on mainframe systems. Less mission-critical, frequently work-group-level, systems have been developed using client/server architectures. The popularity of client/server architectures and businesses' strong desire to achieve more effective computing in more distributed environments as their perspectives became broader and more global led to their expectation that mission-critical systems would be moved away from mainframes and onto client/server architectures.

But moving mission-critical systems from traditional mainframe legacy systems to client/server systems has been challenging. Successful distributed computing depends on workable software distribution, effective performance management and tuning of production systems, established troubleshooting procedures, and proactive code management (Hurwitz, 1996). Organizations have found that managing these mission-critical applications is much more complicated when they are converted to distributed systems. Among the software distribution problems that exist in a distributed processing environment are the following:

- Determining which code must be placed on which workstations and which will be available through a server

- Identifying potential conflicts with code from other applications

- Assuring that sufficient resources are available at all locations to handle the anticipated load

Unless developers anticipate scalability issues and address them as they develop code, moving mission-critical applications to client/server distributed environments is likely to cause serious problems in the transition from pilot phase to production. This has slowed the development of mission-critical client/server systems. Now, Internet applications are causing an upsurge in the need for applications to be interoperable. Troubleshooting such interactions is difficult, and many organizations may not be prepared to undertake such troubleshooting. Increasing use of component libraries (files of shared application modules) increases the need to manage interdependencies that will inevitably develop as these component libraries are shared across applications.

Supporting distributed environments is a very complex undertaking. Understanding the dynamics of different locations' environments and creating a distributed computing network can be very complex. The difficulties of managing distributed computing environments have caused IT managers to rethink their push to move mission-critical systems to client/server solutions. Powerful parallel processing equipment (discussed in the next section) is becoming more readily available, thus making it more attractive to remain centralized on an application or database server.

The difficulties of moving complex, mission-critical applications to a distributed environment using client/server architectures have discouraged many IT managers, and some have withdrawn completely from client/server initiatives, returning to a mainframe environment. However, we expect that each organization will need to achieve a balance between mainframe and client/server platforms, between centralized and distributed solutions, that is closely tailored to the nature of their data and location of business users of the data. As Hurwitz (1996) suggests, data that do not need to be moved often can be centralized on a mainframe. Data to which users need frequent access, complex graphics, and the user interface should be kept close to the users' workstations.

USING PARALLEL COMPUTER ARCHITECTURES

Organizations' attempts to move mission-critical applications to client/server architectures involve building systems that can handle much larger databases than the original client/server projects. Projects that involve very large databases (VLDB) have benefited from the use of parallel computer architectures. Indeed, some projects are possible only because parallel processing of the database gives an acceptably fast response time. The ability to handle high transaction volumes, complex queries, and new data types has proven problematic in many uniprocessor environments (DeWitt and Gray, 1992). But, RDBMSs and the SQL language lend themselves to effecting a parallel environment in two ways (Ferguson, 1994):

1. In most queries, SQL acts as a nonprocedural set processing language. Therefore, queries can be divided into parts, each of which can then be run on a different parallel processor simultaneously.

2. Multiple queries can be run in parallel on parallel processors (see Figure 8-5).

Effective use of parallel computer architectures involves developing an awareness of the processing possibilities that can be exploited in a parallel server environment, not just changing serial algorithms into parallel algorithms. We will introduce two of several multiprocessor hardware architectures that are available; each is optimal for a certain kind of processing.

Figure 8-5
Parallel transactions and queries (adapted from Ferguson, 1994)

(a) Parallel transactions

(b) Parallel query

Figure 8-6
Tightly coupled multiprocessor architecture (adapted from Ferguson, 1994)

Multiprocessor Hardware Architectures

Tightly coupled multiprocessor systems have a common shared memory among all processors (Figure 8-6). This architecture is often called **symmetric multiprocessing (SMP)** and has some advantages (Ferguson, 1994). First, a single copy of the operating system resides in the shared memory and is thus shared across all of the processors. The operating system must be written to operate in such a shared environment so that it can run parts of itself in parallel on any of the processors without developing a tendency to use one processor more heavily than any of the others.

Symmetric multiprocessing (SMP): A parallel processing architecture where the processors share a common shared memory.

A second advantage is that bottlenecks are lessened compared to uniprocessor systems because all processors in symmetric multiprocessing share all the tasks. Even SMP systems may still develop I/O bottlenecks when memory request traffic going to shared memory is heavy, however. Equipping each processor with its own cache memory reduces this problem. Then, it is possible to reduce the volume of shared memory requests by reactivating waiting transactions to run on the processor where their processing was begun. This allows the transaction to reactivate more quickly, with fewer shared memory requests, and possibly to make use of variable information related to the transaction that is still available in the specific processor's memory cache (Ferguson, 1994).

Third, SMP architectures are useful for situations where data must remain in memory during processing to achieve the desired performance level. Problems to be addressed include the possibility of contention for the shared memory, the wide bandwidth required in order to retrieve data into shared memory, and the location of all memory at a single point of failure. I/O contention problems are likely as processors are added in a shared memory environment.

In contrast to SMP architectures, loosely coupled architectures (see Figure 8-7), also referred to as **massively parallel processor (MPP)** architectures or **shared nothing architectures**, set up each CPU with its own dedicated memory. Each node can be a uniprocessor or a multiprocessor. MPP systems thus require a complete copy of the

Massively parallel processor architecture/ Shared nothing architecture (MPP): Massively parallel processing systems where each CPU has its own dedicated memory.

Figure 8-7

Loosely coupled
multiprocessor
architecture (adapted
from Ferguson, 1994)

operating system to be resident in each dedicated memory. Because there is little resource sharing among the processors, the problems of memory contention that occur in SMP systems are unlikely, and it is possible to add nodes (another processor and dedicated memory) in single units. This linear upgradability allows organizations to achieve parallel processing at lower costs, adding processing capability in small increments, as needed. By passing messages across processors to achieve parallelism, these systems can divide up large tasks and spread them over several processors. In fact, it is applications that have large tasks that can benefit from being divided up and worked on simultaneously that are best suited to MPP architectures, rather than applications that can benefit from the use of shared memory. There is a lot of activity in developing MPP technology, and IBM, NCR, Intel, Oracle, Cray, DEC, HP, Encore, and Silicon Graphics and others are currently involved in researching and developing these technologies. Since parallel processing systems are different from traditional systems, it is necessary for companies who consider such systems to reevaluate their database and application design, capacity planning, performance management, operational, and scheduling procedures.

Business Related Uses of SMP and MPP Architectures

Organizations have vast stores of historical operational data of which they are anxious to take advantage, especially valuable information about many aspects of their business, including customers, products, inventories, and sales. Until recently, companies did not have enough computing power at their disposal to be able to take advantage of these stored data (Rudin, 1995). Now, however, parallel processing is enabling organizations to begin to analyze these massive amounts of historical data through the development of data warehouses and data marts. The emergence of parallel processing capabilities underlies the development of data warehousing, which is discussed in detail in Chapter 14. Retail organizations, with large amounts of sales data to analyze, have embraced parallel processing systems.

There are several considerations which organizations should take into account before moving into SMP or MPP systems (Rudin, 1995).

- *Data analysis requirements*   Parallel systems are going to be most effective at solving problems that involve handling large amounts of data (250 GB or larger), executing complex queries, or are used by large numbers of concurrent users. The problems should be addressed only if they are of strategic significance to the organization, or else the significant hardware costs, software development costs, and retraining costs will not be worth it to the organization. For example, retailing applications provide strategic value to retailers. An example is Catalina Marketing's market basket analysis system, which tracks not only what products are purchased but what assortments of products tend to be purchased at the same time. Retailers can use the results of such applications to plan coordinated promotions for related products, shelf space and placements, and pricing decisions.

- *Cost justification*   Remember that parallel systems tend to complement rather than replace existing operational systems. Businesses use them to increase revenues rather than to reduce costs. Therefore, traditional cost justification procedures may not be appropriate. Since many of the applications are intended to improve an organization's marketing strategies, treating the parallel system as an investment in marketing capabilities is appropriate.

- *Traditional technologies*   If the proposed application can be accomplished using traditional, existing technology within the organization, it probably makes sense to continue to rely on that technology. MPP systems are far from mature, and their implementation is sure to challenge any organization. Therefore, even when you are sure that parallel processing would make sense for the problem that the organization wants to address, a feasibility analysis of more mature technologies should be undertaken. It may not be feasible to implement a solution for a problem that is expected to benefit from parallel processing in a uniprocessor environment, but traditional technologies should be ruled out before proceeding with a parallel processing solution.

The data warehousing and data mining applications discussed process queries that access large amounts of data and metadata, using join and aggregation operations. These queries involve many I/O operations and are likely to generate sizable intermediate results sets (Frazer, 1998). At present, there are no object/relational (O/R) databases large enough to qualify as VLDB systems. (See Appendix A to learn about O/R databases.) However, as O/R technology becomes more mature, it will be expected to handle databases at least the size of the current relational implementations, in part because O/R databases handle new data types that are much bulkier to store. O/R databases will deal with complex relationships among instances of the new data types, relationships that go beyond the simple row-and-column structure of the relational model. Parallel processing methods can be expected to enable these coming developments.

USING MIDDLEWARE

Middleware is often referred to as the glue that holds together client/server applications. Simply put, **middleware** is any of several classes of software that allow an application to interoperate with other software without requiring the user to understand and code the low-level operations required to achieve interoperability (Hurwitz, 1998). Middleware has existed for decades—examples are IBM's transaction-processing middleware, CICS, or BEA Systems' Tuxedo for UNIX machines. But the advent of client/server technologies and now Web-oriented development has stimulated new development of commercially available middleware. Universal middleware, one magical software package that could integrate and connect every type of system, would be ideal, of course. At this time, however, such a middleware package

Middleware: Software that allows an application to interoperate with other software without requiring the user to understand and code the low-level operations necessary to achieve interoperability.

is not available. Most organizations use several different middleware packages, sometimes even within one application.

Another consideration is whether the communication involved is synchronous or asynchronous. With synchronous systems, the requesting system waits for a response to the request in real time. An online banking system where the teller checks an account balance before cashing a check is an example of a synchronous system. Asynchronous systems send a request but do not wait for a response in real time. Rather, the response is accepted whenever it is received. Electronic mail is an example of an asynchronous system with which you are probably familiar.

Hurwitz (1998) has provided a helpful classification system containing six categories that organize the many types of middleware that are currently available. Her classifications are based on scalability and recoverability:

- *Asynchronous remote procedure call (RPC)*   The client requests services but does not wait for a response. It will typically establish a point-to-point connection with the server and perform other processing while it waits for the response. If the connection is lost, the client must reestablish the connection and send the request again. This type of middleware has high scalability but low recoverability.

- *Publish/subscribe*   This type of middleware monitors activity and pushes information to subscribers. It is asynchronous—the clients, or subscribers, perform other activities between notifications from the server. The subscribers notify the publisher of information that they wish to receive, and when an event occurs that contains such information, it is sent to the subscriber, who can then elect to receive the information or not. For example, you can supply electronic bookstores with keywords of topics that interest you. Whenever the bookstore adds a book title that is keyword coded with one of your keywords, information about that title will be automatically forwarded to you for consideration. This type of middleware is very useful for monitoring situations where actions need to be taken when particular events occur.

- *Message oriented middleware (MOM)*   MOM is also asynchronous software, sending messages that are collected and stored until they are acted upon, while the client continues with other processing. Workflow applications such as insurance policy applications, which often involve several processing steps, can benefit from MOM. The queue where the requests are stored can be journalized, thus providing some recoverability.

- *Object request brokers (ORBs)*   This type of middleware makes it possible for applications to send objects and request services in an object-oriented system. The ORB tracks the location of each object and routes requests to each object. Current ORBs are synchronous, but asynchronous ORBs are being developed.

- *SQL-oriented data access*   Connecting applications to databases over networks is achieved by using SQL-oriented data access middleware. This middleware also has the capability to translate generic SQL into the SQL specific to the database. Database vendors and companies that have developed multidatabase access middleware dominate this middleware segment.

- *Synchronous RPC*   A distributed program using synchronous RPC may call services available on different computers. This middleware makes it possible to establish this facility without undertaking the detailed coding usually necessary to write an RPC. Examples would include Microsoft Transaction Server and IBM's CICS.

After laying out the preceding classifications, Hurwitz (1998) indicates that the market should consolidate in 1998 and 1999. Already the distinctions are blurring, as SQL-oriented and RPC middleware add awareness of objects and ORBs are adding transaction, queuing, and messaging services.

In client/server systems, database-oriented middleware provides some sort of **application program interface (API)** access to a database. APIs are sets of routines that an application program uses to direct the performance of procedures by the computer's operating system. For example, in achieving access to a database, an API calls library routines that transparently route SQL commands from the front-end client application to the database server. An API might work with existing front-end software, like a third-generation language or custom report generator, and it might include its own facilities for building applications. When APIs exist for several program development tools, then you have considerable independence to develop client applications in the most convenient front-end programming environment yet still draw data from a common server database. Such middleware makes it possible for developers to link an application easily to popular databases.

> **Application program interface (API):** Sets of routines that an application program uses to direct the performance of procedures by the computer's operating system.

Open Database Connectivity (ODBC) is similar to API, but for Windows-based client/server applications. It is most useful for accessing relational data, and not well suited for accessing other types of data, such as ISAM files (LaRue, 1997). Even though ODBC is difficult to program and implement, it has been well accepted because it allowed programmers to make connections to almost any vendor's database without learning proprietary code specific to that database. For a more detailed discussion of ODBC and establishing Internet database connectivity, see Chapter 10.

Java Database Connectivity (JDBC) classes can be used to help an applet access any number of databases without understanding the native features of each database. JDBC defines a call-level interface (CLI) for Java development and borrows from ODBC conventions. OLE-DB adds value to the ODBC standard by providing a single point of access to multiple databases (Linthicum, 1997). Microsoft is planning to make OLE-DB a universal data access standard. Access to legacy data while moving to client/server systems can be achieved by products such as EDA/SQL, which attempt to support many different operating systems, networks, and databases.

Establishing a common language to define interfaces between components and a mechanism to mediate will facilitate developing universal middleware (Keuffel, 1997). The Object Management Group (OMG), established in 1989, is an industry coalition that has produced the Common Object Request Broker Architecture (CORBA), which sets the specification of object-oriented universal middleware. Microsoft has developed a competing model, Distributed Component Object Model (DCOM), but CORBA is a more robust specification because it has been developed to handle many different platforms. Such standards are particularly important on the World Wide Web because of the diversity of the platforms that are connecting.

ESTABLISHING CLIENT/SERVER SECURITY

Client/server database computing implies the existence of a network that connects the client/server components together. In this distributed environment, establishing database security is more complex than in a centralized environment. (See Chapter 13 for a more detailed discussion of database security.) Networks are susceptible to breaches of security through eavesdropping, unauthorized connections, or unauthorized retrieval of packets of information that are traversing the network. Thus, client/server architectures are more susceptible to security threats than centralized systems.

Security measures that should be taken in a client/server environment include measures that are common to securing all systems, but should also include measures taken to secure the more distributed environment of client/server architectures (Bobrowski, 1994):

- *System-level password security*   User names and passwords are typically used to identify and authorize users when they wish to connect to a multiuser client/server system. Security standards should include guidelines for password lengths, password naming conventions, frequency of password changes, and so on. Password management utilities should be included as part of the network and operating systems.

- *Database level password security*   Most client/server DBMSs have database level password security that is similar to system-level password security. It is also possible to pass through authentication information from the operating system authentication capability. Administration that takes advantage of the pass-through capabilities is easier, but external attempts to gain access will also be easier because using the pass-through capabilities reduces the number of password security layers from two to one.

- *Secure client/server communication*   Encryption, transforming readable data (plain text) into unreadable (ciphertext) can help to ensure secure client/server communication. Most clients send database users plain text passwords to database servers. Oracle7 and Sybase SQL Server System 10 both have secure network password transmission capabilities. Encryption of all data that are passed across the network is obviously desired, but the costs are high for encryption software. Encryption also affects performance negatively because of the time required to encrypt and decrypt the data.

CLIENT/SERVER ISSUES

There is no question that the establishment of client/server architectures has affected the database computing environment. But, too often one hears of client/server implementation failures and disillusioned users. In order to succeed, client/server projects should address a specific business problem with well-defined technology and cost parameters. Certain areas should be carefully addressed in order to improve the chances for building a successful client/server application (Linthicum, 1996):

- *Accurate business problem analysis*   Just as is the case with other computing architectures, it is critical to develop a sound application design and architecture for a new client/server system. Developers' tendencies to pick the technology and then fit the application to it seem to be more pronounced in the strong push toward client/server environments that has occurred in the last six years. It is more appropriate to accurately define the scope of the problem and determine requirements, and then use that information to select the technology.

- *Detailed architecture analysis*   It is also important to specify the details of the client/server architecture. Building a client/server solution involves connecting many components, which may not work together easily. One of the often touted advantages of client/server computing, the ability to accept an open systems approach, can be very detrimental if the heterogeneous components chosen are difficult to connect. Besides specifying the client workstations, server(s), network, and DBMS, analysts also should specify network infrastructure, the middleware layer, and the application development tools to be used. At each juncture, analysts should take steps to assure that the tools will connect with the middleware, database, network, and so forth.

- *Avoiding tool-driven architectures*   As above, determine project requirements *before* choosing software tools, and not the reverse. Choosing a tool first and then applying it to the problem risks having a poor fit between problem and tool. Tools selected this way are likely to have been chosen based on an emotional appeal rather than on the appropriate functionality of the tool.

- *Achieving appropriate scalability*   A multitier solution allows client/server systems to scale to any number of users and handle diverse processing loads. But multitiered solutions are significantly more expensive and difficult to build. The tools to develop a multitier environment are still limited, too. Architects should avoid moving to a multitier solution when it's not really needed. Usually, multitier makes sense in environments of more than 100 concurrent users, high-volume OLTP systems, or for real-time processing. Smaller, less intense environments can frequently run more efficiently on traditional two-tier systems, especially if triggers and procedures are used to manage the processing.

- *Appropriate placement of services*   Again, a careful analysis of the business problem being addressed is important when making decisions about the placement of processing services. The move toward thin clients and fat servers is not always the appropriate solution. Moving the application logic to a server, thus creating a fat server, can affect capacity, as end users all attempt to use the application now located on the server. Sometimes it is possible to achieve better scaling by moving application processing to the client. Fat servers do tend to reduce network load because the processing takes place close to the data, and fat servers do lessen the need for powerful clients. Understanding the business problem intimately should help the architect to distribute the logic appropriately.

- *Network analysis*   The most common bottleneck in distributed systems is still the network. Therefore, architects ignore at their peril the bandwidth capabilities of the network that the system must use. If the network is insufficient to handle the amount of information that must pass between client and server, response time will suffer badly, and the system is likely to fail.

- *Be aware of hidden costs*   Client/server implementation problems go beyond the analysis, development, and architecture problems listed above (Atre, 1995). For example, systems that are intended to use existing hardware, networks, operating systems, and DBMSs are often stymied by the complexities of integrating these heterogeneous components to build the client/server system. Training is a significant and recurring expense that is often overlooked. The complexities of working in a multivendor environment can be very costly.

If these issues are addressed appropriately, there are benefits to be won from moving to client/server architectures (Atre, 1995):

- Functionality can be delivered in stages to the end users. Thus, it arrives more quickly as the first pieces of the project are deployed.

- The GUI interfaces common in client server environments encourage users to utilize the applications' functionality.

- The flexibility and scalability of client/server solutions facilitate business process re-engineering.

- More processing can be performed close to the source of data being processed, thereby improving response times and reducing network traffic.

- Client/server architectures allow the development of Web-enabled applications, facilitating the ability of organizations to communicate effectively internally and to conduct external business over the Internet.

SUMMARY

Client/server architectures have offered businesses opportunities to better fit their computer systems to their business needs. Establishing the appropriate balance between client/server and mainframe DBMSs is a matter of much current discussion. Several client/server architectures are discussed in this chapter, including file server architectures, where the file server manages file operations and is shared by each client PC that is attached to its LAN. File servers create a heavy network load, require a full version of the DBMS on each client, and require complex programming in order to manage shared database integrity.

Another approach, the database server architecture, makes the client manage the user interface while the database server manages database storage and access. This architecture reduces network traffic, reduces the power required for each client, and centralizes user authorization, integrity checking, data dictionary maintenance, and query and update processing on the database server.

Three-tier architectures, which include another server in addition to the client and database server layers, allow application code to be stored on the additional server. This approach allows business processing to be performed on the additional server, resulting in a thin client. Advantages of the three-tier architecture can include scalability, technological flexibility, lower long-term costs, better matching of systems to business needs, improved customer service, competitive advantage, and reduced risk. But, higher short-term costs, advanced tools and training, shortages of experienced personnel, incompatible standards, and lack of end-user tools are currently problems with using three-tier or n-tier architectures.

Application partitioning assigns portions of application code to client or server partitions after it is written, in order to achieve better performance and interoperability. Application developer productivity is expected to increase as a result of using application partitioning, but the developer must understand each process intimately in order to place it correctly.

While the hype associated with the widespread adoption of client/server architectures has led some to predict the demise of the mainframe, mission-critical applications have tended to remain on the mainframe. Converting these complex applications to distributed client/server environments has not been easy. The availability of parallel processing solutions is making it more attractive to remain centralized on an application or database server.

Because SQL is a nonprocedural set processing language, it has proven amenable to use in parallel processing environments. Two types of parallel processing have been discussed. Symmetric multiprocessing (SMP) is a tightly coupled multiprocessor system with a common shared memory among all processors. SMP systems are subject to develop I/O bottleneck problems when there is heavy memory request traffic going to shared memory.

Loosely coupled architectures (MPP) set up each CPU with its own dedicated memory. This type of architecture is commonly referred to as a *shared nothing* architecture. Because there is little resource sharing among the MPP processors, the problems of memory contention which occur in SMP systems are unlikely, and it is possible to add nodes in single units, making MPP architectures very scalable.

Middleware is any of several classes of software which allow an application to interoperate with other software without requiring the user to understand and code the low-level operations required to achieve interoperability. Six categories of middleware, based on scalability and recoverability, are discussed. These middleware types are asynchronous remote procedure calls (RPC), publish/subscribe, message-oriented middleware (MOM), object-request brokers (ORBs), SQL-oriented data access middleware, and synchronous RPCs. Recent developments in database-oriented middleware include open database connectivity (ODBC), Java database connectivity (JDBC), and Microsoft's OLE-DB.

Connecting databases to the Web so that browsers may interact with Web sites by placing orders, accessing updated pricing information, and so forth, has also received recent attention. The Web is changing the distribution patterns of data, moving application logic to more centralized servers as browser interfaces are used.

Security is more complex in a client/server environment than in a centralized environment because networks must be secured in addition to the client workstations and the servers. Security measures to be included in a client/server environment include system-level password security, database-level password security, and secure client/server communications.

Client/server issues that should be addressed in order to improve the chances for building a successful client/server application include: accurate business problem analysis, detailed architecture analysis, avoidance of tool-driven architectures, achieving appropriate scalability, appropriate placement of services, adequate network analysis, and awareness of potential hidden costs.

Benefits that may be gained by moving to a client/server environment include deliverance of functionality in stages, flexibility, scalability, less network traffic, and development of Web-enabled applications.

CHAPTER REVIEW

KEY TERMS

Application partitioning
Application program
    interface (API)
Client/server
    architecture
Database server

Fat client
File server
Massively parallel
    processing (MPP)
Middleware
Stored procedure

Symmetric
    multiprocessing
    (SMP)
Thin client
Three-tier architecture

REVIEW   QUESTIONS

1. Define each of the following terms:

   a. application partitioning   e. file server
   b. application program interface (API)   f. middleware
   c. client/server architecture   g. stored procedure
   d. fat client   h. three-tier architecture

2. List several major advantages of the client/server architecture, compared to other computing approaches.

3. Contrast the following terms:

   a. symmetric multiprocessing (SMP); shared nothing architecture (MPP)
   b. file server; database server; three-tier architecture
   c. client/server computing; mainframe computing
   d. fat client; thin client

4. Describe the limitations of file servers.

5. Describe the advantages and disadvantages of database servers.

6. Describe the advantages and disadvantages of three-tier or *n*-tier architectures.

7. How can application partitioning help developers to tailor an application to a particular business situation?

8. Describe six categories of middleware.

9. How is the Web changing distribution patterns of data?

PROBLEMS   AND   EXERCISES

1. Match each of the following terms with the most appropriate definition:

   _____ client/server architecture

   _____ application program
         interface (API)

   _____ fat client

   _____ database server

   _____ file server

   _____ middleware

   _____ three-tiered architecture

   _____ symmetric multiprocessing
         (SMP)

   _____ massively parallel
         processing (MPP)

   _____ thin client

   a. a client that is responsible for processing including application logic and presentation logic

   b. a PC configured for handling the presentation layer and some business logic processing for an application

   c. software that facilitates interoperability, reducing programmer coding effort

   d. architecture where processors share common memory

   e. responsible for database storage and access

   f. systems where the application logic components are distributed.

g. responsible for managing file operations; shared by all attached clients

h. shared nothing architecture

i. software that facilitates communication between front-end programs and back-end database servers

j. three-layer client/server configuration

2. You have been asked to prepare a report that evaluates possible client/server solutions to handle a new customer application system for all branch offices. What business characteristics would you evaluate and what technology characteristics would you evaluate? Why?

3. What managerial issues do you feel are going to be important when introducing a new client/server architecture?

4. Discuss the different levels of security that should be established in a client/server database system.

5. How is the Web affecting client/server database systems?

6. Why is ODBC important? What other connectivity standards are being developed?

7. Historically, what types of applications have moved quickly to client/server database systems? What types have moved more slowly and why? What do you think will happen in the future to the balance of client/server database systems and mainframe database systems?

8. What are the advantages and drawbacks of middleware that is used in connection with database systems?

FIELD EXERCISES

---

1. Investigate the computing architecture of your university. Trace the history of computing at your university and determine what path the university followed to get to its present configurations. Some universities started early with mainframe environments—others started when PCs were available. Can you tell how your university's initial computing environment has affected today's computing environment?

2. On a lesser scale, investigate the computing architecture of one department within your university. Try to find out how well the current system is meeting the department's information processing needs.

3. Interview a systems professional at an organization in your location that you know has offices in other locations. Determine the computing architecture of that organization and find out how well the current system is meeting the department's information processing needs.

4. Locate three sites on the Web that have interactive database systems attached to the site. Evaluate the functionality of the site and discuss how the interactive database system is likely to affect that functionality. If you're not sure where to start, try http://www.amazon.com.

REFERENCES

Anderson, G., and B. Armstrong. 1995. "Client/Server: Where Are We Really?" *Health Management Technology* 16:6 (May): 34, 36, 38, 40, 44.

Atre, S. 1995. "The Hidden Costs of Client/Server." *DBMS* 8:7 (June): 71, 72, 74.

Bobrowski, S. 1994. "Database Security in a Client/Server World." *DBMS* 7:10 (October): 48–50, 54, 58.

DeWitt, D., and J. Gray. 1992. "Parallel Database Systems: The Future of High Performance Database Systems." *Communications of the ACM* 35:6 (June): 85–98.

Ferguson, M. 1994. "Parallel Database the Shape of Things to Come." *Database Programming & Design* 7:10 (October): 32–44.

Frazer, W. D. 1998. "Object/Relational Grows Up." *Database Programming & Design* 11:1 (January): 22–28.

Hurwitz, J. 1996. "Managing Complexity." *DBMS* 9:5 (May): 12, 80.

Hurwitz, J. 1998. "Sorting Out Middleware." *DBMS* 11:1 (January): 10–12.

Keuffel, W. 1997. "CORBA Masterminds Object Management." *DBMS* 10:3 (March): 42–50, 71.

Lam, J. 1997. "Database Connectivity and the Internet." *PC Magazine* (December 16): 249–250, 252, 255, 257.

LaRue, M. 1997. "Database Doorways." *Database Programming & Design* 10:12 (December): 62–67.

Linthicum, D. S. 1996. "Client/Server Collapse." *DBMS* 9:13 (December): 24, 26, 28.

Linthicum, D. S. 1997. "Next-Generation Middleware." *DBMS* 10:10 (October): 69–78.

Panttaja, M. 1996. "Client/Server Redefined." *Database Programming & Design* 9:10 (October): 30–32, 53–55.

Quinlan, T. 1995. "The Second Generation of Client/Server." *Database Programming & Design* 8:5 (May): 31–39.

Rudin, K. 1995. "The Practical Side of Going Parallel." *Database Programming & Design* 8:12 (December): 26–33.

Thompson, C. 1997. "Committing to Three-Tier Architecture." *Database Programming & Design* 10:8 (August): 26–33.

Project Case

PROJECT DESCRIPTION

At the end of Chapter 2, you learned of the Mountain View Community Hospital special study team that is developing a long-term business plan. The planning team of Mr. Heller, Mr. Lopez, Dr. Jefferson, and a consultant have been considering the future technology needs of Mountain View. Currently, patients must negotiate a maze of health plans, administrators, physicians, and clinics, much like the maze shown in Figure 1. They would like to devise a system for Mountain View that integrates all of these data—data from health plans, physicians, and hospital systems—so that accurate real-time information will be available.

The team has heard that many hospitals are just beginning to move their mission-critical, enterprise-level systems off their legacy mainframe systems and onto new client/server systems. They have heard that such systems provide increased flexibility, integration, and functionality. They are wondering if they can integrate Mountain View's present patient accounting, care management, and insurance systems to improve efficiency and support improved hospital systems. The consultant has drafted a potential client/server distributed architecture for the hospital, which is shown in Figure 2. To accomplish the move to client/server, the team has considered three different strategies described in the following paragraphs.

One possibility is to acquire existing client/server application packages and adapt them to fit Mountain View Community Hospital. Taking this approach will allow the existing MIS staff at Mountain View to become familiar with crucial portions of the client/server environment, such as network management, PC configuration management, and distributed-systems management, without having to manage a full-blown, large-scale systems development project in addition to their current work. Most of the packages they have examined, however, require the use of proprietary middleware to achieve client/server connections. The hospital expects to have to continue connection to the legacy systems through the proposed servers and they are not sure how many programs are available that would let them move toward the environment they envision.

Another possibility the planning team is considering is custom development. Some large hospitals have undertaken custom development of their new client/server systems. Considerable risk attends such an undertaking, but the larger hospitals have assumed this risk in order to get the data and information when they need it. The Mountain View team is concerned about

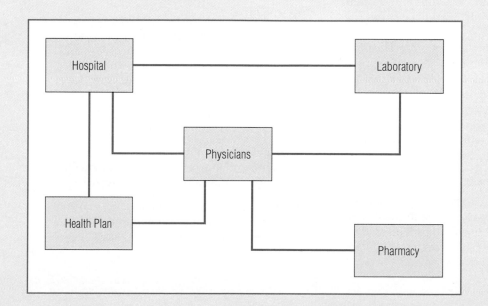

Figure 1
Mountain View Community Hospital's current technology base (adapted from Anderson and Armstrong, 1995)

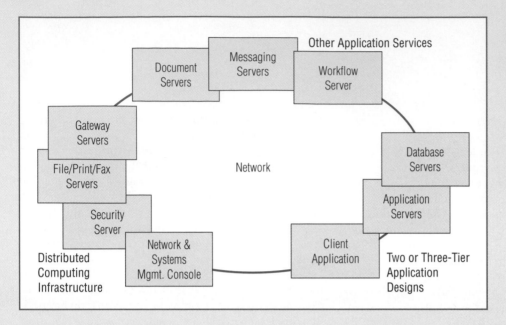

Figure 2
Potential client/server distributed architecture (adapted from Anderson and Armstrong, 1995)

the risk of undertaking such a project and the need for increasing MIS staff that it would entail.

The last possibility being considered would be to layer the client/server applications on top of existing systems. Workflow applications could be used to facilitate the establishment of the front end interface. The need to connect to a data warehouse is also becoming apparent as the team works on the long-range plan, and the team wants to plan the infrastructure now so that the establishment of a data warehouse will be as easy as possible.

Of course, Mountain View Community Hospital could also wait for the technologies to mature and become more widely available. It is expected that by the year 2000, health care alliances will begin to extend their member and patient services beyond their organizational boundaries, to the workplace, schools, and homes. Health plan members will be able to check their claim status, send messages to service representatives, and review coverage. Patients may be able to make their own appointments by accessing appointment schedules. The members of the team are unsure of what the impact of these new services will be in their area, but they expect that some of the other hospitals will be quick to adopt and implement such features. They are wondering if it would be safest to wait and see what develops.

PROJECT QUESTIONS

1. Why do you think the Mountain View team feels that building its own custom client/server applications would be risky?

2. What are some of the possibilities for processing and providing information that could arise if Mountain View were to move to a client/server environment?

3. What activities would have to be planned if Mountain View were to decide to adopt and implement off-the-shelf client/server applications? Select one activity, such as the patient billing system, and think about what is likely to be involved in selecting, installing, and using such a system.

4. What advantages and disadvantages can you see from the third approach, layering the client/server applications on top of existing systems?

5. What advantages and disadvantages can you see from Mountain View remaining with their current systems for the next two years?

PROJECT EXERCISES

1. Outline what you see as the pros and cons of each of the four approaches to moving to a client/server environment: customizing off-the-shelf systems (COTS), custom system development, surrounding and layering, and doing nothing for a while.

2. Now, using the lists developed in the first project exercise, indicate which solution you feel Mountain View Community Hospital should try.

Defend your answer. Indicate what additional information you would like to have to help you with your recommendation.

3. Try to get some material about off-the-shelf client/server hospital systems, such as CAE-NET, SurgiNet, CyCare, or AViiON. Investigate the capabilities of each system, the number of installations, the client operating system used, and so on. Determine which of the systems you have found and learned about might be of interest to Mountain View.

CHAPTER

9

SQL

LEARNING OBJECTIVES

After studying this chapter, you should be able to:

■ Define the following key terms: **relational DBMS (RDBMS), schema, catalog, data definition language, data manipulation language, data control language, referential integrity, base table, scalar aggregate, vector aggregate, join, equi-join, outer join, correlated subquery,** and **trigger.**

■ Interpret the history and role of SQL in database development.

■ Define a database using the SQL data definition language.

■ Write single and multiple table queries using SQL commands.

■ Define three types of join commands and use SQL to write these commands.

■ Write noncorrelated and correlated subqueries, and know when to write each.

■ Establish referential integrity using SQL.

■ Understand common uses of database triggers and stored procedures.

■ Discuss the SQL-92 standard and the proposed SQL3 standard.

INTRODUCTION

Pronounced "S-Q-L" by some and "sequel" by others, SQL has become the de facto standard language used for creating and querying relational databases. The primary purpose of this chapter is to review SQL in depth. SQL is the most common language for relational systems. It has been accepted as an American standard by the American National Standards Institute (ANSI) and is a Federal Information Processing Standard (FIPS). It is also an international standard recognized by the International Organization for Standardization (ISO). The ANSI SQL standards were first published in 1986 and updated in 1989 and 1992 (SQL-92). New SQL3 and

SQL4 standards that will extend SQL-92 capabilities are under development at the time of this writing, but are not expected to be finalized for some time. For complete coverage of SQL-92 along with preliminary understandings of the SQL3 draft, see Date and Darwen (1997). This chapter will conform to SQL-92, with occasional references to predicted SQL3 and SQL4 capabilities.

SQL has been implemented in both mainframe and personal computer systems, so this chapter is relevant to both computing environments. While many of the PC-database packages use a query-by-example (QBE) interface, they also include SQL as an option. In Microsoft Access, for example, it is possible to switch back and forth between the two interfaces; a query that has been built using a QBE interface can be viewed in SQL by clicking a button. This feature may aid the reader in learning SQL syntax. In client/server architectures, SQL commands are executed on the server, and the results are returned to the client workstation.

The first commercial DBMS that supported SQL was Oracle in 1979. Oracle is now available in mainframe, client-server, and PC-based platforms for many operating systems, including DOS, OS/2, various UNIX operating systems, VAX/VMS, VM/CMS, and MVS. IBM's SQL products include DB2 for MVS, DB2 for OS/2, and SQL/400 for the AS/400 operating system. Informix is also available for many operating systems, including DOS, VAX/VMS, and various UNIX systems. Sybase's SQL products, including SQL Server 11, SQL Anywhere and SQL Server Professional are available for IBM RISC/6000, OS/2, Windows NT, and various UNIX systems.

SQL-92 sets a minimum standard for an SQL-92-compliant database. As with each previous standard, vendors have added capabilities to their version of SQL that are not included in the standard. These modifications mean that each vendor's version of SQL must be approached carefully, in order to discern the differences. In this chapter we use Oracle7's version of SQL-92, SQL*Plus, and we have noted when this version of SQL extends the SQL-92 standard. Oracle8 is the most current version of Oracle, but at the time of writing is not widely implemented. Differences between Oracle7 and Oracle8 SQL syntax are minimal, since both implement SQL-92.

HISTORY OF THE SQL STANDARD

The concepts of relational database technology were first articulated in 1970 in a classic paper written by E. F. Codd entitled "A Relational Model of Data for Large Shared Data Banks." Workers at the IBM Research Laboratory in San Jose, California, undertook development of System R, a project whose purpose was to demonstrate the feasibility of implementing the relational model in a database management system. They used a language called Sequel, also developed at the San Jose IBM Research Laboratory. Sequel was renamed SQL during the project, which took place from 1974 to 1979. The knowledge gained was applied in the development of SQL/DS, the first relational database management system available commercially from IBM. SQL/DS was first available in 1981, running on the DOS/VSE operating system. A VM version followed in 1982, and the MVS version, DB2, was announced in 1983.

Because System R was well received at the user sites where it was installed, other vendors began developing relational products that used SQL. One product, ORACLE, from Relational Software, was actually on the market before SQL/DS (1979). Other products included INGRES from Relational Technology (1981), IDM from Britton-Lee (1982), DG/SQL from Data General Corporation (1984), and SYBASE from Sybase Inc. (1986). To provide some directions for the development of RDBMSs, the ANSI and the ISO approved a standard for the SQL relational query language (functions and syntax) proposed originally by the X3H2 Technical Committee on Database (Technical Committee X3H2—Database, 1986; ISO, 1987), often referred to as SQL/86. The 1986 standards have been extended to include an optional Integrity Enhancement Feature (IEF), often referred to as SQL/89. A related standard, Database Language Embedded SQL, was also adopted in the United States in 1989. The ISO and ANSI committees created SQL-92 (Technical Committee X3H2—Database, 1989; ISO, 1989, 1991), which was a more extensive expansion of SQL/86. This standard was ratified in late 1992 and is known as International Standard ISO/IEC 9075:1992, *Database Language SQL.* It was amended in 1994 and 1996. Further extensions are now being considered and are expected to result in SQL3.

There are now many products available that support SQL, and they run on all machine sizes, from small personal computers to large mainframes. The database market is maturing and the rate of significant changes in products may slow, but they will continue to be SQL-based. In 1997 Oracle, with a 37 percent share of the Unix and NT database server and tools market, enjoyed considerable success in the database market. Informix, Sybase, and IBM are Oracle's main competitors, though Microsoft is beginning to move into the corporate database market with SQL Server on Windows NT. Microsoft's Access is very strong at the personal computer level and small business level (*Computerworld,* May 12, 1997). Upcoming product releases, along with Microsoft's move into the corporate database arena, may change the relative strengths of the database management systems by the time you read this book. But all of them will continue to use SQL, and they will follow, to a certain extent, the standards described below.

THE ROLE OF SQL IN A DATABASE ARCHITECTURE

With today's relational DBMSs and application generators, the importance of SQL within the database architecture is not usually apparent to the application users. Many users access database applications with no knowledge of SQL at all. For example, sites on the Web allow users to browse the catalog of the site being visited (see, for example, http://www.llbean.com). The information about an item that is presented, such as size, color, description, or availability, is stored in a database. The information has been retrieved using an SQL query, but the user has not issued an SQL command.

An SQL-based relational database application involves a user interface, a set of tables in the database, and a relational database management system (RDBMS) with an SQL capability. Within the RDBMS, SQL will be used to create the tables, translate user requests, maintain the data dictionary and system catalog, update and maintain the tables, establish security, and carry out backup and recovery procedures. A **relational DBMS (RDBMS)** is a data management system that implements a relational data model, one where data are stored in a collection of tables, and the data relationships are represented by common values, not links. This view of data was illustrated in Chapter 3 for the Pine Valley Furniture database system, and will be used throughout this chapter's SQL example queries.

The original purposes of the SQL standard follow:

1. To specify the syntax and semantics of SQL data definition and manipulation languages

2. To define the data structures and basic operations for designing, accessing, maintaining, controlling, and protecting an SQL database

Relational DBMS (RDBMS): A database management system that manages data as a collection of tables in which all data relationships are represented by common values in related tables.

3. To provide a vehicle for portability of database definition and application modules between conforming DBMSs

4. To specify both minimal (Level 1) and complete (Level 2) standards, which permit different degrees of adoption in products

5. To provide an initial standard, although incomplete, that will be enhanced later to include specifications for handling such topics as referential integrity, transaction management, user-defined functions, join operators beyond the equi-join, and national character sets (among others)

The SQL-92 standard has been widely accepted, and most new products are SQL-92 compliant. However, each vendor's version of SQL also includes enhancements, features, and capabilities that extend their version beyond the baseline standards of SQL-92. For example, Oracle includes a describe command, which lists all attributes, their datatypes, and constraints for a table. This is a very useful feature, especially for students who are becoming familiar with a demonstration database, but it is a command that they will not find if they use another vendor's SQL, such as MS-Access. Thus, the SQL standards have always served as a minimum set of capabilities rather than as a completely specified set of capabilities. What are the advantages and disadvantages of having an SQL standard?

The benefits of such a standardized relational language include the following:

- *Reduced training costs*   Training in an organization can concentrate on one language. A large labor pool of IS professionals trained in a common language reduces retraining when hiring new employees.

- *Productivity*   IS professionals can learn SQL thoroughly and become proficient with it from continued use. The organization can afford to invest in tools to help IS professionals become more productive. And since they are familiar with the language in which programs are written, programmers can more quickly maintain existing programs.

- *Application portability*   Applications can be moved from machine to machine when each machine uses SQL. Further, it is economical for the computer software industry to develop off-the-shelf application software when there is a standard language.

- *Application longevity*   A standard language tends to remain so for a long time; hence there will be little pressure to rewrite old applications. Rather, applications will simply be updated as the standard language is enhanced or new versions of DBMSs are introduced.

- *Reduced dependence on a single vendor*   When a nonproprietary language is used, it is easier to use different vendors for the DBMS, training and educational services, application software, and consulting assistance; further, the market for such vendors will be more competitive, which may lower prices and improve service.

- *Cross-system communication*   Different DBMSs and application programs can more easily communicate and cooperate in managing data and processing user programs.

On the other hand, a standard can stifle creativity and innovation; one standard is never enough to meet all needs, and an industry standard can be far from ideal since it may be the offspring of compromises among many parties. A standard may be difficult to change (because so many vendors have a vested interest in it), so fixing deficiencies may take considerable effort. Another disadvantage of standards is that using special features added to SQL by a particular vendor may result in the loss of some advantages, such as application portability.

The original SQL standard has been widely criticized, especially for its lack of referential integrity rules and certain relational operators. Date and Darwen (1997) express concern that SQL seems to have been designed without adhering to established principles of language design, and "As a result, the language is filled with numerous restrictions, *ad hoc* constructs, and annoying special rules" (p. 8). They feel that the standard is not explicit enough and that the problem of standard SQL implementations will continue to exist. Some of these limitations will be noticeable in this chapter.

THE SQL ENVIRONMENT

Figure 9-1 is a simplified schematic of an SQL environment, consistent with SQL-92 standards. As depicted, an SQL environment includes an instance of an SQL database management system along with the databases accessible by that DBMS and the users and programs that may use that DBMS to access the databases. Each database is contained in a **catalog**, which describes any object that is a part of the database, regardless of which user created that object. Although the term **schema** is not clearly defined in the standard, it may be taken in general to contain descriptions of the objects, such as the base tables, views, constraints, and so on that have been defined for a particular database by a particular user, who owns the objects in the schema. If more than one user has created objects in the database, combining information about all users' schemas will yield information for the entire database. Each catalog must also contain an information schema, which contains descriptions of all schemas in the catalog, tables, views, attributes, privileges, constraints, and domains, along with

Catalog: A set of schemas, which when put together, constitute a description of a database.

Schema: That structure which contains descriptions of objects created by a user, such as base tables, views, constraints, etc., as part of a database.

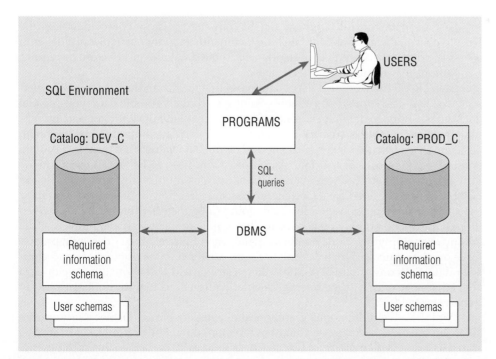

Figure 9-1
A simplified schematic of a typical SQL environment, as described by the SQL-92 standard

Figure 9-2

General syntax of the SELECT statement used in data manipulation language

```
SELECT [ALL|DISTINCT] column_list
FROM table_list
[WHERE conditional expression]
[GROUP BY group_by_column_list]
[HAVING conditional expression]
[ORDER BY order_by_column_list]
```

Data definition language (DDL): Those commands used to define a database, including creating, altering, and dropping tables and establishing constraints.

Data manipulation language (DML): Those commands used to maintain and query a database, including updating, inserting, modifying, and querying data.

Data control language (DCL): Commands used to control a database, including administering privileges and commiting (saving) of data.

other information relevant to the database. The information contained in the catalog is maintained by the DBMS as a result of the SQL commands issued by the users and does not require conscious action by the user to build it. It is part of the power of the SQL language that the issuance of syntactically simple SQL commands may result in complex data management activities being carried out by the DBMS software. Users can browse the catalog contents by using SQL select statements.

SQL commands can be classified into three types. First, there are **data definition language (DDL)** commands. These commands are used to create, alter, and drop tables, and will be covered first in this chapter. In a production database, the ability to use DDL commands will generally be restricted to one or more database administrators in order to protect the database structure from unexpected changes. In development or student databases, DDL privileges will be granted to more users.

Next, there are **data manipulation language (DML)** commands. Many consider the DML commands to be the core commands of SQL. These commands are used for updating, inserting, modifying, and querying the data in the database. They may be issued interactively, so that a result is returned immediately following the execution of the statement, or they may be included within programs written in a 3GL, such as C or COBOL. Embedding SQL commands may provide the programmer with more control over timing of report generation, interface appearance, error handling, and database security. Most of this chapter is devoted to covering basic DML commands, in interactive format. The general syntax of the SQL SELECT command used in DML is shown in Figure 9-2.

Last are **data control language (DCL)** commands. These commands help the DBA to control the database, and include commands to grant or revoke privileges to access the database or particular objects within the database and to store or remove transactions that would affect the database.

Each DBMS has a defined list of data types that it can handle. All contain numeric, string, and date/time-type variables. Some also contain graphic data types, spatial data types, or image data types, which greatly increase the flexibility of data manipulation. When a table is created, the data type for each attribute must be specified. Selection of a particular data type is affected by the data values that need to be stored and the expected uses of the data. A unit price will need to be stored in a numeric format because mathematical manipulations such as multiplying unit price by the number of units ordered are expected. A phone number may be stored as string data, especially if foreign phone numbers are going to be included in the data set. Even though the phone number contains only digits, no mathematical operations, such as adding or multiplying phone numbers, make sense. Since character data will process more quickly, if no arithmetic calculations are expected, store numeric data as character data. Selecting a date field rather than a string field will allow the developer to take advantage of date/time interval calculation functions that cannot be applied to a character field.

With the advent of various graphic and image data types, it is necessary to consider the business needs in deciding how to store data. For example, color may be stored as a descriptive character field, such as 'sand drift' or 'beige'. But such descrip-

TABLE 9-1 Sample Oracle7 Data Types

String	CHAR(*n*)		Fixed-length character data, *n* characters long. Maximum length is 255.
	VARCHAR2(*n*)		Variable-length character data. Maximum size 2000 bytes.
	LONG		Variable-length character data. Maximum size 2 GB. Maximum one per table.
Numeric	NUMBER(*p*, *q*)		Signed decimal number with *p* digits and assumed decimal point *q* digits from right
	INTEGER(*p*)		Signed integer, decimal or binary, *p* digits wide
	FLOAT(*p*)		Floating-point number in scientific notation of *p* binary digits precision
Binary	RAW(*n*)		Variable-length raw binary data. Maximum size 2000 bytes.
Date/time	DATE		Fixed-length date and time data in *dd-mm-yy* form.

tions will vary from vendor to vendor and do not contain the amount of information that could be contained in a spatial data type that includes exact red, green, and blue intensity values. Such data types are now available in universal servers, which handle data warehouses, and can be expected to appear in RDBMSs as well. SQL-92 supports several data types that are not shown in Table 9-1, including TIMESTAMP, REAL, and INTERVAL, and other RDBMSs have included data types such as CURRENCY and LOGICAL. It will be necessary to familiarize yourself with the available data types for each RDBMS with which you work, in order that you can achieve maximum advantage from its capabilities.

We are almost ready to illustrate sample SQL commands. The sample data that we will be using are shown in Figure 9-3. Each table name follows a naming standard that places an underscore and the letter *t* at the end of each table name, such as Order_t or Product_t. While looking at those tables, please take notice of the following:

Customer_ID	Customer_name	Customer_address	City	State	Postal_Code
001	Contemporary Casuals	1355 S. Hines Blvd.	Gainsville	FL	32601
002	Value Furniture	15145 S.W. 17th St.	Plano	TX	75094
003	Home Furnishings	1900 Allard Ave.	Albany	NY	12209
004	Eastern Furniture	1925 Beltline Rd.	Carteret	NJ	7008
005	Impressions	5585 Westcott Ct.	Sacramento	CA	94206
006	Furniture Gallery	325 Flatiron Dr.	Boulder	CO	80514
007	Period Furnishings	394 Rainbow Dr.	Seattle	WA	97954
008	California Classics	816 Peach Rd.	Santa Clara	CA	96915
009	M & H Casual Furniture	3709 First Street	Clearwater	FL	34620
010	Seminole Interiors	2400 Rocky Point Dr.	Seminole	FL	34646
011	American Euro Lifestyles	2424 Missouri Ave. N.	Prospect Park	NJ	7508
012	Battle Creek Furniture	345 Capitol Ave. SW	Battle Creek	MI	49015
013	Heritage Furnishings	66789 College Ave.	Carlisle	PA	17013
014	Kaneohe Homes	112 Kiowai St.	Kaneohe	HI	96744
015	Mountain Scenes	4132 Main Street	Ogden	UT	84403
(AutoNumber)					0

Customer_t : Table

Figure 9-3
Sample Pine Valley Furniture company data

(continues)

Figure 9-3
Continued

Order_line_t : Table		
Order_ID	**Product_ID**	**Quantity**
1001	1	2
1001	2	2
1001	4	1
1002	3	5
1003	3	3
1004	6	2
1004	8	2
1005	4	4
1006	4	1
1006	5	2
1006	7	2
1007	1	3
1007	2	2
1008	3	3
1008	8	3
1009	4	2
1009	7	3
1010	8	10
0	0	0

Order_t : Table		
Order_ID	**Order_Date**	**Customer_ID**
1001	10/21/98	1
1002	10/21/98	8
1003	10/22/98	15
1004	10/22/98	5
1005	10/24/98	3
1006	10/27/98	2
1007	10/27/98	11
1008	10/30/98	12
1009	11/5/98	4
1010	11/5/98	1
0		0

Product_t : Table					
Product_ID	**Product_Name**	**Product_Finish**	**Unit_Price**	**On_hand**	**Product_Description**
1	End Table	Cherry	$175.00	8	
2	Coffee Table	Natural Ash	$200.00	4	
3	Computer Desk	Natural Ash	$375.00	5	Computer Desk 48"
4	Entertainment Center	Natural Maple	$650.00	3	
5	Writer's Desk	Cherry	$325.00	0	
6	8-Drawer Desk	White Ash	$750.00	5	
7	Dining Table	Natural Ash	$800.00	2	
8	Computer Desk	Walnut	$250.00	4	Computer Desk 64"
(AutoNumber)			$0.00	0	

1. Each order must have a valid customer number included in the Order_t table.

2. Each item in an order must have both a valid product number and a valid order number associated with it in the Order_Line_t table.

3. These four tables represent a simplified version of one of the most common sets of relations in business database systems—that of the customer order for products. SQL commands necessary to create the Customer table and the Order table were included in Chapter 3, and are expanded here.

The remainder of the chapter will illustrate DDL, DML, and DCL commands. Figure 9-4 gives an overview of where the various types of commands are used throughout the database development process. We will use the following notation in the illustrative SQL commands:

1. Capitalized words denote the command syntax. Type them exactly as shown, though capitalization may not be required by the RDBMS.

2. Lowercase words denote values that must be supplied by the user.

3. Brackets enclose optional syntax.

4. Ellipses (…) indicate that the accompanying syntactic clause may be repeated as necessary.

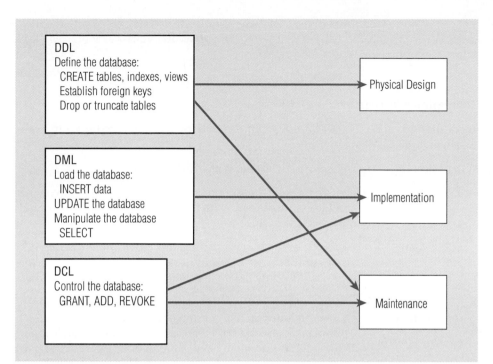

Figure 9-4
DDL, DML, DCL, and the database development process

5. Each SQL command ends with a semicolon (;). In interactive mode, when the user pushes the RETURN key, the SQL command will execute. Be alert for alternative conventions, such as typing GO, or having to include a continuation symbol such as a hyphen at the end of each line used in the command. The spacing and indentations shown here are included for readability and are not a required part of standard SQL syntax.

DEFINING A DATABASE IN SQL

Although SQL-92 does not include a CREATE DATABASE command, most systems have a form of this command that is used for the initial allocation of storage space to contain base tables, views, constraints, indexes, and other database objects. Most systems set aside a significant minimum amount of storage when a database is created. Because of this, the privilege of creating databases may be reserved for the database administrator, and you may need to ask to have a database created. Students at a university may be assigned an account that gives access to an existing database, or they may be allowed to create their own database. In any case, the basic syntax to create a database is CREATE DATABASE *database_name;* and the database will be owned by whoever issues this command, although it is possible for other specified users to work with the database, or even to transfer ownership of the database. Physical storage of the database is dependent on both the hardware and software environment, and is usually the concern of the system administrator. Some physical storage issues may be resolved when the CREATE DATABASE command is issued, depending on the RDBMS being used. Device location(s) for storing the database, maximum datafile sizes, and archiving information are some of the possibilities that can be addressed through the CREATE DATABASE command. Be sure to familiarize yourself with the CREATE DATABASE syntax for your particular RDBMS before attempting to set up a new database.

Generating SQL Database Definitions

In addition to CREATE DATABASE, eight SQL DDL commands are typically available in SQL-92 DBMSs:

CREATE TABLE	Defines a new table and its columns.
DROP TABLE	Destroys a table (definition and contents as well as any views and indexes associated with it). Usually only the table creator may delete the table.
ALTER TABLE	Adds one or more new columns to a table. Some RDBMSs also permit deleting columns or redefining the column's data type. Usually only the table creator may add columns to the table.
CREATE INDEX	Defines an index on one column or a concatenation of columns that enables rapid access to the rows of a table in a sequence or randomly by key value. A table may have many indexes, and each index may be specified to be UNIQUE (primary key) or not and may be sequenced in ascending or descending order.
DROP INDEX	Destroys an index. Usually only the table creator may delete an index of that table.
CREATE VIEW	Defines a logical table from one or more tables or views. Views may not be indexed. There are limitations on updating data through a view, but some updating of data through a view is permitted.
DROP VIEW	Destroys a view definition (and any other views defined from the deleted view.) Usually only the creator of the view's base tables may delete a view.
CREATE SCHEMA	Used to define that portion of a database that a particular user owns. It is possible to run several of the commands above at once under the CREATE SCHEMA command. Multiple CREATE TABLE, CREATE VIEW, and GRANT commands may all be included.

Creating Tables

Once the data model is designed and normalized, the columns needed for each table can be defined using the SQL CREATE TABLE command. The general syntax for CREATE TABLE is shown in Figure 9-5. Here is a series of steps to follow when preparing to create a table:

1. Identify the appropriate datatype, including length, precision, and scale if required, for each attribute.

```
CREATE TABLE tablename
      (column_name datatype [NULL|NOT NULL]
      [DEFAULT default_value] [column_constraint_clause]...
      [,column_name datatype [NULL|NOT NULL]
      [DEFAULT default_value] [column_constraint_clause]...]...
      [table_constraint_clause]...);
```

Figure 9-5
General syntax of the CREATE TABLE statement used in data manipulation language

2. Identify those columns that should accept null values, as discussed in Chapter 7. Column controls that indicate a column cannot be null are established when a table is created and are enforced for every update of the table when data are entered.

3. Identify those columns that need to be unique. When a column control of UNIQUE is established for a column, then the data in that column must have a different value (that is, no duplicate values) for each row of data within that table. Where a column or set of columns is designated as UNIQUE, that column or set of columns is a candidate key, as discussed in Chapter 6. While each base table may have multiple candidate keys, only one candidate key may be designated as a PRIMARY KEY. When a column(s) is specified as the PRIMARY KEY, that column(s) is also assumed to be NOT NULL, even if NOT NULL is not explicitly stated. UNIQUE and PRIMARY KEY are both column constraints.

4. Identify all primary key–foreign key mates, as presented in Chapter 6. Foreign keys can be established immediately, as a table is created, or later by altering the table. The parent table in such a parent–child relationship should be created first, so that the child table will reference an existing parent table when it is created. The column constraint REFERENCES can be used to enforce referential integrity.

5. Determine values to be inserted in any columns for which a default value is desired. DEFAULT, in SQL-92, can be used to define a value that is automatically inserted when no value is inserted during data entry. In Figure 9-6, the command that creates the ORDER_T table has defined a default value of SYSDATE (Oracle's name for the current date) for the DATE attribute.

6. Identify any columns for which domain specifications may be stated that are more constrained than those established by data type. Using CHECK as a column constraint in SQL-92 it may be possible to establish validation rules for values to be inserted into the database. In Figure 9-6, creation of the PRODUCT_T table includes a check constraint, which lists the possible values for PRODUCT_FINISH. Thus, even though an entry of 'White Maple' would meet the varchar datatype constraints, it would be rejected because 'White Maple' is not in the checklist.

7. Create the table and any desired indexes using the CREATE TABLE and CREATE INDEX statements.

In Chapters 3 and 6, SQL database definition commands to create the Customer and Order tables for Pine Valley Furniture were shown that included establishing column constraints within the CREATE TABLE commands. In Figure 9-6, database

```
CREATE TABLE CUSTOMER_T
        (CUSTOMER_ID              INTEGER     NOT NULL,
        CUSTOMER_NAME             VARCHAR(40) NOT NULL,
        CUSTOMER_ADDRESS          VARCHAR(40),
        CITY                      VARCHAR(25),
        STATE                     VARCHAR(2),
        POSTAL_CODE               VARCHAR(10),
CONSTRAINT CUSTOMER_PK PRIMARY KEY (CUSTOMER_ID));

CREATE TABLE ORDER_T
        (ORDER_ID                 INTEGER     NOT NULL,
        ORDER_DATE                DATE        DEFAULT SYSDATE,
        CUSTOMER_ID               INTEGER,
CONSTRAINT ORDER_PK PRIMARY KEY (ORDER_ID),
CONSTRAINT ORDER_FK FOREIGN KEY (CUSTOMER_ID) REFERENCES CUSTOMER_T(CUSTOMER_ID));

CREATE TABLE PRODUCT_T
        (PRODUCT_ID               INTEGER                   NOT NULL,
        PRODUCT_NAME              VARCHAR(40),
        PRODUCT_FINISH            VARCHAR(25)
                     CHECK (PRODUCT_FINISH IN ('Cherry', 'Natural Ash', 'White Ash',
                               'Red Oak', 'Natural Oak', 'Walnut')),
        UNIT_PRICE                DECIMAL(6,2),
        ON_HAND                   INTEGER,
        PRODUCT_DESCRIPTION       VARCHAR(40),
CONSTRAINT PRODUCT_PK PRIMARY KEY (PRODUCT_ID));

CREATE TABLE ORDER_LINE_T
        (ORDER_ID                 INTEGER                   NOT NULL,
        PRODUCT_ID                INTEGER                   NOT NULL,
        QUANTITY                  INTEGER,
CONSTRAINT ORDER_LINE_PK PRIMARY KEY (ORDER_ID, PRODUCT_ID),
CONSTRAINT ORDER_LINE_FK1 FOREIGN KEY(ORDER_ID) REFERENCES ORDER_T(ORDER_ID),
CONSTRAINT ORDER_LINE_FK2 FOREIGN KEY (PRODUCT_ID) REFERENCES PRODUCT_T(PRODUCT_ID));
```

Figure 9-6
SQL database definition commands for Pine Valley Furniture Company

definition commands are shown that include additional column constraints, and primary and foreign keys are given names. For example, the Customer table's primary key is CUSTOMER_ID. The primary key constraint is named CUSTOMER_PK. Now, in Oracle for example, when looking at the DBA_CONSTRAINTS table a database administrator will find it easy to identify the primary key constraint on the customer table because its name, CUSTOMER_PK, will be the value of the constraint_name column. Without the constraint name, a system identifier would be assigned automatically and the identifier would be difficult to read.

Referential integrity: An integrity constraint specifying that the value (or existence) of an attribute in one relation depends on the value (or existence) of a primary key in the same or another relation.

Creating Data Integrity Controls

We have seen the syntax that establishes foreign keys in Figure 9-6. In order to establish **referential integrity** between two tables with a 1:M relationship in the relational data model, the primary key of the table on the one-side will be referenced by a column in the table on the many side of the relationship. Referential integrity means that a value in the matching column on the many side must correspond to a value in the primary key for some row in the table on the one side, or be NULL. The SQL REFERENCES clause prevents a foreign key value from being added if it is not already a valid value in the referenced primary key column, but there are other integrity issues.

If a CUSTOMER_ID value is changed, the connection between that customer and orders placed by that customer will be ruined. The REFERENCES clause prevents making such a change in the foreign key value, but not in the primary key value. This problem could be handled by asserting that primary key values cannot be changed once they are established. In this case, updates to the customer table will be handled in most systems by including an ON UPDATE RESTRICT clause. Then, any updates that would delete or change a primary key value will be rejected unless no foreign key references that value in any child table. See Figure 9-7 for the syntax associated with updates.

Another solution is to pass the change through to the child table(s) by using the ON UPDATE CASCADE option. Then, if a customer ID number is changed, that change will flow through (cascade) to the child table, ORDER_T, and the customer's ID will also be updated in the ORDER_T table.

A third solution is to allow the update on CUSTOMER_T but to change the involved CUSTOMER_ID value in the ORDER_T table to NULL by using the ON UPDATE SET NULL option. In this case, using the SET NULL option would result in losing the connection between the order and the customer, not a desired effect. The most flexible option to use would be the CASCADE option. Were a customer record

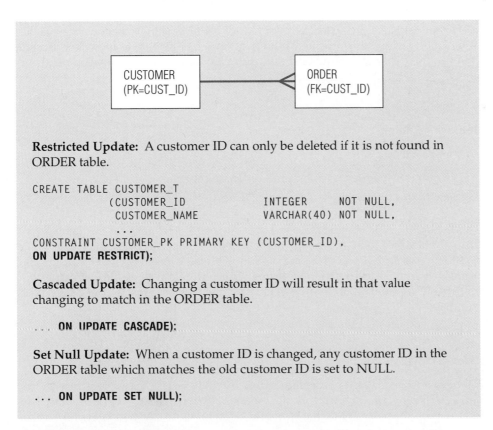

Figure 9-7
Ensuring data integrity through updates

Restricted Update: A customer ID can only be deleted if it is not found in ORDER table.

```
CREATE TABLE CUSTOMER_T
          (CUSTOMER_ID              INTEGER     NOT NULL,
           CUSTOMER_NAME            VARCHAR(40) NOT NULL,
             . . .
CONSTRAINT CUSTOMER_PK PRIMARY KEY (CUSTOMER_ID),
ON UPDATE RESTRICT);
```

Cascaded Update: Changing a customer ID will result in that value changing to match in the ORDER table.

```
. . . ON UPDATE CASCADE);
```

Set Null Update: When a customer ID is changed, any customer ID in the ORDER table which matches the old customer ID is set to NULL.

```
. . . ON UPDATE SET NULL);
```

to be deleted, ON DELETE RESTRICT, CASCADE, or SET NULL are also available. With DELETE RESTRICT, the customer record could not be deleted unless there were no orders from that customer in the ORDER_T table. With DELETE CASCADE, removing the customer would remove all associated order records from ORDER_T. With DELETE SET NULL, the order records for that customer would be set to null before the customer's record is deleted. DELETE RESTRICT would probably make the most sense. Not all SQL RDBMSs provide for primary key referential integrity. In that case, update and delete permissions on the primary key column may be revoked.

Changing Table Definitions

Table definitions may be changed in many SQL RDBMSs by ALTERing column specifications. In Oracle, the ALTER TABLE command may be used to add new columns to an existing table. For example, a customer type column may be added to the CUSTOMER table.

Command: To add a customer type column to the CUSTOMER table.

```
ALTER TABLE CUSTOMER_T
  ADD (TYPE VARCHAR (2));
```

The ALTER TABLE command may include keywords such as ADD and DROP, and allow changing the column's names, datatype, length, and constraints. Usually when adding a new column, its null status will be NULL, in order to deal with data that have already been entered in the table. When the new column is created, it is added to all of the instances in the table and a value of NULL would be the most reasonable. The ALTER command is invaluable for adapting the database to inevitable modifications due to changing requirements, prototyping, evolutionary development, and mistakes.

Removing Tables

To remove a table from a database, use the DROP TABLE command.

Command: To drop a table from a database schema.

```
DROP TABLE CUSTOMER_T;
```

This command will drop the table and save any pending changes to the database. To drop a table, one must either own the table or have been granted the DROP ANY TABLE system privilege. Dropping a table will also cause associated indexes and privileges granted to be dropped. If one wishes to retain the table's structure but remove all of the data that have been entered in the table, use the TRUNCATE TABLE command.

Establishing Synonyms

If table names are long, typographical errors may plague SQL query construction. Try CREATE SYNONYM, which specifies an alternative name for a table or view. This command is often used to define an abbreviation to reduce the number of keystrokes needed when referring to a table or view. DROP SYNONYM will destroy a synonym declaration.

INSERTING, UPDATING, AND DELETING DATA

Once tables and views have been created, it is necessary to populate them with data and maintain those data before queries can be written. The SQL command that is used to populate tables is the INSERT command. If entering a value for every column in the table one could use a command like the following, which was used to add the first row of data to the CUSTOMER_T table. Notice that the data values must be ordered in the same order as the columns in the table.

> **Command:** To insert a row of data into a table where a value will be inserted for every attribute.

```
INSERT INTO CUSTOMER_T VALUES
(001, 'Contemporary Casuals', '1355 S. Himes Blvd.', 'Gainesville',
   'FL', 32601);
```

When data will not be entered into every column in the table, either enter the value NULL for the empty fields or specify those columns to which data are to be added. Here, too, the data values must be in the same order as the columns have been specified in the INSERT command. For example, the following statement was used to insert one row of data into the PRODUCT_T table, since there was no product description for the end table.

> **Command:** To insert a row of data into a table where some attributes will be left null.

```
INSERT INTO PRODUCT_T (PRODUCT_ID, PRODUCT_NAME, PRODUCT_FINISH,
UNIT_PRICE, ON_HAND)
   VALUES (1, 'End Table', 'Cherry', 175, 8);
```

In general, the INSERT command places a new row in a table based on values supplied in the statement, copies one or more rows derived from other database data into a table, or extracts data from one table and inserts them into another. When wanting to populate a table, CA_CUSTOMER_T, that has the same structure as CUSTOMER_T, with only Pine Valley's California customers, one could use the following INSERT command.

> **Command:** Populating a table by using a subset of another table with the same structure.

```
INSERT INTO CA_CUSTOMER_T
   SELECT * FROM CUSTOMER_T
      WHERE STATE = 'CA';
```

Batch Input

The INSERT command is used to enter one row of data at a time. Some versions of SQL have a special command or utility for entering multiple rows of data as a batch: the INPUT command. Oracle7 includes a program, SQL*Loader, which runs from the command line, and can be used to load data from a file into the database. This program is tricky to use and is not included in the scope of this text.

Deleting Database Contents

Rows can be deleted individually or in groups. Suppose Pine Valley Furniture decides that it will no longer deal with customers located in Hawaii. CUSTOMER_T rows for customers with addresses in Hawaii could all be eliminated by the next command.

> **Command:** Deleting rows that meet a certain criterion from the CUSTOMER table.

```
DELETE FROM CUSTOMER_T
  WHERE STATE = 'HI';
```

The simplest form of DELETE eliminates all rows of a table.

> **Command:** Deleting all rows from the CUSTOMER table.

```
DELETE FROM CUSTOMER_T;
```

This form of the command should be used very carefully!

Deletion must also be done with care when rows from several relations are involved. For example, if we delete a CUSTOMER_T row before deleting associated ORDER_T rows, we will have a referential integrity violation. (*Note:* Including the ON DELETE clause with a field definition can mitigate such a problem. Refer back to the DATA INTEGRITY CONTROLS section of this chapter if you've forgotten about ON DELETE.) SQL will actually eliminate the records selected by a DELETE command. Therefore, always execute a SELECT command first to display the records that would be deleted and visually verify that only the desired rows are included.

Changing Database Contents

To update data in SQL we must inform the DBMS what relation, columns, and rows are involved. If an incorrect price is entered for the dining table in the PRODUCT_T table, the following SQL UPDATE statement would establish the correction.

> **Command:** To modify unit price in the PRODUCT table to 775.

```
UPDATE PRODUCT_T
  SET UNIT_PRICE = 775
      WHERE PRODUCT_ID = 7;
```

The SET command can also change a value to NULL; the syntax is SET *columnname* = NULL. As with DELETE, the WHERE clause in an UPDATE command may contain a subquery, but the table being updated may not be referenced in the subquery. Subqueries are discussed later in the chapter.

INTERNAL SCHEMA DEFINITION IN RDBMSs

The internal schema of a relational database can be controlled for processing and storage efficiency. Some techniques used to tune the operational performance of the relational database internal data model include:

1. Choosing to index primary and/or secondary keys to increase the speed of row selection, table joining, and row ordering. Dropping indexes to increase speed of table updating. You may want to review the section in Chapter 7 on selecting indexes.

2. Selecting file organizations for base tables that match the type of processing activity on those tables (for example, keeping a table physically sorted by a frequently used reporting sort key).

3. Selecting file organizations for indexes, which are also tables, appropriate to the way the indexes are used, and allocating extra space for an index file, so that an index can grow without having to be reorganized.

4. Clustering data, so that related rows of frequently joined tables are stored close together in secondary storage to minimize retrieval time.

5. Maintaining statistics about tables and their indexes, so that the DBMS can find the most efficient ways to perform various database operations.

Not all of these techniques are available in all SQL systems. Indexing and clustering are typically available, however, so we discuss these in the following sections.

Creating Indexes

Indexes are created in most RDBMSs to provide rapid random and sequential access to base-table data. Although users do not directly refer to indexes when writing any SQL command, the DBMS recognizes which existing indexes would improve query performance. Indexes can usually be created for both primary and secondary keys and both single and concatenated (multiple-column) keys. In some systems, one can choose between ascending or descending sequences for the keys in an index.

For example, an alphabetical index on CUSTOMER_NAME in the CUS-TOMER_T column in Oracle7 is created here.

Command: To create an alphabetical index on customer name in the CUSTOMER table.

```
CREATE INDEX NAME_IDX ON CUSTOMER_T (CUSTOMER_NAME);
```

Indexes may be created or dropped at any time. If data already exist in the key column(s), index population will automatically occur for the existing data. If an index is defined as UNIQUE (using the syntax CREATE UNIQUE INDEX…) and the existing data violate this condition, the index creation will fail. Once an index is created, it will be updated as data are entered or updated.

When we no longer need tables, views, or indexes, we use the associated DROP statements. For example, the NAME_IDX index above is dropped here.

Command: To remove the index on the customer name in the CUSTOMER table.

```
DROP INDEX NAME_IDX;
```

Although it is possible to index every column in a table, use caution when deciding to create a new index. Each index consumes extra storage space and also requires overhead maintenance time whenever indexed data change value. Together, these costs may noticeably slow retrieval response times and cause annoying delays for on-line users. A system may use only one index even if several are available for keys in a complex qualification. The database designer must know exactly how indexes are used by the particular RDBMS to make wise choices on indexing. Oracle7 includes an *explain plan* tool that can be used to look at the order in which an SQL statement will be processed and the indexes that will be used. The output also includes a cost estimate that can be compared with estimates from running the statement with different indexes in order to determine which is most efficient.

PROCESSING SINGLE TABLES

Four data manipulation language commands are used in SQL. We have talked briefly about three of them (UPDATE, INSERT, and DELETE) and seen several examples of the fourth, SELECT. While the UPDATE, INSERT, and DELETE commands allow modification of the data in the tables, it is the SELECT command, with its various clauses, that allows one to query the data contained in the tables and ask many different questions, or ad hoc queries. The basic construction of an SQL command is fairly simple and easy to learn. Don't let that fool you; SQL is a powerful tool that enables one to specify complex data analysis processes. However, because the basic syntax is relatively easy to learn, it is also easy to write SELECT queries that are syntactically correct but do not answer the exact question that is intended. Before running queries against a large production database, always test queries carefully on a small test set of data to be sure that they are returning the correct results. In addition to checking the query results manually, it is often possible to parse queries into smaller parts, examine the results of these simpler queries, and then recombine them. This will ensure that they act together in the expected way. We begin by exploring SQL queries that affect only a single table. Later, we join tables and use queries that require more than one table.

Clauses of the SELECT Statement

Most SQL data retrieval statements include the following three clauses:

SELECT   Lists the columns (including expressions involving columns) from base tables or views to be projected into the table that will be the result of the command.

FROM   Identifies the tables or views from which columns will be chosen to appear in the result table, and includes the tables or views needed to join tables to process the query.

WHERE   Includes the conditions for row selection within a single table or view, and the conditions between tables or views for joining.

The first two are required, and the third is necessary when only certain table rows are to be retrieved, or multiple tables are to be joined. Our examples for this section are drawn from the data shown in Figure 9-3. As an example, we can display product name and quantity on hand from the PRODUCT relation for all products that have more than four units on hand.

Query: For which products are there more than four units on hand?

```
SELECT PRODUCT_NAME, ON_HAND
   FROM PRODUCT_T
      WHERE ON_HAND > 4;
```

Result:

PRODUCT_NAME	ON_HAND
End Table	8
Computer Desk	5
8-Drawer Desk	5

Every SELECT statement returns a result table when it executes. Two special keywords can be used along with the list of columns to display: DISTINCT and *. If the user does not wish to see duplicate rows in the result, SELECT DISTINCT may be used. In the preceding example, if the *other* computer desk carried by Pine Valley Furniture also had five units in inventory, the results of the query would have duplicate rows. SELECT DISTINCT PRODUCT_NAME would display a result table without the duplicate rows. SELECT *, where * is used as a wildcard to indicate all columns, displays all columns from all the tables or views in the FROM clause.

Also, note that the clauses of a SELECT statement must be kept in order, or syntax error messages will occur and the query will not execute. It may also be necessary to qualify the names of the database objects, according to the SQL version being used. If there is any ambiguity in an SQL command, one must indicate exactly from which table the requested data is to come. For example, in Figure 9-3 CUSTOMER_ID is a column in both CUSTOMER_T and ORDER_T. When one owns the database being used (that is, the user created the tables) and one wants the CUSTOMER_ID to come from CUSTOMER_T, specify it by asking for CUSTOMER_T.CUSTOMER_ID. If one wants CUSTOMER_ID to come from ORDER_T, then ask for ORDER_T.CUSTOMER_ID. Even if one doesn't care which table CUSTOMER_ID comes from, it must be specified because SQL can't resolve the ambiguity without user direction. When using data that were created by someone else, one must also specify the owner of the table by adding the owner's user ID. Now a request to SELECT the CUSTOMER_ID from CUSTOMER_T may look like *OWNER_ID*.CUSTOMER_T.CUSTOMER_ID. The examples in this book will assume that the reader owns the tables being used, as the SELECT statements will be easier to read without the qualifiers. Qualifiers will be included where necessary and may always be included in statements if desired. Problems may occur from leaving out qualifiers, but no problems will occur from including them.

If typing the qualifiers and column names is wearisome, or if the column names will not be meaningful to those who are reading the reports, establish aliases for columns or tables that will then be used for the rest of the query.

Query: What is the address of the customer named Home Furnishings? Use an alias, NAME, for customer name.

```
SELECT CUST.CUSTOMER_NAME AS NAME, CUST.CUSTOMER_ADDRESS
    FROM ownerid.CUSTOMER_T CUST
        WHERE NAME = 'Home Furnishings';
```

will give the result below in many versions of SQL. In Oracle's SQL*Plus, the alias for the column cannot be used in the rest of the SELECT statement, except in a HAVING clause, so CUSTOMER_NAME would have to be used in the last line rather than NAME in order to run. Notice that the column header prints as NAME rather than CUSTOMER_NAME, and that the table alias may be used in the SELECT clause even though it is not defined until the FROM clause.

Result:

NAME	CUSTOMER_ADDRESS
Home Furnishings	1900 Allard Ave.

When using the SELECT clause to pick out the columns for a result table, the columns can be rearranged so that they will be ordered differently in the result table than they were in the original table. In fact, they will be displayed in the same order as they are included in the SELECT statement. Look back at PROD-UCT_T in Figure 9-3 to see the different ordering of the base table from the result table for this query:

Query: List the unit price, product name, and product ID for all products in the PRODUCT table.

```
SELECT UNIT_PRICE, PRODUCT_NAME, PRODUCT_ID
  FROM PRODUCT_T;
```

Result:

UNIT_PRICE	PRODUCT_NAME	PRODUCT_ID
175	End Table	1
200	Coffee Table	2
375	Computer Desk	3
650	Entertainment Center	4
325	Writer's Desk	5
750	8-Drawer Desk	6
800	Dining Table	7
250	Computer Desk	8

8 rows selected.

Using Expressions

Several other things can be done with the basic SELECT…FROM…WHERE clauses with a single table. One may create *expressions*, which are mathematical manipulations of the data in the table, or one may take advantage of stored functions, such as SUM or AVG, to manipulate the chosen rows of data from the table. Perhaps one would like to know the total value of each inventory item. To get the total value, multiply the units on hand by the unit price for each inventory item. Name the resulting expression VALUE. Using SQL*Plus, here are the query and the results.

Query: What is the total value for each product in inventory?

```
SELECT PRODUCT_NAME, UNIT_PRICE, ON_HAND,
   UNIT_PRICE * ON_HAND AS VALUE
      FROM PRODUCT_T;
```

Here UNIT_PRICE is multiplied by ON_HAND, and the multiplication operand is the '*'. Use the '+' for addition, '−' for subtraction, and '/' for division. These operators can be used with any numeric columns. Some systems also have an operand called *modulo*, usually indicated by '%'. A modulo is the integer remainder that results from dividing two integers. For example, 14 % 4 is 2 because 14/4 is 3 with a remainder of 2. Some systems also provide date functions that allow the user to perform calculations with date values. Notice that the results from the above query now show the expression, VALUE.

Result:

```
PRODUCT_NAME            UNIT_PRICE    ON_HAND   VALUE
End Table                      175         8    1400
Coffee Table                   200         4     800
Computer Desk                  375         5    1875
Entertainment Center           650         3    1950
Writer's Desk                  325         0       0
8-Drawer Desk                  750         5    3750
Dining Table                   800         2    1600
Computer Desk                  250         4    1000

8 rows selected.
```

The precedence rules for the order in which complex expressions are evaluated are the same as those used in other programming languages and in algebra. Expressions in parentheses will be calculated first. Where parentheses do not establish order, multiplication and division will be completed first, from left to right, followed by addition and subtraction, also left to right. To avoid confusion, use parentheses to establish order. Where parentheses are nested, the innermost calculations will be completed first.

Using Functions

Functions such as COUNT, MIN, MAX, SUM, and AVG of specified columns in the column list of a SELECT command may be used to specify that the resulting answer table is to contain aggregated data instead of row-level data. All of these functions appear in most SQL implementations.

Query: How many different items were ordered on order number 1004?

```
SELECT COUNT (*)
  FROM ORDER_LINE_T
      WHERE ORDER_ID = 1004;
```

Result:

```
COUNT (*)
        2
```

It seems that it would be simple enough to list the order # 1004 by changing the above query.

Query: How many different items were ordered on order number 1004, and what are they?

```
SELECT ORDER_ID, COUNT (*)
    FROM ORDER_LINE_T
        WHERE ORDER_ID = 1004;
```

But in Oracle, here is the result.

Result:

```
ERROR at line 1:
ORA-00937: not a single-group group function
```

The problem is that ORDER_ID returns a value, 1004, for each of the two rows selected, while COUNT returns one aggregate value, 2, for the set of rows with ID = 1004. In most implementations, SQL cannot return a row value and a set value; one must run two separate queries, one that returns row information and one that returns set information.

Also, it is easy to confuse the functions COUNT (*) and COUNT. The function COUNT (*), used above, counts all rows selected by a query regardless of whether any of the rows contain null values. COUNT tallies only those rows that contain a value; it ignores all null values. So, to tally occurrences, always consider whether to include rows with null values or not. To illustrate this, we will use COUNT and COUNT (*) to count PRODUCT_DESCRIPTION in PRODUCT_T. Look at the two queries and their results. Had we specified any argument other than PRODUCT_DESCRIPTION, the results would have both been 8 because only PRODUCT_DESCRIPTION contains nulls in PRODUCT_T.

> **Query:** How many different product descriptions are included in the PRODUCT table?

```
SELECT COUNT (PRODUCT_DESCRIPTION)
    FROM PRODUCT_T;
```

Result:

COUNT (PRODUCT_DESCRIPTION)
2

> **Query:** How many products are included in the PRODUCT table?

```
SELECT COUNT (*)
    FROM PRODUCT_T;
```

Result:

COUNT (*)
8

SUM and AVG can only be used with numeric columns. COUNT, COUNT (*), MIN, and MAX can be used with any data type. Using MIN on a text column, for example, will find the lowest value in the column, the one whose first column is closest to the beginning of the alphabet. SQL implementations interpret the order of the alphabet differently. For example, some systems may start with A–Z, then a–z, then 0–9 and special characters. Others treat upper and lowercase letters as being equivalent. Yet others start with some special characters, then proceed to numbers, letters, and other special characters. In Oracle7, the language character set is determined when the database is created and cannot be changed without re-creating the database. When a client terminal uses a different character set, Oracle automatically converts the character sets in both directions, changing the database set to that of the client terminal and vice versa. When a direct conversion between sets is not possible, replacement characters are used. Here is the query to ask for the first PRODUCT_NAME in PRODUCT_T alphabetically, which was done using the AMERICAN character set in Oracle 7.3.1.

> **Query:** Alphabetically, what is the first product name in the PRODUCT table?

```
SELECT MIN (PRODUCT_NAME)
  FROM PRODUCT_T;
```

It gives the result shown below, which demonstrates that numbers are sorted before letters in this character set.

Result:

```
MIN(PRODUCT_NAME)
```
8-Drawer Desk

Using Wildcards

The use of the asterisk (*) as a wildcard in a SELECT statement has been previously shown. Wildcards may also be used in the WHERE clause where an exact match is not possible. Here, the keyword LIKE is paired with wildcard characters and usually a string containing the characters that are known to be desired matches. The wildcard character, %, is used to represent any collection of characters. Thus, using LIKE '%Desk' when searching PRODUCT_NAME will find all different types of desks carried by Pine Valley Furniture. The underscore, _, is used as a wildcard character to represent exactly one character, rather than any collection of characters. Thus, using LIKE '_-drawer' when searching PRODUCT_NAME will find any products with specified drawers, such as 3-drawer, 5-drawer, or 8-drawer desks.

Comparison Operators

With the exception of the very first SQL example in this chapter, we have used the equality comparison operator in our WHERE clauses. The first example used the greater than (>) operator. The most common comparison operators for SQL implementations are listed in Table 9-2. You are used to thinking about using comparison operators with numeric data, but you can also use them with character data and dates in SQL. The query shown here asks for all orders placed after 10/24/98.

Query: Which orders have been placed since 10/24/98?

```
SELECT ORDER_ID, ORDER_DATE
  FROM ORDER_T
       WHERE ORDER_DATE > '24-OCT-98';
```

TABLE 9-2 Comparison Operators in SQL

Operator	Meaning
=	Equal to
>	Greater than
>=	Greater than or equal to
<	Less than
<=	Less than or equal to
<>	Not equal to
!=	Not equal to

Notice that the date is enclosed in single quotes and that the format of the date is different from that shown in Figure 9-3, which was taken from MS-Access. The query was run in SQL*Plus.

Result:

ORDER_ID	ORDER_DAT
1006	27-OCT-98
1007	27-OCT-98
1008	30-OCT-98
1009	05-NOV-98
1010	05-NOV-98

Query: What furniture does Pine Valley carry that isn't made of cherry?

```
SELECT PRODUCT_NAME, PRODUCT_FINISH
  FROM PRODUCT_T
      WHERE PRODUCT_FINISH != 'Cherry';
```

Result:

PRODUCT	PRODUCT_FINISH
Coffee Table	Natural Ash
Computer Desk	Natural Ash
Entertainment Center	Natural Maple
8-Drawer Desk	White Ash
Dining Table	Natural Ash
Computer Desk	Walnut

```
6 rows selected.
```

Using Boolean Operators

More complex questions can be answered by adjusting the WHERE clause further. The Boolean or logical operators AND, OR, and NOT can be used to good purpose.

AND   joins two or more conditions and returns results only when all conditions are true.

OR   joins two or more conditions and returns results when any conditions are true.

NOT   negates an expression.

If multiple Boolean operators are used in an SQL statement, NOT is evaluated first, then AND, then OR. For example, consider the following query.

Query: List product name, finish, and unit price for all desks and all tables that cost more than $300 in the PRODUCT table.

```
SELECT PRODUCT_NAME, PRODUCT_FINISH, UNIT_PRICE
  FROM PRODUCT_T
      WHERE PRODUCT_NAME LIKE '%Desk'
          OR PRODUCT_NAME LIKE '%Table'
          AND UNIT_PRICE > 300;
```

All of the desks are listed, even the computer desk that costs less than $300. Only one table is listed; the less expensive ones that cost less than $300 are not included. Looking at the query, the AND will be processed first, returning all tables with a unit price greater than $300. Then the OR is processed, returning all desks, regardless of cost, and all tables costing more than $300.

Result:

PRODUCT_NAME	PRODUCT_FINISH	UNIT_PRICE
Computer Desk	Natural Ash	375
Writer's Desk	Cherry	325
8-Drawer Desk	White Ash	750
Dining Table	Natural Ash	800
Computer Desk	Walnut	250

If we had wanted to return only desks and tables costing more than $300, we should have put parentheses after the WHERE and before the AND.

> **Query:** List product name, finish, and unit price for all desks and tables in the PRODUCT table that cost more than $300.

```
SELECT PRODUCT_NAME, PRODUCT_FINISH, UNIT_PRICE
    FROM PRODUCT_T
        WHERE (PRODUCT_NAME LIKE '%Desk'
            OR PRODUCT_NAME LIKE '%Table')
            AND UNIT_PRICE > 300;
```

Now the results returned are shown below. Only products with unit price greater than $300 are included.

Result:

PRODUCT_NAME	PRODUCT_FINISH	UNIT_PRICE
Computer Desk	Natural Ash	375
Writer's Desk	Cherry	325
8-Drawer Desk	White Ash	750
Dining Table	Natural Ash	800

Ranges

The comparison operators < and > are used to establish a range of values. The keywords BETWEEN or NOT BETWEEN can also be used. For example, to find those products with a unit price between $200 and $300, the following query could be used.

> **Query:** Which products in the PRODUCT table have a unit price between $200 and $300?

```
SELECT PRODUCT_NAME, UNIT_PRICE
    FROM PRODUCT_T
        WHERE UNIT_PRICE > 199 AND UNIT_PRICE < 301;
```

Result:

PRODUCT_NAME	UNIT_PRICE
Coffee Table	200
Computer Desk	250

The same result will be returned by this query.

> **Query:** Which products in the PRODUCT table have a unit price between $200 and $300?

```
SELECT PRODUCT_NAME, UNIT_PRICE
    FROM PRODUCT_T
      WHERE UNIT_PRICE BETWEEN 200 AND 300;
```

> **Result:**
> Same as previous query.

Adding NOT before BETWEEN in this query will return all the other products in PRODUCT_T because their prices are less than $200 or more than $300.

Distinct

Sometimes when returning rows that don't include the primary key, duplicate rows will be returned. For example, look at this query and the results it returns.

> **Query:** What are the order numbers included in the ORDER_LINE table?

```
SELECT ORDER_ID
    FROM ORDER_LINE_T;
```

Eighteen rows are returned, and many of them are duplicates since many orders were for multiple items.

> **Result:**

```
ORDER_ID
──────────
      1001
      1001
      1001
      1002
      1003
      1004
      1004
      1005
      1006
      1006
      1006
      1007
      1008
      1008
      1009
      1009
      1010
      1007
```

```
18 rows selected.
```

If, however, we add the keyword DISTINCT, then only one occurrence of each ORDER_ID will be returned, one for each of the ten orders represented in the table.

Query: What are the order numbers included in the ORDER_LINE table?

```
SELECT DISTINCT ORDER_ID
    FROM ORDER_LINE_T;
```

Result:

```
ORDER_ID
────────
    1001
    1002
    1003
    1004
    1005
    1006
    1007
    1008
    1009
    1010
```

`10 rows selected.`

DISTINCT and its counterpart, ALL, can only be used once in a select statement. It comes after SELECT and before any columns or expressions are listed. If a SELECT statement projects more than one column, only rows that are identical for every column will be eliminated. Thus, if the statement above also includes QUANTITY, 14 rows are returned because there are now only four duplicate rows rather than eight. For example, both items ordered on ORDER_ID 1004 were for two items, so the second pairing of 1004 and 2 will be eliminated.

Query: What are the unique combinations of order number and order quantity included in the ORDER_LINE table?

```
SELECT DISTINCT ORDER_ID, QUANTITY
  FROM ORDER_LINE_T;
```

Result:

```
ORDER_ID        QUANTITY
────────        ────────
    1001            1
    1001            2
    1002            5
    1003            3
    1004            2
    1005            4
    1006            1
    1006            2
    1007            2
    1007            3
    1008            3
    1009            2
    1009            3
    1010           10
```

`14 rows selected.`

IN and NOT IN Lists

To match a list of values, consider using IN.

> **Query:** List all customers who live in warmer states.

```
SELECT CUSTOMER_NAME, CITY, STATE
   FROM CUSTOMER_T
      WHERE STATE IN ('FL', 'TX', 'CA', 'HI');
```

Results:

```
CUSTOMER_NAME                  CITY            ST
Contemporary Casuals           Gainesville     FL
Value Furniture                Plano           TX
Impressions                    Sacramento      CA
California Classics             Santa Clara     CA
M and H Casual Furniture        Clearwater      FL
Seminole Interiors             Seminole        FL
Kaneohe Homes                  Kaneohe         HI

7 rows selected.
```

IN is particularly useful in SQL statements that use subqueries, which will be covered later in this chapter.

Sorting Results: The ORDER BY Clause

Looking at the preceding results, it may seem that it would make more sense to list the California customers, followed by the Floridians, Hawaiians, and Texans. That brings us to the other three basic parts of the SQL statement:

ORDER BY   sorts the final results rows in ascending or descending order

GROUP BY   groups rows in an intermediate results table where the values in those rows are the same for one or more columns.

HAVING   can only be used following a GROUP BY and acts as a secondary WHERE clause, returning only those groups which meet a specified condition.

So, we can order the customers by adding an ORDER BY clause.

> **Query:** List customer, city, and state for all customers in the CUSTOMER table whose address is Florida, Texas, California, or Hawaii. List the customers alphabetically by state, and alphabetically by customer within each state.

```
SELECT CUSTOMER_NAME, CITY, STATE
   FROM CUSTOMER_T
      WHERE STATE IN ('FL', 'TX', 'CA', 'HI')
         ORDER BY STATE, CUSTOMER_NAME;
```

Now the results are easier to read.

Result:

CUSTOMER_NAME	CITY	ST
California Classics	Santa Clara	CA
Impressions	Sacramento	CA
Contemporary Casuals	Gainesville	FL
M and H Casual Furniture	Clearwater	FL
Seminole Interiors	Seminole	FL
Kaneohe Homes	Kaneohe	HI
Value Furniture	Plano	TX

7 rows selected.

Notice that all customers from each state are listed together, and within each state, customer names are alphabetized. The sorting order is determined by the order in which the columns are listed in the ORDER BY clause; in this case, states were alphabetized first, then customer names. If sorting from high to low, use DESC as a keyword placed after the column used to sort.

How are NULLS sorted? SQL-92 stipulates that null values should be placed first or last, before or after columns that have values. Where the NULLS will be placed will depend upon the SQL implementation. SQL*Plus sorts NULLS last.

Categorizing Results: The GROUP BY Clause

GROUP BY is particularly useful when paired with aggregate functions, such as SUM or COUNT. GROUP BY divides a table into subsets (by groups); then an aggregate function can be used to provide summary information for that group. The single value returned by the previous aggregate function examples is called a **scalar aggregate**. When aggregate functions are used in a GROUP BY clause and several values are returned, they are called **vector aggregates**.

Scalar aggregate: A single value returned from an SQL query that includes an aggregate function.

Vector aggregate: Multiple values returned from an SQL query that includes an aggregate function.

Query: Count the number of customers with addresses in each state to which we ship.

```
SELECT STATE, COUNT (STATE)
     FROM CUSTOMER_T
          GROUP BY STATE;
```

Result:

ST	COUNT(STATE)
CA	2
CO	1
FL	3
HI	1
MI	1
NJ	2
NY	1
PA	1
TX	1
UT	1
WA	1

11 rows selected.

It is also possible to nest groups within groups; the same logic is used as when sorting multiple items.

Query: Count the number of customers with addresses in each city to which we ship. List the cities by state.

```
SELECT STATE, CITY, COUNT (CITY)
  FROM CUSTOMER_T
       GROUP BY STATE, CITY;
```

While the GROUP BY clause seems straightforward, it can produce unexpected results if the logic of the clause is forgotten. When a GROUP BY is included, the columns allowed to be specified in the SELECT clause are limited. Only those columns with a single value for each group can be included. In the previous query, each group consists of a city and its state. The SELECT statement includes both the 'city' and 'state' columns. This works because each combination of city and state is one value. But, if the SELECT clause of the first query in this section had also included 'city', that statement would fail because the GROUP BY is only by state. Since states can have more than one city, the requisite that each value in the SELECT clause have only one value in the GROUP BY group is not met, and SQL will not be able to present the city information so that it makes sense. In general, the columns referenced in the SELECT statement must be referenced in the GROUP BY clause, unless the column is an argument for an aggregate function included in the SELECT clause.

Qualifying Results by Categories: The HAVING Clause

The HAVING clause acts like a WHERE clause, but it identifies groups that meet a criterion, rather than rows. Therefore, one usually sees a HAVING clause following a GROUP BY clause.

Query: Find only states with more than one customer.

```
SELECT STATE, COUNT (STATE)
  FROM CUSTOMER_T
       GROUP BY STATE
           HAVING COUNT (STATE) > 1;
```

which returns a result that has removed all those states with one customer as seen above. Remember that using WHERE here would not work because WHERE doesn't allow aggregates; further, WHERE qualifies rows, whereas HAVING qualifies groups.

Result:

ST	COUNT (STATE)
CA	2
FL	3
NJ	2

To include more than one condition in the HAVING clause, use AND, OR, and NOT just as in the WHERE clause. In summary, here is one last command that includes all of the six clauses; remember that they must be used in this order.

Query: List the product finish, average unit price for each finish, and number of products on hand for selected finishes where the average unit price is less than 750 and the quantity on hand is more than 2.

```
SELECT PRODUCT_FINISH, AVG (UNIT_PRICE), SUM (ON_HAND)
  FROM PRODUCT_T
    WHERE PRODUCT_FINISH IN ('Cherry', 'Natural Ash', 'Natural Maple', 'White Ash')
        GROUP BY PRODUCT_FINISH
            HAVING AVG (UNIT_PRICE) < 750
                AND SUM (ON_HAND) > 2
                ORDER BY PRODUCT_FINISH;
```

Result:

PRODUCT_FINISH	AVG(UNIT_PRICE)	SUM(ON_HAND)
Cherry	250	8
Natural Ash	458.333333	11
Natural Maple	650	3

Figure 9-8 shows the order in which SQL processes the clauses of a statement. Arrows indicate the paths that may or may not be followed. Remember, only the SELECT and FROM clauses are mandatory. Notice that the processing order is

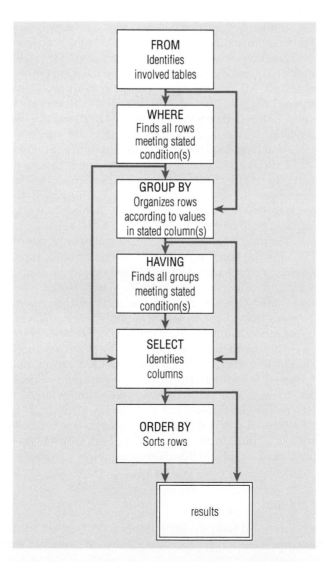

Figure 9-8
SQL statement processing order (adapted from van der Lans, p. 100)

different from the order of the syntax used to create the statement. As each clause is processed an intermediate results table is produced that will be used for the next clause. Users do not see the intermediate results tables; they only see the final results. A query can be debugged by remembering the order shown in Figure 9-8. Take out the optional clauses, then add them back in one at a time in the order that they will be processed. In this way, intermediate results can be seen and, often, problems can be spotted.

PROCESSING MULTIPLE TABLES

Now that we have explored some of the possibilities for working with a single table, it is time to learn how to work with multiple tables simultaneously. The power of the RDBMS is realized when working with multiple tables. Where relationships exist between tables they can be linked together in queries. Remember from Chapter 6 that these relationships are established by including a common column(s) in each table where a relationship is needed. Often this is accomplished by setting up a primary key–foreign key relationship, where the foreign key in one table references the primary key in another and the values in both come from a common domain. We can use these columns to establish the link between two tables by finding common values in the columns. For example, CUSTOMER_ID in ORDER_T matches CUSTOMER_ID in CUSTOMER_T. When we compare them, we learn that Contemporary Casuals placed orders # 1001 and 1010 because Contemporary Casuals' CUSTOMER_ID is 1, and ORDER_T shows that ORDER_ID 1001 and 1010 were placed by customer # 1. In a relational system, data from related tables are combined into one result table or view and then displayed or used as input to a form or report definition.

The linking of related tables varies among different types of relational systems. In SQL, the WHERE clause of the SELECT command is also used for multiple table operations. In fact, SELECT can include references to two, three, or more tables in the same command. As illustrated below, SQL has two ways to use SELECT for combining data from related tables.

Join: A relational operation that causes two tables with a common domain to be combined into a single table or view.

The most frequently used relational operation, which brings together data from two or more related tables into one resultant table, is called a **join**. SQL specifies a join implicitly by referring in a WHERE clause to the matching of common columns over which tables are joined. Two tables may be joined when each one contains a column that share a common domain. The result of a join operation is a single table. Selected columns from all the tables are included. Each row returned contains data from rows in the different input tables where values for the common columns match.

An important rule of thumb in forming join conditions is the following: There should be one WHERE condition for each pair of tables being joined. Thus, if two tables are to be combined, one condition would be necessary, but if three tables (A, B, and C) are to be combined, then two conditions would be necessary because there are two pairs of tables (A-B and B-C), and so forth.

There are several possible types of joins in relational database queries, although each SQL implementation may support only some of these types. Three types of joins are described in this chapter: equi-joins, natural joins, and outer joins.

Equi-join: A join in which the joining condition is based on equality between values in the common columns. Common columns appear (redundantly) in the result table.

Equi-join

With an **equi-join**, the joining condition is based on *equality* between values in the common columns. For example, if we want to know the names of customers who have placed orders, that information is kept in two tables, CUSTOMER_T and ORDER_T. It is necessary to match customers with their orders and then collect the information about name and order number in one table in order to answer our question.

Query: What are the names of all customers who have placed orders?

```
SELECT CUSTOMER_T.CUSTOMER_ID, ORDER_T.CUSTOMER_ID,
CUSTOMER_NAME, ORDER_ID
  FROM CUSTOMER_T, ORDER_T
      WHERE CUSTOMER_T.CUSTOMER_ID = ORDER_T.CUSTOMER_ID;
```

Result:

CUSTOMER_ID	CUSTOMER_ID	CUSTOMER_NAME	ORDER_ID
1	1	Contemporary Casuals	1001
8	8	California Classics	1002
15	15	Mountain Scenes	1003
5	5	Impressions	1004
3	3	Home Furnishings	1005
2	2	Value Furniture	1006
11	11	American Euro Lifestyles	1007
12	12	Battle Creek Furniture	1008
4	4	Eastern Furniture	1009
1	1	Contemporary Casuals	1010

```
10 rows selected.
```

The redundant CUSTOMER_ID columns, one from each table, demonstrate that the customer IDs have been matched, and that matching gives one row for each order placed. The importance of achieving the match between tables can be seen if the WHERE clause is omitted. That query will return all combinations of customers and orders, or 150 rows, which is not a useful result. The number of rows is equal to the number of rows in each table, multiplied together (10 orders × 15 customers = 150 rows).

Also, to demonstrate a difference between Oracle SQL and Access SQL, the syntax for this query as generated by Access is shown here.

Query: What are the names of all customers who have placed orders?

```
SELECT Customer_t.Customer_ID, Order_t.Customer_ID,
Customer_t.Customer_name, Order_t.Order_ID
FROM Customer_t INNER JOIN Order_t ON Customer_t.Customer_ID =
Order_t.Customer_ID;
```

Result:
Same as previous query.

The join is denoted as an *inner join* between CUSTOMER_T and ORDER_T. The WHERE clause is represented by the clause ON Customer_t.Customer_ID = Order_t.Customer_ID.

Natural Join

A **natural join** is the same as an equi-join, except that one of the duplicate columns is eliminated. The natural join is the most commonly used form of join operation. The SQL command to find customer names and order numbers leaves out one CUSTOMER_ID. Notice that CUSTOMER_ID must still be qualified because there is

Natural join: Same as equi-join except one of the duplicate columns is eliminated in the result table.

still ambiguity; CUSTOMER_ID exists in both CUSTOMER_T and ORDER_T, and therefore it must be specified from which table SQL*Plus should pick CUSTOMER_ID.

> **Query:** For each customer who has placed an order, what is the customer's name and order number?

```
SELECT CUSTOMER_T.CUSTOMER_ID, CUSTOMER_NAME, ORDER_ID
   FROM CUSTOMER_T, ORDER_T
      WHERE CUSTOMER_T.CUSTOMER_ID = ORDER_T.CUSTOMER_ID;
```

Note that the order of table names in the FROM clause is immaterial. The query optimizer of the DBMS will decide in which sequence to process each table. Whether indexes exist on common columns will influence the sequence in which tables are processed, as will which table is on the 1 and which is on the M side of 1:M relationships. If a query takes significantly different amounts of time depending on the order in which tables are listed in the FROM clause, the DBMS does not have a very good query optimizer.

Outer Join

Often in joining two tables, we find that a row in one table does not have a matching row in the other table. For example, several CUSTOMER_ID numbers do not appear in the ORDER_T table (see Figure 9-3). We can assume this is because those customers have not placed orders since 10/20/98, or that their orders are not included in our very short sample ORDER_T table. As a result, the equi-join and natural join shown above do not include all of the customers shown in CUSTOMER_T.

Of course the organization may be very interested in identifying those customers who have not placed orders. They may want to contact them to encourage new orders, or they may be interested in analyzing these customers in order to discern why they are not ordering. Using an **outer join** may produce this information: rows that do not have matching values in common columns are also included in the result table. Null values appear in columns where there is not a match between tables.

Not all DBMSs include outer joins, but they are available in both MS-Access and Oracle SQL*Plus. Where an outer join is not available explicitly, use UNION and NOT EXISTS (discussed later in this chapter) to carry out an outer join. Here is an outer join in SQL*Plus.

Outer join: A join in which rows that do not have matching values in common columns are nevertheless included in the result table.

> **Query:** List customer name, identification number, and order number for all customers listed in the CUSTOMER table. Include the customer identification number and name even if there is no order available for that customer.

```
SELECT CUSTOMER_T.CUSTOMER_ID, CUSTOMER_NAME, ORDER_ID
  FROM CUSTOMER_T, ORDER_T
      WHERE CUSTOMER_T.CUSTOMER_ID = ORDER_T.CUSTOMER_ID (+);
```

Notice that (+) has been added to the end of the query. ORDER_T is the table that may have no matches with a row in CUSTOMER_T. The (+) symbol in SQL*Plus indicates that a match (with an all-null row) should also be returned for any row in CUSTOMER_T for which there is not a match. Because the symbol is attached to the table that is on the right of the join equation, this join will sometimes be called a *right outer join.* Access SQL will use the phrase RIGHT JOIN rather than the plus to indicate the right outer join. Compare these results to the results from the equi-join above to see the difference between an outer join and an equi-join.

Result:

CUSTOMER_ID	CUSTOMER_NAME	ORDER_ID
1	Contemporary Casuals	1001
1	Contemporary Casuals	1010
2	Value Furniture	1006
3	Home Furnishings	1005
4	Eastern Furniture	1009
5	Impressions	1004
6	Furniture Gallery	
7	Period Furnishings	
8	California Classics	1002
9	M & H Casual Furniture	
10	Seminole Interiors	
11	American Euro Lifestyles	1007
12	Battle Creek Furniture	1008
13	Heritage Furnishings	
14	Kaneohe Homes	
15	Mountain Scenes	1003

16 rows selected.

The advantage of the outer join is that information is not lost. Here, all customer names were returned whether or not they had placed an order. Had the (+) been attached to CUSTOMER_T, it would be a *left outer join,* and all orders would be returned. (Since referential integrity requires that every order be associated with a valid customer ID, that left outer join would only assure that referential integrity is being enforced.)

> **Query:** List customer name, identification number, and order number for all orders listed in the ORDER table. Include the order number even if there is no customer name and identification number available.

```
SELECT CUSTOMER_T.CUSTOMER_ID, CUSTOMER_NAME, ORDER_ID
    FROM CUSTOMER_T, ORDER_T
    WHERE CUSTOMER_T.CUSTOMER_ID (+) = ORDER_T.CUSTOMER_ID;
```

Unless otherwise stated in this section, all joins will be natural joins.

Below is another sample join query. Let's construct the query that will be necessary to produce a result table that includes the information needed to create an invoice for order #1006. We want the customer information, the order and order line information, and the product information, so we will need to join four tables.

> **Query:** Assemble all information necessary to create an invoice for order number 1006.

```
SELECT CUSTOMER_T.CUSTOMER_ID, CUSTOMER_NAME, CUSTOMER_ADDRESS,
    CITY, STATE, POSTAL_CODE, ORDER_T.ORDER_ID, ORDER_DATE, QUANTITY,
    PRODUCT_NAME, UNIT_PRICE, (QUANTITY * UNIT_PRICE)
    FROM CUSTOMER_T, ORDER_T, ORDER_LINE_T, PRODUCT_T
       WHERE CUSTOMER_T.CUSTOMER_ID = ORDER_T.CUSTOMER_ID
          AND ORDER_T.ORDER_ID = ORDER_LINE_T.ORDER_ID
          AND ORDER_LINE_T.PRODUCT_ID = PRODUCT_T.PRODUCT_ID
          AND ORDER_T.ORDER_ID = 1006;
```

```
CUSTOMER_ID CUSTOMER_NAME   CUSTOMER_ADDRESS      CITY    ST POSTAL_CODE
          2 Value Furniture 15145 S.W. 17th St.   Plano  TX 75094
          2 Value Furniture 15145 S.W. 17th St.   Plano  TX 75094
          2 Value Furniture 15145 S.W. 17th St.   Plano  TX 75094

ORDER_ID ORDER-DAT QUANTITY PRODUCT_NAME          UNIT_PRICE (QUANTITY*UNIT_PRICE)
1006     27-OCT-98    1      Entertainment Center  650                         650
1006     27-Oct-98    2      Writer's Desk         325                         650
1006     27-Oct-98    2      Dining Table          800                        1600
```

Figure 9-9
Results from a 4-table join (edited for readability)

The results of the query are shown in Figure 9-9. Remember, since the join involves four tables, there will be three column joins.

Subqueries

The preceding SQL examples illustrate one of the two basic approaches for joining two tables: the joining technique. SQL also provides the subquery technique, which involves placing an inner query (SELECT, FROM, WHERE) within a WHERE or HAVING clause of another (outer) query. The inner query provides values for the search condition of the outer query. Such queries are referred to as subqueries or nested subqueries, and may be nested multiple times.

Sometimes either the joining or the subquery technique may be used to accomplish the same result, and different people will have different preferences about which technique to use. Other times, only a join or a subquery will work. *The joining technique is useful when data from several relations are to be retrieved and displayed, and the relationships are not necessarily nested.* Let's compare two queries that return the same result. Both answer the question, What is the name and address of the customer who placed order #1008? First, we'll use a join query.

> **Query:** What is the name and address of the customer who placed order number 1008?

```
SELECT CUSTOMER_NAME, CUSTOMER_ADDRESS, CITY, STATE, POSTAL_CODE
  FROM CUSTOMER_T, ORDER_T
      WHERE CUSTOMER_T.CUSTOMER_ID = ORDER_T.CUSTOMER_ID AND
          ORDER_ID = 1008;
```

Now, look at the equivalent query using the subquery technique.

> **Query:** What is the name and address of the customer who placed order number 1008?

```
SELECT CUSTOMER_NAME, CUSTOMER_ADDRESS, CITY, STATE, POSTAL_CODE
      FROM CUSTOMER_T
          WHERE CUSTOMER_T.CUSTOMER_ID =
            (SELECT ORDER_T.CUSTOMER_ID
                FROM ORDER_T
                    WHERE ORDER_ID = 1008);
```

Notice that the subquery, enclosed in parentheses, follows the form learned for constructing SQL queries and this one could stand on its own as an independent query. *The subquery approach may be used for this query because we only need to display data from the table in the outer query.* The value for ORDER_ID does not appear in the query result—it is used as the selection criterion in the outer query. To include data from the subquery in the result, use the join technique since data from a subquery cannot be included in the final results.

We know in advance that the preceding subquery will return at most one value, the CUSTOMER_ID associated with ORDER_ID #1008. The result will be empty if an order with that ID does not exist. A subquery can also return a list of values (with zero, one, or many entries) by using the keyword IN. For example, which customers have placed orders? Here is a query that will answer that question.

Query: Which customers have placed orders?

```
SELECT CUSTOMER_NAME
  FROM CUSTOMER_T
      WHERE CUSTOMER_ID IN
          (SELECT DISTINCT CUSTOMER_ID
              FROM ORDER_T);
```

This query produces the result below. For each customer identified in the ORDER_T table, that customer's name has been returned from CUSTOMER_T.

Result:

```
CUSTOMER_NAME
───────────────────────
Contemporary Casuals
Value Furniture
Home Furnishings
Eastern Furniture
Impressions
California Classics
American Euro Lifestyles
Battle Creek Furniture
Mountain Scenes

9 rows selected.
```

The qualifiers NOT, ANY, and ALL may be used in front of IN or with logical operators such as =, >, and <. Since IN works with zero, one, or many values from the inner query, many programmers simply use IN instead of = for all queries, even if the equal sign would work. The next example shows the use of NOT and it also demonstrates that a join can be used in an inner query.

Query: Which customers have not placed any orders for computer desks?

```
SELECT CUSTOMER_NAME
  FROM CUSTOMER_T
      WHERE CUSTOMER_ID NOT IN
          (SELECT CUSTOMER_ID
              FROM ORDER_T, ORDER_LINE_T, PRODUCT_T
                  WHERE ORDER_T.ORDER_ID =
                          ORDER_LINE_T.ORDER_ID AND
                          ORDER_LINE_T.PRODUCT_ID =
                          PRODUCT_T.PRODUCT_ID
                          AND PRODUCT_NAME = 'Computer Desk');
```

The result shows that 10 of our customers have not yet ordered computer desks. The inner query returned a list of all customers who had ordered computer desks. The outer query listed the names of those customers who were not in the list returned by the inner query.

Two other conditions associated with using subqueries are EXISTS and NOT EXISTS. These keywords are included in an SQL query at the same location where IN would be, just prior to the beginning of the subquery. EXISTS will take a value of *true* if the subquery returns an intermediate results table which contains one or more rows, and *false* if no rows are returned. NOT EXISTS will take a value of *true* if no rows are returned, and *false* if one or more rows are returned. Consider the following SQL statement, which includes EXISTS.

> **Query:** What are the order numbers for all orders that have included furniture finished in natural ash?

```
SELECT DISTINCT ORDER_ID FROM ORDER_LINE_T
WHERE EXISTS
    (SELECT *
      FROM PRODUCT_T
           WHERE PRODUCT_ID = ORDER_LINE_T.PRODUCT_ID
                AND PRODUCT_FINISH = 'Natural Ash');
```

The subquery checks to see if the finish for the product on an order line is natural ash. The main query picks out the order numbers for all orders that have included furniture finished in natural ash. There have been seven such orders, as the result shows.

> **Result:**

```
ORDER_ID
────────
    1001
    1002
    1003
    1006
    1007
    1008
    1009

7 rows selected.
```

When EXISTS or NOT EXISTS is used in a subquery, the select list of the subquery will usually just select all columns (SELECT *) as a placeholder because it doesn't matter which columns are returned. The purpose of the subquery is testing to see if any rows fit the conditions, not to return values from particular columns. The columns that will be returned are determined by the outer query. An EXISTS subquery is almost always a correlated subquery, as described next. Queries containing the keyword NOT EXISTS will return a results table when no rows are found that satisfy the subquery.

In summary, use the subquery approach when qualifications are nested or when qualifications are easily understood in a nested way. While SQL*Plus allows a subquery to return more than one column, most systems allow pairwise joining of *one and only one column* in an inner query with *one* column in an outer query. An exception to this is when a subquery is used with the EXISTS keyword. Data can only be displayed from the table(s) referenced in the outer query. Up to 16 levels of nesting are typically supported. Queries are processed inside out, although another type of subquery, a correlated subquery, is processed outside in.

Correlated Subqueries

In the first subquery example, it was necessary to examine the inner query before considering the outer query. That is, the result of the inner query was used to limit the processing of the outer query. In contrast, **correlated subqueries** use the result of the outer query to determine the processing of the inner query. That is, the inner query is somewhat different for each row referenced in the outer query. In this case, the inner query must be computed for *each* outer row, whereas in the earlier examples, the inner query was computed *only once* for all rows processed in the outer query. Figures 9-10a and 9-10b depict the different processing order that occurs for each of the examples from the previous section on subqueries.

Look at this query, which lists the details of the product that has a higher unit price than any other product in PRODUCT_T.

Correlated subquery: In SQL, a subquery in which processing the inner query depends on data from the outer query.

```
SELECT CUSTOMER_NAME
        FROM CUSTOMER_T
            WHERE CUSTOMER_ID IN

                (SELECT DISTINCT CUSTOMER_ID
                        FROM ORDER_T);
```

Figure 9-10
Subquery processing

(a) Processing a non-correlated subquery

1. The subquery (shown in the box) is processed first and an intermediate results table created:

CUSTOMER_ID
1
8
15
5
3
2
11
12
4

    9 rows selected.

2. The outer query returns the requested customer information for each customer included in the intermediate results table:

CUSTOMER_NAME
Contemporary Casuals
Value Furniture
Home Furnishings
Eastern Furniture
Impressions
California Classics
American Euro Lifestyles
Battle Creek Furniture
Mountain Scenes

    9 rows selected.

(continues)

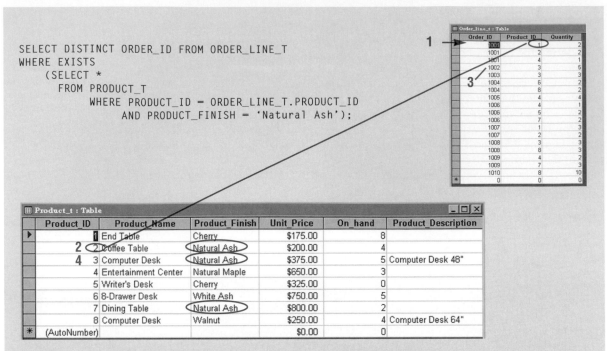

```
SELECT DISTINCT ORDER_ID FROM ORDER_LINE_T
WHERE EXISTS
    (SELECT *
     FROM PRODUCT_T
            WHERE PRODUCT_ID = ORDER_LINE_T.PRODUCT_ID
                AND PRODUCT_FINISH = 'Natural Ash');
```

1. The first order ID is selected from ORDER_LINE_T: ORDER_ID=1001.

2. The subquery is evaluated to see if any product in that order has a natural ash finish. Product 2 does, and is part of the order. EXISTS is valued as *true* and the order ID is added to the result table.

3. The next order ID is selected from ORDER_LINE_T: ORDER_ID=1002.

4. The subquery is evaluated to see if the product ordered has a natural ash finish. It does. EXISTS is valued as true and the order ID is added to the result table.

5. Processing continues through each order ID. Orders 1004, 1005, and 1010 are not included in the result table because they do not include any furniture with a natural ash finish. The final result table is shown in the text.

(b) Processing a correlated subquery

Query: List the details about the product with the highest unit price.

```
SELECT PRODUCT_NAME, PRODUCT_FINISH, UNIT_PRICE
    FROM PRODUCT_T PA
            WHERE UNIT_PRICE > ALL
                (SELECT UNIT_PRICE FROM PRODUCT_T PB
                    WHERE PB.PRODUCT_ID != PA.PRODUCT_ID);
```

Here is the result—the dining table has a higher unit price than any other product.

Result:

PRODUCT_NAME	PRODUCT_FINISH	UNIT_PRICE
Dining Table	Natural Ash	800

The logic of this SQL statement is that the subquery will be executed once for each product to be sure that no other product has a higher unit price. Notice that we are comparing a table to itself and that we are able to do this by giving the table two aliases, PA and PB. First, PRODUCT_ID 1, the end table, will be considered. When the subquery is executed, it will return the prices of every product except the one being considered in the outer query. Then, the outer query will check to see if the unit price for the product being considered is greater than all of the unit prices returned by the subquery. If it is, it will be returned as the result of the query. If not, the next value in the outer query will be considered, and the inner query will return a list of all the unit prices for the other products. The list returned by the inner query changes as each product in the outer query changes; that makes it a correlated subquery. Can you identify a special set of unit prices for which this query will not yield the desired result?

VIEW DEFINITIONS

The often-stated purpose of a view is to simplify query commands, but a view may also provide valuable data security and significantly enhance programming productivity for a database. To highlight the convenience of a view, consider the Pine Valley Invoice of Figure 1-6. Construction of this invoice requires access to the four tables from the Pine Valley database of Figure 9-3: CUSTOMER_T, ORDER_T, ORDER_LINE_T, and PRODUCT_T. A novice database user may make mistakes or be unproductive in properly formulating queries involving so many tables. A view allows us to predefine this association into a single virtual table as part of the database. With this view, a user who wants only customer invoice data does not have to reconstruct the joining of tables to produce the report or any subset of it. Table 9-3 summarizes the pros and cons of using views.

A view, INVOICE_V, is defined by specifying an SQL query that has the view as its result.

Query: What are the data elements necessary to create an invoice for a customer? Save this query as a view named INVOICE_V.

```
CREATE VIEW INVOICE_V AS
  SELECT CUSTOMER_T.CUSTOMER_ID, CUSTOMER_ADDRESS, ORDER_T.ORDER_ID,
  PRODUCT_T.PRODUCT_ID, QUANTITY, and other columns as required
  FROM CUSTOMER_T, ORDER_T, ORDER_LINE_T, PRODUCT_T
  WHERE CUSTOMER_T.CUSTOMER_ID = ORDER_T.CUSTOMER_ID
      AND ORDER_T.ORDER_ID = ORDER_LINE_T.ORDER_ID
      AND PRODUCT_T.PRODUCT_ID = ORDER_LINE_T.PRODUCT_ID;
```

TABLE 9-3 Pros and Cons of Using Views

Positive Aspects	Negative Aspects
Simplify query commands	Use processing time re-creating view each time it is referenced
Help provide data security	
Improve programmer productivity	May or may not be directly updateable
Contains most current base table data	
Uses little storage space	

The SELECT clause specifies, or projects, what data elements (columns) are to be included in the view table. The FROM clause lists the tables and views involved in the view development. The WHERE clause specifies the names of the common columns used to join CUSTOMER_T to ORDER_T to ORDER_LINE_T to PRODUCT_T. Because a view is a table, and one of the relational properties of tables is that the order of rows is immaterial, the rows in a view may not be sorted. But queries that refer to this view may display their results in any desired sequence.

We can see the power of such a view when building a query to generate an invoice for order number 1004. Rather than having to specify the joining of four tables, the query can include all relevant data elements from the view table, INVOICE_V.

Query: What are the data elements necessary to create an invoice for order number 1004?

```
SELECT CUSTOMER_ID, CUSTOMER_ADDRESS, PRODUCT_ID, QUANTITY, and
other columns as required
  FROM INVOICE_V
      WHERE ORDER_ID = 1004;
```

Base table: A table in the relational data model containing the inserted raw data that is likely to correspond to one physical file in secondary storage.

A view is a virtual table; it is constructed automatically as needed by the DBMS, and is not maintained as real data. The real data are stored in **base tables**, those that have been defined by CREATE TABLE commands. A view always contains the most current derived values and is thus superior in terms of data currency to constructing a temporary real table from several base tables. Also, in comparison to a temporary real table, a view consumes very little storage space. A view is costly, however, since its contents must be calculated each time that they are requested.

A view may join multiple tables or views together and may contain derived (or virtual) columns. For example, if a user of the Pine Valley Furniture database only wants to know the total value of orders placed for each furniture product, a view for this can be created from INVOICE_V in Oracle SQL*Plus.

Query: What is the total value of orders placed for each furniture product?

```
CREATE VIEW ORDER_TOTALS_V AS
SELECT PRODUCT_ID PRODUCT, SUM (UNIT_PRICE*QUANTITY) TOTAL
  FROM INVOICE_V
      GROUP BY PRODUCT_ID;
```

Remember, we can assign a different name (an alias) to a view column than the associated base table or expression column name. Here, PRODUCT is a renaming of PRODUCT_ID, local to only this view. TOTAL is the column name given the expression for total sales of each product. The expression can now be referenced via this view in subsequent queries as if it were a column, rather than a derived expression. Defining views based on other views can cause problems. For example, if we redefine INVOICE_V so that UNIT_PRICE is not included, then ORDER_TOTALS_V will no longer work because it won't be able to locate unit prices.

Views can also help to establish security. Tables and columns that are not included will not be obvious to the user of the view. Restricting access to a view with GRANT and REVOKE statements adds another layer of security. For example, granting some users access rights to aggregated data, such as averages, in a view but denying them access to base table, detailed data will not allow them to display the base table data. SQL security commands are explained further in Chapter 13.

Some people advocate the creation of a view for every single base table, even if that view is identical to the base table. They suggest this approach because views can contribute to greater programming productivity as databases evolve. Consider a situation where 50 programs all use the CUSTOMER_T table. Suppose that the Pine Valley Furniture Company database evolves to support new functions that require the CUSTOMER_T table to be renormalized into two tables. If these 50 programs refer directly to the CUSTOMER_T base table, they will all have to be modified to refer to one of the two new tables, or to join the tables together. But if these programs all use the view on this base table, then only the view has to be re-created, saving considerable reprogramming effort. However, views require considerable run-time computer processing since the virtual table of a view is re-created each time the view is referenced. Therefore, referencing a base table through a view rather than directly can add considerable time to query processing. This additional operational cost must be balanced against the potential reprogramming savings from a view.

Updating data directly from a view rather than from base tables is possible under certain limitations. In general, update operations to data in a view are permitted as long as the update is unambiguous in terms of data modification in the base table. But when the CREATE VIEW statement contains any of the following situations, that view may not be updated directly.

1. The SELECT clause includes the keyword DISTINCT. (SELECT clauses are covered in detail beginning with the section entitled PROCESSING SINGLE TABLES.)

2. The SELECT clause contains expressions, including derived columns, aggregates, statistical functions, etc.

3. The FROM clause, or a subquery, or a UNION clause references more than one table.

4. The FROM clause or a subquery references another view that is not updateable.

5. The CREATE VIEW command contains an ORDER BY, GROUP BY, or HAVING clause.

It could happen that an update to an instance would result in it disappearing from the view. Let's create a view named EXPENSIVE_STUFF_V, which lists all furniture products that have a UNIT_PRICE over $300.00. That view will include PRODUCT_ID 5, a writer's desk, which has a unit price of $325. If we update data using EXPENSIVE_STUFF_V and reduce the unit price of the writer's desk to $295.00, then the writer's desk will no longer appear in the EXPENSIVE_STUFF_V virtual table because its unit price is now less than $300.00. If it is desired to track all merchandise with an original price over $300, include a WITH CHECK OPTION clause after the SELECT clause in the CREATE VIEW command. The WITH CHECK OPTION will cause UPDATE or INSERT statements to be rejected when those statements would cause updated or inserted rows to be removed from the view. This option can only be used with updateable views.

Here is the CREATE VIEW statement for EXPENSIVE_STUFF_V.

Query: List all furniture products that have ever had a UNIT_PRICE over $300.

```
CREATE VIEW EXPENSIVE_STUFF_V
   AS
   SELECT PRODUCT_ID, PRODUCT_NAME, UNIT_PRICE
        FROM PRODUCT_T
            WHERE UNIT_PRICE > 300
                WITH CHECK OPTION;
```

When attempting to update the unit price of the writer's desk to $295, using this Oracle SQL*Plus syntax:

```
UPDATE EXPENSIVE_STUFF_V
  SET UNIT_PRICE = 295
      WHERE PRODUCT_ID = 5;
```

Oracle will give the error message shown:

```
ERROR at line 1:
ORA-01402: view WITH CHECK OPTION where-clause violation
```

A price increase on the writer's desk to $350 will take effect with no error message because the view is updateable and the conditions specified in the view are not violated.

Information about views will be stored in the systems tables of the DBMS. In Oracle7, for example, the text of all views is stored in DBA_VIEWS. Users with system privileges can find this information.

Query: What information is available about the view named EXPENSIVE_STUFF?

```
SELECT * FROM DBA_VIEWS WHERE VIEW_NAME = 'EXPENSIVE_STUFF_V';
```

Result:

OWNER	VIEW_NAME	TEXT_LENGTH	TEXT
MPRESCOTT	EXPENSIVE_STUFF_V	103	

```
SELECT PRODUCT_ID, PRODUCT_NAME, UNIT_PRICE
       FROM PRODUCT_T
       WHERE UNIT_PRICE > 300
```

ENSURING TRANSACTION INTEGRITY

Relational DBMSs are no different from other types of database managers in that one of their primary responsibilities is to ensure that data maintenance is properly and completely handled. Data maintenance is defined in units of work called transactions, which involve one or more data manipulation commands. A transaction is the complete set of closely related update commands that must all be done, or none of them done, for the database to remain valid. Consider Figure 9-11. For example, when an order is entered into the Pine Valley database, all of the items ordered should be entered at the same time. Thus, either all ORDER_LINE_T rows from this form are to be entered, along with all the information in ORDER_T, or none of them should be entered. Here, the business transaction is the complete order, not the individual items that are ordered. What we need are commands to define the boundaries of a transaction, to commit the work of a transaction as a permanent change to the database, and to purposely and properly abort a transaction, if necessary. In addition, we need data recovery services to clean up after abnormal termination of database processing in the middle of a transaction. Perhaps the order form is accurate, but in the middle of entering the order, the computer system malfunctions or loses power. In this case, we do not want some of the changes made and not others. It's all or nothing at all, if we want a valid database.

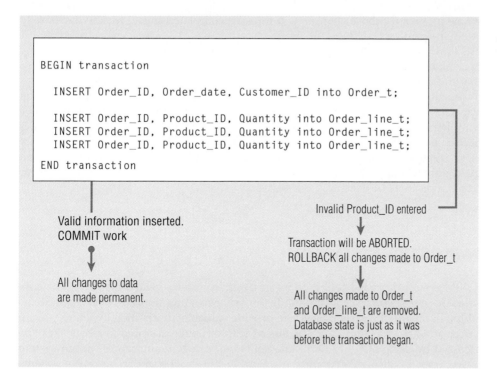

Figure 9-11
An SQL transaction sequence
(in pseudocode)

When a single SQL command constitutes a transaction, most RDBMSs will automatically commit or rollback after the command is run. With a user-defined transaction, however, where multiple SQL commands need to be run and either entirely committed or entirely rolled back, explicit commands to manage the transaction are needed. Many systems will have BEGIN TRANSACTION and END TRANSACTION commands, which are used to mark the boundaries of a logical unit of work. BEGIN TRANSACTION creates a log file and starts recording all changes (insertions, deletions, and updates) to the database in this file. END TRANSACTION or COMMIT WORK takes the contents of the log file and applies them to the database (thus making the changes permanent), and then empties the log file. ROLLBACK WORK asks SQL to empty the log file. There is also an AUTOCOMMIT (ON/OFF) command in many RDBMSs which specifies whether changes are made permanent after each data modification command (ON) or only when work is explicitly made permanent (OFF) by the COMMIT WORK command.

User-defined transactions can improve system performance because transactions will be processed as sets rather than as individual transactions, thus reducing system overhead. When AUTOCOMMIT is set to OFF, changes will not be made automatically until the end of a transaction is indicated. When AUTOCOMMIT is set to ON, changes will be made automatically at the end of each SQL statement; this would not allow for user-defined transactions to be committed or rolled back only as a whole.

SET AUTOCOMMIT is an interactive command, so a given user session can be dynamically controlled for appropriate integrity measures. Each SQL INSERT, UPDATE, and DELETE command typically works on only one table at a time. Some data maintenance requires updating of multiple tables for the work to be complete. Therefore, these transaction integrity commands are important in clearly defining whole units of database changes that must be completed in full for the database to retain integrity.

Further, some SQL systems have concurrency controls that handle the updating of a shared database by concurrent users. These can journalize database changes, so that a database can be recovered after abnormal terminations in the middle of a transaction. They can also undo erroneous transactions. For example, in a banking application, the update of a bank account balance by two concurrent users should be cumulative. Such controls are transparent to the user in SQL; no user programming is needed to ensure proper control of concurrent access to data. To ensure the integrity of a particular database, be sensitive to transaction integrity and recovery issues and make sure that application programmers are appropriately informed of when these commands are to be used.

DATA DICTIONARY FACILITIES

RDBMSs store database definition information in system-created tables; we can consider these system tables as a data dictionary. Becoming familiar with the systems tables for any RDBMS being used will provide valuable information, whether you are a user or a database administrator. Since the information is stored in tables, it can be accessed by using SQL SELECT statements that can generate reports about system usage, user privileges, constraints, etc. Further, a user who understands the systems table structure can extend existing tables or build other tables to enhance the built-in features (for example, to include data on who is responsible for data integrity). A user is, however, often restricted from modifying the structure or contents of the system tables directly, since the DBMS maintains them and depends on them for its interpretation and parsing of queries.

Each RDBMS keeps various internal tables for these definitions. In Oracle7, there are 63 data dictionary views for database administrators to use. Many of these views, or subsets of the DBA view (that information relevant to an individual user), are also available to users who do not possess DBA privileges. Those tables' names begin with USER or ALL rather than DBA. Here is a list of those tables (accessible to DBAs) that keep information about tables, clusters, columns, and security. There are also tables related to storage, objects, indexes, locks, auditing, exports, and distributed environments.

DBA_TABLES	Describes all tables in the database.
DBA_TAB_COMMENTS	Comments on all tables in the database.
DBA_CLUSTERS	Describes all clusters in the database.
DBA_TAB_COLUMNS	Describes columns of all tables, views, and clusters.
DBA_COL_PRIVS	Includes all grants on columns in the database.
DBA_COL_COMMENTS	Comments on all columns in tables and views.
DBA_CONSTRAINTS	Constraint definitions on all tables in the database.
DBA_CLU_COLUMNS	Maps table columns to cluster columns.
DBA_CONS_COLUMNS	Information about all columns in constraint definitions.
DBA_USERS	Information about all users of the database.

DBA_SYS_PRIVS	Describes system privileges granted to users and to roles.
DBA_ROLES	Describes all roles that exist in the database.
DBA_PROFILES	Includes resources limits assigned to each profile.
DBA_ROLE_PRIVS	Describes roles granted to users and to other roles.
DBA_TAB_PRIVS	Describes all grants on objects in the database.

To give an idea of the type of information found in the system tables, consider DBA_USERS. DBA_USERS contains information about the valid users of the database, including user names, user IDs, encrypted passwords, default tablespace, temporary tablespace, date created, and profile assigned. DBA_TAB_COLUMNS has 15 attributes, including owner of each table, table name, column name, data type, data length, precision, and scale, among others. An SQL query against DBA_TAB_COLUMNS to find out who owns PRODUCT_T is shown below.

Query: Who is the owner of the PRODUCT table?

```
SELECT OWNER, TABLE_NAME
   FROM DBA_TABLES
     WHERE TABLE_NAME = 'PRODUCT_T';
```

Result:

OWNER	TABLE_NAME
MPRESCOTT	PRODUCT_T

TRIGGERS AND PROCEDURES

While SQL-92 includes a set of intrinsic operators and functions, such as '+', '–', MAX, MIN, etc., it does not include support for user-defined functions or procedures. Commercial products, recognizing the need for such capabilities, have provided them for some time, and the proposed SQL3 standard includes **trigger** commands. Use of the CREATE ASSERTION command included in Chapter 4 is an example of trigger syntax included in SQL-92. Some vendors have developed proprietary languages (e.g., Sybase's Transact-SQL, Oracle's PL/SQL) in which functions and procedures can be defined. These functions can be invoked from within SQL commands.

> **Trigger:** A named set of SQL statements that are considered (triggered) when a data modification (INSERT, UPDATE, DELETE) occurs. If a condition stated within the trigger is met, then a prescribed action is taken.

Triggers and procedures are very powerful database objects because they are stored in the database and controlled by the DBMS. Thus, the code required to create them is stored in only one location and is administered centrally. This promotes stronger data integrity and consistency of use within the database. Since they are stored once, code maintenance is also simplified (Mullins, 1995).

Both triggers and procedures consist of blocks of procedural code. Trigger code is stored in the database and runs automatically whenever the triggering event, such as an UPDATE, occurs. In contrast, procedures do not run automatically. Procedures are stored blocks of code that have to be called in order to operate (see Figure 9-12). Since triggers are stored and executed in the database, they execute against all applications that access the database. Triggers can also cascade, causing other triggers to fire. Thus, a single request from a client can result in a series of integrity or logic checks being performed on the server without causing extensive network traffic between

Figure 9-12
Triggers contrasted with
stored procedures (adapted
from Mullins, 1995)

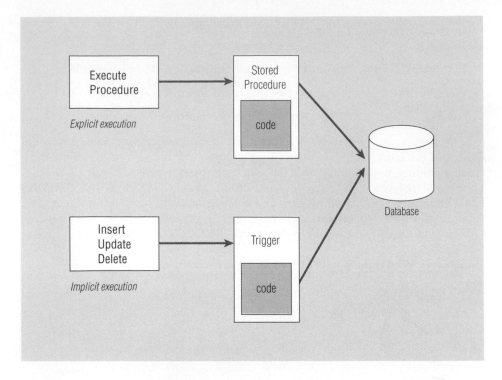

client and server. Triggers can be used to ensure referential integrity, enforce business rules, create audit trails, replicate tables, or activate a procedure (Rennhackkamp, 1996).

Triggers have three parts, the *event,* the *condition,* and the *action,* and these parts are reflected in the coding structure for triggers. A simple example of a trigger written in PL/SQL is shown here:

```
CREATE TRIGGER ORDER_ID_BIR
  BEFORE INSERT ON ORDER_T
  FOR EACH ROW
BEGIN
  SELECT ID_SEQUENCE.NEXTVAL
  INTO :NEW.ORDER_ID
  FROM DUAL;
END ORDER_ID_BIR;
```

This trigger will automatically insert the order number whenever a new order is added. BIR is part of a trigger naming convention and stands for *Before Insert Row.* Triggers may occur either *before* or *after* the statement that aroused the trigger is executed. They may occur on INSERT, UPDATE, or DELETE commands. And they may fire each time a *row* is affected, or they may fire only once per *statement,* regardless of the number of rows affected. In the case illustrated above, the trigger should insert the order number before each order is added. A trigger that checks for inventory level after inventory is updated would be assigned an AUR naming label. The trigger above also requires that a sequence named ID_SEQUENCE has been previously defined, as the next value in this sequence will be used as the next order number.

The developer who wishes to include triggers should be careful. Since triggers fire automatically, unless the trigger includes a message to the user, the user will be unaware that the trigger has fired. Also, triggers can cascade and cause other triggers to fire. For example, a BEFORE UPDATE trigger could require that a row be inserted in another table. If that table has a BEFORE INSERT trigger, it will also fire, possibly with unintended results. It is even possible to create a loop of triggers! So, while triggers have many possibilities, including enforcement of complex business rules, creation of sophisticated auditing logs, and enforcement of elaborate security authorizations, they should be included with care.

SQL3

SQL3 has been under discussion since 1991, before SQL-92 was finalized. It promises to be a significant revision and as such has generated much discussion, and most experts do not expect a final version for some time. See Date and Darwen (1997) for a more comprehensive overview of SQL3. The current draft at the time of that overview was over 1500 pages long. The SQL Standards Home Page (http://www.jcc.com/sql_stnd.html) provides current information about the SQL standards process.

The overall issue in the development of SQL3 has been the inclusion of object technology in the standard. As stated on the SQL Standards Home Page,

> The final standard can be expected to cover generalization and specialization hierarchies, multiple inheritance, user-defined data types, triggers and assertions, support for knowledge-based systems, recursive query expressions, and additional data administration tools. It also includes the specification of abstract data types (ADTs), object identifiers, methods, inheritance, polymorphism, encapsulation, and all of the other facilities normally associated with object data management.

Rather than being one single unified standard like the previous SQL standards, currently SQL3 is divided into eight units, and each is being developed separately. The units include the Call-Level Interface-SQL/CLI and Procedural Extensions-SQL/PSM. Both have been published as standards (CLI-95 and PSM-96). The remaining units are SQL3/CLI, SQL3/PSM, Object-Relational Extensions-SQL/Foundation, Extended Object Extensions-SQL/Object, Host Language Bindings-SQL/Bindings, Distributed Transactions-SQL/Transactions, Temporal Extensions-SQL/Temporal, and Virtual Tables-SQL/VirtualTable. The object orientation of the new standards is apparent from these units.

DBMS standards work began in the late 1960s and the Committee on Data Systems and Languages (CODASYL) produced standards specifications, but no conformance tests or certification procedures were established. The result was that until the late 1980s, DBMSs were unique to each vendor. Conformance tests and certifications were developed by the National Institute of Standards and Technology (NIST) for SQL, however, and these conformance tests are widely regarded as having been instrumental in the establishment of SQL as the de facto standard database management language (Melton, 1997). Now, NIST has announced that it will not be developing any further conformance tests past the current tests through Intermediate SQL-92 and that they will no longer be testing SQL implementations. This development may result in SQL3 never being implemented consistently across vendor products, a result that would seriously undermine organizations' data management options in the future.

SUMMARY

This chapter has introduced the SQL language for relational database definition (DDL), manipulation (DML), and control (DCL), commonly used to define and query relational database management systems (RDBMS). This standard has been criticized for many flaws, and in reaction to these, and to increase the power of the language, extensions are constantly under review by the ANSI X3H2 committee and ISO/IEC JTC1/SC 21/WG3 DBL. The current standard is known as SQL-92. Further developments of the standard are expected to result in SQL3, which will enable the definition and management of persistent, complex objects, and may be completed by late 1999.

The establishment of SQL standards and conformance certification tests has contributed to relational systems being the current dominant form of new database development. Benefits of the SQL standards include reduced training costs, improved productivity, application portability and longevity, reduced dependence on single vendors, and improved cross-system communication.

The SQL environment includes an instance of an SQL DBMS along with accessible databases and associated users and programs. Each database is included in a catalog and has a schema that describes the database objects. Information contained in the catalog is maintained by the DBMS itself, rather than by the users of the DBMS.

The data definition language (DDL) commands of SQL are used to define a database, including its creation and the creation of its tables, indexes, and views. Referential integrity is also established through DDL commands. The data manipulation (DML) commands of SQL are used to load, update, and query the database through use of the SELECT command. Data control language (DCL) commands are used to establish user access to the database through the GRANT, ADD USER, and REVOKE commands.

SQL commands may directly affect the base tables, which contain the raw data, or they may affect a database view which has been created. Changes and updates made to views may or may not be passed on to the base tables. The basic syntax of an SQL SELECT statement contains the following keywords: SELECT, FROM, WHERE, ORDER BY, GROUP BY, and HAVING. SELECT determines which attributes will be displayed in the query results table. FROM determines which tables or views will be used in the query. WHERE sets the criteria of the query, including any joins of multiple tables which are necessary. ORDER BY determines the order in which the results will be displayed. GROUP BY is used to categorize results and may return either scalar aggregates or vector aggregates. HAVING qualifies results by categories.

Equi-joins, natural joins, and outer joins have been considered. Equi-joins are based on equal values in the common columns of the tables which are being joined and will return all requested results including the values of the common columns from each table included in the join. Natural joins return all requested results, but values of the common columns are included only once. Outer joins return all the values in one of the tables included in the join, regardless of whether a match exists in the other table or not.

Nested subqueries, where multiple SELECT statements are nested within a single query, are useful for more complex query situations. A special form of the subquery, a correlated subquery, requires that a value be known from the outer query before the inner query can be processed. Other subqueries process the inner query, return a result to the next outer query, and then that outer query is processed.

Advanced SQL topics include the use of embedded SQL and the use of triggers and procedures. SQL can be included within the context of many third-generation languages including COBOL, C, Fortran, and Ada. The use of embedded SQL allows for the development of more flexible interfaces, improved performance, and improved database security. User-defined functions that run automatically when records are inserted, updated, or deleted are called triggers. Procedures are user-defined code modules, which can be called in order to execute.

Understanding the basic SQL syntax presented in this chapter should enable the reader to start using SQL effectively, and to build a deeper understanding of the possibilities for more complex querying with continued practice.

CHAPTER REVIEW

KEY TERMS

Base table	Data manipulation	Relational DBMS
Catalog	language (DML)	(RDBMS)
Correlated subquery	Equi-join	Scalar aggregate
Data control language	Join	Schema
(DCL)	Natural join	Trigger
Data definition language	Outer join	Vector aggregate
(DDL)	Referential integrity	

REVIEW QUESTIONS

1. Define each of the following terms:

   a. base table

   b. correlated subquery

   c. data definition language

   d. data manipulation language

   e. join

   f. equi-join

   g. natural join

   h. outer join

   i. referential integrity

   j. relational DBMS (RDBMS)

   k. schema

2. Contrast the following terms:

   a. base table; view

   b. equi-join; natural join

   c. natural join; outer join

   d. catalog; schema

3. What is SQL-92? Review the history leading up to SQL-92 and predict the direction of SQL3.

4. Describe a relational DBMS (RDBMS), its underlying data model, data storage structures, and manner of establishing data relationships.

5. List six potential benefits of achieving an SQL standard that is widely accepted.

6. Describe the components and structure of a typical SQL environment.

7. Distinguish among data definition commands, data manipulation commands, and data control commands.

8. Explain how referential integrity is established in databases that are SQL-92 compliant. Explain how the ON UPDATE RESTRICT, ON UPDATE CASCADE, and ON UPDATE SET NULL clauses differ. What happens if the ON DELETE CASCADE clause is set?

9. Explain some possible purposes of creating a view using SQL. In particular, explain how a view can be used to reinforce data security.

10. Explain why it is necessary to limit the kinds of updates performed on data when referencing data through a view.

11. Describe a set of circumstances for which using a view can save reprogramming effort.

12. Drawing on material covered in prior chapters, explain the factors to be considered in deciding whether to create a key index for a table in SQL.

13. Explain and provide at least one example of how one qualifies the ownership of a table in SQL.

14. How is the order in which attributes appear in a result table changed? How are the column heading labels changed?

15. What is the difference between COUNT, COUNT DISTINCT, and COUNT(*) in SQL? When will these three commands generate the same and different results?

16. What is the evaluation order for the Boolean operators (AND, OR, NOT) in an SQL command? How can one be sure that the operators will work in the desired order rather than in this prescribed order?

17. If an SQL statement includes a GROUP BY clause, the attributes that can be requested in the SELECT statement will be limited. Explain that limitation.

18. When is an outer join used instead of a natural join?

19. Explain the processing order of a correlated subquery.

20. Explain the following statement regarding SQL: Any query that can be written using the subquery approach can also be written using the joining approach, but not vice-versa.

21. What is the purpose of the COMMIT command in SQL? How does commit relate to the notion of a business transaction (such as entry of a customer order or issuing a customer invoice)?

PROBLEMS AND EXERCISES

---

1. Match the following terms to the appropriate definitions.

_____ equi-join	a. changes to a table are undone
_____ natural join	b. list of values
_____ outer join	c. description of a database
_____ trigger	d. returns all records of designated table
_____ SQL-92	e. redundant columns are kept
_____ null value	f. changes to a table are made permanent
_____ scalar aggregate	

_____ vector aggregate

_____ COMMIT

_____ catalog

_____ schema

_____ ROLLBACK

_____ host language

g. missing or nonexistent value

h. descriptions of database objects for a database

i. third-generation programming language in which SQL commands are embedded

j. redundant columns are not kept

k. set of SQL statements that execute under stated conditions

l. standard relational query and definition language

m. single value

Problems and Exercises 2 through 10 are based on the class schedule ERD depicted in Figure 4-12 in Chapter 4. The 3NF relations along with some sample data are repeated in Figure 9-13.

2. Write a database description for each of the relations shown, using SQL DDL (shorten, abbreviate, or change any data names as needed for your SQL version). Assume the following attribute data types:

STUDENT_ID (integer, primary key)
STUDENT_NAME (25 characters)
FACULTY_ID (integer, primary key)
FACULTY_NAME (25 characters)
COURSE_ID (8 characters, primary key)
COURSE_NAME (15 characters)
DATE_QUALIFIED (date)
SECTION_ID (integer, primary key)
SEMESTER (7 characters)

3. Use SQL to define the following view:

STUDENT_ID	STUDENT_NAME	COURSE_ID	SECTION_ID	SEMESTER
38214	Letersky	ISM 4212	2714	I-98
54907	Altvater	ISM 4212	2714	I-98
54907	Altvater	ISM 4930	2715	I-98
66324	Aiken	ISM 3113	2713	I-98
...				

4. Before any row can be entered in the SECTION table, the COURSE_ID to be entered must already exist in the COURSE table (referential integrity). Write an SQL assertion that will enforce this constraint.

5. Write SQL retrieval commands for each of the following queries:

a. Display the course ID and course name for all courses with an ISM prefix.

b. Display all courses for which Professor Berndt has been qualified.

c. Display the class roster, including student name, for all students enrolled in section 2714 of ISM 4212.

STUDENT (STUDENT_ID, STUDENT_NAME)

STUDENT_ID	STUDENT_NAME
38214	Letersky
54907	Altvater
66324	Aiken
70542	Marra
...	

IS_QUALIFIED (FACULTY_ID, COURSE_ID, DATE_QUALIFIED)

FACULTY_ID	COURSE_ID	DATE_QUALIFIED
2143	ISM 3112	9/88
2143	ISM 3113	9/88
3467	ISM 4212	9/95
3467	ISM 4930	9/96
4756	ISM 3113	9/91
4756	ISM 3112	9/91
...		

FACULTY (FACULTY_ID, FACULTY_NAME)

FACULTY_ID	FACULTY_NAME
2143	Birkin
3487	Berndt
4756	Collins
...	

SECTION (SECTION_ID, *COURSE_ID*)

SECTION_ID	*COURSE_ID*
2712	ISM 3113
2713	ISM 3113
2714	ISM 4212
2715	ISM 4930
...	

COURSE (COURSE_ID, COURSE_NAME)

COURSE_ID	COURSE_NAME
ISM 3113	Syst Analysis
ISM 3112	Syst Design
ISM 4212	Database
ISM 4930	Networking
...	

IS_REGISTERED (STUDENT_ID, SECTION_ID, SEMESTER)

STUDENT_ID	SECTION_ID	SEMESTER
38214	2714	I-98
54907	2714	I-98
54907	2715	I-98
66324	2713	I-98
...		

Figure 9-13
Class scheduling relations
(missing IS_ASSIGNED)

6. Write an SQL retrieval command to produce the table shown in Problem 3 above. Note the similarity between the view definition (Problem and Exercise 3) and the retrieval command (Problem and Exercise 6). Under what conditions would each of these commands be used?

7. Write an SQL query to answer the following question: Which instructors are qualified to teach ISM 3113?

8. Write an SQL query to answer the following question: Is any instructor qualified to teach ISM 3113 and not qualified to teach ISM 4930?

9. Write SQL queries to answer the following questions: How many students are enrolled in section 2714 during semester I-98? How many students are enrolled in ISM 3113 during semester I-98?

10. Write an SQL query to answer the following question: Which students were not enrolled in any courses during semester I-98?

Problems and Exercises 11 through 20 are based on the entire Pine Valley Furniture database.

11. Write an SQL command to display the order number, customer number, order date, and items ordered for Order #1001.

12. Write an SQL command to display each item ordered for Order #1001, its unit price, and the total price for each item ordered.

13. Write an SQL command to total the cost of Order #1001.

14. Write an SQL command to determine the amount of wood needed for each item ordered for Order #1001. Write another SQL command to determine if enough finished product is on hand to complete Order #1001. If there is not enough finished product on hand, write another SQL query to find if there is enough wood on hand to complete Order #1001.

15. Write an SQL command that will find any customers who have not placed orders.

16. Write an SQL query to produce a list of all the products and the number of times each product has been ordered.

17. Write an SQL query to display customer number, name, and order number for all customers and their orders.

18. Write an SQL query to list the order number and order quantity for all customer orders for which the order quantity is greater than the average order quantity of that product. *Hint:* This involves a correlated subquery.

19. Write an SQL query to determine the least expensive supplier of natural ash.

20. Write an SQL query to list the employees who work in each work center. The results table should be sorted by work center, and then by employee (alphabetically) within each work center.

FIELD EXERCISES

1. Arrange an interview with a database administrator in an organization in your area. When you interview the database administrator, familiarize yourself with one application that is actively used in the organization. Focus your interview questions toward determining end users' involvement with the application and understanding the extent to which end users must be familiar with SQL. For example, if end users are using SQL, what training do they receive? Do they use an interactive form of SQL for their work or do they use embedded SQL?

2. Arrange another interview with a database administrator in your area. Focus the interview toward understanding the environment within which SQL is used in the organization. Inquire about the version of SQL that is used, and determine if the same version is used at all locations. If different versions are used, explore any difficulties that the DBA has had in administering the database. Also inquire about any

proprietary languages, such as Oracle's PL*SQL, which are being used. Again, learn about possible differences in versions used at different locations and explore any difficulties that occur if different versions are installed.

3. Talk with a database developer at a local organization. Explore the developer's use of SQL in her work. Does the developer use any code-generation facilities or does she write all SQL code herself? Is there a CASE tool, such as Designer 2000, that the developer has at her disposal? If possible, get the database developer to demonstrate any CASE tool that is being used.

4. Visit the *Standards Homepage* (http://www.jcc.com/sql_stnd.html) and follow as many links as possible to become familiar with the material which is available on the Web about SQL standards.

5. Compare two versions of SQL to which you have access, such as Microsoft Access and Oracle SQL*Plus. Identify at least five similarities in the SQL code used and three dissimilarities. Do the dissimilarities cause any different results?

REFERENCES

Codd, E. F. 1970. "A Relational Model of Data for Large Relational Databases." *Communications of the ACM* 13 (June): 77–87.

Date, C. J., and H. Darwen. 1997. *A Guide to the SQL Standard.* Reading, MA: Addison-Wesley.

Melton, J. 1997. "A Case for SQL Conformance Testing." *Database Programming & Design* 10 (7): 66–69.

Mullins, C. S. 1995. "The Procedural DBA." *Database Programming & Design* 8 (12): 40–45.

Rennhackkamp, M. 1996. "Trigger Happy." *DBMS* 9 (5): 89–91, 95.

Stedman, C. 1997. "Volatility Rules Database Market." *Computerworld* (May 12, 1997): 8.

Van der Lans, R. F. 1993. *Introduction to SQL,* 2nd ed. Workingham, England: Addison-Wesley.

WEB SITE REFERENCE

Hare, K. W. *SQL Standards Homepage,* http://www.jcc.com/sql_stnd.html, May 14, 1997. [Includes discussion of SQL3 standards developments and links to standards organizations.]

FURTHER READING

American National Standards Institute. http://www.ansi.org, 1996. [Information on the ANSI federation and latest national and international standards.]

Bowman, J. S., S. L. Emerson, and M. Darnovsky. 1996. *The Practical SQL Handbook,* 3rd ed. Reading, MA: Addison-Wesley.

Celko, J. 1997. *Joe Celko's SQL Puzzles & Answers.* San Francisco: Morgan Kaufmann.

IEEE Standards Systems/Network Staff. *IEEE Standards Home Page,* http://standards.ieee.org, 1997. [IEEE Standards Association information.]

ODMG Home Page, http://www.odmg.org/, 1995 (Accessed September 7, 1997.) [Consortium of object-oriented database management system (ODBMS) vendors and interested parties.]

OMG Home Page, http://www.omg.org/, Undated. (Accessed September 7, 1997). [Object Management Group: information about CORBA.]

SW Consulting, SA, *IEC—International Electrotechnical Commission—Home Page (English),* http://www.iec.ch, August 19, 1997. [International standards and conformity assessment body for all fields of electrotechnology.]

Tibbs, A. *Welcome to NCITS,* http://www.ncits.org/, Undated. (Accessed September 7, 1997.) [National Committee for Information Technology Standards—used to be Accredited Standard Committee X3.]

Welcome to ISO Online, http://www.iso.ch, 1997. [Information about the International Organization for Standardization.]

Project Case

Use the SQL data model constructed for Mountain View Community Hospital in Chapter 4 to complete the project questions and project exercises.

PROJECT QUESTIONS

1. What version of SQL will you use to do the project exercises?

2. Which CASE tools are available to be used to do the project exercises?

PROJECT EXERCISES

1. Create in SQL the Mountain View Community Hospital database for the conceptual data model you have constructed in the previous chapters. Use the information provided in the PROJECT CASE sections at the end of Chapters 3, 4, 5, and 6 to help you choose column data types, lengths, indexes, etc.

2. If you did not remember to establish primary and foreign keys in the preceding question, create the SQL assertions necessary to accomplish that.

3. Select at least a portion of your database and populate it with sample data. For example, you may wish to work with the staff, care-center, patient part of your database. Or you may be interested in working with the vendor, medical/surgical items, tests, and patients part of your database. Be prepared to defend the sample test data that you insert into your database. How do the actual values you are using help you to test the functionality of your database?

4. Now write and test some queries that will work using your sample data. Write queries that:

   a. select information from only one of the tables

   b. aggregate information from one attribute in a table

   c. try out the various functions such as MIN, MAX, and AVG

   d. select information from two or more tables

   e. use subquery syntax

   f. return a result table that could be used to produce a hospital report, such as nursing staff assigned to each care center.

10

Database Access from Client Applications

After studying this chapter, you should be able to:

■ Define the following terms: **Query-by-Example (QBE)**, **code generator**, **Object Linking and Embedding (OLE)**, **Component Object Model (COM)**, **ActiveX**, **container**, **dynamic binding**, **Visual Basic for Applications (VBA)**, **event-driven**, **intranet**, **HyperText Markup Language (HTML)**, **Web browser**, and **HTML form**.

■ Explain the capabilities of a Query-by-Example (QBE) interface, its relationship to Microsoft Access97, and its advantages and disadvantages compared to SQL.

■ Define different types of join commands, and be able to use Access97 to construct queries for each of these types of joins.

■ Explain the components, including menus, forms, and reports, of building a client application.

■ Explain conceptually how OLE, COM, OLE-DB, and ActiveX controls are used to achieve database access from client applications.

■ Explain how embedded SQL is used.

■ Explain how VBA is used with Access97 to build client applications.

■ Describe the purpose of, function of, and alternative approaches to writing CGI scripts.

INTRODUCTION

In Chapter 9 you saw examples of SQL, the de facto query language used for data manipulation of relational database implementations. Although SQL's syntax is more easily understood than other languages, it is still complex enough to deter many end users from writing their own queries using SQL. However, over the past few years PCs have gained dramatically in sophistication and processing power, allowing wide adoption of graphical user interfaces (GUIs), and accelerating the acceptance of PCs in the workplace. Windows 3.1, Windows 95, Windows NT, Macintosh, and UNIX-based systems such as Motif and OpenLook have all been well received. GUIs have affected both user interfaces and programming principles. Many new database systems have developed user interfaces that are much more object oriented. PC-based DBMSs such as Microsoft Access, FoxPro, and Paradox have GUI development environments that allow the development of object-oriented GUI interfaces. Even the traditionally character-based interfaces of the larger databases that run on minicomputers and mainframes, such as Oracle, have GUI interfaces that supplement their traditional character-based interfaces. While this chapter is mainly focused on desktop database technologies, examples from both Microsoft Access97 and Oracle 7.3.2 are included to illustrate the more visual interfaces typically available now.

We will investigate in some detail the use of a data manipulation language (DML) that is visually oriented. Such DMLs represent a different style of programming language, called *direct manipulation* (Schneiderman, 1983), which is very visually oriented and different in appearance from the line-mode SQL depicted in Chapter 9. **Query-by-Example (QBE)** is a prime example of a direct-manipulation database language. Most current desktop databases include a QBE interface, and examples are included in this chapter.

Query-by-Example (QBE): A direct manipulation database language that uses a graphical approach to query construction.

The other major recent change in database interfaces has been enabling access to a database through the World Wide Web. Tools and methods commonly used to accomplish this access are also discussed in this chapter. The scope of this chapter does not allow for detailed examples of such components as Common Gateway Interface scripting or CGI scripting, a method that allows programs to run on a Web server using input from any Web browser and making an ODBC connection, but the chapter does address the issues conceptually.

SURVEY OF DESKTOP DATABASE TECHNOLOGY

The desktop RDBMS market currently includes a range of products, from those appropriate for novices to those appropriate for professional database developers. Most manufacturers or vendors claim that their product is suitable for both levels of expertise, but as you would expect, the products vary in ease of use and usability. The current systems generally include extensive on-line help facilities, both passive and interactive, which many users find to be very helpful. Templates to aid in database development and even complete sample databases for common specific purposes are also included. Application generator tools allow even novices to build functional systems, although complex, mission-critical applications must still be built by professional database developers who have a firm grasp of data modeling principles. Most are included in integrated suites that include spreadsheet and word processing applications, such as Lotus or Microsoft Office.

It is not necessary to limit use of these desktop packages only to building smaller, simpler database systems. That is the case where the intent is to use only the desktop package for the entire application, including storage and manipulation of data, because the desktop packages are not as powerful as the larger RDBMSs such as Oracle, Sybase, or Informix. However, the ease of use and inclusion of programming capabilities in the desktop products have led many organizations to use a desktop package, such as Microsoft Access, as a front end attached to a more powerful back-end database such as SQL Server or Oracle. For example, by using pass-through queries, formulated in Access but run against the back-end Oracle database, organizations achieve faster development times but utilize the more robust and powerful RDBMSs for their mission-critical applications.

In the highly competitive desktop database market, new and upgraded versions of the products are introduced often. Because of that, you should read the following brief survey of the current (January 1998) desktop database applications mostly to gain an understanding of the current range of capabilities that are available. Five products are reviewed regularly in the popular press (Technology Buyer's Guide, 1998; Robinson, 1997): Alpha Five, FileMaker Pro, Paradox, Approach, and MS-Access. The companies' current versions of these products are as follows.

Alpha Software: Alpha Five Version 3.0 for Windows 95 and Windows NT

Claris: FileMaker Pro 4.0 for Windows 3.1 and higher and Macintosh

Corel: Paradox 8 for Windows 95 and Windows NT

Lotus: Approach 97 for Windows 95 and Windows NT

Microsoft: Access97 for Windows 95 and Windows NT

Of these products, Alpha Five, Approach, and FileMaker Pro are the easiest for novices to use. Alpha Five is very reasonably priced but is the only product mentioned that is not Web enabled. Approach consistently received reviews that praise its ease of use and full functionality, including the ability to build custom applications using LotusScript. The Macintosh and Windows versions of FileMaker Pro are identical in functionality, and it is the only package mentioned that is available for both environments. FileMaker Pro is the only package mentioned that does not include a database programming language, which limits its use to novices.

Microsoft Access97 and Paradox 8 are more difficult to learn and thus may be more suitable for more experienced users. Access97 has extensive on-line help screens and Wizards that help to counter the sometimes-complex interface. It also includes Visual Basic for Applications (VBA) as its programming language and supports OLE 2.0. Paradox 8 is now well integrated into Corel's WordPerfect Suite 8 Professional. Its interface has been simplified from previous versions to be consistent with Corel's look and feel, making it easier to use for all levels of users. The Enterprise edition includes a Java Runtime version that will run Paradox applications from different platforms, including Windows, Macintosh, DOS, and UNIX. Experienced programmers will also want to consider products such as Visual dBASE and Visual FoxPro, which contain high-end programming tools for building custom applications.

USING QUERY-BY-EXAMPLE

Query-by-Example (QBE) is the most widely available direct-manipulation database query language. Although not an international standard like SQL, QBE has been widely available, especially in the PC-RDBMS market, for many years. As a direct-manipulation query language, it is easy to learn for a wide variety of people wanting to make inquiries against a database. Also, its simplicity makes it a popular language for developing prototypes. Since some database systems, such as Microsoft Access, translate QBE queries into SQL, QBE can be used as at least a first pass at creating SQL code. In this section, you will learn about the history of QBE and many of the querying capabilities of this important database manipulation language.

The History and Importance of QBE

Although QBE (like SQL) was originally developed for mainframe database processing, it has become prevalent in personal computer database systems as well. Query-by-Example was originally developed by Zloof (1977) and was first available for use with SQL/DS and DB2 database systems on IBM mainframes. The success of the first personal computer relational DBMS (PC-RDBMS) that was completely based on QBE, Paradox, encouraged other products to adopt a QBE interface as an option. Most current systems include a variation on QBE.

Coverage of QBE is essential for the understanding of modern database systems. This is true because QBE is considered a highly productive language in which to program. Visual versions of programming languages, such as Visual Basic, Visual C, and Visual Java have transformed the way programs are written. Research studies (for example, Greenblatt and Waxman, 1978; Thomas and Gould, 1975) have shown that even with relatively little training, student subjects find QBE easier to use than SQL or a relational algebra language. Although these studies are more than two decades old, no new database query language has been developed that beats QBE's usability.

QBE is especially useful for end-user database programming. The visual programming environment gives the nonprogramming user a single view of data no matter what database task is performed. As we will see (and as was shown in Chapter 2), queries are developed interactively on a CRT screen in a format that resembles the desired output. In most programs, both queries and results are shown in the same format, usually a spreadsheet-type format.

Complete database applications can be written in QBE, but it is more common to use QBE for interactive querying or updating of a database. That is, QBE is particularly useful for ad hoc database processing. Rather than developing a complete application in QBE, it is more common to use QBE to prototype an application, saving the queries that are developed. These saved queries can then be enhanced by using the application generator tools, such as screen, form, and report generators, and by adding modules of code using the database language associated with the PC-RDBMS to provide custom behaviors.

QBE: The Basics

There is no official standard for QBE as has been defined for SQL (see Chapter 9 for a discussion of the SQL standardization efforts). For this reason, there is no minimal set of capabilities that a query interface must meet to be considered a QBE implementation. However, because QBE has evolved from research on database query languages, because the Windows visual interface has been standardized, and because it is a visual language, all vendors have adopted similar approaches to QBE.

Both data retrieval and data modification can be done via entering keywords, constants, and example data into the cells of a table layout. Because data definitions are stored in internal tables, even data definition is done through a similar table layout interface. In MS-Access97 (used along with Oracle 7.3.2 in this chapter for examples) clicking on an SQL button will reveal the Access SQL code that has been generated as the QBE-based query has been constructed.

Figure 10-1 depicts the original Microsoft Access usability hierarchy. The pyramid conveys that Access will be usable at all levels of programming ability and complexity. At the lowest level of the pyramid are the objects, which allow the creation of tables, queries, forms, and reports without any specific programming knowledge. The use of expressions, or functions, to perform simple processes such as multiplication of fields, validation of data, or enforcement of a specific business rule is possible

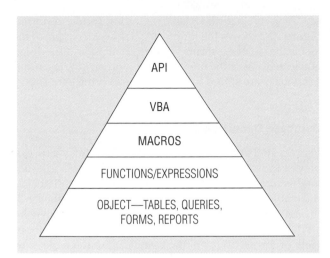

Figure 10-1
The Access usability
hierarchy (adapted from
Prague & Irwin, 1997)

at the next pyramid level. At the next level, macros, users can take advantage of stored modules of Visual Basic for Applications (VBA) code to automate their application, again without explicit knowledge of VBA. At the next level, users can program their own modules of VBA code to custom tailor their own applications. At the top level, Windows API calls (see Chapter 8 for an explanation of APIs) to functions or DLLs written in languages such as C, Java, or Visual Basic can be used to write interfaces to other programs and sources of data.

Figure 10-2 shows the database window for the Pine Valley Furniture Company database. MS-Access97 uses traditional database terminology, including *database, table, record, field,* and *value*. In Access97 the database contains the data and all associ-

Figure 10-2
MS-Access® 97 Database
window (Pine Valley
Furniture Company)

ated objects, including tables, queries, forms, reports, macros, and VBA modules. Figure 10-2 shows the Pine Valley table objects, since the tables tab is depressed. The associated queries, forms, reports, macros, and modules will be listed when their tab is selected. All of the objects (tables, forms, queries, reports, macros, and modules) for a database are stored in a single file with the extension .MDB.

Database Definition

Figures 10-3 and 10-4 illustrate the Pine Valley raw materials table as it can be displayed in Access97. Figure 10-3 shows the table in *Datasheet* view. Each data column on this screen is called a *field*, and each row is called a *record*. This example raw materials table has twenty records. The intersection of each field and record holds a *value*, or *data element*. Figure 10-4 illustrates the *Design* view for the Pine Valley raw materials table. Tables are created in Design view and populated through the Datasheet view or through a form that is attached to the table so that data values entered in the form are passed through to populate the table. In Design view, each field for the table is entered and its data type determined. Common Access97 datatypes are Text, Currency, Date/Time, and Number. There is also a memo field in which a description of each field may be entered. Additional properties for each field can be specified in the fields at the bottom of the Design view window. Properties available depend on the data type that is specified for the field in the top half of the screen. It is here that many data integrity controls can be instituted, including field size, format, default values, validation rules, required fields, and indexes. Movement between the top and bottom parts of the Design view is accomplished by using a mouse or the F6 key. Primary keys are defined by selecting the field or fields that make up the primary key and then clicking on the icon in the database toolbar that has a picture of a key on it. Single-field secondary keys can be created by setting the Indexed property to Yes in the table creation screen. Multiple-field secondary indexes are created by using the Indexes window.

Figure 10-3

The Pine Valley raw materials table in MS-Access97 Datasheet view

Material_ID	Thickness	Size	Grade	Material_description	Footage_on_hand	Unit_price
1	1/4	8x4	B-4	Red Oak	166	$7.89
2	1/2	4x8	A-2	Red Oak	257	$12.05
3	3/4	4x8	A-1	Red Oak	33	$13.67
4	3/4	4x8	C-4	Red Oak	4	$7.66
5	1/4	4x8	A-4	White Oak	72	$7.23
6	3/4	4x8	A-1	White Oak	54	$15.19
7	1/2	4x8	B-4	Walnut	9	$13.02
8	3/4	4x8	A-1	Walnut	58	$15.45
9	3/4	4x8	Shop	Walnut	2	$10.88
10	3/4	4x8	C-2	Natural Ash	11	$15.55
11	1/4	4x8	A-4	White Ash	33	$8.79
12	3/4	4x8	A-1	White Ash	66	$14.26
13	1/2	4x8	A-2	Cherry	2	$15.82
14	1/2	4x8	B-2	Cherry	1	$13.75
15	3/4	4x8	A-1	Cherry	68	$16.72
16	1/4	4x8	A-4	Natural Maple	84	$5.70
17	1/2	4x8	D-3	Natural Maple	165	$7.95
18	3/4	4x8	A-1	Natural Maple	212	$11.13
19	3/4	4x8	B-2	Natural Maple	306	$10.47
20	3/4	4x8	D-3	Natural Maple	302	$9.18
(AutoNumber)					0	$0.00

Raw_Materials_t : Table

Record: 1 of 20

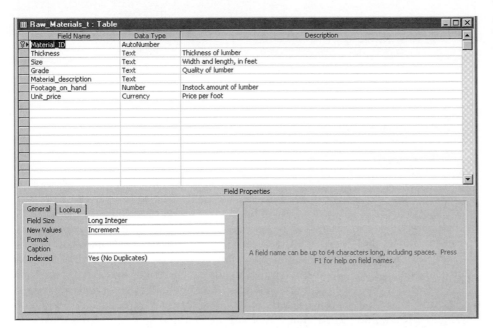

Figure 10-4
The Pine Valley raw materials
table in MS-Access97
Design view

Relationships

Each Access97 database will contain a collection of related tables. When you define
relationships between tables, Access uses these relationships to automatically join
(using the natural join—see Chapter 9 for a definition of natural join) tables in QBE
queries; in this case, the user does not have to write joining statements into the
queries. These relationships can be viewed graphically through the Relationships
screen. Figure 10-5 shows Pine Valley's Relationships screen. Figure 10-5 shows, for
example, that the Product_t table participates in four relationships, including being

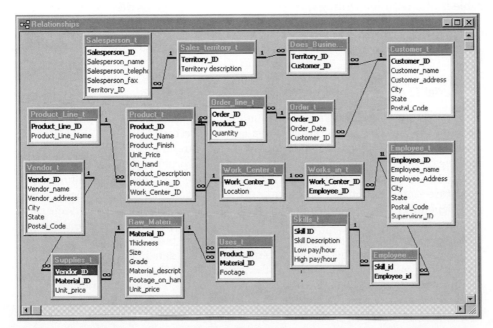

Figure 10-5
Pine Valley data model
from MS-Access97
Relationships screen

on the many-side of a 1:M relationship with Product_Line_t and the one-side of a 1:M relationship with Order_Line_t. Since the Relationship screen shows tables and relationships (not entities and relationships), many-to-many relationships are not allowed. Consequently, M:N relationships appear as associative entity tables in such figures (see table Does_Business_in_t). Referential integrity for your data model can be established as you are creating the relationships shown in this sample data model (see Figure 10-6). You may also specify whether Access should use a natural join or outer join when joining these tables (this is done in a dialogue box that appears by pressing the Join Type button on the screen in Figure 10-6).

The PC screen serves as a window into the Access97 workspace. The workspace holds all the objects you have defined. It is possible to have, for example, many different query forms and data tables active in the workspace at one time. Cursor-movement keys or a mouse are used to move among the different images.

Building Queries Using QBE

With any relational system, the data retrieved as a query result are shown and stored in a table. QBE is no different. What makes QBE unique is that the visual image of a table is also used for writing queries. The visual image gives the user the sense of directly manipulating the data. For most novice users, this visual approach will be more natural, will require less training, and will make programming more efficient.

Single-Table Queries

The simplest form of data retrieval is an unqualified display of the complete contents of one data table. This operation is available in Access97 through the Database window when the Tables tab is depressed by selecting the table to be viewed and clicking on the Open button in the upper right-hand corner of the Database window. Figure 10-3 showed the result of viewing the raw materials table from the Pine Valley Furniture example database. Whether or not such a view may be edited or modified will depend on what user-level security has been set. When user-level security is implemented, users will need to give a password to gain access to the database. Then, depending on the workgroup to which they have been assigned by the administrator, users may be allowed to view, enter, or modify data in the table or not. Such permissions are relatively easy to set at the table level, but they require extensive VBA coding to accomplish at the record level within tables. Standard Windows cursor and mouse movements are employed throughout MS-Access97.

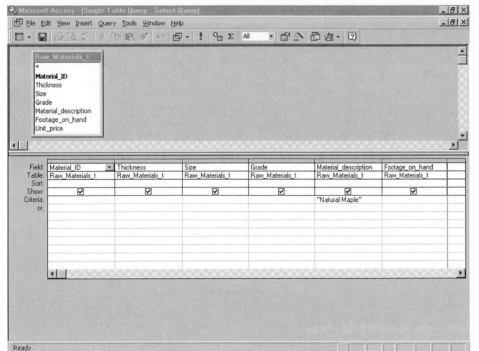

Figure 10-7
MS-Access97 single-table query in design mode (Pine Valley Furniture)

It is also possible to open multiple data table windows and to resize them to a configuration that is most useful to the user. Although viewing table contents can be useful, we usually ask more complex questions of a database. QBE provides a simple, visual method for specifying qualified queries. Data for display may be limited to certain columns and records with desired values, just as was shown in Chapter 9 when using SQL. In fact, the Access SQL that conveys a query constructed in the QBE pane can always be viewed by clicking on the SQL icon.

In Access97, the QBE pane has an upper workspace where data model representations of the tables or queries involved in a query are placed. Previously established relationships will also show automatically. Occasionally, another relationship is needed for a single query, and that relationship can also be established in the QBE pane. The lower part of the QBE pane, called the Query Design Pane or QBE grid, displays a spreadsheet-type form in which the fields needed for the query are placed, along with any sorting and limiting criteria needed for the query. Each column in the QBE grid contains information about a single field from a table or query in the upper pane. Figure 10-7 shows a QBE pane for a single-table select query involving the raw materials table that asks for information about the current inventory of natural maple items. Notice that the result displayed in Figure 10-8 is called a *dynaset*.

Material_ID	Thickness	Size	Grade	Material_description	Footage_on_hand
16 1/4		4x8	A-4	Natural Maple	84
17 1/2		4x8	D-3	Natural Maple	165
18 3/4		4x8	A-1	Natural Maple	212
19 3/4		4x8	B-2	Natural Maple	306
20 3/4		4x8	D-3	Natural Maple	302
(AutoNumber)					0

Record: 1 of 5

Figure 10-8
MS-Access97 dynaset (query result) (Pine Valley Furniture)

Figure 10-9

MS-Access97 single-table
query in SQL view
(Pine Valley Furniture)

```
Single Table Query : Select Query                                    _ □ ×
SELECT Raw_Materials_t.Material_ID, Raw_Materials_t.Thickness,
Raw_Materials_t.Size, Raw_Materials_t.Grade, Raw_Materials_t.Material_description,
Raw_Materials_t.Footage_on_hand
FROM Raw_Materials_t
WHERE (((Raw_Materials_t.Material_description)="Natural Maple"));
```

Although the result looks just like a table, it is not a base table like the raw materials table on which it was based. Rather, it is a *dynamic* or *virtual* set of records and is not stored in the database. Figure 10-9 shows the Access SQL view of this query.

The benefits of a dynaset are that the storage device being used requires less storage space, and that whenever the query is run, it will use the current copy of the database, which will include any records that have been added or updated since the query was last run. Thus, queries behave just like relational views, discussed in Chapter 9. If you need to save the results of the query into a new table, use a make-table query.

Selecting Qualified Records

What if you are only interested in certain records? Figure 10-7 shows the basic approach to entering qualifications for which records to display from a table. Placing conditions under the associated column does this. The condition can be an equality, as in Figure 10-7, or it could involve a range or inequality condition. For example, you could enter <200 under the Footage_on_hand column in Figure 10-7 to learn which sizes and thicknesses of Natural Maple boards you might need to order.

Operators, functions, and expressions can also be used when constructing criteria in queries. Mathematical operators, such as multiplication and division, operate with numeric fields. The relational operators, such as equal, not equal, and less than, can be used with numeric fields, date fields, and text fields. Boolean or logical operators are used for setting conditions in expressions.

Functions are modules of code that always return a value based on a calculation or comparison performed by the function. String, logic, or number values can be returned, depending on the nature of the function. Microsoft Access has many common functions already stored for use, such as *sum* or *average,* or specialized functions may be written in VBA. Expressions are a term or series of terms controlled by operators. Access will try to help with expression syntax by inserting needed characters, such as quotes, if they are left off.

Multiple-Table Queries

A quick review of multiple-table queries in SQL (in Chapter 9) will remind you of the need to specify which tables are needed in the query (in the FROM clause) and to set the equalities between each table that is needed in the query (in the WHERE clause). These links can be time consuming to code in SQL if one is not an excellent keyboarder. In MS-Access97 QBE, these links have been established when the relationships were made explicit in the Relationships screen, and putting the tables needed in the QBE pane will bring those links in automatically, thus eliminating the need to type in each link. This can be a great saving in time and accuracy as a query is devel-

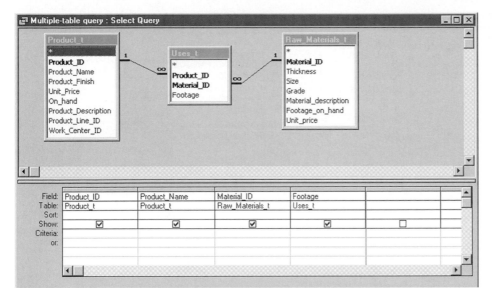

Figure 10-10
MS-Access97: Joining of tables in multiple-table query before criteria have been set

Figure 10-11
MS-Access97: Joining of tables in multiple-table query in SQL, before criteria have been set

oped. Look at Figure 10-10, in which three tables to be used in a query have been added to the QBE pane and the fields required for the query result have been selected and dragged to the QBE grid. No criteria necessary for the final query have been entered directly yet. Figure 10-11 shows you how much of the SQL has already been established just by the simple clicking and dragging which has occurred. Notice that even though the QBE grid does not contain the foreign key columns from the Uses_t table (Product_ID and Material_ID) that have been used to establish the links among the three tables, the correct linkages have been made explicit in the SQL. Notice also how Access SQL varies from the Oracle SQL*Plus used in Chapter 9 (you may want to write the Oracle SQL equivalent to the code in Figure 10-11). The differences make it quite clear that each vendor has its own flavor of SQL.

Another type of multiple-table query uses the outer join. As a reminder, the outer join operator for relational databases works like the natural join, except that rows in the tables being joined that do not have a match in other tables are also included in the result. For example, suppose you wanted to create a list of all the products in Pine Valley Furniture with their corresponding total units sold. A new or unpopular product may not have any entries in the Order_Line_t table. Thus, you must do an outer join of the Product_t and Order_Line_t tables, as is shown in Figure 10-12. The join between the two tables has been clicked on and edited to be an outer join *for this query only*. The arrowhead on the end of the relationship line next to the Order_Line_t table indicates that an outer join is being performed. (As can be seen in Figure 10-13, all products have sales, so no product has a sold value of 0 in the dynaset.) Although we have not discussed grouping and aggregation functions, you can probably see the similarities between how QBE does this and how it is done in

Figure 10-12
MS-Access97 outer join

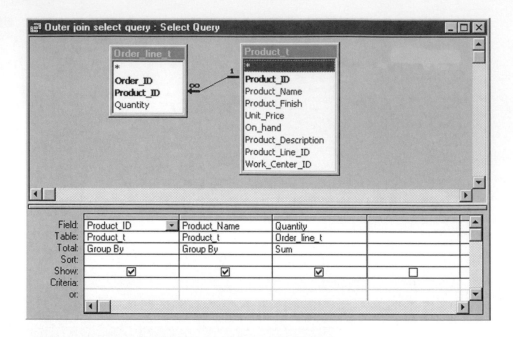

Figure 10-13
Dynaset: Example of outer
join query: List of all
products with total units sold

SQL. The two columns with the Group By phrase in the Total line of the QBE template (Product_ID and Product_Name) will be placed in an SQL Group by clause, and the Sum indication under the Quantity field results in SUM(Quantity) being placed in the select list.

Self-Join

It is not uncommon to find a query that requires a table to be joined with itself. This type of query is called a *self-join* or a *recursive join*. For example, suppose you want to know what orders have been placed that include any of the same products that were ordered on order #1004. Such a query might arise because of, say, a packaging problem with this order, and you need it to find if any other orders have had the same problem. An Access97 QBE query to answer this question appears in Figure 10-14a. A self-join is done by putting two copies of the Order_Line_t table in the QBE pane, setting a relationship between product IDs (see the relationship line connecting the Product_ID fields in the two tables), and setting a criterion of 1004 in one table and a criterion of NOT 1004 in the other table that will return product ID and quantity

Figure 10-14
Example recursive join:
What orders have the same
products as order 1004?

(a) MS-Access97 recursive
join from Pine Valley Furniture

(b) MS-Access97 dynaset
from recursive join in (a)

values. It can be seen in Figure 10-14b that only product number 8 has been ordered on other orders. Three were ordered on order number 1008 and ten were ordered on order number 1010.

Basing a Query on Another Query

It can be difficult even in QBE to answer a question in a single query. One way to deal with such difficult queries is to break a query into multiple steps, save the query generated to answer a particular step, and then base the next query on the saved query rather than the base tables. Such an approach is sometimes similar to using subqueries in SQL. So, basing a query on another query will allow you to compute values for SUM, COUNT, and so on using the dynaset generated by the saved query, thus solving some of the difficulties inherent in using functions with groups of records discussed in Chapter 9.

Suppose you want to find those customers who did not buy anything from Pine Valley Furniture during October 1998. That is, you want to know what customer numbers from records in the Customer_t table are not listed in the records of the Order_t table for October 1998. Figures 10-15 through 10-18 show you how you would answer this question by building one query and then building a second query that uses the first query. The first query (QBE in Figure 10-15 and dynaset result in Figure 10-16) returns the customers who placed orders in October. The QBE for this query was saved in a query named First Query. The second query (QBE in Figure 10-17 and dynaset result in Figure 10-18) then uses an outer join to compare the list of all customers (table Customer_t) with those who placed orders (the virtual table defined by First Query) and returns a dynaset with only those customers who are not found (see the Is Null qualification) in the dynaset from the first query.

Figure 10-15
MS-Access97 base query to be used for next query in Figure 10-17

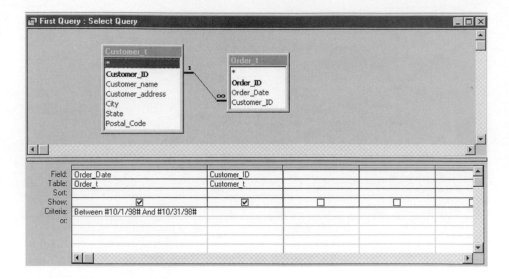

Figure 10-16
MS-Access97 dynaset returned by Figure 10-15 query

Access97 Query Types

All of the Access97 queries illustrated in this chapter have been *select* queries, as were many of the queries illustrated in Chapter 9. However, Access97 supports five other types of queries as well: *SQL, Total, Action, Crosstab,* and *Top(n)* queries. Each type is discussed below.

Most obvious is the fact that Access97 supports *SQL queries*—the conversion of *select* queries to SQL syntax was shown in Figure 10-9. While it is not obvious when using the graphical data definition screens to define a table, as illustrated in Figure 10-4, it is also possible to use *data definition queries* phrased in Access SQL to create, alter, or drop tables and indexes. In addition, there are two types of SQL queries that cannot be represented using Access97's QBE interface. These are *union* and *pass-through* queries. *Union queries* allow the merging of tables that have compatible fields. The union requires that the structure of the tables being combined be identical; that is, each table must have the same columns in the same order in order to combine them. *Pass-through queries* are widely used when Access97 is used as a front-end development tool and attached to a back-end DBMS such as SQL Server or Oracle. These queries send SQL commands directly to the back-end DBMS and must use the syntax of the back-end DBMS rather than Access SQL syntax. Be careful, pass-through queries cannot be converted to other types of queries.

Total queries can be used when one or more of the aggregate functions (average, count, maximum, minimum, and so forth) are needed in a query. To build a total

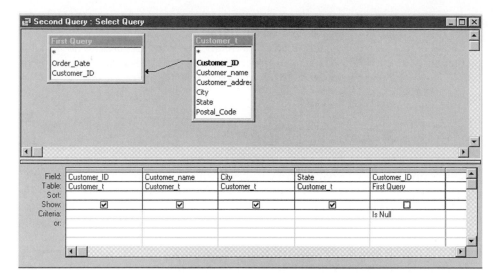

Figure 10-17
MS-Access97 query based
on Figure 10-15 query

Figure 10-18
MS-Access97 dynaset
returned by Figure 10-17
query

query, open a row labeled Total in the QBE pane and select the desired aggregate function from a dropdown list. Totals can also be calculated for groups of records by selecting the Group By option in the Sort row along with the desired aggregate function in the Total row. Applying aggregate functions to groups of records within a column like this is often referred to as establishing control breaks. Records to be used in a total query can be further limited by setting criteria that will return only those records with the desired values.

Crosstab queries are a special type of total query. They are very useful for displaying summarized data, presenting it in a spreadsheet-like format. Each dimension of the dynaset returned from a crosstab query will be grouped by the values of the attributes that are being summarized in the query. For example, a query whose result gives types of customers by state could be created.

Action queries are used to accomplish four specific tasks: creating a new table from the results of a query, deleting specified records from a table or group of tables, appending records from one table to another table, or updating information in a group of records. Action queries cannot be reversed once they execute, because they change, add, or delete data. Therefore, it is especially important to test the query against a test set of data before running the query against production data. Also, a backup of the tables that will be affected by the query should exist before the query is run.

Top(n) queries return only the first *n* rows of a query. This can be very useful when the user is only interested in displaying the best or worst records in a table. To achieve this, create a query that will sort the results so that the desired records are listed first. Then click the sum (Σ) button on the toolbar, click on the combo box next to the Σ button and select or enter a value in the Top Values property cell. Now the query result will display the designated n records.

Each of the query types described has a distinctive icon associated with it that is displayed with the query name in the query windowpane. Once the user becomes familiar with these icons, it is easy to tell at a glance the nature of the query.

BUILDING A CLIENT APPLICATION

Most information systems require easy-to-use menus, input screens, and specialized reports with a variety of summary data and data formatting. Building a client application involves designing a user interface that is as easy to use and as useful as possible. The user interface with most information systems is through customized data entry and display screens (or forms) and printed reports. We illustrated some simple forms and reports in Chapter 1, so you probably have a general feel for such features.

A major trend in information systems has been the transition from character-based user interfaces to graphical, or GUI, user interfaces. This trend has affected both user interfaces and programming principles. In the database arena the trend has resulted in new database systems, such as Access97, being developed using object-oriented concepts. Most traditional industrial strength RDBMSs have at least added GUI tools that create a GUI-based overlay to the original product. Oracle, for example, has the Developer/2000 and Designer/2000 tools, both of which provide GUI interfaces for database design and development.

Application Menus

Up to this point we have concentrated on the salient capabilities of the data retrieval and maintenance commands present in RDBMSs. Primarily, we illustrated the data manipulation commands for single and multiple table operations in both SQL and QBE. This knowledge is very helpful for writing ad hoc, or interactive, data manipulation commands, and for writing programs for processing a database. Using only these query languages, however, you cannot utilize highly stylized screens and reports. Producing the screens and reports requires programming to define the form, report, or menu and its behavior. Current RDMBSs include **code generators** to facilitate screen, report, and menu design. A code generator is a module of a RDBMS that helps you to design an object—screen, report, or menu—and then automatically produces the program instructions required to create the object.

Code generator: A module of a RDBMS that produces the program instructions that define a form, report, or menu. A code generator usually builds these instructions from a visual image of the object drawn by the designer of the object.

Menus are a special form that allows you to tie together the objects of your database application. In Access97, the main menu form is referred to as a switchboard. The switchboard contains user-defined command buttons that establish the behavior of the application for each button that is clicked. It is possible to construct a hierarchy of switchboards. For example, it is possible to create a Print Reports button on the primary switchboard and link it to a subswitchboard that contains buttons linked to each common report required by the application. Access97 contains over 40 macro actions. Each macro is a stored module of VBA code that can be attached to objects and run when the correct events occur. So, for example, clicking on a Print Report button causes the OpenReport or PrintOut macro attached to the button to run, printing out the report. Figures 10-19 and 10-20 show the main switchboard for the example Pine Valley Furniture prototype and the *autoexec* macro attached to the switchboard form. For each Access97 database, one macro named *autoexec* may be

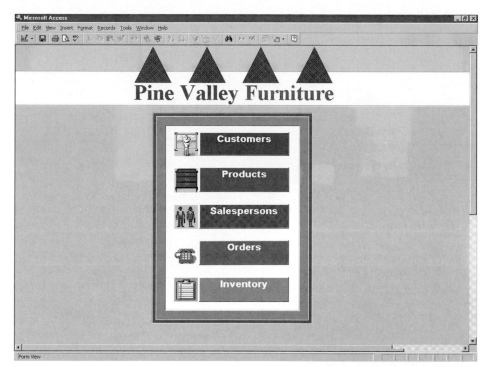

Figure 10-19
Pine Valley Furniture main
switchboard

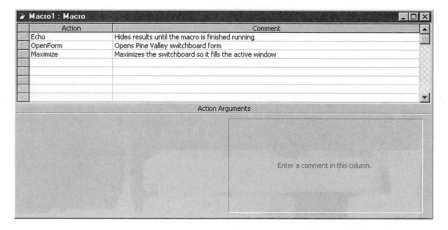

Figure 10-20
The autoexec macro used to
open the Pine Valley Furniture
switchboard

created. This macro will run automatically when the prototype is opened. Usually the main switchboard is opened as part of the autoexec macro, thus causing the main menu to be presented on the screen rather than the database window.

Form Development

Applications also need data entry forms for adding new data or for editing or inspecting existing records. Again, Access97 has two views for forms: Design view and Form view. Design view is the behind-the-scenes view, where the developer designs the look of the form and sets up the properties of the objects (data fields,

Figure 10-21
MS-Access97 Form view for
new product data entry at
Pine Valley Furniture

labels, buttons, etc.) that are placed on the form. Form view is the view that the user
will see and use when the application is complete. Figures 10-21 and 10-22 illustrate
these two views for a form that allows inspection and updating of existing products
and the addition of new products to the product table. Figure 10-22 also shows the
Toolbox toolbar in the lower right corner, which contains icons that lead to utilities to
help construct buttons, drop down lists, and so forth for the form. In the upper right-

Figure 10-22
MS-Access97 Design view
for new product data entry
form at Pine Valley Furniture

hand corner the properties box for the unit price field of the product table is shown. The format properties are displayed, showing that the unit price will be stored as a currency data type, decimal places will be automatically determined, the box and label will always be visible, and so on. Each object on the form has properties associated with it that can be adjusted in the properties box for that object.

Although not shown here, it is also possible to have forms inside forms. In this way, data from several related tables can be displayed on the same screen. Also, forms may have multiple pages, if the content of the form would make one screen too cluttered.

Report Development

The Access Report Wizard can be used to create a report based on a single table or dynaset. It allows you to create a simple report quickly but gives little control over field type or placement. Often, developers use the Wizard to mock up the report quickly and then modify it. It is also possible to start with a blank workspace and develop the report from scratch. A report can be viewed in Design view, Layout Preview, and Print Preview modes.

Access97 follows the banded report design common to other RDBMSs such as Paradox. A report is divided into *bands* or *sections*. Figure 10-23 labels typical Report Writer sections on a Pine Valley report. Figure 10-24 shows the Report Design window. Access97 report sections are these:

- *Report header*   Information included in this section will print only once, at the top of the first page of the report.

- *Page header*   Information included in this section is printed once at the top of each page.

Figure 10-23
MS-Access97 Report Writer sections illustrated on a Pine Valley Report

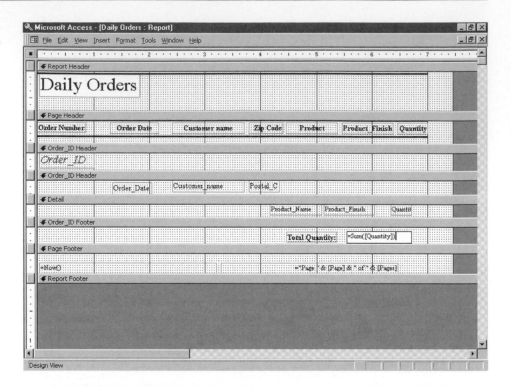

- *Group header*   Information included in this section is printed before the first record of a group is printed as part of the Detail section.

- *Detail*   Information included in this section will be each record included in the table being presented, or each record returned in the dynaset from a query or queries.

- *Group footer*   Information included in this section is printed after the last detail record of a group is printed.

- *Page footer*   Information included in this section is printed once at the bottom of each page.

- *Report footer*   Information included in this section prints once, at the end of the report, after all records have been processed and presented.

It is important to remember that a report is a way to view the records of a table or to view the records that have been returned by a query based on one or more tables. Reports based on more than one table require a query that joins the involved tables and returns the desired records. These records may be selected and ordered by the query. Calculations, such as determining sales tax for an invoice, may be performed in Report Design View by placing the required expression in the appropriate section of the report.

All of the activities described above, including query, menu, form, and report building, can be combined to create an application prototype. It is likely that the final application will need to have some of its components, particularly macros, converted to VBA modules in order to create an application that will be robust in a production environment.

USING OLE, COM, AND ActiveX CONTROLS FOR DATABASE ACCESS

Although the Object Management Group (composed of vendors active in developing object-oriented tools and applications) has created object standards that allow the interoperation of objects across different systems and platforms, Microsoft's **Object Linking and Embedding (OLE)**, **Component Object Model (COM)**, and **ActiveX** specifications have become the de facto standard for establishing interoperability in the Microsoft Windows operating system environment.

Microsoft originally developed OLE as a language-independent binary standard for object sharing (North, 1997). OLE provides interoperability among software components and applications, regardless of programming language or hardware platform. COM provides the underlying infrastructure that permits this object sharing across applications and platforms. COM handles the basic services required to manage the objects, such as memory management, error handling, interface negotiation, and interprocess communication. ActiveX refers to software that provides connectivity using Internet and Web technology. Projects are now underway to allow users to move data among applications such as Lotus Notes, Excel, and SQL databases without coding.

Several terms and many acronyms are associated with OLE. First, an entity that contains linked or embedded objects is called a **container**. Container applications include objects from more than one source application. These objects are identified by OLE object and interface identifiers, which are stored in the Windows registry. Each interface and each object class have a globally unique identifier (GUII), and a class identifier (CLSID) for every standard object class or an interface identifier (IID) for every standard interface.

OLE puts the file to be linked or embedded into the container, along with information about what source program needs to be used to access that file. If both the source program and the container program are OLE compliant, they do not need to know anything else about the other. When a file is linked, the current copy of it will be accessed and displayed as needed. When a file is embedded, the file is brought into the container program and will contain the information stored in the file at the moment that it was embedded, rather than containing the current copy of the file. Linking will keep the size of the container program as small as possible because the object is not added to the container program, but the link must be maintained so the linked object remains available. Embedded objects are always available when needed in the container program, but the object will not be automatically updated and the size of the container program will increase rapidly as multiple objects are embedded.

OLE and ActiveX support **dynamic binding**, which allows determining at run time what functions an interface provides. This happens when the container program accesses the source program, using an interface called Iunknown. If both programs support the interface, Iunknown provides a standard function called QueryInterface, which determines the objects, methods, and properties the source program supports. Thus, OLE and ActiveX provide a standard way to determine the interface to the source program.

Most database applications use a call-level interface (CLI) where the database services functions are kept in a separate library. Some RDBMSs accomplish OLE-based database access by creating an object layer that encapsulates a DBMS CLI (North, 1997). Oracle, Sybase, and SQL Server all take this approach. Microsoft Access uses Data Access Objects (DAO) and ODBCDirect (formerly Remote Data Objects, RDO), which allow system-level data sharing across a variety of databases. The newest element of Microsoft's enterprise OLE strategy is OLE DB, which is intended

Object Linking and Embedding (OLE): A language-independent binary standard for object sharing which provides interoperability among software components and applications, regardless of programming language or hardware platform.

Component Object Model (COM): The infrastructure that underlies OLE and handles the basic services required to manage the objects, such as memory management, error handling, interface negotiation, and interprocess communication.

ActiveX: Software that provides connectivity using Internet and Web technology.

Container: An entity that contains linked or embedded objects.

Dynamic binding: Determining what functions an interface provides at the time it is needed during execution of a program.

to integrate data from different sources, such as SQL databases, legacy databases, and even spreadsheets and project plans.

There are five methods of retrieving data from the server when using MS-Access as a front end to an SQL-based DBMS such as Oracle, Sybase, or SQL Server (Litwin, Getz, and Gilbert, 1997):

- The server may be used as a file server.

- Linked ODBC (Open Database Connectivity) tables may be used. A Microsoft-sponsored standard for database connectivity, ODBC is widely used when connecting Access as a front end to an SQL-based DBMS.

- Jet Data Access Objects (DAO) may be used (ODBC without linked tables).

- SQL pass-through queries may be used.

- ODBCDirect may be used.

Figure 10-25 contrasts these methods visually. Using the server as a *file server* involves moving the Access database to a network server's hard drive. No processing is done on the server—instead the Jet database engine running on the client workstation does the database processing. The Jet database engine is included with Access. This method results in heavy network traffic as the data is moved from the server to the client for all database processing.

Using *Open Database Connectivity (ODBC)* involves the Jet database engine translating the Access queries into a universal SQL dialect that is passed to the ODBC manager, a software component resident on the client workstation. The ODBC manager identifies the correct database server driver and hands the universal SQL statement to the ODBC driver. The ODBC driver translates each query into the SQL appropriate for the SQL server and sends the query to the SQL server, which accesses the SQL database and processes the query. The query result is returned to the client workstation. Since only the SQL query and its final result need to pass between client and server, network traffic is greatly reduced. It is also possible to use ODBC and *Jet Data Access Objects (DAO),* using the ODBC connection information and having Jet open the server database directly. Establishing the data connection in this manner generates heavier overhead loads, however.

SQL pass-through queries require that the SQL dialect understood by the intended SQL database be used when constructing the queries using the Access front end. These queries are then passed through to the SQL server with no translation occurring. This method is popular because eliminating the need to parse the queries into universal SQL and then into the specific SQL database syntax improves the performance of the application. Pass-through queries are also useful if the developer wishes to take advantage of an SQL capability available on the SQL database that does not translate across universal SQL accurately.

ODBCDirect is an alternative approach that sends queries to the database server using an extension to the Jet DAO object model, as mentioned previously. Since this method also results in sending queries directly to the server, performance gains can be realized. To maintain compatibility with DAO, ODBCDirect allows to paths to the database, the Database object, and the Connection object. The Connection object can run asynchronous objects and create temporary QueryDef objects, which are stored queries maintained in the Jet database. The Database object is more compatible with the Jet path (Vaughn, 1997). The actual code used to establish the connections is straightforward. Here is sample code from Vaughn (1997, p. 330) that opens both Connection and Database objects when connecting Access to SQL Server using ODBCDirect:

Figure 10-25
Using MS-Access as a front
end to SQL-based DBMSs
(adapted from Litwin, Getz,
and Gilbert, 1997, p. 917)

```
dim dbs as database
dim cnn as connection

    set dbs = OpenDatabase(" ", _
        dbDriverRequired, false, _
        "ODBC;dsn=DBSer;database=pubs;uid=sa;pwd=pass;")

    set cnn = OpenConnection (" ". _
        dbDriverNoPrompt, false _
        "ODBC;dsn=DBSer;database=pubs;uid=sa;pwd=pass;")
```

where *dsn* stands for data source name, *database* is the database to be connected to, *uid*
is the user's ID, and *pwd* is the user's password. Similar commands are used for
establishing connections to other databases through ODBC.

EMBEDDING SQL IN PROGRAMS

In Chapter 9 we used the interactive, or direct, form of SQL. In that case, one SQL command is entered and executed at a time. It constitutes a logical unit of work, or transaction. The commands necessary to maintain a valid database, such as ROLLBACK

and COMMIT, are transparent to the user in most interactive SQL situations. Another form of SQL is widely used in creating applications on both clients and servers; it is referred to as embedded SQL. SQL commands are embedded into 3GLs (Third Generation Languages) such as Ada, COBOL, C, Fortran, M, Pascal, or PL/I by placing them at appropriate locations in a 3GL host program. Oracle also offers PL/SQL, or Procedural Language SQL, a proprietary language that extends SQL by adding some procedural language features such as variables, types, control structures (including IF-THEN-ELSE loops), functions, and procedures. PL/SQL blocks of code can also be embedded in 3GL programs.

There are several reasons to consider embedding SQL in a 3GL. The first is the possibility of creating a more flexible, accessible interface for the user. Using interactive SQL effectively requires a good understanding of both SQL and the database structure, understanding the typical application user may not have. While many of the RDBMSs come with form, report, and application generators (or such capabilities are available as add-ons), developers frequently envision capabilities that are not easily accomplished with these tools but that can be easily accomplished using a 3GL. Large, complex programs that require access to a relational database may best be programmed in a 3GL, with embedded SQL calls to an SQL database.

Also, it may be possible to improve performance by using embedded SQL. Using interactive SQL requires that each query be converted to executable machine code each time the query is processed. Or, the query optimizer, which runs automatically in a direct SQL situation, may not successfully optimize the query, causing it to run slowly. With embedded SQL the developer has more control of database access and may be able to create significant performance improvements. Knowing when to rely on the SQL translator and optimizer and when to control it through the program depends on the nature of the problem, and making this tradeoff is best accomplished through experience and testing.

A third reason to use embedded SQL would be to improve database security. Restricted access can be achieved by a DBA through the GRANT and REVOKE permissions in SQL, and by creating views. These same restrictions can also be invoked in the embedded SQL application, thus providing another layer of protection. Complex data integrity checks may be more easily accomplished, including cross-field consistency checks.

A program that is using embedded SQL will consist of the *host* program written in a 3GL such as C or COBOL, but there will also be sections of SQL code sprinkled throughout. Each section of SQL code will begin with EXEC SQL, keywords used to indicate an embedded SQL command that will be converted to the host source code when run through the precompiler. You will need a separate precompiler for each host language that you plan to use. Be sure to determine that the 3GL compiler is compatible with your RDBMS's precompiler for each language. Figure 10-26 shows the steps that an embedded SQL program goes through as it is processed.

When the precompiler encounters an EXEC SQL statement, it will translate that SQL command into the host program language. Some, but not all, precompilers will check for correct SQL syntax and generate any required error messages at this point. Others will not generate an error message until the SQL statement actually attempts to execute. Some products' precompilers (DB2, SQL/DS, Ingres) create a separate file of SQL statements that is then processed by a separate utility called a binder, which determines that the referenced objects exist, that the user possesses sufficient privileges to run the statement, and the processing approach that will be used. Other products (Oracle, Informix) interpret the statements at run time rather than compiling

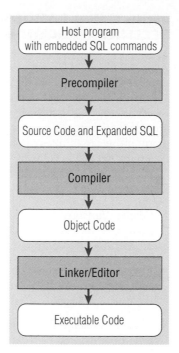

Figure 10-26
Processing an embedded SQL program

them. In either case, the resulting program will contain calls to DBMS routines and the link/editor programs will link them in.

Here is a simple example using C as the host language that will give an idea of what embedded SQL looks like in a program. This example uses a prepared SQL statement, named 'getcust', which will be compiled and stored as executable code in the database. Cust_ID is the primary key of the customer table. Getcust, the prepared SQL statement, returns customer information (c_name, c_address, city, state, postcode) for an order number. A placeholder is used for the order information, which is an input parameter. Customer information is output from the SQL query and stored into host variables using the into-clause. This example assumes that only one tuple is returned from the query.

```
exec sql prepare getcust from
   "select c_name, c_address, city, state, postcode
    from customer_t, order_t
    where customer_t.cust_id = order_t.cust_id and order_id = ?";
   .
   .
   ./* code to get proper value in theOrder */
exec sql execute getcust into :c_name, :c_address, :city, :state,
:postcode using theOrder;
   .
   .
   .
```

If a prepared statement returns multiple tuples, it is necessary to write a program loop using cursors to return a tuple at a time to be stored. Cursors help to eliminate the impedance mismatch between SQL's set-at-a-time processing and procedural languages' record-at-a-time processing.

USING VISUAL BASIC FOR APPLICATIONS (VBA) IN CLIENT APPLICATIONS

Visual Basic for Applications (VBA): The programming language that accompanies Access97.

Access97 allows the novice user to create a prototype of an application, including the database design, menus, forms, and reports. However, there is a limit to what can be accomplished by using the Access macros and the developer is going to be stymied when attempting to include all desired capabilities. While some capabilities require macros, and cannot be accomplished through **Visual Basic for Applications (VBA)**, many more capabilities can be accomplished or enhanced by using VBA in conjunction with Access97. Here are some of the reasons that the Access97 user will want to learn VBA once basic familiarity with Access97 has been achieved (Smith and Sussman, 1997):

- *Complex functionality* can only be accomplished by using VBA. Displaying your own error messages, graying out buttons when they shouldn't be clicked, and so on require VBA coding.

- *Error handling* can only be accomplished by using VBA. Relying on macros in a finished application is dangerous because there is no way for the user to recover if a macro crashes.

- *Faster execution* will be achieved when the application uses VBA modules rather than macros. Code executes faster than macros; this benefit will be more noticeable the larger and more complex the application becomes.

- *Maintenance* is easier because VBA modules are stored with the forms and reports. Macros are stored separately from their related forms and reports. Moving the application to another database will be easier because the VBA modules will move with their forms and reports, since they are stored with them.

- *OLE automation* can be used more completely.

- *More programmatic control* can be achieved by using VBA. Macros cannot pass variables as parameters for another variable and cannot easily control action sequencing.

- *Reading* VBA code is easier than reading macro arguments because you can see the entire module in the Full Module View, which has color-coded text.

An autoexec macro must be created to open a database and macros must also be used to trap certain keystrokes in applications. Beyond that, converting a prototype from macros to VBA modules for a production version of the application will result in a more robust application with more capabilities.

Event-driven: Nonprocedural programming that detects an event when it occurs and generates an appropriate response to that event.

The Windows operating system and Windows applications are **event-driven**. Everything that happens in an Access97 application is a response to an event, such as a mouse click, that Access97 has detected. An event occurs, it is detected, and a response to the event is generated. Thus, Access97 is not procedural—the next event can come from anywhere on the interface screen or from any key on the keyboard. Programming in an event-driven environment consists of creating objects and modifying their properties so they will behave as the programmer wishes for each event that affects the object.

Figure 10-27 shows VBA code that makes the NEXT button on the Product Entry Form disable itself (turn gray) when a new record is displayed. The records for the form come from the Product_t table. Product_ID is the primary key of that table. The value of the current record's Product_ID is determined using Me.Product_ID. If there is no primary key value for the current record, it must be a new record, and the

Figure 10-27
Sample VBA module

NEXT button should be disabled. Because disabling the button that has the focus will cause a run-time error, the focus must first be shifted elsewhere. The focus is shifted to the PREVIOUS button and then the NEXT button is disabled. If the current record is not a new record, the NEXT button remains enabled.

BUILDING INTERNET DATABASE SERVERS

Attaching a database to the Internet or an intranet involves the same logic and processes. An **intranet** is a local network, usually safe within an organizational firewall, that uses HTML technology such as HTTP or FTP protocols. Most database management systems are developing features that make connecting their database to the Internet or an intranet easier. The tools discussed here are available in early 1998; you should investigate new tool availability when you look to attach your first database to the Internet.

Before attempting to connect a database to the Internet, the reader should be familiar with some tools, including **HyperText Markup Language (HTML)**, **Web browsers**, and Web servers (Rowe, 1996). HTML is a simple language used to format documents, link to other Web pages, and communicate between Web browsers wherever they are located. HTML began as a standard that, if followed, results in a document that appears to be the same regardless of the Web browser used. As competition among the browsers, particularly Microsoft Explorer and Netscape, has heated up, each browser has developed nonstandard HTML extensions that do not work on competitors' browsers. While a browser ignores a tag or symbol that it doesn't understand, the tendency to develop nonstandard extensions may erode the usefulness of HTML. Including detailed information about HTML is beyond the scope of this book, but it is highly recommended that any database student make it a point to become familiar with HTML.

One feature of HTML must be discussed here, however: the **HTML form**. It is the HTML form that allows a user to enter information into a Web page and then pass that information on to another page, or to an external program to be processed using the Common Gateway Interface (CGI). Thus, the HTML form is very useful for setting up the criteria for a database select query or for inserting or updating data in a database. Forms have various input formats, such as text boxes, check boxes, radio buttons, pick lists, and pull-down menus.

Intranet: A local network that uses HTML technology such as HTTP or FTP protocols.

HyperText Markup Language (HTML): A simple language used to format documents, link to other Web pages, and communicate between Web browsers.

Web browser: Software that provides the GUI used to display Web site pages and locates those pages and sites on request.

HTML form: An HTML feature that allows a user to enter information into a Web page and then pass that information on to other pages or to an external program such as a database.

Each object of an HTML form is assigned a name when it is created. When the user enters data into the object, that data becomes the value of the object. When the form is submitted to the CGI program, the object name and its value are passed as pairs. These pairs are encoded before they are passed to the CGI program. See Figure 10-28 for a graphic of this process. Since the developer writes the CGI program, it can do whatever is required with the data pairs, reformatting them for insertion into a database or an e-mail message, or whatever is desired.

Web browsers are used to provide the GUI interface and to display the pages. Text, images, sounds, and videos may be automatically recognized and displayed or played when the page loads. Other formats for images, sounds, and videos may also be included, but they require additional external software to process them. Web browsers locate HTML documents by using the Uniform Resource Locator (URL), which indicates on where the document is stored. Web pages are located through the http protocol, while files to be downloaded may be located through a file transfer protocol (ftp).

Web servers are often generic PCs that have a small set of security functions built in. These security functions regulate access to directories and the files resident in those directories. Attempts to access protected directories will result in the Web server requiring username and password verification. A secure Web server also encrypts all messages that pass between the Web server and the user's Web browser, thus reducing the chance that the information can be read while it is being transmitted. Secure Web servers have been an essential part of developing commerce on the Internet because customers have been reluctant to send sensitive information, such as credit card numbers, over the Internet.

Many languages can be used for CGI programming. Three common ones are Unix shell scripts, C, or Perl (Rowe, 1996). Web-enabling capabilities built into DBMSs and authoring programs can make connecting a database to the Internet possible even for nonprogrammers. Cold Fusion is an example of such a program that is currently in fairly wide use. Cold Fusion uses Cold Fusion Markup Language (CFML) as its programming language, which is similar to HTML. For example, the markup tag

Figure 10-28
Calling a CGI program from a Web browser (adapted from Rowe, 1996)

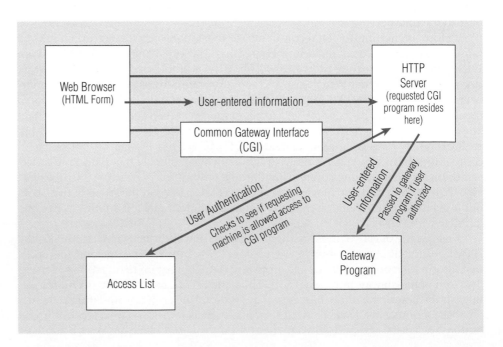

DBQUERY includes Name, Datasource, and SQL as its attributes. This is the tag you will need to send a database query to the database application.

If your Web server has Microsoft's Internet Information Server (IIS) or the ActiveX server installed, use the built-in Web capabilities of Access97 to attach an Access database to the Web. The feature called Publish to the Web Wizard walks the user through selecting the objects wished to be accessible on the Web. Any table, query, form, or report may be selected. One can also develop an HTML template that will be used to provide consistency in Web presentations. If the ActiveX server is used, an ActiveX server page with an .asp extension will be created rather than an .html file.

If it is desired that users be able to see current updated information from the database rather than static stored information, it is necessary to use dynamic HTML. In this case, the system or file data source must be defined and the Access database copied to the Web server, or the database's network location must be defined. Also, the Microsoft Access Desktop Driver should be installed on the Web server, and the folder that contains the dynamic (.idc or .asp) files must have correct permissions set so that users can log on to the ODBC data source for your database and execute the proper scripts. Again, the details of this are beyond the scope of this chapter.

Since Microsoft's IIS has built-in connections to any ODBC database, it can also be used to connect Oracle databases to the Internet. IIS is standard on Windows NT 4.0 and includes Internet Database Connection (IDC) that will access any ODBC-compliant database engine. Again, Web-enabled development packages, such as Spider Technology's NetDynamics, can also be used. These packages are relatively new and are constantly changing, so be sure to look for the latest in this area before committing to a package.

SUMMARY

Current desktop RDBMS products cover a broad range of sophistication, from products suitable for novices to products suitable for professional database developers. Some products are used as a front end attached to more powerful back-end database engines because they are easier to use. Five currently popular desktop RDBMSs include Alpha Five, FileMaker Pro, Paradox, Approach, and Access.

Part of the popularity of the desktop RDBMSs stems from their use of Query-by-Example (QBE) interfaces. QBE provides a visual programming environment commonly used for the development of queries. There is no standard for QBE, so the interfaces differ among the products, but most utilize a data model approach combined with a spreadsheet layout for the result. The Microsoft Access97 QBE interface uses this spreadsheet layout extensively, including for table and query definition, and establishing data relationships.

Defining the tables and building the necessary queries does not result in a completed prototype of the application. Rather, the developer needs to glue the pieces together by building menus for navigation, data entry screens, and reports. In Access97, one *autoexec* macro can be created that runs automatically when the prototype is opened and performs all the desired actions associated with opening the application. Forms for data entry also need to be built, as do reports. It is important to understand that Access97 reports use a *banding* concept, including the report header, page header, group header, detail, group footer, page footer, and report footer bands.

Microsoft's strategies for establishing interoperability in the Microsoft Windows operating system environment include the Component Object Model (COM), which handles the basic service required to manage the objects. Object Linking and Embedding (OLE) overlays COM and provides interoperability among software components and applications, regardless of programming language or hardware platform. ActiveX refers to software that provides connectivity using Internet and Web technology. Both OLE and ActiveX support dynamic binding, which allows determining at run time what functions an interface provides.

Many applications embed SQL in a third-generation host language. This may allow for the creation of a more flexible, accessible user interface. Performance can be improved by embedding SQL. A more secure database can be achieved through embedding SQL in a host language program, also.

The programming language associated with Access97 is Visual Basic for Applications (VBA). Using Access97's macros, which are stored modules of VBA code, works well for prototyping, but building a robust application requires converting these macros to VBA modules. VBA can also be used to accomplish more complex functionality, handle errors, achieve faster execution, easier maintenance, more OLE automation, and more programmatic control.

Attaching a database to the Web requires an understanding of HyperText Markup Language (HTML), particularly HTML forms. These allow a user to enter information into a Web page and then pass that information on to another page, or to an external program to be processed using the Common Gateway Interface (CGI). Common CGI programming languages are Unix shell scripts, C, or Perl. Access97 also has built-in Web capabilities that can be used to attach an Access database to the Web. Microsoft's Internet Information Server (IIS) or its ActiveX server can also be used to attach other databases, such as Oracle, to the Web.

CHAPTER REVIEW

KEY TERMS

ActiveX
code generator
Component Object
    Model (COM)
container
dynamic binding

event-driven
HTML form
HyperText Markup
    Language
    (HTML)
intranet

Object Linking and
    Embedding (OLE)
Query-by-Example (QBE)
Visual Basic for
    Applications (VBA)
Web browser

REVIEW QUESTIONS

1. Define each of the following terms:
   a. ActiveX
   b. Code generator
   c. COM
   d. Container
   e. Dynamic binding
   f. Event-driven
   g. HTML

   h. HTML form
   i. Intranet
   j. OLE
   k. QBE
   l. VBA
   m. Web browser

2. Contrast the following terms:
   a. Object Linking and Embedding (OLE); Common Object Model (COM)
   b. Internet; intranet
   c. Query-by-Example (QBE); line-mode interface

3. Explain the advantages and disadvantages of QBE compared to SQL.

4. What are the components of a system application?

5. How are OLE, COM, OLE-DB and ActiveX controls used to achieve database access from client applications?

6. Why do many applications use embedded SQL?

7. Explain the relationship between Access97 and VBA.

8. Describe the purpose and function of CGI scripts.

PROBLEMS AND EXERCISES

1. Match each of the following terms with the most appropriate definition:

   _____ code generator
   _____ container
   _____ dynamic binding
   _____ event-driven
   _____ HTML form
   _____ OLE
   _____ QBE
   _____ pass-through query

   a. a programming language that involves direct manipulation and is visually oriented
   b. determining what functions an interface provides at the time it is needed during execution of a program
   c. not procedural
   d. a query that uses the syntax of a back-end RDBMS
   e. an entity that contains linked or embedded objects
   f. allows user to enter information into a Web page and passing of that information on to other pages
   g. a module of a RDBMS that produces the program instructions that define a form, report, or menu
   h. standard for object sharing

Problems and Exercises 2–10 are based on the Lakewood College database. Here are the 3NF relations for that application.

STUDENT

STUDENT NO.	STUDENT NAME	MAJOR
38214	Bright	IS
69173	Smith	PM
...	...	...

INSTRUCTOR

INSTRUCTOR NAME	INSTRUCTOR LOCATION
Codd	B 104
Kemp	B 213
Lewis	D 317
…	…

COURSE

COURSE NO.	COURSE TITLE	*INSTRUCTOR NAME*
IS 350	Database	Codd
IS 465	Sys Anal	Kemp
PM 300	Prod Mgt	Lewis
QM 440	Op Res	Kemp
…	…	…

REGISTRATION

STUDENT NO.	COURSE NO.	GRADE
38214	IS 350	A
38214	IS 465	C
69173	IS 465	A
69173	PM 300	B
69173	QM 440	C
…	…	…

2. Develop a full database definition using Access for this database. Assume the following attribute data types:

   STUDENT NO. (integer, primary key)
   STUDENT NAME (25 characters)
   MAJOR (5 characters)
   INSTRUCTOR NAME (25 characters, primary key)
   INSTRUCTOR LOCATION (5 characters)
   COURSE NO. (6 characters, primary key)
   COURSE TITLE (10 characters)
   GRADE (1 character)

3. Develop Access commands for the following:

   a. Validity check on the values of the GRADE field.

   b. Validity check on the format of the COURSE NO. field.

   c. Required value validity checks on all appropriate fields.

4. Before any row can be entered in the REGISTRATION table, the COURSE to be entered must already exist in the COURSE table (referential integrity). Enforce this constraint in Access.

5. Write Access queries for each of the following:
   a. Display the instructor location for the instructor Lewis.
   b. Display the student number and student name for all information systems (IS) majors.
   c. Display the total number of students who are IS majors.

6. Write Access commands to perform the following operations:
   a. Delete all rows for student number 56789 in the REGISTRATION table.
   b. Change the grade for student number 38214 in IS 465 from C to B.

7. Write an Access query to find the minimum grade of all IS majors in IS 465.

8. Write an Access query to find the maximum grade given by each instructor.

9. Create an Access form to enter student registration information.

10. Create a report that shows the grade roster for IS 465.

Problems and Exercises 11–16 are based on the Pine Valley Furniture database.

11. Display the order number, customer number, product number, order date, and order quantity for orders of more than four units of products 3 or 8.

12. Display the customer number, name, and order numbers of all customer orders, and include in this list any customer who has no orders in the database.

13. Write a query that lists all the product descriptions and their associated rooms; include duplicates.

14. Write a query that shows each product and the total quantity ordered for each product, including products that have never been ordered.

15. Display a list of all the products and the number of times each product has been ordered.

16. Display the order number, product number, and order quantity for all customer orders for which the order quantity is greater than the average order quantity of that product. *Hint:* This may require more than one query.

FIELD EXERCISES

1. Locate two similar small businesses in your area that use different computer systems for keeping their records. Compare the functionality and the ease of use of the two systems.

2. Use Access to build a simple application for your own personal use, such as keeping track of your music CDs. After you have created the necessary relations and established their relationships, create at least one data entry form. Also, write any queries necessary to generate the reports you would like to have. Finally, create a menu system and an autoexec macro that opens to the top level of your menu system. Be sure to include navigational aids so that someone else could also use your system easily. Ask a close friend to test your system for ease of use.

3. If you have access to a Web server, create an HTML form for visitors to your site and write a CGI script to pass the information through to your database.

4. Contact a database analyst or systems developer in an organization with which you are familiar. Investigate the use of personal computer and server database systems. What factors are considered in choosing the platform for a database? Does the organization use a mixed platform, in which client-based application modules are written in one language (e.g., QBE) and server application modules are written in another (e.g., SQL)? Why or why not?

REFERENCES

Greenblatt, D., and J. Waxman. 1978. "A Study of Three Database Query Languages." In *Database: Improving Usability and Responsiveness,* ed. B. Schneiderman. New York: Academic Press.

Litwin, P., K. Getz, and M. Gilbert. 1997. Access97 Developer's Handbook. San Francisco: Sybex, Inc.

North, K. 1997. "Understanding OLE." *DBMS* 8:7 (June) 50–51, 54, 56, 60–61, 91.

Robinson. C. 1997. New Products. http://www.pcworld.com/software/database/articles/oct97/1510p128b.html, undated (Accessed January 19, 1998). [From the October 1997 issue of *PC World:* Paradox 8: A Perfect Fit for WordPerfect Suite.]

Rowe, J. 1996. *Building Internet Database Servers with CGI.* Indianapolis: New Riders.

Schneiderman, B. 1983. "Direct Manipulation: A Step Beyond Programming Languages." *IEEE Computer* 16: 57–69.

Smith, R., and Sussman, D. 1997. *Beginning Access97 VBA Programming.* Birmingham, UK: Wrox Press.

Technology Buyer's Guide. 1998. "Digital Entrepreneurs." *Fortune* (Winter): 202–205, 208–210.

Thomas, J. C., and J. D. Gould. 1975. "A Psychological Study of Query by Example." *Proceedings of National Computer Conference.* New York: AFIPS Press.

Vaughn, W. R. 1997. *Hitchhiker's Guide to Visual Basic & SQL Server.* Redmond, WA: Microsoft Press.

Zloof, M. M. 1977. "Query-by-Example: A Data Base Language." *IBM Systems Journal* 16(4): 324–43.

Project Case

Mountain View Community Hospital maintains a small library of current medical journals and books for the use of its healthcare professionals. The library is coordinated by Martha Downes, an administrative assistant in the Patient Records department. Martha is working on an undergraduate degree in business, with a major in management information systems, at the local college. She has recently completed an introductory database course, using Access97 to build a prototype of a hair salon system with three other students in her class. Now she would like to automate the medical library's record-keeping and checkout system, which she has been maintaining manually, also using Access97.

PROJECT QUESTIONS

1. Does it make sense to build this application as a separate, stand-alone application not connected to the rest of Mountain View Hospital's systems?

2. Is Access97 a good choice for a development platform? Assume that her department is already using Access97 for another small departmental system.

3. What advantages can you see to automating the library? What disadvantages?

PROJECT EXERCISES

1. Rough out your idea of what the library system entity-relationship diagram will look like. Your diagram should be able to handle both books and journals, to determine what is checked out and to whom, subscription periods for all journals, and most recent subscription costs.

2. Using Access97 or an RDBMS of your own choosing, define the tables, establish the relationships, and build a simple prototype that would meet Martha's needs.

Distributed Databases

After studying this chapter, you should be able to:

■ Define the following key terms: distributed database, decentralized database, location transparency, synchronous distributed database, asynchronous distributed database, replication transparency, failure transparency, commit protocol, two-phase commit, concurrency transparency, and semijoin.

■ Explain the business conditions that are drivers for the use of distributed databases in organizations.

■ Describe the salient characteristics of the variety of distributed database environments.

■ Explain the potential advantages and risks associated with distributed databases.

■ Explain four strategies for the design of distributed databases, options within each strategy, and the factors to consider in selection among these strategies.

■ State the relative advantages of synchronous and asynchronous data replication and partitioning as three major approaches for distributed database design.

■ Outline the steps involved in processing a query in a distributed database and several approaches used to optimize distributed query processing.

■ Explain the salient features of several distributed database management systems.

INTRODUCTION

When an organization is geographically dispersed, it may choose to store its databases on a central computer or to distribute them to local computers (or a combination of both). A **distributed database** is a single logical database that is spread

> **Distributed database:** A single logical database that is spread physically across computers in multiple locations that are connected by a data communications link.

physically across computers in multiple locations that are connected by a data communications network. We emphasize that a distributed database is truly a database, not a loose collection of files. The distributed database is still centrally administered as a corporate resource while providing local flexibility and customization. The network must allow the users to share the data; thus a user (or program) at location A must be able to access (and perhaps update) data at location B. The sites of a distributed system may be spread over a large area (such as the United States or the world), or over a small area (such as a building or campus). The computers may range from microcomputers to large-scale computers or even supercomputers.

A distributed database requires multiple database management systems, running at each remote site. The degree to which these different DBMSs cooperate, or work in partnership, and whether there is a master site that coordinates requests involving data from multiple sites distinguish different types of distributed database environments.

It is important to distinguish between distributed and decentralized databases. A **decentralized database** is also stored on computers at multiple locations; however, the computers are not interconnected by a network, so that users at the various sites cannot share data. Thus a decentralized database is best regarded as a collection of independent databases, rather than having the geographical distribution of a single database.

Decentralized database:
A database that is stored on computers at multiple locations; however, the computers are not interconnected by a network, so that users at the various sites cannot share data.

Various business conditions encourage the use of distributed databases:

- *Distribution and autonomy of business units*   Divisions, departments, and facilities in modern organizations are often geographically (and possibly internationally) distributed. Often each unit has the authority to create its own information systems, and often these units want local data over which they can have controls.

- *Data sharing*   Even moderately complex business decisions require sharing data across business units, so it must be convenient to consolidate data across local databases on demand.

- *Data communications costs and reliability*   The cost to ship large quantities of data across a communications network or to handle a large volume of transactions from remote sources can be high. It is often more economical to locate data and applications close to where they are needed. Also, dependence on data communications can be risky, so keeping local copies or fragments of data can be a reliable way to support the need for rapid access to data across the organization.

The ability to create a distributed database has existed for over a decade. As you might expect, a variety of distributed database options exist (Bell and Grimson, 1992). Figure 11-1 outlines the range of distributed database environments. These environments are briefly explained by the following:

  I. *Homogeneous*   The same DBMS is used at each node.

    A. *Autonomous*   Each DBMS works independently, passing messages back and forth to share data updates.

    B. *Non-autonomous*   A central, or master, DBMS coordinates database access and update across the nodes.

  II. *Heterogeneous*   Potentially different DBMSs are used at each node.

    A. *Systems*   Supports some or all of the functionality of one logical database.

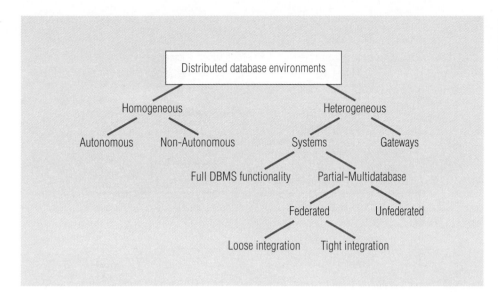

Figure 11-1
Distributed database
environments (adapted from
Bell and Grimson, 1992)

1. *Full DBMS Functionality*   Supports all of the functionality of a distributed database, as discussed in the remainder of this chapter.

2. *Partial-Multidatabase*   Supports some features of a distributed database, as discussed in the remainder of this chapter.

   a. *Federated*   Supports local databases for unique data requests.

      i. *Loose Integration*   Many schemas exist, for each local database, and each local DBMS must communicate with all local schemas.

      ii. *Tight Integration*   One global schema exists that defines all the data across all local databases.

   b. *Unfederated*   Requires all access to go through a central coordinating module.

   B. *Gateways*   Simple paths are created to other databases, without the benefits of one logical database.

A homogeneous distributed database environment is depicted in Figure 11-2. This environment is typically defined by the following characteristics (related to the non-autonomous category described above):

- Data are distributed across all the nodes

- The same DBMS is used at each location

- All data are managed by the distributed DBMS (so there are no exclusively local data)

- All users access the database through one global schema or database definition

- The global schema is simply the union of all the local database schemas

It is difficult in most organizations to force a homogeneous environment, yet heterogeneous environments are much more difficult to manage.

Figure 11-2
Homogeneous distributed
database environment
(adapted from Bell and
Grimson, 1992)

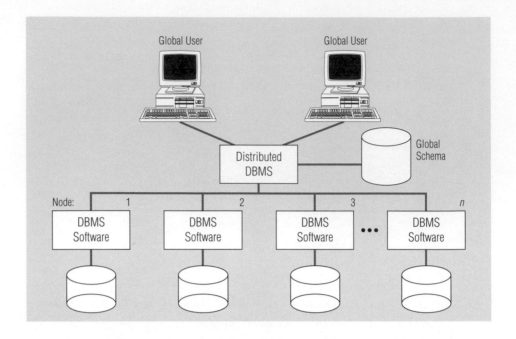

As listed above, there are so many variations of heterogeneous distributed database environments. In the remainder of the chapter, however, a heterogeneous environment will be defined by the following characteristics (as depicted in Figure 11-3):

- Data are distributed across all the nodes.

- Different DBMSs may be used at each node.

Figure 11-3
Heterogeneous distributed
database environment
(adapted from Bell and
Grimson, 1992)

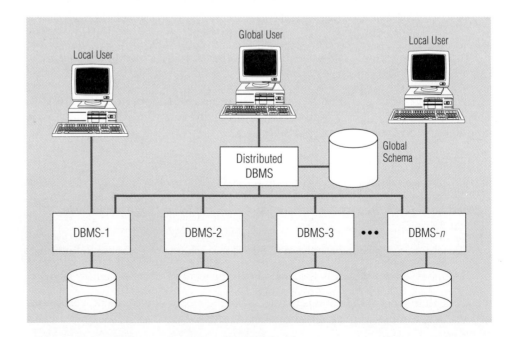

- Some users require only local access to databases, which can be accomplished by using only the local DBMS and schema.

- A global schema exists, which allows local users to access remote data.

Objectives and Trade-offs

A major objective of distributed databases is to provide ease of access to data for users at many different locations. To meet this objective, the distributed database system must provide what is called **location transparency**, which means that a user (or user program) using data for querying or updating need not know the location of the data. Any request to retrieve or update data from any site is automatically forwarded by the system to the site or sites related to the processing request. Ideally, the user is unaware of the distribution of data, and all data in the network appear as a single logical database stored at one site. In this ideal case, a single query can join data from tables in multiple sites as if the data were all in one site.

A second objective of distributed databases is **local autonomy**, which is the capability to administer a local database and to operate independently when connections to other nodes have failed (Date, 1995). With local autonomy, each site has the capability to control local data, administer security, log transactions, and recover when local failures occur, and provide full access to local data to local users when any central or coordinating site cannot operate. In this case, data are locally owned and managed, even though they are accessible from remote sites. This implies that there is no reliance on a central site.

A significant trade-off in designing a distributed database environment is whether to use synchronous or asynchronous distributed technology. With a **synchronous distributed database** technology, all data across the network are continuously kept up-to-date so that a user at any site can access data anywhere on the network at any time and get the same answer. With synchronous technology, if any copy of a data item is updated anywhere on the network, the same update is immediately applied to all other copies or aborted. Synchronous technology ensures data integrity and minimizes the complexity of knowing where the most recent copy of data are located. Synchronous technology can result in unsatisfactorily slow response time since the distributed DBMS is spending considerable time checking that an update is accurately and completely propagated across the network.

Asynchronous distributed database technology keeps copies of replicated data at different nodes so that local servers can access data without reaching out across the network. With asynchronous technology, there is usually some delay in propagating data updates across the remote databases, so some degree of at least temporary inconsistency is tolerated. Asynchronous technology tends to have acceptable response time since updates happen locally and data replicas are synchronized in batches and predetermined intervals, but may be more complex to plan and design to ensure exactly the right level of data integrity and consistency across the nodes.

Compared to centralized databases, there are numerous advantages to either form of a distributed database. The most important are the following:

- *Increased reliability and availability*   When a centralized system fails, the database is unavailable to all users. A distributed system will continue to function at some reduced level, however, even when a component fails. The reliability and availability will depend (among other things) on how the data are distributed (discussed in the following sections).

Location transparency: A design goal for a distributed database, which says that a user (or user program) using data need not know the location of the data.

Local autonomy: A design goal for a distributed database, which says that a site can independently administer and operate its database when connections to other nodes have failed.

Synchronous distributed database: A form of distributed database technology in which all data across the network are continuously kept up-to-date so that a user at any site can access data anywhere on the network at any time and get the same answer.

Asynchronous distributed database: A form of distributed database technology in which copies of replicated data are kept at different nodes so that local servers can access data without reaching out across the network.

- *Local control*   Distributing the data encourages local groups to exercise greater control over "their" data, which promotes improved data integrity and administration. At the same time, users can access nonlocal data when necessary. Hardware can be chosen for the local site to match the local, not global, data processing work.

- *Modular growth*   Suppose that an organization expands to a new location or adds a new work group. It is often easier and more economical to add a local computer and its associated data to the distributed network than to expand a large central computer. Also, there is less chance of disruption to existing users than is the case when a central computer system is modified or expanded.

- *Lower communication costs*   With a distributed system, data can be located closer to their point of use. This can reduce communication costs, compared to a central system.

- *Faster response*   Depending on how data are distributed, most requests for data by users at a particular site can be satisfied by data stored at that site. This speeds up query processing since communication and central computer delays are minimized. It may also be possible to split complex queries into subqueries that can be processed in parallel at several sites, providing even faster response.

A distributed database system also faces certain costs and disadvantages:

- *Software cost and complexity*   More complex software (especially the DBMS) is required for a distributed database environment. We discuss this software later in the chapter.

- *Processing overhead*   The various sites must exchange messages and perform additional calculations to ensure proper coordination among data at the different the sites.

- *Data integrity*   A by-product of the increased complexity and need for coordination is the additional exposure to improper updating and other problems of data integrity.

- *Slow response*   If the data are not distributed properly according to their usage, or if queries are not formulated correctly, response to requests for data can be extremely slow. These issues are discussed later in the chapter.

OPTIONS FOR DISTRIBUTING A DATABASE

How should a database be distributed among the sites (or nodes) of a network? We discussed this important issue of physical database design in Chapter 7, which introduced an analytical procedure for evaluating alternative distribution strategies. In that chapter we noted that there are four basic strategies for distributing databases:

1. Data replication

2. Horizontal partitioning

3. Vertical partitioning

4. Combinations of the above

Figure 11-4
Customer relation for a bank

Acct_Number	Customer_Name	Branch_Name	Balance
200	Jones	Lakeview	1000
324	Smith	Valley	250
153	Gray	Valley	38
426	Dorman	Lakeview	796
500	Green	Valley	168
683	McIntyre	Lakeview	1500
252	Elmore	Lakeview	330

We will explain and illustrate each of these approaches using relational databases. The same concepts apply (with some variations) for other data models, such as hierarchical and network.

Suppose that a bank has numerous branches located throughout a state. One of the base relations in the bank's database is the Customer relation. Figure 11-4 shows the format for an abbreviated version of this relation. For simplicity, the sample data in the relation apply to only two of the branches (Lakeview and Valley). The primary key in this relation is account number (Acct_Number). Branch_Name is the name of the branch where customers have opened their accounts (and therefore where they presumably perform most of their transactions).

Data Replication

An increasingly popular option for data distribution is to store a separate copy of the database at each of two or more sites. Replication may allow an IS organization to move a database off a centralized mainframe onto less expensive, departmental or location-specific servers, close to end users (Koop, 1995). Replication may use either synchronous or asynchronous distributed database technologies, although asynchronous technologies are more typical in a replicated environment. The Customer relation in Figure 11-4 could be stored at Lakeview or Valley, for example. If a copy is stored at every site, we have the case of full replication (which may be impractical except for only relatively small databases).

There are five advantages to data replication:

1. *Reliability* If one of the sites containing the relation (or database) fails, a copy can always be found at another site without network traffic delays. Also, available copies can all be updated as soon as possible as transactions occur, and unavailable nodes will be updated once they return to service.

2. *Fast response* Each site that has a full copy can process queries locally, so queries can be processed rapidly.

3. *Possible avoidance of complicated distributed transaction integrity routines* Replicated databases are usually refreshed at scheduled intervals, so most forms of replication are used when some relaxing of synchronization across database copies is acceptable.

4. *Node decoupling* Each transaction may proceed without coordination across the network. Thus, if nodes are down, busy, or disconnected (e.g., in the case of mobile personal computers), a transaction is handled when the user desires. In

the place of real-time synchronization of updates, a behind-the-scenes process coordinates all data copies.

5. *Reduced network traffic at prime time*   Often updating data happens during prime business hours, when network traffic is highest and the demands for rapid response greatest. Replication, with delayed updating of copies of data, moves network traffic for sending updates to other nodes to non–prime time hours.

Replication has two primary disadvantages:

1. *Storage requirements*   Each site that has a full copy must have the same storage capacity that would be required if the data were stored centrally. Each copy requires storage space (the cost for which is constantly decreasing), and processing time is required to update each copy on each node.

2. *Complexity and cost of updating*   Whenever a relation is updated, it must (eventually) be updated at each site that holds a copy. Synchronizing updating near real time can require careful coordination, as will be clear later under the topic of commit protocol.

For these reasons, data replication is favored where most process requests are read-only and where the data are relatively static, as in catalogs, telephone directories, train schedules, and so on. CD-ROM and DVD storage technology has promise as an economical medium for replicated databases. Replication is used for "noncollaborative data," where one location does not need a real-time update of data maintained by other locations (Thé, 1994). In these applications, data eventually need to be synchronized, as quickly as is practical. Replication is not a viable approach for online applications such as airline reservations, automated teller machine transactions, and other financial activities—applications for which each user wants data about the same, nonsharable resource.

Snapshot Replication   Different schemes exist for updating data copies. Some applications, like those for decision support and data warehousing or mining—which do not require current data—are supported by simple table copying or periodic snapshots. This might work as follows, assuming multiple sites are updating the same data. First, updates from all replicated sites are periodically collected at a master or primary site, where all the updates are made to form a consolidated record of all changes. With some distributed DBMSs, this list of changes is collected in a snapshot log, which is a table of row identifiers for the records to go into the snapshot. Then a read-only snapshot of the replicated portion of the database is taken at the master site. Finally, the snapshot is sent to each site where there is a copy (it is often said that these other sites "subscribe" to the data owned at the primary site). This is called a full refresh of the database (Edelstein, 1995a). Alternatively, only those pages that have changed since the last snapshot can be sent, which is called a differential refresh. In this case, a snapshot log for each replicated table is joined with the associated base to form the set of changed rows to be sent to the replicated sites.

Some forms of replication management allow dynamic ownership of data, in which the right to update replicated data moves from site to site, but at any point in time, only one site owns the right. Dynamic ownership would be appropriate as business activities move across time zones, or where the processing of data follows a work flow across business units supported by different database servers.

A final form of replication management allows shared ownership of data. Shared updates introduces significant issues for managing update conflicts across sites. For example, what if tellers at two bank branches try to update a customer's address at the same time? Asynchronous technology will allow conflicts to exist temporarily. This may be fine as long as the updates are not critical to business operations, and such conflicts can be detected and resolved before real business problems arise.

The cost to perform a snapshot refresh may depend on whether the snapshot is simple or complex. A simple snapshot is one that references all or a portion of only one table. A complex snapshot involves multiple tables, usually from transactions that involve joins (such as the entry of a customer order and associated line items). With some distributed DBMSs, a simple snapshot can be handled by a differential refresh whereas complex snapshots require more time-consuming full refreshes. Some distributed DBMSs support only simple snapshots.

Near Real-Time Replication   For near real-time requirements, store and forward messages for each completed transaction can be broadcast across the network informing all nodes to update data as soon as is possible, without forcing a confirmation to the originating node (as is the case with a coordinated commit protocol, discussed below) before the database at the originating node is updated (Schussel, 1994). One way to generate such messages is by using triggers (discussed in Chapter 9). A trigger can be stored at each local database so that when a piece of replicated data is updated, the trigger executes corresponding update commands against remote database replicas (Edelstein, 1993). With the use of triggers, each database update event can be handled individually and transparently to programs and users. If network connections to a node are down or the node is busy, these messages informing the node to update its database are held in a queue to be processed when possible.

Pull Replication   The schemes explained above for synchronizing replicas are all examples of push strategies. Pull strategies also exist. In a pull strategy, the target, not the source node, controls when a local database is updated. With pull strategies, the local database determines when it needs to be refreshed, and requests a snapshot or the emptying of an update message queue. Pull strategies have the advantage that the local site controls when it needs and can handle updates. Thus, synchronization is less disruptive and occurs only when needed by each site, not when a central master site thinks it is best to update.

Database Integrity with Replication   For both periodic and near real-time replication, consistency across the distributed, replicated database is compromised. Whether delayed or near real-time, the DBMS managing replicated databases still must ensure the integrity of the database. Decision support applications permit synchronization on a table-by-table basis, whereas near real-time applications require transaction-by-transaction synchronization. But in both cases, the DBMS must ensure that copies are synchronized per application requirements.

The difficulty of handling updates with a replicated database also depends on the number of nodes at which updates may occur (Froemming, 1996). In a single-updater environment, updates will usually be handled by periodically sending read-only database snapshots of updated database segments to the nonupdater nodes. In this case the effects of multiple updates are effectively batched for the read-only sites. This would be the situation for product catalogs, price lists, and other reference data for a mobile sales force. In a multiple-updater environment, the most obvious issue is data collisions. Data collisions arise when the independently operating updating nodes are each attempting to update the same data at the same time. In this case, the DBMS must include mechanisms to detect and handle data collisions. For example, the DBMS must decide if processing at nodes in conflict should be suspended until the collision is resolved.

When to Use Replication   Whether replication is a viable alternative design for a distributed database depends on several factors (Froemming, 1996):

1. *Data timeliness*   Applications that can tolerate out-of-date data (whether this be for a few seconds or a few hours) are better candidates for replication.

2. *DBMS capabilities*   An important DBMS capability is whether it will support a query that references data from more than one node. If not, then replication is a better candidate than the partitioning schemes, which are discussed in the following sections.

3. *Performance implications*   Replication means that each node is periodically refreshed. When this refreshing occurs, the distributed node may be very busy handling a large volume of updates. If the refreshing occurs by event triggers (for example, when a certain volume of changes accumulate), refreshing could occur at a time when the remote node is busy doing local work.

4. *Heterogeneity in the network*   Replication can be complicated if different nodes use different operating systems and DBMSs, or, more commonly, use different database designs. Mapping changes from one site to n other sites could mean n different routines to translate the changes from the originating node into the scheme for processing at the other nodes.

5. *Communications network capabilities*   Transmission speeds and capacity in a data communications network may prohibit frequent, complete refreshing of very large tables. Replication does not require a dedicated communications connection, however, so less expensive, shared networks could be used for database snapshot transmissions.

Horizontal Partitioning

With *horizontal partitioning* (see Chapter 7 for a description of different forms of table partitioning), some of the rows of a table (or relation) are put into a base relation at one site, and other rows are put into a base relation at another site. More generally, the rows of a relation are distributed to many sites.

Figure 11-5 shows the result of taking horizontal partitions of the Customer relation. Each row is now located at its home branch. If customers actually conduct most of their transactions at the home branch, the transactions are processed locally and response times are minimized. When a customer initiates a transaction at another branch, the transaction must be transmitted to the home branch for processing and the response transmitted back to the initiating branch (this is the normal pattern for persons using automated teller machines, or ATMs). If a customer's usage pattern changes (perhaps because of a move), the system may be able to detect this change and dynamically move the record to the location where most transactions are being initiated. In summary, horizontal partitions for a distributed database have four major advantages:

1. *Efficiency*   Data are stored close to where they are used and separate from other data used by other users or applications.

2. *Local optimization*   Data can be stored to optimize performance for local access.

Figure 11-5
Horizontal partitions

(a) Lakeview Branch

Acct_Number	Customer_Name	Branch_Name	Balance
200	Jones	Lakeview	1000
426	Dorman	Lakeview	796
683	McIntyre	Lakeview	1500
252	Elmore	Lakeview	330

(b) Valley Branch

Acct_Number	Customer_Name	Branch_Name	Balance
324	Smith	Valley	250
153	Gray	Valley	38
500	Green	Valley	168

3. *Security*   Data not relevant to usage at a particular site are not made available.

4. *Ease of querying*   Combining data across horizontal partitions is easy since rows are simply merged by unions across the partitions.

Thus, horizontal partitions are usually used when an organizational function is distributed, but each site is concerned with only a subset of the entity instances (frequently based on geography).

Horizontal partitions also have two primary disadvantages:

1. *Inconsistent access speed*   When data from several partitions are required, the access time can be significantly different from local-only data access.

2. *Backup vulnerability*   Since data are not replicated, when data at one site become inaccessible or damaged, usage cannot switch to another site where a copy exists; data may be lost if proper backup is not performed at each site.

Vertical Partitioning

With the *vertical partitioning* approach (again, see Chapter 7), some of the columns of a relation are projected into a base relation at one of the sites, and other columns are projected into a base relation at another site (more generally, columns may be projected to several sites). The relations at each of the sites must share a common domain, so that the original table can be reconstructed.

To illustrate vertical partitioning, we use an application for the manufacturing company shown in Figure 11-6. Figure 11-7 shows the Part relation with Part_Number as the primary key. Some of these data are used primarily by manufacturing, while others are used mostly by engineering. The data are distributed to the respective departmental computers using vertical partitioning, as shown in Figure 11-8. Each of the partitions shown in Figure 11-8 is obtained by taking projections (that is, selected columns) of the original relation. The original relation in turn can be obtained by taking natural joins of the resulting partitions.

In summary, the advantages and disadvantages of vertical partitions are identical to those for horizontal partitions, with the exception that combining data across vertical partitions is more difficult than across horizontal partitions. This

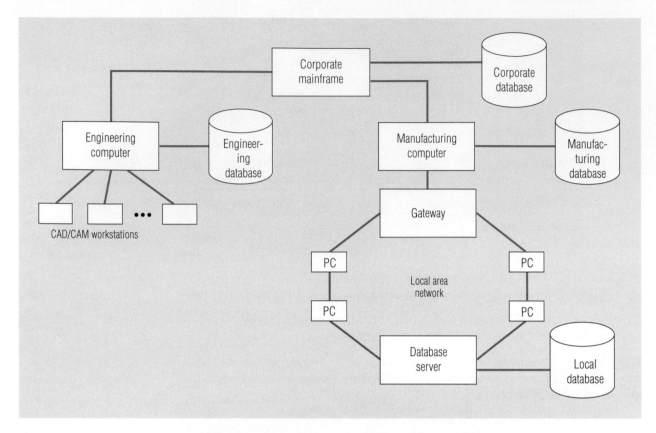

Figure 11-6
Distributed processing system for a manufacturing company

Figure 11-7
Part relation

Part_Number	Name	Cost	Drawing_Number	Qty_on_Hand
P2	Widget	100	123-7	20
P7	Gizmo	550	621-0	100
P3	Thing	48	174-3	0
P1	Whatsit	220	416-2	16
P8	Thumzer	16	321-0	50
P9	Bobbit	75	400-1	0
P6	Nailit	125	129-4	200

difficulty arises from the need to match primary keys or other qualifications to join rows across partitions. Horizontal partitions support an organizational design in which functions are replicated, often on a regional basis, while vertical partitions are typically applied across organizational functions with reasonably separate data requirements.

Figure 11-8 Vertical partitions

(a) Engineering

Part_Number	Drawing_Number
P2	123-7
P7	621-0
P3	174-3
P1	416-2
P8	321-0
P9	400-1
P6	129-4

(b) Manufacturing

Part_Number	Name	Cost	Qty_On_Hand
P2	Widget	100	20
P7	Gizmo	550	100
P3	Thing	48	0
P1	Whatsit	220	16
P8	Thumzer	16	50
P9	Bobbit	75	0
P6	Nailit	125	200

Combinations of Operations

To complicate matters further, there are almost unlimited combinations of the preceding strategies. Some data may be stored centrally, while other data are replicated at the various sites. Also, for a given relation, both horizontal and vertical partitions may be desirable for data distribution. Figure 11-9 is an example of a combination strategy:

1. Engineering Parts, Accounting, and Customer data are each centralized at different locations.

2. Standard parts data are partitioned (horizontally) among the three locations.

3. The Standard Price List is replicated at all three locations.

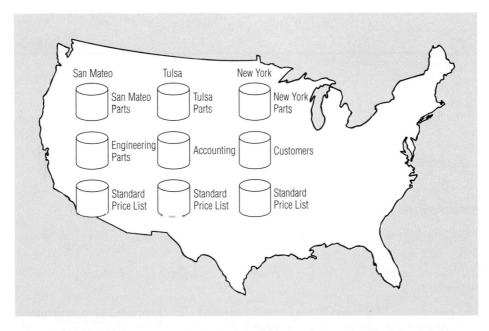

Figure 11-9
Data distribution strategies (Source: Copyright © *Database Programming & Design*, April 1989, Vol. 2, No. 4. Reprinted by permission of Miller Freeman Publications.)

TABLE 11-1   Comparison of Distributed Database Design Strategies

Strategy	Reliability	Expandability	Communications Overhead	Manageability	Data Consistency
Centralized	**POOR:** Highly dependent on central server	**POOR:** Limitations are barriers to performance	**VERY HIGH:** High traffic to one site	**VERY GOOD:** One, monolithic site requires little coordination	**EXCELLENT:** All users always have same data
Replicated with snapshots	**GOOD:** Redundancy and tolerated delays	**VERY GOOD:** Cost of additional copies may be less than linear	**LOW to MEDIUM:** Not constant, but periodic snapshots can cause bursts of network traffic	**VERY GOOD:** Each copy is like every other one	**MEDIUM:** Fine as long as delays are tolerated by business needs
Synchronized replication	**EXCELLENT:** Redundancy and minimal delays	**VERY GOOD:** Cost of additional copies may be low and synchronization work only linear	**MEDIUM:** Messages are constant, but some delays are tolerated	**MEDIUM:** Collisions add some complexity to manageability	**MEDIUM to VERY GOOD:** Close to precise consistency
Integrated partitions	**VERY GOOD:** Effective use of partitioning and redundancy	**VERY GOOD:** New nodes get only data they need without changes in overall database design	**LOW to MEDIUM:** Most queries are local but queries which require data from multiple sites can cause a temporary load	**DIFFICULT:** Especially difficult for queries that need data from distributed tables, and updates must be tightly coordinated	**VERY POOR:** Considerable effort, and inconsistencies not tolerated
Decentralized with independent partitions	**GOOD:** Depends on only local database availability	**GOOD:** New sites independent of existing ones	**LOW:** Little if any need to pass data or queries across the network (if one exists)	**VERY GOOD:** Easy for each site, until there is a need to share data across sites	**LOW:** No guarantees of consistency, in fact pretty sure of inconsistency

The overriding principle in distributed database design is that data should be stored at the sites where they will be accessed most frequently (although other considerations, such as security, data integrity, and cost, are also likely to be important). The data administrator plays a critical and central role in organizing a distributed database in order to make it distributed, not decentralized.

Selecting the Right Data Distribution Strategy

Based on the prior sections, a distributed database can be organized in five unique ways:

1. totally centralized at one location accessed from many geographically distributed sites

2. partially or totally replicated across geographically distributed sites, with each copy periodically updated with snapshots

3. partially or totally replicated across geographically distributed sites, with near real-time synchronization of updates

4. partitioned into segments at different geographically distributed sites, but still within one logical database and one distributed DBMS

5. partitioned into independent, nonintegrated segments spanning multiple computers and database software.

None of these four approaches is always best. Table 11-1 summarizes the comparative features of these five approaches using the key dimensions of reliability, expandability for adding nodes, communications overhead or demand on communications network, manageability, and data consistency. A distributed database designer needs to balance these factors to select a good strategy for a given distributed database environment. The choice of which strategy is best in a given situation depends on several factors.

- *Organizational forces*   funding availability, autonomy of organizational units, and the need for security

- *Frequency and locality or clustering of reference to data*   In general, data should be located close to the applications that use those data.

- *Need for growth and expansion*   The availability of processors on the network will influence where data may be located and applications can be run, and may indicate the need for expansion of the network.

- *Technological capabilities*   Capabilities at each node and for DBMSs, coupled with the costs for acquiring and managing technology, must be considered. Storage costs tend to be low, but the costs for managing complex technology can be great.

- *Need for reliable service*   Mission-critical applications and very frequently required data encourage replication schemes.

DISTRIBUTED DBMS

To have a distributed database, there must be a database management system that coordinates the access to data at the various nodes. We will call such a system a *distributed DBMS*. Although each site may have a DBMS managing the local database at that site, a distributed DBMS is also required to perform the following functions (Elmasri and Navathe, 1989):

1. Keep track of where data are located in a distributed data dictionary.

2. Determine the location from which to retrieve requested data and the location at which to process each part of a distributed query.

3. If necessary, translate the request at one node using a local DBMS into the proper request to another node using a different DBMS and data model, and return data to the requesting node in the format accepted by that node.

4. Provide data management functions such as security, concurrency and deadlock control, query optimization, and failure recovery.

5. Provide consistency among copies of data across the remote sites.

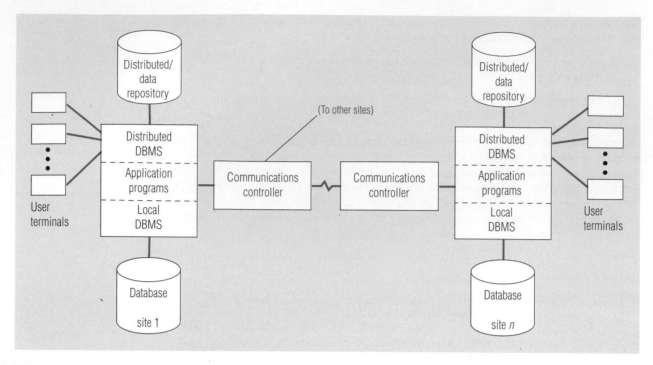

Figure 11-10
Distributed DBMS
architecture

Conceptually, there could be different DBMSs running at each local site, with one master DBMS controlling the interaction across database parts. Such an environment is called a *heterogeneous distributed database,* as defined earlier in the chapter. Although ideal, complete heterogeneity is not practical today; limited capabilities exist with some products when each DBMS follows the same data architecture (for example, relational).

Figure 11-10 shows one popular architecture for a computer system with a distributed DBMS capability. Each site has a local DBMS that manages the database stored at that site. Also, each site has a copy of the distributed DBMS and the associated distributed data dictionary/directory (DD/D). The distributed DD/D contains the location of all data in the network, as well as data definitions. Requests for data by users or application programs are first processed by the distributed DBMS, which determines whether the transaction is local or global. A **local transaction** is one in which the required data are stored entirely at the local site. A **global transaction** requires reference to data at one or more nonlocal sites to satisfy the request. For local transactions, the distributed DBMS passes the request to the local DBMS; for global transactions, the distributed DBMS routes the request to other sites as necessary. The distributed DBMSs at the participating sites exchange messages as needed to coordinate the processing of the transaction until it is completed (or aborted, if necessary). This process may be quite complex, as we will see.

Local transaction: In a distributed database, a transaction that requires reference only to data that are stored at the site where the transaction originates.

Global transaction: In a distributed database, a transaction that requires reference to data at one or more nonlocal sites to satisfy the request.

The DBMS (and its data model) at one site may be different from that at another site; for example, site A may have a relational DBMS, while site B has a network DBMS. In this case, the distributed DBMS must translate the request so that it can be processed by the local DBMS. The capability for handling mixed DBMSs and data models is a state-of-the-art development that is beginning to appear in some commercial DBMS products.

In our discussion of an architecture for a distributed system (Figure 11-10), we assumed that copies of the distributed DBMS and DD/D exist at each site (thus the DD/D is itself an example of data replication). An alternative is to locate the distributed DBMS and DD/D at a central site, and other strategies are also possible. However, the centralized solution is vulnerable to failure and therefore is less desirable.

A distributed DBMS should isolate users as much as possible from the complexities of distributed database management. Stated differently, the distributed DBMS should make transparent the location of data in the network as well as other features of a distributed database. Four objectives of a distributed DBMS, when met, ease the construction of programs and the retrieval of data in a distributed system. These objectives, which are described below, are the following: location transparency, replication transparency, failure transparency, and concurrency transparency. To fully understand failure and concurrency transparency, we also discuss the concept of a commit protocol. Finally, we describe query optimization, which is an important function of a distributed DBMS.

Location Transparency

Although data are geographically distributed and may move from place to place, with *location transparency* users (including programmers) can act as if all the data were located at a single node. To illustrate location transparency, consider the distributed database in Figure 11-9. This company maintains warehouses and associated purchasing functions in San Mateo, California; Tulsa, Oklahoma; and New York City. The company's engineering offices are in San Mateo and sales offices in New York City. Suppose that a marketing manager in San Mateo, California, wanted a list of all company customers whose total purchases exceed $100,000. From a terminal in San Mateo, with location transparency the manager could enter the following request:

```
SELECT *
  FROM CUSTOMER
  WHERE TOTAL_SALES > 100,000;
```

Notice that this SQL request does not require the user to know where the data are physically stored. The distributed DBMS at the local site (San Mateo) will consult the distributed DD/D and determine that this request must be routed to New York. When the selected data are transmitted and displayed in San Mateo, it appears to the user at that site that the data were retrieved locally (unless there is a lengthy communications delay!).

Now consider a more complex request that requires retrieval of data from more than one site. For example, consider the Parts logical file in Figure 11-9, which is geographically partitioned into physically distributed database files stored on computers near their respective warehouse location: San Mateo parts, Tulsa parts, and New York parts. Suppose that an inventory manager in Tulsa wishes to construct a list of orange-colored parts (regardless of location). This manager could use the following query to assemble this information from the three sites:

```
SELECT DISTINCT PART_NUMBER, PART_NAME
  FROM PART
  WHERE COLOR = 'Orange'
  ORDER BY PART_NO;
```

In forming this query, the user need not be aware that the parts data exist at various sites (assuming location transparency) and that therefore this is a global transaction. Without location transparency, the user would have to reference the parts data at each site separately and then assemble the data (possibly using a UNION operation) to produce the desired results.

If the DBMS does not directly support location transparency, a database administrator can accomplish virtual location transparency for users by creating views (see Chapter 9 for a discussion of views in SQL). For the distributed database of Figure 11-9, the following view virtually consolidates part records into one table:

```
CREATE VIEW ALL_PART AS
  (SELECT PART_NUMBER, PART_NAME FROM SAN_MATEO_PART
   UNION
   SELECT PART_NUMBER, PART_NAME FROM TULSA_PART
   UNION
   SELECT PART_NUMBER, PART_NAME FROM NEW_YORK_PART);
```

where the three part table names are synonyms for the tables at three remote sites.

The preceding examples concern read-only transactions. Can a local user also update data at a remote site (or sites)? With today's distributed DBMS products, a user can certainly update data stored at one remote site, such as the Customer data in this example. Thus a user in Tulsa could update bill-of-material data stored in San Mateo. A more complex problem arises in updating data stored at multiple sites, such as the Vendor file. We discuss this problem in the next section.

To achieve location transparency, the distributed DBMS must have access to an accurate and current data dictionary/directory that indicates the location (or locations) of all data in the network. When the directories are distributed (as in the architecture shown in Figure 11-9), they must be synchronized so that each copy of the directory reflects the same information concerning the location of data. Although much progress has been made, true location transparency is not yet available in most systems today.

Replication Transparency

Replication transparency:
A design goal for a distributed database, which says that although a given data item may be replicated at several nodes in a network, a programmer or user may treat the data item as if it were a single item at a single node. Also called *fragmentation transparency*.

Although the same data item may be replicated at several nodes in a network, with **replication transparency** (sometimes called *fragmentation transparency*) the programmer (or other user) may treat the item as if it were a single item at a single node.

To illustrate replication transparency, see the Standard Price List file (Figure 11-9). An identical copy of this file is maintained at all three nodes (full replication). First, consider the problem of reading part (or all) of this file at any node. The distributed DBMS will consult the data directory and determine that this is a local transaction (that is, it can be completed using data at the local site only). Thus the user need not be aware that the same data are stored at other sites.

Now suppose that the data are replicated at some (but not all) sites (partial replication). If a read request originates at a site that does not contain the requested data, that request will have to be routed to another site. In this case the distributed DBMS should select the remote site that will provide the fastest response. The choice of site will probably depend on current conditions in the network (such as availability of communications lines). Thus the distributed DBMS (acting in concert with other network facilities) should dynamically select an optimum route. Again, with replication transparency the requesting user need not be aware that this is a global (rather than local) transaction.

A more complex problem arises when one or more users attempt to update replicated data. For example, suppose that a manager in New York wants to change the price of one of the parts. This change must be accomplished accurately and concurrently at all three sites, or the data will not be consistent. With replication transparency, the New York manager can enter the data as if this were a local transaction and be unaware that the same update is accomplished at all three sites. However, to guarantee that data integrity is maintained, the system must also provide concurrency transparency and failure transparency, which we discuss next.

Failure Transparency

Each site (or node) in a distributed system is subject to the same types of failure as in a centralized system (erroneous data, disk head crash, and so on). However, there is the additional risk of failure of a communications link (or loss of messages). For a system to be robust, it must be able to *detect* a failure, *reconfigure* the system so that computation may continue, and *recover* when a processor or link is repaired.

Error detection and system reconfiguration are probably the functions of the communications controller or processor, rather than the DBMS. However, the distributed DBMS is responsible for database recovery when a failure has occurred. The distributed DBMS at each site has a component called the **transaction manager** that performs the following functions:

Transaction manager: In a distributed database, a software module that maintains a log of all transactions and maintains an appropriate concurrency control scheme.

1. Maintains a log of transactions and before and after database images.

2. Maintains an appropriate concurrency control scheme to ensure data integrity during parallel execution of transactions at that site.

For global transactions, the transaction managers at each participating site cooperate to ensure that all update operations are synchronized. Without such cooperation, data integrity can be lost when a failure occurs. To illustrate how this might happen, suppose (as we did earlier) that a manager in New York wants to change the price of a part in the Standard Price List file (Figure 11-9). This transaction is global: every copy of the record for that part (three sites) must be updated. Suppose that the price list records in New York and Tulsa are successfully updated; however, due to transmission failure, the price list record in San Mateo is not updated. Now the data records for this part are in disagreement, and an employee may access an inaccurate price for that part.

With **failure transparency**, either all the actions of a transaction are committed or none of them are committed. Once a transaction occurs, its effects survive hardware and software failures. In the vendor example, when the transaction failed at one site, the effect of that transaction was not committed at the other sites. Thus the old vendor rating remains in effect at all sites until the transaction can be successfully completed.

Failure transparency: A design goal for a distributed database, which guarantees that either all the actions of each transaction are committed or else none of them is committed.

Commit Protocol

To ensure data integrity for update operations, the cooperating transaction managers execute a **commit protocol**, which is a well-defined procedure (involving an exchange of messages) to ensure that a global transaction is either successfully completed at each site or else aborted. The most widely used protocol is called a **two-phase commit**. A two-phase commit works something like arranging a meeting between many people. First, the site originating the global transaction or an overall coordinating site (like the person trying to schedule a meeting) sends a request to each of the sites that will process some portion of the transaction. In the case of scheduling a meeting, the message might be "Are you available at a given date and time?" Each site processes the subtransaction (if possible), but does not immediately commit (or store) the result to the local database. Instead, the result is stored in a temporary file. In our meeting analogy, each person writes the meeting on his or her calendar in pencil. Each site does, however, lock (prohibit other updating) its portion of

Commit protocol: An algorithm to ensure that a transaction is successfully completed, or else it is aborted.

Two-phase commit: An algorithm for coordinating updates in a distributed database.

the database being updated (as each person would prohibit other appointments at the same tentative meeting time). Each site notifies the originating site when it has completed its subtransaction. When all sites have responded, the originating site now initiates the two-phase commit protocol:

1. A message is broadcast to every participating site, asking whether that site is willing to commit its portion of the transaction at that site. Each site returns an "OK" or "not OK" message. This would be like a message that each person can or cannot attend the meeting. This is often called the prepare phase. An OK says that the remote site promises to allow the initiating request to govern the transaction at the remote database.

2. The originating site collects the messages from all sites. If all are "OK," it broadcasts a message to all sites to commit the portion of the transaction handled at each site. If one or more responses are "not OK," it broadcasts a message to all sites to abort the transaction. This is often called the commit phase. Again, our hypothetical meeting arranger would confirm or abort plans for the meeting depending on the response from each person. It is possible for a transaction to fail during the commit phase (that is, between commits among the remote sites), even though it passed the prepare phase; in this case, the transaction is said to be in limbo. A limbo transaction can be identified by a timeout or polling. With a timeout (no confirmation of commit for a specified time period), it is not possible to distinguish between a busy or failed site. Polling can be expensive in terms of network load and processing time.

This description of a two-phase commit protocol is highly simplified. For a more detailed discussion of this and other protocols, see Date (1995).

With a two-phase commit strategy for synchronizing distributed data, committing a transaction is slower than if the originating location were able to work alone. Recent improvements in this traditional approach to two-phase commit are aimed at reducing the delays caused by the extensive coordination inherent in this approach. Three improvement strategies have been developed (McGovern, 1993):

• *Read-only commit optimization*   This approach identifies read-only portions of a transaction and eliminates the need for confirmation messages on these portions. For example, a transaction might include checking an inventory balance before entering a new order. The reading of the inventory balance within the transaction boundaries can occur without the callback confirmation.

• *Lazy commit optimization*   This approach allows those sites which can update to proceed to update, and other sites which cannot immediately update are allowed to "catch up" later.

• *Linear commit optimization*   This approach permits each part of a transaction to be committed in sequence, rather than holding up a whole transaction when subtransaction parts are delayed from being processed.

Concurrency Transparency

The problem of concurrency control for a single (centralized) database is discussed in depth in Chapter 13. When multiple users access and update a database, data integrity may be lost unless locking mechanisms are used to protect the data from the effects of concurrent updates. The problem of concurrency control is more complex in a distributed database, since the multiple users are spread out among multiple sites and the data are often replicated at several sites, as well.

The objective of concurrency management is easy to define but often difficult to implement in practice. Although the distributed system runs many transactions concurrently, **concurrency transparency** allows each transaction to appear as if it were the only activity in the system. Thus when several transactions are processed concurrently, the results must be the same as if each transaction were processed in serial order.

The transaction managers (introduced above) at each site must cooperate to provide concurrency control in a distributed database. Three basic approaches may be used: locking and versioning, which will be explained in Chapter 13 as concurrency control methods in any database environment, and timestamping. A few special aspects of locking in a distributed database are discussed in Date (1995). The next section reviews the timestamping approach.

Timestamping   With this approach, every transaction is given a globally unique timestamp, which generally consists of the clock time when the transaction occurred and the site ID. **Timestamping** ensures that even if two events occur simultaneously at different sites, each will have a unique timestamp.

The purpose of timestamping is to ensure that transactions are processed in serial order, thereby avoiding the use of locks (and the possibility of deadlocks). Every record in the database carries the timestamp of the transaction that last updated it. If a new transaction attempts to update that record and its timestamp is *earlier* than that carried in the record, the transaction is assigned a new timestamp and restarted. Thus, a transaction cannot process a record until its timestamp is *later* than that carried in the record, and therefore it cannot interfere with another transaction.

To illustrate timestamping, suppose that a database record carries the timestamp 168, which indicates that a transaction with timestamp 168 was the most recent transaction to successfully update that record. A new transaction with timestamp 170 attempts to update the same record. This update is permitted, since the transaction's timestamp is later than the record's current timestamp. When the update is committed, the record timestamp will be reset to 170. Now, suppose instead that a record with timestamp 165 attempts to update the record. This update will not be allowed, since the timestamp is earlier than that carried in the record. Instead, the transaction timestamp will be reset to that of the record (168), and the transaction will be restarted.

The major advantage of timestamping is that locking and deadlock detection (and the associated overhead) are avoided. The major disadvantage is that the approach is conservative, in that transactions are sometimes restarted even when there is no conflict with other transactions.

Query Optimization

With distributed databases, the response to a query may require the DBMS to assemble data from several different sites (although with location transparency, the user is unaware of this need). A major decision for the DBMS is how to process a query, which is affected by both the way a user formulates a query and the intelligence of the distributed DBMS to develop a sensible plan for processing. Date (1983) provides an excellent yet simple example of this problem. Consider the following situation adapted from Date. A simplified procurement (relational) database has the following three relations:

SUPPLIER (SUPPLIER_NUMBER, CITY)	10,000 records, stored in Detroit
PART (PART_NUMBER, COLOR)	100,000 records, stored in Chicago
SHIPMENT(SUPPLIER_NUMBER, PART_NUMBER)	1,000,000 records, stored in Detroit

Concurrency transparency: A design goal for a distributed database, with the property that although a distributed system runs many transactions, it appears that a given transaction is the only activity in the system. Thus, when several transactions are processed concurrently, the results must be the same as if each transaction were processed in serial order.

Timestamping: In distributed databases, a concurrency control mechanism that assigns a globally unique timestamp to each transaction. Timestamping is an alternative to the use of locks in distributed databases.

TABLE 11-2 Query-Processing Strategies in a Distributed Database Environment (Adapted from Date, 1983)

Method	Time
Move PART relation to Detroit, and process whole query at Detroit computer.	16.7 minutes
Move SUPPLIER and SHIPMENT relations to Chicago, and process whole query at Chicago computer.	28 hours
JOIN SUPPLIER and SHIPMENT at the Detroit computer, PROJECT these down to only tuples for Cleveland suppliers, and then for each of these, check at the Chicago computer to determine if associated PART is red.	2.3 days
PROJECT PART at the Chicago computer down to just the red items, and for each, check at the Detroit computer to see if there is some SHIPMENT involving that PART and a Cleveland SUPPLIER.	20 seconds
JOIN SUPPLIER and SHIPMENT at the Detroit computer, PROJECT just SUPPLIER_NUMBER and PART_NUMBER for only Cleveland SUPPLIERs, and move this qualified projection to Chicago for matching with red PARTs.	16.7 minutes
Select just red PARTs at the Chicago computer and move the result to Detroit for matching with Cleveland SUPPLIERs.	1 second

and a query is made (in SQL) to list the supplier numbers for Cleveland suppliers of red parts:

```
SELECT      SUPPLIER.SUPPLIER_NUMBER
FROM        SUPPLIER, SHIPMENT, PART
WHERE       SUPPLIER.CITY = 'Cleveland'
  AND       SHIPMENT.PART_NUMBER = PART.PART_NUMBER
  AND       PART.COLOR = 'Red';
```

Each record in each relation is 100 characters long, there are 10 red parts, a history of 100,000 shipments from Cleveland, and a negligible query computation time compared with communication time. Also, there is a communication system with a data transmission rate of 10,000 characters per second and 1 second access delay to send a message from one node to another.

Date identifies six plausible query-processing strategies for this situation and develops the associated communication times; these strategies and times are summarized in Table 11-2. Depending on the choice of strategy, the time required to satisfy the query ranges from 1 second to 2.3 days! Although the last strategy is best, the fourth strategy is also acceptable.

In general, this example indicates that it is often advisable to break a query in a distributed database environment into components that are isolated at different sites, then determine which site has the potential to yield the fewest qualified records, and then move this result to another site where additional work is performed. Obviously, more than two sites require even more complex analyses and more complicated heuristics to guide query processing.

A distributed DBMS typically uses the following three steps to develop a query processing plan (Özsu and Valduriez, 1992):

1. *Query decomposition*   In this step, the query is simplified and rewritten into a structured, relational algebra form.

2. *Data localization*   Here, the query is transformed from a query referencing data across the network as if the database were in one location into one or more fragments which each explicitly reference data at only one site.

3. *Global optimization*   In this final step, decisions are made about the order in which to execute query fragments, where to move data between sites, and where parts of the query will be executed.

Certainly, the design of the database interacts with the sophistication of the distributed DBMS to yield the performance for queries. A distributed database will be designed based on the best possible understanding of how and where the data will be used. Given the database design (which allocates data partitions to one or more sites), however, all queries, whether anticipated or not, must be processed as efficiently as possible.

One technique used to make processing a distributed query more efficient is to use what is called a **semijoin** operation (Elmasri and Navathe, 1989). In a semijoin, only the joining attribute is sent from one site to another, and then only the required rows are returned. If only a small percentage of the rows participate in the join, then the amount of data being transferred is minimal.

For example, consider the distributed database in Figure 11-11. Suppose that a query at Site 1 asks to display the Cust_Name, SIC, and Order_Date for all customers in a particular Zip_Code range and an Order_Amount above a specified limit. Assume that 10 percent of the customers fall in the Zip_Code range and 2 percent of the orders are above the amount limit. A semijoin would work as follows:

Semijoin: A joining operation used with distributed databases in which only the joining attribute from one site is transmitted to the other site, rather than all the selected attributes from every qualified row.

1. A query is executed at Site 1 to create a list of the Cust_No values in the desired Zip_Code range. So 10,000 customers * .1, or 1,000 rows satisfy the Zip_Code qualification. Thus, 1,000 rows of 10 bytes each for the Cust_No attribute (the joining attribute), or 10,000 bytes, will be sent to Site 2.

2. A query is executed at Site 2 to create a list of the Cust_No and Order_Date values to be sent back to Site 1 to compose the final result. If we assume roughly the same number of orders for each customer, then 40,000 rows of the Order table will match with the customer numbers sent from Site 1. If we assume any customer order is equally likely to be above the amount limit, then 800 rows (40,000 * .02) of the Order table rows are relevant to this query. For each row, the Cust_No and Order_Date need to be sent to Site 1, or 14 bytes * 800 rows, thus 11,200 bytes.

Figure 11-11
Distributed database, one table at each of two sites

Site 1		Site 2	
Customer table		Order table	
Cust_No	10 bytes	Order_No	10 bytes
Cust_Name	50 bytes	Cust_No	10 bytes
Zip_Code	10 bytes	Order_Date	4 bytes
SIC	5 bytes	Order_Amount	6 bytes
10,000 rows		400,000 rows	

The total data transferred is only 21,200 bytes using the semijoin just described. Compare this total to simply sending the subset of each table needed at one site to the other site:

- To send data from Site 1 to Site 2 would require sending the Cust_No, Cust_Name, and SIC (65 bytes) for 1000 rows of the Customer table (65,000 bytes) to Site 2.

- To send data from Site 2 to Site 1 would require sending Cust_No and Order_Date (14 bytes) for 8000 rows of the Order table (112,000 bytes).

Clearly, the semijoin approach saves network traffic, which can be a major contributing factor to the overall time to respond to a user's query.

A distributed DBMS uses a cost model to predict the execution time (for data processing and transmission) of alternative execution plans. The cost model is performed before the query is executed based on general network conditions; consequently the actual cost may be more or less, depending on the actual network and node loads, database reorganizations, and other dynamic factors. Thus, the parameters of the cost model should be periodically updated as general conditions change in the network (for example, as local databases are redesigned, network paths are changed, and DBMSs at local sites are replaced).

Evolution of Distributed DBMS

Distributed database management is still an emerging, rather than established technology. Current releases of distributed DBMS products do not provide all of the features described in the previous sections. For example, some products provide location transparency for read-only transactions but do not yet support global updates. To illustrate the evolution of distributed DBMS products, we briefly describe three stages in this evolution: remote unit of work, distributed unit of work, and distributed request. Then, in the next section, we review the major features of leading distributed DBMSs (present in these packages at the time of writing this text).

In the following discussion the term *unit of work* refers to the sequence of instructions required to process a transaction. That is, it consists of the instructions that begin with a "begin transaction" operation and end with either a "commit" or a "rollback" operation.

Remote Unit of Work   The first stage allows multiple SQL statements to be originated at one location and executed as a single unit of work on a *single* remote DBMS. Both the originating and receiving computers must be running the same DBMS. The originating computer does not consult the data directory to locate the site containing the selected tables in the remote unit of work. Instead, the originating application must know where the data reside and connect to the remote DBMS prior to each remote unit of work. Thus the remote unit of work concept does not support location transparency.

A remote unit of work allows updates at the single remote computer. All updates within a unit of work are tentative until a commit operation makes them permanent or a rollback undoes them. Thus transaction integrity is maintained for a single remote site; however, an application cannot assure transaction integrity when more than one remote location is involved. Referring to the database in Figure 11-9, an application in San Mateo could update the Part file in Tulsa and transaction integrity would be maintained. However, that application could not simultaneously update the Part file in two or more locations and still be assured of maintaining transaction integrity. Thus the remote unit of work also does not provide failure transparency.

Distributed Unit of Work   A distributed unit of work allows various statements within a unit of work to refer to *multiple* remote DBMS locations. This approach supports some location transparency, since the data directory is consulted to locate the DBMS containing the selected table in each statement. However, all tables in a *single* SQL statement must be at the same location. Thus, a distributed unit of work would not allow the following query, designed to assemble parts information from all three sites in Figure 11-9:

```
SELECT DISTINCT    PART_NUMBER, PART_NAME
FROM               PART
WHERE              COLOR = 'ORANGE'
ORDER BY           PART_NUMBER
```

Similarly, a distributed unit of work would not allow a single SQL statement that attempts to update data at more than one location. For example, the following SQL statement is intended to update the part file at three locations:

```
UPDATE    PART
SET       UNIT_PRICE = 127.49
WHERE     PART_NUMBER = 12345
```

This update (if executed) would set the unit price of part number 12345 to $127.49 at Tulsa, San Mateo, and New York (Figure 11-9). The statement would not be acceptable as a distributed unit of work, however, since the single SQL statement refers to data at more than one location. The distributed unit of work does support protected updates involving multiple sites, provided that each SQL statement refers to a table (or tables) at one site only. For example, suppose in Figure 11-9 we want to increase the balance of part number 12345 in Tulsa and at the same time decrease the balance of the same part in New York (perhaps to reflect an inventory adjustment). The following SQL statements could be used:

```
UPDATE    PART
SET       BALANCE = BALANCE - 50
WHERE     PART_NUMBER = 12345 AND LOCATION = 'TULSA'
UPDATE    PART
SET       BALANCE = BALANCE + 50
WHERE     PART_NUMBER = 12345 AND LOCATION = 'NEW YORK';
```

Under the distributed unit of work concept, either this update will be committed at both locations, or else it will be rolled back and (perhaps) attempted again. We conclude from these examples that the distributed unit of work supports some (but not all) of the transparency features described earlier in this section.

Distributed Request   The distributed request allows a single SQL statement to refer to tables in more than one remote DBMS, overcoming a major limitation of the distributed unit of work. The distributed request supports true location transparency, since a single SQL statement can refer to tables at multiple sites. However, the distributed request may or may not support replication transparency or failure transparency. It will probably be some time before a true distributed DBMS, one that supports all of the transparency features we described earlier, appears on the market.

DISTRIBUTED DBMS PRODUCTS

Most of the leading vendors of database management systems have a distributed version. In most cases, to utilize all distributed database capabilities, one vendor's DBMS must be running at each node (a homogeneous distributed database environment). Client/server forms of a distributed database are arguably the most common form in existence today. In a client/server environment (see Chapter 8 for an explanation of client/server databases), it is very easy to define a database with tables on several nodes in a local or wide area network. Once a user program establishes a linkage with each remote site, and suitable database middleware is loaded, full location transparency is achieved. So, in a client/server database form, distributed databases are readily available to any information systems developer, and heterogeneity of DBMS is possible.

Although their approaches are constantly changing, it is illustrative to overview how different vendors address distributed database management. Probably the most interesting aspect of the following sections is the differences across products. These differences (summarized in Table 11-3) suggest how difficult it is to select a distributed DBMS product, since the exact capabilities of the DBMS must be carefully matched with the needs of an organization. Also, with so many options, and with each product handling distributed data differently, it is almost impossible to outline general principles for managing a distributed database. The design of any distributed database requires careful analysis of both the business's needs and the intricacies of the DBMS. Thompson (1997) also recommends that a distributed DBMS product should be used only when you really need a distributed DBMS. Do not use a distributed DBMS to create a backup database for a mission-critical application; easier solutions, such as RAID (see Chapter 7), exist for simpler needs.

IBM Corporation and DB2

One of IBM's distributed database products is called DataPropagator Relational (DPropR), which works in conjunction with IBM's DB2 family of relational DBMSs on a variety of operating system platforms. DataPropagator uses a primary site for all updates, with asynchronous updates sent to other read-only sites. By a primary site we mean that all updates occur first at a specified site, and all remote sites are refreshed usually at the same time. Thus, the primary site serves as one official database of record for the organization. The data to be replicated across sites are identified and registered in a data dictionary at the primary site. Sites other than the primary site subscribe to receive the data they want (Edelstein, 1995b).

A powerful capability of DataPropagator is that the data for which a remote site subscribes need not be simple subsets of the primary site data. Rather, a site can subscribe to a simple subset or to the result of a query. For example, a remote bank branch could subscribe to a table that is the result of joining customer and account data for only accounts assigned to that branch. This capability would be especially powerful for decision support databases, which contain aggregations and summaries of base data.

IBM is also developing a standard, distributed relational database architecture (DRDA), which will facilitate heterogeneous, distributed databases. However, as a proprietary standard, it may not have broad influence on the industry. IBM provides DataJoiner, which allows a user of an IBM database product to access databases managed by products from other vendors. DataJoiner (a type of middleware) provides a basic level of heterogeneous, distributed database support for users of an IBM DBMS.

Table 11-3   Distributed DBMSs

Vendor	Product	Important Features
IBM	DataPropagator Relational	• Works with DB2 • Primary site and asynchronous updates • Read-only sites subscribe to primary site • Subscription to subset or query result
	Distributed Relational Database Architecture (DRDA)	• Heterogeneous databases
	DataJoiner	• Middleware to access non–IBM databases
Sybase	Replication Server	• Primary site and distributed read-only sites • Update to read-only site as one transaction • Hierarchical replication • Data and stored procedures replicated
	SQL Anywhere	• Mobile databases
	OmniSQL	• Heterogeneous databases
Oracle	Table Snapshot Option	• Periodic snapshots sent to read-only sites
	Symmetric Replication option	• Asynchronous with multiple updateable copies • Differential refresh • DBA controls replication • Two-phase commit
Computer Associates	CA-Ingres/Replicator	• All database copies updateable • Hierachical replication • DBA registers data for replication and other sites subscribe • Master/slave form allows slave to be an Ingres database
	Ingres/Net and Ingres/Star	• Decomposes query to distributed, homogeneous sites • Two-phase commit • Also used with non–Ingres databases
Microsoft	SQL Server	• Primary site and distributed read-only sites • Publish and subscribe, with articles and publications • One database can pass copies of publications to other sites • Mobile databases

Sybase Inc.

The Sybase Replication Server was one of the first replication-based distributed DBMSs. As with the case for IBM, Sybase's solution also is based on a primary site for updates and distributed read-only databases. Unique to the Sybase Replication Server approach is that all the updated row information sent to a remote site is sent as one transaction, so it is easy to control the integrity of a remote site refresh—either all the data in the refresh are processed, or the refresh is aborted through normal transaction aborting procedures of the local DBMS. Replication Server also supports hierarchical replication, so a corporate primary site can refresh divisional sites, which then can refresh local databases, for example. Different times can be used for each level of refreshing. A site subscribes to a copy of a table, or to any row and column subsets of a table using a typical SQL WHERE clause. Replication can also involve stored procedures of a database, not just data. This is a very powerful feature that allows a database to behave the same way on any site. This feature can reduce the update traffic on the network. For example, if one update causes other database changes, then the remote site needs to receive only the first update and the stored procedures, and all spawned updates will be locally generated at the replicated site. Sybase also provides SQL Anywhere, which is a tool loaded on a mobile computer that allows a mobile database to be a fully functioning node in a distributed database.

Another Sybase distributed database product is OmniSQL, which is a gateway to Sybase, DB2, Oracle, and a few other DBMSs. With OmniSQL, all the data across these heterogeneous databases appear to be on one server. The user is able to use one SQL syntax, and OmniSQL translates the query recognizing the unique features and syntax of the target DBMS. A join may involve tables from several sites, but there are limited synchronization controls.

Oracle Corporation

Oracle provides several options for distributed database replication. The original Table Snapshot option supports the distribution of periodic snapshots of a database table to be sent to other read-only nodes in the distributed database network. In addition, the newer Symmetric Replication option, a form of asynchronous distributed database technology, allows multiple master (or updateable) copies of a full table, and all changes to any one of the masters are broadcast to all of the other masters. A second version of the Symmetric Replication option extends the Table Snapshot option to allow target sites for a snapshot to also update data in the local database copy. All updates eventually flow back to a master database, for further distribution to all replicas (so there are no peer-to-peer refreshes). Snapshots can be a full refresh of a table (or its subset) or of joined tables. Oracle supports a "fast refresh," which we earlier in the chapter called a differential refresh. A fast refresh must be based on only one table. Oracle does not use the publish-and-subscribe approach to defining replicas. Instead, the database administrator identifies the portions of the database to be replicated (this includes not only data but also any database object, such as a view, trigger, and so forth). Replica schemas are thus controlled by a global database administrator. Oracle also uses stored procedures as the way to propagate changes across replicated sites. All the forms of asynchronous technology are an integral part of the Oracle product.

In addition, Oracle supports a two-phase commit approach to synchronizing copies of data. This synchronous distributed database technology supports distributed queries and transactions, synchronous replication, and is a standard component of Oracle.

Computer Associates International and Ingres

The CA-Ingres/Replicator uses yet a different approach. Replicator does not require a master or primary site; thus all copies of data are updateable. Replicator supports hierarchical replication. A database administrator registers what data in a database may be replicated, and other sites subscribe to a replication service. Replicator implements three forms of replication: peer-to-peer, in which any copy is updateable, and a Conflict Resolver module determines which update is the official update across all the databases; the traditional master/slave in which one database is the only one that can be updated; and a master/slave, in which the slave can be a non–Ingres database.

Ingres/Net and Ingres/Star work together to provide operational access to a distributed, homogeneous database of Ingres sites. Ingres/Star breaks a query into subqueries corresponding to the nodes in the distributed database. It then transmits each subquery to the instance of Ingres at each of the relevant sites. Ingres/Star at the initiating site then collects the results sent to it from each remote site processing a subquery, and returns the consolidated result to the originating process. A two-phase commit protocol is used to synchronize data across nodes. Ingres/Star can also be used with DB2, IMS, and other non–CA DBMSs.

Microsoft Corporation and SQL Server

SQL Server uses the primary-site approach, in which the database at one site is the only one that can receive updates. SQL Server also uses the publish-and-subscribe approach utilized by several of the other distributed DBMS products. An interesting concept with SQL Server is how far it takes the publish-and-subscribe analogy. Data published for replication are packaged into an "article." An article is a row and/or column subset of a table at the primary site. Articles are grouped into a "publication," which is transmitted to subscriber sites as a logical unit of work. There can be only one subscriber to a publication on a given site, but the subscriber database can pass along its copy of the publication to other databases at the same site. For a mobile database (a database on a laptop computer or a microprocessor server on a dial-up network), SQL Server works in conjunction with ODBC drivers and the Jet engine available with Access and Visual Basic.

SUMMARY

This chapter covered various issues and technologies for distributed databases. We saw that a distributed database is a single logical database that is spread across computers in multiple locations connected by a data communications network. A distributed database is contrasted with a decentralized database, in which distributed data are not interconnected. In a distributed database, the network must allow users to share the data as transparently as possible, yet must allow each node to operate autonomously, especially when network linkages are broken or specific nodes fail. Business conditions today encourage the use of distributed databases: dispersion and autonomy of business units (including globalization of organizations), need for data sharing, and the costs and reliability of data communications. A distributed database environment may be homogeneous, involving the same DBMS at each node, or heterogeneous, with potentially different DBMSs at different nodes. Also, a distributed database environment may keep all copies of data and related data in immediate synchronization, or may tolerate planned delays in data updating through asynchronous methods.

There are numerous advantages to distributed databases. The most important of these are the following: increased reliability and availability of data, local control by users over their data, modular (or incremental) growth, reduced communications costs, and faster response to requests for data. There are also several costs and disadvantages of distributed databases: software is more costly and complex, processing overhead often increases, maintaining data integrity is often more difficult, and if data are not distributed properly, response to requests for data may be very slow.

There are several options for distributing data in a network: data replication, horizontal partitioning, vertical partitioning, and combinations of these approaches. With data replication, a separate copy of the database (or part of the database) is stored at each of two or more sites. Data replication can result in improved reliability and faster response, can be done simply under certain circumstances, allows nodes to operate more independently (yet coordinated) of each other, and reduces network traffic; however, additional storage capacity is required, and immediate updating at each of the sites may be difficult. Replicated data can be updated by taking periodic snapshots of an official record of data and sending the snapshots to replicated sites. These snapshots can involve all data or only the data that have changed since the last snapshot. With horizontal partitioning, some of the rows of a relation are placed at one site, and other rows are placed in a relation at another site (or several sites). On the other hand, vertical partitioning distributes the columns of a relation among different sites. The objectives of data partitioning include improved performance and security. Combinations of data replication and horizontal and vertical partitioning are often used. Organizational factors, frequency and location of queries and transactions, possible growth of data and node, technology, and the need for reliability influence the choice of a data distribution design.

To have a distributed database, there must be a distributed DBMS that coordinates the access to data at the various nodes. Requests for data by users or application programs are first processed by the distributed DBMS, which determines whether the transaction is local (can be processed at the local site), remote (can be processed at some other site), or global (requires access to data at several nonlocal sites). For global transactions, the distributed DBMS consults the data directory and routes parts of the request as necessary, and then consolidates results from the remote sites.

A distributed DBMS should isolate users from the complexities of distributed database management. By location transparency, we mean that although data are geographically distributed, they appear to users as if all of the data were located at a single node. By replication transparency, we mean that although a data item may be stored at several different nodes, the user may treat the item as if it were a single item at a single node. With failure transparency, either all the actions of a transaction are completed at each site, or else none of them are committed. Distributed databases can be designed to allow temporary inconsistencies across the nodes, when immediate synchronization is not necessary. With concurrency transparency, each transaction appears to be the only activity in the system. Failure and concurrency transparency can be managed by commit protocols, which coordinate updates across nodes, locking data, and timestamping.

A key decision made by a distributed DBMS is how to process a global query. The time to process a global query can vary from a few seconds to many hours depending on how intelligent the DBMS is in producing an efficient query-processing plan. A query-processing plan involves decomposing the query into a structured set of steps, identifying different steps with local data at different nodes in the distributed database, and finally choosing a sequence and location for executing each step of the query.

Few (if any) distributed DBMS products provide all forms of transparency, all forms of data replication and partitioning, and the same level of intelligence in distributed query processing. These products are, however, improving rapidly as the business pressures for distributed systems increase. Leading vendors of relational database products have introduced distributed versions, with tools to help a database administrator design and manage a distributed database.

C H A P T E R   R E V I E W

K E Y   T E R M S

Asynchronous
    distributed database
Commit protocol
Concurrency
    transparency
Decentralized database
Distributed database

Failure transparency
Global transaction
Local autonomy
Local transaction
Location transparency
Replication transparency
Semijoin

Synchronous distributed
    database
Timestamping
Transaction manager
Two-phase commit

R E V I E W   Q U E S T I O N S

1. Define each of the following terms:
    a. distributed database
    b. location transparency
    c. two-phase commit
    d. global transaction
    e. local autonomy
    f. timestamping
    g. transaction manager

2. Contrast the following terms:
    a. distributed database; decentralized database
    b. homogeneous distributed database; heterogeneous distributed database
    c. location transparency; local autonomy
    d. asynchronous distributed database; synchronous distributed database
    e. horizontal partition; vertical partition
    f. publish; subscribe
    g. full refresh; differential refresh
    h. push replication; pull replication
    i. local transaction; global transaction

3. Briefly describe three business conditions which are encouraging the use of distributed databases.

4. Explain two types of homogeneous distributed databases.

5. Briefly describe five major characteristics of homogeneous distributed databases.

6. Briefly describe four major characteristics of heterogeneous distributed databases.

7. Briefly describe five advantages for distributed databases compared to centralized databases.

8. Briefly describe four costs and disadvantages for distributed databases.

9. Briefly describe five advantages to the data replication form of distributed databases.

10. Briefly describe two disadvantages to the data replication form of distributed databases.

11. Explain under what circumstances a snapshot replication approach appears to be best.

12. Explain under what circumstances a near real-time replication approach appears to be best.

13. Briefly describe five factors that influence whether data replication is a viable distributed database design strategy for an application.

14. Explain the advantages and disadvantages of horizontal partitioning for distributed databases.

15. Explain the advantages and disadvantages of vertical partitioning for distributed databases.

16. Briefly describe five factors that influence the selection of a distributed database design strategy.

17. Briefly describe five unique functions performed by a distributed database management system.

18. Briefly explain the effect of location transparency on an author of an ad hoc database query.

19. Briefly explain the effect of replication transparency on an author of an ad hoc database query.

20. Briefly explain in what way two-phase commit can still fail to create a completely consistent distributed database.

21. Briefly describe three improvements to the two-phase commit protocol.

22. Briefly describe the three steps in distributed query processing.

23. Briefly explain the conditions that suggest the use of a semijoin will result in faster distributed query processing.

PROBLEMS AND EXERCISES

1. Match the following terms to the appropriate definition:

_____ replication transparency

_____ unit of work

_____ global transaction

_____ concurrency transparency

_____ replication

_____ failure transparency

a. guarantees that all or none of the updates occur in a transaction across a distributed database

b. the appearance that a given transaction is the only transaction running against a distributed database

c. treating copies of data as if there were only one copy

d. references data at more than one location

e. sequence of instructions required to process a transaction

f. a good database distribution strategy for read-only data

Problems and Exercises 2–4 refer to the distributed database shown in Figure 11-9.

2. Name the type of transparency (location, replication, failure, concurrency) that is indicated by each statement.

   a. End users in New York and Tulsa are updating the Engineering Parts database in San Mateo at the same time. Neither user is aware that the other is accessing the data, and the system protects the data from lost updates due to interference.

   b. An end user in Tulsa deletes an item from the Standard Price List at the site. Unknown to the user, the distributed DBMS also deletes that item from the Standard Price List in San Mateo and New York.

   c. A user in San Mateo initiates a transaction to delete a part from San Mateo parts and simultaneously to add that part to New York parts. The transaction is completed in San Mateo but due to transmission failure is not completed in New York. The distributed DBMS automatically reverses the transaction at San Mateo and notifies the user to retry the transaction.

   d. An end user in New York requests the balance on hand for part number 33445. The user does not know where the record for this part is located. The distributed DBMS consults the directory and routes the request to San Mateo.

3. Consider the Standard Price List in Figure 11-9.

   a. Write an SQL statement that will increase the Unit_Price of Part_Number 56789 by 10%.

   b. Indicate whether the statement you wrote in part (a) is acceptable under each of the following protocols:
      i. Remote unit of work
      ii. Distributed unit of work
      iii. Distributed request

4. Consider the four parts databases in Figure 11-9.

   a. Write an SQL statement that will increase the Balance in Part_Number 56789 in San Mateo Parts by 10 percent, and another SQL statement that will decrease the Balance in Part_Number 12345 in New York Parts by 10 percent.

   b. Indicate whether the statement you wrote in part (a) is acceptable under each of the following protocols:
      i. Remote unit of work
      ii. Distributed unit of work
      iii. Distributed request

5. Speculate on why you think a truly heterogeneous distributed database environment is so difficult to achieve. What specific difficulties exist in this environment?

6. Explain the major factors at work in creating the drastically different results for the six query-processing strategies outlined in Table 11-2.

7. Do any of the six query-processing strategies in Table 11-2 utilize a semijoin? If so, explain how a semijoin is used. If not, explain how you might use a semijoin to create an efficient query-processing strategy or why the use of a semijoin will not work in this situation.

8. Consider the SUPPLIER, PART, and SHIPMENT relations and distributed database mentioned in the section on Query Optimization in this chapter.

   a. Write a global SQL query (submitted in Chicago) to display the Part_Number and Color for every part that is not supplied by a supplier in Columbus.

    b. Design three alternative query-processing strategies for your answer to part (a).

    c. Develop a table similar to Table 11-2 to compare the processing times for these three strategies.

    d. Which of your three strategies was best and why?

    e. Would data replication or horizontal or vertical partitioning of the database allow you to create an even more efficient query-processing strategy? Why or why not?

9. Consider the following normalized relations for a database in a large retail store chain:

STORE (Store_ID, Region, Manager_ID, Square_Feet)
EMPLOYEE (Employee_ID, Where_Work, Employee_Name, Employee_Address)
DEPARTMENT (Department_ID, Manager_ID, Sales_Goal)
SCHEDULE (Department_ID, Employee_ID, Date)

Assume that a data communications network links a computer at corporate head-quarters with a computer in each retail outlet. The chain includes 50 stores with an average of 75 employees per store. There are 10 departments in each store. A daily schedule is maintained for 5 months (the previous 2 months, the current month, and next 2 months). Further assume that

- Each store manager updates the employee work schedule for her or his store roughly five times per hour.

- The corporation generates all payroll checks, employee notices, and other mailings for all employees for all stores.

- The corporation establishes a new sales goal each month for each department.

- The corporation hires and fires store managers and controls all information about store managers; store managers hire and fire all store employees and control all information about employees in that store.

    a. Would you recommend a distributed database, a centralized database, or a set of decentralized databases for this retail store chain?

    b. Assuming that some form of distributed database is justified, what would you recommend as a data distribution strategy for this retail store chain?

FIELD EXERCISES

1. Visit an organization that has installed a distributed database management system. Explore the following questions:

    a. Does the organization have a truly distributed database? If so, how are the data distributed: replication, horizontal partitioning, vertical partitioning?

    b. What commercial distributed DBMS products are used? What were the reasons the organization selected these products? What problems or limitations has the organization found with these products?

    c. To what extent does this system provide each of the following:

       i. Location transparency

       ii. Replication transparency

       iii. Concurrency transparency

       iv. Failure transparency

       v. Query optimization

    d. What are the organization's plans for future evolution of distributed databases?

e. Talk with a database administrator in the organization to explore how decisions are made concerning the location of data in the network. What factors are considered in this decision? Are any analytical tools used? If so, is the database administrator satisfied that the tools help to make the processing of queries efficient?

2. Using the Web site for this text, investigate the latest distributed database product offerings from the DBMS vendors mentioned in this chapter. Update the description of the features for one of the distributed DBMS products listed.

3. Visit an organization that has installed a client/server database environment. Explore the following questions:

   a. What distributed database features do the client/server DBMSs in use offer?

   b. Is the organization attempting to achieve the same benefits from a client/server environment as are outlined in this chapter for distributed databases? Which of these benefits are they achieving? Which cannot be achieved with client/server technologies?

REFERENCES

Bell, D. and J. Grimson. 1992. *Distributed Database Systems*. Reading, MA: Addison-Wesley.

Date, C. J. 1983. *An Introduction to Database Systems*. Vol. 2. Reading, MA: Addison-Wesley.

Date, C. J. 1995. *An Introduction to Database Systems*. 6th ed. Reading, MA: Addison-Wesley.

Edelstein, H. 1993. "Replicating Data." *DBMS* 6 (June): 59–64.

Edelstein, H. 1995a. "The Challenge of Replication, Part I." *DBMS* 8 (March): 46–52.

Edelstein, H. 1995b. "The Challenge of Replication, Part II." *DBMS* 8 (April): 62–70, 103.

Elmasri, R., and S. B. Navathe. 1989. *Fundamentals of Database Systems*. Menlo Park, CA: Benjamin/Cummings.

Froemming, G. 1996. "Design and Replication: Issues with Mobile Applications—Part 1." *DBMS* 9 (March): 48–56.

Koop, P. 1995. "Replication at Work." *DBMS* 8 (March): 54–60.

McGovern, D. 1993. "Two-Phased Commit or Replication." *Database Programming & Design* 6 (May): 35–44.

Özsu, M. T., and P. Valduriez. 1992. "Distributed Database Systems: Where Were We?" *Database Programming & Design* 5 (April): 49–55.

Schussel, G. 1994. "Database Replication: Watch the Data Fly." *Client/Server Today* (October): 80–90.

Thé, L. 1994. "Distribute Data Without Choking the Net." *Datamation* (January 7): 35–38.

Thompson, C. 1997. "Database Replication: Comparing Three Leading DBMS Vendors' Approaches to Replication." *DBMS* 10 (May): 76–84.

Project Case

In the Mountain View Community Hospital case in Chapter 7, you made some physical database design decisions for a centralized database. Refer to your answers to Project Questions and Project Exercises in that case segment.

PROJECT DESCRIPTION

Mountain View Community Hospital is growing in several ways. First, the hospital will be opening its first satellite outpatient surgical unit in the Golf Estates suburb. Second, the hospital has been acquiring the practices of several doctor groups in the community and will be providing all patient record-keeping and billing services for these offices and clinics. Given these significant changes, the hospital information systems staff members are considering using distributed computing and databases.

PROJECT QUESTIONS

1. What additional kinds of information, besides the information collected to make the physical database design decisions in the case in Chapter 7, do you need to decide if Mountain View Community should use distributed database technology?

2. What additional kinds of information, besides the information collected to make the physical database design decisions in the case in Chapter 7, do you need to design a distributed database for Mountain View Community?

3. Are there opportunities for data replication, horizontal partitioning, and vertical partitioning of a distributed database for Mountain View Community? If you are not sure, what other information would you need to answer this question?

PROJECT EXERCISES

Most of the data maintenance for the Mountain View Community Hospital database is local at the site of patient activity. For example, over 80 percent of changes to data represented in Case Figure 1 in Chapter 7 are

made from doctor offices, 10 percent will be made at the main hospital, and 10 percent at the satellite surgical unit. Also, most queries are local (for example, a physician at a doctor's office will look up what treatments have been performed on a patient when that patient is in the office). But, because medical service questions usually require rapid response, the doctors are concerned about the performance of a distributed database.

On the other hand, administrative queries are almost exclusively centralized at the administrative offices located at the main hospital. Queries to produce statements, summaries of treatment statistics for state health agency inquiries, and physician productivity and profitability questions all are submitted by administrative staff at the hospital.

One proposal for the design of Mountain View's distributed database is to horizontally partition physician, patient, procedure, and consumption data and distribute these to the local physician office computer. For example, records for all the physicians in one practice, all the patients for whom any of these doctors are the primary care physician, and all the associated activity data will be stored on one computer at the doctors' office. Treatment and Item data are to be replicated across the sites. The main hospital computer and the surgical unit's computer are to maintain a copy of all data, since all the data need to be accessible when a patient is being treated at the hospital or surgical unit and data links to the offices are down.

1. What form of data replication integrity control would you recommend for this distributed database and why?

2. What would you recommend as a global query optimization plan for each of the following queries:

   a. What is the total number of units consumed of each Item during the last month?

   b. How many patients has each physician treated in each of the following categories over the past month: doctor offices, surgical unit, main hospital?

   c. Grouped by physician medical specialty, how many of each kind of treatment has each physician prescribed?

12

Object-Oriented Database Development

After studying this chapter, you should be able to:

■ Concisely define each of the following key terms: **atomic literal, collection literal, set, bag, list, array, structured literal,** and **extent.**

■ Create logical object-oriented database schemas using the object definition language (ODL).

■ Transform conceptual UML class diagrams to logical ODL schemas by mapping classes (abstract and concrete), attributes, operations (abstract and concrete), association relationships (one-to-one, one-to-many, and many-to-many), and generalization relationships.

■ Identify the type specifications for attributes, operation arguments, and operation returns.

■ Create objects and specify attribute values for those objects.

■ Understand the steps involved in implementing object-oriented databases.

■ Understand the syntax and semantics of the object query language (OQL).

■ Use OQL commands to formulate various types of queries.

■ Gain an understanding of the types of applications object-oriented databases have been applied to.

INTRODUCTION

In Chapter 5, we introduced you to object-oriented data modeling. You learned how to conceptually model a database using UML class diagrams. In this chapter, we will describe how such conceptual object-oriented models can be transformed into logical schemas that can be directly implemented using an object database management system (ODBMS).

This chapter was written by Professor Atish P. Sinha, University of Dayton.

As you will learn later, although relational databases are effective for traditional business applications, they have severe limitations when it comes to storing and manipulating complex data and relationships. In this chapter, we will show how to implement applications within an object-oriented database environment.

In this chapter, we will adopt the Object Model proposed by the Object Database Management Group (ODMG) for defining and querying an object-oriented database (OODB). For developing logical schemas, we will specifically use the object definition language (ODL), a data definition language for OODBs specified in the ODMG 2.0 standard (Cattell and Barry, 1997). Just as an SQL data definition language (DDL) schema can be implemented in an SQL-compliant relational DBMS (see Chapter 9), a logical schema created using ODL can be implemented in an ODMG-compliant ODBMS.

We will use examples similar to the ones you saw earlier in Chapter 5 to show how to map conceptual UML class diagrams into logical ODL schemas. You will learn how to map classes (abstract and concrete), attributes, operations (abstract and concrete), association relationships (unary and binary), and generalization relationships from a UML class diagram into corresponding ODL constructs.

Recall from Chapter 9 that, in addition to the DDL component, SQL has a data manipulation language (DML) component that allows users to query or manipulate the data inside a relational database. A similar language, called object query language (OQL), has been specified in the ODMG 2.0 standard to query object databases (Cattell and Barry, 1997). We will describe how various types of queries can be formulated using OQL.

In Chapter 5, we showed a conceptual object-oriented model for the Pine Valley Furniture Company. In this chapter, we will transform this conceptual model into a logical ODL schema. Finally, we will discuss the types of applications for which ODBMSs are well suited and describe briefly some of the applications developed using existing ODBMS products.

OBJECT DEFINITION LANGUAGE

In Chapter 9, you learned how to use the SQL data definition language (DDL) to specify a logical schema for a relational database. Similarly, the object definition language (ODL) allows you to specify a logical schema for an object-oriented database. ODL is a programming language–independent specification language for defining OODB schemas. Just as an SQL DDL schema is portable across SQL-compliant relational DBMSs, an ODL schema is portable across ODMG-compliant ODBMSs.

Defining a Class

Figure 12-1 shows a conceptual UML class diagram (see Chapter 5 for an explanation of the notation for a class diagram) for a university database, an example with which all readers are familiar. For the time being, we will focus on the Student and Course classes, and their attributes. In ODL, a class is specified using the *class* keyword, and an attribute is specified using the *attribute* keyword. The Student and Course classes are defined as follows:

```
class Student {
    attribute string name
    attribute Date dateOfBirth
```

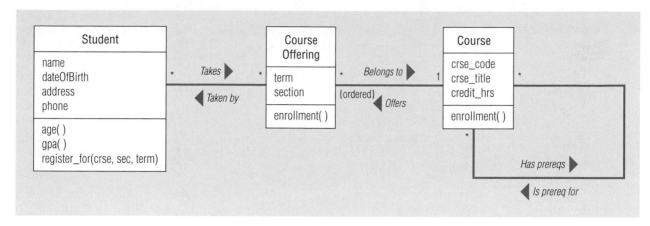

Figure 12-1
UML class diagram for a university database

```
    attribute string address
    attribute string phone
// plus relationship and operations...
}

class Course {
    attribute string crse_code
    attribute string crse_title
    attribute short credit_hrs
// plus relationships and operation...
```

We have highlighted the ODL keywords in bold. We have added comments (preceded by the "//" sign) to indicate that we need to add the relationships and operations (see Figure 12-1) to the classes at a later stage. Note that next to an attribute keyword, we have specified the type of the attribute followed by the attribute's name.

Defining an Attribute

An attribute's value is either a literal or an *object identifier*. As we discussed in Chapter 5, each object has a unique identifier. Because an object retains its identifier over its lifetime, the object remains the same despite changes in its state. In contrast, literals do not have identifiers and, therefore, cannot be individually referenced like objects. Literals are embedded inside objects. You can think of literal values as constants. For example, the string Mary Jones, the character C, and the integer 20 are all literal values.

The Object Model supports different literal types, including atomic literals, collection literals, and structured literals. Examples of **atomic literal** types are string, char (character), boolean (true or false), float (real number), short (short integer), and long (long integer).

A **collection literal** is a collection of elements, which themselves could be of any literal or object type. The collection literal types supported by the ODMG Object Model include *set, bag, list,* and *array.* A **set** is an unordered collection of elements without any duplicates. A **bag** is an unordered collection of elements that may contain duplicates. In contrast to sets and bags, a **list** is an ordered collection of elements. An **array** is a dynamically sized ordered collection of elements that can be located by position.

Atomic literal: A constant that cannot be decomposed into any further components.

Collection literal: A collection of literals or object types.

Set: An unordered collection of elements without any duplicates.

Bag: An unordered collection of elements that may contain duplicates.

List: An ordered collection of elements.

Array: A dynamically sized ordered collection of elements that can be located by position.

Structured literal: A fixed
number of named elements,
each of which can be of literal
or object type.

A **structured literal**, also known as *structure*, consists of a fixed number of named elements, each of which could be of literal or object type. The Object Model supports the following predefined structures: Date, Interval, Time, and Timestamp. In addition, it supports user-defined structures, examples of which will be given later.

Let us now go back to the ODL schema for the university database. The attributes name, address, and phone of Student, and crse_code and crse_title of Course are all of string type. A string attribute can store a string of alphanumeric characters enclosed within double quotes. The attribute credit_hrs of Course is short because its value is always an integer less than 2^{16}. In addition to these atomic literal types, the schema also specifies the structured literal type Date for the dateOfBirth attribute of Student.

Defining User Structures

In addition to the structured data types provided by ODL, you can define structures yourself by using the *struct* keyword. For example, you can define a structure called Address that consists of four components—street_address, city, state, and zip—all of which are string attributes.

```
struct Address {
    string street_address
    string city
    string state
    string zip
}
```

Similarly, you can define Phone as a structure consisting of an area code and a personal_number. Note that the latter is specified as a long integer, because it is more than 2^{16}.

```
struct Phone {
    short area_code
    long personal_number
}
```

Defining Operations

We can also define the operations for the two classes. In ODL, you specify an operation using parentheses after its name. The ODL definition for Student is now as follows:

```
class Student {
    attribute string name
    attribute Date dateOfBirth
//user-defined structured attributes
    attribute Address address
    attribute Phone phone
//plus relationship
//operations
    short age()
    float gpa()
    boolean register_for(string crse, short sec, string term)
}
```

We have defined all three operations shown in Figure 12-1: age, gpa, and register_for. The first two are query operations. The register_for operation is an update operation that registers a student for a section (sec) of a course (crse) in a given term. Each of these arguments, shown within parentheses, is preceded by its type.[1] We also have to specify the return type for each operation. For example, the return types for age and gpa are short (short integer) and float (real number), respectively. The return type for the register_for operation is boolean (true or false), indicating if the registration was successfully completed or not. If the operation does not return any value, the return type is declared as void.

Defining a Range for an Attribute

If you know all the possible values that an attribute can have, you can enumerate those values in ODL. For example, if you know that the maximum number of sections for a course is 8, you can use the keyword *enum* before the attribute name (section) within the CourseOffering class and the possible values after the name.

```
class CourseOffering {
   attribute string term
   attribute enum section {1, 2, 3, 4, 5, 6, 7, 8}
//operation
   short enrollment()
}
```

Defining Relationships

Finally, we will add the relationships shown in Figure 12-1 to the ODL schema. There are two binary relationships and one unary relationship. As discussed in Chapter 5, a relationship is inherently bidirectional. In Figure 12-1, we have provided names for both directions of a relationship. For example, we have named the relationship between Student and Course Offering *Takes* when traversing from the former to the latter, and *Taken by* when traversing in the reverse direction. We use the ODL keyword *relationship* to specify a relationship.

```
class Student {
   attribute string name
   attribute Date dateOfBirth
   attribute Address address
   attribute Phone phone
// relationship between Student and CourseOffering
   relationship set<CourseOffering> takes inverse CourseOffering::taken_by
//operations
   short age()
   float gpa()
   boolean register_for(string crse, short sec, string term)
}
```

---

[1]If the strict ODL syntax is followed, the argument type has to be preceded by the keyword "in", "out", or "inout", specifying the argument as an input, output, or input/output, respectively. We have chosen not to show this specification for the sake of simplicity.

Within the Student class, we have defined the "takes" relationship, using the relationship keyword. The name of the relationship is preceded by the class the relationship targets: CourseOffering. Because a student can take multiple course offerings, we have used the keyword "set" to indicate that a Student object is related to a set of CourseOffering objects. This relationship specification represents the traversal path from Student to CourseOffering.

The ODMG Object Model requires that a relationship be specified in both directions. In ODL, the *inverse* keyword is used to specify the relationship in the reverse direction. The inverse of "takes" is "taken_by" from CourseOffering to Student. In the class definition for Student, we have named this traversal path (taken_by), preceded by the name of the class from where the path originates (CourseOffering), along with a double colon (::). In the class definition for CourseOffering shown below, the relationship is specified as "taken_by," with the inverse being "takes" from Student. Because a course offering can be taken by many students, the relationship links a set of Student objects to a given CourseOffering object. For a many-to-many relationship such as this, therefore, you must specify a collection (set, list, bag, or array) of objects on both sides.

```
class CourseOffering {
   attribute string term
   attribute enum section {1, 2, 3, 4, 5, 6, 7, 8}
// many-to-many relationship between CourseOffering and Student
   relationship set<Student> taken_by inverse Student::takes
// one-to-many relationship between CourseOffering and Course
   relationship Course belongs_to inverse Course::offers
//operation
   short enrollment()
}
```

The ODBMS would automatically enforce the *referential integrity* of the relationships you specify in an ODL schema (Bertino and Martino, 1993; Cattell and Barry, 1997). For instance, if you delete a Student object, the ODBMS will automatically dereference its links to all CourseOffering objects. It will also dereference links from all CourseOffering objects back to that Student object. If you link a Student object to a set of CourseOffering objects, the ODBMS will automatically create inverse links. That is, it will create a link from each of the CourseOffering objects back to the Student object in question.

We have specified another relationship, "belongs_to," for the CourseOffering class, with the inverse being "offers" from Course. Because a course offering belongs to exactly one course, the destination of the belongs_to traversal path is Course, implying that a CourseOffering object can be linked to only one Course object. In specifying the "one" side of an association relationship, therefore, you simply specify the destination object type, and not a collection (e.g., set) of an object type.

We show below how to specify the relationships and operation for Course. We have specified the offers relationship within Course, with the inverse being belongs_to. But because the course offerings are ordered within a course (according to section number within a given term), we have used *list*, as opposed to *set*, to denote the ordering within the collection. Both directions of the unary relationship shown in Figure 12-1, has_prereqs and is_prereq_for, begin and terminate in the Course class, as specified in the Course definition below.

```
class Course {
   attribute string crse_code
   attribute string crse_title
   attribute short credit_hrs
```

```
class Student {
( extent students)
  attribute string name
  attribute Date dateOfBirth
  attribute Address address
  attribute Phone phone
  relationship set<CourseOffering> takes inverse CourseOffering::taken_by
  short age()
  float gpa()
  boolean register_for(string crse, short sec, string term)
}

class CourseOffering {
( extent courseofferings)
  attribute string term
  attribute enum section {1, 2, 3, 4, 5, 6, 7, 8}
  relationship set<Student> taken_by inverse Student::takes
  relationship Course belongs_to inverse Course::offers
  short enrollment()
}

class Course {
( extent courses)
  attribute string crse_code
  attribute string crse_title
  attribute short credit_hrs
  relationship set<Course> has_prereqs inverse Course::is_prereq_for
  relationship set<Course> is_prereq_for inverse Course::has_prereqs
  relationship list<CourseOffering> offers inverse CourseOffering::belongs_to
  short enrollment()
}
```

Figure 12-2
ODL schema for university database

```
// unary relationship for prerequisite courses
   relationship set<Course> has_prereqs inverse Course::is_prereq_for
   relationship set<Course> is_prereq_for inverse Course::has_prereqs
// binary relationship between Course and CourseOffering
   relationship list<CourseOffering> offers inverse CourseOffering::belongs_to
//operation
   short enrollment()
}
```

The complete schema for the university database is shown in Figure 12-2. Notice that we have introduced the ODL keyword *extent* to specify the extents of the classes. The **extent** of a class is the set of all instances of the class within the database (Cattell and Barry, 1997). For example, the extent called students refers to all the Student instances in the database.

Extent: The set of all instances of a class within the database.

Defining an Attribute with an Object Identifier as Its Value

In all the examples that you have seen so far, an attribute's value is always a literal. Recall that we said that it could also be an object identifier. For instance, there could

Figure 12-3 UML class diagram for an employee project database

(a) Many-to-many relationship with an association class

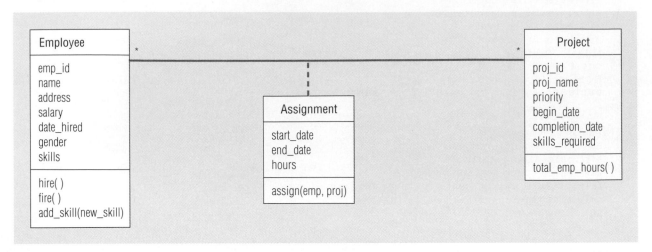

be an attribute called "dept" within Course that represents the department offering a course. Instead of storing the department's name, the attribute could store the identifier for a Department object. We need to make the following changes:

```
class Course {
// the dept attribute's value is an object identifier
    attribute Department dept
// other attributes, operations, and relationships...
}

class Department {
    attribute short dept_number
    attribute string dept_name
    attribute string office_address
}
```

The type of the dept attribute is Department, implying that the attribute's value is an object identifier for an instance of Department. This is akin to representing a unidirectional relationship, from Course to Department. The ODBMS, however, does not automatically maintain the referential integrity of such unidirectional relationships specified through attributes. If most of the references in user queries are from Course to Department (e.g., finding the name of the department offering a given course), not vice versa, and referential integrity is not an issue, then representing such a relationship in one direction using an attribute reference provides a more efficient alternative.

Defining Many-to-Many Relationships, Keys, and Multivalued Attributes

Figure 12-3a shows a many-to-many relationship between Employee and Project. To make an assignment, you need an Employee object, as well as a Project object. Hence we have modeled Assignment as an association class with features of its own. The features include the start_date, end_date, and hours attributes, and the assign operation. In Figure 12-3b, we have broken the many-to-many relationship between

(b) Many-to-many relationship broken into two many-to-many relationships

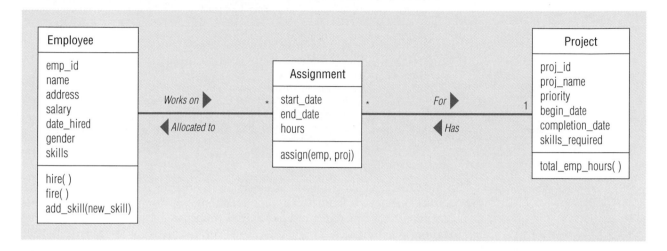

Employee and Project into two one-to-many relationships, one from Employee to Assignment and the other from Project to Assignment. Although we could have specified the many-to-many relationship directly in ODL, we could not have captured the features special to Assignment unless we decomposed the relationship into two one-to-many relationships.

The class diagram shown in Figure 12-3b can now be transformed into the following ODL schema:

```
class Employee {
(   extent employees
// emp_id is the primary key for Employee
    key emp_id)
    attribute short emp_id
    attribute string name
    attribute Address address
    attribute float salary
    attribute Date date_hired
    attribute enum gender {male, female}
// multivalued attribute
    attribute set<string> skills
    relationship set<Assignment> works_on inverse Assignment::allocated_to
// the following operations don't return any values
    void hire()
    void fire()
    void add_skill(string new_skill)
}

class Assignment {
(   extent assignments)
    attribute Date start_date
    attribute Date end_date
    attribute short hours
    relationship Employee allocated_to inverse Employee::works_on
    relationship Project for inverse Project::has
// the following operation assigns an employee to a project
    void assign (short emp, string proj)
}
```

```
class Project {
(  extent projects
// proj_id is the primary key for Project
   key proj_id)
   attribute string proj_id
   attribute string proj_name
   attribute enum priority {low, medium, high}
   attribute Date begin_date
   attribute Date completion_date
//multivalued attribute
   attribute set<string> skills_required
   relationship set<Assignment> has inverse Assignment::for
   long total_emp_hours()
}
```

In the ODL schema, we have specified the candidate keys for Employee and Project using the keyword called *key*. Note that each Employee or Project instance in an object database is inherently unique; that is, you do not require an explicit identifier to enforce the uniqueness of objects. However, specifying a key ensures that no two objects belonging to a class have the same value for the key attribute(s). The scope of uniqueness is confined to the extent of the class. Hence, before specifying a key for a class, you must specify its extent. The emp_id attribute must have a unique value for each Employee object; the same applies to proj_id of Project. ODL also supports compound keys, that is, keys consisting of more than one attribute. For example, if an employee is uniquely identified by name and address, then you could specify the key as follows:

```
keys {name, address}
```

The schema above also illustrates how to define a multivalued attribute, an attribute that may have multiple values at a given point in time. The skills attribute of Employee and the skills_required attribute of Project are each specified as a set of string values.

Defining Generalization

ODL supports unary and binary association relationships, but not relationships of higher degree. It allows you to represent generalization relationships using the *extends* keyword. In Figure 12-4, we have shown a UML class diagram you had seen earlier in Chapter 5. Three subclasses—Hourly Employee, Salaried Employee, and Consultant—are generalized into a superclass called Employee. The ODL schema corresponding to the class diagram is given below:

```
class Employee {
(  extent employees)
   attribute short emp_number
   attribute string name
   attribute Address address
   attribute float salary
   attribute Date date_hired
   void print_label()
}
```

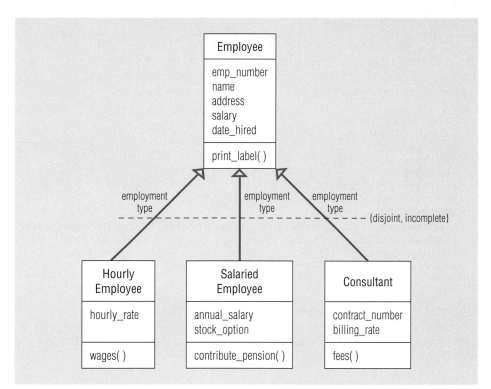

Figure 12-4
UML class diagram showing
employee generalization

```
class HourlyEmployee extends Employee {
(  extent hrly_emps)
   attribute float hourly_rate
   float wages()
}

class SalariedEmployee extends Employee {
(  extent salaried_emps)
   attribute float annual_salary
   attribute boolean stock_option
   void contribute_pension()
}

class Consultant extends Employee {
(  extent consultants)
   attribute short contract_number
   attribute float billing_rate
   float fees()
}
```

The subclasses HourlyEmployee, SalariedEmployee, and Consultant extend the more
general Employee class by introducing new features. For example, HourlyEmployee
has two special features, hourly_rate and wages, in addition to the common set of features inherited from Employee. All the classes, including Employee, are concrete,
implying that they can have direct instances. Employee is a concrete class because the
subclasses are incomplete.

Defining an Abstract Class

Figure 12-5 shows an example of an abstract class called Student, which cannot have any direct instances. That is, a student has to be an instance of Graduate Student or of Undergraduate Student (note the "complete" constraint among the subclasses). In the logical schema, we specify Student as an abstract class as follows:

```
abstract class Student {
(  extent students
   key stu_number)
   attribute long stu_number
   attribute string name
   attribute Date dateOfBirth
   attribute Address address
   attribute Phone phone
   relationship set<CourseOffering> takes inverse CourseOffering::taken_by
   boolean register_for(string crse, short section, string term)
// abstract operation
   abstract float calc_tuition()
}
```

Notice that the calc_tuition operation of Student is abstract, implying that, at this level, the operation's form is specified but not its implementation. We have used the *abstract* keyword to specify both the abstract class and the abstract operation.[2] The subclasses are defined as follows:

```
class GraduateStudent extends Student {
(  extent grads)
   attribute char undergrad_major
   attribute GRE gre_score
   attribute GMAT gmat_score
   float calc_tuition()
}

class UndergradStudent extends Student {
(  extent undergrads)
   attribute SAT sat_score
   attribute ACT act_score
   float calc_tuition()
}
```

Because both of the subclasses are concrete, the calc_tuition operations within them must also be concrete. Therefore, although each subclass inherits the form of the operation from Employee, it still has to provide the method. The calc_tuition operation is specified separately within each subclass, thereby illustrating polymorphism. The fact that it is concrete is indicated by the absence of the *abstract* keyword.

Defining Other User Structures

The schema definition contains user-defined structures such as GRE, GMAT, SAT, and ACT, which specify the types for the various test scores. While a predefined

---

[2]ODL does not currently support the "abstract" keyword for classes and operations. The syntax we have used parallels that of Java, which clearly differentiates an abstract class/operation from a concrete class/operation.

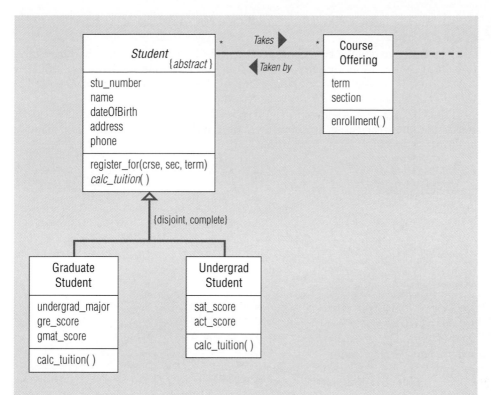

Figure 12-5
UML class diagram showing student generalization

structure such as Date or Time allows you to readily use it for attribute specification, you can define additional structures that could be used for the same purpose. We define the structures for the test scores as follows:

```
struct GRE {
    Score verbal_score
    Score quant_score
    Score analytical_score
}

struct GMAT {
    Score verbal_score
    Score quant_score
}

struct SCORE {
    short scaled_score
    short percentile_score
}

struct SAT { ... }

struct ACT { ... }
```

The GRE structure consists of a verbal score, a quantitative score, and an analytical score, while the GMAT structure does not have an analytical score. The type of each of these scores, in turn, is a structure called SCORE, which consists of a scaled score (e.g., 680) and a percentile score (e.g., 95%).

OODB DESIGN FOR PINE VALLEY FURNITURE COMPANY

In Chapter 5, we developed a conceptual object-oriented model for the Pine Valley Furniture Company in the form of a class diagram (see Figure 5-18). We will now transform this conceptual model into a logical ODL schema, which may be used to implement an object-oriented database system for the company.

The ODL schema is shown in Figure 12-6. By now you should be able to clearly understand how each class, attribute, operation, and relationship in the class diagram

Figure 12-6

ODL schema for Pine Valley Furniture Company database

```
class Salesperson {
(  extent salespersons
   key salespersonID)
   attribute string salespersonID
   attribute string salespersonName
   attribute Phone salespersonFax
   relationship SalesTerritory serves inverse
       SalesTerritory::represented_by
   float totalCommission()
}

class SalesTerritory {
(  extent salesterritories
   key territoryID)
   attribute char territoryID
   relationship set<Salesperson> represented_by
       inverse Salesperson::serves
   relationship set<Customer> consists_of inverse
       Customer::does_business_in
}

class Customer {
(  extent customers
   key customerID)
   attribute string customerID
   attribute string customerName
   attribute Address customerAddress
   attribute float balance
   relationship set<SalesTerritory>
       does_business_in inverse
       SalesTerritory::consists_of
   relationship list<Order> submits inverse
       Order::submitted_by
   void mailInvoice(float amount)
   void receivePaymt(float amount)
}

class Order {
(  extent orders
   key orderID)
   attribute string orderID
   attribute Date orderDate
   relationship Customer submitted_by inverse
       Customer::submits
   relationship list<OrderLine> contains inverse
       OrderLine::contained_in
   float orderTotal()
}

class OrderLine {
(  extent orderlines)
   attribute short quantity
   relationship Order contained_in inverse
       Order::contains
   relationship Product specifies inverse
       Product::specified_in
   long orderlineTotal()
}

class Product {
(  extent products
   key productID)
   attribute string productID
   attribute string productDescr
   attribute char productFinish
   attribute float unitPrice
   relationship ProductLine belongs_to inverse
       ProductLine::includes
   relationship set<OrderLine> specified_in
       inverse OrderLine::specifies
   relationship set<WorkCenter> produced_at
       inverse WorkCenter::produces
   relationship set<RawMaterial> uses inverse
       RawMaterial::used_in
   float totalSales()
   boolean assignProd(string line)
}

class ProductLine {
(  extent productlines)
   attribute string productLineName
   relationship list<Product> includes inverse
       Product::belongs_to
   float totalSales()
}

class WorkCenter {
(  extent materialID
   key workCenterID)
   attribute char workCenterID
   attribute string location
   relationship set<Product> produces inverse
       Product::produced_by
   relationship list<Employee> employs inverse
       Employee::works_in
}
```

```
class RawMaterial {                          class Employee {
(  extent rawmaterials                       (  extent employees
   key materialID)                              key employeeID)
   attribute string materialID                  attribute string employeeID
   attribute enum unitOfMeasure {piece, box,    attribute string employeeName
       carton, lb, oz, gallon, litre}           attribute Address employeeAddress
   attribute float standardCost                 relationship set<WorkCenter> works_in inverse
   relationship set<Product> used_in inverse        WorkCenter::employs
       Product::uses                            relationship set<skill> has inverse
   relationship set<Supply> listed_in inverse       Skill::possessed_by
       Supply::lists                            relationship Employee supervised_by inverse
}                                                   Employee::supervises
                                                relationship set<Employee> supervises inverse
class Supply {                                      Employee::supervised_by
(  extent supplies)                             boolean checkSkills(string product)
   attribute float unitPrice                 }
   relationship RawMaterial lists inverse
       RawMaterial::listed_in
   relationship Vendor provided_by inverse   class Skill {
       Vendor::provides                      (  extent skills)
}                                               attribute string skillName
                                                relationship set<Employee> possessed_by inverse
class Vendor {                                      Employee::has
(  extent vendors)                           }
   attribute string vendorName
   attribute Address vendorAddress
   relationship set<Supply> provides inverse
       Supply::provided_by
}
```

has been mapped to an equivalent ODL construct in the logical schema. A few points need some mention, however. The definitions of the Address and Phone structures are not shown in the figure because they were given previously. Notice that the type for the salespersonFax attribute of Salesperson is Phone, indicating that the attribute shares the same type as phone. Also, although the class diagram does not specify any of the collections as ordered, we ordered some of them in the ODL schema. For example, the collection of order lines contained within an Order object is specified as a list, implying that the order line objects are ordered or sorted.

Another thing to note is how we mapped the two many-to-many relationships, each with an association class, into two one-to-many relationships. The first one is between Order and Product with an association class called OrderLine. In the logical schema, we defined a class called OrderLine that participates in two one-to-many relationships, one with Order and the other with Product. The other many-to-many relationship with an association class is *Supplies,* which was similarly mapped into two one-to-many relationships, one between Vendor and Supply, and the other between RawMaterial and Supply.

CREATING OBJECT INSTANCES

When a new instance of a class is created, a unique object identifier is assigned. You may specify an object identifier with a unique tag name. For example, we can create a new course object called MBA 669 as follows:

```
MBA669 course {}
```

This creates a new instance of Course. The object tag name, MBA699, can be used to reference this object. We have not specified the attribute values for this object at this point. Suppose you want to create a new student object and initialize some of its attributes.

```
Cheryl student {name "Cheryl Davis", dateOfBirth 4/5/77}
```

This creates a new student object with a tag name of Cheryl and initializes the values of two attributes. You can also specify the values for the attributes within a structure as in the following example:

```
Jack student {
    name "Jack Warner", dateOfBirth 2/12/74,
    address {street_address "310 College Rd", city "Dayton",
            state "Ohio", zip 45468}
    phone {area_code 937, personal_number 228-2252}}
```

For a multivalued attribute, you can specify a set of values. For example, you can specify the skills for an employee called Dan Bellon as follows:

```
Dan employee {emp_id 3678, name "Dan Bellon",
                skills {"Database design", "OO Modeling"}}
```

Establishing links between objects for a given relationship is also easy. Suppose you want to store the fact that Cheryl is taking three courses in fall 1999. You can write:

```
Cheryl student {takes {OOAD99F, Telecom99F, Java99F}}
```

where OOAD99F, Telecom99F, and Java99F are tag names for three course offering objects. This definition creates three links for the "takes" relationship, from the object tagged Cheryl to each of the course offering objects.

Consider another example. To assign Dan to the TQM project, we write:

```
assignment {start_date 2/15/99, allocated_to Dan, for TQM}
```

Notice that we have not specified a tag name for the assignment object. Such objects will be identified by the system-generated object identifiers. The assignment object has a link to an employee object (Dan) and another link to a project object (TQM).

OBJECT QUERY LANGUAGE

We will now describe the Object Query Language (OQL), which has been set forth as an ODMG standard for querying OODBs. OQL allows you a lot of flexibility in formulating queries. You can write a simple query such as

Jack.dateOfBirth

which returns Jack's birth date, a literal value, or

Jack.address

which returns a structure with values for street address, city, state, and zip. If instead we want to simply find in which city Jack resides, we can write

Jack.address.city

Like SQL, OQL uses a select-from-where structure to write more complex queries. Consider, for example, the ODL schema for the university database given in Figure 12-2. We will see how to formulate OQL queries for this database. Because of the strong similarities between SQL and OQL, the explanations in the following sections are quite brief. For further explanations, you may want to review Chapter 9 on SQL and Chapter 5 on object modeling. The more interested reader is referred to the chapter on OQL in Cattell and Barry (1997).

Basic Retrieval Command

Suppose we want to find the title and credit hours for MBA 664. Parallel to SQL, those attributes are specified in the select clause, and the extent of the class that has those attributes is specified in the from clause. In the where clause, we specify the condition that has to be satisfied. In the query shown below, we have specified the extent courses of the Course class and bound the extent to a variable called c in the from clause. We have specified the attributes crse_title and credit_hrs for the extent (i.e., set of all Course instances in the database) in the select clause, and stated the condition, c.crse_code = "MBA 664", in the where clause.

```
select c.crse_title, c.credit_hrs
from courses c
where c.crse_code = "MBA 664"
```

Because we are dealing with only one extent, we could have left out the variable c without any loss in clarity. However, as with SQL, if you are dealing with multiple classes that have common attributes, you must bind the extents to variables so that the system can unambiguously identify the classes for the selected attributes.

Including Operations in Select Clause

We can invoke operations in an OQL query similar to the way we specify attributes. For example, to find the age of John Marsh, a student, we invoke the "age"operation in the select clause.

```
select s.age
from students s
where s.name = "John Marsh"
```

The query returns an integer value, assuming that there is only one student with that name. In addition to literal values, a query can also return objects with identity. For example, the query

```
select s
from students s
where s.gpa >= 3.0
```

returns a collection of student objects for which the gpa is greater than or equal to 3.0. Notice that we have used the gpa operation in the where clause.

If we want to formulate the same query, but only for those students who do not reside in Dayton, we can use the *not* operator as in SQL:

```
select s
from students s
where s.gpa >= 3.0
and not (s.address.city = "Dayton")
```

Instead of using "not", we could have specified the new condition as follows:

```
s.address.city != "Dayton"
```

where ! is the inequality operator.

Now suppose that we want to find the ages of all students whose gpa is less than 3.0. This query is:

```
select s.age
from students s
where s.gpa < 3.0
```

Finding Distinct Values

The preceding query will return a collection of integers. It is possible that there is more than one student with the same age. If you want to eliminate duplicates, you can reformulate the query using the distinct keyword as shown below:

```
select distinct s.age
from students s
where s.gpa < 3.0
```

Querying Multiple Classes

In an OQL query, you can traverse the paths for the relationships defined in the schema. The following query finds the course codes of all courses that were offered in fall 1998.

```
select distinct y.crse_code
from courseofferings x,
     x.belongs_to y
where x.term = "Fall 1998"
```

We have used *distinct* in the select clause because a course may have had multiple offerings in the given term. In the *from* clause, we have specified a path from a CourseOffering object to a Course object using the "belongs_to" relationship between them. The variable "y" gets bound to the Course object where the path represented by x.belongs_to terminates.

Suppose that we want to find the number of students enrolled in section 1 of the MBA 664 course. The enrollment operation is available in CourseOffering, but the course code is available in Course. The query given below traverses from CourseOffering to Course using the belongs_to relationship. The variable "y" represents the destination object for the x.belongs_to path.

```
select x.enrollment
from courseofferings x,
  x.belongs_to y
where y.crse_code = "MBA 664"
and x.section = 1
```

The following query traverses two paths, one using the "takes" relationship and the other using the "belongs_to" relationship, to find the codes and titles of all courses taken by Mary Jones.

```
select c.crse_code, c.crse_title
from students s
  s.takes x,
  x.belongs_to c
where s.name = "Mary Jones"
```

We can also select a structure consisting of multiple components. For example, the following query returns a structure with age and gpa as its attributes.

```
select distinct struct(name: s.name, gpa: s.gpa)
from students s
where s.name = "Mary Jones"
```

Writing Subqueries

You can use a select statement within a select statement. To select course codes, course titles, and course offerings for which the enrollment is less than 20, you can write the following OQL command:

```
select distinct struct (code: c.crse_code, title: c_crse_title,
    (select x
    from c.offers x
    where x.enrollment < 20 ))
    from courses c
```

This query returns a collection of distinct structures, each of which contains string values for course code and course title, and an object identifier for a CourseOffering object.

You can also use a select statement within the from clause (by the way, this is possible also in SQL, but this was not illustrated in Chapter 9). In the example below, we have written a query that retrieves the names, addresses, and gpa's for those students over 30 with gpa more than or equal to 3.0.

```
select x.name, x.address, x.gpa
from (select s from students s where s.gpa >= 3.0) as x
where x.age > 30 )
```

Calculating Summary Values

OQL supports all the aggregate operators that SQL does: count, sum, avg, max, and min. For example, we can find the number of students in the university by using the count operator as follows:

```
count(students)
```

We could have also written this query as

```
select count (*)
from students s
```

Let us now consider the schema for the employee-project database that we saw earlier. Suppose we want to find the average salary of female employees in the company. We use the avg function to do that in the following query:

```
select avg_salary_female: avg (e.salary)
from employees e
where e.gender = female
```

To find the maximum salary paid to an employee, we use the max function:

```
max (select salary from employees)
```

To find the total of all employee salaries, we use the sum function:

```
sum (select salary from employees)
```

Calculating Group Summary Values

As in SQL, you can partition a query response into different groups. In the following query, we have used the group command to form two groups based on gender: male and female. The query calculates the minimum salary for each of the two groups.

```
select min (e.salary)
from employees e
group by e.gender
```

If we want to group the projects based on their priority levels, we can write the following query:

```
select *
from projects p
group by    low:          priority = low
            medium:       priority = medium
            high:         priority = high
```

This query returns three groups of project objects, labeled by the priority of the group: low, medium, and high.

Qualifying Groups   As with SQL, we can use the *having* command to impose a condition or filter on each group as a whole. For example, in the following query, we filter only those groups for which a total of more than 50 hours have been logged in.

```
select *
from projects p
group by    low:          priority = low
            medium:       priority = medium
            high:         priority = high
having sum(select x.hours from p.has x) > 50
```

Using a Set in a Query

Sometimes you will have to find whether an element belongs to some set. To do that, you should use the *in* keyword. Suppose we want to find the IDs and names of those employees who are skilled in database design or object-oriented modeling. Note that skills is a multivalued attribute, implying that it stores a set of values. In the where clause, we have used "in" to check if database design or object-oriented modeling is one of the elements in an employee's skill set.

```
select emp_id, name
from employees
where "Database Design" in skills
or "OO Modeling" in skills
```

Similarly, we can find those employees who have worked in a project whose ID is TQM9.

```
select e.emp_id, e.name
from employees e,
  e.works_on a,
  a.for p
where "TQM9" in p.proj_id
```

To find those projects that do not require C++ programming skills, we can write:

```
select *
from projects p
where not ("C++ Programming" in p.skills_required)
```

Finally, you can use the existential quantifier *exists* and the universal quantifier *for all*. The following query finds those employees who have been assigned to at least one project.

```
select e.emp_id, e.name
from employees e
where exists e in (select x from assignments y
                        y.allocated_to x)
```

The select statement inside the where clause returns a set of employee objects (i.e., their identifiers) allocated to all the assignments. The exists quantifier then checks if an employee object bound in the from clause is in that set. If so, that employee's ID and name are included in the response, otherwise not.

If we want to find the employees who have worked only on projects beginning in 1998, we can use the *for all* quantifier as follows:

```
select e.emp_id, e.name
from employees e,
  e.works_on a
where for all a: a.start_date >= 1/1/98
```

In the from clause, the query finds a set of assignment objects that an employee object is linked to through the "works_on" relationship. In the where clause, it applies the condition (start_date >= 1/1/98) to all the objects in the set using the for all quantifier. Only if the condition is satisfied by all those objects, are the employee's ID and name included in the query response.

CURRENT ODBMS PRODUCTS AND THEIR APPLICATIONS

With the growing need in organizations to store and manipulate complex data (e.g., image, audio, and video) and relationships, in applications ranging from computer-aided design and manufacturing (CAD/CAM) to geographic information systems to multimedia, ODBMS products are gaining popularity. But more than anything else, industry analysts believe that Internet and Web-based applications are responsible for the sudden renewed interest in ODBMSs (King, 1997; Watterson, 1998).

ODBMSs allow organizations to store diverse components (objects) associated with their Web sites (Watterson, 1998). The proliferation of complex data types on the Web and the need to store, index, search, and manipulate such data have provided ODBMS technology an edge over other database technologies. To counter this emerging technology, major relational database vendors such as Oracle, Informix, IBM, and Sybase have come up with universal databases, also known as object-relational DBMSs (ORDBMSs), as a possible alternative. An ORDBMS is a hybrid relational DBMS that somehow incorporates complex data as objects (King, 1997; also see Appendix A). However, these systems raise concerns relating to performance and scalability. Moreover, the fundamental mismatch between relational and object technology may induce many firms to adopt the pure ODBMS option.

The types of applications for which ODBMSs are particularly useful include bill-of-materials data (see Figure 5-16), telecommunications data supporting navigational access, healthcare, engineering design, finance and trading, multimedia, and geographic information systems. Several commercial ODBMS products are currently available. Examples include ObjectStore (the current market leader), O_2, Versant, GemStone, Objectivity, and Jasmine (see Table 12-1).

Watterson (1998) provides several examples of real-world applications of ODBMSs. Lucent Technologies' Customer Support Division used GemStone to share information globally on customers' switches. Motorola used Objectivity to store complex celestial information for one of its satellite networks. Groupe Paradis, a retirement-plan management company in France, uses O_2 to access over 100 gigabytes of data spread across several databases. And companies like GTE, Southwest Airlines, and Time-Warner have used ObjectStore to develop dynamic Web applications that require integrating pieces of information from various sources on the fly.

Industry experts predict that ODBMSs represent the most promising of the emerging database systems. While for traditional business applications, relational DBMSs are expected to maintain their hold on the market, the data for many applications, such as the ones described above, cannot be easily flattened to two-dimensional database tables. Also, accessing the data from various tables requires you to perform joins, which could become very costly.

SUMMARY

In this chapter, you learned how to implement an object-oriented database system using the object definition language. We introduced you to the syntax and semantics of ODL. You learned how to transform a conceptual schema, represented in the form of a UML class diagram, to a logical schema, defined using ODL constructs. You further learned how to populate an OODB by creating new instances and specifying attribute values for those instances. We also introduced you to OQL, a language

Table 12-1   ODBMS Products

Company	Product	Web Site
Computer Associates	Jasmine	http://www.cai.com/products/jasmine
Franz	AllegroStore	http://www.franz.com
Fujitsu Software	Jasmine	http://www.fsc.fujitsu.com
Gemstone Systems	GemStone/S	http://www.gemstone.com
Matisse Software	ADB	http://www.matisse.com
neoLogic	neoAccess	http://neologic.com
O_2 Technology	O_2	http://www.o2tech.com
Object Design	ObjectStore	http://www.odi.com
Objectivity	Objectivity/DB	http://www.objectivity.com
Object Systems	ITASCA	http://www.iprolink.ch/ibex.com
Ontos	Ontos Integrator	http://www.ontos.com
Persistence	Persistence Live Object Server	http://www.persistence.com
Poet Software	Poet Object Server	http://www.poet.com
Unisys	Osmos	http://www.osmos.com
Versant	Versant ODBMS	http://www.versant.com

Other Links Related to ODBMS Products

Barry & Associates	http://www.odbmsfacts.com
Cetus links	http://www.uax.es/uax/oop/allpages.html
International Data Corp. (Bulletin 14065)	http://www.idcresearch.com
Doug Barry's *The Object Database Handbook*	http://wiley.com
Object database newsgroup	news://comp.databases.object
Rick Cattell's *The Object Database Standard ODMG 2.0*	http://www.mkp.com
Object Database Management Group`	http://www.odmg.org

designed for querying OODBs. Using OQL, we showed you how to write various types of OODB queries.

The chapter also discussed the types of applications for which ODBMSs are well suited. It briefly described some of the applications for which current ODBMSs have been used.

While Chapter 5 provided you with the conceptual underpinnings of OODB design, this chapter provides you with the knowledge required to actually implement an object-oriented database system using an ODMG-compliant ODBMS.

CHAPTER REVIEW

KEY TERMS

Array	Collection literal	Set
Atomic literal	Extent	Structured literal
Bag	List	

REVIEW QUESTIONS

1. Define each of the following terms:
   a. object class
   b. relationship
   c. extent
   d. atomic literal
   e. structured literal

2. Contrast the following terms:
   a. list; bag
   b. set; array
   c. collection literal; structured literal

3. Explain the concept of an object identifier. How is an object identifier different from a primary key in a relational system?

4. What is the purpose of the *struct* keyword in ODL?

5. What is the purpose of the *enum* keyword in ODL?

6. Explain the meaning of the term *relationship set* for many of the relationships in Figure 12-2.

7. Explain the hazards of representing a relationship in ODL by implying that an attribute's value is an object identifier rather by using the relationship clause.

8. Explain the meaning of the *extends* keyword in ODL.

9. Explain the parallels and differences between SQL and OQL.

PROBLEMS AND EXERCISES

1. Develop an ODL schema for the following problem situation. A student, whose attributes include studentName, Address, phone, and age, may engage in multiple campus-based activities. The university keeps track of the number of years a given student has participated in a specific activity and, at the end of each academic year, mails an activity report to the student showing his participation in various activities.

2. Develop an ODL schema for a real estate firm that lists property for sale. The following describes this organization:
   - The firm has a number of sales offices in several states; location is an attribute of sales office.
   - Each sales office is assigned one or more employees. Attributes of employee include employeeID and employeeName. An employee must be assigned to only one sales office.
   - For each sales office, there is always one employee assigned to manage that office. An employee may manage only the sales office to which she is assigned.
   - The firm lists property for sale. Attributes of property include propertyName and location.
   - Each unit of property must be listed with one (and only one) of the sales offices. A sales office may have any number of properties listed, or may have no properties listed.

- Each unit of property has one or more owners. Attributes of owner are ownerName and address. An owner may own one or more units of property. For each property that an owner owns, an attribute called percentOwned indicates what percentage of the property is owned by the owner.

3. Develop an ODL schema for some organization that you are familiar with—Boy Scouts/Girl Scouts, sports team, etc. Include at least four association relationships.

4. Develop an ODL schema for the following situation (state any assumptions you believe you have to make in order to develop the schema): Stillwater Antiques buys and sells one-of-a-kind antiques of all kinds (for example, furniture, jewelry, china, and clothing). Each item is uniquely identified by an item number and is also characterized by a description, asking price, condition, and open-ended comments. Stillwater works with many different individuals, called clients, who sell items to and buy items from the store. Some clients only sell items to Stillwater, some only buy items, and some others both sell and buy. A client is identified by a client number, and is also described by a client name and client address. When Stillwater sells an item in stock to a client, the owners want to record the commission paid, the actual selling price, sales tax (tax of zero indicates a tax exempt sale), and date sold. When Stillwater buys an item from a client, the owners want to record the purchase cost, date purchased, and condition at time of purchase.

Problems and Exercises 5–14 all pertain to the ODL schema in Figure 12-2. Write OQL queries for these exercises.

5. Find the names and phone numbers of all those students who took only one course in fall 1998.

6. Find the code and title of all courses that were offered in both the winter 1998 and fall 1998 terms.

7. Find the total enrollment for all sections of the MBA 664 course being offered in winter 1999.

8. Find the prerequisite courses (code and title) for the MIS 385 course.

9. Find all those students who reside in Cincinnati and who took the MBA 665 course in fall 1998.

10. Find the total credit hours for all prerequisite courses for the MIS 465 course.

11. Find the average age and gpa of students, grouped by the city they live in.

12. Find the courses (code and title) taken by Sean Chen in winter 1999.

13. Find the names and phone numbers of all students who are taking sections 1 and 2 of the MBA 665 course in winter 1999.

14. Find the minimum enrollment among all the sections of each 3 credit-hour course being offered in the winter 1999 term. The response should by grouped by course and the group label should be crse_code.

FIELD EXERCISES

---

1. Interview a database administrator in a company with which you are familiar. Ask this person to explain the potential benefits of an ODBMS for that organization. Are they planning to use an ODBMS? Why or why not?

2. Visit the World Wide Web site for this textbook. From that site, visit several sites for vendors of ODBMSs. Prepare a summary of one of the products you find. How does its DDL compare to the ODL in this chapter? How does its query language compare to the OQL explained in this chapter? What claims does the vendor make about the relative advantages of their product versus other ODBMS or relational products?

REFERENCES

Bertino, E., and Martino, L. 1993. *Object-Oriented Database Systems: Concepts and Architectures.* Wokingham, England: Addison-Wesley.

Cattell, R. G. G., and D. K. Barry. (Eds.) 1997. *The Object Database Standard: ODMG 2.0.* San Francisco: Morgan Kaufmann.

King, N. H. 1997. "Object DBMSs: Now or Never." *DBMS* (July): 42–99.

Watterson, K. 1998. "When It Comes to Choosing a Database, the Object Is Value." *Datamation* (December/January): 100–107.

Project Case

Review the project description found in the Project Case in Chapter 5. Refer to this description and your answer to Project Exercises for that case in responding to the following exercises.

PROJECT EXERCISES

1. Develop an ODL schema for your answer to Project Exercise 1 from Chapter 5.

2. Write three questions that would be typical of applications using this schema and develop OQL commands for each of these queries.

Data Administration

CHAPTER 13

Data and Database Administration

CHAPTER 14

Data Warehouse

Part V Overview

Parts II through IV have prepared you to develop useful and efficient databases. Part V introduces some additional, important database design and management issues. These issues include database security, backup, and recovery; controlling concurrent access to data; preserving data quality; advanced topics in database performance tuning; and one of the most actively discussed database topics today—data warehousing. Following Part V are three appendices, covering the object-relational data model, advanced normal forms, and data structures.

You are likely to conclude from reading this text that data are a corporate asset, just as personnel, physical resources, and financial resources are corporate assets. As such, data and information are resources that are too valuable to be managed casually. Data administration activities have been developed to help achieve organizations' goals for the effective management of data.

In Chapter 13 you will learn about the critical activities of data and database administration. You will learn the meaning of critical concepts and terms, including concurrency control, deadlock, encryption, information repository, locking, recovery, system catalog, transaction, and versioning. You will learn about the role of both

- a *data administrator*—the person who takes overall responsibility for data, metadata, and policies about data use, and

- a *database administrator*—the person who is responsible for physical database design and for dealing with the technical issues, such as security enforcement, database performance, and backup and recovery, associated with managing a database.

Data and database administration activities occur throughout the database development process. A data administrator plays a stronger role during early stages of database development and in the overall planning of data resources. A database administrator plays a stronger role during physical database design, implementation, and operation.

Given the remarkable developments in information technology during the last few years, one would expect that most organizations would have highly developed systems for delivering required information to their managers and other users. Surprisingly, this is seldom the case. Managers are often frustrated by their inability to access or use the data and information they require.

This situation of managerial frustration is a consequence of the fragmented way in which organizations have developed information systems—and their supporting databases—for many years. Throughout this text we have emphasized a carefully planned approach to systems development that would lead to an integrated set of databases. However, the reality is that most organizations have resorted to a "one-thing-at-a-time" approach for developing their systems. This approach has inevitably led to a hodge podge of uncoordinated and often inconsistent databases on a variety of hardware and software platforms.

In addition, most systems are developed or purchased to support *operational processing*, with little or no thought given to the *informational processing* (or analytical tools) required to support decision making. As we explain in Chapter 14, the processing performed and the types of data required are very different for these two types of processing.

Data warehouses consolidate and integrate information from many different sources and format it into a meaningful context for making accurate business decisions. Data warehousing has evolved to meet these needs without disturbing existing operational processing.

Chapter 14 provides an overview of data warehousing. In this chapter you will learn key concepts and terms, including data mart, reconciled data, derived data, star schema, snowflake schema, on-line analytical processing, data mining, and data visualization. Data warehousing is an exceptionally broad topic that would normally require an entire text. We have chosen to emphasize the areas of data architecture and database design, which we consider of greatest importance in a database textbook. First we describe the overall concept of a data warehouse, and how the warehouse relates to existing operational systems. Next we describe the three-tier data architecture, which is most appropriate for most data warehouse environments. We then address the problem of extracting data from existing operational systems and loading them into a data warehouse. Finally, we discuss how users interact with the data warehouse including on-line analytical processing, data mining, and data visualization.

13

Data and Database Administration

After studying this chapter, you should be able to:

■ Define the following key terms: **data administration, database administration, database security, encryption, database recovery, transaction, concurrency control, locking, deadlock, versioning, system catalog,** and **information repository**.

■ List several major functions of data administration and of database administration.

■ Describe the changing roles of the data administrator and database administrator in the current business environment.

■ Describe the role of data dictionaries and information repositories and how they are used by data administration.

■ Describe the function of a database management system (DBMS) and the major components of a DBMS.

■ Compare the optimistic and pessimistic systems of concurrency control.

■ Describe the problem of database security, and list five techniques that are used to enhance security.

■ Describe the problem of database recovery, and list four basic facilities that are included with a DBMS to recover databases.

■ Describe the problem of tuning a database to achieve better performance, and list 5 areas where changes may be made when tuning a database.

INTRODUCTION

The critical importance of data to organizations is now recognized. Data are a corporate asset, just as personnel, physical resources, and financial resources are corporate assets. As such, data and information are resources that are too valuable to be managed casually. The development of information technology has made effective management of corporate data far more possible. Data administration activities have been developed to help achieve organizations' goals for the effective management of data. Effective data administration provides support for managerial decision making at all levels in the organization.

Ineffective data administration, on the other hand, leads to poor data utilization, and can be characterized by the following conditions, which are all too common in organizations:

1. Multiple definitions of the same data entity and/or inconsistent representations of the same data elements in separate databases, making integration of data across different databases hazardous.

2. Missing key data elements, whose loss eliminates the value of existing data.

3. Low data quality levels due to inappropriate sources of data or timing of data transfers from one system to another, thus reducing the reliability of the data.

4. Inadequate familiarity with existing data, including awareness of data location and meaning of stored data, thus reducing the capability to use the data to make effective strategic or planning decisions.

Data administration: A high-level function that is responsible for the overall management of data resources in an organization, including maintaining corporate-wide definitions and standards.

Database administration: A technical function that is responsible for physical database design and for dealing with technical issues such as security enforcement, database performance, and backup and recovery.

Organizations have responded to these data utilization issues with different strategies. Some have created a function called **data administration**. The person who heads this function is called the data administrator, or information resource manager, and takes responsibility for the overall management of data resources. A second function, that of **database administration**, has been regarded as responsible for physical database design and for dealing with the technical issues, such as security enforcement, database performance, and backup and recovery, associated with managing a database. Other organizations combine the data administration and database administration functions. The rapidly changing pace of business has caused the roles of the data administrator and the database administrator (DBA) to change, in ways that are discussed below.

THE CHANGING ROLES OF DATA AND DATABASE ADMINISTRATORS

Two factors are driving the changes in the data administration and database administration roles: the availability of more technologies and platforms that must be managed concurrently at many organizations, and the increased pace of business changes (Quinlan, 1996). Against the background of these changes, it is important to understand traditional role distinctions. This will help us to understand the ways in which the roles are being blended in organizations that have different information technology architectures.

Data Administration

Databases are shared resources that belong to the entire enterprise; they are not the property of a single function or individual within the organization. Data administration is the custodian of the organization's data, in much the same sense that the controller is custodian of the financial resources. Like the controller, the data administrator must develop procedures to protect and control the resource. Also, data administration must resolve disputes that may arise when data are centralized and shared among users, and must play a significant role in deciding where data will be stored and managed. Data administration is a high-level function that is responsible for the overall management of data resources in an organization, including maintaining corporate-wide data definitions and standards.

Data administration is responsible for a wide range of functions, including database planning, analysis, design, implementation, maintenance, and protection. Data administration is also responsible for improving database performance and for providing education, training, and consulting support to users. The data administrator must interact with top management, users, and computer applications specialists.

Selecting the data administrator and organizing the function are extremely important. The data administrator must be a highly skilled manager capable of resolving differences that normally arise when significant change is introduced into an organization. The data administrator should be a respected, senior-level middle manager selected from within the organization, rather than a technical computer expert or a new individual hired for the position.

The manager of the data administration function requires a high level of both managerial and technical skills. On the one hand, this person must be capable of eliciting the cooperation of users, who may resist the idea of giving up their private data to a shared database. Also, these users must be convinced of the benefits of adhering to a set of standard definitions and procedures for accessing the database. On the other hand, the data administrator must be capable of managing a technical staff and dealing with technical issues such as query optimization and concurrency control.

Database Administration

Typically, the role of database administration is taken to be a more hands-on, physical involvement with the management of a database or databases. Database administration is a technical function that is responsible for physical database design and for dealing with technical issues such as security enforcement, database performance, and backup and recovery. The database administrator should be involved in every phase of database development, from database planning through the analysis, design, and implementation stages, and on through operation, maintenance, and modification. The DBA carries through the standards and procedures established by the data administrator, including enforcing programming standards, data standards, policies, and procedures. In organizations where there is not a separate database administration function, the DBA also assumes the responsibilities of the data administrator.

Just as the data administrator needs a wide variety of job skills, so does the DBA. A broad technical background, including a sound understanding of current hardware architectures and capabilities and a solid understanding of data processing, is essential. An understanding of the database development life cycle, including traditional and prototyping approaches, is also necessary. Strong design and data modeling skills are essential at the conceptual, logical, and physical levels. But managerial skills are also critical; the DBA must manage other IS personnel as the database is analyzed, designed, and implemented, and the DBA must also interact with and provide support for the end users who are involved with the design and usage of the database.

There are no universally accepted data administration and database administration structures, and organizations vary widely in their approaches to data administration. As business practices change, the roles are also changing within organizations. There is, however, a core set of database administration functions that must be met in every organization, regardless of the database administration structure they have chosen. These functions may be spread across data administrators and database administrators, or at the other extreme, all of these functions may be handled by a single DBA. Some of the functions are organization-level functions, and those tend to be classed as data administration functions in organizations that distinguish between data administration and database administration. Other functions are much more specific to a database or application, and they tend to be classed as database administration functions. In any case, though, effective data administration requires that the following functions be addressed:

- *Data policies, procedures, and standards*   Every database application requires protection established through consistent enforcement of data policies, procedures, and standards. Data policies are statements that make explicit the goals of data administration, such as, "Every user must have a password." Data procedures are written outlines of actions to be taken in order to perform a certain activity. Backup and recovery procedures, for example, should be communicated to all involved employees. Data standards are explicit conventions and behaviors that are to be followed and that can be used to help evaluate database quality. Naming conventions for database objects should be standardized for programmers, for example. Also, increased use of external data sources and increased access to organizational databases from outside the organization have increased the importance of employees' understanding of data administration policies, procedures, and standards.

- *Planning*   A key data administration function is involvement with the development of the organization's information architecture. Effective data administration requires both the understanding of the needs of the organization for information, and the ability to contribute to the development of an information architecture that will meet the diverse needs of the typical organization. It is crucial that those involved in data administration understand the information requirements of the organization and be able to contribute to the development of the information architecture that will meet those needs.

- *Data conflict resolution*   Databases are intended to be shared, and usually involve data from several different departments of the organization. Ownership of data is a ticklish issue at least occasionally in every organization. Those in data administration are well placed to resolve data ownership issues because they are not typically associated with a certain department. Establishing procedures for resolving such conflicts is essential. If the data administration function has been given sufficient authority to mediate and enforce the resolution of the conflict, they may be very effective in this capacity.

- *Internal marketing*   While the importance of data and information to the organization has become more widely recognized within the organization, it is not necessarily true that an appreciation for data administration standards has also evolved. The importance of following established procedures and policies must be proactively instituted through data administrators. Effective internal marketing may reduce resistance to change and data ownership problems.

- *Managing the data repository*   Repositories contain the metadata that describe an organization's data and data processing resources. Information repositories are replacing data dictionaries in many organizations. While data dictionaries are simple data-element documentation tools, information repositories are used by data administrators and other information specialists to manage the total information-processing environment. The repository is an essential tool for data administration and is used throughout the entire database system life cycle. An information repository serves as a source of information for each of the following:

1. Users who must understand data definitions, business rules, and relationships among data objects

2. Automated CASE tools that are used to specify and develop information systems

3. Applications that access and manipulate data (or business information) in the corporate databases

4. Database management systems, which maintain the repository and update system privileges, passwords, object definitions, etc.

- *Selection of hardware and software*   The evaluation and selection of hardware and software is critical to an organization's success. The increasingly rapid development of new hardware and software and the rapid change within organizations creates a very demanding situation. A vendor's database that is the most appropriate product available when the choice of platform is made may turn out to be an unfortunate choice if a competitor releases a new version that has different and more appropriate functionality. The current vendor may even go out of business, resulting in a production database that is a nightmare to maintain. Database administrators are being expected to know more about hardware architectures and to be able to administer both in-house-developed applications and off-the-shelf applications, as organizations strive to meet their information needs more rapidly.

- *Managing data security, privacy, and integrity*   Protecting the security, privacy, and integrity of the organizational databases rests with the database administration function. More detailed explanations of the ways in which privacy, security, and integrity are assured are included later in the chapter. Here it is important to realize that the advent of the Internet and intranets to which databases are attached, along with the possibilities for distributing data and databases to multiple sites, have complicated the management of data security, privacy, and integrity.

- *Data backup and recovery*   The DBA must ensure that backup procedures are established that will allow the recovery of all necessary data, should a loss occur through application failure, hardware failure, physical or electrical disaster, or human error or malfeasance. Common backup and recovery strategies are also discussed later in this chapter. These strategies must be fully tested and evaluated at regular intervals.

Reviewing these data administration functions should convince any reader of the importance of proper data administration, both at the organizational and the project level. Failure to take the proper steps can greatly reduce an organization's ability to operate effectively, and may even result in its going out of business. Pressures to reduce application development time must always be reviewed to be sure that necessary quality is not being forgone in order to react more quickly, for such shortcuts are likely to have very serious repercussions.

Changing Approaches to Data Administration

The traditional approach to database management follows practices that enforce the quality and integrity of the data. Movement from each stage of the development process is monitored and sign-offs are generally required when moving from one phase to the next. Usually the databases involved must handle heavy transaction loads, are mission critical, and have high availability. It may take a year or more for a database project to be completed under such circumstances. The database development process was described in Chapter 2 and included these activities: enterprise modeling, conceptual data modeling, logical database design, physical database design and creation, database implementation, and database maintenance. Figure 13-1 presents a breakdown of the major functions within each of the life-cycle phases. This figure also shows which of the functions are traditionally considered to be data administration activities and which are database administration activities. Notice that data administration is normally responsible for the following functions: database planning, conceptual design, and logical database design. Database administration is typically responsible for physical database design and much of database implementation, operation, and maintenance. Several functions, such as specifying database access policies, conducting user training, and managing growth and change, may be the responsibility of both groups.

The actual allocation of responsibilities between data administration and database administration varies from one organization to the next. Organizations that employ separate data administration functions often have mainframe-based databases that have been developed using established systems development methodologies, including development of logical and physical data models. Operating from an existing database infrastructure that includes carefully specified database standards and backup and disaster recovery procedures, database development is generally carefully controlled. Many organizations now, though, have blended the data administration and database administration roles together. These organizations emphasize the capability to build a database quickly, tuning it for maximum performance and being able to restore it to production quickly when problems develop. These databases are more likely to be departmental, client/server databases that are developed quickly using newer development approaches such as prototyping, which allow changes to be made more quickly. Awareness of changing hardware capabilities also affects database administration behavior. Hot-swappable drives (which can be plugged in and restored without powering down) make it quicker to replace a corrupted 100-gigabyte drive than to restore it. Dropping storage costs have resulted in Level 5 RAID systems (redundant arrays of inexpensive disks) and mirroring becoming common. DBAs must know more about hardware architectures and be able to tune devices effectively. The blending of data administration and database administration roles also means that DBAs in such organizations must be able to create and enforce data standards and policies. DBAs in such environments are expected to deliver high-quality, robust systems quickly. Across all organizations, database administrators will be expected to maintain required quality levels while decreasing the time required to build a reliable system. Quinlan (1996) has suggested some changes in data administration and database administration practices that can be made at each stage of the traditional database development life cycle to accomplish these goals:

- *Database planning*   Improve selection of technology by selectively evaluating possible products. Be sure to consider each technology's fit with the enterprise data model, seeking to find ways to reduce time required in later stages as a result of careful selection of technology at the database planning stage.

Figure 13-1
Functions of data
administration and
database administration

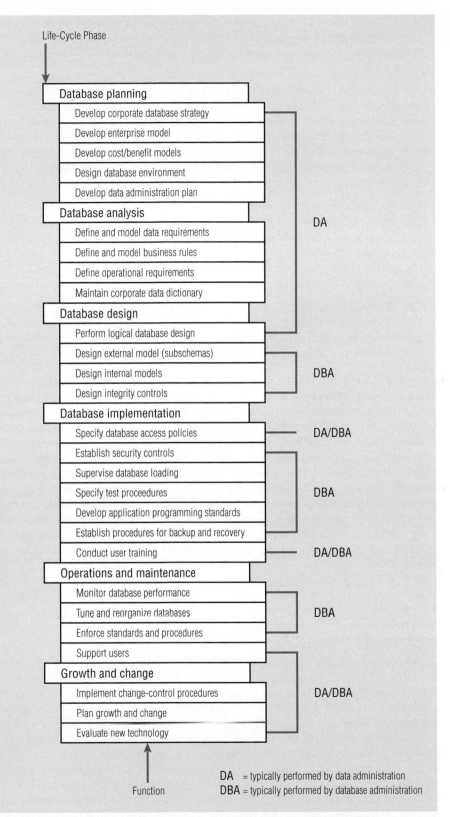

- *Database analysis*   Try to work on physical design in parallel with development of the logical and physical models. Prototyping the application now may well lead to changes in the logical and physical data models earlier in the development process.

- *Database design*   Prioritize application transactions by volume, importance, and complexity. These transactions are going to be most critical to the application. Specifications for them should be reviewed as quickly as the transactions are developed. Logical data modeling, physical database modeling, and prototyping may occur in parallel. DBAs should strive to provide adequate control of the database environment while allowing the developers space and opportunity to experiment.

- *Database implementation*   Institute database change-control procedures so that development and implementation are supported rather than slowed. Wherever possible, segment the model into modules that can be analyzed and implemented more quickly. Find ways to test the system more quickly without compromising quality. Testing may be moved earlier in the development; use testing and change control tools to build and manage the test and production environments.

- *Operation and maintenance*   Review all timesaving measures that have been taken to ensure that database quality has not been compromised. Consider using third-party tools and utilities wherever possible to save work; other tools such as Lotus Notes may reduce the need for meetings, thus saving time.

The DBA role has emerged in the last ten years with the advent of shared databases. In the next ten years, the role will continue to evolve. Most see the DBA role as becoming more specialized, evolving into specialties such as distributed database/network capacity planning DBAs, server programming DBAs, off-the-shelf customizing DBAs, or warehousing DBAs (Dowgiallo et al., 1997). The ability to work with multiple databases, communication protocols, and operating systems will be highly valued. Those DBAs who gain broad experience and develop the ability to adapt quickly to changing environments will have many opportunities. It is possible that some current DBA activities, such as tuning, will be replaced by decision support systems able to tune systems by analyzing usage patterns. Opportunities in large companies to continue working with very large databases (VLDBs) and opportunities in small and midsize companies to manage desktop and midrange servers should remain strong.

MODELING ENTERPRISE DATA

In the current business environment DBAs are pressured to adapt to change while providing high-quality systems quickly. Key to achieving these expectations is developing an enterprise architecture or Information Systems Architecture, as described briefly in Chapter 2. The author of ISA (Zachman, 1987) sees the development of information systems to be similar to other complex product development and manufacturing processes. He has studied those processes in order to apply their principles and procedures to development of an information systems enterprise architecture. Building an enterprise architecture enables an organization to make the step from business strategy to implementation more effectively. Zachman (1997, p. 48) defines an enterprise architecture as "that set of descriptive representations (that is, models) that are relevant for describing an enterprise such that it (the enterprise) can be produced to management's requirements (quality) and maintained over the period of its useful life (change)."

All too often in systems development, the enterprise view has been de-emphasized as developers concentrated on building a piece of the enterprise system. It has often been problematic to fit these pieces together into a smoothly functioning enterprise system. Some systems are no longer relevant when completed, or do not remain relevant for long. System maintenance is a major portion of the overall cost of a new system. Problems such as the Year 2000 problem, currently estimated by the Gartner Group at $400 billion worldwide, arise from past failures to address data element definitions within the enterprise architecture.

Ideally, every database development project should fit within the enterprise architecture. This means developing conceptual data models that are congruent with the needs of the business and that are then translated into logical data models, physical data models, and implemented systems. Such congruence has been clearly promoted and is a part of every database design life cycle. But the conceptual data models must also fit across Zachman's framework, meshing with the business process model, business network logistics, work flow models within the enterprise, the enterprise master schedule, and the enterprise business plan. Each component, such as the conceptual data model, has an architectural structure of its own, but it must also fit with the architectural structures of the other components of the framework. The enterprise-wide impacts of execution of each component must be considered, and problems and discontinuities resolved.

Organizations that articulate an enterprise architecture and develop standards and procedures to ensure that systems development projects fit within that enterprise architecture should experience benefits. Code can be reused, systems mesh together rather than conflicting with each other, and business objectives are met. As the articulation and incorporation of business rules becomes more sophisticated, those organizations with an articulated enterprise architecture should be able to implement those business rules more consistently and more quickly than similar organizations who have not developed an enterprise architecture. Such possibilities provide obvious strategic benefits to organizations in today's competitive environment.

PLANNING FOR DATABASES

The initial phase of the database development life cycle is planning. It is at this point that a proposed system should be carefully considered from the viewpoint of the enterprise architecture. Database design occurs within the constraints of the enterprise information system. During the planning phase, an initial assessment of the proposed database system is made. The proposed system should contribute to meeting the business's goals and strategies, which have been developed as part of the enterprise architecture. The other components of the Scope layer in the enterprise architecture are also important:

- What data will be included? Have they previously been identified as being important to the business?

- What processes will the system perform? Have these processes been identified as important organization processes?

- What business locations will the system affect? Should the locations identified be affected by such as system, or have some locations that will be unintentionally affected been identified?

- Which work units and people will be affected by the system, and what is the nature of these effects? What effects on work units beyond the work unit requesting the new system have been identified?

- How will the system fit with significant business events? Will the new system fit with existing schedules?

The initial assessment will also include consideration of continuing use of the existing system, modifying the existing system, or replacing the existing system. The decision will rest with the extent to which flaws in the current system exist, and the possibilities for correcting those flaws.

If a new system is a possibility, then a feasibility study should be conducted. The feasibility study should address the technical aspects of the project, including hardware and software purchase or development costs, operating environment, system size and complexity, and level of experience with similar systems. At this point it is not necessary to identify particular vendors or products, but classes of implementation, such as PC or mainframe hardware, database model, and programming language should be considered. The feasibility study should also address the estimated costs of the project, both tangible and intangible. Costs should be identified as one-time costs associated with the project or recurring costs that will continue throughout the life of the system. Operational feasibility, an assessment of the likelihood that the project will meet its expected objectives, should also be determined. The likelihood of completing the project within the expected time schedule should also be estimated. Any potential legal or contractual problems should be identified now. And, political implications of the project should be considered. Key stakeholder support for the project will greatly improve its prospects of success.

Once the feasibility information has been collected, a formal review of the project that includes all interested parties can be conducted. The focus of this review is to verify all information and assumptions in the baseline plan that has been developed before moving ahead with the project. After the project is approved, problems defined during the planning phase will be studied further during the analysis phase of the project.

MANAGING DATA SECURITY

Database security:
Protection of the data against accidental or intentional loss, destruction, or misuse.

The goal of **database security** is the protection of data from accidental or intentional threats to its integrity and access. The database environment has grown more complex, with distributed databases located on client/server architectures rather than mainframes. Access to data has become more open through the Internet and corporate intranets. As a result, managing data security effectively has also become more difficult and time consuming. As noted earlier in the chapter, data administration is responsible for developing overall policies and procedures to protect databases. The facilities that data administrators have to use in establishing adequate data security are discussed below, but first it is important to review potential threats to data security.

Threats to Data Security

Threats to data security may be direct threats to the database. For example, those who gain unauthorized access to a database may then browse, change, or even steal the data to which they have gained access. Focusing on database security alone,

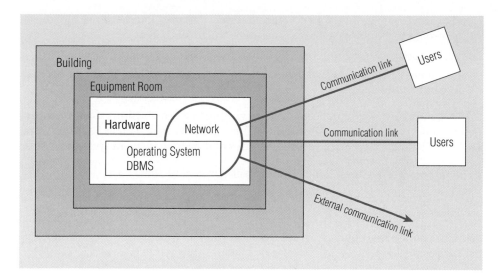

Figure 13-2
Possible locations of data
security threats

however, will not ensure a secure database. All parts of the system must be secure, including the database, the network, the operating system, the building(s) in which the database resides physically, and the personnel who have any opportunity to access the system. Figure 13-2 diagrams many of the possible locations for data security threats. Accomplishing this level of security requires careful review, establishment of security procedures and policies, and implementation and enforcement of those procedures and policies. The following threats must be addressed in a comprehensive data security plan:

- *Accidental losses, including human error, software, and hardware-caused breaches*
  Establishing operating procedures such as user authorization, uniform software installation procedures, and hardware maintenance schedules are examples of actions that may be taken to address threats from accidental losses. As in any effort that involves human beings, some losses are inevitable, but well thought out policies and procedures should reduce the amount and severity of losses. Of potentially more serious consequence are the threats that are not accidental.

- *Theft and fraud* These activities are going to be perpetrated by people, quite possibly through electronic means, and may or may not alter data. Attention here should focus on each possible location shown in Figure 13-2. For example, control of physical security, so that unauthorized personnel are not able to gain access to the machine room, should be established. Data access policies that restrict altering data immediately prior to a payroll run will help to secure the data. Establishment of a firewall to protect unauthorized access to inappropriate parts of the database through outside communication links is another example of a security procedure that will hamper people who are intent on theft or fraud.

- *Loss of privacy or confidentiality* Loss of privacy is usually taken to mean loss of protection of data about individuals, while loss of confidentiality is usually taken to mean loss of protection of critical organizational data, which may have strategic value to the organization. Failure to control privacy of information may lead to blackmail, bribery, public embarrassment, or stealing of user passwords. Failure to control confidentiality may lead to loss of competitiveness.

- *Loss of data integrity* When data integrity is compromised, data will be invalid or corrupted. Unless data integrity can be restored through established backup and recovery procedures, an organization may suffer serious losses or make incorrect and expensive decisions based on the invalid data.

- *Loss of availability* Sabotage of hardware, networks, or applications may cause the data to become unavailable to users, which again may lead to severe operational difficulties.

A comprehensive data security plan will include establishing administrative policies and procedures, physical protections, and data management software protections. The most important security features of data management software follow:

1. Views or subschemas, which restrict user views of the database

2. Authorization rules, which identify users and restrict the actions they may take against a database

3. User-defined procedures, which define additional constraints or limitations in using a database

4. Encryption procedures, which encode data in an unrecognizable form

5. Authentication schemes, which positively identify a person attempting to gain access to a database

6. Backup, journaling, and checkpointing capabilities, which facilitate recovery procedures

Views

In Chapter 9 we defined a view as a subset of the database that is presented to one or more users. A view is created by querying one or more of the base tables, producing a dynamic result table for the user at the time of the request. Thus, a view is always based on the current data in the base tables that it is built from. The advantage of a view is that it can be built to present only the data to which the user requires access, effectively preventing the user from viewing other data that may be private or confidential. The user may be granted the right to access the view, but not to access the base tables upon which the view is based. So, confining a user to a view may be more restrictive for that user than allowing him access to the involved base tables.

For example, we could build a view for a Pine Valley employee that provides information about materials needed to build a Pine Valley furniture product without providing other information, such as unit price, that is not relevant to the employee's work. This command creates a view that will list the wood required and the wood available for each product:

```
CREATE VIEW MATERIALS_V
    AS
    SELECT PRODUCT_T.PRODUCT.ID, PRODUCT_NAME, FOOTAGE,
    FOOTAGE_ON_HAND
        FROM PRODUCT_T, RAW_MATERIALS_T, USES_T
            WHERE PRODUCT_T.PRODUCT_ID = USES_T.PRODUCT_ID
            AND RAW_MATERIALS_T.MATERIAL_ID =
            USES_T.MATERIAL_ID;
```

The contents of the view created will be updated each time the view is accessed, but here are the current contents of the view, which can be accessed with the SQL command

```
SELECT * FROM MATERIALS_V;

PRODUCT_ID PRODUCT_NAME              FOOTAGE FOOTAGE_ON_HAND
           1 End Table                    4               1
           2 Coffee Table                 6              11
           3 Computer Desk               15              11
           4 Entertainment Center        20              84
           5 Writer's Desk               13              68
           6 8-Drawer Desk               16              66
           7 Dining Table                16              11
           8 Computer Desk               15               9
8 rows selected.
```

The user can write SELECT statements against the view, treating it as though it were a table. Although views promote security by restricting user access to data, they are not adequate security measures, because unauthorized persons may gain knowledge of or access to a particular view. Also, several persons may share a particular view; all may have authority to read the data, but only a restricted few may be authorized to update the data. Finally, with high-level query languages, an unauthorized person may gain access to data through simple experimentation. As a result, more sophisticated security measures are normally required.

Authorization Rules

Authorization rules are controls incorporated in the data management system that restrict access to data and also restrict the actions that people may take when they access data. For example, a person who can supply a particular password may be authorized to read any record in a database but cannot necessarily modify any of those records.

Fernandez, Summers, and Wood (1981) have developed a conceptual model of database security. Their model expresses authorization rules in the form of a table (or matrix) that includes subjects, objects, actions, and constraints. Each row of the table indicates that a particular subject is authorized to take a certain action on an object in the database, perhaps subject to some constraint. Figure 13-3 shows an example of such an authorization matrix. This table contains several entries pertaining to records in an accounting database. For example, the first row in the table indicates that anyone in the Sales Department is authorized to insert a new customer record in the

Authorization rules:
Controls incorporated in the data management systems that restrict access to data and also restrict the actions that people may take when they access data.

Figure 13-3
Authorization matrix

Subject	Object	Action	Constraint
Sales Dept.	Customer record	Insert	Credit limit LE $5000
Order trans.	Customer record	Read	None
Terminal 12	Customer record	Modify	Balance due only
Acctg. Dept.	Order record	Delete	None
Ann Walker	Order record	Insert	Order amt LT $2000
Program AR4	Order record	Modify	None

Figure 13-4

Implementing authorization rules

(a) Authorization table for subjects (salespersons)

	Customer records	Order records
Read	Y	Y
Insert	Y	Y
Modify	Y	N
Delete	N	N

	Salespersons (password BATMAN)	Order entry (password JOKER)	Accounting (password TRACY)
Read	Y	Y	Y
Insert	N	Y	N
Modify	N	Y	Y
Delete	N	N	Y

(b) Authorization table for objects (order records)

database, provided that the customer's credit limit does not exceed $5,000. The last row indicates that the program AR4 is authorized to modify order records without restriction. Data administration is responsible for determining and implementing authorization rules that are implemented at the database level. Authorization schemes can also be implemented at the operating system level or the application level.

Most contemporary database management systems do not implement an authorization matrix such as the one shown in Figure 13-3; they normally use simplified versions. There are two principal types: authorization tables for subjects and authorization tables for objects. Figure 13-4 shows an example of each type. In Figure 13-4a, for example, we see that salespersons are allowed to modify customer records but not delete these records. In Figure 13-4b, we see that users in Order Entry or Accounting can modify order records, but salespersons cannot. A given DBMS product may provide either one or both of these types of facilities.

Authorization tables such as those shown in Figure 13-4 are attributes of an organization's data and their environment; they are therefore properly viewed as metadata. Thus, the tables should be stored and maintained in the repository. Since authorization tables contain highly sensitive data, they themselves should be protected by stringent security rules. Normally, only selected persons in data administration have authority to access and modify these tables.

For example, in Oracle7, the privileges included in Figure 13-5 can be granted to users at the database or table level. INSERT and UPDATE can be granted at the column level. Where many users, such as those in a particular job classification, need similar privileges, roles may be created that contain a set of privileges, and then all of the privileges can be granted to a user simply by granting the role. To grant the ability to read the product table and update prices to a user with the login ID of smith, the following SQL command may be given:

```
GRANT SELECT, UPDATE (unit_price) ON PRODUCT_T TO SMITH;
```

There are eight data dictionary views that contain information about privileges that have been granted. In this case, DBA_TAB_PRIVS contains users and objects for

Figure 13-5
Oracle7 privileges

Privilege	Capability
SELECT	Query the object.
INSERT	Insert records into the table/view. Can be given for specific columns.
UPDATE	Update records in table/view. Can be given for specific columns.
DELETE	Delete records from table/view.
ALTER	Alter the table.
INDEX	Create indexes on the table.
REFERENCES	Create foreign keys that reference the table.
EXECUTE	Execute the procedure, package, or function.

every user who has been granted privileges on objects, such as tables. DBA_COL_PRIVS contains users who have been granted privileges on columns of tables.

User-Defined Procedures

Some DBMS products provide user exits (or interfaces) that allow system designers or users to create their own **user-defined procedures** for security, in addition to the authorization rules we have just described. For example, a user procedure might be designed to provide positive user identification. In attempting to log on to the computer, the user might be required to supply a procedure name in addition to a simple password. If valid password and procedure names are supplied, the system then calls the procedure, which asks the user a series of questions whose answers should be known only to that password holder (such as mother's maiden name).

User-defined procedures: User exits (or interfaces) that allow system designers to define their own security procedures in addition to the authorization rules.

Encryption

For highly sensitive data such as company financial data, data encryption can be used. **Encryption** is the coding or scrambling of data so that humans cannot read them. Some DBMS products include encryption routines that automatically encode sensitive data when they are stored or transmitted over communications channels. For example, encryption is commonly used in electronic funds transfer (EFT) systems. Other DBMS products provide exits that allow users to code their own encryption routines.

Encryption: The coding or scrambling of data so that humans cannot read them.

Any system that provides encryption facilities must also provide complementary routines for decoding the data. These decoding routines must be protected by adequate security, or else the advantages of encryption are lost, and they also require significant computing resources.

Authentication Schemes

A long-standing problem in computer circles is how to positively identify persons who are trying to gain access to a computer or its resources. The first line of defense is the use of passwords, which provides some protection. However, people assigned passwords for different devices quickly devise ways to remember these passwords, ways that tend to decrease the effectiveness of the password scheme. The passwords get written down, where others may find them. They get shared with other users; it is not unusual for an entire department to use one common password for access. Passwords get included in automatic logon scripts, which removes the inconvenience of remembering them and typing them but also eliminates their effectiveness. And passwords usually traverse a network in cleartext, not encrypted, so if intercepted they may be easily interpreted. Also, passwords cannot, of themselves, ensure the security of a computer and its databases, because they give no indication of who is trying to gain access. The current distributed and networked environments require additional security measures. Different approaches and combinations of approaches are being tried to deal with this problem.

Biometric device: Measures or detects personal characteristics such as fingerprints, voice prints, eye pictures, or signature dynamics.

First, industry has developed devices and techniques to positively identify any prospective user. The most promising of these appear to be **biometric devices**, which measure or detect personal characteristics such as fingerprints, voice prints, eye pictures, or signature dynamics. The use of retina prints has declined because of concerns about possible damaging effects to the eye by the laser optics used to capture a retina print. To implement the biometric approach, several companies have developed a smart card that embeds an individual's unique biometric data (such as fingerprints or hand geometry) permanently on the card. To access a computer, the user inserts the card into a reader device (a biometric device) that reads the person's fingerprint or other characteristic. The actual biometric data are then compared with the stored data, and the two must match for the user to gain computer access. A lost or stolen card would be useless to another person, since the biometric data would not match.

Another approach is the use of third-party mediated authentication systems, which establish user authenticity through a trusted authentication agent, such as Kerberos. Developed at MIT, Kerberos is primarily used in application-level protocols, such as TELNET or FTP, to provide user-to-host security. Kerberos works by providing a secret key (Kerberos ticket) to a user that can then be embedded in any other network protocol. Any process which implements that protocol can then be certain of the source of the request. Sun Microsystems also has an authentication mechanism, called DES Authentication, which is based on the sender encrypting a timestamp when the message is sent, which is then checked against the receiver's internal clock. This requires agreement between the agents as to the current time and both must be using the same encryption key. Liability issues have kept third-party authentication schemes from achieving widespread acceptance. Public key, certificate-based authentication schemes which issue to parties identification certificates that they can then exchange without further involvement of a third party are also being used. Such digital certificates will be used extensively in electronic commerce transactions involving credit card or digital cash purchases.

A last piece of the authentication problem is establishing nonrepudiation. That is, after a message has been sent, the user should not be able to repudiate having sent the message, or say that it was not sent. Biometric devices coupled with the sending of messages are used to establish nonrepudiation.

BACKING UP DATABASES

Database recovery: Mechanisms for restoring a database quickly and accurately after loss or damage.

Database recovery is data administration's response to Murphy's law. Inevitably, databases are damaged or lost because of some system problem that may be caused by human error, hardware failure, incorrect or invalid data, program errors, computer viruses, or natural catastrophes. Since the organization depends so heavily on its database, the database management system must provide mechanisms for restoring a database quickly and accurately after loss or damage.

Basic Recovery Facilities

A database management system should provide four basic facilities for backup and recovery of a database:

1. **Backup facilities**, which provide periodic backup copies of the entire database

2. **Journalizing facilities**, which maintain an audit trail of transactions and database changes

3. A **checkpoint facility**, by which the DBMS periodically suspends all processing and synchronizes its files and journals

4. A **recovery manager**, which allows the DBMS to restore the database to a correct condition and restart processing transactions

Backup Facilities The DBMS should provide backup facilities that produce a backup copy (or *save*) of the entire database. Typically, a backup copy is produced at least once per day. The copy should be stored in a secured location where it is protected from loss or damage. The backup copy is used to restore the database in the event of hardware failure, catastrophic loss, or damage. Some DBMSs provide backup utilities for the DBA to use to make backups; other systems assume the DBA will use the operating system commands to perform backups. Since performing the nightly backup for a particular database is repetitive, creating a script that automates regular backups will save time and result in fewer backup errors.

With large databases, regular backups may be impractical, as the time required to perform the backup may exceed that available. Or, a database may be a critical system that must always remain available. As a result, backups may be taken of dynamic data regularly, but backups of static data, which don't change frequently, may be taken less often. Incremental backups, which record changes made since the last full backup, but which do not take so much time to complete, may also be taken on an interim basis, allowing for longer periods of time between full backups. Determining backup strategies, thus, must be based on the demands being placed on the database systems.

Journalizing Facilities A DBMS must provide journalizing facilities to produce an audit trail of **transactions** and database changes. In the event of a failure, a consistent database state can be reestablished using the information in the journals together with the most recent complete backup. As Figure 13-6 shows, there are two basic journals, or logs. The first is the **transaction log**, which contains a record of the essential data for each transaction that is processed against the database. Data that are typically recorded for each transaction include the transaction code or identification, time of the transaction, terminal number or user ID, input data values, records accessed, and records modified.

The second kind of log is the **database change log**, which contains before- and after-images of records that have been modified by transactions. A **before-image** is simply a copy of a record before it has been modified, and an **after-image** is a copy of the same record after it has been modified.

Some systems also keep a security log, which can alert the DBA to any security violations that occur or are attempted.

Backup facilities: An automatic dump facility that produces a backup copy (or *save*) of the entire database.

Journalizing facilities: An audit trail of transactions and database changes.

Transaction: A discrete unit of work that must be completely processed or not processed at all within a computer system. Entering a customer order is an example of a transaction.

Transaction log: Contains a record of the essential data for each transaction that is processed against the database.

Database change log: Contains before- and after-images of records that have been modified by transactions.

Before-image: A copy of a record (or page of memory) before it has been modified.

After-image: A copy of a record (or page of memory) after it has been modified.

Figure 13-6
Database audit trail

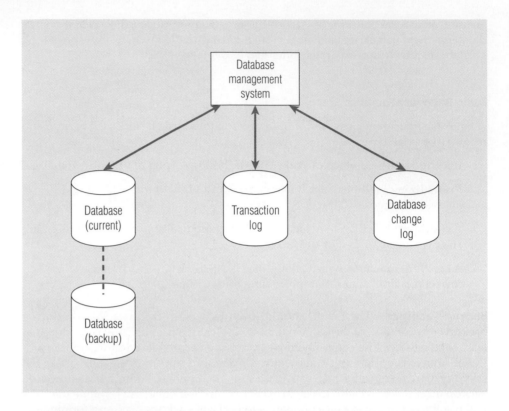

Checkpoint Facility   A **checkpoint facility** in a DBMS periodically refuses to accept any new transactions. All transactions in progress are completed, and the journal files are brought up to date. At this point, the system is in a quiet state, and the database and transaction logs are synchronized. The DBMS writes a special record (called a checkpoint record) to the log file, which is like a snapshot of the state of the database. The checkpoint record contains information necessary to restart the system. Any dirty data blocks (pages of memory that contain changes that have not yet been written out to disk) are written from memory to disk storage, thus ensuring that all changes made prior to taking the checkpoint have been written to long-term storage.

A DBMS may perform checkpoints automatically (which is preferred) or in response to commands in user application programs. Checkpoints should be taken frequently (say, several times an hour). When failures do occur, it is often possible to resume processing from the most recent checkpoint. Thus, only a few minutes of processing work must be repeated, compared with several hours for a complete restart of the day's processing.

Recovery Manager   The **recovery manager** is a module of the DBMS that restores the database to a correct condition when a failure occurs, and resumes processing user requests. The type of restart used depends on the nature of the failure. The recovery manager uses the logs shown in Figure 13-6 (as well as the backup copy, if necessary) to restore the database.

Recovery and Restart Procedures

The type of recovery procedure that is used in a given situation depends on the nature of the failure, the sophistication of the DBMS recovery facilities, and operational policies and procedures. Following is a discussion of the techniques that are most frequently used.

Switch   In order to be able to switch to an existing copy of the database, the database must be mirrored. That is, at least two copies of the database must be kept and updated simultaneously. When a failure occurs, processing is switched to the duplicate copy of the database. This strategy allows for the fastest recovery and has become increasingly popular as the cost of long-term storage has dropped. Level 1 RAID systems implement mirroring. Rather than being stored on a large drive, the database is distributed across several smaller, less expensive disks and mirrored to a second set of such disks. When a disk failure occurs, the system immediately switches to the mirrored disk. The defective or damaged disk can then be removed and a new disk put in place. That disk can be rebuilt from the mirrored disk with no disruption in service to the user. Such disks are referred to as being hot-swappable. This strategy does not protect against loss of power or catastrophic damage to both databases, though.

Restore/Rerun   The **restore/rerun** technique involves reprocessing the day's transactions (up to the point of failure) against the backup copy of the database. The most recent copy of the database (say, from the previous day) is mounted, and all transactions that have occurred since that copy (which are stored on the transaction log) are rerun.

Restore/rerun: Involves reprocessing the day's transactions (up to the point of failure) against the backup copy of the database.

The advantage of restore/rerun is its simplicity. The DBMS does not need to create a database change journal, and no special restart procedures are required. However, there are two major disadvantages. First, the time to reprocess transactions may be prohibitive. Depending on the frequency of making backup copies, several hours of reprocessing may be required. Processing new transactions will have to be deferred until recovery is completed, and if the system is heavily loaded, it may be impossible to catch up. The second disadvantage is that the sequencing of transactions will often be different from when they were originally processed, which may lead to quite different results. For example, in the original run, a customer deposit may be posted before a withdrawal. In the rerun, the withdrawal transaction may be attempted first and may lead to sending an insufficient funds notice to the customer. For these reasons, restore/rerun is not a sufficient recovery procedure and is generally used only as a last resort in database processing.

Transaction Integrity   A database is updated by processing transactions that result in changes to one or more database records. If an error occurs during the processing of a transaction, the database may be compromised, and some form of database recovery is required. Thus, to understand database recovery, we must first understand the concept of transaction integrity.

A business transaction is a sequence of steps that constitute some well-defined business activity. Examples of business transactions are "Admit Patient" in a hospital and "Enter Customer Order" in a manufacturing company. Normally, a business transaction requires several actions against the database. For example, consider the transaction "Enter Customer Order." When a new customer order is entered, the following steps may be performed by an application program:

1. Input order data (keyed by user).

2. Read CUSTOMER record (or insert record if a new customer).

3. Accept or reject the order. If Balance Due plus Order Amount does not exceed Credit Limit, accept the order; otherwise, reject it.

Figure 13-7
Basic recovery techniques

(a) Rollback

(b) Rollforward

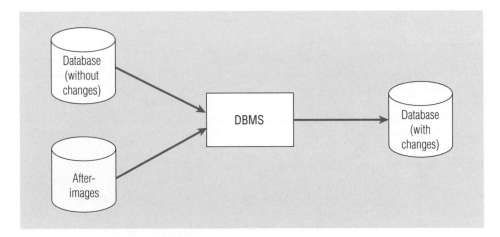

4. If the order is accepted, Increase Balance Due by Order Amount. Store the updated CUSTOMER record. Insert the accepted ORDER record in the database.

In processing a transaction, we want the changes to the database to be made only if the transaction is processed successfully, in its entirety. In this case, we say that the changes are committed. If the transaction fails at any point, we say that it has aborted, and we do not want any of the changes to be made. For example, suppose that the program accepts a new customer order, increases Balance Due, and stores the updated CUSTOMER record. However, suppose that the new ORDER record is not inserted successfully (perhaps there is a duplicate Order No. key, or perhaps there is insufficient physical file space). In this case, we want the transaction to abort.

To maintain transaction integrity, the DBMS must provide facilities for the user or application programmer to define **transaction boundaries**—that is, the logical beginning and end of a transaction. The DBMS should then commit changes for successful transactions and reject changes for aborted transactions.

Backward Recovery With **backward recovery** (also called **rollback**), the DBMS backs out of or undoes unwanted changes to the database. As Figure 13-7a shows, before-images of the records that have been changed are applied to the database. As a result, the database is returned to an earlier state; the unwanted changes are eliminated.

Transaction boundaries:
The logical beginning and end of transactions.

Backward recovery (rollback): Used to back out or undo unwanted changes to the database. Before-images of the records that have been changed are applied to the database, and the database is returned to an earlier state. Used to reverse the changes made by transactions that have been aborted or terminated abnormally.

Backward recovery is used to reverse the changes made by transactions that have aborted, or terminated abnormally. To illustrate the need for backward recovery (or UNDO), suppose that a banking transaction will transfer $100 in funds from the account for customer A to the account for customer B. These steps are performed:

1. The program reads the record for customer A and subtracts $100 from the account balance.

2. The program then reads the record for customer B and adds $100 to the account balance. Now the program writes the updated record for customer A to the database. However, in attempting to write the record for customer B, the program encounters an error condition (such as a disk fault) and cannot write the record. Now the database is inconsistent—record A has been updated but record B has not—and the transaction must be aborted. An UNDO command will cause the recovery manager to apply the before-image for record A to restore the account balance to its original value (the recovery manager may then restart the transaction and make another attempt).

Forward Recovery   With **forward recovery** (also called **rollforward**), the DBMS starts with an earlier copy of the database. Applying after-images (the results of good transactions) quickly moves the database forward to a later state (see Figure 13-7b). Forward recovery is much faster and more accurate than restore/rerun, for the following reasons:

1. The time-consuming logic of reprocessing each transaction does not have to be repeated.

2. Only the most recent after-images need to be applied. A database record may have a series of after-images (as a result of a sequence of updates), but only the most recent, "good" after-image is required for rollforward.

The problem of different sequencing of transactions is avoided, since the results of applying the transactions (rather than the transactions themselves) are used.

Forward recovery (rollforward): Starts with an earlier copy of the database. After-images (the results of good transactions) are applied to the database, and the database is quickly moved forward to a later state.

Types of Database Failure

A wide variety of failures can occur in processing a database, ranging from the input of an incorrect data value to complete loss or destruction of the database. Four of the most common types of problems are aborted transactions, incorrect data, system failure, and database loss or destruction. Each of these types of problems is described in the following sections, and possible recovery procedures are indicated (see Table 13-1).

Aborted Transactions   As we noted earlier, a transaction frequently requires a sequence of processing steps to be performed. An aborted transaction terminates abnormally. Some reasons for this type of failure are human error, input of invalid data, hardware failure, and deadlock (covered in the next section). A common type of hardware failure is the loss of transmission in a communications link when a transaction is in progress.

When a transaction aborts, we want to "back out" the transaction and remove any changes that have been made (but not committed) to the database. The recovery manager accomplishes this by backward recovery (applying before-images for the transaction in question). This function should be accomplished automatically by the

Aborted transaction: A transaction in progress that terminates abnormally.

Table 13-1   Responses to Database Failure

Type of Failure	Recovery Technique
Aborted transaction	Rollback (preferred) Rollforward/rerun transactions to state just prior to abort
Incorrect data (update inaccurate)	Rollback (preferred) Reprocess transactions without inaccurate data updates Compensating transactions
System failure (database intact)	Switch to duplicate database (preferred) Rollback Restart from checkpoint
Database destruction	Switch to duplicate database (preferred) Rollforward Reprocess transactions

DBMS, which then notifies the user to correct and resubmit the transaction. Other procedures, such as rollforward or transaction reprocessing, could be applied to bring the database to the state it was in just prior to the abort occurrence, but rollback is the preferred procedure in this case.

Incorrect Data   A more complex situation arises when the database has been updated with incorrect, but valid, data. For example, an incorrect grade may be recorded for a student, or an incorrect amount input for a customer payment.

Incorrect data are difficult to detect and often lead to complications. To begin with, some time may elapse before an error is detected and the database record (or records) corrected. By this time, numerous other users may have used the erroneous data, and a chain reaction of errors may have occurred as various applications made use of the incorrect data. In addition, transaction outputs (such as documents and messages) based on the incorrect data may be transmitted to persons. An incorrect grade report, for example, may be sent to a student or an incorrect statement sent to a customer.

When incorrect data have been introduced, the database may be recovered in one of the following ways:

1. If the error is discovered soon enough, backward recovery may be used. (However, care must be taken to ensure that all subsequent errors have been reversed.)

2. If only a few errors have occurred, a series of compensating transactions may be introduced through human intervention to correct the errors.

3. If the first two measures are not feasible, it may be necessary to restart from the most recent checkpoint before the error occurred, and subsequent transactions processed without the error.

Any erroneous messages or documents that have been produced by the erroneous transaction will have to be corrected by appropriate human intervention (letters of explanation, telephone calls, etc.)

System Failure   In a system failure, some component of the system fails, but the database is not damaged. Some causes of system failure are power loss, operator error, loss of communications transmission, and system software failure.

When the system crashes, some transactions may be in progress. The first step in recovery is to back out those transactions using before-images (backward recovery). Then, if the system is mirrored, it may be possible to switch to the mirrored data and rebuild the corrupted data on a new disk. If the system is not mirrored, it may not be possible to restart because status information in main memory has been lost or damaged. The safest approach is to restart from the most recent checkpoint before the system failure. The database is rolled forward by applying after-images for all transactions that were processed after that checkpoint.

Database Destruction   In the case of **database destruction**, the database itself is lost, or destroyed, or cannot be read. A typical cause of database destruction is a disk drive failure (or head crash).

Database destruction: The database itself is lost, or destroyed, or cannot be read.

Again, using a mirrored copy of the database is the preferred strategy for recovering from such an event. If there is no mirrored copy, a backup copy of the database is required. Forward recovery is used to restore the database to its state immediately before the loss occurred. Any transactions that may have been in progress when the database was lost are restarted.

CONTROLLING CONCURRENT ACCESS

Databases are shared resources. We must expect and plan for the likelihood that several users will attempt to access and manipulate data at the same time. With concurrent processing involving updates, a database without **concurrency control** will be compromised due to interference between users. There are two basic approaches to concurrency control: a pessimistic approach (involving locking) and an optimistic approach (involving versioning). We summarize both of these approaches in the following sections.

Concurrency control: The process of managing simultaneous operations against a database so that data integrity is maintained and the operations do not interfere with each other in a multiuser environment.

Most DBMSs run in a multiuser environment, with the expectation that users will be able to share the data contained in the database. If users are only reading data, no data integrity problems will be encountered, because no changes will be made in the database. However, if one or more users are updating data, then potential problems with maintaining data integrity arise. When more than one transaction is being processed against a database at the same time, the transactions are considered to be concurrent. The actions that must be taken to ensure that data integrity is maintained are called currency control actions. Remember that the CPU can process only one instruction at a time. As new transactions are submitted while other processing is occurring against the database, the transactions are usually interleaved, with the CPU switching among the transactions so that some portion of each transaction is performed as the CPU addresses each transaction in turn. Because the CPU is able to switch among transactions so quickly, most users will not notice that they are sharing CPU time with other users.

The Problem of Lost Updates

The most common problem encountered when multiple users attempt to update a database without adequate concurrency control is that of lost updates. Figure 13-8 shows a common situation. John and Marsha have a joint checking account and both want to withdraw some cash at the same time, each using an ATM terminal in a different location. Figure 13-8 shows the sequence of events that might occur, in the absence of a concurrency control mechanism. John's transaction reads the account

Figure 13-8
Lost update (no concurrency control in effect)

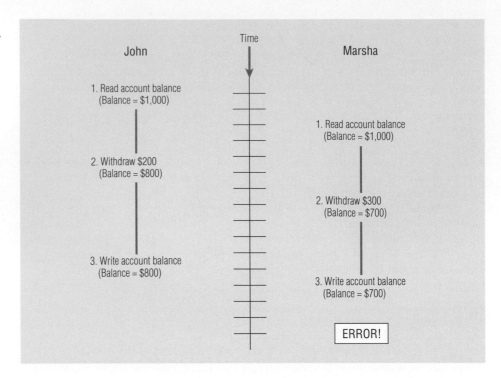

balance (which is $1,000) and he proceeds to withdraw $200. Before the transaction writes the new account balance ($800), Marsha's transaction reads the account balance (which is still $1,000). She then withdraws $300, leaving a balance of $700. Her transaction then writes this account balance, which replaces the one written by John's transaction. The effect of John's update has been lost due to interference between the transactions, and the bank is unhappy.

Another, similar type of problem that may occur when concurrency control is not established is the **inconsistent read problem**. This problem occurs when one user reads data that have been partially updated by another user. The read will be incorrect, and is sometimes referred to as a dirty read or an unrepeatable read.

Inconsistent read problem: An unrepeatable read, one that occurs when one user reads data that have been partially updated by another user.

Serializability

Concurrent transactions need to be processed so that they do not interfere with each other. If one transaction were entirely processed at a time before another transaction, no interference would occur. Procedures that process transactions so that the outcome is the same as this are called serializable. Processing transactions using a serializable schedule will give the same results as if the transactions had been processed one after the other. Schedules are designed so that transactions that will not interfere with each other can still be run in parallel. For example, transactions that request data from different tables in a database will not conflict with each other and can be run concurrently without causing data integrity problems. Serializability is achieved by different means, but locking mechanisms are the most common type of concurrency control mechanism. With **locking**, any data that are retrieved by a user for updating must be locked, or denied to other users, until the update is complete or aborted. Locking data is much like checking a book out of the library—it is unavailable to others until the borrower returns it.

Locking: Any data that are retrieved by a user for updating must be locked, or denied to other users, until the update is completed or aborted.

Locking Mechanisms

Figure 13-9 shows the use of record locks to maintain data integrity. John initiates a withdrawal transaction from an ATM. Since John's transaction will update this record, the application program locks this record before reading it into main memory. John proceeds to withdraw $200, and the new balance ($800) is computed. Marsha has initiated a withdrawal transaction shortly after John, but her transaction cannot access the account record until John's transaction has returned the updated record to the database and unlocked the record. The locking mechanism thus enforces a sequential updating process that prevents erroneous updates.

Locking Level   An important consideration in implementing concurrency control is choosing the locking level. The **locking level** (also called **granularity**) is the extent of the database resource that is included with each lock. Most commercial products implement locks at one of the following levels:

Locking level (granularity): The extent of the database resource that is included with each lock.

Figure 13-9
Updates with locking (concurrency control)

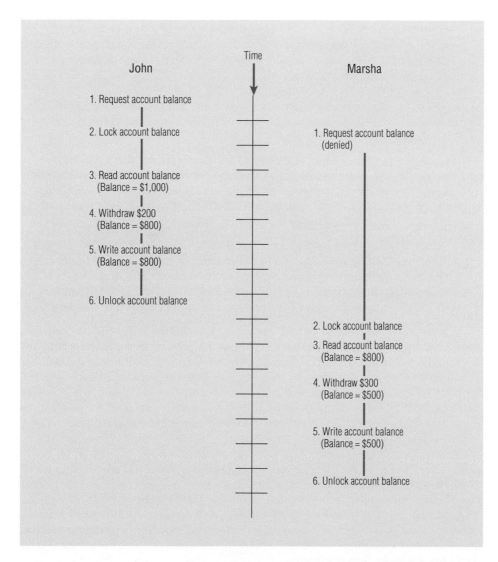

John

1. Request account balance

2. Lock account balance

3. Read account balance
   (Balance = $1,000)

4. Withdraw $200
   (Balance = $800)

5. Write account balance
   (Balance = $800)

6. Unlock account balance

Time

Marsha

1. Request account balance
   (denied)

2. Lock account balance

3. Read account balance
   (Balance = $800)

4. Withdraw $300
   (Balance = $500)

5. Write account balance
   (Balance = $500)

6. Unlock account balance

1. *Database*   The entire database is locked and becomes unavailable to other users. This level has limited application, such as during a backup of the entire database (Rodgers, 1989).

2. *Table*   The entire table containing a requested record is locked. This level is appropriate mainly for bulk updates that will update the entire table, such as giving all employees a 5 percent raise.

3. *Block or page*   The physical storage block (or page) containing a requested record is locked. This level is the most commonly implemented locking level. A page will be a fixed size (4K, 8K, etc.) and may contain records of more than one type.

4. *Record level*   Only the requested record (or row) is locked. All other records, even within a table, are available to other users. It does impose some overhead at run time when several records are involved in an update.

5. *Field level*   Only the particular field (or column) in a requested record is locked. This level may be appropriate when most updates affect only one or two fields in a record. For example, in inventory control applications the quantity-on-hand field changes frequently, but other fields (such as description and bin location) are rarely updated. Field-level locks require considerable overhead and are seldom used.

Types of Locks   So far, we have discussed only locks that prevent all access to locked items. In reality, the database administrator can generally choose between two types of locks: shared and exclusive.

Shared lock (S lock or read lock): Allows other transactions to read but not update a record or other resource.

1. **Shared locks**   Shared locks (also called S locks, or read locks) allow other transactions to read (but not update) a record or other resource. A transaction should place a shared lock on a record or data resource when it will only read but not update that record. Placing a shared lock on a record prevents another user from placing an exclusive lock on that record.

Exclusive lock (X lock or write lock): Prevents another transaction from reading and therefore updating a record until it is unlocked.

2. **Exclusive locks**   Exclusive locks (also called X locks, or write locks) prevent another transaction from reading (and therefore updating) a record until it is unlocked. A transaction should place an exclusive lock on a record when it is about to update that record (Descollonges, 1993). Placing an exclusive lock on a record prevents another user from placing any type of lock on that record.

Figure 13-10 shows the use of shared and exclusive locks for the checking account example. When John initiates his transaction, the program places a read lock on his account record, since he is reading the record to check the account balance. When John requests a withdrawal, the program attempts to place an exclusive lock (write lock) on the record, since this is an update operation. However, as you can see in the figure, Marsha has already initiated a transaction that has placed a read lock on the same record. As a result, his request is denied; remember that if a record is a read lock, another user cannot obtain a write lock.

Deadlock: An impasse that results when two or more transactions have locked a common resource, and each waits for the other to unlock that resource.

Deadlock   Locking solves the problem of erroneous updates but may lead to another problem, called **deadlock**: an impasse that results when two or more transactions have locked a common resource, and each must wait for the other to unlock that resource. Figure 13-10 shows a simple example of deadlock. John's transaction is waiting for Marsha's transaction to remove the read lock from the account record, and vice versa. Neither person can withdraw money from the account, even though the balance is more than adequate.

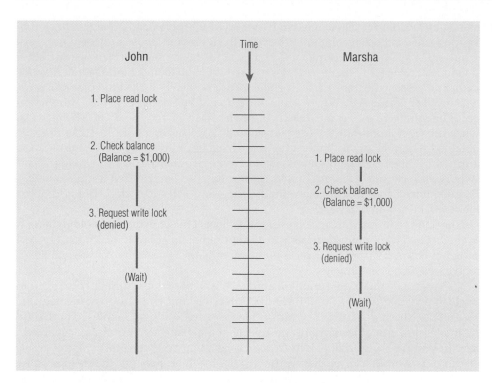

Figure 13-10
The problem of deadlock

Figure 13-11 shows a slightly more complex example of deadlock. In this example, User A has locked record X and User B has locked record Y. User A then requests record Y (intending to update) and User B requests record X (also intending to update). Both requests are denied, since the requested records are already locked. Unless the DBMS intervenes, both users will wait indefinitely.

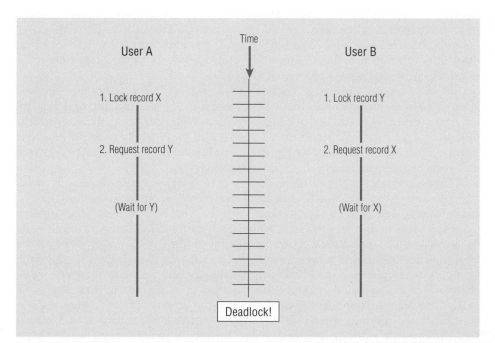

Figure 13-11
Another example of deadlock

Deadlock prevention: User programs must lock all records they require at the beginning of a transaction (rather than one at a time).

Two-phase locking protocol: A procedure for acquiring the necessary locks for a transaction where all necessary locks are acquired before any locks are released, resulting in a growing phase where locks are acquired and a shrinking phase where they are released.

Deadlock resolution: Allows deadlocks to occur but builds mechanisms into the DBMS for detecting and breaking the deadlocks.

Managing Deadlock   There are two basic ways to resolve deadlocks: deadlock prevention and deadlock resolution. When **deadlock prevention** is employed, user programs must lock all records they will require at the beginning of a transaction, rather than one at a time. In Figure 13-11, User A would have to lock both records X and Y before processing the transaction. If either record is already locked the program must wait until it is released. Where all locking operations necessary for a transaction occur before any resources are unlocked, a **two-phase locking** protocol is being used. Once any lock obtained for the transaction is released, no more locks may be obtained. Thus, the phases in the two-phase locking protocol are often referred to as a growing phase (where all necessary locks are acquired) and a shrinking phase (where all locks are released). Locks do not have to be acquired simultaneously. Frequently some locks will be acquired, processing will occur, and then additional locks will be acquired as needed.

Locking records in advance prevents deadlock. Unfortunately, it is often difficult to predict in advance what records will be required to process a transaction. A typical program has many processing parts and may call other programs. As a result, deadlock prevention is not always practical.

The second, and more common, approach is to allow deadlocks to occur but to build mechanisms into the DBMS for detecting and breaking the deadlocks. Essentially, these **deadlock resolution** mechanisms work as follows. The DBMS maintains a matrix of resource usage, which, at a given instant, indicates what subjects (users) are using what objects (resources). By scanning this matrix, the computer can detect deadlocks as they occur. The DBMS then resolves the deadlocks by "backing out" one of the deadlocked transactions. Any changes made by that transaction up to the time of deadlock are removed, and the transaction is restarted when the required resources become available. We will describe the procedure for backing out shortly.

Versioning

Versioning: There is no form of locking. Each transaction is restricted to a view of the database as of the time that transaction started, and when a transaction modifies a record, the DBMS creates a new record version instead of overwriting the old record.

Locking as described here is often referred to as a *pessimistic* concurrency control mechanism, because each time a record is required, the DBMS takes the highly cautious approach of locking the record so that other programs cannot use it. In reality, in most cases other users will not request the same documents, or they may only want to read them, which is not a problem (Celko, 1992).

A newer approach to concurrency control, called **versioning**, takes the *optimistic* approach that most of the time other users do not want the same record, or if they do, they only want to read (but not update) the record. With versioning, there is no form of locking. Each transaction is restricted to a view of the database as of the time that transaction started, and when a transaction modifies a record, the DBMS creates a new record version instead of overwriting the old record.

The best way to understand versioning is to imagine a central records room, corresponding to the database (Celko, 1992). The records room has a service window. Users (corresponding to transactions) arrive at the window and request documents (corresponding to database records). However, the original documents never leave the records room. Instead, the clerk (corresponding to the DBMS) makes copies of the requested documents and timestamps them. Users then take their private copies (or versions) of the documents to their own workplace and read them and/or make changes. When finished, they return their marked-up copies to the clerk. The clerk merges the changes from marked-up copies into the central database. When there is no conflict (for example, when only one user has made changes to a set of database records), that user's changes are merged directly into the public (or central) database.

Figure 13-12
The use of versioning

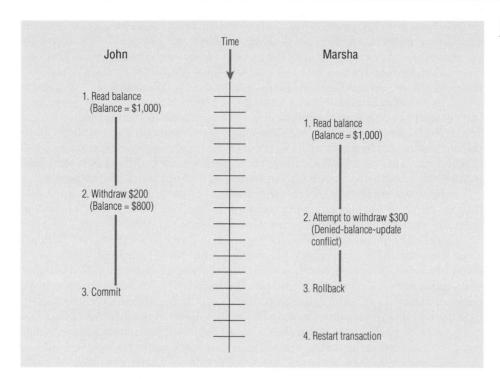

Suppose instead that there is a conflict; for example, two users have made conflicting changes to their private copy of the database. In this case, the changes made by one of the users are committed to the database. (Remember that the transactions are timestamped, so that the earlier transaction can be given priority.) The other user must be told that there was a conflict, and his work cannot be committed (or incorporated into the central database). He must check out another copy of the data records and repeat the previous work. Under the optimistic assumption, this type of rework will be the exception rather than the rule.

Figure 13-12 shows a simple example of the use of versioning for the checking account example. John reads the record containing the account balance, successfully withdraws $200, and the new balance ($800) is posted to the account with a COMMIT statement. Meanwhile, Marsha has also read the account record and requested a withdrawal, which is posted to her local version of the account record. However, when the transaction attempts to COMMIT it discovers the update conflict, and her transaction is aborted (perhaps with a message such as, "Cannot complete transaction at this time"). She can then restart the transaction, working from the correct starting balance of $800.

The main advantage of versioning over locking is performance improvement. Read-only transactions can run concurrently with updating transactions, without loss of database consistency.

MANAGING DATA QUALITY

High-quality data, that is, data that are accurate, consistent, and available in a timely fashion are essential to the management of organizations today. Organizations must strive to identify the data that are relevant to their decision making, to develop business policies and practices that ensure the accuracy and completeness of the data, and to facilitate enterprise-wide data sharing.

Establishment of a business information advisory committee consisting of representatives from each major business unit who have the authority to make business policy decisions can contribute to the establishment of high data quality (Moriarty, 1996). These committee members act as liaisons between IT and their business unit, and consider not only their functional unit's data needs but also enterprise-wide data needs. The members need to have a strong interest in managing information as a corporate resource, an in-depth understanding of the business of the organization, and good negotiation skills. Such members are sometimes referred to as **data stewards**, people who have the responsibility to ensure that organizational applications properly support the organization's enterprise goals. They must also ensure that the data that are captured are accurate and consistent throughout the organization, so that users throughout the organization can rely on the data.

Establishing enterprise-wide data quality standards is not easy, and there are even some business structures and practices that tend to inhibit data quality (Moriarty, 1996). Where organizations establish strategic business units that compete with each other within the enterprise, data sharing may be difficult as each strategic business unit strives to protect its competitive position. Regulated industries such as banking and telecommunications may be legally limited in the amount of data that can be shared. Another threat to maintaining high data quality may occur when data entry is conducted under an incentive plan or quota system that is based on volume of work completed. Then, achieving high speeds of data entry may override concerns about accuracy of data entry. Where data that need to be shared are collected from more than one business unit, the potential for inaccurate and inconsistent data skyrockets. Policies must be developed to handle each of the concerns listed above.

In addition to handling such concerns, any organization needs to address five areas with regard to achieving high data quality:

1. Security policy and disaster recovery

2. Personnel controls

3. Physical access controls

4. Maintenance controls

5. Data protection and privacy

Data steward: A person assigned the responsibility of ensuring that organizational applications properly support the organization's enterprise goals.

Security Policy and Disaster Recovery

Every organization, no matter its size, should establish comprehensive security policies and make detailed disaster recovery plans. The security policies will determine how the organization is going to maintain a secure system. Disaster recovery plans will determine how the organization will continue to function should an emergency situation, such as a flood or fire, arise.

Written security policies should be established that provide guidelines where security measures will be necessary. Responsibilities and duties of the employees with regard to those policies should be established, and the consequences should the policies not be followed stated. Last, general procedures to be taken to implement the guidelines should be stated. These general procedures will be implemented through more specific procedures, which are the most likely part of the security policy to change over time, as new uses for technology develop and new products for enforcing a secure environment are developed.

Disaster recovery plans should be worked out in detail prior to the occurrence of any disaster that may be foreseen, and if possible, tested. In 1993, for example, when Hurricane Andrew devastated the Miami area, many Tampa Bay organizations activated their hurricane disaster recovery plans. As a result, some organizations discovered that their plans to move data tapes to safer locations by using regularly scheduled airline flights would not be practical, and they used the opportunity to improve their hurricane disaster recovery plans. Contingency plans must consider data, equipment, personnel, and management issues involved in transferring operations to another location and safeguarding operations. Copies of the plans should be kept in multiple locations and reviewed periodically.

Larger organizations may arrange for space (a cold site) that can be used in the event of a disaster, either in the same general physical area, or in an area remote from the organization site being covered. Sometimes, an organization will invest in a warm site, which contains the equipment necessary to establish computer operations. And some organizations maintain a hot site, where their operations are conducted in duplicate, so that if one system encounters problems, an immediate switch can be made to the hot site.

Personnel Controls

Adequate controls of personnel must be developed and followed, for the greatest threat to business security is often internal rather than external. In addition to the security authorization and authentication procedures discussed earlier in this chapter, organizations should develop procedures to ensure a selective hiring process that validates potential employees' representations about their backgrounds and capabilities. Monitoring to ensure that personnel are following established practices, taking regular vacations, working with other employees, and so forth, should be followed. Employees should be trained in those aspects of security and quality that are relevant to their jobs, and be encouraged to be aware of and follow standard security and data quality measures. Standard job controls, such as separating duties so no one employee has responsibility for an entire business process, or keeping application developers from having access to production systems, should also be enforced. Should an employee need to be let go, there should be an orderly set of procedures to remove authorizations and authentications and to notify other employees of the status change.

Physical Access Controls

Limiting access to particular areas within a building is usually a part of controlling physical access. Sensitive equipment, including hardware and peripherals, such as printers (which may be used to print classified reports) can be controlled by placement in secure areas. Other equipment may be locked to a desk or cabinet, or may have an alarm attached. Backup data tapes should be kept in fireproof data safes and/or kept off-site at a safe location. Procedures that make explicit the schedules for moving media and disposing of media, and that establish labeling and indexing of all materials stored, and so forth, must be established.

Placement of computer screens so that they cannot be seen from outside the building may also be important. Control procedures for areas external to the office building should also be developed. Companies frequently use security guards to control access to their buildings, or use a card swipe system or handprint recognition system to automate employee access to the building. Visitors may be given an identification card and required to be accompanied throughout the building.

Maintenance Controls

An area of control that helps to maintain data quality but that is often overlooked is maintenance control. Organizations should review external maintenance agreements for all hardware and software they are using to ensure that appropriate response rates are agreed to for maintaining data quality. It is also important to consider reaching agreements with the developers of all critical software so that the organization can get access to source code should the developer go out of business or stop supporting the programs. One way to accomplish this is by having a third party hold the source code, with an agreement that it will be released if such a situation develops.

Data Protection and Privacy

Concerns about the rights of individuals to not have personal information collected and disseminated casually or recklessly have intensified as more of the population has become familiar with computers and as communications among computers have proliferated. Information privacy legislation generally gives individuals the right to know what data have been collected about them, and to correct any errors in those data. As the amount of data exchanged continues to grow, the need is also growing to develop adequate data protection. Also important are adequate provisions to allow the data to be used for legitimate legal purposes, so that organizations who need the data can access them and rely upon their quality.

DATA DICTIONARIES AND REPOSITORIES

Data dictionary: A repository of information about a database that documents data elements of a database.

An integral part of relational DBMSs is the **data dictionary**, which stores metadata, or information about the database, including attribute names and definitions for each table in the database. The data dictionary is usually a part of the **system catalog** that is generated for each database. The system catalog describes all database objects, including table-related data such as table names, table creators or owners, column names and data types, foreign keys and primary keys, index files, authorized users, user access privileges, and so forth. The system catalog is created by the database management system and the information is stored in systems tables, which may be queried in the same manner as any other data table, if the user has sufficient access privileges.

System catalog: A system-created database that describes all database objects, including data dictionary information, but also includes user access information.

Data dictionaries may be either active or passive. An active data dictionary is managed automatically by the database management software. Active systems are always consistent with the current structure and definition of the database because they are maintained by the system itself. Most relational database management systems now contain active data dictionaries that can be derived from their system catalog. A passive data dictionary is managed by the user(s) of the system, and is modified whenever the structure of the database is changed. Since this modification must be performed manually by the user, it is possible that the data dictionary will not be current with the current structure of the database. However, the passive data dictionary may be maintained as a separate database. This may be desirable during the design phase, as it allows developers to remain independent from using a particular RDBMS for as long as possible. Also, passive data dictionaries are not limited to information that can be discerned by the database management system. Since passive data dictionaries are maintained by the user, they may be extended to contain information about organizational data that is not computerized.

Repositories

While data dictionaries are simple data-element documentation tools, information repositories are used by data administrators and other information specialists to manage the total information processing environment. The **information repository** is an essential component of both the development environment and the production environment. In the application development environment, people (either information specialists or end users) use CASE tools, high-level languages, and other tools to develop new applications. CASE tools may tie automatically to the information repository. In the production environment, people use applications to build databases, keep the data current, and extract data from databases. Each of these activities requires that the information repository be accessed and that it be current.

As indicated above, CASE tools often generate information that should be a part of the information repository, as do documentation tools, project management tools, and of course the database management software itself. When they were first developed, the information recorded by each of these products was not easily integrated. Now, however, there has been an attempt to make this information more accessible and shareable. The **Information Repository Dictionary System (IRDS)** is a computer software tool that is used to manage and control access to the information repository. It provides facilities for recording, storing, and processing descriptions of an organization's significant data and data processing resources (Lefkovitz, 1985). When systems are compliant with IRDS, it is possible to transfer data definitions among the data dictionaries generated by the various products. IRDS has been adopted as a standard by the International Standards Organization (1990), and includes a set of rules for storing data dictionary information and for accessing it.

Figure 13-13 shows the three components of a repository system architecture (Bernstein, 1996). First is an information model. This model is a schema of the information stored in the repository, which can then be used by the tools associated with

Information repository:
Stores metadata that describe an organization's data and data processing resources. Manages the total information processing environment. Combines information about an organization's business information and its application portfolio.

Information Repository Dictionary System (IRDS):
A computer software tool that is used to manage and control access to the information repository.

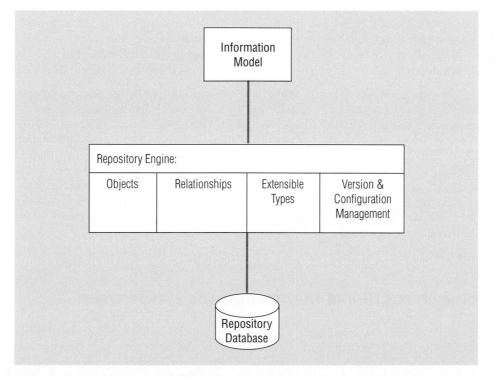

Figure 3-13
Three components of repository system architecture (Adapted from Bernstein, 1996)

the database to interpret the contents of the repository. Next is the repository engine, which manages the repository objects. Services such as reading and writing repository objects, browsing, and extending the information model are included. Last is the repository database, where the repository objects are actually stored. Notice that the repository engine supports five core functions (Bernstein, 1996):

- *Object management*   Object-oriented repositories store information about objects. As databases become more object-oriented, developers will be able to use the information stored about database objects in the information repository. The repository can be based on an object-oriented database or it can add the capability to support objects.

- *Dynamic extensibility*   The repository information model defines types, which should be easy to extend, that is, to add new types or to extend the definitions of those that already exist. This capability can make it easier to integrate a new software tool into the development process.

- *Relationship management*   The repository engine contains information about object relationships that can be used to facilitate the use of software tools that attach to the database.

- *Version management*   During development it is important to establish version control. The information repository can be used to facilitate version control for software design tools. Version control of objects is more difficult to manage than version control of files, since there are many more objects than files in an application, and each version of an object may have many relationships.

- *Configuration management*   It is also necessary to group the versioned objects into configurations that represent the entire system, which are also versioned. It may help you to think of a configuration as similar to a file directory, except configurations can be versioned and they contain objects rather than files. Repositories often use checkout systems to manage objects, versions, and configurations. A developer who wishes to use an object checks it out, makes the desired changes, and then checks the object back in. At that time, a new version of the object will be created and the object will become available to other developers.

As object-oriented database management systems become more available, and as object-oriented programming associated with relational databases increases, the importance of the information repository is also going to increase, since object-oriented development requires the use of the metadata contained in the information repository. Also, the metadata and application information generated by different software tools will be more easily integrated into the information repository now that the IRDS standard has been accepted. Although information repositories have already been included in the enterprise-level development tools, the increasing emphasis on object-oriented development should lead to more widespread use of information repositories.

OVERVIEW OF TUNING THE DATABASE FOR PERFORMANCE

Effective database support results in a reliable database where performance is not subject to interruption from hardware, software, or user problems and where optimal performance is achieved. Tuning a database is not an activity that is undertaken at the time of DBMS installation and/or at the time of implementation of a new application and then disregarded. Rather, tuning is an ongoing part of managing any database, as hardware and software configurations change, and as user activity changes. Five areas of DBMS management that should be addressed when trying to maintain a well-tuned database are addressed here: installation of the DBMS, memory usage, input/output contention, CPU usage, and application tuning. The extent to which the database administrator can affect each of these areas will vary across DBMS products. Oracle7 will be used as the exemplar DBMS throughout this section, but it should be noted that each product has its own set of tuning capabilities.

Tuning a database application requires familiarity with the system environment, the DBMS, the application, and the data used by the application. It is here that the skills of even an experienced database administrator are tested. Achieving a quiet environment, one that is reliable and allows users to secure desired information in a timely manner, requires skills and experience that are obtained by working with databases over time. The areas discussed below are quite general and are intended to provide an initial understanding of the scope of activities involved in tuning a database rather than providing the type of detailed understanding necessary to tune a particular database application.

Installation of the DBMS

Correct installation of the DBMS product is essential to any environment. Products often include README files, which may include detailed installation instructions, revisions of procedures, notification of increased disk space needed for installation, and so on. A quick review of any README files may save time during the installation process and result in a better installation. General installation instructions should also be reviewed. Failing to make such a review may result in default parameter values being set during installation that are not optimal for the situation. Some possible considerations are listed here.

Before beginning installation, the database administrator should ensure that adequate disk space is available. It is possible that the space allocation recommendations are low, as changes made to a DBMS tend to make it larger, but the documentation may not reflect that change. To be safe, allocate at least 20 percent more space than suggested. After installation, review any log files generated during the installation process. Their contents will reveal installation problems that were not noticed, or provide assurance that the installation proceeded as expected.

Allocation of disk space for the database should also receive consideration. For example, some UNIX backup systems have trouble with data files that exceed a gigabyte in size. Keeping data files under 1 gigabyte will avoid possible problems. Allocation of data files in standard sizes will make it easier to balance I/O, as data file locations can be swapped more easily should a bottleneck need to be resolved.

Memory Usage

Efficient usage of main memory involves understanding how the DBMS uses main memory, what buffers are being used, and what needs the programs in main memory have. For example, Oracle7 has seven background processes that reside in memory when a database is running that handle database management functions. Some operating systems require a contiguous chunk of memory to be able to load Oracle, and a system with insufficient memory will have to free up memory space first. Oracle maintains in main memory a data dictionary cache that ideally should be large enough so that at least 90 percent of the requests to the data dictionary can be located in the cache rather than having to retrieve information from disk. Each of these is an example of typical memory management issues that should be considered when tuning a database.

Input/Output (I/O) Contention

Achieving maximum I/O performance is one of the most important aspects of tuning a database. Database applications are very I/O intensive—a production database will usually both read and write large amounts of data to disk as it works. While CPU clock speeds have increased dramatically, I/O speeds have not increased proportionately, and increasingly complex distributed database systems have further complicated I/O functioning.

Understanding how data are accessed by end users is critical to managing I/O contention. When hot spots, physical disk locations that are accessed repeatedly, develop, understanding the nature of the activity that is causing the hot spot affords the database administrator a much better chance of reducing the I/O contention being experienced. Oracle7 allows the DBA to control the placement of tablespaces, which contain data files. The DBA's in-depth understanding of user activity facilitates her ability to reduce I/O contention by separating datafiles that are being accessed together. Where possible, large database objects that will be accessed concurrently may be striped across disks to reduce I/O contention and improve performance. An overall objective of distributing I/O activity evenly across disks and controllers should guide the DBA in tuning I/O.

CPU Usage

Most database operations are going to require CPU work activity. Because of this, it is important to evaluate CPU usage when tuning a database. Using multiple CPUs allows query processing to be shared when the CPUs are working in parallel, and performance may be dramatically improved. DBAs need to maximize the performance of their existing CPUs while planning for the gains that may be achieved with each new generation of CPUs.

Monitoring CPU load so that typical load throughout a 24-hour period is known provides DBAs with basic information necessary to begin to rebalance CPU loading. The mixture of online and background processing may need to be adjusted for each environment. For example, establishing a rule that all jobs that can be run in off-hours *must* be run in off-hours will help to unload the machine during peak working hours. Establishing user accounts with limited space will help manage the CPU load also.

Application Tuning

The previous sections have concentrated on activities to tune the DBMS. Examining the applications that end users are using with the database may also increase performance. While normalization to at least 3NF is expected in many organizations that are using relational data models, carefully planned denormalization may improve performance, often by reducing the number of tables that must be joined when running an SQL query.

Examination and modification of the SQL code in an application may also lead to performance improvement. Queries that do full table scans should be avoided, for example, because they are not selective and may not remain in memory very long. This necessitates more retrievals from long-term storage. Multitable joins should be actively managed when possible with the DBMS being used, as the type of join can dramatically affect performance, especially if a join requires a full table join.

Similarly, statements containing views and those containing subqueries should be actively reviewed. Tuning of such statements so that components are resolved in the most efficient manner possible may achieve significant performance gains.

The preceding brief mentions of potential areas where database performance may be affected should convince the reader of the importance of effective database management and tuning. As a DBA achieves an in-depth understanding of a DBMS and the applications for which responsibility is assigned, the importance of tuning the database for performance should become apparent. Hopefully this brief section on database tuning will whet the reader's appetite for learning more about one or more database products in order to develop tuning skills.

SUMMARY

The importance of managing data is emphasized in this chapter. The functions of data administration, which takes responsibility for the overall management of data resources, include developing procedures to protect and control data, resolving data ownership and use issues, and developing and maintaining corporate-wide data definitions and standards. The functions of database administration, on the other hand, are those associated with the direct management of a database or databases, including database design issues and technical issues such as security enforcement, database performance, and backup and recovery. The data administration and database administration roles are changing in today's business environment, with pressure being exerted to maintain data quality while building high-performing systems quickly. Key to achieving these expectations is developing an enterprise architecture (ISA) and performing adequate database planning.

Threats to data security include accidental losses, theft and fraud, loss of privacy, loss of data integrity, and loss of availability. A comprehensive data security plan will address all of these potential threats, partly through the establishment of views, authorization rules, user-defined procedures, and encryption procedures.

Database recovery and backup procedures are another set of essential data administration activities. Basic recovery facilities that should be in place include backup facilities, journalizing facilities, checkpoint facilities, and a recovery manager. Depending on the type of problem encountered, backward recovery (rollback) or forward recovery (rollforward) may be needed.

The problems of managing concurrent access in multiuser environments must also be addressed. If concurrency controls are not established, lost updates may occur, which will cause data integrity to be impaired. Locking mechanisms, including shared and exclusive locks, can be used. Deadlocks may also occur in multiuser environments, and may be managed by various means, including using a two-phase locking protocol or other deadlock resolution mechanism. Versioning is an optimistic approach to concurrency control.

There are five areas of concern when maintaining high data quality: security policy and disaster recovery, personnel controls, physical access controls, maintenance controls, and data protection and privacy concerns.

Managing the data dictionary, which is part of the system catalog in most relational database management systems, and the information repository help the DBA maintain high-quality data and high-performing database systems. The establishment of the Information Repository Dictionary System (IRDS) standard has helped with the development of repository information that can be integrated from multiple sources, including the DBMS itself, CASE tools, and software development tools.

Effective data administration is not easy and encompasses all of the areas summarized above. Increasing emphasis on object-oriented development methods and rapid development are changing the data administration function, but better tools to achieve effective administration and database tuning are becoming available.

CHAPTER REVIEW

KEY TERMS

Aborted transaction
After-image
Authorization rules
Backup facilities
Backward recovery
    (rollback)
Before-image
Biometric device
Checkpoint facility
Concurrency control
Data administration
Data dictionary
Data steward
Database administration
Database change log

Database destruction
Database recovery
Database security
Deadlock
Deadlock prevention
Deadlock resolution
Encryption
Exclusive lock
Forward recovery
    (rollforward)
Inconsistent read
    problem
Information repository
Journalizing facilities
Locking

Locking level
    (granularity)
Recovery manager
Restore/rerun
Shared lock
System catalog
Transaction
Transaction boundaries
Transaction log
Two-phase locking
    protocol
User-defined procedures
Versioning

REVIEW QUESTIONS

1. Define each of the following terms:
    a. Data administration
    b Database administration
    c. Data steward
    d. Information repository
    e. Locking
    f. Versioning
    g. Deadlock
    h. Transaction
    i. Encryption

2. Compare and contrast the following terms:
   a. data administration; database administration
   b. repository; data dictionary
   c. deadlock prevention; deadlock resolution
   d. backward recovery; forward recovery
   e. active data dictionary; passive data dictionary
   f. optimistic concurrency control; pessimistic concurrency control
   g. shared lock; exclusive lock
   h. before-image; after-image
   i. two-phase locking protocol; versioning
   j. authorization; authentication

3. What is the function of a data steward?

4. Briefly describe six stages in the life cycle of a typical database sytem.

5. Describe the changing roles of the data administrator and database administrator in the current business environment.

6. List four common problems of ineffective data administration.

7. List four job skills necessary for system data administration or data administrators. List four job skills necessary for project data administration or database administrators.

8. List and describe eight functions that should be addressed in order to achieve effective database administration.

9. What changes can be made in data administration at each stage of the traditional database development life cycle in order to deliver high-quality, robust systems more quickly?

10. List and discuss five areas where threats to data security may occur.

11. Explain how creating a view may increase data security. Also explain why one should not rely completely on using views to enforce data security.

12. What is the difference between an authentication scheme and an authorization scheme?

13. What is the advantage of optimistic concurrency control, compared with pessimistic concurrency control?

14. What is the difference between shared locks and exclusive locks?

15. What is the difference between deadlock prevention and deadlock resolution?

16. Briefly describe four DBMS facilities that are required for database backup and recovery.

17. What is transaction integrity? Why is it important?

18. List and describe four common types of database failure.

19. List and describe five areas that should be addressed in order to achieve high data quality.

20. What is an Information Resource Dictionary System (IRDS)?

PROBLEMS AND EXERCISES

1. Match the following terms to the appropriate definitions.

    _____ Backup facilities

    _____ Biometric device

    _____ Checkpoint facility

    _____ Database recovery

    _____ Database security

    _____ Granularity

    _____ Recovery manager

    _____ Rollback

    _____ Rollforward

    _____ System catalog

    a. protects data from loss or misuse

    b. reversal of abnormal or aborted transactions

    c. describes all database objects

    d. automatically produce a saved copy of an entire database

    e. application of after-images

    f. might analyze your signature

    g. restoring a database after a loss

    h. DBMS module that restores a database after a failure

    i. extent to which a database is locked for a transaction

    j. records database state at moment of synchronization

2. Fill in the two authorization tables for Pine Valley Furniture Company below, based on the following assumptions (enter Y for yes or N for no):

Authorizations for Inventory Clerks

	Inventory Records	Receivables Records	Payroll Records	Customer Records
Read				
Insert				
Modify				
Delete				

Authorizations for Inventory Records

	Salespersons	A/R Personnel	Inventory Clerks	Carpenters
Read				
Insert				
Modify				
Delete				

(1) Salespersons, managers, and carpenters may read inventory records but may not perform any other operations on these records.

(2) Persons in Accounts Receivable and Accounts Payable may read and/or update (insert, modify, delete) receivables records and customer records.

(3) Inventory clerks may read and/or update (modify, delete) inventory records. They may not view receivables records or payroll records. They may read but not modify customer records.

3. Five recovery techniques are listed below. For each situation described, decide which recovery technique is most appropriate.

(1) Backward recovery

(2) Forward recovery (from latest checkpoint)

(3) Forward recovery (using backup copy of database)

(4) Reprocessing transactions

(5) Switch

a. A phone disconnection occurs while a user is entering a transaction.

b. A disk drive fails during regular operations.

c. A lightning storm causes a power failure.

d. An incorrect amount is entered and posted for a student tuition payment. The error is not discovered for several weeks.

e. Data entry clerks have entered transactions for two hours after a full database backup when the database becomes corrupted. It is discovered that the journalizing facility of the database has not been activated since the backup was made.

4. Whitlock Department Stores runs a multiuser DBMS on a local area network file server. Unfortunately, at the present time the DBMS does not enforce concurrency control. One Whitlock customer had a balance due of $250.00 when the following three transactions related to this customer were processed at about the same time:

(1) Payment of $250.00.

(2) Purchase on credit of $100.00.

(3) Merchandise return (credit) of $50.00.

Each of the three transactions read the customer record when the balance was $250.00 (that is, before any of the other transactions were completed). The updated customer record was returned to the database in the order shown above.

a. What balance *will* be included for the customer after the last transaction was completed?

b. What balance *should* be included for the customer after the three transactions have been processed?

5. For each of the situations described below, indicate which of the following security measures is most appropriate:

(1) authorization rules

(2) encryption

(3) authentication schemes

a. A national brokerage firm uses an electronic funds transfer (EFT) system to transmit sensitive financial data between locations.

b. An organization has set up an off-site computer-based training center. The organization wishes to restrict access to the site to authorized employees. Since each employee's use of the center is occasional, it does not wish to provide the employees with keys to access the center.

    c. A manufacturing firm uses a simple password system to protect its database but finds it needs a more comprehensive system to grant different privileges (such as read, versus create or update) to different users.

    d. A university has experienced considerable difficulty with unauthorized users who access files and databases by appropriating passwords from legitimate users.

6. Metro Marketers, Inc., wants to build a data warehouse for storing customer information that will be used for data marketing purposes. Building the data warehouse will require much more capacity and processing power than they have previously needed, and they are considering Oracle and Red Brick as their database and data warehousing products. As part of their implementation plan, Metro has decided to organize a data administration function. At present, they have four major candidates for the data administrator position:

    a. Monica Lopez, a senior database administrator with five years of experience as an Oracle database administrator managing a financial database for a global banking firm, but no data warehousing experience.

    b. Gerald Bruester, a senior database administrator with six years of experience as an Informix database administrator managing a marketing-oriented database for a Fortune 1000 food products firm. Gerald has been to several data warehousing seminars over the last twelve months and is interested in being involved with a data warehouse.

    c. Jim Reedy, currently project manager for Metro Marketers. Jim is very familiar with Metro's current systems environment and is well respected by his co-workers. He has been involved with Metro's current database system but has not had any data warehousing experience.

    d. Marie Weber, a data warehouse administrator with two years of experience using a Red Brick–based application that tracks accident information for an automobile insurance company.

Based on this limited information, rank the four candidates for the data administration position. Support your rankings by indicating your reasoning.

7. Referring to Problem and Exercise 6, rank the four candidates for the position of data warehouse administrator at Metro Marketing. Again, support your rankings.

8. Referring to Problem and Exercise 6, rank the four candidates for the position of database administrator at Metro Marketing. Again, support your rankings.

9. What concerns would you have if you accept a job as a database administrator and discover that the database users are entering one common password to log on to the database each morning when they arrive for work? You also learn that they leave their workstations connected to the database all day, even when they are away from their machines for an extended period of time.

10. An organization has a database server with three disk devices. The accounting and payroll applications share one of these disk devices and are experiencing performance problems. You have been asked to investigate the problem and tune the databases. What might you suggest to reduce I/O contention?

11. You take a new job as a database administrator at an organization that has a globally distributed database. You are asked to analyze the performance of the database and as part of your analysis discover that all of the processing for regional monthly sales reports is being conducted at the corporate headquarters location. Operations are categorized by five regions: Eastern United States, Western United States, Canada, South America, and Mexico. Data for each region are kept on a server located at the regional headquarters. What would you try to improve the time needed to create the monthly sales reports?

FIELD EXERCISES

1. Visit an organization that has implemented a database approach. Evaluate each of the following:
   a. The organizational placement of system data administration and project data administration
   b. The assignment of responsibilities for system data administration and project data administration
   c. The background and experience of the person chosen as head of data administration
   d. The status and usage of an information repository (passive, active-in-design, active-in-production)

2. Visit an organization that has implemented a database approach and interview an MIS department employee who has been involved in disaster recovery planning about the organization's disaster recovery plans. Before you go for the interview, think carefully about the relative probabilities of various disasters for the organization you are visiting. For example, is the area subject to earthquakes or other natural disasters? What type of damage might the physical plant be subject to? Or what is the background and training of the employees who must use the system? Find out about the organization's disaster recovery plans, and ask specifically about any potential problems you have identified.

3. Visit an organization that has implemented a database approach and interview them about the security measures that they take routinely. Evaluate each of the following:
   a. database security measures
   b. network security measures
   c. operating system security measures
   d. physical plant security measures
   e. personnel security measures

4. Identify an organization that handles large, sporadic data loads. For example, organizations that have implemented data warehouses may have large data loads as they populate their data warehouses. Determine what measures the organization has taken to handle these large loads as part of their capacity planning.

5. Databases tend to grow larger over time, not smaller, as new transaction data are added. Interview at least three companies who use databases extensively and identify their criteria and procedures for purging or archiving old data. Find out how often data are purged, and what type of data are purged. Identify the data each organization archives and how long those data are archived.

REFERENCES

Bernstein, P. A. 1996. "The Repository: A Modern Vision." *Database Programming & Design* 9:12 (December): 28–35.

Celko, J. 1992. "An Introduction to Concurrency Control." *DBMS* 5:9 (September): 70–83.

Descollonges, M. 1993. "Concurrency for Complex Processing." *Database Programming & Design* 6:1 (January): 66–71.

Dowgiallo, E., H. Fosdick, Y. Lirov, A. Langer, T. Quinlan, and C. Young. 1997. "DBA of the Future." *Database Programming & Design* (June): 33–41.

Fernandez, E. B., R. C. Summers, and C. Wood. 1981. *Database Security and Integrity.* Reading, MA: Addison-Wesley.

Lefkovitz, H. C. 1985. *Proposed American National Standards Information Resource Dictionary System,* Wellesley, MA: QED Information Sciences.

Moriarty, T. 1996. "Better Business Practices." *Database Programming & Design* 9:7 (September): 59–61.

Rodgers, U. 1989. "Multiuser DBMS Under UNIX." *Database Programming & Design* 2:10 (October): 30–37.

Quinlan, T. 1996. "Time to Reengineer the DBA?" *Database Programming & Design* 9:3 (March): 29–34.

Zachman, J. A. 1987. "A Framework for Information Systems Architecture." *IBM Systems Journal* 26:3 (March): 276–92.

Zachman, J. A. 1997. "Enterprise Architecture: The Issue of the Century." *Database Programming & Design* 10:3 (March): 44–53.

Project Case

At the end of Chapter 2, you learned of the Mountain View Community Hospital special study team that is developing a long-term business plan. You may remember that Mr. Heller, Mr. Lopez, Dr. Jefferson, and a consultant are the members of this team. They are trying to build a plan that will meet the hospital's goals of high-quality health care, cost containment, and expansion into new services, such as Dr. Browne's anticipated Geriatric Medicine department.

Mr. Heller, Director of Information Systems, regularly reads journals and magazines that he finds helpful, such as *Computerworld, Health Management Technology,* and *Healthcare Informatics.* His reading has made him aware of the movement toward implementing computer-based patient records (CPR) systems in leading hospitals in large metropolitan areas, and he is wondering if Mountain View should be planning now for future implementation of CPR. From his reading he has deduced that there are two perspectives on CPR. Until recently, CPR has been regarded as a way of replacing the existing manual systems of patient care record keeping, but use of the term is now changing. Many articles now refer to CPR as an integrated patient care information system to be accessible by hospital administrators, physicians, caregivers, and healthcare management organizations. A CPR system may well involve integrating health care information from diverse systems such as bedside terminals, laboratory systems, and administrative systems. Systems that achieve this degree of integration and accessibility are not expected to be available until the early 2000s.

Such systems will be a significant change in the way health care information is collected and used. Establishing CPR will provide an infrastructure for physicians to be able to access all medical records of their patients, even though those records are distributed over many locations, including various physician, hospital, laboratory, and insurance records. Eventually, if CPR integration is successful, nonredundant healthcare information across a patient's life will be available.

PROJECT QUESTIONS

1. Does CPR seem to have the potential to help Mountain View achieve its goals of achieving high-quality care and cost containment? Support your answers with examples of how you think these goals may or may not be achieved.

2. Establishing patient record security has always been a primary requirement of healthcare record keeping. What data security issues would you expect Mountain View to encounter if they decide to implement a CPR system that is accessible by physicians in the community, by laboratories, and by healthcare organizations?

3. Clinical decisions are the basis of over 70 percent of healthcare expenditures in the United States. In what ways could a CPR system aid clinical decision making and thus help to contain healthcare expenditures?

4. If CPR systems will not be widely available until after 2000, should Mr. Heller expend efforts now to consider such systems? Why or why not?

5. Is an integrated CPR system likely to be a good innovation for Mountain View to adopt, or do you think that it is an innovation that will be more suited to larger communities and larger hospitals? Are there any environmental situations, such as an agreement by physicians practicing at the hospital to adopt the system, that you would want to exist before you would advise Mountain View to adopt a CPR system?

PROJECT EXERCISES

1. If a CPR system were installed at Mountain View, list all the possible types of users that would need authorization to use the system. Include user groups external to the hospital that would be likely to be included in an integrated CPR system.

2. For each user type listed above, indicate what permissions (read, insert, delete, modify) you would grant.

3. In this case, Mr. Heller is beginning to engage in the planning activity described in the chapter as a typical data administration task. Outline briefly

the issues that you feel he should include in his deliberations.

4. Legal questions such as data ownership, authentication, and admissibility have not yet been answered for CPR systems. If Mountain View decides to press ahead with plans for implementing a CPR system, what steps would they have to take in order to address each of these issues? Is there any way that they could press ahead if these issues have not been resolved? Does any one of these issues seem less important to you than the others? Why?

Data Warehouse

LEARNING OBJECTIVES

After studying this chapter, you should be able to:

■ Define the following key terms: **data warehouse, data mart, reconciled data, derived data, transient data, periodic data, star schema, snowflake schema, on-line analytical processing, data mining,** and **data visualization**.

■ Give two important reasons why an "information gap" often exists between the information manager's need and the information generally available.

■ List two major reasons why most organizations today need data warehousing.

■ Name and briefly describe the three levels in a data warehouse architecture.

■ List five characteristics normally associated with the reconciled data layer.

■ List the four main steps of data reconciliation.

■ Describe the two major components of a star schema.

■ Estimate the number of rows and total size in bytes of a fact table, given reasonable assumptions concerning the database dimensions.

INTRODUCTION

Everyone agrees that readily available high-quality information is vital in business today. Consider the recent comments of two data management experts:

> Information is pivotal in today's business environment. Success is dependent on its early and decisive use. A lack of information is a sure sign for failure. The rapidly changing environment in which business operates demands ever more immediate access to data. (Devlin, 1997)

> Many corporations are actively looking for new technologies that will assist them in becoming more profitable and competitive. Gaining competitive advantage requires

that companies accelerate their decision making process so that they can respond quickly to change. One key to this accelerated decision making is having the right information, at the right time, easily accessible. (Poe, 1996)

In light of this strong emphasis on information and the recent advances in information technology, you might expect most organizations to have highly developed systems for delivering information to managers and other users. Yet this is seldom the case. In fact, despite having mountains of data, few organizations have more than a fraction of the information they need. Managers are often frustrated by their inability to access or use the data and information they need.

Modern organizations are said to be drowning in data but starving for information. Despite the mixed metaphor, this statement seems to portray quite accurately the situation in many organizations. What is the reason for this state of affairs? Let's examine two important (and related) reasons why an information gap has been created in most organizations.

The first reason for the information gap is the fragmented way in which organizations have developed information systems—and their supporting databases—for many years. The emphasis in this text is on a carefully planned, architectural approach to systems development that should produce an integrated set of databases. However, in reality constraints on time and resources cause most organizations resort to a "one-thing-at-a-time" approach to developing systems. This approach inevitably produces a hodgepodge of uncoordinated and often inconsistent databases. Usually databases are based on a variety of hardware and software platforms. In this environment it is extremely difficult if not impossible for managers to locate and use accurate information.

The second reason for the information gap is that most systems are developed to support operational processing, with little or no thought given to the information or analytical tools needed for decision making. *Operational processing,* also called transaction processing, captures, stores, and manipulates data to support daily operations of the organization. *Informational processing* is the analysis of summarized data or other forms of information to support decision making. The processing that is performed and the types of data required are very different for these two types of processing, as explained in the following section. Most systems that are developed internally or purchased from outside vendors are designed to support operational processing, with little thought given to informational processing.

Bridging the information gap are *data warehouses* which consolidate and integrate information from many different sources and arrange it in a meaningful format for making accurate business decisions (Martin, 1997a). They support executives, managers, and business analysts in making complex business decisions through applications such as the analysis of trends, target marketing, competitive analysis, and so on. Data warehousing has evolved to meet these needs without disturbing existing operational processing.

This chapter provides an overview of data warehousing. This exceptionally broad topic normally requires an entire text. In fact, most texts on the topic are devoted to just a single aspect, such as data warehouse design or administration. We focus on the two areas that are essential: data architecture and database design. You will learn first how the data warehouse relates to existing operational systems. Described next is the three-tier data architecture, which is most appropriate for most data warehouse environments. Then we address the problem of extracting data from existing operational systems and loading them into a data warehouse. Finally, you will see how users interact with the data warehouse including on-line analytical processing, data mining, and data visualization.

BASIC CONCEPTS OF DATA WAREHOUSING

A **data warehouse** is a subject-oriented, integrated, time-variant, nonvolatile collection of data used in support of management decision making processes (Inmon and Hackathorn, 1994). The meaning of each of the key terms in this definition is the following:

1. *Subject-oriented*   A data warehouse is organized around the key subjects (or high-level entities) of the enterprise. Major subjects may include customers, patients, students, and products.

2. *Integrated*   The data housed in the data warehouse are defined using consistent naming conventions, formats, encoding structures, and related characteristics.

3. *Time-variant*   Data in the data warehouse contain a time dimension so that they may be used as a historical record of the business.

4. *Nonvolatile*   Data in the data warehouse are loaded and refreshed from operational systems, but cannot be updated by end users.

Data warehouse: A subject-oriented, integrated, time-variant, nonvolatile collection of data used in support of management decision-making processes.

Data warehousing is the process whereby organizations extract meaning from their informational assets through the use of data warehouses (Barquin, 1996). Data warehousing is a recent initiative in information technology. Since it began about 10 years ago, it has evolved so rapidly that data warehousing is now one of the hottest topics in information systems. Studies repeatedly show that over 90 percent of larger companies either have a data warehouse or are starting one. A 1996 study of 62 data warehousing projects showed an average return on investment of 321 percent, with an average payback period of 2.73 years. Users are expected spend nearly $200 billion on data warehouse technology over the next 5 years (Burwen, 1997).

A Brief History

Data warehousing emerged as a result of advances in the field of information systems over several decades. Some key advances were the following:

- Improvements in database technology, particularly the development of the relational data model and relational database management systems (DBMS)

- Advances in computer hardware, particularly the emergence of affordable mass storage and parallel computer architectures

- The emergence of end-user computing, facilitated by powerful, intuitive computer interfaces and tools

- Advances in middleware products that enable enterprise database connectivity across heterogeneous platforms (Hackathorn, 1993)

The key discovery that triggered the development of data warehousing was the recognition (and subsequent definition) of the fundamental differences between operational (or production) systems, and informational (or decision support) systems. In 1988 Devlin and Murphy published the first article describing the architecture of a data warehouse, based on this distinction. In 1992 Inmon published the first book describing data warehousing and has subsequently become the most prolific author in this field.

The Need for Data Warehousing

Two major factors drive the need for data warehousing in most organizations today:

1. Business require an integrated, company-wide view of high-quality information.

2. The information systems department must separate informational from operational systems in order to dramatically improve performance in managing company data.

Need for a Company-Wide View   Data in operational systems are typically fragmented and of poor quality. They are also generally distributed on a variety of incompatible hardware and software platforms. For example, one file containing customer data may be located on a Unix-based server running an Oracle DBMS, while another is located on an IBM mainframe running the DB2 DBMS. Yet for decision-making purposes it is often necessary to provide a single, corporate view of that information.

To better understand the difficulty of deriving a single corporate view, look at the simple example shown in Figure 14-1. This figure shows three tables, each containing some student data. There is a STUDENT_DATA table, a STUDENT_EMPLOYEE table, and a STUDENT_HEALTH table. Each table contains some unique data con-

Figure 14-1

Examples of heterogeneous data

STUDENT_DATA

Student_No	Last_Name	MI	First_Name	Telephone	Status	• • •
123-45-6789	Enright	T	Mark	483-1967	Soph	
389-21-4062	Smith	R	Elaine	283-4195	Jr	

STUDENT_EMPLOYEE

Student_ID	Address	Dept	Hours	• • •
123-45-6789	1218 Elk Drive, Phoenix, AZ 91304	Soc	8	
389-21-4062	134 Mesa Road, Tempe, AZ 90142	Math	10	

STUDENT_HEALTH

Name	Telephone	Insurance	ID	• • •
Mark T. Enright	483-1967	Blue Cross	123-45-6789	
Elaine R. Smith	555-7828	?	389-21-4062	

cerning students, but even common data (such as student names) are stored using different formats.

Suppose you want to develop a profile for each student, consolidating all data in a single file format. Some of the issues that you must resolve are as follows:

- *Inconsistent key structures*   The primary key of the first two tables is some version of the student social security number, while the primary key of STUDENT_HEALTH is Student_Name.

- *Synonyms*   In STUDENT_DATA the primary key is named Student_No, while in STUDENT_EMPLOYEE it is named Student_ID (we discussed how to deal with synonyms in Chapter 6).

- *Free-form fields versus structured fields*   In STUDENT_HEALTH, Student_Name is a single field. In STUDENT_DATA, Student_Name (a composite attribute) is broken into its component parts: Last_Name, MI, and First_Name.

- *Inconsistent data values*   Elaine Smith has one telephone number in STUDENT_DATA, but a different number in STUDENT_HEALTH. Is this an error, or does this person have two telephone numbers?

- *Missing data*   The value for Insurance is missing (or null) for Elaine Smith in the STUDENT_HEALTH table. How will this value be located?

This simple example illustrates the nature of the problem of developing a single corporate view but fails to capture the complexity of that task. A real-life scenario would likely have dozens (if not hundreds) of files, and thousands (or millions!) of records. We will return to the issue of complexity and size later in this chapter.

Need to Separate Operational and Informational Systems   An operational system is a system that is used to run a business in real time, based on current data. Examples of operational systems are sales order processing, reservation systems, and patient registration. Operational systems must process large volumes of relatively simple read/write transactions, while providing fast response.

Informational systems are designed to support decision making based on stable point-in-time or historical data. They are also designed for complex read-only queries or data-mining applications. Examples of informational systems are sales trend analysis, customer segmentation, and human resources planning.

The key differences between operational and informational systems are shown in Table 14-1. These two types of processing have very different characteristics in nearly every category of comparison. In particular, notice that they have quite different communities of users. Operational systems are used by clerks, administrators,

Operational system: A system that is used to run a business in real time, based on current data.

Informational systems: Systems designed to support decision making based on stable point-in-time or historical data, and designed for complex and read-only queries or data mining applications.

Table 14-1   Comparison of Operational and Informational Systems

Characteristic	Operational Systems	Informational Systems
Primary purpose	Run the business on a current basis	Support managerial decision making
Type of data	Current representation of state of the business	Historical or point-in-time (snapshots)
Primary users	Clerks, salespersons, administrators	Managers, business analysts, customers
Scope of usage	Narrow vs. simple updates and queries	Broad vs. complex queries and analysis
Design goal	Performance	Ease of access and use

salespersons, and others who must process business transactions. Informational systems are used by managers, executives, business analysts, and (increasingly) by customers who are searching for status information or who are decision makers.

Data Warehouse Principle 1

For most organizations today, it is essential to separate informational processing from operational processing by creating a data warehouse.

Supporting the first Data Warehouse Principle are three primary factors:

1. A data warehouse centralizes data (at least logically) that are scattered throughout disparate operational systems and makes them readily available for decision-support applications.

2. A properly designed data warehouse adds value to data by improving their quality and consistency.

3. A separate data warehouse eliminates much of the contention for resources that results when informational applications are confounded with operational processing.

DATA WAREHOUSE ARCHITECTURES

The basic architectures used most often with data warehouses are first, a generic two-level physical architecture for entry-level data warehouses; second, an expanded three-level architecture that is increasingly used in more complex environments; and finally, the three-level data architecture that is associated with three-level physical architecture.

Generic Two-Level Architecture

A generic architecture for a data warehouse is shown in Figure 14-2. Building this architecture requires four basic steps:

1. Data are extracted from the various source system files and databases. In a large organization there may be dozens or even hundreds of such files and databases.

2. The data from the various source systems are transformed and integrated before being loaded into the data warehouse.

3. The data warehouse is a read-only database organized for decision support. It contains both detailed and summary data.

4. Users access the data warehouse by means of a variety of query languages and analytical tools.

An Expanded Data Warehouse Architecture

The architecture shown in Figure 14-2 represents the earliest data warehouse applications but is still widely used today. It works well in small- to medium-sized com-

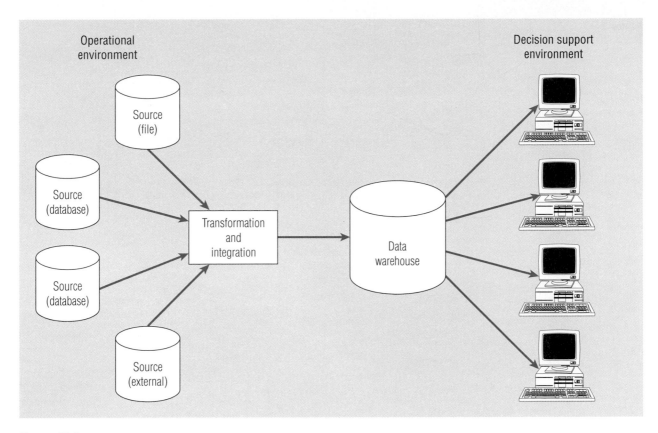

Figure 14-2
Generic data warehouse architecture

panies with a limited number of hardware and software platforms and a relatively homogeneous computing environment. However, for larger companies with a large number of data sources and a heterogeneous computing environment, this approach leads to problems in maintaining data quality and managing the data extraction processes (Devlin, 1997). These problems, together with the trend toward distributed computing, led to the expanded architecture shown in Figure 14-3. The architecture shown in Figure 14-3 is referred to as a three-level architecture, where the three levels are the following:

1. Operational systems and data

2. Enterprise data warehouse

3. Data marts

An **enterprise data warehouse** (EDW) is a centralized, integrated data warehouse that is the control point and single source of all data made available to end users for decision-support applications. Its purpose is twofold:

1. The EDW serves as a control point for assuring the quality and integrity of data before making it available to end users.

2. It provides a historical record of the business, for time-sensitive data.

Enterprise data warehouse:
A centralized, integrated data warehouse that is the control point and single source of all data made available to end users for decision-support applications.

Figure 14-3
Three-layer architecture

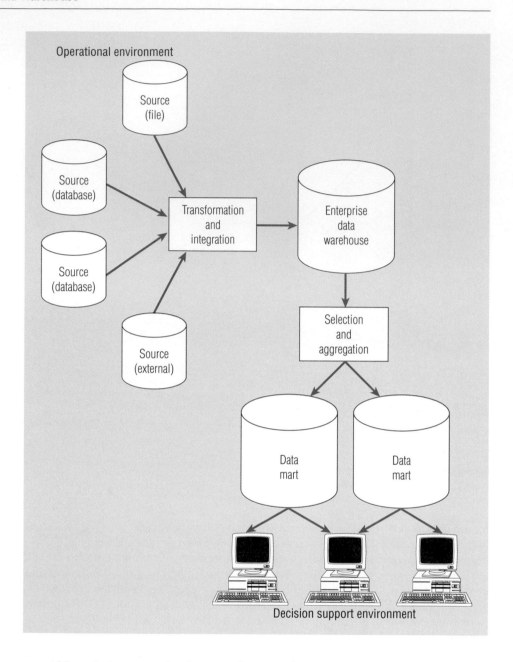

Although the enterprise data warehouse is the single source of all data for decision support, it is not typically accessed directly by end users. It is simply too large and too complex for users to navigate for most decision-support applications. Instead, users access the data that have been derived from the data warehouse and stored in data marts. Users may access the data indirectly through the process of drill-down, as explained below.

A **data mart** is a data warehouse that is limited in scope. Its contents are obtained by selecting and (where appropriate) summarizing data from the enterprise data warehouse. Each data mart is customized for the decision-support applications of a particular end-user group. An organization may have a marketing data mart, a finance data mart, and so on.

Data mart: A data warehouse that is limited in scope, whose data are obtained by selecting and (where appropriate) summarizing data from the enterprise data warehouse.

> ### Data Warehouse Principle 2
>
> Large organizations with many heterogeneous data sources should adopt a three-level data warehouse architecture.

Three factors support the approach described by the second Data Warehouse Principle:

1. The enterprise data warehouse and the data mart serve very different purposes and have very different data architectures, as we will see in the next section.

2. Transforming heterogeneous source data into a format that is appropriate for decision making is a highly complex process that is best performed in two steps.

3. Using data marts allows the organization to customize decision-support data for each end-user group, and to exploit the advantages of distributed processing.

Three-Layer Data Architecture

Figure 14-4 shows a three-layer data architecture:

1. Operational data are stored in the various operational systems throughout the organization (and sometimes in external systems).

2. Reconciled data are the type of data stored in the enterprise data warehouse.

3. Derived data are the type of data stored in each of the data marts.

Reconciled data are detailed, historical data intended to be the single, authoritative source for all decision-support applications. Reconciled data are generally not intended to be accessed directly by end users.

Derived data are data that have been selected, formatted, and aggregated for end-user decision-support applications.

We discuss reconciled data and derived data in the next two sections. Two components shown in Figure 14-4 play critical roles in the data architecture; they are the enterprise data model and metadata.

Role of the Enterprise Data Model   In Figure 14-4 we show the reconciled data layer linked to the enterprise data model. Recall from Chapter 2 that the enterprise data model presents a total picture explaining the data required by an organization. If the reconciled data layer is to be the single, authoritative source for all data required for decision support, it must conform to the design specified in the enterprise data model. Thus the organization needs to develop an enterprise data model before it can design a data warehouse. Otherwise there is a strong risk that a data warehouse it constructs will fail to meet user needs and that the effort will fail.

Role of Metadata   Figure 14-4 also shows a layer of metadata linked to each of the three data layers. Recall from Chapter 1 that metadata are data that describe the properties or characteristics of other data. Following is a brief description of the three types of metadata shown in Figure 14-4.

1. *Operational metadata* describe the data in the various operational systems (as well as external data) that feed the enterprise data warehouse. Operational

Reconciled data: Detailed, historical data intended to be the single, authoritative source for all decision-support applications and not generally intended to be accessed directly by end users.

Derived data: Data that have been selected, formatted, and aggregated for end-user decision-support applications.

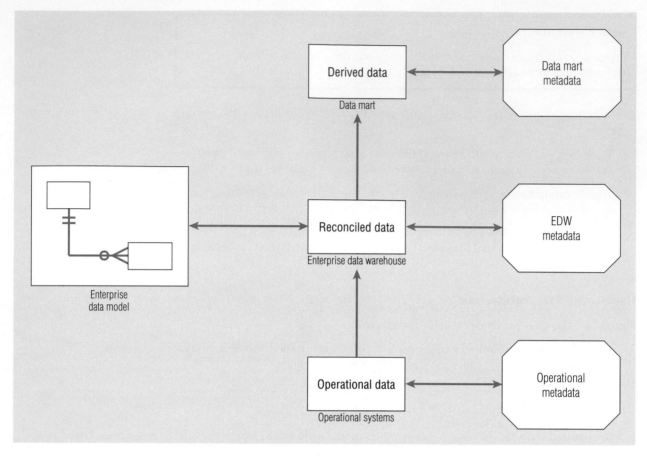

Figure 14-4
Three-layer data architecture

metadata typically exist in a number of different formats and unfortunately are often of poor quality.

2. *Enterprise data warehouse (EDW) metadata* are derived from (or at least consistent with) the enterprise data model. EDW metadata describe the reconciled data layer as well as the rules for transforming operational data to reconciled data.

3. *Data mart metadata* describe the derived data layer and the rules for transforming reconciled data to derived data.

SOME DATA CHARACTERISTICS

In order to better understand the data in each of these layers, you need to learn some basic characteristics of data as they are stored in databases.

Status versus Event Data

The difference between status data and event data is shown in Figure 14-5. The figure shows a typical log entry recorded by a database management system when processing a business transaction for a banking application. This log entry contains both

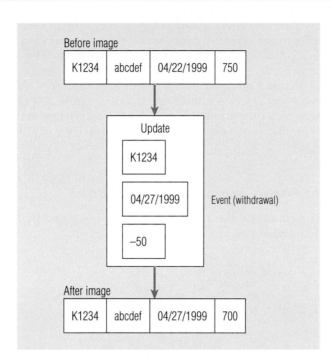

Figure 14-5
Example of DBMS log entry

status and event data: The "before image" and "after image" represent the *status* of the bank account before and then after a withdrawal. Data representing the withdrawal (or update event) are shown in the middle of the figure.

A transaction, as defined in Chapter 13, is a business activity that causes one or more business events to occur at a database level (Devlin, 1997). An **event** is a database action (create, update, or delete) that results from a transaction. Notice that a transaction may lead to one or more events. The withdrawal transaction in Figure 14-5 leads to a single event, which is the reduction in the account balance from 750 to 700. On the other hand, the transfer of money from one account to another would lead to two events: a withdrawal event and a deposit event.

Event: A database action (create, update, or delete) that results from a transaction.

Both status data and event data can be stored in a database. However, in practice most of the data stored in databases (including data warehouses) are status data. Event data, which represent transactions, may be stored for a short time but are then deleted or archived to save storage space. Both status and event data are typically stored in database logs (such as represented in Figure 14-5) for backup and recovery purposes. As will be explained below, the database log plays an important role in filling the data warehouse.

Transient versus Periodic Data

In data warehouses it is often necessary to maintain a record of when events occurred in the past. This is necessary, for example, to compare sales on a particular date or during a particular period with the previous year's sales on the same date or during the same period.

Most operational systems are based on the use of transient data. **Transient data** are data in which changes to existing records are written over previous records, thus destroying the previous data content. Records are deleted without preserving the previous contents of those records.

Transient data: Data in which changes to existing records are written over previous records, thus destroying the previous data content.

You can easily visualize transient data by again referring to Figure 14-5. If the after image is written over the before image, the before image (containing the previous balance) is lost. However, since this is a database log both images are normally preserved.

Periodic data: Data that are never physically altered or deleted, once they have been added to the store.

Periodic data are data that are never physically altered or deleted once added to the store. The before and after images in Figure 14-4 represent periodic data. Notice that each record contains a timestamp that indicates the date (and time, if needed) when the most recent update event occurred (we introduced the use of timestamps in Chapter 3).

An Example of Transient and Periodic Data

A more detailed example comparing transient and periodic data is shown in Figures 14-6 and Figure 14-7.

Figure 14-6
Transient operational data

Table X (10/01)

Key	A	B
001	a	b
002	c	d
003	e	f
004	g	h

Table X (10/02)

Key	A	B
001	a	b
▶ 002	r	d
003	e	f
▶ 004	y	h
▶ 005	m	n

Table X (10/03)

Key	A	B
001	a	b
002	r	d
▶ 003	e	t
▶ ¦_ _ _ _ _ _ _¦		
005	m	n

Figure 14-7
Periodic warehouse data

Table X (10/01)

Key	Date	A	B	Action
001	10/01	a	b	C
002	10/01	c	d	C
003	10/01	e	f	C
004	10/01	g	h	C

Table X (10/02)

	Key	Date	A	B	Action
	001	10/01	a	b	C
	002	10/01	c	d	C
▶	002	10/02	r	d	U
	003	10/01	e	f	C
	004	10/01	g	h	C
▶	004	10/02	y	h	U
▶	005	10/02	m	n	C

Table X (10/03)

	Key	Date	A	B	Action
	001	10/01	a	b	C
	002	10/01	c	d	C
	002	10/02	r	d	U
	003	10/01	e	f	C
▶	003	10/03	e	t	U
	004	10/01	g	h	C
	004	10/02	y	h	U
▶	004	10/03	y	h	D
	005	10/02	m	n	C

Transient Data   Figure 14-6 shows a relation (Table X) that contains four records. The table has three attributes: a primary key and two nonkey attributes A and B. The values for each of these attributes on the date 10/01 are shown in the figure. For example, for record 001 the value of attribute A on this date is a.

On date 10/02 three changes are made to the table (changes to rows are indicated by arrows to the left of the table). Record 002 is updated, so that the value of *A* is changed from *c* to *r*. Record 004 is also updated, so the value of *A* is changed from *g* to *y*. Finally, a new record (with key 005) is inserted into the table.

Notice that when records 002 and 004 are updated, the new records replace the previous records. Therefore the previous values are lost—there is no historical record of these values. This is characteristic of transient data.

More changes are made to the records on date 10/03 (to simplify the discussion, we assume that only one change can be made to a given record on a given date). Record 003 is updated, and record 004 is deleted. Notice that there is no record to indicate that record 004 was ever stored in the database. The way the data are processed in Figure 14-5 is characteristic of the transient data typical in operational systems.

Periodic Data   One typical objective for a data warehouse to maintain a historical record of key events, or to create a time series for particular variables such as sales. This often requires storing periodic data, rather than transient data. Figure 14-7 shows the table used in 14-6, now modified to represent periodic data. The following changes have been made in Figure 14-7:

1. Two new columns have been added to Table X.

    a. The column named Date is a timestamp that records the most recent date when a row has been modified.

    b. The column named Action is used to record the type of change that occurred. Possible values for this attribute are C (Create), U (Update), and D (Delete).

2. Once a record has been stored in the table, that record is never changed or deleted. When a record is changed, both the before image and the after image are stored in the table. Although a record may be *logically* deleted, a historical version of the deleted record is maintained in the database.

Now let's examine the same set of actions that occurred in Figure 14-6. Assume that all four records were created on the date 10/01, as shown in the first table.

In the second table (for 10/02), rows 002 and 004 have been updated. The table now contains both the old version (for 10/01) and the new version (for 10/02) for these rows. The table also contains the new row (005) that was created on 10/02.

The third table (for 10/03) shows the update to row 003, with both the old and new versions. Also, row 004 is deleted in this table. This table now contains *three* versions of row 004: the original version (from 10/01), the updated version (from 10/02), and the deleted version (from 10/03). The D in the last row for record 004 indicates that this record has been logically deleted, so that it is no longer available to users or their applications.

If you examine Figure 14-7 you can see why data warehouses tend to grow very rapidly. Storing periodic data can impose large storage requirements. A corollary is that users must choose very carefully the key data that require this form of processing.

THE RECONCILED DATA LAYER

As indicated in Figure 14-4, we use the term *reconciled data* to refer to the data layer associated with the enterprise data warehouse. This is the term used by IBM in a 1993 paper describing data warehouse architectures. Although the term is not widely used, it accurately describes the nature of the data that should appear in the enterprise data warehouse and the way they are derived.

Characteristics of Reconciled Data

Reconciled data are intended to provide a single, authoritative source for data that support decision making. Ideally normalized, this data layer is detailed, historical, comprehensive, and quality controlled.

1. *Detailed*   The data are detailed (rather than summarized), providing maximum flexibility for various user communities to structure the data to best suit their needs.

2. *Historical*   The data are periodic (or point-in-time) to provide a historical perspective.

3. *Normalized*   The data are fully normalized (that is, third normal form or higher). (We discussed normalization in Chapter 6.) Normalized data provide greater integrity and flexibility of use than denormalized data. Denormalization is not necessary to improve performance, since reconciled data are usually accessed periodically using batch processes.

4. *Comprehensive*   Reconciled data reflect an enterprise-wide perspective, whose design conforms to the enterprise data model.

5. *Quality controlled*   Reconciled data must be of unquestioned quality and integrity, since they are summarized into the data marts and used for decision making.

Notice that these characteristics of reconciled data are quite different from the typical operational data from which they are derived. Operational data are typically detailed, but they differ strongly in the other four dimensions described above.

1. Operational data are transient, rather than historical.

2. They are not normalized. Depending on their roots, operational data may never have been normalized or may have been denormalized for performance reasons.

3. Rather than being comprehensive, operational data are generally restricted in scope to a particular application.

4. Operational data are often of poor quality, with numerous types of inconsistencies and errors.

The data reconciliation process is responsible for transforming operational data to reconciled data. Because of the sharp differences between these two types of data, clearly data reconciliation is the most difficult and technically challenging part of building a data warehouse. Fortunately several sophisticated software products are available to assist with this activity.

The Data Reconciliation Process

Data reconciliation occurs in two stages during the process of filling the enterprise data warehouse.

Figure 14-8

Steps in data reconciliation

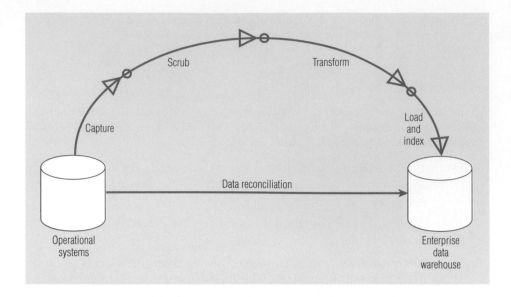

1. An initial load, when the EDW is first created

2. Subsequent updates (normally performed on a periodic basis) to keep the EDW current and/or to expand it

   Data reconciliation can be visualized as a process shown in Figure 14-8, consisting of four steps: capture, scrub, transform, and load and index. In reality, the steps may be combined in different ways. For example, data capture and scrub might be combined as a single process, or scrub and transform might be combined. We discuss capture, scrub, and load and index next, followed by a thorough discussion of transform.

Capture   Extracting the relevant data from the source files and databases used to fill the EDW is called capture. Usually, not all of the data contained in the various operational systems are required, but just a subset. Capturing the subset of data is based on an extensive analysis of both the source and target systems, which is best performed by a team directed by data administration and composed of both end users and data warehouse professionals.

The two generic types of data capture are static capture and incremental capture. Static capture is used to fill the data warehouse initially, and incremental capture is used for ongoing warehouse maintenance.

Static capture: A method of capturing a snapshot of the required source data at a point in time.

Static capture is a method of capturing a snapshot of the required source data at a point in time. The view of the source data is independent of the time when it was created.

Incremental capture: A method of capturing only the changes that have occurred in the source data since the last capture.

Incremental capture captures only the changes that have occurred in the source data since the last capture. The most common method is log capture. Recall that the database log contains after images that record the most recent changes to database records (see Figure 14-5). With log capture, only after images that are logged after the last capture are selected from the log.

Scrub   Data in operational systems are often of poor quality. Some of the errors and inconsistencies typical of these data are as follows:

1. Misspelled names and addresses

2. Impossible or erroneous dates of birth

3. Fields used for purposes for which they were never intended

4. Mismatched addresses and area codes

5. Missing data

Let's consider some examples of such errors. Customer names are often used as primary keys or as search criteria in customer files. However, these names are often misspelled or spelled in various ways in these files. For example, the name "The Coca-Cola Company" is the correct name for the soft-drink company. This name may be entered in customer records as "Coca-Cola," "Coca Cola," "TCCC," and so on. In one study, a company found that the name "McDonald's" could be spelled 100 different ways!

Another type of data pollution occurs when a field is used for purposes not intended. For example, in one bank a record field was designed to hold a telephone number. However, branch managers who had no other use for this field instead stored the interest rate in it. Another example, reported by a major UK bank, was even more bizarre. The data scrubbing program turned up a customer on their files whose occupation was listed as "steward on the Titanic"! (Devlin, 1997).

You may wonder why such errors are so common in operational data. The quality of operational data is largely determined by their value to the organization responsible for gathering them. Unfortunately, it often happens that the data-gathering organization places a low value on some data whose accuracy is important to downstream applications, such as data warehousing.

Given the common occurrence of errors, the worst thing a company can do is simply to copy operational data to the data warehouse. Instead, it is important to improve the quality of the source data through a technique called data scrubbing. **Data scrubbing** (also called data cleansing) is a technique using pattern recognition and other artificial intelligence techniques to upgrade the quality of raw data before transforming them and moving the data to the data warehouse.

> **Data scrubbing:** A technique using pattern recognition and other artificial intelligence techniques to upgrade the quality of raw data before transforming and moving the data to the data warehouse. Also called data cleansing.

Data Warehouse Principle 3

A successful data warehouse effort requires that a formal program in total quality management (TQM) be implemented as part of the data management effort.

Total quality management (TQM) focuses on defect prevention, rather than defect correction. Although data scrubbing can help upgrade data quality, it is not a long-term solution to the data quality problem. For a good discussion of TQM applied to data management, see English (1997).

Load and Index   The last step in filling the enterprise data warehouse is to load the selected data into the target data warehouse and to create the necessary indexes. The two basic modes for loading data to the target EDW are refresh and update.

Refresh mode is an approach to filling the data warehouse that employs bulk rewriting of the target data at periodic intervals. That is, the target data are written initially to fill the warehouse. Then at periodic intervals the warehouse is rewritten, replacing the previous contents.

> **Refresh mode:** An approach to filling the data warehouse that employs bulk rewriting of the target data at periodic intervals.

Update mode is an approach in which only changes in the source data are written to the data warehouse. To support the periodic nature of warehouse data, these new records are usually written to the data warehouse without overwriting or deleting previous records (see Figure 14-7).

> **Update mode:** An approach in which only changes in the source data are written to the data warehouse.

As you would expect, refresh mode is generally used to fill the warehouse when it is first created. Update mode is then generally used for ongoing maintenance of the target warehouse. Refresh mode is used in conjunction with static data capture, while update mode is used in conjunction with incremental data capture.

With both the refresh and update modes, it is necessary to create and maintain the indexes that are used to manage the warehouse data. A type of indexing called *bit-mapped indexing* is often used in a data warehouse environment. Although this topic is beyond the scope of this chapter, you can learn more about bit-mapped indexing in Winter (1996).

DATA TRANSFORMATION

Data transformation:
The component of data reconciliation that converts data from the format of the source operational systems to the format of the enterprise data warehouse.

Data transformation (or transform) is at the very center of the data reconciliation process. **Data transformation** is the component of data reconciliation that converts data from the format of the source operational systems to the format of the enterprise data warehouse. Data transformation accepts data from the data capture component (after data scrubbing, if it applies), then maps the data to the format of the reconciled data layer, and then passes them to the load and index component.

Data transformation may range from a simple change in data format or representation to a highly complex exercise in data integration. Following are three examples that illustrate this range:

1. A salesperson requires a download of customer data from a mainframe database to her laptop computer. In this case the transformation required is simply mapping the data from EBCDIC to ASCII representation, which can easily be performed by off-the-shelf software.

2. A manufacturing company has product data stored in three different inherited systems—a manufacturing system, a marketing system, and an engineering application. The company needs to develop a consolidated view of these product data. Data transformation involves several different functions, including resolving different key structures, converting to a common set of codes, and integrating data from different sources. These functions are quite straightforward, and most of the necessary software can be generated using a standard commercial software package with a graphical interface.

3. A large health care organization manages a geographically dispersed group of hospitals, clinics, and other care centers. Because many of the units have been acquired through acquisition over time, the data are heterogeneous and uncoordinated. For a number of important reasons, the organization needs to develop a data warehouse to provide a single corporate view of the enterprise. This effort will require the full range of transformation functions described below, including some custom software development.

It is important to understand the distinction between the functions performed in data scrubbing and the functions performed in data transformation. The goal of data scrubbing is to correct errors in data *values* in the source data, whereas the goal of data transformation is to convert the data *format* from the source to the target system. Note that it is essential to scrub the data before they are transformed since, if there are errors in the data before they are transformed, the errors will remain in the data after transformation.

Data Transformation Functions

Data transformation encompasses a variety of different functions. These functions may be classified broadly into two categories: record-level functions and field-level functions. In most data warehousing applications, a combination of some or even all of these functions is required.

Record-Level Functions   Operating on a set of records, such as a file or table, are the record-level functions most important: selection, joining, normalization, and aggregation.

Selection (also called *subsetting*) is the process of partitioning data according to predefined criteria. For data warehouse applications, selection is used to extract the relevant data from the source systems that will be used to fill the data warehouse. In fact, selection is typically a part of the capture function discussed earlier.

Selection: The process of partitioning data according to predefined criteria.

When the source data are relational, SQL SELECT statements can be used for selection (see Chapter 9 for a detailed discussion). For example, recall that incremental capture is often implemented by selecting after images from the database log that have been created since the previous capture. A typical after image was shown in Figure 14-5. Suppose that the after images for this application are stored in a table named ACCOUNT_HISTORY. Then the after images that have been created after 12/31/99 can be selected with the following statements:

```
SELECT *
FROM    ACCOUNT_HISTORY
WHERE   Create_Date > 12/31/99;
```

Joining combines data from various sources into a single table or view. Joining data is an important function in data warehouse applications, since it is often necessary to consolidate data from various sources. For example, an insurance company may have client data spread throughout several different files and databases. When the source data are relational, SQL statements can be used to perform a join operation (see Chapter 9 for details).

Joining: The process of combining data from various sources into a single table or view.

Joining is often complicated by factors such as the following:

1. Often the source data are not relational, in which case SQL statements cannot be used. Instead, procedural language statements must be coded.

2. Even for relational data, primary keys for the tables to be joined are often from different domains. These keys must then be reconciled before a SQL join can be performed.

3. Source data may contain errors, which makes join operations hazardous.

Normalization is the process of decomposing relations with anomalies to produce smaller, well-structured relations (see Chapter 6 for a detailed discussion). As indicated earlier, source data in operational systems are often denormalized (or simply not normalized). The data must therefore be normalized as part of data transformation.

Aggregation is the process of transforming data from a detailed level to a summary level. For example, in a retail business, individual sales transactions can be summarized to produce total sales by store, product, date, and so on. Since (in our model) the enterprise data warehouse contains only detailed data, aggregation is not normally associated with this component. However, aggregation is an important function in filling the data marts, as explained below.

Aggregation: The process of transforming data from a detailed to a summary level.

Figure 14-9
Single-field transformation

(a) Basic representation

(b) Algorithmic
transformation

(c) Table look-up

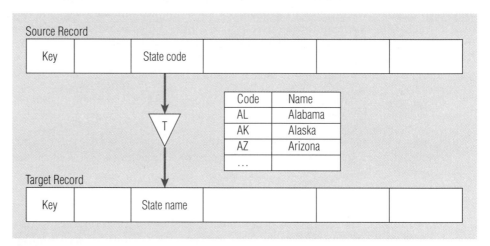

Field-Level Functions   A field-level function converts data from a given format in a source record to a different format in a target record. Field-level functions are of two types: single-field and multifield.

A *single-field* transformation converts data from a single source field to a single target field. Figure 14-9a is a basic representation of this type of transformation (designated by the letter "T" in the diagram). An example of a single-field transformation is converting a measurement from imperial to metric representation.

As shown in Figures 14-9b and c, there are two basic methods for performing a single-field transformation: algorithmic and table lookup. An algorithmic transformation is performed using a formula or logical expression. Figure 14-9b shows a conversion from Fahrenheit to Celsius temperature using a formula. When a simple algorithm does not apply, a lookup table can be used instead. Figure 14-9c shows the use of a table to convert state codes to state names (this type of conversion is common in data warehouse applications).

A *multifield* transformation converts data from one or more source fields to one or more target fields. This type of transformation is very common in data warehouse applications. Two multifield transformations are shown in Figure 14-10.

Figure 14-10a is an example of an many-to-one transformation (in this case, two source fields are mapped to one target field). In the source record, the combination of employee name and telephone number is used as the primary key. This combination is awkward and may not uniquely identify a person. Therefore in creating a target record, the combination is mapped to a unique employee identification (Emp_ID). A lookup table would be created to support this transformation. A data scrubbing program might be employed to help identify duplicates in the source data.

Figure 14-10b is an example of a one-to-many transformation (in this case, one source field has been converted to two target fields). In the source record, a product

Figure 14-10
Multifield transformation

(a) A M:1 relationship

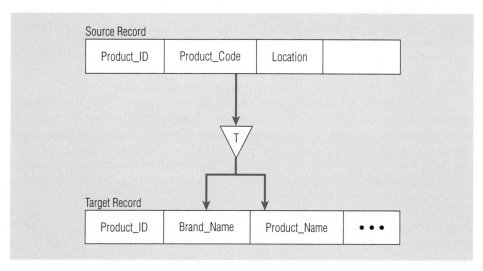

(b) A 1:M relationship

code has been used to encode the combination of brand name and product name (the use of such codes is common in operational data). However, in the target record it is desired to display the full text describing product and brand names. Again, a lookup table would be employed for this purpose.

More Complex Transformations   In Figure 14-10, the multifield transformations both involve only one source record and one target record. More generally, multifield transformations may involve more than one source record and/or more than one target record. In the most complex cases, these records may even originate in different operational systems and in different time zones (Devlin, 1997).

Tools to Support Data Reconciliation

As you can readily see, data reconciliation is an extremely complex and challenging process. A variety of closely integrated software applications must be developed (or acquired) to support this process. Fortunately, a number of powerful software tools are available to assist organizations in developing these applications. In this section we describe three categories of such tools: data quality, data conversion, and data cleansing (for a more detailed discussion, see Williams, 1997). Table 14-2 summarizes the tools in each of these three categories.

Data Quality Tools   These tools are intended to assess the quality of data in existing systems and compare them to the requirements of the data warehouse. Thus the tools are useful during an early stage of warehouse development. Two such tools listed in Table 14-2 are Analyze (QDB Solutions, Inc.) and WizRules (WizSoft, Inc.). The product named Analyze is used to assess the quality of data and related business rules and to make recommendations for cleansing and organizing data prior to extraction and transformation. The product also monitors the quality of data on an ongoing basis.

WizRules is a rules discovery tool that searches through records in existing tables and discovers the rules associated with the data. For example, a rule might state the following: "If Customer_Name is Able or Baker, then City is San Diego; probability 0.95. This rule exists in 50 records." The product also identifies records that deviate from the established rules.

Data Conversion Tools   The next set of tools shown in Table 14-2 are data conversion tools. These tools generally perform three mainstream functions: extract, transform, and load and index. Such tools listed in Table 14-2 include Extract (Evolutionary Technologies International), InfoSuite (Platinum Technology, Inc.), Passport (Carleton Corp.), and Prism (Prism Solutions, Inc.). In addition to the three functions listed above, Passport provides some data scrubbing functions.

The tools in this category are basically program-generation tools. They accept as input the schema (or file descriptions) of the source and target files, and the business rules that are to be used for data transformation. Typical business rules would include formulas, algorithms, and lookup tables (such as those shown in Figure 14-9). The tools then generate the program code necessary to perform the transformation functions on an ongoing basis. The tools are quite sophisticated and typically employ some artificial intelligence features.

Data-Cleansing Tools   The last category contains one tool designed specifically to provide data cleansing and related functions. Integrity (Vality Technology, Inc.) is

Table 14-2   Tools to Support Data Reconciliation

Product Name	Company	Description
Analyze	QDB Solutions, Inc. www.qdb.com	Data quality assessment
WizRules	WizSoft, Inc. www.wizsoft.com	Rules discovery
Extract	Evolutionary Technologies www.evtech.com	Extract, transform, load and index
InfoSuite	Platinum Technology, Inc. www.platinum.com	Extract, transform, load and index
Passport	Carleton Corp. www.carleton.com	Extract, scrub, transform, load and index
Prism	Prism Solutions, Inc. www.prismsolutions.com	Extract, transform, load and index
Integrity	Vality Technology, Inc. www.vality.com	Quality analysis, data scrubing

designed to perform data quality analysis, data cleansing, and data reengineering (that is, discovering business rules and relationships among entities).

THE DERIVED DATA LAYER

We turn now to the derived data layer. This is the data layer associated with data marts (see Figure 14-4). It is the layer with which users normally interact for their decision-support applications. In this section we first discuss the characteristics of the derived data layer and the way that it is derived from the reconciled data layer. We then introduce the star schema (or dimensional model), which is the data model most commonly used today to implement this data layer.

Characteristics of Derived Data

Earlier we defined derived data as data that have been selected, formatted, and aggregated for end-user decision-support applications. As shown in Figure 14-4, the source of the derived data is the reconciled data described earlier. Derived data are generally optimized for the needs of particular user groups such as departments, work groups, or even individuals. A common mode of operation is to select the relevant data from the enterprise data warehouse on a daily basis, format and aggregate those data as needed, then load and index those data in the target data marts.

The objectives that are sought with derived data are quite different from the objectives of reconciled data. Typical objectives are the following:

1. Provide ease of use for decision-support applications.

2. Provide fast response for user queries or requests for information.

3. Customize data for particular target user groups.

4. Support ad-hoc queries and data-mining applications.

To satisfy these needs, we usually find the following characteristics in derived data:

1. Both detailed data and aggregate data are present.

    a. Detailed data are often (but not always) periodic—that is, they provide a historical record.

    b. Aggregate data are formatted to respond quickly to predetermined (or common) queries.

2. Data are distributed to departmental servers.

3. The data model that is most commonly used is the star schema, which is a relational-like model. Proprietary models are also sometimes used.

The Star Schema

Star schema: A simple database design in which dimensional data are separated from fact or event data. A dimensional model is another name for star schema.

A **star schema** is a simple database design (particularly suited to ad-hoc queries) in which dimensional data (describing how data are commonly aggregated) are separated from fact or event data (describing individual business transactions) (Devlin, 1997). Another name that is often used is the dimensional model (Kimball, 1996). Although the star schema is suited to ad-hoc queries (and other forms of informational processing), it is not suited to on-line transaction processing and therefore is not generally used in operational systems.

Fact Tables and Dimension Tables   A star schema consists of two types of tables: fact tables and dimension tables. *Fact tables* contain factual or quantitative data about a business such as units sold, orders booked, and so on. *Dimension tables* hold descriptive data about the business. The simplest star schema consists of one fact table, surrounded by several dimension tables. Typical business dimensions are Product, Customer, and Period. This structure is shown in Figure 14-11, which contains four dimension tables.

Each dimension table has a one-to-many relationship to the central fact table. Each dimension table generally has a simple primary key, as well as several nonkey attributes. The primary key in turn is a foreign key in the fact table (as shown in Figure 14-11). The primary key of the fact table is a composite key that consists of the concatenation of all of the foreign keys (four keys in Figure 14-11). The relationship between each dimension table and the fact table provides a join path that allows users to query the database easily, using SQL statements for either predefined or ad-hoc queries. Nonkey attributes are generally called data columns, as shown in Figure 14-11.

By now you have probably recognized that the star schema is not a new data model, but instead a particular implementation of the relational data model. The fact table plays the role of an associative entity that links the instances of the various dimensions. To review associative entities see Chapter 3, and for an example of the use of an associative entity see Figure 3-13.

Example Star Schema   A simple example of a star schema is shown in Figure 14-12. This example has three dimension tables: PRODUCT, PERIOD, and STORE, and one fact table, named SALES. The fact table is used to record three business facts: total

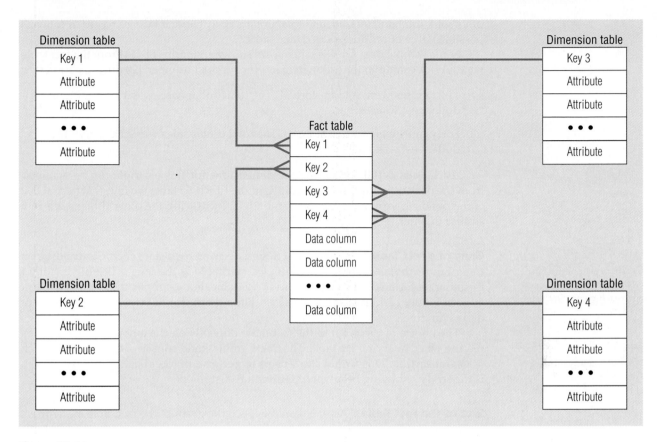

Figure 14-11
Components of a star schema

Figure 14-12
Star schema example

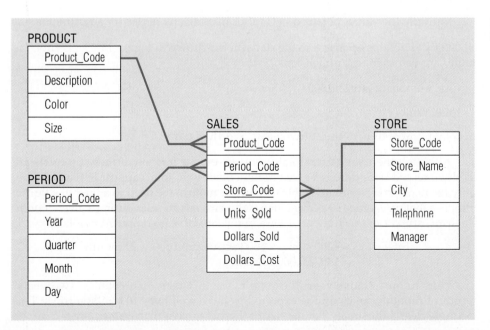

units sold, total dollars sold, and total dollars cost. These totals are recorded for each possible value of product, period, and store.

Some sample data for this schema are shown in Figure 14-13. From the fact table we find (for example) the following facts for product number 110 during period 002:

1. Thirty units were sold in store S1. The total dollar sales was 1500, and total dollar cost was 1200.

2. Forty units were sold in store S3. The total dollar sales was 2000, and total dollar cost was 1200.

Additional detail concerning the dimensions for this example can be obtained from the dimension tables. For example, in the PERIOD table we find that period 002 corresponds to year 1999, quarter 1, month 5. Try tracing the other dimensions in a similar manner.

Grain of a Fact Table   An important design decision for a star schema is deciding on the grain of the fact table. The **grain** of a fact table is the length of time (or other meaning) associated with each record in the table. For example, the grain of the fact table in Figure 14-13 is *monthly item totals*. Finer grain would be weekly item totals or daily item totals.

Grain: The length of time (or other meaning) associated with each record in the table.

The choice of the grain of the fact table depends on the amount of detail users require when querying the table. The finest grain would consist of the details for each sales transaction. This would allow users to perform **market basket analysis**, which is the study of buying behavior of individual customers.

Market basket analysis: The study of buying behavior of individual customers.

Size of the Fact Table   As you would expect, the grain of the fact table has a direct impact on the size of that table. We can estimate the number of rows in the fact table as follows:

1. Estimate the number of possible values for each dimension associated with the fact table (in other words, the number of possible values for each foreign key in the fact table).

2. Multiply the values obtained in (1) after making any necessary adjustments.

Let's apply this approach to the star schema shown in Figure 14-13. Assume the following values for the dimensions:

total number of stores: 1000

total number of products: 10,000

total number of periods: 24 (two years' worth of data)

Although there are 10,000 total products, only a fraction of these products are likely to record sales during a given month. Since item totals appear in the fact table only for items that record sales during a given month, we need to adjust this figure. Suppose that on average 50 percent (or 5,000) items record sales during a given month. Then an estimate of the number of rows in the fact table is computed as follows:

$$\text{total rows} = 1000 \text{ stores} \times 5000 \text{ active products} \times 24 \text{ months}$$
$$= 120{,}000{,}000 \text{ rows (!)}$$

Thus in our relatively small example, the fact table that contains two years' worth of monthly totals can be expected to have well over 100 million rows. This example clearly illustrates that the size of the fact table is many times larger than the

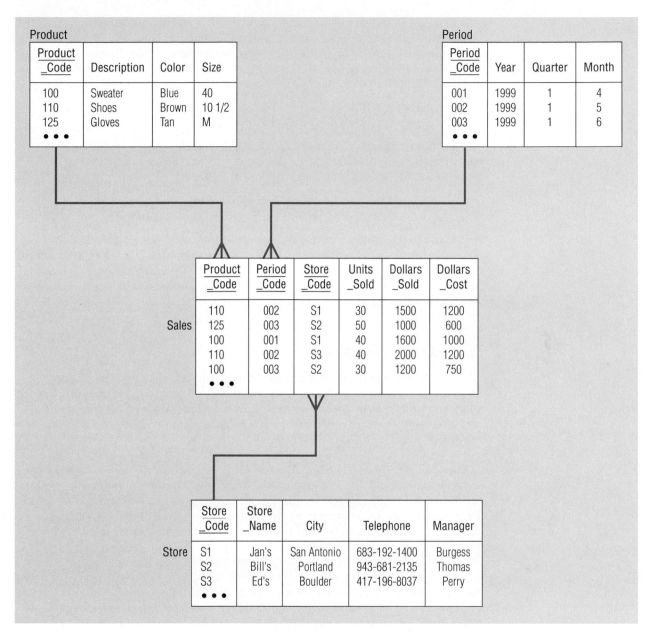

Figure 14-13
Star schema with sample data

dimension tables. For example, the STORE table has 1000 rows, the PRODUCT table 10,000 rows, and the PERIOD table 720 rows.

If we know the size of each field in the fact table, we can further estimate the size (in bytes) of that table. The fact table (named SALES) in Figure 14-13 has six fields. If each of these fields averages four bytes in length, we can estimate the total size of the fact table as follows:

$$\text{total size} = 120{,}000{,}000 \text{ rows} \times 6 \text{ fields} \times 4 \text{ bytes/field}$$
$$= 2{,}880{,}000{,}000 \text{ bytes or } 2.88 \text{ gigabytes}$$

The size of the fact table depends on both the number of dimensions and the grain of the fact table. Suppose that after using the database shown in Figure 14-13 for a short period of time, the marketing department requests that *daily* totals be accumulated in the fact table (this is a typical evolution of a data mart). With the grain of the table changed to daily item totals, the number of rows is computed as follows:

$$\text{total rows} = 1000 \text{ stores} \times 2000 \text{ active products} \times 720 \text{ days (two years)}$$
$$= 1,440,000,000 \text{ rows}$$

In the preceding calculation we have assumed that 20 percent of all products record sales on a given day. The database can now be expected to contain well over 1 *billion* rows. The database size is calculated as follows:

$$\text{total size} = 1,440,000,000 \text{ rows} \times 6 \text{ fields} \times 4 \text{ bytes/field}$$
$$= 34,560,000,000 \text{ bytes (or 34.56 gigabytes)}$$

Many large retailers (such as Wal-Mart, K-Mart, and Sears) now have data warehouses (or data marts) whose design resembles the one shown in Figures 14-12 and 14-13. The size of most of these data warehouses is in the multiple-terabyte range, and growing rapidly as marketing people continue to press for more dimensions and an ever-finer grain in the fact table.

Variations of the Star Schema

The simple star schema introduced above is adequate for many applications. However, various extensions to this schema are often required to cope with more complex modeling problems. In this section we briefly describe two such extensions: multiple fact tables and the snowflake schema. For a discussion of additional extensions and variations, see Poe (1996).

Multiple Fact Tables   It is often desirable for performance or other reasons to define more than one fact table in a given star schema. For example, suppose that various users require different levels of aggregation (in other words, a different table grain). Performance can be improved by defining a different fact table for each level of aggregation. The obvious tradeoff is that storage requirements may increase dramatically with each new fact table.

Figure 14-14 shows the star schema for the previous example (Figure 14-12), with two fact tables. One fact table is for daily sales, the other for monthly sales. We have previously calculated the estimated size of each of these tables. Designers of the data mart would have to decide whether the increased storage requirements are justified by the prospective performance improvement.

Snowflake Schema   Sometimes a dimension in a star schema forms a natural hierarchy. A geographic hierarchy is a typical example of this situation. For example, consider a dimension named Market. The following geographic hierarchy may exist:

1. There are several markets within a state.

2. There are several states within a region.

3. There are several regions within a country.

   When a dimension participates in a hierarchy, the designer has two basic choices:

1. Include all of the information for the hierarchy in a single table. In this case the table is said to be *denormalized*—that is, it is not in third normal form.

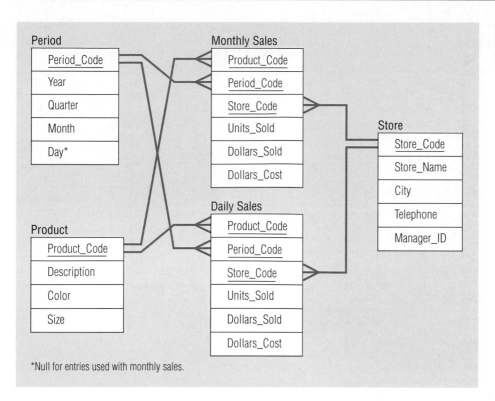

Figure 14-14
Star schema with two
fact tables

2. Normalize the tables (discussed in Chapter 6). Normalizing the tables results in an expanded schema called the snowflake schema.

A **snowflake schema**, named for its shape, is an expanded version of a star schema in which all of the tables are fully normalized. An example of a snowflake schema is shown in Figure 14-15. In this example, each product is a member of a product group. When PRODUCT is normalized, a separate table called PRODUCT GROUP is created. Notice that there is a 1:M relationship between PRODUCT GROUP and PRODUCT.

In this same figure a separate table is created for STORE MANAGER, so that these tables are also normalized. The relationship between STORE and STORE MANAGER is 1:1 mandatory.

Should dimensions with hierarchies be decomposed, as shown in this example? The advantages claimed for this approach are reduced storage space and improved flexibility. The major disadvantage is poor performance, particularly when browsing the database. Kimball (1996) warns: "Do not snowflake your dimensions, even when they are large. If you do snowflake your dimensions, prepare to live with poor browsing performance."

Proprietary Databases   A number of vendors have developed proprietary databases for decision-support applications. Such databases are often called *multidimensional*. Data are first summarized or aggregated, then stored in the multidimensional database for predetermined queries or other analytical operations.

Multidimensional databases usually store data in some form of array, similar to that used in the star schema. The advantage of a multidimensional database is very fast performance, provided that the system is used for the type of queries for which it was optimized. One disadvantage of a multidimensional database is that it is often

Snowflake schema: An expanded version of a star schema in which all of the tables are fully normalized.

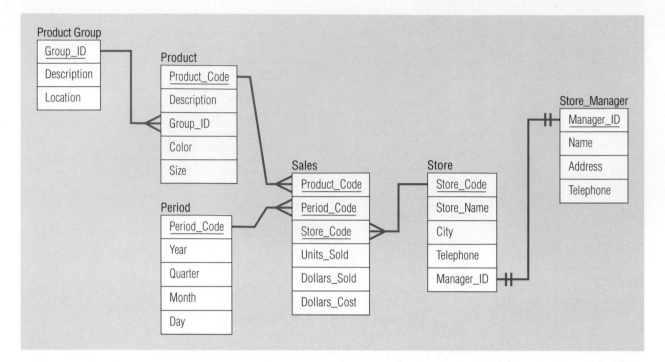

Figure 14-15
Example of snowflake schema

limited in the size of the database it can accommodate. Another disadvantage is that it is not as flexible as a star schema (or other relational database).

Independent versus Dependent Data Marts

Dependent data mart:
A data mart filled exclusively from the enterprise data warehouse and its reconciled data layer.

Independent data mart:
A data mart filled with data extracted from the operational environment, without benefit of a reconciled data layer.

The final topic of this section is whether it is possible (or desirable) to build data marts that are independent of an enterprise data warehouse. A **dependent data mart** is one filled exclusively from the enterprise data warehouse and its reconciled data layer. This is the approach illustrated in Figure 14-4 and described throughout this chapter. However, it is also possible to conceive at least of an independent data mart (in fact, some vendors advocate this approach). An **independent data mart** is one filled with data extracted from the operational environment, without benefit of a reconciled data layer.

Although independent data marts might have an initial appeal, they suffer from a number of disadvantages (Meyer, 1997):

1. There can be no assurance that the data from different data marts are semantically consistent, since each set is derived from different sources.

2. There is no capability to drill down to greater detail in the enterprise data warehouse.

3. Data redundancy increases because the same data are often stored in the various data marts.

4. There is lack of integration of data from an enterprise perspective, since that is the responsibility of the enterprise data warehouse.

5. Creating an independent data mart may require cross-platform joins that are difficult (at best) to perform.

6. Different users have different requirements for the currency of data in data marts, which might lower the quality of data that is made available.

Data Warehouse Principle 4

Any organization that plans to develop more than one data mart should employ the dependent data mart approach.

Note that this principle does not preclude a phased approach to developing an enterprise data warehouse and the data marts that depend on it. For a phased (or iterative) approach to building a data warehouse, see Inmon (1997).

THE USER INTERFACE

"Build it and they will come" is a strategy that may work in some contexts but cannot be relied upon with data warehouses and data marts. Even a well-designed data mart, loaded with relevant data, may not be used unless users are provided with a powerful, intuitive interface that allows them to easily access and analyze those data. In this section we provide a brief introduction to contemporary interfaces for data warehouses.

A variety of tools are available to query and analyze data stored in data warehouses and data marts. These tools may be classified as follows:

1. Traditional query and reporting tools

2. On-line analytical processing (OLAP) tools

3. Data-mining tools

4. Data-visualization tools

Traditional query and reporting tools include spreadsheets, personal computer databases, and report writers and generators. For reasons of space (and since they are covered elsewhere) we do not describe these tools in this chapter. We describe the remaining three categories of tools after discussing the role of metadata.

Role of Metadata

The first requirement for building a user-friendly interface is a set of metadata that describes the data in the data mart in business terms that users can easily understand. We show the association of metadata with data marts in the overall three-level data architecture in Figure 14-4.

The metadata associated with data marts are often referred to as a "data catalog," "data directory," or some similar term. Metadata serve as kind of a "yellow pages" directory to the data in the data marts. The metadata should allow users to easily answer questions such as the following:

1. What subjects are described in the data mart? (Typical subjects are customers, patients, students, products, courses, and so on.)

2. What dimensions and facts are included in the data mart? What is the grain of the fact table?

3. How are the data in the data mart derived from the enterprise data warehouse data? What rules are used in the derivation?

4. How are the data in the enterprise data warehouse derived from operational data? What rules are used in this derivation?

5. What reports and predefined queries are available to view the data?

6. What drill-down and other data analysis techniques are available?

7. Who is responsible for the quality of data in the data marts, and to whom are requests for changes made?

On-Line Analytical Processing (OLAP) Tools

A relatively new class of tools has been developed to provide users with multidimensional views of their data, then to easily analyze the data using a graphical interface. In the simplest case, data are viewed as a simple three-dimensional cube.

On-line analytical processing (or OLAP) is the use of a set of graphical tools that provides users with multidimensional views of their data and allows them to analyze the data using simple windowing techniques. The term on-line analytical processing is intended to contrast with the more traditional term *on-line transaction processing*. The differences between these two types of processing were summarized in Table 14-1. The term "multidimensional analysis" is often used as a synonym for OLAP.

An example of a "data cube" (or multidimensional view) of data that is typical of OLAP is shown in Figure 14-16. This view corresponds quite closely to the star schema introduced in Figure 14-12. Two of the dimensions in Figure 14-16 correspond to the dimension tables (PRODUCT and PERIOD) in Figure 14-12, while the third dimension (named measures) corresponds to the data in the fact table (named SALES) in Figure 14-12.

On-line analytical processing (OLAP):
The use of a set of graphical tools that provides users with multidimensional views of their data, and allows them to analyze the data using simple windowing techniques.

Figure 14-16
Slicing a data cube

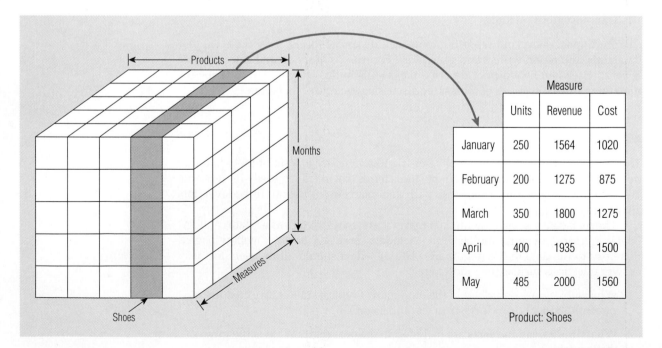

	Measure		
	Units	Revenue	Cost
January	250	1564	1020
February	200	1275	875
March	350	1800	1275
April	400	1935	1500
May	485	2000	1560

Product: Shoes

Figure 14-17
Example of drill-down

(a) Summary report

Brand	Package size	Sales
SofTowel	2-pack	$75
SofTowel	3-pack	$100
SofTowel	6-pack	$50

(b) Drill-down with color added

Brand	Package size	Color	Sales
SofTowel	2-pack	White	$30
SofTowel	2-pack	Yellow	$25
SofTowel	2-pack	Pink	$20
SofTowel	3-pack	White	$50
SofTowel	3-pack	Green	$25
SofTowel	3-pack	Yellow	$25
SofTowel	6-pack	White	$30
SofTowel	6-pack	Yellow	$20

Slicing a Cube   Figure 14-16 also shows a typical OLAP operation—slicing the data cube to produce a simple two-dimensional table or view. In Figure 14-16, this slice is for the product named "shoes." The resulting table shows the three measures (units, revenues, and cost) for this product by period (or month). Other views can easily be developed by the user by means of simple "drag and drop" operations. This type of operation is often called "slicing and dicing" the cube.

Another operation closely related to slicing and dicing is data pivoting. This term refers to rotating the view for a particular data point, to obtain another perspective. For example, Figure 14-16 shows sales of 400 units of shoes for April. The analyst could pivot this view to obtain (for example) the sales of shoes by store for the same month.

Drill-Down   Another type of operation often used in multidimensional analysis is *drill-down*—that is, analyzing a given set of data at a finer level of detail. An example of drill-down is shown in Figure 14-17. Figure 14-17a shows a summary report for the total sales of three package sizes for a given brand of paper towels—2-pack, 3-pack, and 6-pack. However, the towels come in different colors, and the analyst wants a further breakdown of sales by color within each of these package sizes. Using an OLAP tool, this breakdown can be easily obtained using a "point-and-click" approach with a mouse device.

The result of the drill-down is shown in Figure 14-17b. Notice that a drill-down presentation is equivalent to adding another column to the original report (in this case, a column was added for the attribute "color").

Table 14-3   Data-Mining Techniques

Technique	Function
Case-based reasoning	Derives rules from real-world case examples
Rule discovery	Searches for patterns and correlations in large data sets
Signal processing	Identifies clusters of observations with similar characteristics
Neural nets	Develops predictive models based on principles modeled after the human brain
Fractals	Compresses large databases without losing information

Executing a drill-down (as in this example) may require that the OLAP tool "reach back" to the data warehouse to obtain the detail data necessary for the drill-down. This type of operation can be performed by an OLAP tool (without user participation) only if an integrated set of metadata is available to that tool. Some tools even permit the OLAP tool to reach back to the operational data if necessary for a given query.

Data-Mining Tools

Data mining: Knowledge discovery using a sophisticated blend of techniques from traditional statistics, artificial intelligence, and computer graphics (Weldon, 1996).

With on-line analytical processing, users are searching for answers to questions they have raised—for example, "Are health care costs greater for single or married persons?" With data mining, users are looking for patterns or trends in a collection of facts or observations. **Data mining** is knowledge discovery using a sophisticated blend of techniques from traditional statistics, artificial intelligence, and computer graphics (Weldon, 1996).

The goals of data mining are threefold:

1. *Explanatory.* To explain some observed event or condition, such as why sales of pickup trucks have increased in Colorado

2. *Confirmatory.* To confirm a hypothesis, such as whether two-income families are more likely to buy family medical coverage than single-income families

3. *Exploratory.* To analyze data for new or unexpected relationships, such as what spending patterns are likely to accompany credit card fraud.

Data-Mining Techniques   Several different techniques are commonly used for data mining. See Table 14-3 for a summary of the most common of these techniques. The choice of an appropriate technique depends on the nature of the data to be analyzed, as well as the size of the data set. Data mining can be performed against either the data marts or the enterprise data warehouse (or both).

Data-Mining Applications   Data-mining techniques have been successfully used for a wide range of real-world applications. A summary of some of the typical types of applications, with examples of each type, is presented in Table 14-4. Data-mining applications are growing rapidly, for the following reasons:

Table 14-4 Typical Data-Mining Applications (Adapted from Zaitz, 1997)

Type of Application	Example
Profiling populations	Developing profiles of high-value customers, credit risks, and credit-card fraud.
Analysis of business trends	Identifying markets with above average (or below average) growth.
Target marketing	Identifying customers (or customer segments) for promotional activity.
Usage analysis	Identifying usage patterns for products and services.
Campaign effectiveness	Comparing campaign strategies for effectiveness.
Product affinity	Identifying products that are purchased concurrently, or the characteristics of shoppers for certain product groups.

1. The amount of data in data warehouses and data marts is growing exponentially, so that users require the type of automated techniques provided by data-mining tools to mine the knowledge in these data.

2. New data-mining tools with expanded capabilities are continually being introduced.

3. Increasing competitive pressures are forcing companies to make better use of the information and knowledge contained in their data.

Data Visualization

Often the human eye can best discern patterns when data are represented graphically. **Data visualization** is the representation of data in graphical and multimedia formats for human analysis. Benefits of data visualization include the ability to better observe trends and patterns, and to identify correlations and clusters. Data visualization is often used in conjunction with data mining and other analytical techniques.

Data visualization: The representation of data in graphical and multimedia formats for human analysis.

SUMMARY

Despite the vast quantities of data collected in organizations today, most managers have difficulty obtaining the information they need for decision making. Two major factors contribute to this "information gap." First, data are often heterogeneous and inconsistent as a result of the piecemeal system development approaches that have commonly been used. Second, systems are developed (or acquired) primarily to satisfy operational objectives, with little thought given to the information needs of managers.

There are major differences between operational and informational systems, and between the data that appear in those systems. Operational systems are used to run the business on a current basis, and the primary design goal is to provide high performance to users who process transactions and update databases. Informational systems are used to support managerial decision making, and the primary design goal is to provide ease of access and use for information workers.

The purpose of a data warehouse is to consolidate and integrate data from a variety of sources, and to format those data in a context for making accurate business decisions. A data warehouse may be formally defined as an integrated and consistent store of subject-oriented data obtained from a variety of sources and formatted into a meaningful context to support decision making in an organization.

Most data warehouses today follow a three-layer architecture. The first layer consists of data distributed throughout the various operational systems. The second layer is an enterprise data warehouse, which is a centralized, integrated data warehouse that is the control point and single source of all data made available to end users for decision-support applications. The third layer is a series of data marts. A data mart is a data warehouse whose data are obtained by selecting and (where appropriate) summarizing data from the enterprise data warehouse. Each data mart is designed to support the decision-making needs of a department or other work group.

The data layer in the enterprise data warehouse is called the reconciled data layer. The characteristics of this data layer (ideally) are the following: it is detailed, historical, normalized, comprehensive, and quality-controlled. Reconciled data are obtained by filling the enterprise data warehouse from the various operational systems. Reconciling the data requires four steps: capturing the data from the source systems; scrubbing the data (to remove inconsistencies); transforming the data (to convert it to the format required in the data warehouse); and loading and indexing the data in the data warehouse. Reconciled data are not normally accessed directly by end users.

The data layer in the data marts is referred to as the derived data layer. These are the data that are accessed by end users for their decision-support applications. Derived data are obtained by populating a data mart with data that have been selected and (as appropriate) aggregated from the enterprise data warehouse.

Data are most often stored in a data mart using a variation of the relational model called the star schema, or dimensional model. A star schema is a simple database design where dimensional data are separated from fact or event data. A star schema consists of two types of tables: dimension tables and fact tables. The size of a fact table depends in part on the grain (or level of detail) in that table. Fact tables with over one billion rows are common in data warehouse applications today. There are several variations of the star schema, including models with multiple fact tables, and snowflake schemas that arise when one or more dimensions have a hierarchical structure.

A variety of end-user interfaces are available to access and analyze decision-support data. On-line analytical processing (or OLAP) is the use of a set of graphical tools that provides users with multidimensional views of their data (data are normally viewed as a cube). OLAP facilitates data analysis operations such as slice-and-dice, data pivoting, and drill-down. Data mining is a form of knowledge discovery that uses a sophisticated blend of techniques from traditional statistics, artificial intelligence, and computer graphics.

C H A P T E R   R E V I E W

K E Y   T E R M S

Aggregation
Data mart
Data mining
Data scrubbing
Data transformation
Data visualization
Data warehouse
Dependent data mart
Derived data
Enterprise data
    warehouse

Event
Grain
Incremental capture
Independent data mart
Informational systems
Joining
Market basket analysis
On-line analytical
    processing (OLAP)
Operational system
Periodic data

Reconciled data
Refresh mode
Selection
Snowflake schema
Star schema
Static capture
Transient data
Update mode

R E V I E W   Q U E S T I O N S

1. Define each of the following terms:
   a. data warehouse
   b. data mart
   c. reconciled data
   d. derived data
   e. on-line analytical processing
   f. data mining
   g. star schema
   h. snowflake schema
   i. grain
   j. static capture
   k. incremental capture
   l. event

2. Contrast the following terms:
   a. static capture; incremental capture
   b. transient data; periodic data
   c. data warehouse; data mart
   d. data scrubbing; data transformation
   e. reconciled data; derived data
   f. fact table; dimension table
   g. star schema; snowflake schema
   h. independent data mart; dependent data mart

3. Name the two major factors that necessitate data warehousing in many organizations today.

4. List four data warehouse principles that are introduced in this chapter.

5. Briefly describe the three components of a three-level data warehouse architecture.

6. List three types of metadata that appear in a three-layer data warehouse architecture, and briefly describe the purpose of each type.

7. List five typical characteristics of reconciled data.

8. List and briefly describe four steps in the data reconciliation process.

9. List five errors and inconsistencies that are commonly found in operational data.

10. Briefly describe three types of operations that can easily be performed with OLAP tools.

P R O B L E M S   A N D   E X E R C I S E S

---

1. Match the following terms and definitions:

_____ event	a. previous data content is lost
_____ periodic data	b. detailed, historical data
_____ data mart	c. converts data formats
_____ star schema	d. corrects errors in source data
_____ data mining	e. data are not altered or deleted
_____ reconciled data	f. a database action (e.g., create)
_____ dependent data mart	g. limited scope data warehouse
_____ data visualization	h. dimension and fact tables
_____ transient data	i. form of knowledge discovery
_____ snowflake schema	j. filled from data warehouse
_____ data transformation	k. results from hierarchical dimensions
_____ data scrubbing	l. data represented in graphical formats

2. Examine the three tables with student data shown in Figure 14-1. Design a single table format that will hold all of the data (nonredundantly) that are contained in these three tables. Choose column names that you believe are most appropriate for these data.

3. The table below shows some simple student data as of the date 06/20:

Key	Name	Major
001	Amy	Music
002	Tom	Business
003	Sue	Art
004	Joe	Math
005	Ann	Engineering

The following transactions occur on 06/21:
1. Student 004 changes major from 'Math' to 'Business'.
2. Student 005 is deleted from the file.
3. New student 006 is added to the file. Name is 'Jim', Major is 'Phys Ed'.

The following transactions occur on 06/22:
1. Student 003 changes major from 'Art' to 'History'.
2. Student 006 changes major from 'Phys Ed' to 'Basket Weaving'.

Your assignment is in two parts:

a. Construct tables for 06/21 and 06/22 reflecting the above transactions, assuming that the data are transient (refer to Figure 14-6).

b. Construct tables for 06/21 and 06/22 reflecting the above transactions, assuming that the data are periodic (refer to Figure 14-7).

4. Millennium College wants you to help design a star schema to record grades for courses completed by students. There are four dimension tables, with attributes as follows:

- Course_Section. Attributes: Course_ID, Section_Number, Course_Name, Units, Room_ID, Room_Capacity. During a given semester the college offers an average of 500 course sections.

- Professor. Attributes: Prof_ID, Prof_Name, Title, Department_ID, Department_Name.

- Student. Attributes: Student_ID, Student_Name, Major. Each course section has an average of 40 students.

- Period. Attributes: Semester_ID, Year. The database will contain data for 30 periods (a total of 10 years).

The only fact that is to be recorded in the fact table is Course_Grade.

a. Design a star schema for this problem. See Figure 14-12 for the format you should follow.

b. Estimate the number of rows in the fact table, using the assumptions stated above.

c. Estimate the total size of the fact table (in bytes), assuming that each field has an average of 5 bytes.

5. Having mastered the principles of normalization described in Chapter 6, you recognize immediately that the star schema you developed for Millennium College (Problem 4) is not in third normal form. Using these principles, convert the star schema to a snowflake schema. What impact (if any) does this have on the size of the fact table for this problem?

6. You are to construct a star schema for Simplified Automobile Insurance Company (see Kimball, 1996 for a more realistic example). The relevant dimensions, dimension attributes, and dimension sizes are as follows:

- Insured Party. Attributes: Insured_Party_ID, Name. There is an average of two insured parties for each policy and covered item.

- Coverage Item. Attributes: Coverage_Key, Description. There is an average of 10 covered items per policy.

- Agent. Attributes: Agent_ID, Agent_Name. There is one agent for each policy and covered item.

- Policy. Attributes: Policy_ID, Type. The company has approximately one million policies at the present time.

- Period. Attributes: Date_Key, Fiscal_Period.

Facts to be recorded for each combination of these dimensions are: Policy_Premium, Deductible, and Number_of_Transactions.

a. Design a star schema for this problem. See Figure 14-12 for the format you should follow.

b. Estimate the number of rows in the fact table, using the assumptions stated above.

c. Estimate the total size of the fact table (in bytes), assuming an average of 5 bytes per field.

7. Simplified Automobile Insurance Company would like to add a Claims dimension to its star schema (see Problem 5). Attributes of Claim are: Claim_ID, Claim_Description, and Claim_Type. Attributes of the fact table are now: Policy_Premium, Deductible, and Monthly_Claim_Total.

   a. Extend the star schema from Problem 5 to include these new data.

   b. Calculate the estimated number of rows in the fact table, assuming that the company experiences an average of 2000 claims per month.

FIELD EXERCISES

---

1. Visit an organization that has developed a data warehouse, and interview the data administrator or other key participant. Discuss the following issues:

   a. How satisfied are users with the data warehouse? In what ways has it improved their decision making?

   b. Does the warehouse employ a two-tier or three-tier architecture?

   c. Does the architecture employ one or more data marts? If so, are they dependent or independent?

   d. What end-user tools are employed? Is data mining used?

   e. What were the main obstacles or difficulties overcome in developing the data warehouse environment?

2. Visit the following Internet Web sites. Browse these sites for additional information on data warehouse topics, including case examples of warehouse implementations, descriptions of the latest warehouse-related products, and announcements of conferences and other events.

   a. Data-warehouse.com: http://www.data-warehouse.com

   b. The Data Warehousing Institute: http://www.dw-institute.com

   c. Knowledge Discovery Mine: http://www.kdnuggets.com

   d. Data Mining Institute: http://www.datamining.org

   e. Data Warehousing Information Center:
      http://www.pwp.starnetinc.com/larryg/index.html

   f. Data Mining and Knowledge Discovery Journal:
      http://www.research.microsoft.com/research/datamine

REFERENCES

Barquin, R. 1996. "On the First Issue of *The Journal of Data Warehousing*." *The Journal of Data Warehousing* 1 (July): 2–6.

Burwen, M. 1997. "Syndicated Study of Data Warehousing Market." *DM Review* 7 (September): 58, 59.

Devlin, B. 1997. *Data Warehouse: From Architecture to Implementation*. Reading, MA: Addison Wesley Longman.

Devlin, B., and P. Murphy. 1988. "An Architecture for a Business Information System." *IBM Systems Journal* 27 (No. 1): 60–80.

English, L. 1997. "The New Philosophy of Data Quality." *DM Review* 7 (July/August): 14, 15.

Griffin, J. 1997. "Fast Payback Projects." *DM Review* 7 (December): 10, 11.

Hackathorn, R. 1993. *Enterprise Database Connectivity.* New York: John Wiley & Sons.

IBM. 1993. "Information Warehouse Architecture." SC26-324-00. White Plains, NY: IBM Corp.

Inmon, B. 1997. "Iterative Development in the Data Warehouse." *DM Review* 7 (November): 16, 17.

Inmon, W. 1992. *Building the Data Warehouse.* Wellesley, MA: QED Information Sciences.

Inmon, W. H., and R. D. Hackathorn. 1994. *Using the Data Warehouse.* New York: John Wiley & Sons.

Kimball, R. 1996. *The Data Warehouse Toolkit.* New York: John Wiley & Sons.

Martin, J. 1997a. "New Tools for Decision Making." *DM Review* 7 (September): 80.

Martin, J. 1997b. "Web Warehousing." *DM Review* 7 (November): 10.

Meyer, A. 1997. "The Case for Dependent Data Marts." *DM Review* 7 (July/August): 17–24.

Poe, V. 1996. *Building a Data Warehouse for Decision Support.* Upper Saddle River, NJ: Prentice-Hall.

Weldon, J. L. 1996. "Data Mining and Visualization." *Database Programming & Design* 9 (May): 21–24.

Williams, J. 1997. "Tools for Traveling Data." *DBMS* 10 (June): 69–76.

Winter, R. 1996. "Birds, Bees, and Bitmaps." *Database Programming & Design* 9 (June): 55–57.

Zaitz, J. 1997. "Data Mining Neural Clusters." *DM Review* 7 (July/August): 91, 92.

FURTHER READING

Bischoff, J., and T. Alexander. 1997. *Data Warehouse: Practical Advice from the Experts.* Upper Saddle River, NJ: Prentice-Hall.

Goodhue, D., M. Mybo, and L. Kirsch. 1992. "The Impact of Data Integration on the Costs and Benefits of Information Systems." *MIS Quarterly* 16 (September): 293–311.

Jenks, B. 1997. "Tiered Data Warehouse." *DM Review* 7 (October): 54–57.

Project Case

PROJECT DESCRIPTION

In most respects, Mountain View Community Hospital has followed a carefully planned approach to designing, selecting, and installing its information systems. The organization developed an enterprise data model to guide its database development (see Chapters 3 and 4). The hospital installed computer systems to support most of the routine operations in the organization. For example, there are systems for patient accounting, administrative services, and financial management. Most of these systems were acquired from outside vendors after a careful selection process.

Despite this careful planning, management is aware that there are some deficiencies and limitations in the present hospital information systems. Two typical problems that have been noted are the following:

1. Data are often duplicated in different files and databases, in different formats, and even in different media. For example, one set of patient data (used for billing purposes) resides in a patient accounting system based on a relational database. On the other hand, most patient medical records are maintained in a manual system (one folder per patient).

2. The systems are designed primarily to support operational (or transaction) processing, but are not generally well suited to provide management information or to support analytical studies that are increasingly required for modern hospital management.

The health care industry in general (including hospitals such as Mountain View Community) is being driven by the trend to managed care to gain better and more centralized access to its clinical, operational, and financial information (Griffin, 1997). A typical hospital data warehouse may contain four types of data: patient records; doctor, clinic, and hospital records; drug and pharmaceutical company records; and HMO and insurance company records (Martin, 1997b).

To address these concerns, managers at Mountain View Community Hospital would like to investigate whether the techniques of data warehousing might be successfully applied in their organization. Because the

hospital is small, they realize that they could not justify a large-scale data warehouse development project. Nevertheless, they would like to develop a small prototype to test the concept. After some investigation they decide to develop two small prototype data marts:

1. A data mart that will record summary information regarding tests and procedures performed by physicians at the hospital.

2. A more detailed data mart that will record the details of tests and procedures performed by physicians for individual patients.

PROJECT QUESTIONS

1. What are some of the advantages that a hospital such as Mountain View Community might realize from a data warehouse and/or data mart?

2. Suppose that a hospital decides to develop a data mart using a star schema. List several dimensions that you would expect to find represented in this schema.

3. Should Mountain View Community Hospital consider developing a data mart (such as those proposed) without an established data warehouse? What are the risks associated with that approach? Do you think that an organization can develop a prototype data mart to investigate "proof-of-concept," without an established data warehouse? Discuss some of the likely advantages and disadvantages of this approach.

PROJECT EXERCISES

1. Summary data mart.

   a. Design a star schema:

      Physician dimension:

         Physician_ID (pk): 5 bytes
         Physician_Name: 10 bytes
         Specialty: 5 bytes
         Physician_Address: 10 bytes
         Physician_Telephone: 5 bytes

Treatment dimension:

Treatment_ID (pk): 3 bytes
Treatment_Description: 6 bytes

Period dimension:

Period_ID (pk): 2 bytes
Month: 1 byte
Year: 2 bytes

Treatment (fact) table:

Grain: monthly summary of treatments and average treatment costs, by physician and treatment
Monthly_Total: 3 bytes
Average_Cost: 5 bytes

b. Calculate the expected number of rows in the fact table and its estimated size (bytes).

Assumptions:

1. Treatments: approximately 500 *different* treatments are performed at the hospital. During a typical month, approximately 30 percent (or 150 different treatments) are performed.
2. Physicians: each treatment is performed by one physician.
3. Periods: If a full-scale data mart is developed, it is anticipated that 36 periods (or 3 years) of data will be accumulated.

2. Detailed data mart.

a. Design a star schema.

Physician dimension: same as above

Treatment dimension: same as above

Period dimension:

Period_ID (pk): 3 bytes
Date: 5 bytes

Patient dimension:

Patient_ID (pk): 5 bytes
Patient_Name: 10 bytes
Patient_Address: 10 bytes
Patient_Telephone: 5 bytes

Treatment (fact) table:

Grain: detail for each treatment occurrence administered to a patient by a physician
Treatment_Cost: 4 bytes
Treatment_Result: 20 bytes
Doctors_Order: 10 bytes

b. Calculate the expected number of rows in the fact table and its estimated size (bytes).

Assumptions:

1. Treatments. An average of 200 total treatments are performed for patients on a given day (this is based on an average patient census of 200, and an average of two treatments per patient per day).
2. Patients. Each treatment is performed for one patient. To simplify matters, assume that a given treatment may only be performed once by a given physician and for a particular patient on a given day.
3. Physicians. Each treatment is performed by one physician.
4. Periods. If a full-scale data mart is developed, it is anticipated that approximately 1000 days (nearly three years) of data will be collected.

c. Why is it necessary to assume that a given treatment may be performed only once by a given physician for a given patient on a given day? Suggest a way to overcome this limitation.

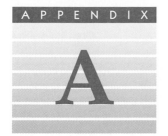

A

Object-Relational Databases

In this textbook we have described the two models most widely used for the design and implementation of databases: relational and object-oriented. The relational model (with its associated relational database management systems) is the model most often used for implementing mainstream business applications today. Some of the strengths of this model are the following:

- data independence, described in Chapter 1

- powerful query language (SQL), described in Chapter 9

- mature relational database management system technology, including features such as online backup and recovery and flexible concurrency control (described in Chapter 13)

Despite these strengths, we noted in Chapter 5 (as well as in other chapters) that the relational data model is not well suited to handling complex data types such as images, audio, video, and spatial (or geographical) data. Thus the object-oriented data model was introduced primarily to manage these complex data types (this model is described in Chapters 5 and 12). The market for object-oriented database management systems has grown slowly, yet the technology is extremely promising for applications such as Web servers that incorporate multimedia data types. The weaknesses of object-oriented database systems (at least until recently) have been the lack of important features found in relational systems such as query capability, online backup and recovery, and flexible concurrency control.

In summary, relational and object-oriented database systems each have certain strengths as well as certain weaknesses. In general the weaknesses of one type of system tend to be a strength of the other (and vice versa). This has led the industry to develop a new generation of hybrid database system—the object-relational system—that seeks to combine the best features of both models. Most of the major DBMS vendors have released a version of an object-relational database. In this appendix we present a brief description of this type of system, including its advantages and disadvantages.

BASIC CONCEPTS AND DEFINITIONS

An **object-relational database management system** (or **ORDBMS**) is a database engine that supports both relational and object-oriented features in an integrated

> **Object-relational database management system:** A database engine that supports both relational and object-oriented features in an integrated fashion.

Table A-1   Complex Data Types

Data type	Description	Example applications
Image	Bit-mapped representation	Documents, photographs, medical images, fingerprints
Graphic	Geometric objects	CAD, CAM, CASE, presentation graphics
Spatial	Geographic objects	Maps
Recursive	Nested objects	Bills of materials
Audio	Sound clips	Music, animation, games
Video	Video segments, movies	Training films, product demonstrations, movies
Array	Subscripted variables	Time series, multidimensional data
Computational-intensive	Data requiring extensive computations	Data mining, financial instruments (e.g., derivatives)

fashion (Frank, 1995). Thus the user can (at least ideally) define, manipulate, and query both relational data and objects while using common interfaces (such as SQL).

Two other terms that are used for object-relational databases are extended relational and universal server. The term *extended relational* (an older term) derives from the fact that the first versions of these types of systems were developed by adding object-oriented features onto existing relational DBMSs. The term *universal server* (a more contemporary term) is based on the stated objective of managing *any* type of data (including user-defined data types) with the same server technology.

Features of an ORDBMS

As indicated above, the intent with ORDBMS is to combine the best features of the relational and object database models. Following are the main features usually included:

1. An enhanced version of SQL that can be used to create and manipulate both relational tables and object types or classes

2. Support for traditional object-oriented functions including inheritance, polymorphism, user-defined (or abstract) data types, and navigational access

Complex Data Types

There are three main categories of data types in SQL: NUMERIC, CHARACTER, and TEMPORAL. NUMERIC types include DECIMAL and INTEGER, while TEMPORAL types include DATE and TIME (Celko, 1995).

Modern business applications often require storing and manipulating complex data types that are not easily handled by relational systems. Some of the more common of these complex data types are shown in Table A-1. For each data type, this table provides a brief description and one or more typical applications. For example, the Graphic data type consists of geometric objects such as points, lines, and circles; typical applications are for computer-assisted design (CAD), computer-assisted manufacturing (CAM), computer-assisted software engineering (CASE) tools, and presentation graphics (such as charts and graphs).

ENHANCED SQL

The most powerful feature of an ORDBMS is that it uses an extended version of a relational query language (such as SQL) to define, fetch, and manipulate data (Cattell, 1994). In fact, the third generation of the SQL standard (called SQL3) is currently under development by the language development committees. The primary theme of SQL3 is the addition of support for object technology (Melton, 1995).

A Simple Example

Suppose that an organization wants to create a relation named EMPLOYEE to record employee data (see Figure A-1). Traditional relational attributes in this table are the following: Emp_ID, Name, Address, and Date_of_Birth. In addition, the organization would like to store a photograph of each employee that will be used for identification purposes. This attribute (which will be defined as an object) is named Emp_Photo in Figure A-1. When the data for a particular employee are retrieved, the employee photo will be displayed with the remaining data.

SQL3 will provide statements to create both tables and data types (or object classes). For example, the SQL CREATE TABLE statement for EMPLOYEE might appear as follows:

```
CREATE TABLE EMPLOYEE
   Emp_ID INTEGER NOT NULL,
   Name CHAR(20) NOT NULL,
   Address CHAR(20),
   Date_of_Birth DATE NOT NULL,
   Emp_Photo TYPE IMAGE NOT NULL);
```

In this example IMAGE is a data type (or class), and Emp_Photo is an object of that class. IMAGE may be either a predefined class or a user-defined class. If it is a user-defined class, a SQL CREATE CLASS statement is used to define the class. The user can also define methods that operate on the data defined in a class. For example,

Emp_ID	Name	Address	Date_of_Birth	Emp_Photo
12345	Charles	112 Main	04/27/1973	
34567	Angela	840 Oak	08/12/1967	
56789	Thomas	520 Elm	10/13/1975	

Figure A-1
Relation with complex object

one method of IMAGE is Scale( ), which can be used to expand or reduce the size of the photograph.

Content Addressing

One of the most powerful features of the relational SQL language is the ability to select a subset of the records in a table that satisfy stated qualifications. For example, in the EMPLOYEE relation a simple SQL statement will select records for all employees whose date of birth is on or before 12/31/1940 (see Chapter 9 for examples). In contrast, "pure" object database systems do not have this query capability. Instead, access to objects is navigational—that is, each object has a unique object identifier (see Chapter 5).

Content addressing: The facility that allows a user to query a database to select all records and/or objects that satisfy a given set of qualifications.

The ORDBMS products extend relational's content addressibility to complex objects (Norman and Bloor, 1996). **Content addressing** is the facility that allows a user to query a database (or database table) to select all records and/or objects that satisfy a given set of qualifications.

SQL3 includes extensions for content addressing with complex data types. Let's see how content addressing might be applied in the EMPLOYEE table. Remember that each employee record contains (or is at least linked to) a photo of that employee. A user might want to pose the following query: given a photograph of a person, scan the EMPLOYEE table to determine if there is a close match for any employee to that photo, then display the data (including the photograph) of the employee or employees selected (if any). Suppose the electronic image of a photograph is stored in a location called My_Photo. Then a simple query for this situation might appear as follows:

```
SELECT *
  FROM EMPLOYEE
  WHERE My_Photo LIKE Emp_Photo;
```

Content addressing in an ORDBMS is a very powerful feature that allows users to search for matches to multimedia objects such as images, audio or video segments, and documents. One obvious application for this feature is searching databases for fingerprint or voiceprint matches.

ADVANTAGES OF THE OBJECT-RELATIONAL APPROACH

For applications that require complex processing or significant query activity on large datasets, the object-relational approach offers several advantages compared to relational database systems (Moxon, 1997):

1. *Reduced network traffic*   Queries that employ methods to scan data can be executed entirely on the server, without the need to send large quantities of data back to the clients.

2. *Application and query performance*   The methods that process large datasets can exploit large parallel servers to significantly improve performance.

3. *Software maintenance*   The fact that data and methods are stored together on the server greatly simplifies the task of software maintenance.

4. *Integrated data and transaction management*   All transaction integrity, concurrency, and backup and recovery are handled within the database engine.

Table A-2   ORDBMS Vendors and Products

Vendor	ORDBMS Product	Extender technology
IBM	DB2 Universal Database	DB2 Extenders
Informix	Universal Server	Data Blades
Oracle	Oracle 8	Data Cartridges
Computer Associates	ODB-II (Jasmine)	none

ORDBMS VENDORS AND PRODUCTS

A list of the major vendors and the ORDBMS products they provide is shown in Table A-2. The table also shows the extender technology (or framework) that is provided by each vendor that allows users to define their own data types, as well as the methods that manipulate those data.

REFERENCES

Cattell, R. 1994. *Object Data Management: Object-Oriented and Extended Relational Database Systems.* Reading, MA: Addison-Wesley, pp. 303–304.

Celko, J. 1995. *Instant SQL Programming.* Chicago: Wrox Press, pp. 54–55.

Frank, M. 1995. "Object-Relational Hybrids." *DBMS* 8 (July): 46–56.

Melton, J. 1995. "A Case for SQL Conformance Testing." *Database Programming & Design* 10 (7): 66–69.

Moxon, B. 1997. "Database out of This Universe". *DB2 Magazine* 2 (Fall): 9–16.

Norman, M., and R. Bloor. 1996. "To Universally Serve." *Database Programming & Design* 9 (July): 26–35.

Advanced Normal Forms

In Chapter 6 we introduced the topic of normalization and described first through third normal forms in detail. Relations in third normal form (3NF) are sufficient for most practical database applications. However, 3NF does not guarantee that all anomalies have been removed. As indicated in Chapter 6, several additional normal forms are designed to remove these anomalies: Boyce-Codd normal form, fourth normal form, and fifth normal form (see Figure 6-21). We describe Boyce-Codd normal form and fourth normal form in this appendix.

BOYCE-CODD NORMAL FORM

When a relation has more than one candidate key, anomalies may result even though that relation is in 3NF. For example, consider the STUDENT_ADVISOR relation shown in Figure B-1. This relation has the following attributes: SID (student ID), Major, Advisor, and Maj_GPA. Sample data for this relation are shown in Figure B-1a, and the functional dependencies are shown in Figure B-1b.

As shown in Figure B-1b, the primary key for this relation is the composite key consisting of SID and Major. Thus the two attributes Advisor and Maj_GPA are functionally dependent on this key. This reflects the constraint that although a given student may have more than one major, for each major a student has exactly one advisor and one GPA.

There is a second functional dependency in this relation: Major is functionally dependent on Advisor. That is, each advisor advises in exactly one major. Notice that this is *not* a transitive dependency. In Chapter 6 we defined a transitive dependency as a functional dependency between two nonkey attributes. In contrast, in this example a key attribute (Major) is functionally dependent on a nonkey attribute (Advisor).

Anomalies in STUDENT_ADVISOR

The STUDENT_ADVISOR relation is clearly in 3NF, since there are no partial functional dependencies and no transitive dependencies. Nevertheless, because of the functional dependency between Major and Advisor there are anomalies in this relation. Consider the following examples:

Figure B-1
Relation in 3NF, but not BCNF

(a) Relation with sample data

STUDENT_ADVISOR

SID	Major	Advisor	Maj_GPA
123	Physics	Hawking	4.0
123	Music	Mahler	3.3
456	Literature	Michener	3.2
789	Music	Bach	3.7
678	Physics	Hawking	3.5

(b) Functional dependencies
in STUDENT_ADVISOR

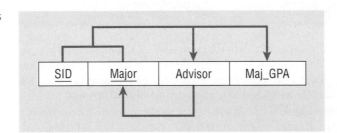

1. Suppose that in Physics the advisor Hawking is replaced by Einstein. This change must be made in two (or more) rows in the table (update anomaly).

2. Suppose we want to insert a row with the information that Babbage advises in Computer Science. This, of course, cannot be done until at least one student majoring in Computer Science is assigned Babbage as an advisor (insertion anomaly).

3. Finally, if student number 789 withdraws from school, we lose the information that Bach advises in Music (deletion anomaly).

Definition of Boyce-Codd Normal Form (BCNF)

Boyce-Codd normal form:
A relation in which every determinant is a candidate key.

The anomalies in STUDENT_ADVISOR result from the fact that there is a determinant (Advisor) that is not a candidate key in the relation. R. F. Boyce and E. F. Codd identified this deficiency and proposed a stronger definition of 3NF that remedies the problem. We say a relation is in **Boyce-Codd normal form (BCNF)** if and only if every determinant in the relation is a candidate key. STUDENT_ADVISOR is not in BCNF because although the attribute Advisor is a determinant, it is not a candidate key (only Major is functionally dependent on Advisor).

Converting a Relation to BCNF

A relation that is in 3NF (but not BCNF) can be converted to relations in BCNF using a simple two-step process. This process is shown in Figure B-2.

In this first step, the relation is modified so that the determinant in the relation which is not a candidate key becomes a component of the primary key of the revised relation. The attribute that is functionally dependent on that determinant becomes a

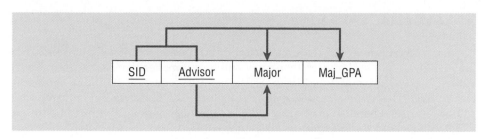

Figure B-2
Converting a relation to BCNF relations

(a) Revised STUDENT_ADVISOR relation (2NF)

(b) Two relations in BCNF

(c) Relations with sample data

STUDENT

SID	Advisor	Maj_GPA
123	Hawking	4.0
123	Mahler	3.3
456	Michener	3.2
789	Bach	3.7
678	Hawking	3.5

ADVISOR

Advisor	Major
Hawking	Physics
Mahler	Music
Michener	Literature
Bach	Music

nonkey attribute. This is a legitimate restructuring of the original relation because of the functional dependency.

The result of applying this rule to STUDENT_ADVISOR is shown in Figure B-2a. The determinant Advisor becomes part of the composite primary key. The attribute Major, which is functionally dependent on Advisor, becomes a nonkey attribute.

If you examine Figure B-2a you will discover that the new relation has a partial functional dependency (Major is functionally dependent on Advisor, which is just one component of the primary key). Thus the new relation is in first (but not second) normal form.

The second step in the conversion process is to decompose the relation to eliminate the partial functional dependency, as we learned in Chapter 6. This results in two relations, as shown in Figure B-2b. These relations are in 3NF. In fact the relations are also in BCNF, since there is only one candidate key (the primary key) in each relation. Thus we see that if a relation has only one candidate key (which therefore becomes the primary key), then 3NF and BCNF are equivalent.

The two relations (now named STUDENT and ADVISOR) with sample data are shown in Figure B-2c. You should verify that these relations are free of the anomalies that were described for STUDENT_ADVISOR. You should also verify that you can recreate the STUDENT_ADVISOR relation by joining the two relations STUDENT and ADVISOR.

FOURTH NORMAL FORM

When a relation is in BCNF, there are no longer any anomalies that result from functional dependencies. However, there may still be anomalies that result from multivalued dependencies (defined below). For example, consider the table shown in Figure B-3a. This user view shows for each course the instructors who teach that course, and the textbooks that are used (these appear as repeating groups in the table). In this table the following assumptions hold:

1. Each course has a well-defined set of instructors (for example, Management has four instructors).

2. Each course has a well-defined set of textbooks that are used (for example, Finance has two textbooks).

3. The textbooks that are used for a given course are independent of the instructor for that course. For example, the same two textbooks are used for Management regardless of which of the three instructors is teaching Management.

In Figure B-3b this table has been converted to a relation by filling in all of the empty cells. This relation (named OFFERING) is in first normal form. Thus, for each course, all possible combinations of instructor and text appear in OFFERING. Notice

Figure B-3
Data with multivalued dependencies

(a) Table of courses, instructors, and textbooks

Course	Instructor	Textbook
Management	White Green Black	Drucker Peters
Finance	Gray	Jones Chang

(b) Relation in BCNF

OFFERING

Course	Instructor	Textbook
Management	White	Drucker
Management	White	Peters
Management	Green	Drucker
Management	Green	Peters
Management	Black	Drucker
Management	Black	Peters
Finance	Gray	Jones
Finance	Gray	Chang

TEACHER

Course	Instructor
Management	White
Management	Green
Management	Black
Finance	Gray

TEXT

Course	Textbook
Management	Drucker
Management	Peters
Finance	Jones
Finance	Chang

that the primary key of this relation consists of all three attributes (Course, Instructor, and Textbook). Since there are no determinants other than the primary key, the relation is actually in BCNF. Yet it does contain much redundant data that can easily lead to update anomalies. For example, suppose that we want to add a third textbook (author: Middleton) to the Management course. This change would require the addition of *three* new rows to the relation in Figure B-3b, one for each Instructor (otherwise that text would apply only to certain instructors).

Multivalued Dependencies

The type of dependency shown in this example is called a **multivalued dependency**, which exists when there are at least three attributes (for example, A, B, and C) in a relation, and for each value of A there is a well-defined set of values of B and a well-defined set of values of C. However, the set of values of B is independent of set C, and vice versa.

To remove the multivalued dependency from a relation, we divide the relation into two new relations. Each of these tables contains two attributes that have a multivalued relationship in the original relation. Figure B-4 shows the result of this decomposition for the OFFERING relation of Figure B-3b. Notice that the relation called TEACHER contains the Course and Instructor attributes, since for each course there is a well-defined set of instructors. Also, for the same reason TEXT contains the attributes Course and Textbook. However, there is no relation containing the attributes Instructor and Course since these attributes are independent.

A relation is in **fourth normal form (4NF)** if it is in BCNF and contains no multivalued dependencies. You can easily verify that the two relations in Figure B-4 are 4NF and are free of the anomalies described earlier. Also, you can verify that you can reconstruct the original relation (OFFERING) by joining these two relations.

Multivalued dependencies:
The type of dependency that exists when there are at least three attributes in a relation (say A, B, and C) and for each value of A there is a well-defined set of values of B and a well-defined set of values of C. However, the set of values of B is independent of set C, and vice versa.

Fourth normal form:
A relation in BCNF which contains no multivalued dependencies.

HIGHER NORMAL FORMS

At least two higher-level normal forms have been defined: fifth normal form (5NF) and domain-key normal form (DKNF). Fifth normal form deals with a property called "lossless joins." According to Elmasri and Navathe (1994), "these cases occur very rarely and are difficult to detect in practice." For this reason (and also because fifth normal form has a complex definition), we do not describe 5NF in this text.

Domain-key normal form (DKNF) is an attempt to define an "ultimate normal form" that takes into account all possible types of dependencies and constraints (Elmasri and Navathe, 1994). Although the definition of DKNF is quite simple, according to these authors "its practical utility is quite limited." For this reason we do not describe DKNF in this text.

For more information concerning these two higher normal forms see Elmasri and Navathe (1994) and Dutka and Hanson (1989).

REFERENCES

Dutka, A., and H. Hanson. 1989. *Fundamentals of Data Normalization*. Reading, MA: Addison-Wesley.

Elmasri, R., and S. Navathe. 1994. *Fundamentals of Database Systems*. Reading, MA: Addison-Wesley, pp. 440, 443.

Data Structures

Data structures are the basic building blocks of any physical database architecture. No matter what file organization or DBMS you use, data structures are used to connect related pieces of data. Although many modern DBMSs hide the underlying data structures, the tuning of a physical database requires understanding the choices a database designer can make about data structures. This appendix addresses the fundamental elements of all data structures and overviews some common schemes for storing and locating physical elements of data.

POINTERS

A pointer was introduced in Chapter 7. As described in that chapter, a pointer is used generically as any reference to the address of another piece of data. In fact, there are three types of pointers, as illustrated in Figure C-1:

1. *Physical address pointer* Contains the actual, fully resolved disk address (device, cylinder, track, and block number) of the referenced data. A physical pointer is the fastest way to locate another piece of data, but it is also the most restrictive: if the address of the referenced data changes, all pointers to it must also be changed. Physical pointers are commonly used in legacy database applications with network and hierarchical database architectures.

2. *Relative address pointer* Contains the relative position (or "offset") of the associated data from some base, or starting, point. The relative address could be a byte position, a record, or a row number. A relative pointer has the advantage that when the whole data structure changes location, all relative references to that structure are preserved. Relative pointers are used in a wide variety of DBMSs; a common use is in indexes in which index keys are matched with row identifiers (a type of relative pointer) for the record(s) with that key value.

3. *Logical key pointer* Contains meaningful data about the associated data element. A logical pointer must be transformed into a physical or relative pointer by some table lookup, index search, or mathematical calculation to actually locate the referenced data. Foreign keys in a relational database are often logical key pointers.

Figure C-1
Types of pointers

(a) Physical address pointer

(b) Relative address pointer
for *R*th record in file

(c) Logical key pointer for
record with key

Table C-1 summarizes the salient features of each of these three types of pointers. A database designer may be able to choose which type of pointer to use in different situations in a database. For example, a foreign key in a relation can be implemented using any of these three types of pointers. In addition, when a database is damaged,

Table C-1   Comparison of Types of Pointers

	Type of Pointer		
Characteristic	**Physical**	**Relative**	**Logical**
Form	Actual secondary memory (disk) address	Offset from reference point (beginning of file)	Meaningful business data
Speed of access	Fastest	Medium	Slowest
Sensitivity to data movement	Most	Only sensitive to relative position changes	Least
Sensitivity to destruction	Very	Very	Often can be easily reconstructed
Space requirement	Fixed, usually short	Varies, usually shortest	Varies, usually longest

a database administrator who understands what types of pointers are used may be able to rebuild broken links between database contents.

DATA STRUCTURE BUILDING BLOCKS

All data structures are built from several alternative basic building blocks for connecting and locating data. Connecting methods allow movement between related elements of data. Locating methods allow data within a structure to first be placed or stored and then found.

There are only two basic methods for *connecting* elements of data:

1. *Address sequential connection*   A successor (or related) element is placed and located in the physical memory space immediately following the current element (see Figures C-2a and c). Address sequential connections perform best for reading the entire set of data or reading the next record in the stored sequence. In contrast, address sequential structures are inefficient for retrieving arbitrary records and data update (add, delete, and change) operations. Update operations are also inefficient because the physical order must be constantly maintained, which usually requires immediate reorganization of the whole set of data.

2. *Pointer sequential connection*   A pointer (or pointers) is stored with one data element to identify the location of the successor (or related) data element (see Figures C-2b and d). Pointer sequential is more efficient for data update operations because data may be located anywhere as long as links between related data are maintained. Another major feature of pointer sequential schemes is the ability to maintain many different sequential linkages among the same set of data by using several pointers. We review various common forms of pointer sequential schemes (linear data structures) shortly.

Also, there are two basic methods for *placement* of data relative to the connection mechanism:

1. *Data direct placement*   The connection mechanism links an item of data directly with its successor (or related) item (see Figures C-2a and b). Direct placement has the advantage of immediately finding the data once a connection is traversed. The disadvantage is that the actual data are spread across large parts of disk storage because space for the actual data must be allocated among the connection elements.

2. *Data indirect placement*   The connection mechanism links pointers to the data, not the actual data (see Figures C-2c and d). The advantage of indirect placement is that scanning a data structure for data with specified characteristics is usually more efficient because the scanning can be done through compact entries of key characteristics and pointers to the associated data. Also, the connection and placement of data are decoupled, so the physical organization of the data records can follow the most desirable scheme (for example, physically sequential for a specified sorting order). The disadvantage is the extra access time required to retrieve both references to data and the data, and the extra space required for pointers.

Any data structure, file organization, or database architecture uses a combination of these four basic methods.

Figure C-2
Basic location methods

(a) Address sequential
connection (sequential)

(b) Pointer sequential
connection (simple chain
or list)

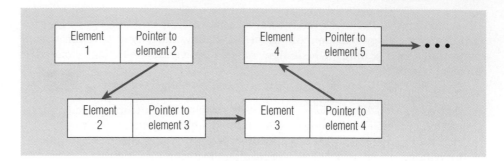

(c) Address sequential,
data indirect connection
(key index)

(d) Pointer sequential, data indirect connection (chain key index)

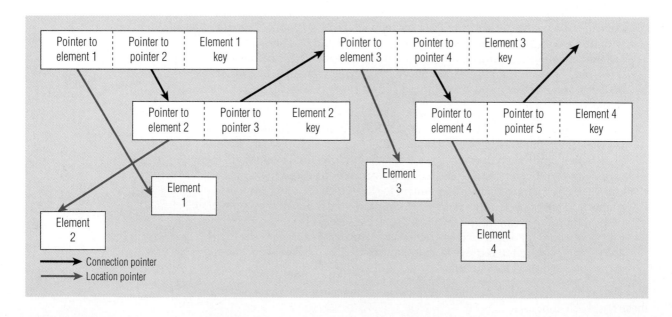

LINEAR DATA STRUCTURES

Pointer sequential data structures have been popular for storing highly volatile data, typical of what is found in operational databases. Transactional data (such as customer orders or personnel change requests) and historical data (such as product price quotes and student class registrations) make up a large portion of operational databases. Also, because users of operational databases want to view data in many different sequences (for example, customer orders in sequence by order date, product numbers, or customer numbers), the ability to maintain several chains of pointers running through the same data can support a range of user needs with one set of data.

The ability of a linear data structure to handle data updates is illustrated in Figure C-3. Figure C-3a shows how easy it is to insert a new record into a linear (or chain) structure. This figure illustrates a file of product records. For simplicity, we represent each product record by only the product number and a pointer to the next product record in sequence by product number. A new record is stored in an available location (S) and patched into the chain by changing pointers associated with the records in locations R and S. In Figure C-3b the act of deleting a record is equally easy, as only the pointer for the record in location R is changed. Although there is extra space to store the pointers, this space is minimal compared to what may be hundreds

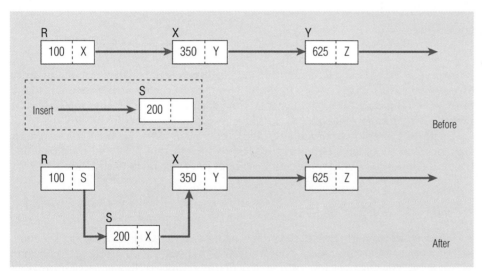

Figure C-3
Maintaining a pointer sequential data structure

(a) Insertion

(b) Deletion

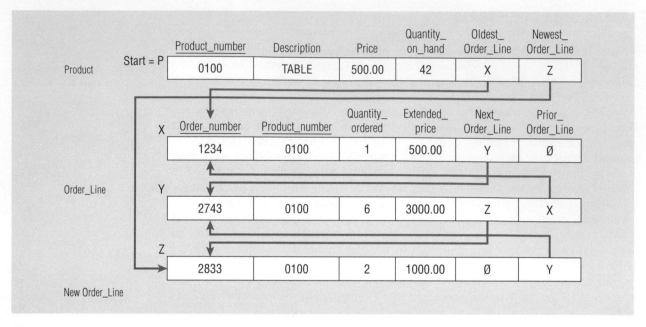

Figure C-4
Example of a queue with bidirectional pointers

of bytes needed to store all the product data (product number, description, quantity on hand, standard price, and so forth). It is easy to find records in product number order given this structure, but the actual time to retrieve records in sequence can be extensive if logically sequential records are stored far apart on disk.

With this simple introduction to linear data structures, we now consider four specific versions of such structures: stacks, queues, sorted lists, and multilists. We conclude this section with some cautions about linear, chain data structures.

Stacks

A stack has the property that all record insertions and deletions are made at the same end of the data structure. Stacks exhibit a last-in-first-out (LIFO) property. A common example of a stack is a vertical column of plates in a cafeteria. In business information systems, stacks are used to maintain unprioritized or unsorted records (for example, the line items associated with the same customer order).

Queues

A queue has the property that all insertions occur at one end and all deletions occur at the other end. A queue exhibits a first-in-first-out (FIFO) property. A common example of a queue is a check-out lane at a grocery store. In business information systems, queues are used to maintain lists of records in chronological order of insertion. For example, Figure C-4 illustrates a chained queue of Order Line records kept in order of arrival for a common Product record in Pine Valley Furniture.

In this example, the Product record acts as the head-of-chain node in the data structure. The value of the Oldest_order_line field is a pointer to the oldest (first entered) Order Line record for product 0100. The Next_order_line field in the Order_Line record contains the pointers to the next record in reverse chronological sequence. The value Ø in a pointer is called a null pointer and signifies the end of the chain.

This example also introduces the concept of a bidirectional chain, which has both forward and backward pointers. The benefit of next and prior pointers is that data in the records can be retrieved and presented in either forward or backward order, and the code to maintain the chain is easier to implement than with single-directional chains.

Sorted Lists

A sorted list has the property that insertions and deletions may occur anywhere within the list; records are maintained in logical order based on a key field value. A common example of a sorted list is a telephone directory. In business information systems, sorted lists occur frequently. Figure C-5a illustrates a single-directional, pointer sequential sorted list of Order records related to a Customer record, in which records are sorted by Delivery_date.

Maintaining a sorted list is more complex than maintaining a stack or queue because insertion or deletion can occur anywhere in a chain which may have zero or many existing records. To guarantee that insertions and deletions always occur in the interior of the chain, "dummy" first and last records are often included (see Figure C-5b). Figure C-5c shows the result of inserting a new Order into the sorted list of Figure C-5b. To perform the insertion, the list is scanned starting from the address in the pointer First_order. Once the proper position in the chain is found, there must be a rule for deciding where to store a record with a duplicate key value, if duplicates are allowed, as in this example. Usually this location for a duplicate record will be first among the duplicates because this requires the least scanning.

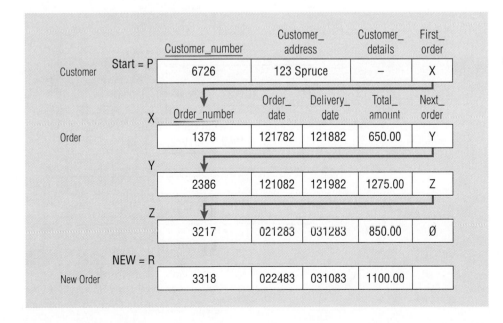

Figure C-5
Example of a sorted list

(a) Before new Order insertion and without dummy first and dummy last Orders

(b) Before new Order insertion and with dummy first and dummy last Orders

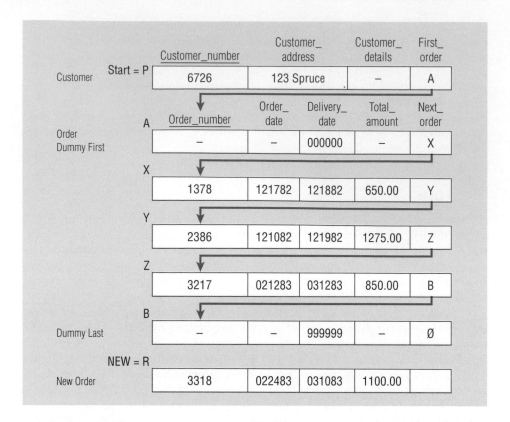

(c) After new Order insertion (Circled numbers next to pointers indicate the step number in the associated maintenance procedure that changes pointer value.)

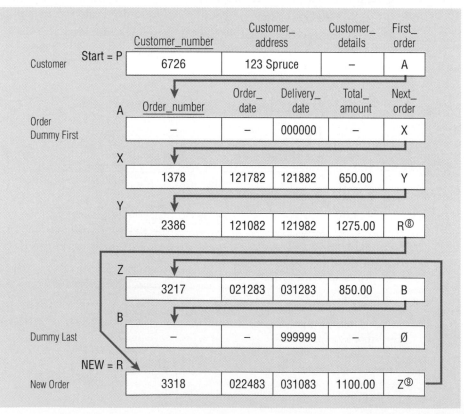

Figure C-6
Outline of record
insertion code

```
/*    Establish position variables beginning values */
1     PRE ← First_order(START)
2     AFT ← Next_order(PRE)
/*    Skip/scan through chain until proper position is found */
3     DO WHILE Delivery_date(AFT) < Delivery_date(NEW)
         4   PRE ← AFT
         5   AFT ← Next_order(AFT)
6     ENDO
7     [If Delivery_date(AFT) = Delivery_date(NEW)
      then indicate a Duplicate Error and terminate procedure]
/*    Weld in new chain element */
8     Next_order(PRE) ← NEW
9     Next_order(NEW) ← AFT
```

If you use a file organization or DBMS which supports chains, and in particular sorted lists, you will not have to write the code to maintain lists. Rather, this code will exist within the technology you use. Your program will simply issue an insert, delete, or update command, and the support software will do the chain maintenance. Figure C-6 contains an outline of the code needed to insert a new record in the sorted list of Figure C-5b. In this outline, position variables PRE and AFT are used to hold the values of the predecessor and successor, respectively, of the new Order record. Step 7 is included in brackets to show where a check for duplicate keys would appear if required. The symbol ← means replace the value of the variable on the left with the value of the variable on the right. Steps 8 and 9, which change pointer values, in Figure C-5 show exactly which pointers would change for the example of this figure. You may want to desk check this routine by manually executing it to see how variables' values are set and changed.

Multilists

A multilist data structure is one for which more than one sequence is maintained among the same records. Thus, multiple chains are threaded through the same records, and records can be scanned in any of the maintained sequences without duplicating the data records. The tradeoff for this flexible accessing is the extra storage space and maintenance for each chain. With a multilist, it is possible to walk through one association and in the middle decide to follow another. For example, while accessing the Order records for a given Customer (one list), we could find all the Orders to be delivered on the same day of delivery for a given Order record. Such a multilist is depicted in Figure C-7.

A multilist provides some of the same benefits of multiple indexes (see Chapter 7 for a discussion of primary and secondary key indexes). The major disadvantages of multilists, and the main reasons they are not used in relational DBMSs, is that the cost to scan a list is high compared to accessing an index, and there is no quick way to respond to multiple key qualifications with multilists (for example, find all the orders for customers in the Northwest region and products in the Paper product line). For this and other reasons, indexes have generally replaced linear data structures in modern database technologies. However, legacy applications may still use technologies employing single- and multilist structures.

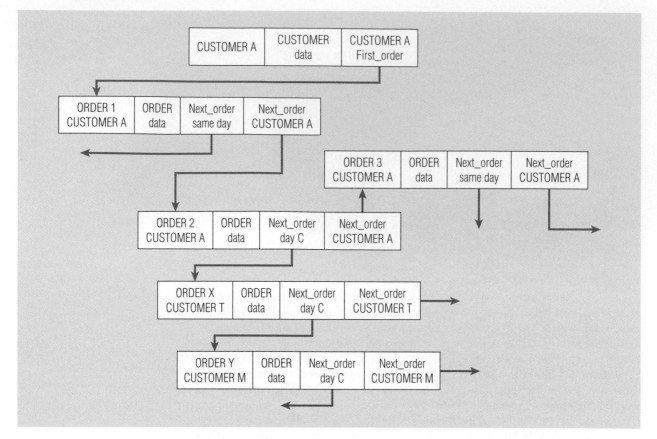

Figure C-7
Example of multilist
structures

HAZARDS OF CHAIN STRUCTURES

Besides the limitation of chains that prohibits their use in quickly responding to multiple-key qualifications, chains also have the following hazards and limitations:

1. Long chains can take an enormous amount of time to scan because records in sequence are not necessarily stored physically close to one another.

2. Chains are vulnerable to being broken. If an abnormal event occurs in the middle of a chain maintenance routine, the chain can be partially updated and the chain becomes incomplete or inaccurate. Some safety measures can be taken to cope with such mistakes, but these measures add extra storage or processing overhead.

TREES

The problem that a linear data structure may become long and hence time consuming to scan is an inherent issue with any linear structure. Fortunately, nonlinear structures, which implement a divide-and-conquer strategy, have been developed. A popular type of nonlinear data structure is a tree. A tree (see Figure C-8) is a data structure that consists of a set of nodes that branch out from a node at the top of the

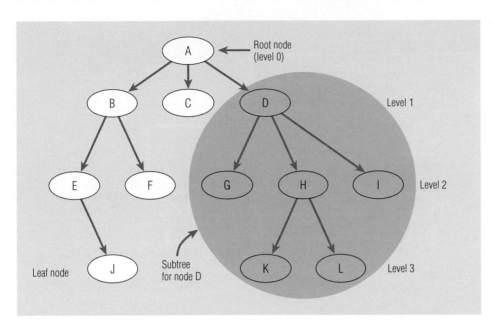

Figure C-8
Example of a tree
data structure

tree (thus the tree is upside down!). The root node is the node at the top of a tree. Each node in the tree, except the root node, has exactly one parent and may have zero, one, or more than one child nodes. Nodes are defined in terms of levels: the root is level zero, and the children of this node are at level one, and so on.

A leaf node is a node in a tree that has no child nodes (e.g., nodes J, F, C, G, K, L, and I in Figure C-8). A subtree of a node consists of that node and all the descendants of that node.

Balanced Trees

The most common use of trees in database management systems today is as a way to organize the entries within a key index. As with linear data structures, the database programmer does not have to maintain the tree structure because this is done by the DBMS software. However, a database designer may have the opportunity to control the structure of an index tree to tune the performance of index processing.

The most common form of tree used to build key indexes is a balanced tree, or B-tree. In a B-tree, all leaves are the same distance from the root. For this reason, B-trees have a predictable efficiency. B-trees support both random and sequential retrieval of records. The most popular form of B-tree is the B+-tree. A B+-tree of degree m has the following special balanced tree property:

- Every node has between $m/2$ and m children (m is an integer greater than or equal to 3 and usually odd), except the root (which does not obey this *lower* bound)

It is this property that leads to the dynamic reorganization of nodes, which we illustrate later in this section.

VSAM (virtual sequential access method), an access method supported by many operating systems, is based on the B+-tree data structure. VSAM is a more modern version of ISAM (indexed sequential access method). There are two primary differences

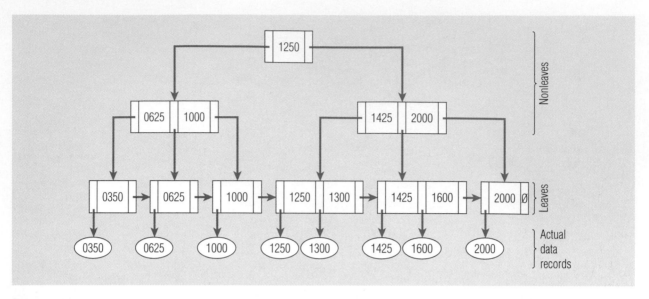

Figure C-9
Example of a B+-tree

between ISAM and VSAM: (1) the location of index entries under ISAM are limited by the physical boundaries of a disk drive, whereas in VSAM index entries may span the physical boundaries, and (2) an ISAM file needs to be occasionally rebuilt when its structure becomes inefficient after many key additions and deletions, whereas in VSAM the index is dynamically reorganized in incremental ways when segments of the index become unwieldy.

An example of a B+-tree (of degree 3) appears in Figure C-9 for the Product file of Pine Valley Furniture. In this diagram, each vertical arrow represents the path followed for values that are equal to the number to the left of the arrow, but less than the number to the right of the arrow. For example, in the nonleaf node that contains the values 625 and 1000, the middle arrow leaving the bottom of this node is the path followed for values equal to 625 but less than 1000. Horizontal arrows are used to connect the leaf nodes so that sequential processing can occur without having to move up and down through the levels of the tree.

Suppose you wanted to retrieve the data record for product number 1425. Notice that the value in the root node is 1250. Because 1425 is greater than 1250, you follow the arrow to the right of this node down to the next level. In this node you find the target value (1425), so you follow the middle arrow down to the leaf node that contains the value 1425. This node contains a pointer to the data record for product number 1425, so this record can now be retrieved. You should trace a similar path to locate the record for product number 1000. Because the data records are stored outside the index, multiple B+-tree indexes can be maintained on the same data.

A B+-tree also easily supports the addition and deletion of records. Any necessary changes to the B+-tree structure are dynamic and retain the properties of a B+-tree. Consider the case of adding a record with key 1800 to the B+-tree in Figure C-9. The result of this addition is shown in Figure C-10a. Since node 1 still has only three children (the horizontal pointer does not count as a child pointer), the B+-tree in Figure C-10a still satisfies all B+-tree properties. Now consider the effect of adding another record, this time with key 1700, to the B+-tree in Figure C-10a. An initial result of this insertion appears in Figure C-10b. In this case, node 1 violates the degree

Figure C-10
Inserting records in a B+-tree

(a) Insertion of record 1800

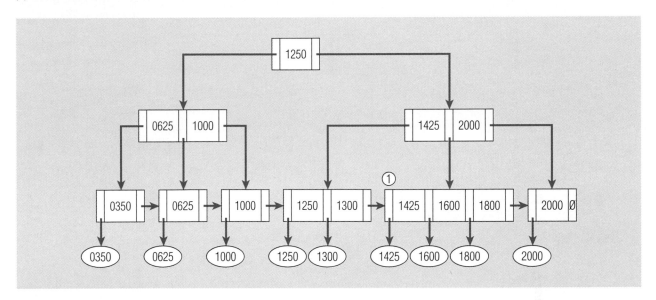

(b) Initial attempt to insert record 1700

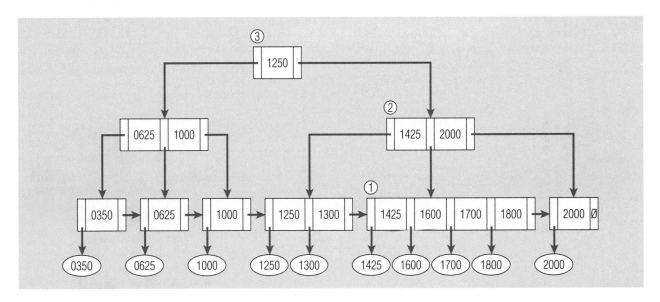

limitation, so this node must be split into two nodes. Splitting node 1 will cause a new entry in node 2, which then will make this node have four children, one too many. So, node 2 must also be split, which will add a new entry to node 3. The final result is shown in Figure C-10c.

(c) Final B+-tree after insertion of record 1700

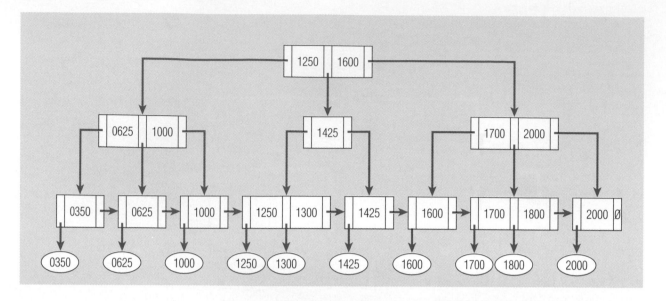

An interesting situation occurs when the root becomes too large (has more than m children). In this case, the root is split, which adds an additional level to the tree. The deletion of a record causes an entry in a leaf to be eliminated. If this elimination causes a leaf to have fewer than $m/2$ children, that leaf is then merged with an adjacent leaf; if the merged leaf is too large (more than m children), the merged leaf is split, resulting simply in a less skewed redistribution of keys across nodes. The result is that a B+-tree is dynamically reorganized to keep the tree balanced (equal depth along any path from the root) and with a limited number of entries per node (which controls the bushiness, or width, of the tree).

If you are interested in learning more about B-trees, see Comer (1979), a classic article on B-tree properties and design.

REFERENCES

Comer, D. 1979. "The Ubiquitous B-tree." *ACM Computing Surveys* 11 (June): 121–37.

Glossary of Terms

Note: The Chapter or Appendix in which a term is defined is listed in parentheses after the definition.

Aborted transaction   A transaction in progress that terminates abnormally. (13)

Abstract class   A class that has no direct instances, but whose descendants may have direct instances. (5) *See also* Concrete class.

Abstract operation   Defines the form or protocol of the operation, but not its implementation. (5)

Access method   An operating system algorithm for storing and locating data in secondary memory. (7) *See also* File organization.

ActiveX   Software that provides connectivity using Internet and Web technology. (10) *See also* Component Object Model (COM), Object Linking and Embedding (OLE).

After-image   A copy of a record (or page of memory) after it has been modified. (13) *See also* Before-image, Database recovery.

Aggregation   A part-of relationship between a component object and an aggregate object. (5) *See also* Composition. The process of transforming data from a detailed to a summary level. (14) *See also* Data transformation.

Alias   An alternative name used for an attribute. (6) *See also* Synonyms.

Anomalies   Errors or inconsistencies that may result when a user attempts to update a table that contains redundant data. There are three types of anomalies: insertion, deletion, and modification anomalies. (6) *See also* Normalization, Well-structured relation.

Application partitioning   The process of assigning portions of application code to client or server partitions after it is written, in order to achieve better performance and interoperability (ability of a component to function on different platforms). (8)

Application program interface (API)   Sets of routines that an application program uses to direct the performance of procedures by the computer operating system. (8) *See also* Client/server architecture, Middleware.

Array   A dynamically sized ordered collection of elements that can be located by position. (12) *See also* Bag, List, Set.

Association   A relationship between object classes. (5)

Association class   An association that has attributes or operations of its own or that participates in relationships with other classes. (5)

Association role   The end of an association where it connects to a class. (5)

Associative entity   An entity type that associates the instances of one or more entity types and contains attributes that are peculiar to the relationship between those entity instances. (3)

Asynchronous distributed database   A form of distributed database technology in which copies of replicated data are kept at different nodes so that local servers can access data without reaching out across the network. (11) *See also* Synchronous distributed database.

Atomic literal   A constant that cannot be decomposed into any further components. (12) *See also* Collection literal, Structured literal.

Attribute   A property or characteristic of an entity type that is of interest to the organization. For relational databases, an attribute is a named column of a relation. (3) *See also* Composite attribute, Derived attribute, Multivalued attribute, Simple attribute.

Attribute inheritance   A property that subtype entities inherit values of all attributes of the supertype. (4) *See also* Generalization, Specialization.

Authorization rules   Controls incorporated in the data management systems that restrict access to data and also restrict the actions that people may take when they access data. (13)

Backup facilities   An automatic dump facility that produces a backup copy (or *save*) of the entire database. (13) *See also* Database recovery.

Backward recovery (rollback)   Used to back out or undo unwanted changes to a database. Before-images of the records that have been changed are applied to the database, and the database is returned to an earlier state. Used to reverse the changes made by transactions that have been aborted or terminated abnormally. (13) *See also* Forward recovery.

Bag   An unordered collection of elements that may contain duplicates. (12) *See also* Array, List, Set.

Base table   A table in the relational data model containing the inserted raw data that is likely to correspond to one physical file in secondary storage. (9) *See also* User view.

Before-image   A copy of a record (or page of memory) before it has been modified. (13) *See also* After-image, Database recovery.

Behavior   Represents how an object acts and reacts. (5) *See also* Method, Operation.

Binary relationship   A relationship between the instances of two entity types. (3) *See also* Ternary relationship, Unary relationship.

Biometric device   Measures or detects personal characteristics such as fingerprints, voice prints, eye pictures, or signature dynamics. (13)

Bitmap index   A table of bits in which each row represents the distinct values of a key and each column is a bit, which when on indicates that the record for that bit column position has the associated field value. (7)

Blocking factor   The number of physical records per page. (7)

Boyce-Codd normal form   A relation in which every determinant is a candidate key. (B)

Business function   A related group of business processes that support some aspect of the mission of an enterprise. (2)

Business rule   A statement that defines or constrains some aspect of the business. It is intended to assert business structure or to control or influence the behavior of the business. (4) *See also* Constraint, Operational constraints, Structural constraints.

Candidate key   An attribute, or combination of attributes, that uniquely identifies a row in a relation. (6) *See also* Primary key.

Cardinality constraint   Specifies the number of instances of one entity that can (or must) be associated with each instance of another entity. (3) *See also* Constraint, Maximum cardinality, Minimum cardinality.

Catalog   A set of schemas, which when put together, constitute a description of a database. (9)

Checkpoint facility   A facility by which the DBMS periodically refuses to accept any new transactions. The system is in a quiet state, and the database and transaction logs are synchronized. (13) *See also* Database recovery.

Class   *See* Object class.

Class diagram   Shows the static structure of an object-oriented model: the object classes, their internal structure, and the relationships in which they participate. (5) *See also* Object diagram.

Class-scope attribute   An attribute of a class which specifies a value common to an entire class, rather than a specific value for an instance. (5)

Client/server architecture   A local area network-based environment in which database software on a server (called a database server or database engine) performs database commands sent to it from client workstations, and application programs on each client concentrate on user interface functions. (2)

Client/server systems   A networked computing model that distributes processes between clients and servers, which supply the requested services. In a database system, the database generally resides on a server that processes the DBMS. The clients may possess the application systems or request services from another server that holds the application programs. (8)

Code generator A module of a RDBMS that produces the program instructions that define a form, report, or menu. A code generator usually builds these instructions from a visual image of the object drawn by the designer of the object. (10)

Collection literal A collection of literals or object types. (12) *See also* Array, Atomic literal, Bag, List, Set, Structured literal.

Commit protocol An algorithm to ensure that a transaction is successfully completed, or else it is aborted. (11) *See also* Timestamping, Two-phased commit.

Completeness constraint A type of constraint that addresses the question whether an instance of a supertype must also be a member of at least one subtype. (4) *See also* Disjointness constraint.

Component Object Model (COM) The infrastructure that underlies OLE and handles the basic services required to manage the objects, such as memory management, error handling, interface negotiation, and interprocess communication. (10). *See also* ActiveX, Object Linking and Embedding (OLE).

Composite attribute An attribute that can be broken down into component parts. (3) *See also* Attribute.

Composite identifier An identifier that consists of a composite attribute. (3)

Composite key A primary key that consists of more than one attribute. (6)

Composition A part object which belongs to only one whole object, and which lives and dies with the whole object. (5) *See also* Aggregation.

Computer-aided software engineering (CASE) Software tools that provide automated support for some portion of the systems development process. (2)

Conceptual schema A detailed, technology independent specification of the overall structure of a database. (2) *See also* Physical schema, User view

Concrete class A class that can have direct instances. (5) *See also* Abstract class.

Concurrency control The process of managing simultaneous operations against a database so that data integrity is maintained and the operations do not interfere with each other in a multiuser environment. (13) *See also* Incomplete read problem.

Concurrency transparency A design goal for a distributed database, with the property that although a distributed system runs many transactions, it appears that a given transaction is the only activity in the system. Thus, when several transactions are processed concurrently, the results must be the same as if each transaction were process in serial order. (11) *See also* Failure transparency, Location transparency, Replication transparency.

Constrained object An entity, attribute, or relationship on which operations (such as create, delete, update, or read) are limited. (4) *See also* Constraining object, Operational constraint.

Constraining object An entity, attribute, or relationship that influences the ability to perform an operation (create, delete, update, or read) on another object. (4) *See also* Constrained object, Operational constraint.

Constraint A rule that cannot be violated by database users. (1) *See also* Business rule, Cardinality constraint.

Constraint base An organized collection of rules (or constraints), usually stored in a repository. (4) *See also* Operational constraints, Structural constraints.

Constructor operation An operation that creates a new instance of a class. (5)

Container An entity that contains linked or embedded objects. (10) *See also* Object Linking and Embedding (OLE).

Content addressing The facility that allows a user to query a database to select all records and/or objects that satisfy a given set of qualifications. (A)

Correlated subqueries In SQL, a subquery in which processing the inner query depends on data from the outer query. (9)

Data Facts, text, graphics, images, sound, and video segments that have meaning in the users' environment. (1)

Data administration A high-level function that is responsible for the overall management of data resources in an organization, including maintaining corporate-wide definitions and standards. (13) *See also* Database administration, Data steward.

Data control language (DCL) Commands used to control a database, including administering privileges and committing (saving) of data. (9) *See also* Data definition language (DDL), Data manipulation language (DML).

Data definition language (DDL) Those commands used to define a database, including creating, altering, and dropping tables and establishing constraints. (9)

See also Data control language (DCL), Data manipulation language (DML).

Data dictionary   A repository of information about a database which documents data elements of a database. (13)

Data independence   The separation of data descriptions from the application programs that use the data. (1)

Data manipulation language (DML)   Those commands used to maintain and query a database, including updating, inserting, modifying, and querying data. (9) *See also* Data control language (DCL), Data definition language (DDL).

Data mart   A data warehouse that is limited in scope, whose data are obtained by selecting and (where appropriate) summarizing data from the enterprise data warehouse. (14) *See also* Dependent data mart, Independent data mart.

Data mining   Knowledge discovery using a sophisticated blend of techniques from traditional statistics, artificial intelligence, and computer graphics. (14) *See also* Data visualization, Data warehouse, On-line analytical processing.

Data scrubbing   A technique of using pattern recognition and other artificial intelligence techniques to upgrade the quality of raw data before they are transformed and moved to the data warehouse. Also called data cleansing. (14)

Data steward   A person assigned the responsibility of ensuring that organizational applications properly support the organization's enterprise goals. (13) *See also* Data administration, Database administration.

Data transformation   The component of data reconciliation that converts data from the format of the source operational systems to the format of the enterprise data warehouse. (14) *See also* Selection.

Data type   A detailed coding scheme recognized by system software, such as a DBMS, for representing organizational data. (7) *See also* Field.

Data visualization   The representation of data in graphical and multi-media formats for human analysis. (14) *See also* Data mining, On-line analytical processing.

Data warehouse   An integrated decision support database whose content is derived from the various operational databases. (1) A subject-oriented, integrated, time-variant, nonvolatile collection of data used in support of management decision-making processes.

(14) *See also* Data mart, Data mining, Derived data, Enterprise data warehouse, Informational system, On-line analytical processing, Operational system, Reconciled data, Star schema.

Database   An organized collection of logically related data. (1)

Database administration   A technical function that is responsible for physical database design and for dealing with technical issues such as security enforcement, database performance, and backup and recovery. (13) *See also* Data administration, Data steward.

Database application   An application program (or set of related programs) that is used to perform a series of database activities (create, read, update, and delete) on behalf of database users. (1)

Database change log   Contains before- and after-images of records that have been modified by transactions. (13) *See also* Database recovery.

Database destruction   The database itself is lost, or destroyed, or cannot be read. (13)

Database management system (DBMS)   A software application that is used to create, maintain, and provide controlled access to user databases. (1)

Database recovery   Mechanisms for restoring a database quickly and accurately after loss or damage. (13) *See also* Backup facilities, Backward recovery, Checkpoint facility, Forward recovery, Journalizing facilities, Recovery manager, Transaction log.

Database security   Protection of the data against accidental or intentional loss, destruction, or misuse. (13) *See also* Authorization rules, Biometric device, Encryption, User-defined procedures.

Database server   A computer that is responsible for database storage, access, and processing in a client/server environment. Some people also use this term to describe a two-tier client/server environment. (8)

Deadlock   An impasse that results when two or more transactions have locked a common resource, and each waits for the other to unlock that resource. (13) *See also* Locking.

Deadlock prevention   User programs must lock all records they require at the beginning of a transaction (rather than one at a time). (13)

Deadlock resolution   Allows deadlocks to occur but builds mechanisms into the DBMS for detecting and breaking the deadlocks. (13)

Decentralized database A database that is stored on computers at multiple locations; however, the computers are not interconnected by a network, so that users at the various sites cannot share data. (11) *See also* Distributed database.

Degree The number of entity types that participate in a relationship. (3)

Denormalization The process of transforming normalized relations into unnormalized physical record specifications. (7) *See also* Horizontal partitioning, Vertical partitioning.

Dependent data mart A data mart that is populated exclusively from the enterprise data warehouse and its reconciled data layer. (14) *See also* Independent data mart.

Derived attribute An attribute whose values can be calculated from related attribute values. (3)

Derived data Data that have been selected, formatted, and aggregated for end user decision support applications. (14) *See also* Data warehouse, Reconciled data.

Derived fact A fact that is derived from other facts or rules, using an algorithm or inference. (4)

Determinant The attribute on the left-hand side of the arrow in a functional dependency. (6)

Disjoint rule Specifies that if an entity instance (of the supertype) is a member of one subtype, it cannot simultaneously be a member of any other subtype. (4) *See also* Disjointness constraint, Overlap rule.

Disjointness constraint A constraint that addresses the question whether an instance of a supertype may simultaneously be a member of two (or more) subtypes. (4) *See also* Completeness constraint.

Distributed database A single logical database that is spread physically across computers in multiple locations that are connected by a data communications link. (11) *See also* Asynchronous distributed database, Decentralized database, Synchronous distributed database.

Domain constraint A specification of the characteristics of the data values that can be associated with one or more attributes. (4) *See also* Structural constraints.

Dynamic binding Determining what functions an interface provides at the time it is needed during execution of a program. (10)

Encapsulation The technique of hiding the internal, implementation details of an object from its external view. (5)

Encryption The coding or scrambling of data so that humans cannot read them. (13) *See also* Database security.

Enhanced entity-relationship model The model that has resulted from extending the original E-R model with new modeling constructs. (4)

Enterprise data model A graphical model that shows the high-level entities for the organization and the relationships among those entities. (1)

Enterprise data modeling The first step in database development, in which the scope and general contents of organizational databases are specified. (2) *See also* Enterprise data model.

Enterprise data warehouse A centralized, integrated data warehouse that is the control point and single source of all data made available to end users for decision support applications. (14)

Entity A person, place, object, event, or concept in the user environment about which the organization wishes to maintain data. (3) *See also* Associative entity, Strong entity, Weak entity.

Entity instance A single occurrence of an entity type. (3) *See also* Entity, Entity type.

Entity integrity rule No primary key attribute (or component of a primary key attribute) can be null. (6)

Entity-relationship diagram (E-R diagram) A graphical representation of an entity-relationship model. (3)

Entity-relationship model A logical representation of the data for an organization or for a business area. (3) *See also* Enhanced entity-relationship model.

Entity type A collection of entities that share common properties or characteristics. (3) *See also* Entity instance.

Equi-join A join in which the joining condition is based on equality between values in the common columns. Common columns appear (redundantly) in the result table. (9) *See also* Natural join, Outer join.

Event A database action (create, update, or delete) that results from a transaction. (14) *See also* Data warehouse, Periodic data, Transient data.

Event-driven Nonprocedural programming that detects an event when it occurs and generates an appropriate response to that event. (10)

Exclusive lock (X lock or write lock)   Prevents another transaction from reading and therefore updating a record until it is unlocked. (13) *See also* Shared lock.

Extended relational   *See* Object-relational database management system.

Extent   The set of all instances of a class within the database. (12)

External schema   *See* User view.

Fact   An association between two or more terms. (4) *See also* Derived fact.

Failure transparency   A design goal for a distributed database, which guarantees that either all the actions of each transaction are committed or else none of them is committed. (11) *See also* Concurrency transparency, Location transparency, Replication transparency.

Fat client   A client PC that is responsible for processing, including presentation logic, extensive application and business rules logic, and many DBMS functions. (8) *See also* Thin client.

Field   The smallest unit of named application data recognized by system software. (7) *See also* Data type.

File organization   A technique for physically arranging the records of a file on secondary storage devices. (7) *See also* Hashing file organization, Indexed file organization, Sequential file organization.

File server   A device that manages file operations and is shared by each of the client PCs attached to the LAN. (8)

First normal form   A relation which contains no multivalued attributes. (6) *See also* Anomalies, Normalization, Second normal form, Third normal form, Well-structured relation.

Foreign key   An attribute in a relation of a database that serves as the primary key of another relation in the same database. (6) *See also* Recursive foreign key.

Forward recovery (rollforward)   Starts with an earlier copy of the database. After-images (the results of good transactions) are applied to the database, and the database is quickly moved forward to a later state. (13) *See also* Backward recovery.

Fourth normal form (4NF)   A relation in BCNF which contains no multivalued dependencies. (B)

Fragmentation transparency   *See* Replication transparency.

Functional decomposition   An iterative process of breaking down the description of a system into finer and finer detail in which one function is described in greater detail by a set of other, supporting functions. (2)

Functional dependency   A constraint between two attributes or two sets of attributes. (6) *See also* Anomalies, Normal form, Normalization, Well-structured relation.

Generalization   The process of defining a more general entity type (object class) from a set of more specialized entity types (object classes). (4) *See also* Attribute inheritance, Specialization, Subtype, Supertype.

Global transaction   In a distributed database, a transaction that requires reference to data at one or more nonlocal sites to satisfy the request. (11) *See also* Local transaction.

Grain   The length of time (or other meaning) associated with each record in the table. (14) *See also* Star schema.

Hashed file organization   The address for each record is determined using a hashing algorithm. (7)

Hashing algorithm   A routine that converts a primary key value into a relative record number (or relative file address). (7) *See also* Hashed file organization.

Homonym   An attribute that may have more than one meaning. (6)

Horizontal partitioning   Distributing the rows of a table into several separate files. (7) *See also* Denormalization, Vertical partitioning.

HTML form   An HTML feature that allows a user to enter information into a Web page and then pass that information on to other pages or to an external program such as a DBMS. (10)

HyperText Markup Language (HTML)   A simple language used to format documents, link to other Web pages, and communicate between Web browsers. (10)

Identifier   An attribute (or combination of attributes) that uniquely identifies individual instances of an entity type. (3) *See also* Composite identifier, Primary key.

Identifying owner   The entity type on which the weak entity type depends. (3)

Identifying relationship   The relationship between a weak entity type and its owner. (3)

Inconsistent read problem   An unrepeatable read, one that occurs when one user reads data that have been partially updated by another user. (13) *See also* Concurrency control.

Incremental capture   A method of capturing only the changes that have occurred in the source data since the last capture. (14) *See also* Data warehouse, Static capture.

Incremental commitment   A strategy in systems development projects in which the project is reviewed after each phase and continuation of the project is rejustified in each of these reviews. (2)

Independent data mart   A data mart that is populated with data extracted from the operational environment, without benefit of a reconciled data layer. (14) *See also* Dependent data mart.

Index   A table or other data structure used to determine the location of rows in a file that satisfy some condition. (7) *See also* Bitmap index, Indexed file organization, Primary key, Secondary key.

Indexed file organization   The records are stored either sequentially or nonsequentially and an index is created that allows software to locate individual records. (7) *See also* Indexed nonsequential, Indexed sequential.

Indexed nonsequential   Storage of records in no particular order using an index to find each record. (7) *See also* Indexed file organization, Indexed sequential.

Indexed sequential   Storage of records sequentially by primary key value (within each data block) using a simple index (called a block index). (7) *See also* Indexed file organization, Indexed nonsequential.

Information   Data that have been processed in such a way as to increase the knowledge of the person who uses the data. (1)

Information engineering   A formal, top-down methodology that uses a data orientation to create and maintain information systems. (2) *See also* Top-down planning.

Information repository   Stores metadata that describe an organization's data and data processing resources. Manages the total information processing environment. Combines information about an organization's business information and its application portfolio. (13)

Information Repository Dictionary System (IRDS)   A computer software tool that is used to manage and control access to the information repository. (13)

Information systems architecture (ISA)   A conceptual blueprint or plan that expresses the desired future structure for the information systems in an organization. (2)

Informational systems   Systems designed to support decision making based on stable point-in-time or historical data, and designed for complex and read-only queries or data mining applications. (14) *See also* Data warehouse, Operational system.

Inheritance   *See* Attribute inheritance.

Intranet   A local network that uses HTML technology such as HTTP or FTP protocols. (10)

Join   A relational operation that causes two tables with a common domain to be combined into a single table. (9) *See also* Equi-join, Natural join.

Joining   The process of combining data from various sources into a single table or view. (14) *See also* Data transformation, Selection.

Journalizing facilities   An audit trail of transactions and database changes. (13) *See also* Database recovery.

List   An ordered collection of elements. (12) *See also* Array, Bag, Set.

Local autonomy   A design goal for a distributed database, which says that a site can independently administer and operate its database when connections to other nodes have failed. (11)

Local transaction   In a distributed database, a transaction that requires reference only to data that are stored at the site where the transaction originates. (11) *See also* Global transaction.

Location transparency   A design goal for a distributed database, which says that a user (or user program) using data need not know the location of the data. (11) *See also* Concurrency transparency, Failure transparency, Replication transparency.

Locking   Any data that are retrieved by a user for updating must be locked, or denied to other users, until the update is completed or aborted. (13) *See also* Concurrency control, Deadlock, Exclusive lock, Shared lock, Two-phase locking protocol.

Locking level (granularity)   The extent of the database resource that is included with each lock. (13)

Market basket analysis   The study of buying behavior of individual customers. (14) *See also* Data warehouse.

Massively parallel processing (MPP)   Many parallel processing systems where each CPU has its own dedicated memory. Also called shared nothing architecture. (8)

Maximum cardinality   The maximum number of instances of one entity that may be associated with a single occurrence of another entity. (3) *See also* Minimum cardinality.

Metadata   Data that describe the properties or characteristics of other data. (1)

Method   The implementation of an operation. (5) *See also* Overriding.

Middleware   Software that allows an application to interoperate with other software without requiring the user to understand and code the low-level operations necessary to achieve interoperability. (8)

Minimum cardinality   The minimum number of instances of one entity that may be associated with each instance of another entity. (3) *See also* Maximum cardinality.

Multiple classification   An object is an instance of more than one class. (5)

Multiplicity   Indicates how many objects participate in a given relationship. (5)

Multivalued attribute   An attribute that may take on more than one value for a given entity instance. (3)

Multivalued dependency   The type of functional dependency that exists in a relation when there are at least three attributes in that relation (say A, B, and C) and for each value of A there is a well-defined set of values of B and well-defined set of values of C. However, the set of values of B is independent of set C, and vice versa. (A) *See also* Fourth normal form (4NF).

Natural join   The same as equi-join except that one of the duplicated columns is eliminated in the result table. (9) *See also* Outer join.

Normal form   A state of a relation that results from applying simple rules regarding functional dependencies (or relationships between attributes) to that relation. (6) *See also* Anomalies, First normal form, Functional dependency, Normalization, Second normal form, Third normal form, Well-structured relation.

Null   A value that may be assigned to an attribute when no other value applies, or when the applicable value is unknown. (6)

Object   An entity that has a well-defined role in the application domain, and has state, behavior, and identity. (5) *See also* Object class.

Object class   A set of objects that share a common structure and a common behavior. (5)

Object diagram   A graph of instances that are compatible with a given class diagram. (5) *See also* Class diagram.

Object Linking and Embedding (OLE)   A language-independent binary standard for object sharing which provides interoperability among software components and applications, regardless of programming language or hardware platform. (10)

Object-relational database management system   A database engine that supports both relational and object-oriented features in an integrated fashion. Also called extended relational and universal server. (A)

On-line analytical processing (OLAP)   The use of a set of graphical tools that provides users with multidimensional views of their data, and allows them to analyze the data using simple windowing techniques. (14) *See also* Data mining, Data warehouse.

Operation   A function or a service that is provided by all the instances of a class. (5) *See also* Abstract operation, Behavior, Constructor operation, Method, Polymorphism, Query operation, Update operation.

Operational constraints   Business rules that constrain the ongoing operations of the organization. These operations are often characterized by a series of transactions that represent business events. (4) *See also* Structural constraints.

Operational system   A system that is used to run a business in real time, based on current data. (14) *See also* Data warehouse, Informational system.

Outer join   A join in which rows that do not have matching values in common columns are nevertheless included in the result table. (9) *See also* Equi-join, Natural join.

Overlap rule   Specifies that an entity instance can simultaneously be a member of two (or more) subtypes. (4) *See also* Disjoint rule, Disjointness constraint.

Overriding The process of replacing a method inherited from a superclass by a more specific implementation of that method in a subclass. (5)

Page The amount of data read or written in one secondary memory (disk) input or output operation. For I/O with a magnetic tape, the equivalent term is record block. (7) *See also* Blocking factor.

Partial functional dependency A functional dependency in which one or more nonkey attributes (such as Name) are functionally dependent on part (but not all) of the primary key. (6) *See also* Second normal form.

Partial specialization rule Specifies that an entity instance of the supertype is allowed not to belong to any subtype. (4) *See also* Completeness constraint, Total specialization rule.

Periodic data Data that are never physically altered or deleted, once they have been added to the store. (14) *See also* Data warehouse, Event, Transient data.

Physical file A named portion of secondary memory (a magnetic tape or hard disk) allocated for the purpose of storing physical records. (7)

Physical record A group of fields stored in adjacent memory locations and retrieved together as a unit. (7)

Physical schema Specifications for how data from a conceptual schema are stored in a computer's secondary memory. (2) *See also* Conceptual schema, User view.

Pointer A field of data that can be used to locate a related field or record of data. (7)

Polymorphism The same operation may apply to two or more classes in different ways. (5)

Primary key An attribute (or combination of attributes) that uniquely identifies each row in a relation. (6) *See also* Composite key, Foreign key, Identifier, Index, Secondary key.

Project A planned undertaking of related activities to reach an objective that has a beginning and an end. (2)

Prototyping An iterative process of systems development in which requirements are converted to a working system that is continually revised through close work between analysts and users. (2) *See also* Systems development life cycle (SDLC).

Query-by-Example (QBE) A direct manipulation database language that uses a graphical approach to query construction. (10)

Query operation An operation that accesses the state of an object but does not alter the state. (5)

Read lock *See* Shared lock.

Reconciled data Detailed, historical data intended to be the single, authoritative source for all decision support applications and not generally intended to be accessed directly by end users. (14) *See also* Data warehouse, Derived data.

Recovery manager A module of the DBMS that restores the database to a correct condition when a failure occurs, and resumes processing user requests. (13) *See also* Database recovery.

Recursive foreign key A foreign key in a relation that references the primary key values of that same relation. (6)

Redundant Arrays of Inexpensive Disks (RAID) A set, or array, of physical disk drives that appear to the database user (and programs) as if they form one large logical storage unit. (7) *See also* Stripe.

Referential integrity An integrity constraint specifying that the value (or existence) of an attribute in one relation depends on the value (or existence) of a primary key in the same or another relation. (9)

Referential integrity constraint A rule that states that either each foreign key value must match a primary key value in the other relation or else the foreign key value must be null. (6)

Refresh mode An approach for populating the data warehouse that employs bulk rewriting of the target data at periodic intervals. (14) *See also* Update mode.

Relation A named, two-dimensional table of data. (6)

Relational DBMS (RDBMS) A database management system that manages data as a collection of tables in which all data relationships are represented by common values in related tables. (9) *See also* Foreign key, Normalization, Primary key, Relation.

Relationship instance An association between (or among) entity instances, where each relationship instance includes exactly one entity from each participating entity type. (3)

Relationship type A meaningful association between (or among) entity types. (3) *See also* Binary relationship, Relationship instance, Ternary relationship, Unary relationship.

Replication transparency   A design goal for a distributed database, which says that although a given data item may be replicated at several nodes in a network, a programmer or user may treat the data item as if it were a single item at a single node. Also called fragmentation transparency. (11) *See also* Concurrency transparency, Failure transparency, Location transparency.

Repository   A centralized knowledge base of all data definitions, data relationships, screen and report formats, and other system components. (1 and 2)

Restore/rerun   Involves reprocessing the day's transactions (up to the point of failure) against the backup copy of the database. (13) *See also* Database recovery.

Rollback   *See* Backward recovery.

Rollforward   *See* Forward recovery.

S lock   *See* Shared lock.

Scalar aggregate   A single value returned from an SQL query that includes an aggregate function. (9) *See also* Vector aggregate.

Schema   That structure which contains descriptions of objects created by a user, such as base tables, views, constraints, etc., as part of a database. (9) *See also* Relational DBMS.

Second normal form   A relation that is in first normal form and has every nonkey attribute fully functionally dependent on the primary key. (6) *See also* Anomalies, Functional dependency, Normalization, Partial functional dependency, Third normal form, Well-structured relation.

Secondary key   One field or a combination of fields for which more than one record may have the same combination of values. (7) *See also* Index, Primary key.

Security   *See* Database security.

Selection   The process of partitioning data according to predefined criteria. (14) *See also* Data transformation, Joining.

Semijoin   A joining operation used with distributed databases in which only the joining attribute from one site is transmitted to the other site, rather than all the selected attributes from every qualified row. (11)

Sequential file organization   The records in the file are stored in sequence according to a primary key value. (7)

Set   An unordered collection of elements without any duplicates. (12)

Shared lock (S lock or read lock)   Allows other transactions to read but not update a record or other resource. (13) *See also* Exclusive lock, Locking.

Shared nothing architecture   *See* Massively parallel processing (MPP).

Simple attribute   An attribute that cannot be broken down into smaller components. (3)

Snowflake schema   An expanded version of a star schema in which all of the tables are fully normalized. (14)

Specialization   The process of defining one or more subtypes (subclasses) of the supertype (superclass), and forming supertype/subtype (superclass/subclass) relationships. (4) *See also* Attribute inheritance, Generalization.

Star schema   A simple database design in which dimensional data are separated from fact or event data. A dimensional model is another name for star schema. (14) *See also* Data warehouse, Grain, Market basket analysis, Snowflake schema.

State   Encompasses an object's properties (attributes and relationships) and the values those properties have. (5)

Static capture   A method of capturing a snapshot of the required source data at a point in time. (14) *See also* Data warehouse, Incremental capture.

Stripe   The set of pages on all disks in a RAID which are the same relative distance from the beginning of the disk drive. (7)

Strong entity type   An entity that exists independently of other entity types. (3)

Stored procedure   A module of code, usually written in a proprietary language such as Oracle's PL/SQL or Sybase's Transact-SQL, that implements application logic or a business rule and is stored on the server, where it runs when it is called. (8)

Structural constraints   Business rules that define the static structure of the organization. The three primary types are definitions, domains, and relationships. (4) *See also* Operational constraints.

Structured literal   A fixed number of named elements, each of which can be a literal or object type. (12) *See also* collection literal.

Subquery   A query in SQL whose results are used in the search condition of another SQL query. (9) *See also* Correlated subqueries.

Subtype   A subgrouping of the entities in an entity type that is meaningful to the organization and that shares common attributes or relationships distinct from other subgroupings. (4) *See also* Generalization, Specialization, Supertype.

Subtype discriminator   An attribute of the supertype whose values determine the target subtype or subtypes. (4)

Supertype   A generic entity type that has a relationship with one or more subtypes. (4) *See also* Generalization, Specialization, Subtype.

Supertype/subtype hierarchy   A hierarchical arrangement of supertypes and subtypes, where each subtype has only one supertype. (4)

Symmetric multiprocessing (SMP)   A parallel processing architecture where the processors share a common shared memory. (8)

Synchronous distributed database   A form of distributed database technology in which all data across the network are continuously kept up-to-date so that a user at any site can access data anywhere on the network at any time and get the same answer. (11) *See also* Asynchronous distributed database.

Synonyms   Two (or more) attributes having different names but the same meaning, as when they describe the same characteristic of an entity. (6) *See also* Alias.

System catalog   A system-created database which describes all database objects, including data dictionary information, but also includes user access information. (13)

Systems development life cycle (SDLC)   The traditional methodology used to develop, maintain, and replace information systems. (2) *See also* Prototyping.

Term   A word or phrase that has a specific meaning for the business. (4) *See also* Fact, Structural constraints.

Ternary relationship   A simultaneous relationship among the instances of three entity types. (3) *See also* Binary relationship, Unary relationship.

Thin client   A PC configured for handling user interfaces and some application processing, and usually with no or limited local data storage. (8)

Third normal form   A relation that is in second normal form and has no transitive dependencies present. (6) *See also* Anomalies, First normal form, Functional dependency, Normalization, Second normal form, Transitive dependency, Well-structured relation.

Three-tier architecture   A client/server configuration that includes three layers: a client layer and two server layers. While the nature of the server layers differs, a common configuration is an application server. (8)

Time stamp   A time value that is associated with a data value. (3)

Timestamping   In distributed databases, a concurrency control mechanism that assigns a globally unique time stamp to each transaction. Timestamping is an alternative to the use of locks in distributed databases. (11)

Top-down planning   A generic information systems planning methodology that attempts to gain a broad understanding of the information system needs of the entire organization. (2) *See also* Information engineering.

Total specialization rule   Specifies that each entity instance of the supertype must be a member of some subtype in the relationship. (4) *See also* Completeness constraint, Partial specialization rule.

Transaction   A discrete unit of work that must be completely processed or not processed at all within a computer system. Entering a customer order is an example of a transaction. (13)

Transaction boundaries   The logical beginning and end of transactions. (13)

Transaction log   Contains a record of the essential data for each transaction that is processed against the database. (13) *See also* Database recovery.

Transaction manager   In a distributed database, a software module that maintains a log of all transactions and maintains an appropriate concurrency control scheme. (11)

Transient data   Data for which changes to existing records are written over previous records, thus destroying the previous data content. (14) *See also* Data warehouse, Event, Periodic data.

Transitive dependency   A functional dependency between two (or more) nonkey attributes. (6) *See also* Third normal form.

Trigger   A named set of SQL statements that are considered (triggered) when a data modification (INSERT, UPDATE, DELETE) occurs. If a condition stated within the trigger is met, then a prescribed action is taken. (9)

Two-phase commit   An algorithm for coordinating updates in a distributed database. (11)

Two-phase locking protocol   A procedure for acquiring the necessary locks for a transaction where all necessary locks are acquired before any locks are released, resulting in a growing phase where locks are acquired and a shrinking phase where they are released. (13)

Unary relationship   A relationship between the instances of a single entity type. (3) *See also* Binary relationship, Ternary relationship.

Universal server   *See* Object-relational database management system.

Update mode   An approach in which only changes in the source data are written to the data warehouse. (14) *See also* Refresh mode.

Update operation   An operation that alters the state of an object. (5)

User-defined procedures   User exits (or interfaces) that allow system designers to define their own security procedures in addition to the authorization rules. (13)

User view   A logical description of some portion of the database that is required by a user to perform some task. (1) *See also* Conceptual database.

Vector aggregate   Multiple values returned from an SQL query that includes an aggregate function. (9) *See also* Scalar aggregate.

Versioning   There is no form of locking. Each transaction is restricted to a view of the database as of the time that transaction started, and when a transaction modifies a record, the DBMS creates a new record version instead of overwriting the old record. (13)

Vertical partitioning   Distributing the columns of a table into several separate files. (7) *See also* Denormalization, Horizontal partitioning.

Visual Basic for Applications (VBA)   The programming language that accompanies Access97. (10)

Weak entity type   An entity type whose existence depends on some other entity type. (3)

Web browser   Software that provides the GUI used to display Web site pages and locates those pages and sites on request. (10)

Well-structured relation   A relation that contains minimum redundancy and allows users to insert, modify, and delete the rows in a table without errors or inconsistencies. (6) *See also* Anomalies, Normalization.

Write lock   *See* Exclusive lock.

X lock   *See* Exclusive lock.

Glossary of Acronyms

ANSI   American National Standards Institute

API   Application Program Interface

ASCII   American Standards Code for Information Interchange

BCNF   Boyce-Codd Normal Form

CAD/CAM   Computer-Aided Design/Computer-Aided Manufacturing

CASE   Computer-Aided Software Engineering

CD-ROM   Compact Disk-Read-Only Memory

COBOL   COmmon Business Oriented Language

CODASYL   Committee On DAta SYstem Languages

COM   Component Object Model

CRT   Cathode Ray Tube

CSF   Critical Success Factor

DA   Data Administrator (or Data Administration)

DBA   Database Administrator (or Database Administration)

DBC   Database Computer

DBD   Database Description

DBMS   Database Management System

DBTG   Data Base Task Group

DB2   Data Base2 (an IBM Relational DBMS)

DCL   Device Control Language

DDL   Data Definition Language

DFD   Data Flow Diagram

DK/NF   Domain-Key Normal Form

DL/I   Data Language I (part of IMS)

DML   Data Manipulation Language

DOS   Disk Operating System

E-R   Entity-Relationship

EER   Extended Entity-Relationship

ERD   Entity-Relationship Diagram

FORTRAN   FORmula TRANslator

GUI   Graphical User Interface

HDAM   Hierarchical Direct Access Method

HIDAM   Hierarchical Indexed Direct Access Method

HISAM   Hierarchical Indexed Sequential Access Method

HSAM   Hierarchical Sequential Access Method

HTML   HyperText Markup Language

IBM   International Business Machines

I-CASE   Integrated Computer-Aided Software Engineering

ID   Identifier

IDMS/R   Integrated Database Management System/Relational (a relational DBMS from Computer Associates)

IDS   Integrated Data System (an early network DBMS)

IMS   Information Management System (an IBM hierarchical DBMS; current version is IMS/ESA, or Information Management System/Extended System Architecture)

IRDS   Information Repository Dictionary System

IRM   Information Resource Management

IS   Information System

ISA   Information Systems Architecture

ISAM   Indexed Sequential Access Method

ISO   International Standards Organization

LAN   Local Area Network

LDB   Logical Database

LDBR   Logical Database Record

MB   Million Bytes

MIS   Management Information System

M:1   Many-to-One

MPP   Massively Parallel Processing

M:N   Many-to-Many

ODBMS   Object Database Management System

OLAP   On-line Analytical Processing

OLE   Object Linking and Embedding

O-O   Object-Oriented

OODM   Object-Oriented Data Model

OSAM   Overflow Sequential Access Method

OS/2   Operating System/2

PAL   Paradox Application Language

PC   Personal Computer

PCB   Program Communication Block

PC-DBMS   Personal Computer-Database Management System

PC-RDBMS   Personal Computer-Relational Database Management System

PDBR   Physical Database Record

P.K.   Primary Key

QBE   Query-by-Example

RAID   Redundant Arrays of Inexpensive Disks

RDBMS   Relational Database Management System

SAM   Sequential Access Method

SDLC   Systems Development Life Cycle

SMP   Symmetric Multiprocessing

SQL   Structured Query Language

SQL/DS   Structured Query Language/Data System (an IBM relational DBMS)

UDF   User-Defined Function

UML   Unified Modeling Language

VBA   Visual Basic for Applications

VSAM   Virtual Storage Access Method

1:1   One-to-One

1:M   One-to-Many

1NF   First Normal Form

2NF   Second Normal Form

3NF   Third Normal Form

4NF   Fourth Normal Form

5NF   Fifth Normal Form

Index

Note: **Boldface** terms are defined on the page that is boldfaced.

Aborted transaction, 503–504
Abstract class, 183
   See also Concrete class
Abstract operation, 185
Access97. *See* Microsoft Access97
Access method, 267–268
   See also File organization(s)
ActiveX, 401, 409
   See also Component Object Model, Object
      Linking and Embedding
ADD (SQL), 336
After-image, 499
   See also Before-image, Database recovery
Aggregation, 187–191, **547**
   propagation in, 191
   recursive, 190
   See also Composition, Data transformation
Alias, 242
   See also Synonyms
ALTER TABLE (SQL), 285, 332, 336
ANALYZE command (Oracle), 286
Analyze (data quality tool), 550, 551
Ancestors, 182
Anomalies, 217
   deletion, 217, 239
   example, 239
   insertion, 217, 239
   modification, 217, 239
   See also Normalization, Well-structured
      relation
ANY operator (SQL), 359
Application development, 9, 22
Application partitioning, 304
Application program interface (API), 311
   See also Client/server architecture,
      Middleware
Array, 455
   See also Bag, List, Set
Association classes, 177–180
Association role, 174
Associations, 174–177
   derived, 180–181
Associative entities (gerunds), 90, **99**–101, 103,
   219, 224–227

Associative relation, 224
Asynchronous distributed database, 421
Atomic literal, 455
Atre, S., on client/server implementation,
   313–314
Attribute(s), 93–97
   class-scope, **184**, 185
   composite, **94**–95, 96, 219–220
   derived, 90, **95**–97, 180–181
   domains and, 153–154
   multivalued, 90, **95**, 210, 220
   in ODL, 455–456, 459–462
   on relationships, 99, 100
   sample definitions of, 151
   simple (atomic), **95**, 96
   stored, 95–97
Attribute inheritance, **133**
Authorization rules, 495–497

Babad, Y.M., on missing data, 260
Back-end. *See* Server(s)
Back-end functions, 301
Backup and recovery, 25, 487, 498–505
   basic facilities for, 499–500
   recovery and restart procedures,
      500–503
   types of failure, 503–505
Backup facilities, **499**
Backward recovery (rollback), **502**–503
Bag, **455**
   See also Array, List, Set
Balanced trees (B-tree), 271, 595–598
   B+-tree, 271, 595–597
Bands (sections), 399
Barquin, R., on data warehousing, 531
Barry, D.K.
   on extent of class, 459
   on object query language, 454, 469
   on ODBMS, 458
Base table, **364**–366
Before-image, **499**
BEGIN TRANSACTION (SQL), 367
Behavior, **171**
   See also Method, Operation

Bell, D., on distributed database systems, 418,
   419, 420
Bernstein, P.A., on repository system
   architecture, 515–516
Bertino, E., on ODBMS, 458
BETWEEN clause (SQL), 347
Bill-of-materials, 101, 190, 229
Binary relationship(s), 90, 102, **104**, 175,
   222–224, 225
   many-to-many (M:N), 223–224
   one-to-many (1:M), 222–223
   one-to-one (1:1), 224
Biometric device, **498**
Bitmap index, **271**–272
Bitmapped indexing, 546
Blaha, M.
   on abstract class, 183
   on ancestors and descendants, 182
   on binary association, 176
   on class-cope attribute, 184
   on design activity, 169
   on discriminators, 181
   on encapsulation, 173
   on modeling, 168
   object-oriented modeling language defined
      by, 170
   on objects, 171
   on polymorphism, 186
   on propagation, 191
   on query operation, 173, 174
Blocking factor, **261**
Bloor, R., on content addressing, 576
Bobrowski, S., on client/server security, 312
Booch, G.
   on abstract class, 183
   on encapsulation, 173
   object-oriented modeling language defined
      by, 170
   on objects, 171
   on polymorphism, 186
Boolean operators, 346–347
Boyce-Codd normal form (BCNF), 234,
   579–581, **580**
Bruce, T.A., on selecting identifiers, 97

B-trees. *See* Balanced trees (B-tree)
Burwen, M., on data warehousing, 531
Business function, 41, 42
Business rules, 43, 130, **145**–159
　benefits of, 169–170
　classification of, 147–148
　declarative approach to, 154–155
　example, 156–159, 191–194
　in object-oriented modeling, 191, 192
　operational constraints, 147–148, 154–159
　paradigm, 146
　phases of, 168–169
　scope of, 146–147
　structural constraints, 147, 148–154
　　definitions, 148–152
　　domains, 153–154

CA-Ingres/Replicator, 443, 444–445
Call-level interface (CLI), 401
Candidate key, 235–236
　See also Primary key
Capture, 544
Cardinality constraint, 105–107, 108
　in E-R diagram, 90
　mandatory, 106
　maximum, 106
　minimum, 106
　optional, 106
CASE. *See* Computer-aided software
　　engineering (CASE)
Catalog, 327
Cattell, R.G.G.
　on extent of class, 459
　on object query language, 454, 469
　on ODBMS, 458
Celko, J.
　on SQL data types, 574
　on versioning, 510
CFML. *See* Cold Fusion Markup Language
　　(CFML)
CGI. *See* Common Gateway Interface (CGI)
Chain structures. *See* Linear data structures
CHECK operator (SQL), 333
Checkpoint facility, 500
Chen, P.P-S., on entity-relationship model, 86
Chouinard, P., on supertype/subtype
　　relationships, 231
Christerson, M.
　on object-oriented design phase, 169
　object-oriented modeling language defined
　　by, 170
Class(es), 168, **171**–**172**
　abstract, 183
　association, 177–180
　concrete, 183
　Java Database Connectivity (JDBC), 311
　in ODL, 454–455
Class diagram, 172, 173
Classification, multiple, 187
Class-scope attribute, 184, 185
CLI. *See* Call-level interface (CLI)
Client
　fat, 299
　thin, 302
Client/server architecture, 29, **58**
Client/server database, 29
Client/server systems, 297–321
　application partitioning, 304

architectures, 298–304
　database server, 301–302
　file server, 299–300
　n-tier, 302–304
　parallel computer, 306–309
　three-tier, 302–304
　issues in, 312–314
　mainframe's role in, 305–306
　middleware, 309–311
　security in, 311–312
　trends in, 297–298
　See also Database(s)
Client tier, 57
Coad, P., on object-oriented modeling, 169–170
Codd, E.F.
　on relational database model, 208
　relational database technology and, 324
　relational model defined by, 27, 28
Code generator, 396
　by CASE, 50
Coding techniques, 257–259
Cold Fusion, 408–409
Cold Fusion Markup Language (CFML), 408
Collection literal, 455
Collisions, data, 425
Comer, D., on B-trees, 598
Commitment, incremental, 53
Commit protocol, 435–436
COMMIT (SQL), 404
Committee on Data Systems and Languages
　　(CODASYL), 371
Common Gateway Interface (CGI), 407–409
Common Object Request Broker Architecture
　　(CORBA), 311
Comparison operators, in SQL, 345–346
Completeness constraint, 137–138
Complete subclasses, 183
Component Object Model (COM), 401
Composite attributes, 94–95, 96, 219–220
Composite entity. *See* Associative entities
　　(gerunds)
Composite identifier, 96–97
Composite key, 209
Composition, 189–190
Compression techniques, 257–259
Computer-aided software engineering (CASE),
　　25, **50**
　information repository and, 515
　integrated (I-CASE), 50–51
　lower CASE, 51
　role in database development, 50–51
　upper CASE, 51
Computer Associates International and Ingres
　distributed DBMS products, 443, 444–445
　ORDBMS products of, 577
Conceptual data model, 46, 47
Conceptual schema, 47, **54,** 55
　See also Conceptual data model
Concrete class, 183
Concurrency control, 505–511
　inconsistent read problem, 506
　locking, 507
　locking level (granularity), 507–508
　lock types, 508–510
　lost updates, 505–506
　optimistic vs. pessimistic, 510
　serializability, 506
　versioning, 510–511

Concurrency transparency, 436–**437**
Conflict, organizational, 25
Constrained object, 155–159
Constraining object, 155–159
Constraint(s), 23
　cardinality, 90, **105**–107, 108
　completeness, 137–138
　disjointness, 138–141
　integrity, 146, 213–215
　operational, 147–148, 154–159
　structural, 147, 148–154
　　definitions, 148–152
　　domains, 153–154, 213
Constraint base, 154–155
Constraint specification language, 155
Constructor operation, 173
Container, 401
Content addressing, 576
CORBA. *See* Common Object Request Broker
　　Architecture (CORBA)
Corporate planning objects, 41, 42
Correlated subquery, 361–363
COUNT function (SQL), 343, 344, 351
CPU usage, 518
CREATE ASSERTION command (SQL), 159, 369
CREATE DATABASE (SQL), 331–332
CREATE INDEX (SQL), 274–275, 332, 339
CREATE SCHEMA (SQL), 332
CREATE SYNONYM (SQL), 336–337
CREATE TABLE (SQL), 215, 332–333
CREATE VIEW (SQL), 332
Crosstab queries, 395
Currency control, 505

DAO. *See* Data Access Objects (DAO)
Darwen, H.
　on SQL, 327
　on SQL3, 371
Data, 4–**5,** 538–542
　conflict resolution, 486
　connecting elements of, 587
　consistency, 22
　derived, 537
　duplication of, 9
　event, 538–539
　incorrect, 504
　information vs., 5–6
　loading of, 48
　missing, 260
　periodic, 540–542
　policies, 486
　procedures, 486
　quality of, 23
　reconciled, 537
　redundancy, 21
　reference, 262, 265
　replication of. *See* Replication, data
　sharing of, 9, 22
　standards, 22, 486
　status, 538–539
　summary, 241
　time-dependent, 107–110
　transient, 539–542
　See also Data model; Data security; Integrity
Data Access Objects (DAO), 401
Data administration, 484
　See also Database administration, Data
　　steward

Data administrator, 26, 51, 482
Data and database administration, 69, 482,
    483–528
  backup and recovery, 25, 487, 498–505
    basic facilities for, 499–500
    recovery and restart procedures, 500–503
    types of failure, 503–505
  concurrency control, 505–511
    inconsistent read problem, 506
    locking, 507
    locking level (granularity), 507–508
    lock types, 508–510
    lost updates, 505–506
    optimistic vs. pessimistic, 510
    serializability, 506
    versioning, 510–511
  data dictionaries, 514
  data security, 492–498
    authentication schemes, 497–498
    authorization rules, 495–497
    encryption, 497
    threats to, 492–494
    user-defined procedures, 497
    views and, 494–495
  functions of, 488–490
  modeling enterprise data, 490–491
  planning for databases, 491–492
  quality management, 511–514
    data protection and privacy, 514
    maintenance controls, 514
    personnel controls, 513
    physical access controls, 513
    security policy and disaster recovery,
        512–513
  repositories, 515–516
  requirements for effective, 485, 486–487
  roles of administrators, 484–490
  tuning database for performance, 516–519
Database(s), 4, 26
  administering. *See* Data and database
      administration
  analyzing requirements, 61–63
  approach, 10–15, 20–25
  client/server, 29
  costs and risks of, 24–25
  decentralized, 418
  department, 18–19, 56
  enterprise, 19–20
  implementation of, 46, 48
  maintenance of, 46, 48
  object-oriented, 29
  personal computer, 15–16, 56
  proprietary (multidimensional), 557
  relational, 11–14
  security, 492–498
  workgroup, 16–17, 56
  See also Client/server architecture;
      Distributed database(s)
Database administration, 484
Database administrator, 51, 482
Database analysis, 489, 490
Database analysts, 51
Database application, 14–20
Database change log, 499
Database design, 64–67, 489, 490
  See also Logical database design; Physical
      database design
Database destruction, 504, **505**

Database development process, 37–82
  CASE and, 50–51
  example, 58–69
  within information systems development,
      38–44
    alternative approaches, 48–50
  personnel management, 51–53
  repository and, 50–51
  systems development life cycle (SDLC),
      45–48
  three-schema architecture in, 53–57
  three-tiered database location architecture,
      56–58
Database environment, 25–27
Database implementation, 489, 490
Database Language Embedded SQL, 325
Database level password security, 312
Database management systems (DBMS), 26
  evolution of, 27–29
  installation of, 517
  new technologies, 298
  trends, 298
  See also Distributed DBMS; Object-relational
      database management system
      (ORDBMS); Relational DBMS
      (RDBMS)
Database model
  hierarchical, 282, 283
  multidimensional, 283, 284–285
  network, 282–284
  object-oriented, 283, 284
  relational, 283, 284
Database planning, 486, 488, 489
Database recovery, 498
  See also Backup and recovery
Database security, 492–498
  authentication schemes, 497–498
  authorization rules, 495–497
  encryption, 497
  policy on, 512–513
  threats to, 492–494
  user-defined procedures, 497
  views and, 494–495
  See also Security
Database server, 301–302
Database technology, desktop, 382–383
Data-cleansing tools, 550–551
Data collisions, 425
Data control language, 328, 331
Data conversion tools, 550
Data definition, in QBE, 386–387
Data definition language, 328, 331
Data definition queries, 394
Data dictionary, 368–369, **514**
  See also Repository(ies)
Data direct placement, 587
Data independence, 21
Data indirect placement, 587
Data integrity, 259–260
Data Joiner, 443
Data manipulation language, 328, 331
Data mart, 536–537
  independent vs. dependent, 558–559
Data mart metadata, 538
Data mining, 562–563
Data model, 54
  conceptual, 46, 47
  definitions for, 150

enterprise, 10–11, 537
  relational, 28
  See also Entity-relationship (E-R) model;
      Relational data model
DataPropagator Relational (DPROP R), 442, 443
Data quality tools, 550
Data scrubbing, 544–545
Data steward, 512
Data structure(s)
  building blocks, 587–588
  linear, 589–594
    hazards of, 594
    multilists, 593–594
    queues, 590–591
    sorted lists, 591–593
    stacks, 590
  pointers, 267, 585–587
  relational, 209
  trees, 271, 594–598
Data transformation, 546–551
  functions of, 547–550
Data types, 255, **257**–259
  in oracle, 258
  Oracle7, 329
  of ORDBMS, 574
Data visualization, 563
Data warehouse, 14, **19**, 482, 529–571, **531**
  architectures, 534–538
    expanded, 534–536
    three-level, 537–538
    two-level, 534
  data mart, 536–537
    independent vs. dependent, 558–559
  data transformation, 546–551
    functions of, 547–550
  derived data layer, 551–559
  history of, 531
  information gap and, 530
  need for, 532–534
  reconciled data layer, 542–546, 550–551
  star schema, 552–558
    components of, 552, 553, 554–556
    example, 552–554
    variations of, 556–558
  user interface for, 559–563
    data mining tools, 562–563
    data visualization, 563
    metadata and, 559–560
    **on-line analytical processing (OLAP)
        tools**, 560–562
Date, C.J.
  on local autonomy, 421
  on locking in distributed database, 437
  on query optimization, 437, 438
  on SQL, 327
  on SQL3, 371
  on two-phase commit protocol, 436
David, M., on object-oriented databases, 29
DBMS. *See* Database management systems
      (DBMS)
DBQUERY, 409
DCOM. *See* Distributed Component Object
      Model (DCOM)
Deadlock, 508–510
Deadlock prevention, 510
Deadlock resolution, 510
Decentralized database, 418
DEFAULT operator (SQL), 333

Default value, 259
Definitions, 148–152
  components of, 148–149
  for data model, 150
  precision of, 150–152
Degree, 101
DELETE command (SQL), 336, 338
Deletion anomalies, 217, 239
Denormalization, 261–267, **262**
  horizontal partitioning by, 265–266
  opportunities for, 262–264
  vertical partitioning by, 266–267
Department databases, 18–19, 56
Department server, 57
Dependency(ies)
  multivalued, 582
  transitive, 238–240, 242–243
  See also Functional dependency
Dependent data mart, 558
Derived attributes, 90, **95–97,** 180–181
Derived data, 537, 551–559
  characteristics of, 551–552
Derived fact, 149
Descendants, 182
  disjoint, 183
  overlapping, 183
Descollonges, M., on exclusive locks, 508
Descriptors, 220
Desktop database technology, 382–383
Determinant, 235
Devlin, B., 529
  on data pollution, 545
  on data transformation, 550
  on data warehousing architecture, 531, 535
  on star schema, 552
  on transactions, 539
DeWitt, D., on uniprocessor environments, 306
DG/SQL, 324
Dictionary, data, 368–369, **514**
Dimension tables, 552, 553
Disaster recovery, 512–513
Discriminator, subtype, 141–143
Disjoint descendant, 183
Disjointness constraints, 138–141
Disjoint rule, 138–139, 140, 141
Disjoint subtypes, 141–142
Disk space considerations, 517
DISTINCT (SQL), 348–349
Distributed Component Object Model (DCOM), 311
Distributed database(s), 417–431
  asynchronous, 421
  combined operations on, 429–430
  data replication, 423–426
    database integrity with, 425–426
    near real-time, 425
    pull, 425
    snapshot, 424–425
    when to use, 426
  heterogeneous, 418–419, 420, 432
  homogeneous, 418–420
  objectives and trade-offs, 421–422
  partitioning
    horizontal, 426–427
    vertical, 427–429
  selecting data distribution strategy, 430–431
  synchronous, 421

Distributed DBMS, 431–446
  architecture, 432
  commit protocol, 435–436
  concurrency transparency, 436–437
  evolution of, 440
  failure transparency, 435
  location transparency, 421, 433–434
  query optimization in, 437–440
  replication transparency, 434–435
  vendors of, 442–445
Distributed environments, 305
Distributed Processing Technology, 281
Distributed Relational Database Architecture (DRDA), 442, 443
Distributed request, 441
Distributed systems. *See* Client/server systems
Distributed unit of work, 441
DK/NF. *See* Domain-key normal form (DKNF)
Domain constraint, 153–154, 213
Domain-key normal form (DKNF), 584
Domains, attributes and, 153–154
Dowgiallo, E., on DBA, 526
Downsizing, 298
Drawing tools, 50
Drill-down, 561–562
DROP INDEX (SQL), 332
DROP (SQL), 336
DROP TABLE (SQL), 332, 336
DROP VIEW (SQL), 332
Dutka, A.F.
  on functional dependency, 235
  on higher normal forms, 584
  on keys, 235
  on transitive dependencies, 239
Dynamic binding, 401
Dynasty, 304

Eddy, F.
  on abstract class, 183
  on ancestors and descendants, 182
  on binary association, 176
  on class-cope attribute, 184
  on design activity, 169
  on discriminators, 181
  on encapsulation, 173
  on modeling, 168
  object-oriented modeling language defined by, 170
  on objects, 171
  on polymorphism, 186
  on propagation, 191
  on query operation, 173, 174
Edelstein, H., on data replication, 424, 425, 442
Elmasri, R.
  on constraints, 137
  on distributed database management systems, 431
  on higher normal forms, 584
  on inconsistent databases, 154
  on relationship instance, 99
  on semijoin, 439
  on supertype/subtype hierarchy, 143
Encapsulation, 173
Encryption, 497
END TRANSACTION (SQL), 367
End-user computing, 27
English, L., on TQM, 545

Enhanced entity-relationship (EER) model, 129–145, **130**
  supertype/subtype relationships, 130–145
    basic concepts and notation, 130–133
    constraints in, 137–145
    generalization, 133–136, **134**
    specialization, 136–137
  transformed into relations. *See under* Relation(s)
Enhanced SQL, 575
Enterprise databases, 19–20
Enterprise data model, 10–11, 537
Enterprise data modeling, 28
Enterprise data warehouse, 535
Enterprise data warehouse metadata, 538
Enterprise modeling, 41–44, 46–47
Enterprise server, 57
Entity(ies), 11, 42, 43–44, **89–92**
  associative. *See* Associative entities (gerunds)
  in E-R diagram, 89–92
  regular, 218, 219–220
  sample definitions of, 150
  strong, 90
  weak, 90, **92,** 218, 221–222
Entity instance (instance), 91
Entity integrity, 213–214
Entity-relationship diagram. *See* E-R diagram
Entity-relationship (E-R) model, 85–127, **87**
  constructs, 89–97
    attributes, 93–97
    entities, 89–92
    entity types, 91–93
  example, 111–117
  notation, 89
  relationships, 97–111
    basic concepts and definitions in, 98–101
    cardinality constraints, 105–107, 108
    degree of, 101–105
    multiple, 110–111
    time-dependent data, 107–110
  See also Enhanced entity-relationship (EER) model
Entity type, 91–93
  strong, 92
  weak, 92
Equi-join, 354–355
E-R diagram, 11, 41, **87**
  cardinality in, 90
  sample, 87–89
  transformed into relations. *See under* Relation(s)
E-R model. *See* Entity-relationship (E-R) model
Evans, M.
  on entity-relationship model, 86
  on participation constraints, 104
Event, 539
Event data, 538–539
Event-driven, 406
Exclusive lock (X lock; write lock), 508, 509
EXEC SQL (SQL), 404
EXISTS operator (SQL), 360
Exists quantifier (OQL), 473
Expressions, in SQL, 342–343
Extended relational server. *See* Object-relational database management system (ORDBMS)
Extent, 459
External schema, 55
Extract (conversion tool), 550, 551

Fact, **148**–149
   derived, 149
Fact tables, 552, 553
   grain of, 554
   multiple, 556, 557
   size of, 554–555
Failure, system, 504–505
Failure transparency, **435**
Fat client, **299**
Ferguson, M.
   on parallel environment, 306
   on symmetric multiprocessing (SMP), 307, 308
Field(s), **257**–260
   data integrity, 259–260
   data types, **257**–259
   fixed-length, 261
   transformation of, 548–550
   variable-length, 261
Fifth normal form (5NF), 233, 234, 584
File access, parallel processing to improve, 276–282
FileMaker Pro 4.0, 383
File organization(s), 255, **268**–272
File organization(s)
   comparative features of, 273
   hashed, 270, **272**
   indexed, **268**–272
   sequential, **268**, 269
File processing system, 7–10, 28
   disadvantages of, 8–10
Files. *See under* Physical database design
File server, **299**–300
Finkelstein, R., on denormalization, 262
First normal form (1NF), 233, 234, **237**
Fixed-length fields, 261
Fleming, C.C., on relational database model, 208
For all quantifier (OQL), 473
Foreign key, **210**
   recursive, **228**
FOREIGN KEY REFERENCES (SQL), 216
Form, 67–68
   development of, 397–399
   normal, **233**
Fort, 304
Forward recovery (rollforward), **503**
Fosdick, H., on DBA, 526
Fourth normal form (4NF), 234, **582**–583
Fowler, M.
   on attributes, 193
   on composition, 189
   on multiple classification, 187
   on query operation, 173
   on role name, 174
Fragmentation transparency (replication transparency), **434**–435
Frank, M., on ORDBMS, 574
Frazer, W.D., on data warehousing, 309
Froemming, G., on data replication, 425, 426
From clause (OQL), 470
FROM clause (SQL), 364
Front-end. *See* Client
Front-end functions, 301
Fry, J.P., on entity-relationship model, 86
Functional decomposition, **41**–42
Functional dependency, **235**–236
   between nonkeys, 237

   partial, **237**
   transitive, **238**–240, 242–243
Functions, in SQL, 343–345

Gantt chart, 52
GemStone, 474
Generalization(s), 133–136, **134**, 181–186
   example, 135
   in ODL, 462–463
   specialization combined with, 137
   See also Supertype/subtype relationships
George, J.F.
   on client/server architecture, 58
   on data modeling, 86
   on field specifications, 257
   on planning matrixes, 44
   on project team management, 53
   on system development life cycle (SDLC), 45
Gerunds. *See* Associative entities (gerunds)
Getz, K., on Access97 data retrieval, 402, 403
Gilbert, M., on Access97 data retrieval, 402, 403
Global transaction, **432**
Gottesdiener, E., on business rules, 146
Gould, J.D., on QBE, 384
Grain, **554**
Granularity (locking level), **507**–508
Gray, J., on uniprocessor environments, 306
Greenblatt, D., on QBE, 384
Grimson, J., on distributed database systems, 418, 419, 420
GROUP BY clause (SQL), 351–352
Group command (OQL), 472

Hackathorn, R.D., on data warehousing, 531, 559
Hanson, H.H.
   on functional dependency, 235
   on higher normal forms, 584
   on keys, 235
   on transitive dependencies, 239
Hardware selection, 487
Hash clash, 272
Hashed file organization, 270, **272**
Hashing algorithm, **272**
HAVING clause (SQL), 341, 352–354
Having command (OQL), 472
Hierarchical database model, 282, 283
Hierarchy, supertype/subtype, **143**–145
Hoffer, J.A.
   on client/server architecture, 58
   on data modeling, 86
   on field specifications, 257
   on missing data, 260
   on planning matrixes, 44
   on project team management, 53
   on system development life cycle (SDLC), 45
Homonym, **242**
Horizontal partitioning, **265**–266, 426–427
Hurwitz, J.
   on mainframe legacy systems, 305
   on middleware, 309, 310, 311
HyperText Markup Language (HTML), **407**

IBM Corp.
   distributed DBMS products, 442–443
   ORDBMS products of, 577

I-CASE. *See* Integrated-CASE (I-CASE)
Identifier, **96**
   assigned, 225–226
   composite, **96**–97
   object, 455
   unassigned, 224–225
Identifying owner, **92**–93
Identifying relationship, **93**
IDM, 324
IEF. *See* Integrity Enhancement Feature (IEF)
Incomplete subclasses, 183
Inconsistent read problem, **506**
Incorrect data, 504
Incremental capture, **544**
Incremental commitment, **53**
Independent data mart, **558**
Index(es), 255, **268**, **274**–276
   bitmap, **271**–272, 546
   multiple, 270–271
   primary key, 274–275
   of reconciled data, 545–546
   in relational DBMS, 339–340
   rules for choosing, 275–276
   secondary key, 275
Indexed file organization, **268**–272
Indexed nonsequential, **270**
Indexed sequential, **270**
Information, **5**
   data vs., 5–6
Informational processing, 482, 530
Informational systems, **533**–534
Information engineering, **40**
   phases of, 40–44
Information gap, 530
Information repository, **515**
   See also Repository(ies)
Information Repository Dictionary System (IRDS), **515**
Information Systems Architecture (ISA), **39**, 490
   components of, 39
   matching user needs to, 59–61
Information systems planning. *See* IS planning
Informix, ORDBMS products of, 577
InfoSuite, 550, 551
INGRES, 324
Ingres/Net and Ingres/Star, 443, 445
Inheritance, 168, 182, 186–187, 188
   attribute, **133**
   multiple, 187, 188
In keyword (OQL), 473
Inmon, W.H.
   on data warehousing, 531, 559
   on normalized databases, 261
   on snowflake schema, 557
IN operator (SQL), 350, 359
INPUT command (SQL), 337
Input/output (I/O) contention, 518
INSERT command (SQL), 337
Insertion anomalies, 217, 239
Instance, relationship, **99**
Instance (entity instance), **91**
Integrated-CASE (I-CASE), 50–51
Integrity
   data, 259–260
   entity, **213**–214
   management of, 487
   referential, 260, **334**, 458

Integrity, *continued*
transaction, 366–368, 501–502
See also Data integrity
Integrity constraints, 146, 213–215
referential, 214–215
See also Business rules
Integrity (data quality tool), 551
Integrity Enhancement Feature (IEF), 325
Internal marketing, 486
Internet database servers, 407–409
Internet Information Server (IIS), 409
Intranet, 407
IRDS. *See* Information Repository Dictionary
System (IRDS)
ISA. *See* Information Systems Architecture (ISA)
IS planning, 40–44
matrices, 43–44
objects, 41, 42
Iunknown, 401

Jacobson, I.
on object-oriented design phase, 169
on object-oriented modeling, 170
object-oriented modeling language defined
by, 170
Jasmine, 474
Java Database Connectivity (JDBC) classes, 311
Jet Data Access Objects, 402
Join, 354–358
equi-join, 354–355
lossless, 584
natural, 355–356
outer, 356–358, 391–392
semijoin, 439
Joining, 547
in data transformation, 547
Jonsson, P.
on object-oriented design phase, 169
on object-oriented modeling, 170
object-oriented modeling language defined
by, 170
Jordan, A., on data warehousing, 23
Journalizing facilities, 499

Kerberos, 498
Keuffel, W., on middleware, 311
Key(s), 209–210, 235–236
candidate, 235–236
composite, 209
foreign, 210
recursive, 228
in ODL, 460–462
primary, 64, **209**
secondary, 268
Kimball, R., on dimensional model, 552
King, N.H., on object DBMS, 474
Koop, P., on data replication, 423

Lambert, B., on data warehouses, 4
Langer, A., on DBA, 526
La Rue, M., on ODBC, 311
Lefkovitz, H.C., on IRDS, 515
Legacy systems, 25
LIKE (SQL), 345
Linear data structures, 589–594
hazards of, 594
multilists, 593–594
queues, 590–591

sorted lists, 591–593
stacks, 590
Linthicum, D.S.
on client/servers, 312
on JDBC, 311
Lirov, Y., on DBA, 526
List, 455
sorted, 591–593
See also Array, Bag, Set
Litwin, P.K., on Access97 data retrieval,
402, 403
Loading reconciled data, 545–546
Local area network (LAN)
file server, 299
limitations of, 300
types of, 298–302
Local autonomy, 421
Local transaction, 432
Location transparency, 421, 433–434
Locking, 506
Locking level (granularity), 507–508
Locks, types of, 508–510
Logical database design, 46, 47–48, 206, 207–251
EER and E-R diagrams transformed into
relations, 218–232
associative entities, 224–227
binary relationships, 222–224, 225
regular entities, 219–220
supertype/subtype relationships,
231–232, 233
ternary and *n*-ary relationships, 229–231
unary relationships, 227–229
weak entities, 221–222
merging relations, 241–243
normal forms, 237–241
normalization, 232–236, **233**
functional dependency, 235–236
keys, 235–236
steps in, 233–234
objective of, 208
See also Relational data model
Logical database model. *See* Relational data
model
Logical key pointer, 585–586
Loop relationship, in network database model
See also Unary (recursive) relationship
Loosely coupled architectures, 307
Lorensen, W.
on abstract class, 183
on ancestors and descendants, 182
on binary association, 176
on class-cope attribute, 184
on design activity, 169
on discriminators, 181
on encapsulation, 173
on modeling, 168
object-oriented modeling language defined
by, 170
on objects, 171
on polymorphism, 186
on propagation, 191
on query operation, 173, 174
Lossless joins, 584
Lost updates, 505–506
Lower CASE, 51

McGovern D., on two-phase commit protocol,
436

Macros, in Access97, 396–397, 406
Mainframe, client/server systems and, 305–306
Maintenance, 489, 490
program, 10
Maintenance controls, 513
Mandatory cardinality, 106
Market basket analysis, 554
Marketing, internal, 486
Martin, J., on data warehouses, 530
Martino, L., on ODBMS, 458
**Massively parallel processor
architecture/shared nothing architecture
(MPP)**, 307–309
MAX function (SQL), 343, 344
Maximum cardinality, 106
Melton, J., on SQL, 371
Memory usage, 517–518
Menus, application, 396–397
Message oriented middleware (MOM), 310
Metadata, 6–7, 537–538, 559–560
Method (or service), 185
Meyer, A., on data marts, 530
Microsoft Access, 67, 325
data retrieval in, 402
functions, 390
Microsoft Access97, 383
form development in, 397–399
macros in, 396–397, 406
multiple-table queries in, 390–392
outer join in, 391–392
QBE in, 384–386, 394–396
Query Design Pane, 389
query types in, 394–396
Report Wizard, 399–400
self-join in, 392–393
single-table queries in, 388–390
switchboard, 396
VBA with, 406
Microsoft Corp., 401
distributed DBMS products, 443, 445
Middleware, 309–311
MIN function (SQL), 343, 344
Minimum cardinality, 106
Missing data, 260
Modification anomalies, 217, 239
Moriarty, T.
on business information advisory committee,
512
on repository, 51
Moxon, B., on SQL3, 575
Mullins, C.S., on triggers and procedures, 369,
370
Multidimensional database model, 283, 284–285
Multidimensional (proprietary) databases, 557
Multidimensional table view, 283
Multifield transformation, 549–550
Multilists, 593–594
Multiple classification, 187
Multiple inheritance, 187, 188
Multiplicity, 174–176
Multiprocessor hardware architectures, 307–308
Multivalued attribute(s), 95, 210, 220
in E-R diagram, 90
Multivalued dependencies, 582
Murphy, P., on data warehousing architecture,
531, 535

n-ary relationships, 229–231

National Institute of Standards and Technology (NIST), 371
Natural join, 355–356
Navathe, S.B.
   on constraints, 137
   on distributed database management systems, 431
   on higher normal forms, 584
   on inconsistent databases, 154
   on relationship instance, 99
   on semijoin, 439
   on supertype/subtype hierarchy, 143
Near real-time replication, 425
Network analysis, 313
Network database model, 282–284
Normal form(s), 233, 579–584
   Boyce-Codd (BCNF), 234, 579–581, **580**
   domain-key (DKNF), 584
   fifth (5NF), 233, 234, 584
   first (1NF), 233, 234, **237**
   fourth (4NF), 234, **582**–583
   second (2NF), 233, 234, **237**–238
   third (3NF), 233, 234, **238**–240
Normalization, 47, 232–236, **233,** 547
   functional dependency, 235–236
   keys, 235–236
   steps in, 233–234
   See also Denormalization
Norman, M., on content addressing, 576
North, K., on OLE, 401
NOT operator (SQL), 216, 359
n-tier architectures, 302–304
Null, 214
NULL (SQL), 216, 351
Null value control, 259

O$_2$, 474
Object(s), 168, **171**–172
   behavior of, 171
   constrained, 155–159
   constraining, 155–159
   state of, 171
Object Database Management Group (ODMG), 454
Object design, 169
Object diagram, 172, 173
   example, 178
Object identifier, 455
Objectivity (ODBMS), 474
Object Linking and Embedding (OLE), 401–402
Object Management Group (OMG), 311, 401
Object-oriented database development, 453–479
   example, 466–467
   object definition language (ODL), 454–465
      abstract class in, 464
      attribute in, 455–456, 459–462
      class in, 454–455
      generalization in, 462–463
      keys in, 460–462
      operations in, 456–457
      range for attribute in, 457
      relationships in, 457–459, 460–462
      user structures in, 456, 464–465
   object instances, 467–468
   Object Query Language (OQL), 468–473
      finding distinct values, 470
      multiple classes, 470–471

retrieval command, 469
   select clause, 469–470
   sets in query, 473
   subqueries in, 471
   summary values, 471–472
   products and applications, 474
Object-oriented database model, 283, 284
Object-oriented databases, 29
Object-oriented modeling, 167–203
   aggregation, 187–191
   association classes, 177–180
   associations, 174–177
   benefits of, 169–170
   business rules in, 191, 192
   classes, 168, **171**–172
   derived attributes, derived associations, and derived roles, 180–181
   example, 191–194
   generalizations, 181–186
   inheritance, 168, 182, 186–187, 188
   objects, 168, **171**–172
   operation types, 173–174
   overriding, 186–187
   phases of, 168–169
   Unified Modeling Language (UML), 170–171
Object-relational database management system (ORDBMS), 474, **573**–577
   advantages of, 576
   content addressing in, 576
   data types of, 574
   enhanced SQL in, 575
   example, 575–576
   features of, 574
   vendors and products, 577
Object request brokers (ORBs), 310
ObjectStore, 474
OBS Universal Database, 577
ODBCDirect, 401, 402–403
ODB-II (Jasmine), 577
ODMG. *See* Object Database Management Group (ODMG)
OLE. *See* Object Linking and Embedding (OLE)
OLE DB, 401–402
OMG. *See* Object Management Group (OMG)
OmniSQL, 443, 444
On-line analytical processing (OLAP), 14, **560**–562
Online transaction processing (OLTP), 302
Open Database Connectivity (ODBC), 311, 402
Operation, 173, 489, 490
Operational constraints, 147–148, 154–159
   in relational data model, 215
Operational metadata, 537–538
Operational processing, 482, 530
Operational system, 533
Optimization, overriding for, 187
Optional cardinality, 106
ORACLE, 324
Oracle, 325
   ANALYZE command, 286
   database definition commands, 272–273
   data types in, 258
   row clustering, 272
Oracle7, data types in, 329
Oracle Corp.
   distributed DBMS products, 443, 444
   ORDBMS products of, 577
ORBs. *See* Object request brokers (ORBs)

ORDBMS. *See* Object-relational database management system (ORDBMS)
ORDER BY clause (SQL), 276, 350–351
Ordering, 215
Organizational conflict, 25
Outer join, 356–358, 391–392
Overgaard, G.
   on object-oriented design phase, 169
   object-oriented modeling language defined by, 170
Overlapping descendant, 183
Overlapping subtypes, 142–143
Overlap rule, 139–141, 142
Overriding, 186–187
   for extension, 186
   for optimization, 187
   for restriction, 187–188
Owner, identifying, 92–93
Özsu, M.T., on query processing, 438

Page, 260
Paradox 8, 383
   See also Query-by-Example (QBE)
Parallel computer architecture, 306–309
Parallel processing, 276–282
Park, E.K.
   on entity-relationship model, 86
   on participation constraints, 104
Partial functional dependency, 237
Partial specialization rule, 137, 138, 139
Partitioning
   advantages and disadvantages of, 266
   application, 304
   horizontal, 265–266, 426–427
   vertical, 266–267, 427–429
Passport (conversion tool), 550, 551
Pass-through queries, 394, 402
Password security, 312
Periodic data, 540–542
Personal computer databases, 15–16, 56
Personnel, specialized, 24
Personnel controls, 513
PERT chart, 52
Physical access controls, 513
Physical address pointer, 585–586
Physical database design, 46, 48, 206, 253–294
   architecture selection, 255, 282–285
   data volume and usage analysis, 255–256
   denormalization, 261–267, **262**
      horizontal partitioning by, 265–266
      opportunities for, 262–264
      vertical partitioning by, 266–267
   fields, 257–260
      data integrity, 259–260
      data types, 257–259
   indexes, 255, 274–276
   physical files, 267–274
      access methods, 267–268
      clustering, 272–274
      controls for, 274
      file organization, 255, **268**–272
      pointer, 267
   physical records, 255, **260**–261
   process of, 254–255
   query performance optimization, 255, 285–286
Physical records, 255, **260**–261
Physical schema, 55

Planning, database, 486, 488, 489
Planning matrix, 43–44
Poe, V., 530
    on star schema extensions and variations, 556
Pointer, **267**, 585–587
Pointer sequential connection, 89, 587, 588
Polymorphism, 185, **186**
Premerlani, W.
    on abstract class, 183
    on ancestors and descendants, 182
    on binary association, 176
    on class-scope attribute, 184
    on design activity, 169
    on discriminators, 181
    on encapsulation, 173
    on modeling, 168
    object-oriented modeling language defined
        by, 170
    on objects, 171
    on polymorphism, 186
    on propagation, 191
    on query operation, 173, 174
Primary key, 64, **209**
    in relational database model, 209
Primary key index, 274–275
PRIMARY KEY operator (SQL), 216, 333
Prism (conversion tool), 550, 551
Privacy, 514
    management of, 487
Program-data dependence, 8–9
Program maintenance, 10
Programmers, 51
Project, **51**–53
Proprietary (multidimensional) databases, 557
Prototyping, **49**–50
Publish/subscribe middleware, 310
Pull replication, 425

Quality management, 511–514
    data protection and privacy, 514
    maintenance controls, 514
    personnel controls, 513
    physical access controls, 513
    security policy and disaster recovery, 512–513
Query(ies)
    action, 395
    crosstab, 395
    data definition, 394
    parallel, 306
    pass-through, 394, 402
    top(n), 395–396
    total, 394–395
    union, 394
Query-by-Example (QBE), 68–69, **382**, 383–396
    in Access97, 384–386, 394–396
    data definition, 386–387
    history of importance of, 384
    multiple-table queries, 390–392
    query based on other queries, 393
    query building using, 388
    record selection, 390
    relationships in, 387–388
    self-join (recursive join) queries, 392–393
    single-table queries, 388–390
QueryInterface, 401
Query operation, **173**–174
Query optimization, in distributed DBMS,
    437–440

Queues, 590–591
Quinlan, T.
    on application partitioning tools, 304
    on application servers, 302
    on data administration, 454, 488
    on DBA, 526

RAID. *See* Redundant Arrays of Inexpensive
    Disks (RAID)
Range control, 259
Range for attribute in ODL, 457
Ranges, in SQL, 347–348
Rapid application development (RAD), 48–49
Read lock (S lock; shared lock), **508**, 509
Reconciled data, **537**
Reconciliation, data, 542–546
    data transformation and, **546**–551
    support tools, 550–551
Records
    clustering, 272–274
    physical, 255, **260**–261
    transformation of, 547
Recovery, disaster, 512–513
    See also Backup and recovery
Recovery manager, **500**
Recursive foreign key, **228**
Recursive join (self-join) queries, 392–393
Recursive relationship. *See* Unary (recursive)
    relationship
Recursive structure. *See* Repeating group
Redman, T.C., on data quality, 23
**Redundant Arrays of Inexpensive Disks
    (RAID)**, 276–282, **277**
    levels of, 278–281
    performance of, 281–282
Reference data, 262, 265
REFERENCES clause (SQL), 333, 335
Referential integrity, 260, **334**, 458
Referential integrity constraint, **214**–215
Refresh mode, 545
Regular entities, 218, 219–220
Relation(s), **209**
Relation
    associative, 224
    converting to BCNF, 580–581
    EER and E-R diagrams transformed into,
        218–232
        associative entities, 224–227
        binary relationships, 222–224, 225
        regular entities, 219–220
        supertype/subtype relationships,
          231–232, 233
        ternary and *n*-ary relationships, 229–231
        unary relationships, 227–229
        weak entities, 221–222
    merging (view integration), 241–243
    properties of, 210
    well-structured, **217**
    See also Table(s)
Relational database, 11–14
    example, 211–213
    implementation of, 13–14
Relational database model, 283, 284
    components of, 208
Relational data model, 28, 208–217
    data structure, 209
    definitions, 208
    integrity constraints in, 213–215

    keys, 209–210
    table definitions, 215–216
    well-structured relations, **217**
Relational data structures, 209
Relational DBMS (RDBMS), **325**
    data dictionary, 368–369
    data maintenance, 366
    indexes in, 339–340
    internal schema definitions in, 338–340
Relational tables, 215–216
Relationship(s), 11, 97–111
    attributes on, 99, 100
    cardinality, 90
    degree, **101**–105
    in E-R diagram, 90
    identifying, **93**
    many-to-many (M:N), 103
        with nonkey attributes, 262, 264
    n-ary, 229–231
    in ODL, 457–459, 460–462
    one-one-one, 262, 263
    in QBE, 387–388
    See also Binary relationship(s);
        Supertype/subtype relationships;
        Ternary relationship; Unary (recursive)
        relationship
Relationship instance, **99**
Relationship type, **98**–99
Relative access method, 267
Relative address pointer, 585–586
Remote procedure call (RPC), 310
Remote unit of work, 440–441
Rennhackkamp, M., on triggers, 370
Repeating group
    in first normal form, 237
    in relational database model, 211
Replication, data, 267, 423–426
    advantages and disadvantages of, 266
    database integrity with, 425–426
    near real-time, 425
    pull, 425
    snapshot, 424–425
    when to use, 426
Replication server, 443–444
**Replication transparency (fragmentation
    transparency)**, **434**–435
Report, 68
Repository(ies), 21, **25**, **51**, 515–516
    information, **515**
    management of, 486–487
Request, distributed, 441
Restore/rerun, **501**
Robinson, C., on desktop database applications,
    383
Rogers, U., on denormalization, 262
Roles, derived, 180–181
Rollback (backward recovery), **502**–503
ROLLBACK command (SQL), 403–404
Rollforward (forward recovery), **503**
Ross, R.G., on business rules, 154, 155, 159
Rotating Parity Array, 281
Rowe, J., on Internet database servers, 407, 408
Rudin, K., on SMP or MPP systems, 308
Rumbaugh, J.
    on abstract class, 183
    on ancestors and descendants, 182
    on binary association, 176
    on class-cope attribute, 184

on design activity, 169
on discriminators, 181
on encapsulation, 173
on modeling, 168
object-oriented modeling language defined
    by, 170
on objects, 171
on polymorphism, 186
on propagation, 191
on query operation, 173, 174

Scalability, 302
Scalar aggregate, **351**
Schema, **327**
    conceptual, 47, **54**, 55
    external, 55
    physical, **55**
    in RDBMS, 338–340
    snowflake, **556–557**, 558
    star. *See* Star schema
Schneiderman, B., on direct manipulation, 382
Schumacher, R.
    on bitmap storage, 271
    on index limits, 276
    on server technology, 285, 286
Schussel, G., on data replication, 425
Scrubbing, data, **544–545**
SDLC. *See* Systems development life cycle
    (SDLC)
Secondary key, **268**
Secondary key index, 275
Second normal form (2NF), 233, 234, **237–238**
Sections (bands), 399
Security
    in client/server systems, 311–312
    embedded SQL and, 404
    management of, 487
    See also Database security
Select clause (OQL), 469–470
Selection (subsetting), **547**
SELECT statement (SQL), 328, 340–342, 352, 354,
    364
Self-join (recursive join) queries, 392–393
Semijoin, **439**
Sequential access method, 267–268
Sequential file organization, **268**, 269
Server(s)
    database (database engine), 16, 58, **301**–302
    department, 57
    enterprise, 57
    file, 299–300
    Internet database, 407–409
    web, 408
Set, **455**
Sets in query, 473
Shared lock (S lock; read lock), **508**, 509
Shared nothing architecture. *See* Massively
    parallel processor architecture
Simple (atomic) attribute, **95**, 96
Single-field transformation, 548–549
Smith, R., on Access97, 406
SMP. *See* Symmetric multiprocessing (SMP)
Snapshot replication, 424–425
Snowflake schema, **556–557**, 558
Software selection, 487
Song, I-Y.
    on entity-relationship model, 86
    on participation constraints, 104

Sorted lists, 591–593
Sowa, J.F., on ISA, 39
Specialization, **136–137**, 181
    example, 136
SQL, 323–380
    in Access97, 394
    ADD, 336
    ALL operator, 349, 359
    ALTER TABLE, 285, 332, 336
    ANY operator, 359
    AUTOCOMMIT, 367
    AVG function, 343, 344
    batch input, 337–338
    BEGIN TRANSACTION, 367
    BETWEEN clause, 347
    CHECK operator, 333
    COMMIT, 404
    COUNT function, 343, 344, 351
    CREATE ASSERTION command, 159, 369
    CREATE DATABASE, 331–332
    CREATE INDEX, 274–275, 332, 339
    CREATE SCHEMA, 332
    CREATE SYNONYM, 336–337
    CREATE TABLE, 215, 332–333
    CREATE VIEW, 332
    database definition, 331–337
        changing table definitions, 336
        commands, 332
        data integrity controls, 334–336
        establishing synonyms, 336–337
        removing tables, 336
        table creation, 332–334
    data dictionary, 368–369
    DEFAULT operator, 333
    DELETE command, 336, 338
    DISTINCT, 348–349
    DROP, 336
    DROP INDEX, 332
    DROP TABLE, 332, 336
    DROP VIEW, 332
    dynamic, 304
    embedded, 403–405
    END TRANSACTION, 367
    enhanced, 575
    environment, 327–331
    EXEC SQL, 404
    EXISTS operator, 360
    FOREIGN KEY REFERENCES, 216
    FROM clause, 364
    GROUP BY clause, 351–352
    HAVING clause, 341, 352–354
    history of, 324–325
    IN operator (SQL), 350, 359
    INPUT command, 337
    INSERT command, 337
    inserting, updating, and deleting data,
        337–338
    internal schema definitions in RDBMS,
        338–340
    LIKE, 345
    MAX function, 343, 344
    MIN function, 343, 344
    NOT operator, 216, 359
    NULL, 216, 351
    ORDER BY clause, 276, 350–351
    PRIMARY KEY operator, 216, 333
    procedures, 369–371
    processing multiple tables, 354–363

correlated subqueries, **361**–363
    equi-join, **354**–355
    natural join, **355**–356
    outer join, **356**–358
    subqueries, 358–360
processing single tables, 340–349
    Boolean operators, 346–347
    comparison operators, 345–346
    expressions, 342–343
    functions, 343–345
    ranges, 347–348
    wildcards, 345
REFERENCES clause, 333, 335
role in database architecture, 325–327
ROLLBACK command, 403–404
SELECT statement, 328, 340–342, 352, 354,
    364
static, 304
SUM function, 343, 344, 351
table definitions, 215–216
transaction integrity, 366–368
triggers, **369**–371
UNION operator, 266
UNIQUE operator, 274–275, 333
UPDATE clause, 335
view in, 363–366
WHERE clause, 345, 346, 352, 354, 355, 364
SQL3, 371, 575
SQL/86, 325
SQL Anywhere, 443, 444
SQL-oriented data access, 310
SQL Server, 443, 445
Stacks, 590
Star schema, **552–558**
    components of, 552, 553, 554–556
    example, 552–554
    variations of, 556–558
Star-schema view, 283
State, **171**
Static capture, **544**
Status data, 538–539
Stored attributes, 95–97
Stored procedure, **301**–302
Storey, V.C., on entity-relationship model, 86
Stripe, **277**
Strong entity, 90
Strong entity type, **92**
Structural constraints, **147**, 148–154
    definitions, 148–152
    domains, 153–154
Structured literal, **456**
Structured query language (SQL). *See* SQL
Subclasses, 183
Subquery(ies), 358–360
    correlated, **361**–363
    in OQL, 471
Subsetting (selection), **547**
Subtype(s), **130**
    disjoint, 141–142
    overlapping, 142–143
    See also Generalization(s);
        Supertype/subtype relationships
Subtype discriminator, **141**–143
SUM function (SQL), 343, 344, 351
Summary data, 241
Superclass, 182
Supertype, **130**
Supertype/subtype hierarchy, **143**–145

Supertype/subtype relationships, 130–145, 231–232, 233
  basic concepts and notation, 130–133
  constraints in, 137–145
    completeness, 137–138
    discriminators, 141–143
    disjointness, 138–141
    hierarchies, 143–145
    generalization, 133–136, **134**
    specialization, 136–137
  in view integration, 243
Sussman, D., on Access97, 406
Switch, 501
Switchboard, Access97, 396
SYBASE, 324
Sybase Inc., distributed DBMS products, 443–444
Symmetric multiprocessing (SMP), 307
Symmetric Replication Option, 443, 444
Synchronous distributed database, 421
Synchronous remote procedure call, 310
Synonyms, 242
  in SQL, 336–337
  in view integration, 242
System catalog, 514
System developers, 26
System failure, 504–505
System-level password security, 312
System R., 324
Systems analysts, 51
Systems development life cycle (SDLC), 45–48

Table(s)
  base, 364–366
  code look-up, 258–259
  dimension, 552, 553
  fact, 552, 553
    grain of, 554
    multiple, 556, 557
    size of, 554–555
  relational, 215–216
  in relational database model, 210–211, 215–216
  in SQL
    changing definitions, 336
    creating, 332–334
    multiple, 354–363
    removing, 336
    single, 340–349
  See also Relation(s)
Table Snapshot Option, 443, 444
Teorey, T.J., on entity-relationship model, 86
Term, 148
Ternary relationship, 90, 102, **104**–105, 107, 108, 175, 180, 229–231
Thin client, 302
Third Generation Languages (3GLs), 404
Third normal form (3NF), 233, 234, **238**–240
Thomas, J.C., on QBE, 384
Thompson, C.
  on client/server architecture, 58
  on distributed DBMS products, 442
  on three-tier architectures, 302, 303
Three-tier architecture, 302–304

Time stamp, 108
Timestamping, 437
Top-down planning, 40
Top(n) queries, 395–396
Total quality management (TQM), 545
Total queries, 394–395
Total specialization rule, 137, 138
Transaction(s), 499
  aborted, 503–504
  global, 432
  local, 432
  parallel, 306
  See also Backward recovery (rollback);
      Forward recovery (rollforward);
      Recovery manager; Transaction(s)
Transaction boundaries, 502
Transaction integrity, 366–368, 501–502
Transaction log, 499
Transaction manager, 435
Transaction processing (TP) monitor, 302
Transient data, 539–542
Transitive dependency, 238–240
  example, 238–240
  in view integration, 242–243
Transparency
  concurrency, 436–**437**
  failure, 435
  location, 421, 433–434
  replication (fragmentation), 434–435
Trees, 271, 594–598
Trigger, 369–371, 425
Two-phase commit, 435
Two-phase locking protocol, 510

Unary (recursive) relationship, 90, **101**–104, 175, 227–229
  many-to-many (M:N), 228–229
  one-to-many (1:M), 227–228
Unified Modeling Language (UML), 170–171
Uniform Resource Locator (URL), 408
UNION operator (SQL), 266
Union queries, 394
UNIQUE operator (SQL), 274–275, 333
Unit of work
  distributed, 441
  remote, 440–441
Universal server. *See* Object-relational database management system (ORDBMS)
Universal Server (Informix), 577
UPDATE clause (SQL), 335
Update mode, 545
Update operation, 174
Updates, lost, 505–506
Upper CASE, 51
User-defined procedures, 497
User interface, 26, 559–563
  data mining tools, 562–563
  data visualization, 563
  metadata and, 559–560
  on-line analytical processing (OLAP) tools, 560–562
Users, 51
User structures, in ODL, 456, 464–465
User view, 22, 47, 54

Valacich, J.S.
  on client/server architecture, 58
  on data modeling, 86
  on field specifications, 257
  on planning matrixes, 44
  on project team management, 53
  on system development life cycle (SDLC), 45
Valduriez, P., on query processing, 438
Variable-length fields, 261
Vaughn, W.R., on ODBCDirect, 402
Vector aggregate, 351
Versant, 474
Versioning, 510–511
Vertical partitioning, 266–267, 427–429
Viehman, P., on physical database design and efficiency, 276
View(s)
  data security and, 494–495
  in SQL, 363–366
View integration, 241–243
Virtual sequential access method (VSAM), 595–596
Visual Basic for Applications (VBA), 383, **406**–407
Visual Gen, 304
Visualization, data, 563
Visual programming tools, 50
von Halle, B.
  on business rules, 146
  on relational database model, 208

Watterson, K., on object DBMS, 474
Waxman, J., on QBE, 384
Weak entities, 90, **92,** 218, 221–222
Weak entity type, 92
Web browsers, 407, 408
Web servers, 408
Weldon, J.L., on data mining, 562
Well-structured relation, 217
WHERE clause (SQL), 345, 346, 352, 354, 355, 364
Wildcards, in SQL, 345
Williams, J., on data reconciliation tools, 550
Windows operating system, 406
Winter, R.
  on bitmap indexing, 546
  on large databases, 4
WizRules, 550, 551
Workgroup databases, 16–17, 56
Write lock (X lock; exclusive lock), 508, 509

X lock (write lock; exclusive lock), 508, 509

Yang, D., on entity-relationship model, 86
Year 2000 problem, 154, 491
Young, C., on DBA, 526
Yourdon, E., on object-oriented modeling, 169–170

Zachman, J.A.
  on ISA, 39
  on IS development, 490
Zaitz, J., on data mining, 563
Zloof, M.M., on QBE, 384